TEACHING STUDENTS
WITH MODERATE AND SEVERE DISABILITIES

Teaching Students with
MODERATE AND SEVERE DISABILITIES

DIANE M. BROWDER
FRED SPOONER

THE GUILFORD PRESS
New York   London

Printed in the United States of America

This book is printed on acid-free paper.

Last digit is print number: 9 8 7 6 5 4

The authors have checked with sources believed to be reliable in their efforts to provide information that is complete and generally in accord with the standards of practice that are accepted at the time of publication. However, in view of the possibility of human error or changes in behavioral, mental health, or medical sciences, neither the authors, nor the editor and publisher, nor any other party who has been involved in the preparation or publication of this work warrants that the information contained herein is in every respect accurate or complete, and they are not responsible for any errors or omissions or the results obtained from the use of such information. Readers are encouraged to confirm the information contained in this book with other sources.

Library of Congress Cataloging-in-Publication Data

Browder, Diane M.
   Teaching students with moderate and severe disabilities / Diane M. Browder and Fred Spooner.
      p. cm.
   Includes bibliographical references and index.
   ISBN 978-1-60623-991-9 (hardcover: alk. paper)
   1. Students with disabilities—Education.   2. Students with disabilities—Life skills guides.
3. Children with disabilities—Education.   4. Teachers of children with disabilities.
5. Special education teachers.   I. Spooner, Fred.   II. Title.
   LC4065.B76 2011
   371.9—dc22
                                                          2010045008

To our families, for their ongoing encouragement and support

To our research staff, who help generate the ideas
and make them teacher-friendly

and

To the students with severe disabilities and their teachers,
who have taught us what is important

About the Authors

Diane M. Browder, PhD, is the Lake and Edward P. Snyder Distinguished Professor of Special Education at the University of North Carolina at Charlotte. She has over two decades of experience conducting research and writing on assessment and instruction for students with severe developmental disabilities, with a recent focus on teaching reading, math, and science. She received the 2009 Distinguished Researcher Award from the American Educational Research Association Special Education Special Interest Group and was the 2009 First Citizens Bank Scholar at the University of North Carolina at Charlotte. She also was recognized by the state of North Carolina for Outstanding Service to the Schools. Dr. Browder currently serves as co-principal investigator (with Fred Spooner) for the Institute of Education Sciences What Works Clearinghouse research-to-practice guides in intellectual disability. She has provided professional development and consultation to states across the nation and has been an international keynote speaker.

Fred Spooner, PhD, is Professor in the Department of Special Education and Child Development at the University of North Carolina at Charlotte. He has over two decades of experience conducting research and writing on instructional practices for students with severe developmental disabilities, alternate assessment, and validating evidence-based practices. He currently serves as co-principal investigator (with Diane M. Browder) for the Institute of Education Sciences What Works Clearinghouse research-to-practice guides in intellectual disability. Dr. Spooner has held numerous editorial posts, including coeditor of *TEACHING Exceptional Children* and *Teacher Education and Special Education,* and is currently coeditor of the *Journal of Special Education* and associate editor of *Research and Practice for Persons with Severe Disabilities.*

Contributing Authors

Lynn Ahlgrim-Delzell, PhD, Department of Educational Leadership, College of Education, University of North Carolina at Charlotte, Charlotte, North Carolina

Joshua Baker, PhD, School of Education, Piedmont College, Athens, Georgia

Bree Jimenez, PhD, Department of Special Education and Child Development, College of Education, University of North Carolina at Charlotte, Charlotte, North Carolina

Victoria F. Knight, PhD, Department of Special Education and Rehabilitation Counseling, University of Kentucky, Lexington, Kentucky

Irene Meier, PhD, Department of Special Services, Fairfax County Public Schools, Fairfax, Virginia

Candice Meyer, PhD, English, Reading, and Humanities Division, Central Piedmont Community College, Charlotte, North Carolina

Pamela J. Mims, PhD, Department of Human Development and Learning, College of Education, East Tennessee State University, Johnson City, Tennessee

Sharon Richter, PhD, Department of Language, Reading, and Exceptionalities, Appalachian State University, Boone, North Carolina

Katherine Trela, PhD, Extended Content Standards, Programs for Exceptional Children, Charlotte–Mecklenburg Schools, Charlotte, North Carolina

Nicole Uphold, PhD, Department of Special Education, Illinois State University, Normal, Illinois

Shawnee Wakeman, PhD, Department of Special Education and Child Development, College of Education, University of North Carolina at Charlotte, Charlotte, North Carolina

Tracie-Lynn Zakas, MS, Specialized Grant Liaison, Charlotte–Mecklenburg Schools, Charlotte, North Carolina

Preface

J ada, Beth, and Marcus are three individuals with developmental disabilities who have been important people in my (D. M. B.) life. They were born in different eras, and so the experiences we had together also were from different worlds. Marcus (not his real name) grew up in an institution, and I was a part of his life when he was in his early teens. The radical idea at the time was that individuals like Marcus could be full members of the community, go to school, and have normal lives. The activities Marcus and I did together were often new for both of us. I remember his delight in learning that he could ask for something using manual signing and our shared joy in trying new places in the community. I think my favorite moment was when we went through an automatic car wash and both laughed as the water sprayed through a partially opened window. I was Marcus's "recreational therapist," and 2 years after I worked with him, at the age of 14, he got to go to school for the first time in his life when Public Law 94-142 (the Education of All Handicapped Children Act) became law.

Many of you met Beth through videos I shared at workshops and through vignettes in my earlier books. Beth is my niece with Angelman syndrome, and her parents have always been gracious about letting me share her story. Besides my early mentors Marti Snell and Adelle Renzaglia, Beth was my most important teacher. Each new idea I learned through the research literature Beth and I would try during "Aunt Diane's Summer Camp." Beth taught me about why and how some AAC (augmentative and alternative communication) methods work better than others; how powerful systematic instruction can be in improving quality of life (such as when she learned to walk up the stairs); why positive behavior support makes life better for all concerned; the benefits of planning with a team; and why choice and self-determination are important (as a Browder, Beth was born with strong self-determination genes!). Beth had the best of community-based life skills instruction and received school services from the time she was a toddler. She now is an adult and has a great supported living situation. I also learned from Beth—and from my experiences working with school-age students with autism and adults in supported living—the benefits of thoughtful planning.

Jada (not her real name) is the person who taught me what early literacy instruction can achieve. When I first met Jada, the teacher was introducing Jada to her first-ever literacy lessons. Jada had an individualized education plan (IEP) that contained many essential life skills—self-feeding, toileting, communicating basic needs—but there was no expectation that she would learn to read. To be honest, we ourselves did not begin with that goal, but Jada outpaced our expectations. During read-alouds she demonstrated remarkable comprehension and began to recognize pictures and words. Jada was one of the first students in the Early Literacy Skills Builder curriculum developed at the University of North Carolina at Charlotte. Not only did she master all levels, but she transitioned into Reading Mastery and now reads and comprehends passages. She also mastered her basic self-care in those years, but we would have underestimated her if that had been all we expected. One reason Jada seemed an unlikely candidate to learn to read was that her communication skills were extremely limited when she began elementary school. At the age of 5, she had no speech and was inconsistent recognizing pictures. She learned to use pictures and words to show what she knew across her school subjects, and she began to make speech sounds in her early work on phonics. Her speech became comprehensible enough to use for sounding out words. Jada now is applying these skills in learning science, math, and other content. As she enters the transition years and begins learning skills for a future job, Jada will have more options because she can read.

Like many of you, our ongoing experiences with individuals with severe developmental disabilities and their teachers have taught us to target increasingly ambitious goals. This book reflects our most ambitious expectations to date—that students with moderate and severe developmental disabilities will make progress in the general curriculum, while also mastering essential life skills, to build a strong foundation for life in the community. Entering the school door for the first time was exciting for Marcus, walking up the school stairs and taking off her coat were milestones for Beth, and learning to read broke new ground for Jada; and we envision a future in which students with moderate and severe disabilities have new leisure, community, and job options because they have both the skills and supports to negotiate their daily lives and the academic knowledge to engage more fully in their world.

This volume is a follow-up to *Curriculum and Assessment for Students with Moderate and Severe Disabilities* (Browder, 2001). The current book covers the new guidelines and resources that have emerged on teaching academic content. What we include on assessment provides the core of what educators need—assessment for IEPs, progress monitoring, alternate assessment, planning positive behavior support, and transition assessment. In some cases, examples and passages from the earlier book were retained to preserve key information, but most of the information in this book is new.

Although there are several excellent texts on severe disabilities, our goal is to provide an alternative with balanced coverage of both academic and life skills learning. There are specific chapters on reading, mathematics, science, and social studies, as well as on foundations and on life skills. We considered subtitling the book *Finding the Balance* because this is the challenge we know teachers face with today's changing curricular priorities. In nearly every chapter, we articulate the challenge for balance that educators face (e.g., between teaching daily living and academic skills) and some possible ways to respond. The ideas in these chapters come from both research and practice. Wherever possible, we have highlighted research that provides support for the guidelines offered. We think it is important for teachers to have guidance that has some evidence of effectiveness. We then built on this research base using ideas from our work with teachers in the schools. We invited a contributor for every chapter who has tried, or helped teachers to try, the chapter's guidelines. To illustrate the ideas, we offer brief vignettes. Unless indicated as being true, these are fictional examples. But they are not fantasy. That is, we have used composites of real people and real experiences to illustrate a point, although the example itself is not a specific event. It always has been important to us to honor people with severe disabilities by sharing individuals' achievements with as much authenticity as possible.

This book reflects our roots in applied behavior analysis, as well as research. We also share the value that individuals with severe disabilities should have full inclusion in school and society and opportunities for self-determination. We hope to promote these goals by offering examples of teaching in general education settings, promoting student-led planning, and using community-based job options. Realizing that we have a way to go to achieve these values for all students, we also have tried to offer guidelines with enough flexibility for the wide range of contexts and disability challenges educators may encounter.

This book is written both for preservice personnel preparation and as a resource for experienced professionals. We use the term *teacher* when we are describing an activity typically implemented by a frontline professional in a classroom. Other times we use the terms *team* and *educator* to reinforce the fact that many of the ideas will be implemented by a transdisciplinary team. Before sending this book to press, we field-tested the chapters in both undergraduate- and graduate-level preservice teacher licensure programs and received positive feedback. We hope that you will find the book similarly useful whether you are new to teaching, new to teaching students with moderate and severe disabilities, or just ready for some new ideas. We would be delighted to hear what worked for you.

DIANE M. BROWDER
FRED SPOONER

Acknowledgments

This book reflects the synergy of the research teams in the General Curriculum Projects at the University of North Carolina at Charlotte and the teachers with whom we have worked for the past decade from around the country. We are grateful for all we have learned in our work together with the goal that "all students benefit." We especially want to acknowledge the contributors who by initial agreement served as third authors. This is not an edited book but a "hybrid" in which we wrote every chapter with the contribution of someone who brought unique skills and experiences to the topic. These contributions were outstanding, and we acknowledge the key role of the contributors to each chapter. We also urge that future writers cite the chapters, rather than the book as a whole, so that these contributors' names are acknowledged. We express our gratitude to Bethany Smith, Melissa Hudson, and Susan Flynn, doctoral students at the University of North Carolina at Charlotte, who invested long hours in proofreading the chapters and finding references and other resources. We appreciate the helpful staff at The Guilford Press and their unwavering encouragement to complete this project. Finally, we acknowledge our families for their flexibility and support, especially in the final crunch weeks before submission.

Contents

PART THREE. LIFE SKILLS AND QUALITY OF LIFE

TEACHING STUDENTS
WITH MODERATE AND SEVERE DISABILITIES

PART ONE

EDUCATIONAL FOUNDATIONS

CHAPTER 1

~

Introduction

DIANE M. BROWDER, FRED SPOONER, AND IRENE MEIER

Ryan is a 6-year-old who is a member of Annette Harris's first-grade class. Ryan has cerebral palsy and uses a wheelchair for ambulation. Ryan also has a severe intellectual disability and does not use speech. He communicates socially by smiling and will look at a person or object to invite others to talk with him. He is learning to recognize pictures to communicate his needs and wishes and to "show what he knows" during reading and other instruction. Ms. Harris has a log that she sends home to his mother daily to show what Ryan has done that day in school. The paraprofessional for the class, Mr. Mahler, is helping Ryan learn to prepare the report by selecting pictures of his daily activities. Ryan participates in nearly all the first-grade activities. Because Ms. Harris uses small groups, learning centers, and lots of hands-on activities, there is usually a way for Ryan to be involved in learning. Ms. Harris works closely with a team in planning for Ryan. The special education teacher, Ms. Walker, who supports several children with disabilities in the K–3 classes, helps adapt materials, provides advice on how to make lessons inclusive of Ryan, and provides some systematic instruction to Ryan during key times of the day. A school nurse checks in daily with Ryan because of his complex medical needs. Ryan's speech therapist works on his communication goals in both an individual session and during classroom times when he can generalize these skills. Similarly, his physical therapist both provides some individual training and helps Ms. Harris incorporate special equipment and therapy goals in the course of Ryan's day.

The field of special education is much younger than some other areas of education, with the first law guaranteeing a free and appropriate education for all children with disabilities having been passed just over 30 years ago (Public Law 94-142; Education for All Handicapped Children Act, 1975). Although services for students with disabilities were emerging in the schools and community prior to the mid-1970s, students with severe disabilities often were omitted from these options. In the past 30 years, more attention has been focused on developing educational programs for students with more severe disabilities. This chapter provides information on who the students are, what the law requires that students receive, and what experts recommend as the qualities that form the foundation of a strong educational program.

WHO ARE STUDENTS WITH MODERATE AND SEVERE DISABILITIES?

Problems with Terminology

The problem that arises in describing any subgroup of a population is that such descriptions overlook the unique qualities of the individual and the many other subgroups to which the student belongs. In describing Ryan at the beginning of this chapter, the reader gains a brief perspective on his educational day. A name for the disability (intellectual disability, cerebral palsy) and some characteristics about Ryan's disability are also provided (e.g., use of wheelchair, health problems, nonverbal communication). The reader gets a small glimpse of his personality (social smiling and engaging others in conversation by looking at them or at objects), but each of these descriptors is only part of the picture of Ryan. For example, this paragraph could have been written from many other perspectives. If Ryan could write it himself, he might want the reader to know about his interests (e.g., popular music, swimming, puppies) or his family or friends. His school nurse might write about Ryan's specific medical diagnoses and health care needs. His grandmother would describe Ryan's Cherokee heritage and their tribal ties. Ryan's younger brother would want you to know about the dinosaur bedspreads in the room they share and how Ryan sometimes keeps him awake by snoring. His father might describe how Ryan has taught him to see life with deeper appreciation. To get to know Ryan requires learning much more than the label for his disability, and the label might actually bring to mind stereotypes that are not true of Ryan. For this reason, it might seem advantageous to avoid the use of a label altogether. Most of the time in planning for Ryan, there will be no need to use the label for his disability. His individual characteristics, not his label, will be the point of focus. In contrast, there are at least three situations in which Ryan's label will be relevant and needed. First, under the law, Ryan will need a formal classification to receive special education and related services. Second, Ryan's teachers and his parents will use the label to locate information related to his needs (e.g., information on physical and intellectual disability). Third, Ryan is a participant in a research study. The researchers will report outcomes using Ryan's label to build new knowledge about how to educate students who share the same or similar characteristics to Ryan (Luckasson & Reeve, 2001). The researchers will not use Ryan's name to protect confidentiality.

Given that labels are sometimes needed, some guidelines should be followed in using them ethically. First, educators should use what is called "person-first" terminology. These terms avoid reference to the disability alone (e.g., "the disabled") and emphasize the individuality of those who share this one characteristic of disability (e.g., "individuals with disabilities"). The best way to emphasize a person-first perspective in referring to a specific child is to use the child's name ("Ryan") rather than the disability ("the child who is disabled"). A second guideline is to respect individuals' and their families' choices of how to refer to their own disabilities. Some individuals may find the term *severe* uninformative or pessimistic or the term *intellectual* confusing. They may prefer the term *developmental disability* or simply *disability*. As Collins (2007) notes, some individuals may prefer to refer to themselves simply as "deaf" versus "individual who is deaf." A third guideline is to use the most current terminology for the disability. Because disability labels have become stigmatizing, the terminology for disability groups has evolved over time. Some of the terms now considered pejorative (*imbecile, retarded, moron, feebleminded*) were at one time considered professional classifications. Professional associations have also changed names to avoid such terms as *handicap* and *mental retardation*. The American Association on Mental Retardation (AAMR) became the American Association on Intellectual and Developmental Disabilities (AAIDD). In its earliest years, the organization was called the Association of Medical Officers of American Institutions for Idiotic and Feeble Minded Persons (in 1876) and the Association for the Study of the Feeble Minded (in 1906; Collins, 2007). The advocacy organization TASH began as the American Association for the Education of the Severely/Profoundly Handicapped (AAESPH) in 1974. Now, it simply uses TASH. Similarly, the former Association for Retarded Citizens is now simply the ARC. The term *handicap* refers to a limitation created by the lack of accommodations in an environment and not to the disability per se (Vergason & Anderegg, 1997). A person who is not disabled may have a handicap because of the restrictions of the environment. For example, a very short person may find it challenging to reach office supplies in a closet with high shelves. Accommodations for disabilities, such as those provided in restrooms and parking lots, should be designated as "accessible" rather than "handicapped." The term *mental retardation* is being replaced because the term *retarded* has negative connotations. For example, media have used this term in pejorative ways (e.g., in comedies in which the character is told to quit "acting retarded").

Current Terminology

Handleman (1986) proposed the term *severe developmental disabilities* as an umbrella term to refer to individuals with autism, severe intellectual disability, and multiple disabilities. A developmental disability is one that (1) is manifested before the age of 22, (2) is chronic and severe, (3) can be attributed to a mental or physical impairment or both, (4) results in substantial functional limitations in major life activities, and (5) requires lifelong need for special services that are individually planned and coordinated (Handleman, 1986). With appropriate supports over time, the life functioning of the person will improve (AAMR, 2002). Throughout this book we use the term *developmental disabilities* to refer to this umbrella group of individuals who may have intellectual disability, autism spectrum disorders, or sensory or physical disabilities combined with either of these.

For many educators, the term *intellectual disability* is replacing the term *mental retardation*. Individuals with intellectual disability have limitations in both intellectual functioning and adaptive behavior, and the disability originates before age 18 (AAIDD Ad Hoc Committee on Terminology and Classification, 2010). The term *mental retardation* continues to be used in federal law referring to educating students with disabilities (the Individuals with Disabilities Education Act [IDEA]) and may be the classification that educators will see on students' psychological assessments. Individuals with intellectual disability may or may not have a recognizable syndrome, such as Down or Angelman syndrome. Intellectual disability can vary in severity and in the level of support that students require. Educators have used terms such as *educable* for a milder disability, *trainable* for moderate, and *severe/profound* for students with the most severe disabilities. Because we believe that all students are educable, we avoid the term *trainable*. In this book, we use the term *students with moderate and severe intellectual disability* to refer to those who need what AAMR has called extensive and pervasive supports (Luckasson et al., 1992). Our focus includes those students sometimes referred to as having "the most severe disabilities" or a "profound intellectual disability," and we use the umbrella term "severe disability" to be inclusive of these students.

Students with autism spectrum disorders have a range of intellectual disability, from gifted to disabled. The Autism Society of America (ASA) defines autism spectrum disorders (ASD) as a complex developmental disability that usually appears during the first 3 years of life and is the result of a neurological disorder that affects the normal functioning of the brain (Autism Society of America, n.d.). Mirenda and Iacono (2009) describe three primary symptoms of ASD as (1) significant difficulties with social interaction, (2) delayed or abnormal functioning in verbal and nonverbal communication, and (3) unusual patterns of behavior. Other variations that fall under the ASD umbrella include (1) pervasive developmental disorder (PDD), or "atypical autism," which has many of the same characteristics as autism but not all the criteria associated with the disorder; (2) Rett disorder, which is similar to autism but presents only in girls; and (3) Asperger syndrome, which does not include the usual language barriers associated with autism and generally is associated with high intellectual ability, although struggles with social interaction are apparent (Autism Society of America, n.d.). Although individuals with ASD present with a wide range of intellectual abilities, the majority of individuals with ASD have some degree of intellectual disability. In this book, our focus is on students with ASD who also have moderate to severe intellectual disability.

Some students with moderate to severe intellectual disability also have physical or sensory disabilities, such as cerebral palsy or visual or hearing impairments. Like those with ASD, students with these sensory or physical disabilities may range in intellectual ability from gifted to severely impaired. We focus on students who have multiple disabilities that include a moderate or severe intellectual disability.

Another term found in the law is *students with significant cognitive disabilities*. A student with significant cognitive disability (SCD) is defined by Browder and Spooner (2006) as "one who (a) is one who requires substantial modifications, adaptations, or supports to meaningfully access the grade-level content; (b) requires intensive individualized instruction in order to acquire and generalize knowledge; and (c) is working toward alternate achievement standards for grade-level content" (p. xviii). This term refers to students who participate in alternate assessments based on alternate achievement standards; this is a broader population of students than those with severe disabilities (Browder & Spooner, 2006).

In this book, we use the term *severe disabilities* as shorthand for students who have moderate and severe developmental disabilities. As described and shown in Figure 1.1, *developmental disability* also is an umbrella term to refer to students with intellectual disability, ASD, and multiple disabilities. Table 1.1 provides a summary of terms for students with severe disabilities with recommendations on when to use each term.

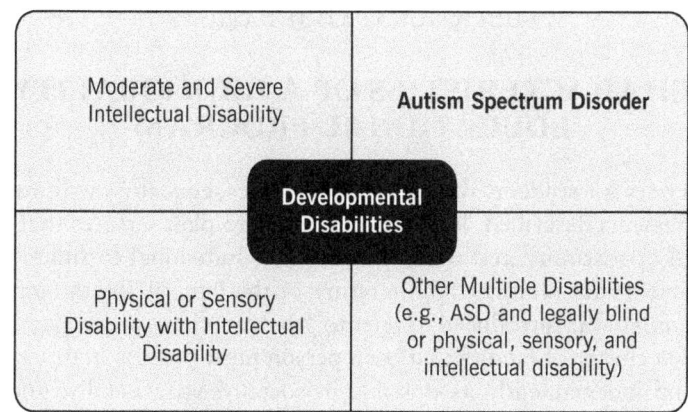

FIGURE 1.1. Developmental disabilities is a general term for these subgroups.

TABLE 1.1. Recommended Terminology for Use in Describing Students with Severe Disabilities

Term (students with . . .)	Reference group	When to use
Significant cognitive disabilities	Students who participate in alternate assessment based on alternate achievement standards; many, but not all, of these students have moderate to severe developmental disabilities.	When referring to students who take alternate assessments based on alternate achievement standards; sometimes also used as a general term for students with severe disabilities.
Developmental disabilities	An umbrella term for students with intellectual disability, autism spectrum disorders, and multiple disabilities, including intellectual disability.	When referring generally to students with autism, intellectual disability, and multiple disabilities that may be mild to severe.
Severe disabilities	An umbrella term for students with moderate and severe developmental disabilities.	As shorthand for moderate and severe development disabilities.
Intellectual disability	Students who have limitations in intellectual functioning and adaptive behavior; onset before age 18.	Instead of older term *mental retardation*; may specify level as mild, moderate, severe (*severe* replaces older term, *severe/profound*).
Autism spectrum disorders	Includes students who have symptoms of significant difficulties with social interaction, delayed verbal and nonverbal communication, and unusual patterns of behavior; usually apparent before 3 years of age.	To refer to students who may have any one of these cluster of disabilities; the term *autism* is sometimes also used generally.
Physical disabilities	Students who have disabilities that affect mobility and motor functioning (e.g., cerebral palsy, muscular dystrophy).	When a broad term is needed for physical disabilities; when possible, use the more precise disability (e.g., type of cerebral palsy).
Sensory disabilities	Students who have disabilities that affect vision, hearing, or both (e.g., deaf, hearing impaired, blind, visually impaired, deaf/blind).	When a broad term is needed for both hearing and visual impairments; when possible, use the more precise disability (e.g., type of hearing impairment).

CHARACTERISTICS OF A HIGH-QUALITY EDUCATIONAL PROGRAM

In planning services for students with severe disabilities, educators will want to attend to the legal requirements described. It is also important to plan services that will provide a full educational opportunity and that will allow the individual to function as independently as possible as an adult. In the literature of the late 1970s, the term *criterion of ultimate functioning* was introduced to refer to "the ever changing, expanding, localized, and personalized cluster of factors that each person must possess in order to function as productively and independently as possible in socially, vocationally, and domestically integrated adult community environments" (Brown, Nietupski, & Hamre-Nietupski, 1976, p. 8). Educators began to refer to skills and activities such as making purchases while shopping or learning to dress as "functional" because they related to this criterion of adult functioning. Because research on effective interventions was just emerging,

Donnellan (1984) suggested applying the *criterion of the least dangerous assumption* by choosing practices that would have the least dangerous effect on students' independent adult functioning. For example, it is less dangerous to assume that a student can use money skills in real community environments if he or she has opportunities to practice these skills in these contexts than it is to assume that generalization will occur. Donnellan and Neel (1986) proposed that the combination of the criteria of ultimate functioning and of the least dangerous assumption, although two separate concepts, could be used in evaluating program decisions.

In 1987, Meyer, Eichinger, and Park-Lee outlined a social validation study of program quality indicators in educational services for school-age students with severe disabilities. The survey respondents included four expert groups in the areas of (1) behavior therapy, (2) services for students who were deaf–blind, (3) mental retardation, and (4) severe disabilities (experts identified by TASH). In addition, stakeholders such as state special education directors and parents of students with disabilities were included in the sample. Respondents identified five criteria for best practice in providing services for students with severe disabilities, including (1) integration, (2) individualized professional practices and home–school instructional strategies, (3) staff development, (4) data-based instruction, and (5) criterion of ultimate functioning. Since this survey in the late 1980s, many experts in the field have built on these concepts to describe best practices for the field (Collins, 2007; Kennedy & Horn, 2004; Snell & Brown, 2006; Westling & Fox, 2004).

The quality indicators have evolved partly because educators have had new expectations for what students will learn. Browder, Spooner, Ahlgrim-Delzell, et al. (2003) and Browder et al. (2004) described the evolution of curricular expectations for students with severe disabilities. As shown in Figure 1.2, when the first public programs for students with severe disabilities were formed in the 1970s, educators adapted early childhood or infant curricula with the idea that education could be planned based on a student's "mental age." This developmental model was rejected in the 1980s with the emergence of the concept of the criterion of ultimate functioning. Applying this criterion, educators planned for functional life skills instruction, including teaching both in and for community settings. Social inclusion and self-determination were integrated with this functional curriculum in the 1990s. Educators planned ways for students to be full members of their schools, including learning with typical peers. They also promoted students' choice mak-

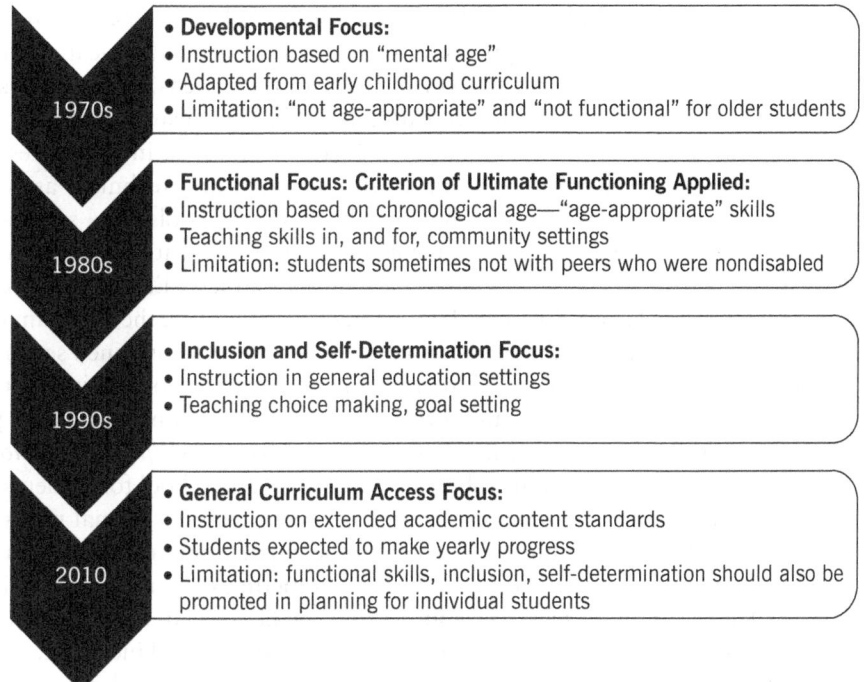

FIGURE 1.2. Changing expectations for students with severe disabilities.

ing, goal setting, and self-directed learning. Inclusion, self-determination, and functional skills all continue to be priorities in the current era. The newest thinking also is that students should have opportunities to learn general curriculum content.

Based on these changing expectations, on the research by Meyer et al. (1987), and on current writing by experts in severe disabilities (e.g., Collins, 2007; Kennedy & Horn, 2004; Snell & Brown, 2006; Westling & Fox, 2004), we would recommend the following eight criteria as current indicators of high-quality educational programs for students with severe disabilities: (1) inclusive practices, (2) positive home–school relationship, (3) collaborative teaming, (4) systematic instruction, (5) positive behavior support, (6) self-determination, (7) teaching academic skills, and (8) teaching functional skills.

Inclusive Practices

According to Alper and Ryndak (1996), full inclusion has been defined as "the practice of educating students with moderate to severe disabilities alongside their chronological age peers without disabilities in general classrooms within their home neighborhood schools" (p. 3). Full inclusion encompasses social and physical integration into activities that occur in school that are educational, recreational, and social. Inclusion, as opposed to full inclusion, refers to the "placement of special education students in general education settings" (Sailor & Roger, 2005, p. 503). Some students may be included for some portion of their school day. How much time students spend in general education settings is an individualized education plan (IEP) team placement decision, as described in Chapter 3.

The ideal is that all students with severe disabilities will be full members of their neighborhood schools, including having opportunities to learn in general education classes with instruction that has been developed to be inclusive of their needs. The reality is that only a small percentage of students with severe disabilities have inclusive school programs (Smith, 2007). This discrepancy may be due to a variety of factors, including resource allocation, professional development, administrative support, and technical assistance for planning inclusion. Given that research shows how some schools have successfully included students with severe disabilities as members of general education classes (Agran, Cavin, Wehmeyer, & Palmer, 2006; Giangreco, Dennis, Cloninger, Edelman, & Schattman, 1993; McDonnell, Mathot-Buckner, Thornson, & Fister, 2001), the IEP team needs a strong rationale for planning special education in a full-time self-contained setting.

An important part of this work is the planning needed to focus on the instructional priorities of the student with moderate and severe disabilities. Inclusion is more than planning for the student to be present in general educational settings (*temporal inclusion*). It also is more than encouraging social membership in the class and school for students with moderate and severe disabilities (*social inclusion*). To meet their educational needs, students also must have the opportunity to learn from the curriculum and to address their unique instructional needs (*instructional inclusion*). Sometimes the adapted curricular priorities of students with more severe disabilities and the fast-paced academic priorities of general education can seem to create a "mismatch" for instructional inclusion. Careful planning is needed to determine how to meet the individual needs of students with more severe disabilities in general educational settings.

Schools that want to promote the belonging of all students should begin by outlining what the outcomes will be once all students are included. Based on his earlier work, Giangreco (2006) outlined characteristics of inclusive education. First, students with disabilities attend the district school that they would attend if they were not disabled, appropriate supports are available, and all students are welcome in the general education program. Second, students with disabilities are educated with age-appropriate peers in classes in which the proportion of students with disabilities is related to the proportion in the community. Third, shared educational experiences take place in general education classes and integrated community settings. Fourth, students receive educational services that are individually designed to balance academic–functional and social–personal domains of learning.

In a review of the literature, Alper and Ryndak (1992) found that students with severe disabilities who are fully included have more opportunities for social interaction, more appropriate behavior models, improved communication and social skills, and more friendships. Teachers develop higher expectations as students access more age-appropriate curricular content. Finally, students may increase their chances for increased participation in lifelong integrated activities.

One of the challenges of providing inclusive programs for students with severe disabilities is identifying how students' needs for intensive instructional and personal support will be met. Ryndak (1996) suggests meeting instructional needs by using cooperative learning strategies, small-group instruction, and peer partnering with peer tutoring and study buddies. Research on peer supports shows this to be an especially viable strategy to support students in inclusive settings (Cushing & Kennedy, 1997, 2004). Carter, Cushing, Clark, and Kennedy (2005) conducted a study with three middle school students with severe disabilities and six general education students. Peers were taught strategies, including how to adapt materials, provide instruction on IEP goals, implement behavior plans, give feedback to the student, and promote communication between the students with disabilities and their peers in the classroom. Results indicated that students with disabilities increased social interaction when two peers were provided versus one peer, but this did not affect their interactions with other students in the class. Peer supports also increased the alignment of the student's activities with the general curriculum.

Home–School Collaboration

Chen and Miles (2004) note that "teachers not only must have instructional skills for teaching children but also must have the competency to work effectively with families" (p. 31). Although schools today appear to be child focused, there is a need to be more family focused and to utilize a family-centered approach when working with students with severe disabilities (Childre, 2004). Family and educator collaborative practices are more likely to be positive when a family-centered approach is used. According to Powell, Batsche, Ferro, Fox, and Dunlap (1997), major principles for establishing a family-centered approach are: (1) building trust, (2) maintaining open communication, (3) enabling and empowering family and student, and (4) using a collaborative problem-solving approach.

One way to build trust and open communication is to strive to understand and respect the family's cultural perspective. One way to build strong relationships with families is to gain more understanding about multicultural perspectives. Hall (1976), as cited in Browder and Lim (2001), uses the concept of "high-context" and "low-context" cultures to describe how communication patterns may differ. In a high-context culture, members will share a well-defined pattern of interaction through established hierarchies and situational cues, prefer nonconfrontational responses, and place greater value on personal style and relations. Even though high-context cultures place greater emphasis on well-defined roles and formality, their members also value a personal approach to communication and relations because they may need longer time to "warm up" to meeting and knowing others. There is a belief in high-context cultures that relationships take time and trust before personal disclosure can happen. Professionals who do not share this cultural perspective may judge parents from high-context cultures as evasive, passive, and "beating around the bush." In contrast, low-context cultures emphasize and encourage direct expressions of messages and feelings. European American cultures are generally low-context cultures. Freedom to say what one thinks is viewed as an individual right. Unlike high-context cultures, in which much significance is placed on the process of interaction before trust and personal rapport can be built, low-context cultures value interactions that focus on achieving desired outcomes through expedience, direction, and "getting the job done" (Hanson, Lynch, & Wayman, 1990). Members of high-context cultures may interpret such interactions as cold and impersonal. Hall's (1976; cited in Browder & Lim, 2001) schema is just one of many options for understanding how culture may influence communication.

Culture not only influences the style of communication but can also influence how families view and manage the student's disability (Gartner, Lipsky, & Turnbull, 1991). Mary (1990) found that Hispanic American mothers reported a self-sacrificing attitude and spousal denial of disabilities more than did individuals in some other ethnic groups. Marion (1980) found that Mexican American and African American parents were more likely to report feelings of protection and acceptance as opposed to shock and grief about their child's disability. Chan (1986) noted that some Asian families viewed disability as a source of shame. Harry (1992) and Fowler (1998) note that most Native American languages do not have words for disability and tend to be more inclusive of individuals with disabilities. Of course, individual members of an ethnic group may differ in their personal perspectives. For example, whereas some may find a disability to be a source of shame, others may be strong advocates for disability rights. One way to build trust with families and to understand their individual perspectives is to invite them to share their stories about how they have come to understand their child's disability. Professionals also need to remember that families have the most extensive history with, and knowledge of, the child. Through careful listening, the professional may gain insights about what motivates the student, what skills need to be developed, and what does not work or is not appropriate for the child's cultural context. Readers are encouraged to study resources such as Lynch and Hanson's (1998) book and to attend professional development workshops on cultural diversity to understand more about working with culturally diverse families.

PROFESSIONALS WHO HAVE FAMILY MEMBERS WITH DISABILITIES

Professionals who also have family members with severe disabilities have a unique perspective on the challenges that can exist in home–school communication. After attending many IEP meetings as a teacher or an expert, they may be confused to discover how much more difficult it can be to be heard as a parent or other family member. Expectations for parents to be fully participating members of the team may need to be cultivated. I (D. M. B.) once accompanied a colleague who was both a professional and a parent to an IEP meeting to make what seemed to be reasonable requests for transition planning. To our shock, the school system had selected a large conference table, invited extra people, and seated the two of us on one side and the twelve of them on the other. We did reach some good decisions that day, but it took some time to reestablish the trust that was strained by the context. When my niece was first diagnosed with a severe disability over 25 years ago, the team would not permit her parents to attend their multidisciplinary team meeting to review their findings but would permit me because of my credentials as a professional. I was not expected to contribute to the discussion, even though I had spent many more hours with her than anyone in the room and had training in infant assessment. I am now grateful for these experiences because they caused me to reexamine my own professional views about parents as partners.

Collaborative Teaming

For students with severe disabilities to experience school success, a certain degree of collaborative teaming among professionals is required (Ryndak, 1996). A collaborative team has been defined by Ryndak (1996) as "a group of equal individuals who voluntarily work together in a spirit of willingness and mutual reward to problem solve and accomplish one or more common and mutually agreed upon goals by contributing their own knowledge and skills and participating in shared decision making, while focusing on the efficiency of the whole team" (p. 85). A collaborative team functions differently than does a transdisciplinary team in that the members focus on the student's needs and work together to accomplish their goals as a team rather than individually (Thousand & Villa, 2000). In collaborative teaming, professionals brainstorm to meet a student's needs in many environments, including school, home, and the community. The team shares roles and responsibilities and treats the student as a "whole" rather than just focusing on the student's needs in their particular disciplines. Collaborative teams plan services in locations that would be considered "natural." For example, collaborative services are delivered in locations at which the target skill may naturally occur (e.g., an occupational therapist works with the student while he or she is eating in the cafeteria) rather than working on skills in isolation.

One of the benefits of collaborative teaming for students with severe disabilities is that the students have an increased number of practice trials during the instructional day, which may result in a faster acquisition and generalization of skills. A second benefit is that collaborative teams provide information to parents relative to instructional strategies and applications to real-life situations. A third benefit is that collaborative teams problem solve and provide technical and moral support to each other, to the classroom teacher, and to families and students (Armbruster & Howe, 1985, Ferguson, Meyer, Jeanchild, Juniper, & Zingo, 1992). The use of collaborative teaming, including cross-disciplinary instruction and flexible scheduling, has often been recommended as a best practice for this population of students (Ryndak, 1996; Snell & Brown, 2006; Westling & Fox, 2004).

Evidence-Based Instructional Practices

Students with severe disabilities may acquire new skills through a variety of instructional methods, as described in Chapter 4. One of the most effective strategies found in the research is systematic instruction. Systematic instruction has been defined as "teaching focused on specific, measurable responses that may either be discrete (singular) or a response chain (e.g., task analysis), and that are established through the use of defined methods of prompting and feedback based on the principles and research of applied behavior analysis" (Browder, 2001, p. 95). One aspect of systematic instruction is using a defined prompting and fading schedule to promote acquisition of a new response. For example, the system of least prompts refers to a hierarchy in which a teacher presents a series of prompts from least to most intrusive. If there is no response or an incorrect response, prompts are then given from the least to the most intrusive until the student gives the correct response (Ault, Wolery, Doyle, & Gast, 1989). Doyle, Wolery, Ault, and Gast (1988) found that the system of least prompts was successful in teaching students of different ages and with a variety of diagnoses tasks across various domains. Demchak's (1990) review identified four methods for prompt fading that included not only the system of least prompts but also most-to-least prompts, graduated guidance, and time delay. Each of these systems is described in detail in Chapter 4. As noted in this chapter, systematic instruction is not confined to one-to-one instruction or self-contained settings but can be used in the community, in general education classes, and in small-group contexts.

Positive Behavior Support Strategies

Positive behavior support (PBS) has been used as an effective practice for managing challenging behaviors in students with disabilities, including severe intellectual disability (Cooper, Heron, & Heward, 2007). In general, PBS involves using educative strategies to decrease inappropriate behaviors and increase appropriate behaviors (Horner, Albin, Todd, & Sprague, 2006). PBS strategies have been proven to be effective with students with developmental disabilities (Carr, Dunlap, et al., 1999), including severe intellectual disability (Snell & Brown, 2006) and autism (Horner, Carr, Strain, Todd, & Reed, 2002). Snell (2005) reported that although PBS has experienced success, there is still a research-to-practice gap for students with severe disabilities.

Carr, Dunlap, et al. (1999) conducted a comprehensive review of 107 studies involving PBS. Two hundred and twenty-two participants, with the largest percentage having mental retardation, were identified in the studies between the years 1985 and 1996. The investigation focused on the following variables: (1) demographics, (2) assessment, (3) interventions, and (4) outcomes. Results of the comprehensive review indicated that the field has been growing over the years, primarily in the areas of assessment and interventions focused on remediating environmental deficiencies. PBS strategies can be utilized for people with serious behavioral problems and are effective in reducing behavioral problems in one-half to two-thirds of cases. Success rates appear to improve to almost double when the intervention is predicated on the functional assessment. Chapter 12 provides more information on PBS.

Self-Determination

The importance of self-determination for students with disabilities has been substantiated in the literature, although students with severe disabilities have not always had the opportunity to learn these skills (Algozzine, Browder, Karvonen, Test, & Wood, 2001; Martin, Van Dycke, Greene, et al., 2006; Wehmeyer & Schwartz, 1998b; Wood, Fowler, Uphold, & Test, 2005). Self-determination has been defined as "a combination of skills, knowledge, and beliefs that enable a person to engage in goal-directed, self-regulated, autonomous behavior" (Field, Martin, Miller, Ward, & Wehmeyer, 1998, p. 2). These skills include (1) choice making, (2) decision making, (3) goal setting and attainment, (4) problem solving, (5) self-awareness, (6) self-regulation, and (7) participation in the IEP process (Agran, Blanchard, Wehmeyer, & Hughes, 2001; Allen, Smith, Test, Flowers, & Wood, 2001; Van Reusen & Bos, 1990). Wehmeyer (2005) has proposed that the definition of self-determination for students with severe disabilities be that "self-determined behavior refers to volitional acts that enable one to act as the primary causal agent in one's life and to maintain or improve one's quality of life" (p. 117).

Regardless of the severity of disability, all individuals should be active participants as much as possible in exercising choice over the decisions affecting their lives (Brown, Belz, Corsi, & Wenig, 1993). According to Wehmeyer and Schwartz (1998b), people who are self-determined have better outcomes related to their quality of life. Research has demonstrated that students of varying age ranges and disabilities can be taught self-determination and self-advocacy skills (Algozzine et al., 2001; Wood et al., 2005).

General Curriculum Access

For students with disabilities to learn general curriculum content, the instructional plan will need to have a strong focus on academic domains such as language arts, mathematics, science, and social studies. The overarching topic of general curriculum access was addressed by Spooner, Dymond, and Kennedy (2006) in a special issue of *Research and*

Practice for Persons with Severe Disabilities. In that issue, Spooner, Dymond, Smith, and Kennedy (2006) described some of what we knew at that point in time and what we needed to know about accessing the general curriculum. They delineated approaches (i.e., peer supports, self-determination, universal design for learning [UDL], and teaching and assessing content standards), in addition to benefits and pitfalls (e.g., promise, varying definitions, evolving approaches, impact on postschool outcomes). As Browder, Wakeman, Spooner, Ahlgrim-Delzell, and Algozzine (2006) note, teaching academics simply because students can learn them is not the primary rationale. Instead, it is important to realize that these educational opportunities increase competence for adult living. Students with disabilities can learn and do much more than we once believed. With increased learning, students have increased opportunities. For example, having some reading ability increases job options. Providing academic content instruction also promotes educational equality. Students who are nondisabled do not have to master skills such as making their beds before learning such skills as how to read. Similarly, students with severe disabilities should not be held to a double standard of having to learn all life skills before learning academic content. Gaining skills in general curriculum content can also increase opportunities for self-determination by providing students with more tools to gain information and demonstrate ability.

In teaching academic content, the focus is on teaching the standards for the students' age and grade level (i.e., aligning instruction with age-appropriate academic content; Browder, Spooner, Wakeman, Trela, & Baker, 2006). Although students may lack many basic skills, by applying what skills they do have, they may be able to access the grade-appropriate content and continue to develop literacy and numeracy. For example, students who cannot yet read may access a sixth-grade novel through a read-aloud of a text summary. The student might use existing picture identification skills to indicate his or her understanding of the passage (Browder, Trela, & Jimenez, 2007).

Unfortunately, students with severe disabilities have sometimes lacked the educational opportunity to learn any academics. Koppenhaver and Yoder (1993) reported that students with severe disabilities did not have sufficient opportunities to participate in literacy activities in school. The reasons for this could be the low expectations that children with severe disabilities could learn to read and the difficulty in making reading materials accessible for this population of students. Much of the research in math instruction for students with moderate to severe disabilities also has reflected expectations that students could learn only a few functional skills of money management. Models for teaching grade-level content, especially in science and social studies, are only now emerging. This book includes chapters on each of the major content domains—language arts, mathematics, science, and social studies—as well as an additional chapter on teaching comprehension across the content areas.

Functional Skills and Transition

Functional skills are those that are used in daily living in the home and community and on the job. Westling and Fox (2004) recommend that the teaching of functional skills should occur on a daily basis and that functional objectives should be incorporated into a student's IEP. Functional skills promote the criterion of ultimate functioning for students to become as independent as possible. Brown et al. (1976) delineated four domains for functional curriculum planning, including community, domestic, vocational, and recreational skills. As students get older, home and community skills grow in importance, and the focus becomes increased independence in the home and community (Bambara, Browder, & Koger, 2006). Some recommended practices for teaching functional skills follow: (1) Objectives should be focused on increasing independence or self-determination while teaching integrated skills. (2) Skills should be taught in the home, school, or community environment (naturalistic settings) within functional contexts. (3) Skills should be taught that focus not only on initial acquisition of skills but also on maintenance and generalization of skills. (4) Data should be kept on student performance, and results of the data should drive the decisions to change instruction (Westling & Fox, 2004).

Teaching functional skills is one way to prepare students to transition to adult living. A high-quality program for students with severe disabilities will also include other areas of transition planning. Although the unemployment rate for students with severe disabilities is extremely high (Newman, Wagner, Cameto, & Knokey, 2009; Wehman, Kregel, & Seyfarth, 1985b), and although there is limited empirical evidence suggesting that transition practices lead to successful adult outcomes for students with the most severe disabilities (Baer, McMahan, & Flexer, 2004; Inge & Moon, 2006), individuals with severe disabilities have demonstrated that they can work community jobs (Test et al., 2009; Wagner, Marder, et al., 2003; Wagner, Cadwallader, & Marder, 2003; Wehman, Hill, Wood, & Parent, 1987; White & Weiner, 2004). A high-quality transition plan will include instruction in job skills, incorporating community-based experiences for older students. Wehman, Moon, Everson, Wood, and Barcus (1988) recommend that, in addition to employment, transition planning include consideration of postsecondary education, residential plans, financial income needs, recreation and leisure, medical needs, transportation, advocacy or legal needs, personal, home, and money management, and personal counseling (e.g., sex education). Planning across these areas includes not only considering skills needed for the IEP, as described in Chapter 3, but also creating opportunities to learn to apply skills in real-life contexts.

LEGAL REQUIREMENTS FOR EDUCATION OF STUDENTS WITH SEVERE DISABILITIES

The opinions of advocates and experts about what characterizes high-quality programs for students with disabilities have helped to shape current federal law and policy. Federal law governing students with disabilities has guaranteed all students with disabilities a free appropriate public education since the Education for All Handicapped Children Act was passed in 1975. The Individuals with Disabilities Education Improvement Act of 2004 (IDEA) continued to guarantee this right. The special education services to be provided are outlined through the development of an IEP (described in Chapter 3). Like earlier versions of this federal law, IDEA (2004) provided procedural safeguard provisions for parents (20 U.S.C. § 615). Parents have recourse, through dispute resolution, to file a petition for an administrative hearing if they believe a school district did not follow legal procedures or if they disagreed with district decisions involving identification, evaluation, or placement of the child (Yell, 2006).

Methodology is a prominent dispute area, particularly for young students with autism (Katsiyannis & Maag, 2001; Mandlawitz, 2002). The courts across the nation have consistently deferred to the educational teams regarding methodology decisions (*Lachman v.*

Illinois State Board of Education, 1988), but costly litigation continues to occur regarding methodological considerations, particularly for young children with autism. A second area of dispute may occur when a parent believes that his or her child has been denied a free appropriate public education (FAPE; Drasgow, Yell, & Robinson, 2001). The FAPE standard was first defined in the *Rowley* case as being "reasonably calculated to enable a child to receive educational benefit" (*Board of Education of the Hendrick Hudson Central School District, Westchester County, et al. v. Rowley*, 1982). This standard has been tested repeatedly in cases involving students with significant cognitive disabilities and the provision of both special education and related services.

A third area of dispute may occur when parents disagree with school districts regarding a child's placement in his or her least restrictive environment (LRE; DeMitchell & Kerns, 1997; Thomas & Rapport, 1998; Yell & Drasgow, 1999). According to IDEA (2004), the definition of least restrictive environment is as follows: "to the maximum extent appropriate, children with disabilities, including children in public or private institutions and other care facilities, are educated with children who are not disabled." The law also states that students should be removed from the regular education environment "only when the nature and severity of the disability of the child is such that education in regular classes with supplementary aids and services cannot be achieved satisfactorily" [20 U.S.C.§ 612 (a)(5)(A)].

School districts enter into litigation with parents of students with disabilities for a variety of reasons (Yell & Drasgow, 2000). Many of these disputes can be addressed by developing high-quality programs for students (described in the next section). For example, a major area of dispute may occur when a parent believes that his or her child has been denied FAPE (Drasgow, Yell, & Robinson, 2001). According to IDEA (2004), FAPE is defined as

> special education and related services that (A) have been provided at public expense, under public supervision and without charge; (B) meet the standards of the state educational agency; (C) include an appropriate preschool, elementary school, or secondary school education in the State involved; and (D) are provided in conformity with the individualized education program required under 614(d). [20 U.S.C. § 602 (9)(A-D)]

Parents also may disagree with a school district regarding a child's placement in the least restrictive environment (LRE; DeMitchell & Kerns, 1997; Thomas & Rapport, 1998; Yell & Drasgow, 1999). According to IDEA (2004), least restrictive environment is defined as " to the maximum extent appropriate, children with disabilities, including children in public or private institutions and other care facilities, are educated with children who are not disabled." The law also reflects that students should not be removed from the regular education environment except "only when the nature and severity of the disability of the child is such that education in regular classes with supplementary aids and services cannot be achieved satisfactorily" [20 U.S.C.§ 612 (a)(5)(A)].

According to Yell (1995), five elements related to inclusion are grounded in federal regulations: (1) The individual needs of the student determine his or her least restrictive environment. (2) Districts are not required to place a student in an integrated setting before recommending a segregated placement. (3) Each district should make a continuum of alternative placements available to students. (4) If students are placed in segregated placements, then they should be integrated to the maximum extent appropriate to meet their individual needs. (5) The potential disruptive effect on the students without disabilities should be considered.

The courts have considered many of these elements when making decisions in LRE cases involving students with severe disabilities. For example, in *Oberti v. Board of Education of the Borough of Clementon School District* (1993), the third U.S. Circuit Court of Appeals ordered full inclusion of a young child with Down syndrome because, it said, the district had reached the decision regarding a segregated placement without considering the range of supplemental aids and services. The court concluded that the use of the supplemental aids and services might have helped the student to be successful in a general education placement. In this case, the court considered three factors in making its decision. First, it considered whether or not the district made a reasonable effort to accommodate the child in a general education classroom. Second, it investigated what educational benefits were available to the child in the general educational classroom if appropriate supplemental aids and services were provided as compared with the potential benefits that would have been provided in a segregated class. Third, it questioned whether there were any possible negative effects on the education of students in the class if the child were included. In addition, the court considered the young age of the student (age 8) as a significant factor in favor of inclusion.

In *Sacramento City Unified School District Board of Education v. Rachel H.* (1994), the court considered similar factors as in *Oberti*, but it also considered the cost of including a student in a general education classroom. In this case, the district was unable to demonstrate that placing the student in general education classes would burden the district financially. Crockett and Kaufmann (1999) refer to LRE, FAPE, and evidence-based practices as the "holy trinity" of special education law. A key concept in the literature is that following the legal tenets of LRE and FAPE may not be all that is required of districts to prevent disputes. Researchers in the field of special education and special education law make reference to the fact that validated or evidence-based practices should be followed by school districts as well (Heflin & Simpson, 1998; Crockett, 2000; Crockett & Kaufmann, 1999; Etscheidt, 2003; Yell & Drasgow, 2000). Chapter 4 provides information on evidence-based practices for students with severe disabilities.

Litigation may also occur in the area of related services (Bartlett, 2000). According to IDEA (2004), "the term related services means transportation, and such developmental, corrective, and other supportive services . . . as may be required to assist a child to benefit from special education." Some examples of related services outlined in the statute are speech–language pathology, audiology, interpreting services, psychological services, occupational and physical therapy, therapeutic recreation services, social work, nursing, counseling, orientation and mobility, medical services designed for evaluative purposes [20 U.S.C.§ 602(26)(A)]. In *Irving Independent School District v. Tatro* (1984), the U.S. Supreme Court ruled that clean, intermittent catheterization for a child with spina bifida was considered a related service and not an excluded medical service under federal law. In this landmark case, the U.S. Supreme Court established a "bright line" test stating that districts must provide health-care-related services if the child needs these services during the day so that he or she may attend school and benefit from education. The services must be able to be performed by nonphysicians and would therefore be considered a related service under IDEA rather than a medical service (Norlin, 2007).

Finally, one of the most frequent sources of litigation has been parents' desire for a specific type of instruction for young students with autism (Katsiyannis & Maag, 2001; Mandlawitz, 2002). Parents' requests for discrete trial training based on Lovaas therapy (discrete-trial training in a highly structured environment) often results in school districts entering into litigious situations with parents because of the cost of the therapy. Etscheidt (2003) reviewed 68 legal cases published between 1997 and 2002 representing 28 states involving parents of students with autism who have challenged, through litigation, the appropriateness of districts' proposed programs for their children. Results of the investigation revealed three major factors that influenced the determination that an IEP had been reasonably calculated to confer educational benefit under the *Rowley* standard: First, the goals developed should match the needs identified by the evaluation. Second, the IEP team participants should be qualified to make appropriate placement decisions for students identified with autism. Third, the methodology selected by the district should be able to achieve goals outlined in the child's IEP.

Educators who are planning for students with disabilities need to remember three important points about the law and potential for litigation. First, the best way to avoid litigation is to provide a high-quality program using the quality indicators described in the prior section. Rather than focusing on what minimal standards will suffice, educators should do strategic planning for continuous quality enhancement. Second, when disputes with parents occur, the optimal starting point is to resolve differences through a well-implemented IEP meeting. If the issues cannot be resolved, school systems still have two options prior to a hearing. Under IDEA (2004), there are now three distinct types of dispute resolution including: *resolution, mediation,* or an *administrative hearing* [20 U.S.C § 615 (2)(b)(5-7); (2)(e)(2)(a); (2)(f)(2)(1)(A)]. Both resolution and mediation are legislative processes designed to settle disagreements between parents and school districts before a hearing occurs. Hazelkorn, Packard, and Douvanis (2008) found that 76% of districts surveyed believed that mediation permits a better discussion of the issues than an administrative hearing. Third, both educators and parents can benefit from training in team collaboration. Communication breakdowns may be avoided by establishing that all are committed to the student's education and by ensuring that participants have specific skills in conflict resolution. If differences cannot be resolved, there may still be the increased likelihood of both parties accepting a third party's assistance in resolution.

DEVELOPING HIGH-QUALITY SERVICES FOR STUDENTS WITH SEVERE DISABILITIES

Educators may realize that the services for students with severe disabilities in their classroom, school, or school system lack some of the criteria experts propose for quality. To begin the process of strategic planning for quality enhancement, the first step is to conduct a self-study. The quality indicators proposed in this chapter can create a checklist for planning this evaluation, as shown in Figure 1.3.

Since the 1980s, American businesses and schools have considered principles of "total quality management" (TQM) to enhance their work (Marchese, 1991). TQM is both a philosophy and a set of tools for creating a "culture of quality." It requires a shift in thinking from individualism and "If it works, don't fix it" to teamwork and constant improvement. The principles of TQM can be helpful in responding to the outcomes of a self-study. The following are some of the principles of TQM with examples of how each can be applied when responding to data received from alternate assessments of students with moderate and severe disabilities.

Quality indicator	Our strengths	Our weaknesses	Our goals for this planning period
Promotion of inclusion for all students			
Communication between home and school			
Collaboration as a team			
Positive behavior support			
Evidence-based instruction			
Access to and learning in general curriculum/ alternate assessment outcomes			
Student learning of functional skills/ transition outcomes			
Our other criteria:			

FIGURE 1.3. Checklist of indicators of program quality for students with severe disabilities.

Making Quality the Goal

The starting point in quality enhancement is to set the goal of having a high-quality program. When disappointing results are obtained in a self-study or external evaluation, energy can be wasted belittling the evaluation itself or making excuses for the failure to achieve the standards. Although there may be real issues with the evaluation and resources available, a team that is committed to excellence will respond to these challenges with problem solving rather than not responding at all.

Customer-Driven Services

A common TQM expression is "delight the customer." The goal of excellence is to surpass customer needs and expectations, turning to customers themselves to define quality. Encouraging self-determination and family-centered services are two ways to make special education services customer driven. The district or school can form a quality enhancement team that includes families and students with disabilities to develop program improvement plans.

Continuous Improvement

In TQM, quality enhancement is not episodic but continuous. Planning teams are always seeking ways to do their work better. There is no finish line in the journey toward quality. Once formed, a quality enhancement team will become an ongoing part of planning for the educational programs of a school or district. Also, these teams will not be dead committees but dynamic groups who solve specific problems and are empowered to make things happen.

Making Processes Work Better

As a problem-solving team, those most directly involved with the process need to be included in creating solutions. For example, teachers, therapists, paraprofessionals, and others who work with students with moderate and severe disabilities often can recognize what led to a disappointing alternate assessment or transition outcome. For example, was there a mismatch between the curriculum and the performance indicators of the alternate assessment? Were there no opportunities for community-based job training? Through these discussions, the team can create specific action steps to improve program quality.

SUMMARY

Although special education, at some level, has been around for about 200 years (dating back to Itard's work in France with Victor, the Wild Boy of Aveyron, in 1797), the first legal requirements for public educational services were enacted less than 35 years ago. Prior to the mid-1970s students with severe disabilities were categorically excluded from public school programs. With the law came labels, and labels have been viewed by many as a double-edged sword, because people are unique individuals. This is especially true for individuals with severe disabilities, as they probably are more different than alike; but services cannot be accessed without a label (federal law requires labeling to be eligible for special education services). Person-first language is important when referring to individuals with disabilities, as they are people first! Organizations serving and advocating for individuals with disabilities (e.g., AAIDD, TASH, ARC) have changed their names over the course of their organizational lives in an attempt to keep pace with the times and reflect current terminology.

Individuals with severe disabilities will need the best quality educational services in order to function as independently as possible as adults (e.g., full educational opportunity to promote adult independent functioning). As a consequence of changing expectations and research specifically aimed at increasing both academic and life skill functioning, we have recommended eight criteria as quality indicators: (1) inclusive practices, (2) positive home–school relationship, (3) collaborative teaming, (4) systematic instruction, (5) positive behavior support, (6) self-determination, (7) teaching academic skills, and (8) teaching functional skills.

Advocates and experts have significantly influenced the legal requirements for eligibility and reception of educational services for students with severe disabilities. Unfortunately, the provision of many services (e.g., FAPE) has been decided by litigation. An overarching goal is to provide high-quality services to improve quality of life for individuals with severe disabilities.

APPLICATIONS

1. Go to your state's education website and find out what terms are used for students with disabilities in your state. Which of these apply to students with severe disabilities? To what extent does your state use the most current terminology?

2. Watch how media (television, movies, Internet) describe individuals with disabilities. To what extent do the media use the most current terms? People-first language? How might you influence the media's portrayal of individuals with disabilities?

3. Interview the parents of a student with severe disabilities about their child's history. What have been their challenges and joys? How did they discover the child had a disability? What are the most important qualities and abilities of their child that they want others to recognize? If possible, choose a family whose culture differs from your own.

4. Using the quality indicator checklist shown in Figure 1.3, rate the strengths and weaknesses of the school system in which you live or work. What would you recommend as goals for the future?

5. Interview a special education administrator about the goal of full inclusion for students with severe disabilities. Does their school system have students who are fully included, and, if so, what made this possible? If not, what do they consider to be the barriers?

CHAPTER 2

Alternate Assessment

DIANE M. BROWDER, FRED SPOONER, AND SHAWNEE WAKEMAN

Some schools have a banner across their entryway announcing that the school is a "School of Excellence." The local papers provide "report cards" on school performance. These are signs of the current educational focus on school accountability. Schools must meet state and federal requirements for students to show proficiency on state standards. This proficiency is measured through large-scale state assessments. Anna is a student with severe disabilities who goes to Conifer Elementary School. Her performance also "counts" in the school's accountability, but she will take an alternate assessment based on alternate achievement standards. Some students with disabilities in her school will take the general assessment that all students take. A few will take these tests with accommodations, such as extended time. All students, including Anna, will have assessments that are derived from the state's academic content standards for their grade level. This chapter describes how the IEP team decides which assessment students will take and the characteristics of alternate assessments based on alternate achievement standards.

To understand the intense requirements of assessments that most schools now must administer, it is helpful to review some recent history in school reform. As Bolt and Roach (2009) describe, Americans have experienced several waves of school reform focusing on such goals as organizational structures, compensatory education, and special curricular innovations (e.g., "new" math). Two of the long-standing goals of reform have been to close the achievement gap for low-achieving students and to prepare all students for the workplace.

The most recent wave of school reform has focused on the articulation of standards that all students should achieve. By the end of the 1990s, most states had educational standards, assessments to measure these standards, and a system for school accountability. These systems were a part of the "standards-based reform" of America's educational system that occurred over a period of more than 40 years. This reform movement can be traced back to the Elementary and Secondary Education Act (ESEA, 1965), which created the services that many teachers now know as "Title I." Some years later, the report *A Nation at Risk* (National Commission on Excellence in Education, 1983) criticized the problems with America's educational system, including the substandard content and low expectations for what students should learn in classrooms. In response to these criticisms, Goals 2000: Educate America Act (1994) articulated eight goals for the educational system related to academic standards, student progress, and student support. One important requirement within this act was for states to use national standards created by subject-based national organizations (e.g., National Council of Teachers of Mathematics [NCTM], National Council of Teachers of English [NCTE]) as a guide for their own state standards (Watt, 2005). The Improving America's Schools Act (1994), a reauthorization of ESEA, reinforced the efforts of Title I, which mandated holding all students to high standards, including the use of state-developed content and performance standards and an evaluation system of yearly student progress. But it was not until the reauthorization of the IDEA in 1997 that all students with disabilities were required to have access to the general curriculum and to be included in state and district large-scale assessments. This initiative was continued in the 2004 IDEA. Finally, the reauthorization of ESEA, the No Child Left Behind Act of 2001 (NCLB, 2002), reinforced the inclusion of students with disabilities in standards-based reform, as these students were identified as a subgroup to be measured for adequate yearly progress (AYP) in grades 3–8 and high school as a part of the state accountability system. This act gave states flexibility to assess students with disabilities using alternate assessments based on modified or alternate achievement standards. This chapter focuses on alternate assessments based on alternate achievement standards, assessments designed to measure the performance of students with significant cognitive disabilities.

CHECK FOR UNDERSTANDING

Did you take large-scale assessments in elementary or secondary school? What were they called? Do you know if and how students with disabilities were included? Have policies changed since you were in school? How might you find out?

THE CHARACTERISTICS OF STATES' ALTERNATE ASSESSMENTS

All states have developed alternate assessments based on alternate achievement standards (AA–AAS). One way to understand these systems is to go to a state's education website and look for information on accountability. Most of these websites have links to information on AA–AAS. The following questions may be useful in discovering the policies for your state.

• *Question 1: How will the alternate assessment information be used?* Some states focus assessment primarily on *school* accountability (e.g., schoolwide contingencies based on student scores), others target *student* accountability (e.g., graduation or promotion contingent on test scores), and others incorporate both. NCLB (2002) required that all students' scores be included in determining the percentage of students who had made AYP. All assessments have some definition of proficiency. For example, students might need to get 83% of items correct on a math assessment. Students who score at or above this cut score are considered proficient in this content area; those who score below are not. Assessment scores are divided into at least three categories to show how close to the proficiency target students score (e.g., "distinguished" for scores in the defined above-target range, "proficient" for scores in the defined target range, and "novice" for scores in the defined below-target range). If there are 100 students in a grade level in a school and 75 score at or above the proficiency score in a content area (e.g., mathematics), then a public report is made that 75% of students were proficient in this content. Depending on the percentage of students who were required to be proficient at that grade level for that school, the report will discuss whether students in that grade at the school met the requirements of AYP (e.g., if it was necessary that 75% of fourth graders were proficient in mathematics to meet AYP, then it would be reported for the school that the fourth-grade students met AYP in mathematics). NCLB (2002) required that reporting of AYP be further specified for specific subgroups, such as students with disabilities, specific ethnic groups, and English language learners.

Most of the students with disabilities in the above-mentioned school probably took the mathematics assessment with or without some accommodations, such as extended time (see Byrnes, 2008, for information regarding accommodations). For example, suppose that there are 100 students in grade 3 at the school. Of those students, 10 have disabilities. Nine of the ten students took the general assessment, and five of those students met the level of proficiency. Some (in this example, one) students may not have been able to participate in the general assessment with accommodations, so they participated in an AA–AAS. The format of this assessment probably differs from the general assessment, this situation is described later in the chapter. Whatever the format, some level of proficiency was also specified, and each student met or did not meet this standard. If one student in the school took the AA–AAS and met proficiency, his or her score would count toward the proficiency level set to reach the overall AYP for mathematics for that grade level. When a school meets its target for proficiency, there often is some form of public recognition (e.g., the designation of a "School of Excellence"). When a school does not meet this goal, there may be the need for some changes in the school, such as curricular reform, professional development, or enhanced tutoring programs for students.

Sometimes the assessments are also used for student accountability, such as requirements for promotion and graduation. For students taking the AA-AAS, the individual student's performance may provide information for IEP planning. For example, a student who has fallen below expectations for proficiency in mathematics may need additional opportunities to use technology, to gain core math skills, or to learn content related to the grade level.

• *Question 2: Who takes AA–AAS in my state? What alternative might students take, and who decides?* Eligibility guidelines concerning who can participate in the AA-AAS versus the general assessment vary from state to state. Pennsylvania (Pennsylvania Department of Education, 2010) requires that the student be in grades 3–8 or 11 and have a significant cognitive disability. The student must also require intensive instruction to learn, extensive adaptations and supports to participate in daily life, and substantial modifications to the general education curriculum. He or she must also participate in the general education curriculum in a way that differs substantially in form and substance from that of other students. Federal guidelines forbid using the student's diagnosis or disability label as an eligibility criterion. Although many students with moderate and severe developmental disabilities do participate in AA–AAS, a state cannot make an a priori assumption that all will do so. Instead, the IEP team decides how each student will participate in statewide assessments. Federal guidelines allow states to offer five options to IEP teams, as shown in Table 2.1. Not all states have all options as shown.

Alternate assessments that will be measured against alternate achievement standards are for students with "significant cognitive disabilities." Although federal law does not define the characteristics of these students using traditional disability categories, there is some research related to the characteristics of the students who are participating in the AA–AAS. In a survey of special education teachers in three states, Towles-Reeves, Kearns, Kleinert, and Kleinert (2007) asked about the characteristics of students who participated in the AA–AAS. Teachers indicated that many students used symbolic communication (63% or more), could read sight words or simple sentences (33% or more), and could solve computational problems with or without a calculator (37% or more). Teachers also indicated that most students considered for the survey did not have vision (15% or less), hearing (6% or less), or motor (24% or less) concerns.

• *Question 3: What will be assessed?* Many states' first alternate assessments focused on functional domains such as leisure, daily living, vocational, and self-help skills, which may or may not have had any relationship to the academic content standards expected for the general population (Thompson & Thurlow, 2001). A few years later, states were forced to rethink the content of their alternate assessments. With the implementation of NCLB (2002), this population of students was required to participate in AA–AAS (as clarified in the December 9, 2003, final rule; U.S. Department of Education, 2003) that measured student performance in the academic content areas of math, reading, and science. States continued to have the flexibility to decide what components or standards would be used to measure student performance. Thompson, Johnstone, Thurlow, and Altman (2005) surveyed state directors of exceptional-children programs about the content of their AA–AAS. Very few states ($n = 4$) reported using anything other than academic content standards in 2003–2004 to define the content of the items within the AA–AAS.

TABLE 2.1. Assessment Options Offered by States to IEP Teams

Assessment option	Must states offer this option for students with disabilities?
General assessment	Yes—required
General assessment with accommodations	Yes—required
Alternate assessment measured against grade-level achievement standards	No—optional
Alternate assessment measured against modified achievement standards	No—optional
Alternate assessment measured against alternate achievement standards	Yes—required

With the focus on the core academic content areas that is prevalent in today's alternate assessments, educators will likely find assessments with content in math, language arts, and science. Some will have additional areas of content to be assessed, such as social studies. Most will parallel their state's general assessment. For example, if eighth graders take general assessments in reading, writing, and mathematics, the alternate assessment for students with significant cognitive disabilities will likely focus on content that links to eighth-grade standards from these areas also. Many states define how grade-level content standards will be extended for students who take AA–AAS. This information may be called "extended standards" or "curricular frameworks." One of the most important tasks for a teacher who will have students taking the AA–AAS is to identify the appropriate grade-level standards and any extensions for ongoing instructional planning (for more information, see Chapter 3 on IEPs).

Although the content will align, the target for achievement will differ. Some prioritization will occur in creating the AA–AAS to focus on the most essential standards and alternative ways of showing proficiency. For example, if a content standard says that students will identify points on a coordinate plane, the alternate assessment task might include x and y axes with smaller number ranges (e.g., 1–10), picture cues (e.g., people for number of people), and manipulatives for showing the answer (e.g., chip placed on graph vs. pencil dot). In some states, these tasks are created by test developers or vendors and assigned to all students in the state. In others, the tasks are developed by teachers, and evidence of student performance is included in a portfolio. Still others use some combination of tasks, such as offering a task bank from which teachers select what to assess.

• *Question 4: How will the alternate assessment be conducted?* Roeber (2002) described three major types of alternate assessment: (1) performance assessments, (2) portfolios, and (3) checklists. For a performance assessment, the state creates an alternate assessment with preselected tasks that are given to all students. Teachers receive the assessment during some window of time and must complete the tasks with their students before a deadline. The advantages of these systems are that the teacher does not need to create the assessment and that the tasks are likely well aligned to the content priorities within the state. The disadvantage is that when the IEP team prioritizes the content for instruction, it may not match what the state decides is most critical for the assessment. Sometimes this disadvantage is addressed by giving the tasks early in the school year. Other states offer information on priorities. In the second format, portfolio assessments, the teacher selects the content of the assessments following some state guidelines. The portfolio may include data sheets, student work samples, and other permanent products. The advantage of this approach is that the tasks can be derived directly from instruction, supported by the student's IEP, and used for ongoing instructional decision making. The disadvantages include the amount of time required to build the portfolio and the chance of misinterpretation or misunderstanding (e.g., lack of alignment) of the standards in the tasks by the teachers. States often address these disadvantages through professional development. A third format type is the use of a state-developed checklist. In this model, the teacher summarizes performance previously observed during classroom instruction and assessments. The advantages of the checklist are that it can be the least time-consuming and that the items can be aligned with standards. The disadvantage is that checklists may not reflect actual student performance, as they can be subjective. States address this disadvantage by having two licensed individuals familiar with the student complete the checklist and/or include evidence of student performance for certain tasks with the checklist. Thompson et al. (2005) reported that in 1999, 28 states used a portfolio or body-of-evidence format to assess student performance (typically teacher developed). By 2005, only 12 states reported using portfolios, 13 reported using a body-of-evidence format with a standardized set of performance-based items (performance assessment), and 7 reported using a rating scale or checklist format. Table 2.2 provides examples of these different alternate assessment formats.

- *Question 5: How will the alternate assessment be scored?* Three primary methods are used to score the alternate assessments: (1) teachers score their own assessments, (2) other teachers scores the assessments (e.g., at a state-organized scoring event), and (3) someone not involved in the assessment conducts the scoring (e.g., a test coordinator in the school system; a test company the state hires). Early research suggested that there may have been issues with the reliability of teacher-scored alternate assessment (Kleinert, Kearns, & Kennedy, 1997). Reliability can be improved by having clearly defined scoring criteria and providing training in the application of these criteria.

Some states also use a second observer who takes data concurrently as the teacher assesses and scores the students. In addition, other states use an independent second rater for checklist assessments, as described earlier. This procedure can promote more reliable scoring and discourage biased or dishonest scoring.

- *Question 6: What evidence exists that the scores of an alternate assessment are reliable and valid?* NCLB (2002) required that states' alternate assessments be technically

TABLE 2.2. Examples of Three Different Alternate Assessment Formats

Performance assessment: State-developed	Portfolio assessment: Teacher-developed entries	Checklist: State-developed
1. After participating in a read-aloud of a grade-appropriate passage, the student selects a picture of the main character given three standardized choices, and the teacher records the student's response on a bubble sheet.	1. The teacher creates an adapted book to use with the student. She implements a shared reading in which she reads some portions and the student uses augmentative and alternative communication to read a repeated story line. The student selects a picture of the main character, given three teacher-made choices, and the teacher records the student's response on a data sheet.	1. Toward the end of the school year, the teacher and the speech–language pathologist individually score the student's overall performance using a 3-point rating scale (*always*, *sometimes*, and *rarely*) for the item "Identifies the main character of a story."
2. After being shown a graph in the testing booklet and having the teacher read the item, the student selects an answer given four standardized choices and the teacher records the student's response on a bubble sheet.	2. The teacher gives the student a partially completed object graph and reads a word problem. The student selects an object to complete the graph. The teacher takes a picture of the completed graph for the portfolio.	2. Toward the end of the school year, the teacher and the inclusion math teacher individually score the overall student's performance using a 4-point rating scale (*always*, *frequently*, *occasionally*, and *rarely*) for the item "Interprets information presented in a graph" and includes a sample of the student's work in the submission.

adequate and show evidence of both reliability and validity. Reliability means that the scores are consistent or free from error. For example, when students are given the same item twice or two items that address the same construct, students should perform about the same on both items. In addition, when two teachers score a student's performance on a task, their scores should be comparable. Validity is the ability to make inferences about a student's performance using the outcomes of a test or other measure. There are many types of validity that are used together to make an argument about the overall validity of a test or measure. One common type is content validity—that is, does the test measure what it is intended or supposed to measure? Some research suggests that alternate assessments sometimes lack adequate psychometric properties (Johnson & Arnold, 2004). For example, issues within AA–AAS related to reliability may stem from including prompted student responses in the assessment score or assessing a skill using only one opportunity for student response. Kohl, McLaughlin, and Nagle (2006) surveyed 16 states and found that only 9 had conducted validity studies of their AA–AAS and that little specific information was available from these. Recently, the National Alternate Assessment Center (NAAC; *www.NAACPartners.org*; 2005) provided states with a technical manual to guide a self-study of the quality of their AA–AAS. States may provide information from these self-studies, as well as other validity studies, on their websites. For example, there may be information on interrater reliability for the scoring of the alternate assessment in the technical manual of the AA–AAS.

Documenting this technical quality may be especially important given that research has suggested possible benefits of AA–AAS. Ysseldyke, Dennison, and Nelson (2003) found that these assessments not only increased participation of students in testing programs but also created higher expectations and improved instruction. Flowers, Ahlgrim-Delzell, Browder, and Spooner (2005), Karvonen, Flowers, Browder, Wakeman, and Algozzine (2006), and Kleinert, Kennedy, and Kearns (1999) also found some benefits in their studies with teachers. In contrast, teachers also reported the burden of conducting alternate assessments. Browder, Karvonen, Davis, Fallin, and Courtade-Little (2005) found that providing professional development to teachers enhanced alternate assessment scores. Although alternate assessments may improve educational services for students with disabilities, they may also compete with instructional time and provide little useful information if their technical adequacy is poor and if teachers do not receive adequate professional development in how to develop and administer assessment items.

• *Question 7: Does the alternate assessment system promote learning in the general curriculum?* Some research suggests that increased access to the general curriculum may improve alternate assessment outcomes (Roach & Elliott, 2006). That is, if students have the opportunity to learn mathematics, science, language arts, and other academic content, they are more likely to do well on assessment of this content. Unfortunately, the alignment between instruction, assessment, and the state standards is not always clear. That is, what the students are learning, what the students are supposed to learn, and what the test assesses are not always the same. In their review of research on alternate assessment, Towles-Reeves, Kleinert, and Muhomba (2009) reported that much more needs to be studied on both the technical adequacy of alternate assessments and how they improve access to the general curriculum. One way to improve this access for students is through aligning instruction, assessment, and standards; which is discussed next. Before we move on to the topic of alignment, the story of Helen Stevens (based on the experiences of some teachers in North Carolina with whom we worked closely) offers some guidance for teachers in finding balance in alternate assessment.

FINDING THE BALANCE: LEARNING TO MANAGE ALTERNATE ASSESSMENT

Helen Stevens is a special education teacher in a state that had a changing alternate assessment system. In her first experience, she was asked to prepare a portfolio of her students' achievements using the students' IEP goals. Because Helen tracked the students' IEP progress using ongoing data sheets, she was able to do so. What was new for Helen was the pressure for her students to achieve their goals by the deadline for the portfolio, in March. Using the data-based decision guidelines (described in Chapter 4), she began to closely monitor progress and change instruction to promote mastery. Although not all students met their goals, more students met proficiency. In her third year with the portfolios, the state required that the tasks selected for the portfolios be math, reading, and science and link to the grade-level content standards rather than to the IEP goals. This was a major shift for Helen's instruction. She obtained professional development to gain new competence in teaching these academic goals and formed partnerships with general education teachers. She developed data sheets for each student for specific academic tasks that linked to general curriculum content for his or her grade level. Using the methods she knew in systematic instruction and data-based decisions, she continued to promote positive outcomes on the alternate assessments. She worried about how the IEP goals would be met, as she seemed to spend all of her time on teaching and documenting these alternate assessment tasks. The next year she sought out some new information on how to develop standards-based IEPs with her planning team. Now her system was more coordinated, with less of a gap between IEP goals, the academic priorities, and the tasks in the portfolios. She found that she could address many of the students' special therapy and functional life skill needs in the context of naturally occurring routines such as lunch and going outside. She found, however, that the portfolio tasks were still consuming large portions of her teaching time, and so she realized that she would have to be sure that the tasks to be submitted would be meaningful priorities for her students. Then the state decided to use performance assessments to reduce the time teachers spent on alternate assessments and to have tasks with closer links to the state standards. Helen celebrated the day she finished preparing her last portfolio, but she planned to maintain some of the positive innovations they had created, such as tracking ongoing progress in academic content. The first year of the performance assessment was a shock to Helen. Although this new method did not consume the entire school year, it did take most of her teaching day during the 6-week window she had to complete them with her students. She also was shocked to realize that she had not taught many of the skills reflected in the assessment. Her students performed poorly in the first year of this new system. Helen realized that she needed to follow the curricular guide provided by the state much more closely and with more consultation with the general education teacher to understand the academic content. For example, she thought teaching students to identify circles and triangles was appropriate geometry for her eighth graders, even though she knew the general education class was learning far more complex concepts. Now she realized that the state performance tasks were setting much higher expectations for learning the content of eighth-grade geometry. Helen was not the only teacher surprised by the changes, and the state offered professional development in the coming year in standards-based instruction. Although it took Helen a while to get used to the idea of teaching students with severe disabilities content that she had to study herself to prepare (e.g., What is "rise, run, and slope"?), she was surprised to realize that some students grasped the new content after a few demonstrations with concrete materials. For others, she returned to her systematic instruction with repeated trials to promote progress. For all of them, she began assessing progress using tasks similar to those they would encounter on the alternate assessment so they could learn to "show what they know." This also helped her realize what types of assistive technology the students needed and to have adequate time in the school year to teach students to use it. Working with the general education teacher to plan universally designed lessons, promoting more inclusive opportunities for shared learning in general education, and setting priorities using the state's extended standards made her academic goals even richer in content. Helen will tell you that the way she balanced the changing demands of alternate assessment was to recognize the importance of using student performance data to inform the content of her teaching and to work to make the assessment beneficial to her students. She has not changed her commitment to effective instruction of content that has a priority for the lives of her students, but she has gained some new insights about what to teach and how to help students learn to show what they know.

ALIGNMENT: LINKING ASSESSMENT AND INSTRUCTION TO STATE STANDARDS

What the Research Shows

Alignment can be formally defined as the degree of agreement, overlap, or intersection between standards, instruction, and assessments (Webb, 1997). For AA–AAS, this means the overlap between the state standards for the students' grade, what students are taught, and the content on the alternate assessment. Alignment studies of AA–AAS (Almond & Bechard, 2005; Browder et al., 2004; Flowers, Browder, & Ahlgrim-Delzell, 2006; Johnson & Arnold, 2004; Roach, Elliott, & Webb, 2005) suggest that this agreement has not always been optimal. That is, students are not always being taught the material that is being tested or that is in the state content standards, and the material being tested has not always matched the state standards. To be fair, students need the opportunity to learn the content that will be on the state assessment. Research also shows that teachers struggle to know how to extend the state standards for students with severe disabilities and may oversimplify the content (Karvonen, Wakeman, Flowers, & Browder, 2007). To address these alignment challenges, Browder, Wakeman, et al. (2007) developed a conceptual model of what it means to target alternate achievement of grade-level content standards. Their seven criteria formed the bases for an alignment model called links for academic learning (LAL; Flowers, Wakeman, Browder, & Karvonen, 2007). This model has been applied to help states evaluate how well the components within their alternate assessment systems align (i.e., content standards, instruction, and AA–AAS; Flowers, Wakeman, Browder, & Karvonen, 2009). A full explanation of this model can be found in Flowers et al. (2007) (available at *www.naacpartners.org* and *education.uncc.edu/access*).

FROM RESEARCH TO PRACTICE

The alignment criteria developed by Browder et al. (2007) and delineated further by Flowers et al. (2009) to study states' alternate assessments also can be used by teachers to understand how to link instruction with state standards. Table 2.3 provides an overview of the eight alignment criteria teachers can use to guide their instructional planning.

Criterion 1: The Content Is Academic

For the first criterion, teachers must ask themselves if the focus of the content is academic in nature. A clashing of values may lead teachers to force a square peg (i.e., a functional daily living task) into a round hole (i.e., an academic task). For example, learning the steps of hand washing is an important task for students related to hygiene. However, if the task is purported to address microbiology and germs without any specific instruction in those scientific concepts, the task is functional and meaningful but not academic.

Instruction that is intended to be academic must explicitly represent a strand within the content domains of reading, writing, mathematics, or science. Using guidance from the national curricular professional societies (i.e., NCTE, NCTM, and the National Research Council) to define what is "academic" provides a framework for considering whether an instructional or assessment task is truly academic in its intent or not. It is important to recognize, however, that some tasks may be precursors of or foundational

TABLE 2.3. Criteria for Instruction and Assessment That Link to Grade-Level Content

Criteria	What teachers can do
1. The content is academic and includes the major domains/strands of the content area as reflected in state and national standards (e.g., reading, math, science).	1. Study the academic content (e.g., textbooks, curricular websites) and collaborate with the general education teacher to be sure that instructional activities reflect academic content.
2. The content is referenced to the student's assigned grade level (based on chronological age).	2. Use the grade-level content standards to plan priorities for instruction. Ask general educators which are the most important standards.
3. The focus of achievement maintains fidelity to the content of the original grade-level standards (content centrality) and, when possible, the specified performance (performance centrality).	3. Be sure there is a match between the skill or concept targeted for instruction and the original standard. Check with the general education teacher to be sure that there is a link between the content of the standard and the content of the instruction.
4. The content differs from grade level in range, balance, and depth of knowledge but matches high expectations set for students with significant cognitive disabilities.	4. Alternate achievement is not the same as grade-level achievement. Although fewer content standards may be targeted within instruction and the AA–AAS than in grade-level instruction and assessments, purposefully address a range of skills and performance expectations that vary in complexity in instructional activities and assessments.
5. There is some differentiation in content across grade levels or grade bands.	5. Plan for vertical sequences of content from grade to grade and within a grade using the state standards as a guide.
6. The expected achievement is that the students will show learning of grade-referenced academic content.	6. Define active responses that the student will learn to make independently to show mastery of the content—not just "exposure" or prompted responses. Include data to show a change in performance (e.g., baseline data of minimal performance to mastery; generalization of the concept)
7. The potential barriers to demonstrating what students know and can do are minimized in the assessment.	7. Plan adaptations so that students with sensory or physical impairments, as well as different communication needs, can participate in the curriculum and show learning.
8. The instructional program promotes learning in the general curriculum.	8. Be sure the overall educational program continues to use best practices such as effective instructional strategies, planning for inclusion and working with nondisabled peers, promoting self-determination, and use of assistive technology.

to the skills or knowledge represented in grade-level content standards. For example, students may need to learn preliteracy skills, such as orienting a book and turning the pages, in conjunction with standards that may address other reading competencies. Although these foundational skills may not be considered academic (i.e., they do not fit within a strand of the content domain), they may be necessary for the student to gain access to the content. Foundational skills are not what have been called "access skills"—motor responses such as grasp and release or passive responses such as being exposed to content.

Although foundational skills are considered important to capture progress toward a standard, these alone will likely not count toward measuring proficiency in the AA–AAS.

The content of alternate assessments, as described earlier, changed from emphasizing a functional curriculum to focusing on the academic material required for reporting AYP. A shift in thinking about content has been occurring broadly within special education. Nolet and McLaughlin (2000) explained that special education students have historically received an alternate curriculum but can receive access to a general curriculum through diversified instruction. Browder, Spooner, Algozzine, et al. (2003) and Browder et al. (2004) described the evolution of curricular expectations for students with significant cognitive disabilities that led to the expectation for general curriculum access. As shown in Table 2.4, the first curricular approach in the 1970s adapted early childhood or infant curricula. This developmental model was rejected in the 1980s with the emergence of a functional, life skills approach. Social inclusion and self-determination were integrated with the functional curriculum in the 1990s. Although this approach is still valued today, the 2000s brought an additive focus on academic content reflected in state standards.

Criterion 2: Content Is Referenced to the Student's Grade Level

Thinking about academic content by starting with the grade-level standards can be new for some educators. By focusing on the priorities and essence of the student's grade-level or grade-band content standards when planning their instruction, teachers promote a high degree of alignment between these two components within the AA–AAS system.

TABLE 2.4. A Summary of Changing Curricular Expectations for Students with Significant Cognitive Disabilities

Time frame	Curricular focus	Conceptual foundation	Examples of assessments	Relationship to prior era
1970s	Developmental curriculum	Mental age can be used to plan interventions.	Checklist of infant and early child development	First public education services for the population
1980s	Functional curriculum	Use students' chronological age; teach for community living.	Ecological inventory of skills needed in job site; checklist of functional skills	Replaced the focus on mental age; new thinking is "age appropriateness"
1990s	Social inclusion and self-determination	Students should be full members of schools and have choices.	Person-centered plans with goals; preference assessments	Complemented functional curriculum but more in inclusive settings
2000–Present	Learning in the general curriculum	All students should have instruction in state academic content standards.	Alternate assessments with alternate achievement; but also ongoing IEP	Continued importance of person-centered planning and functional skills, but increased focus on academic learning

Note. From Browder, Wakeman, and Flowers (2009). Copyright 2009 by Paul H. Brookes Publishing Co., Inc. Reprinted by permission.

Criterion 3: Fidelity to Grade-Level Content and Performance

Extending content and defining performance for the heterogeneous population of students who participate in AA–AAS is challenging and can produce targets for learning that "miss the mark." In the LAL model, experts rate the quality of the content link for content centrality (Achieve, Inc., 2002) using a 3-point scale (i.e., *near, far, none*). AA–AAS items are evaluated based on how closely they match the content within the corresponding content standard that is identified as the target standard. Educators could use a similar scale (potentially dichotomous) when determining how closely their instruction targets the content within the content standard it is intended to exemplify. For example, if the content standard is to identify the forces that cause the weathering of rocks and the instructional activity models the effects of wind, water, and temperature on soil and sand, the educator and general education science partner could discuss whether the content is a match or not. In this case there would be a match. If, however, the task was to identify a picture of a rock, it is likely that, although that may be a foundational skill to the content standard, it would not be a match to that standard. An item can be academic but not have content centrality for several reasons. It may be mismatched to the wrong grade-level standard (e.g., misidentification or misunderstanding of the content). The misunderstanding of the content standards can also lead to a misconception that is illustrated in the instructional activity (e.g., a lesson that uses "All magnets stick to metal" as the concept statement). Sometimes the target item has been overextended or "watered down" so that the link is lost, which would be the case in the preceding rock example. Sometimes due to back mapping or retrofitting, the content is the functional activity rather than the academic content. The use of a functional context for the academic items within AA–AAS and instruction should be encouraged, but the test is whether the response the student is learning to make shows learning of academic content.

As the content of the standard and instruction is the primary concern, it should be noted that the expected performance within the standard should not be ignored. Performance centrality (Achieve, inc., 2002) is also reviewed in the LAL model by the content experts in relation to judging the degree of equivalent performance (i.e., *all, some, none*) between the content standards and the alternate assessment items or tasks. Educators should note the necessity that their instruction provide opportunities for a range of performance expectations, including changes in complexity within their overall instruction. This can be challenging as educators consider how to design activities and lessons that stretch students with significant cognitive disabilities toward higher levels of performance. Because the expectation is alternate achievement, it is expected that *some* of the performance from the content standards will be found in the instructional tasks designed by educators. For guidance, educators can refer to the NAAC (2005) introduction of "Is it plumb? Is it square?" to consider whether instructional targets link to state standards. For example, if the content standard is "Compare and contrast the main characters in two or more novels of fictional literature," for content centrality, the alternate assessment item should incorporate an activity with at least two novels. Many students can also be taught to compare and contrast characters within a story, a novel, a movie, and so on. A student with extensive communication challenges may identify the main character, for example, but not be able to compare and contrast across novels. Whenever possible, a performance match of an extended content standard is the goal and may require some decisions about whether enough attention has been given to the use of assistive technology and symbol options for more students to show what they know.

Criterion 4: The Content Differs in Range, Balance, and Depth of Knowledge

This criterion includes considerations of what proportion of the standards are represented in the AA–AAS and the instructional content (range of knowledge), what the weight or emphasis given to content standards in the AA–AAS and instruction is (balance), and what the relationship between the content standards, instruction, and AA–AAS items means in terms of the expectation for knowledge (depth of knowledge [DOK]). The range and balance in instructional planning should match the state's priorities, with consideration given to some coverage of the major strands of academic content covered at the student's grade level. The LAL is based on the assumption that the DOK level between the alternate assessment items and any extended standards should match, but the DOK level of the alternate assessment items and extended standards should be skewed to lower levels than the state standards. This is a key difference between grade-level achievement and alternate achievement. Educators should consider this difference when planning instruction and designing assessments.

Criterion 5: Differentiation across Grade Levels or Grade Bands

An important issue to consider is the degree to which instruction and assessment reflect different skills and knowledge for students as they progress through the grade levels. Think back to the example of Helen earlier in the chapter. One struggle she encountered was the need for different tasks and expectations for her middle school students. No longer was teaching geometric shapes—naming circles and triangles—a task aligned to the standards appropriate for her students. Although teaching those skills as a foundation may be appropriate, it is important to recognize the need to move students beyond those skills and address content in the grade-level standards. It is just as important to consider whether the actual alternate assessment tasks show changing expectations over time and are age-appropriate. For example, students may learn to recognize and use coins in elementary school, but there should be some change in expectation by middle and secondary levels (e.g., using dollars, recognizing prices). Extending standards for access for students with significant cognitive disabilities should not lead to achievement of the same academic skills year after year.

In addition, a review of the materials used in the instruction and assessment tasks is necessary to promote differentiation. There are a few ways to do this. First, determine whether the materials are adapted from materials used to teach content in general education classrooms. An example would be adapting the novel *Swiss Family Robinson* by streamlining the text, highlighting and repeating vocabulary terms within and across chapters, and including picture or object supports with text. Are the materials neutral and appropriate for students at all grades? An example would be using text and experiments having to do with planting a garden. Below-grade-level materials, such as counting teddy bears in seventh grade, reading *The Very Hungry Caterpillar* in fifth grade, or coloring a workbook sheet in high school, should *not* be used in either instruction or assessment tasks. A second way to show different expectations across grades is to include new skills or expand the expectation of content in broader or deeper terms. For example, whereas students in one grade may focus on counting sets and number recognition, students in the next grade may use counters to solve simple addition problems. As students master a skill, educators should build on that mastery and ask students to take the skill or knowledge further in a progression rather than teaching skills that splinter into isolated tasks. Again it is important to note that repeating the skill or task year after year does not ensure that the student will ever master that skill. Educators should use systematic instructional procedures to evaluate student progress with a task and adjust instruction to support progress (see Chapter 4 for ways to adjust instruction).

Criterion 6: Expected Achievement of Students Is Learning Grade-Referenced Academic Content

States' alternate achievement standards, or what is counted in the scoring of the AA–AAS, must link to grade-level content. The LAL assumes that what is actually counted toward a score that will be classified as "proficient" should be clearly linked to academic content. Inferences about student learning are more difficult to make when these scores incorporate aspects of teacher or program performance. The strongest inference can be made that the student learned the content if: (1) there is evidence that the student did not already have the skill (e.g., through use of pretest, baseline, or previous years' learning); (2) the skill is performed without teacher prompting; and (3) the skill is performed across materials and lessons to show mastery of the concept rather than rote memory of one specific response. Educators should be keenly aware of what they are doing to support students in instruction compared with what the state counts as mastery of an assessment item. Prompting students (with either stimulus or response prompts) in instruction provides the scaffolding to allow students to become independent responders and is very appropriate and important to promote student success. Prompting in an assessment convolutes the score by influencing information about what a student can do independently. For example, if a child selects a picture for the main idea by pointing or eye gazing, it can be determined that it was the child's performance. On the other hand, if a student selects the picture while the teacher points to the correct answer or allows a peer to select the correct response, then something other than the student's performance is being measured. Educators must know how to fade prompts to encourage students to give independent responses in both instructional and assessment tasks (see Chapter 4 for methods of fading prompts).

Criterion 7: Barriers to Performance

Jorgensen (2005) discussed using the "least dangerous assumption" for students with significant disabilities. This idea is best actualized in the AA–AAS system when consideration is given to how *all* students can engage and participate not only in the AA–AAS itself but also in the instruction of the content standards assessed within the AA–AAS. Because of complex disabilities that students with significant cognitive disabilities sometimes have, it can be difficult to demonstrate achievement. This may be especially true if the only means to show learning is through symbolic representation, such as words and pictures. Some students may need to show learning in a meaningful context using everyday objects. Consideration also needs to be given to how students with sensory and physical challenges can both access the instruction and assessment materials and show learning. The LAL examines whether the alternate assessment items or tasks are difficult because of the knowledge and skills they target or for other reasons not related to the item or task content, such as sensory and physical challenges. In addition, educators must provide all students with opportunities to actively participate in instruction. Barriers that prevent students from this engagement could be detrimental to their acquisition of content and the ability to demonstrate what they know. This criterion considers whether student performance accurately reflects the intended content standard rather than the disability.

Criterion 8: The Instructional Program Promotes Learning in the General Curriculum

Finally, the LAL gives specific consideration to the alignment of instruction with content standards. Educators can reflect on their use of best-practice indicators with this population of students, including the use of assistive technology, inclusion opportunities in general education contexts, applications of content knowledge and skills in functional activities, self-determination, and collaboration with general educators. This reflection does not end here; educators can continue to examine the alignment of their instruction with the prioritized state standards, as well as the AA–AAS. Wakeman, Bechard, Karvonen, and Almond (2009) developed a self-study guide for educators in which teachers use evidence to evaluate their efforts for alignment within the AA–AAS system. As in Helen's case, educators must be purposeful in their efforts to address their areas of need by identifying supports in the form of professional development, other special educators, and general education partners.

WORK IT ACROSS

Browder, Ahlgrim-Delzell, Courtade-Little and Snell (2006) describe and illustrate how instruction can be differentiated for students at a presymbolic, early (concrete) symbolic, and expanded (abstract) symbolic level. Whereas students at an abstract symbolic level have mastered some sight words, numbers, and other symbols that can be applied to demonstrating knowledge of an academic concept, students at a concrete symbolic level will probably need symbols that have immediate applicability to the context. Students at a presymbolic level will be learning symbol use (e.g., the meaning of pictures) concurrently with academic content and may need alternative ways to show what they know as well. This idea was developed by Browder, Spooner, et al. (2006) into a procedure known as "Work It Across." To Work It Across to extend a state standard, the teacher begins by identifying a prioritized content standard for students. Collaboration with a general education teacher may illuminate a lesson or activity that is used to address the standard with students without disabilities. By beginning with the general education teacher's lesson plan, the special educator is less likely to misinterpret the standard, to overstretch the content within the standard, or to create a task that does not address that standard. Figure 2.1 is an example of a Work It Across. It is important to note that once the teacher has an aligned task that addresses the standard, the teacher works the task (and content

English Language Arts (ELA): Writing

Grade-level standard: 7–4.3. Create multiple-paragraph compositions that include a central idea with supporting details and use appropriate transitions between paragraphs.

Grade level: 7

On-grade-level expectation (not adapted)	Abstract symbolic	Concrete symbolic	Beginning with symbols (primarily communicates nonsymbolically)
		Teaching activities	
Present elements of a good paragraph. Have students highlight each part, including main or central idea, transitional words, and supporting details. Generate compositions with each element. Review peer's work for elements and provide feedback.	Chunk this task into two or more lessons (central or main idea and supporting details). Present the students with a three-sentence paragraph on a familiar topic. Have the students read the paragraph. Define for the students what a main or central idea is. Discuss how they can identify which idea is the main one from the paragraph. Use a colored highlighter to identify the central idea within the paragraph. Do several more paragraphs with either teacher leading or student identifying and giving reasons why he or she selected that sentence or idea. Allow independent practice and review of this skill. Present original paragraph and have students again identify central idea. With a different colored highlighter, indicate the other supporting details and define those. Have students highlight on their copies. Present previous examples of paragraphs and have students identify and highlight those supporting details. Present new paragraphs and ask students to identify both the central idea and supporting details within those paragraphs. Allow independent practice and review.	Chunk this task into two or more lessons (central or main idea and supporting details). Present the students with a two-sentence paragraph using picture supports on a familiar topic. Have the students read the paragraph if possible. Define for the students what a main or central idea is. Discuss how they can identify which idea is the main one from the paragraph. Use a colored highlighter to identify the central idea within the paragraph. Do several more picture-supported paragraphs with either teacher leading or student identifying and giving reasons why he or she selected that sentence or idea. Allow independent practice and review of this skill. Present original paragraph and have students again identify central idea. With a different colored highlighter indicate the other, supporting detail sentence and define the details. Have students highlight on their copies. Present previous examples of paragraphs and have students identify and highlight those supporting details. Present new picture-supported paragraphs and ask students to identify both the central idea and the supporting detail sentence within those paragraphs. Allow independent practice and review.	Present student with option of two or three topics to write about. Let student choose the topic (choice can be presented in object or picture form and choice can be made by stating, pointing, reaching, eye gazing, etc.). Present the student with the selected topic object or picture and ask "What do you want to tell me about _____?" while providing two options: "I like _____" or "The _____ is _____". Have the student choose the sentence (e.g., student puts picture of object into the sentence blank[s]). If the second option is chosen, have descriptors that can be placed into the second blank (such as "my favorite food," etc.). Explain that this is the central or main idea for the paragraph and define it for the student. Present the student with a supporting detail sentence, such as "I like it because _____" or "It makes me feel _____" or "It is _____". Repeat the steps of allowing the student to select the sentence and insert his or her selection. Explain to the student that this sentence is a supporting detail about his or her topic and define what a detail is. Read the sentences the student generates back to the student. Publish work (on the bulletin board).

	and	*and/or*
Create a paragraph using transitional words and a central idea with supporting details.	Review the central idea and supporting details. Model writing about a topic with a main idea and supporting details. Ask students to identify those in your paragraph. Present the student with options (if needed) or the opportunity to generate a topic to write about. Have students as a group write about the topic with a central idea and supporting details. (Provide students with a topic sentence and have them generate supporting details if necessary to start the process.) Have students copy or type the completed paragraph from the board if possible. Finally, ask students to suggest a topic (provide selection if needed). Have students generate a central idea and at least two supporting details (dictate to scribe if needed, use assistive technology, or write independently). Have students read their work to you or to a peer. Publish the work (on the bulletin board).	Review the central idea and supporting details. Model writing about a topic with a main idea and a supporting detail sentence using pictures and words. Ask students to identify those elements in your paragraph. Present the student with options (if needed) or the opportunity to generate a topic to write about. Have students as a group write to the topic for central idea and supporting details. (Provide students with a topic sentence and have students add a supporting detail sentence if necessary to start the process, or use a stem such as "I like _____.") Finally, ask students to suggest a topic (provide selection and/or stem of sentence if needed). Have students generate a central idea and at least one supporting detail sentence (dictate to scribe, or use assistive technology). Have students read their work (or central idea only or supporting detail only) with or to you or a peer if possible. Publish the work (on the bulletin board).
How student shows mastery		
1. Students will generate or select a topic to write about. 2. Students will generate at least a three-sentence paragraph with a main or central idea/topic sentence and two supporting details.	1. Students will generate or select a topic to write about. 2. Students will generate or dictate to ascribe at least a two-sentence paragraph with a main or central idea/topic sentence and one supporting detail.	1. Students will select a topic to write about. 2. Students will fill in a blank using pictures or objects to complete the main or central idea and supporting detail sentences.

Extended Indicator (for AA–AAS): Create a paragraph that uses transitional words and includes a central idea with supporting details.

FIGURE 2.1. Work It Across.

from the standard) across the page for each level of symbolic communication used. This consideration of what the students need in terms of presentation and assessment of content ensures that all students have the opportunity to engage in the lesson and show what they know. This type of consideration then translates to the AA–AAS in making sure that all students have access to the content within the assessment (i.e., what is being asked of them) and have response options that allow them to participate with the items (i.e., opportunities to respond using their levels of communication).

SUMMARY

Although federal policy continues to evolve, the changes created by NCLB had a lasting impact on services for students with severe disabilities. It required schools to be accountable for all students' learning in core academic areas; thus changes were needed so that all students could have access to general curriculum content. Alternate assessment was the tool used to ensure that schools were accountable for students who could not participate in the general assessment. These alternate assessments could be measured against alternate achievement standards. To implement an alternate assessment, educators need to understand their state systems. The questions provided in this chapter can guide a self-study to gain this understanding using your state's education website. Being effective in preparing students for alternate assessments also requires understanding state standards and ensuring that assessment and instruction align with these standards. This chapter provided eight criteria from links for academic learning to help educators gain a deeper understanding of alignment. Finally, to teach to a standard requires being able to extend that standard to students' current symbolic level. The "Work It Across" example provides a tool to help plan for students' participation in grade-aligned content. The chapters in this book on standards-based IEPs, language arts, mathematics, and science offer additional information for planning this grade-appropriate instruction.

APPLICATIONS

1. Find your state's education website and the link to the state accountability system. Then locate the link for alternate assessment. The link may be called "alternate assessment," or you may need to use the acronym (e.g., PASA-ALT) or name for the system (e.g., Extend 1). Find the answer to each question posed in this chapter for your state's alternate assessment. If you are working on this exercise in a college class, you might "jigsaw" this assignment by having different people find the answers to different questions and then compiling your answers.

2. Take the "alignment quiz" in Figure 2.2. Can you explain why the answer to each question is "no"? (Hint: The numbers line up with each of the criteria shown in Table 2.3; i.e., Question 1 has something to do with Criteria 1; Question 2 with Criteria 2, and so on).

Does each statement reflect alignment with general curriculum content? Circle Yes or No (explain why, if the answer is No).

1. To target a standard on "identifying influences on weather patterns" in science, the teacher developed a plan to teach Francis to push the button to open an umbrella.

   Yes   No   Why? _____

2. The special education supervisor in a school system advised teachers to use the standards from whatever grade level best suited the student's current functioning. In planning for an eighth grader named Calvin, the team decided to use the kindergarten standards.

   Yes   No   Why? _____

3. To teach the geometry standard "finding the points on a coordinate plane," the teacher decided to have Anna discriminate between circles and triangles.

   Yes   No   Why? _____

4. In Mr. West's fourth-grade class, students were expected to read chapter books independently and develop a book report. He decided this expectation was not applicable to Cara because she could not read.

   Yes   No   Why? _____

5. Jeremy worked on identifying a quarter, nickel and dime in third grade . . . and in fifth grade . . . and in ninth grade . . . and in 12th grade.

   Yes   No   Why? _____

6. The inclusion specialist working with Cara in Mr. West's class decided she can participate in the book report expectation by having a peer do the report for her. When the class read the chapter books, she had the peer turn the pages for Cara.

   Yes   No   Why? _____

7. In this state, the students who met the criteria for proficiency on the alternate assessment were able to complete a paper-and-pencil test that involved circling words and numbers. Students without these skills were assumed not to have achieved the standards.

   Yes   No   Why? _____

8. When a state learned that student achievement should be the focus for state alternate assessments, they eliminated the rubric previously used to evaluate whether students had access to assistive technology, general education contexts, self-determination, and peer supports. Teachers were told "these issues are no longer considered relevant for this population." The professional development was changed to focus on how to document outcomes for the alternate assessment.

   Yes   No   Why? _____

FIGURE 2.2. Understanding alignment quiz.

CHAPTER 3

Standards-Based Individualized Education Plans and Progress Monitoring

DIANE M. BROWDER, FRED SPOONER, AND BREE JIMENEZ

Ms. Lim is a special education teacher at Wilson Middle School. In the year ahead, she will be providing support for students with severe disabilities both in their general education classes and in supplemental instruction in her classroom. As she begins to schedule IEP team meetings, she is overwhelmed at what she must achieve for the 10 students on her planning caseload. She wants to consider their academic, therapy, and functional needs. She needs to use the state standards for their grade level and to coordinate with multiple general education teachers. The students need to be prepared to participate in the state's alternate assessment in the spring. She wants to identify appropriate forms of progress monitoring to be sure the students are on track to master the priority content. Ms. Lim's mentor suggests that she allow more time to develop the first student's plan and then use the strategies learned to complete the remaining plans. This chapter gives information Ms. Lim can use in creating a working process for developing and monitoring IEPs.

The Individuals with Disabilities Education Improvement Act of 2004 (IDEA) requires that all students receiving special education services have an IEP. The IEP is a working plan for the delivery of these special education services. As such, it is both a specific document that must meet certain legal requirements and an ongoing reference for daily instruction. The IEP is developed by a multidisciplinary team that must include the local education agency (LEA) representative, at least one special education teacher, at least one regular education teacher (if the child is or may be participating in the regular education environment), someone who can interpret the assessment results, related service providers as requested by the parents or agency (e.g., occupational therapist, physical therapist, speech–language pathologist), parents or guardians, and student (whenever appropriate). IDEA requires that the student must be invited if over the age of 16, but all students should be included in the development of their IEPs and included in the team's meetings to the extent possible. This chapter provides information on how to teach students with severe disabilities to participate in the development of their IEPs. Often the special education teacher will lead the IEP process, but students may be able to lead all or part of the meeting as their goal-setting and leadership skills develop. To develop effective IEPs, teachers need: (1) knowledge of the federal and state regulations for IEPs, (2) guidelines for developing a standards-based IEP, and (3) a process for assessment and planning. Once the IEP is developed, strategies are needed to monitor progress. These components of the IEP process are described in the following sections.

FOLLOWING FEDERAL AND STATE REQUIREMENTS FOR IEP DEVELOPMENT

The IEP is the written commitment for a student's special education and related services. As a legal document, the IEP must address the requirements of federal law. Most states also require specific formats and specify content to be included in the IEP. Sometimes a local school system will have further guidelines for the development of the IEP and written document. Teachers who are new to a state or a school system or to being special education teachers will need to pursue professional development offered for meeting these guidelines. This chapter provides the requirements for the IEP specified by the most current legislation, IDEA (2004). Updates can be found through the Council for Exceptional Children (*www.cec.sped.org*). Most state education agency websites have a section for special education services that includes guidelines for the IEP.

In general, the IEP should reflect a group planning process. To be consistent with federally mandated procedures, the written statements in the IEP are developed by the IEP team, using information from assessments conducted in all areas of the student's disabilities. According to IDEA (2004), Section 514 (d)(1)(A), the IEP must include:

1. The student's present level of academic achievement and functional performance, including:
   a. How the child's disability affects involvement and progress in general education curriculum;
   b. For preschool children, how the disability affects the child's participation in appropriate activities; and
   c. For children with disabilities who take alternate assessments aligned to alternate achievement standards, a description of benchmarks or short-term objectives.
2. A statement of measurable annual goals, including academic and functional goals, designed to:
   a. Meet the child's needs that result from the child's disability to enable the child to be involved in and make progress in the general education curriculum; and
   b. Meet each of the child's other educational needs that result from the child's disability.
3. A description of how the child's progress toward meeting the annual goals will be measured and when periodic progress will be provided.

4. A statement of the special education and related services and supplementary aids and services, based on peer-reviewed research to the extent practicable, to be provided to the child and a statement of the program modifications or supports for school personnel that will be provided for the child:
   a. To advance appropriately toward attaining the annual goals,
   b. To be involved in and make progress in the general education curriculum and participate in extracurricular and nonacademic activities, or
   c. To be educated and participate with other children with disabilities and nondisabled children.

5. An explanation of the extent, if any, to which the child will not participate with nondisabled children in the regular class.

6. A statement of any individual appropriate accommodations that are necessary to measure the academic achievement and functional performance of the child on state and district-wide assessments,
   a. And, if the IEP team determines that the child will take an alternate assessment, a statement of why the child cannot participate in the regular assessment and why the particular alternate assessment is appropriate for the child.

7. The projected date for the beginning of the services and modifications and the anticipated frequency, location, and duration of the services.

8. Beginning no later than when the child is 16:
   a. Appropriate measurable postsecondary goals based upon age-appropriate transition assessments related to training, education, employment, and, where appropriate, independent living skills;
   b. The transition services (including courses of study) needed to assist the child in reaching these goals; or
   c. Beginning not later than 1 year before the child reaches the age of majority under state law, a statement that the child has been informed of the child's rights under this title that will transfer to the child on reaching the age of majority,

- Additional considerations, depending on the student's unique needs:
  - Student's behavioral needs and whether positive behavior interventions are needed;
  - Language needs of a student with limited English proficiency;
  - Provision of instruction in Braille is appropriate for a student who is blind or visually impaired; or
  - Communication needs and modes of the student, especially if he or she is deaf or hard of hearing. (U.S. Department of Education, 2003)

Figure 3.1 provides an example of an IEP that contains the components just described. This is a standards-based IEP, which is described in the next section.

Most states provide the specifics of how to meet these requirements through state regulations and procedures. For example, the IEP will often have a section on assessment participation, in which the team checks an option and a box for stating the rationale. These IEP templates help the planning team respond to all of the federal and state requirements. Some states or school systems use IEP development software to expedite the process. A few examples of these can also be found on the Internet (*www.iepware.com*; *www.superschoolsoftware.com*; *www.classplus.com*). Although the IEP team should use the system provided by the state or school system, it also is important to understand

(text resumes on page 53)

INDIVIDUALIZED EDUCATION PLAN

Student's Name: Jabrill

DOB 4/23/1998   School Year 2010–2011   GRADE 7

IEP Initiation/Duration Dates   FROM 9/21/10–9/20/11

THIS IEP WILL BE IMPLEMENTED DURING THE REGULAR SCHOOL TERM UNLESS NOTED IN EXTENDED SCHOOL YEAR SERVICES.

STUDENT PROFILE

Jabrill is a seventh-grade student who is included in general education classes for science, social studies, and English language arts with accommodations and supports. Jabrill spends part of his school day in a special education setting for intensive support in math and additional academic and functional skills. Due to his cerebral palsy, Jabrill receives physical therapy for mobility and occupational therapy to increase his fine motor skills to participate in classroom activities. Jabrill is able to speak verbally; however, he is difficult to understand. He does use assistive technology to augment his speech during classroom lessons and to participate in academic assignments.

Jabrill will work on seventh-grade academic skills using extended standards. He can identify a large number of sight words and guess new words by applying his knowledge of initial letter sounds but comprehends only a small portion of them. Reading comprehension has been identified by his teacher last year, as well as his family, as a priority. Jabrill relies on read-alouds to learn the grade-level content. He can complete assessments using word/picture selections in a multiple-choice format or by answering questions orally using his communication device. Math has been a special challenge, and Jabrill does not yet identify numbers or count consistently.

Jabrill is able to identify his name, address, and personal information but is not able to communicate them when asked. His family is concerned about his safety in the environment due to his inability to communicate with his community (when not given a choice of response options). Jabrill participates in Special Olympics and bowled in the state competition.

Jabrill is social and has many school friends. He does not always recognize when to stop socializing. Jabrill will often speak out loud, laugh with excitement, and talk to peers during classroom lessons. Although teachers and peers remind him to wait his turn or raise his hand to talk, these behaviors often disrupt the learning environment. His general education teachers have asked for a plan to manage these disruptions.

Parent Notification		
Attempt #1: Letter 9/4/10	Attempt #2: Phone call 9/8/10	Attempt #3: reminder notice sent home with student on 9/18/10
Parent response: will attend as per phone call on 9/9/10		

SPECIAL INSTRUCTIONAL FACTORS

Items checked "YES" will be addressed in the IEP:

- Does the student have behavior which impedes his/her learning or the learning of others?   Yes ☒   No ☐
- Does the student have limited English proficiency?   Yes ☐   No ☒
- Does the student need instruction in Braille and the use of Braille?   Yes ☐   No ☒
- Does the student have communication needs (deaf or hearing impaired only)?   Yes ☐   No ☒

(cont.)

FIGURE 3.1. Sample of an IEP.

- Does the student need assistive technology devices and/or services?   Yes ☒   No ☐
- Does the student require specially designed physical education?   Yes ☒   No ☐
- Is the student working toward alternate achievement standards and participating   Yes ☒   No ☐
  in the alternate assessment?
- Are transition services addressed in the IEP?   Yes ☐   No ☒

AREA: ENGLISH LANGUAGE ARTS

Present Level of Educational Performance:

A review of classroom assessments and progress monitoring data indicate that Jabrill learned 30 vocabulary words in the prior school year but demonstrated comprehension of only 10. He has strong skills in recognizing the initial sound in words and can sometimes guess new words using this skill. Jabrill uses word-to-picture matching to show comprehension but needs many trials of instruction to master each vocabulary word. He does not yet comprehend passages. During read-alouds of adapted texts for chapter books, Jabrill is able to identify the main character but is not able to identify the setting, theme, and author's purpose. To complete written work, Jabrill selects words or phrases from a list related to the topic. Currently, he chooses these randomly and does not yet compose sentences without peer or teacher assistance. Jabrill can use an adapted keyboard to activate special software on the computer but cannot use an adapted mouse to access the Internet to research new topics. Jabrill received a score of "proficient" on last year's state alternate assessment in language arts.

Measurable Annual Goals related to meeting the student's needs:

Given seventh-grade literature that has been adapted with text summaries and picture cues, Jabrill will increase comprehension of literature adapted from the seventh-grade curriculum by applying vocabulary, story elements, and passage-reading skills.
Priority Seventh-Grade-Level Standards:

- The learner will explore and respond to a variety of print and nonprint texts.
- The learner will synthesize and use information from a variety of sources.
- The learner will respond to various literary genres using interpretive and evaluative processes.

Short-Term Objectives/Benchmarks:

1. Jabrill will acquire at least 50 new vocabulary words from seventh- and eighth-grade literature and use pictures/definitions to comprehend 90% of them. *Assessment: Repeated trials of matching word to picture or word to definition.*
2. Jabrill will identify the elements of a story, including setting, theme, and author's purpose, in grade-appropriate adapted text with all steps of the task analysis correct by the end of the first quarter. He will generalize this skill across at least three novels and two other types of text (e.g., news article, biography). *Assessment: Story elements task analysis.*
3. Jabrill will read already known words in longer passages by:
   - Reading phrases correctly with 100% accuracy. *Assessment: repeated trials of phrase to be read.*
   - Reading one sentence with 100% accuracy. *Assessment: repeated trials of sentence to be read.*
   - Reading two-sentence paragraphs with 90% accuracy. *Assessment: repeated trials of number of words read when presented with two sentences.*
   - Reading four-sentence paragraphs with 90% accuracy. *Assessment: repeated trials of number of words read when presented with four sentences.*
4. After silently reading a passage, Jabrill will answer three out of four comprehension questions correctly. *Assessment: Repeated trials of comprehension questions.*
5. Jabrill will expand his text comprehension skills during read-alouds or silent reading to include application, connections, and synthesis questions with three out of four correct across three or more texts. *Assessment: Repeated trial of each form of question.*

(cont.)

FIGURE 3.1. *(cont.)*

6. Jabrill will compose a sentence that states an opinion using his known vocabulary on three out of four opportunities. *Assessment: repeated-opportunity checklist of sentences written independently.*
7. Jabrill will use an adapted mouse to gain access to the Internet and navigate websites to research topics in three out of four trials. *Assessment: Task analysis of Internet search.*

AREA: Math

Present Level of Educational Performance:

Jabrill finds math his most difficult subject. After years of instruction, he still cannot count consistently. He has learned to use one-to-one correspondence. He does read numerals using his keen symbol recognition skills but cannot match the numeral to a set of objects. Because of his experiences with math, Jabrill becomes loud and disruptive during math lessons. He needed to leave math class most days last year to calm down. His parents have asked that he receive more intensive special education services in the area of mathematics. Jabrill also does not have functional math skills such as making a purchase, although he likes the social activity of shopping or dining out with others. Jabrill received a score of "novice" in the state alternate assessment in mathematics for sixth grade. He needs to learn to apply any new skills to the grade-level content to be assessed in the seventh grade. An adaptation for mathematics (use of Excel) will be submitted to the state for approval for use in the seventh-grade alternate assessment if it proves successful in the first quarter.

Measurable Annual Goals related to meeting the student's needs:

Given the accommodation of mathematics computer software, Jabrill will perform grade-linked math problems and demonstrate understanding of the solutions.
Priority Seventh-Grade-Level Standards:
- Use proportional reasoning to find missing values in problems.
- Use concepts of percent to solve problems.
- Use arithmetic operations to solve problems involving integers.

Short-Term Objectives/Benchmarks:

1. Using his number recognition skills, Jabrill will complete all steps needed to enter numbers to add or subtract facts found in read-alouds of word problems using Excel software with 100% of steps correct. *Assessment: Task analysis of computation in Excel.*
2. Using his skill in recognizing symbols, Jabrill will complete all steps needed to create tables and graphs in Excel software for read-alouds of word problems with 100% of steps correct. *Assessment: Task analysis of tables/graphs in Excel.*
3. Applying his emerging reading comprehension skills, Jabrill will answer three out of four questions correctly to "explain his work" in mathematics. *Task Analysis: repeated-trials assessment.*
4. Using skills mastered for Excel, Jabrill will solve problems adapted from the seventh-grade text (missing values, percent, problems with integers) presented as read-aloud word problems with 90% accuracy. *Assessment: Permanent product of math problem solutions.*
5. In an inclusive computer lab, Jabrill will generalize his emerging math skills with peers who are doing similar tasks with at least 90% of problems solved correctly. *Assessment: Permanent product of math problem solutions.*

AREA: Science

Present Level of Educational Performance:

Jabrill can answer questions to complete a KWHL chart (what I KNOW, WANT to know, HOW I will find out more, what I LEARNED), when directed by the teacher or a peer. Jabrill is very interested in fossils

(cont.)

FIGURE 3.1. *(cont.)*

and enjoys learning about anything to do with the Earth's materials. Jabrill can listen to science text and answer comprehension questions, but his content knowledge is limited. Jabrill is able to answer literal questions immediately after text is read but often is not able to generalize the information to gain the "big idea" or concept of the science unit. Jabrill needs daily embedded systematic instruction to master science vocabulary and concepts. His love of competition (Special Olympics) can be incorporated in having him work toward an experiment to be entered into the school's science fair.

Measurable Annual Goals related to meeting the student's needs:

Given adapted tests and a KWHL chart, Jabrill will demonstrate knowledge of prioritized seventh-grade science content and the skills needed to self-direct inquiry science experiments.
Priority Seventh-Grade-Level Standards:
- Understand the properties of matter and changes that occur when matter interacts in an open and closed container.
- Predict weather conditions and patterns based on information obtained from weather data.
- Identify general functions of the major systems of the human body and ways that these systems interact with each other to sustain life.

Short-Term Objectives/Benchmarks:

1. Jabrill will complete a KWHL chart independently to direct himself during an inquiry science lesson in three out of four opportunities by the second quarter *Assessment: Task analysis of KWHL chart.*
2. Jabrill will develop an experiment by selecting the experiment from a choice of science fair options from a website of examples (teacher/parents help procure materials), then conducting the experiment steps and recording results of each trial with 100% accuracy over the course of the investigation by the end of the third quarter. (The science fair is usually held at the beginning of the fourth quarter.) *Assessment: Rubric for rating outcomes of trial experiments.*
3. Jabrill will complete adapted chapter tests for seventh-grade science that include defining vocabulary (match word to definition or picture) with 90% accuracy across all quarters. *Assessment: Permanent product-adapted chapter tests; progress monitoring using repeated-trial data from embedded daily systematic instruction.*
4. Jabrill will complete adapted chapter tests for seventh-grade science that include concept statements of the big ideas of the chapter with 90% correct across all quarters. *Assessment: Permanent product-adapted chapter tests; progress monitoring using repeated-trial data from embedded daily systematic instruction.*

AREA: Social Studies

Present Level of Educational Performance:

Jabrill applies his strong word-recognition skills to read and guess words in the social studies text. He is able to demonstrate factual recall given three to four options immediately after the passage is read aloud. He is very interested in learning about other people and often will choose a book from the library on other cultures. Jabrill understands that a map tells us about a place, but he cannot use it to gain information.

Measurable Annual Goal related to meeting the student's needs:

Given adapted seventh-grade social studies text, Jabrill will use tools to access information and demonstrate comprehension of other settings, people, and resources (cultures).
Priority Seventh-Grade-Level Standards:
- The learner will use geographic tools to answer geographic questions.
- The learner will access the relationship between physical environments and cultures of selected societies and regions.
- The learner will recognize the common characteristics of different cultures.

(cont.)

FIGURE 3.1. *(cont.)*

Short-Term Objectives/Benchmarks:

1. When presented with a map, globe, or model used during the unit of instruction, Jabrill will identify oceans versus land (first quarter), North and South America (second quarter), Europe and Asia (third quarter), and Australia and Antarctica (fourth quarter) in three out of four trials. *Assessment: Repeated-trial assessment of finding information on a map, globe, or model.*
2. Using a graphic organizer, Jabrill will correctly identify three out of four big ideas for each of 4 major cultures—one culture per quarter. *Assessment: Repeated trials of filling in graphic organizer using social studies vocabulary.*
3. Jabrill will complete adapted chapter tests that include multiple-choice questions on at least four out of six big ideas tested with at least one chapter test meeting criteria each quarter. *Assessment: Permanent product of chapter tests.*

AREA: Related Services

Present Level of Educational Performance:

Jabrill has cerebral palsy; he is able to move his arms but with restricted range of motion. He is able to complete most gross-motor and fine-motor tasks without assistance but is not able to write using a paper and pencil. He is able to use an adapted keyboard to create a permanent product and is able to paste words and pictures into a blank when given an adapted worksheet. Jabrill is unable to button his own clothing or begin a zipper.

Jabrill is able to walk unassisted, but his mobility is challenged when presented with uneven surfaces or stairs. Jabrill is able to hold a bowling ball and roll it on a ramp to participate in Special Olympics activities but is not able to move the ramp to determine where he wants the ball to roll.

Measurable Annual Goal related to meeting the student's needs:

Given opportunities to learn and apply new skills in his daily routines, Jabrill will master five new gross-motor and fine-motor skills to participate in academic and community settings.

Short-Term Objectives/Benchmarks:

1. Jabrill will use a pencil or marker to circle or checkmark his response to questions provided on paper in three out of four trials by the end of the first quarter. *Assessment: Repeated-trial observations.*
2. Jabrill will successfully button a button and begin a zipper on 100% of opportunities by the end of the second quarter. *Assessment: Therapy observation.*
3. Jabrill will use an adapted mouse to navigate educational software in three out of four trials by the end of the third quarter. *Assessment: Repeated-trial observations.*
4. When presented with uneven ground, Jabrill will walk 10 steps without assistance by the end of the fourth quarter. *Assessment: Frequency count of steps.*
5. When presented with a bowling ramp, Jabrill will move the ramp to either the left or right to determine the direction he would like the ball to go in three out of four trials by the end of the fourth quarter. *Assessment: Repeated-trial assessment.*

AREA: Social Behavior

Present Level of Educational Performance:

Jabrill enjoys being part of the general education classes (except for math). He socializes by calling out student's names, saying "Hey," and making small nonverbal jokes (e.g., pretending to sleep). The problem is that Jabrill does not discriminate when to socialize. He often yells out answers in class, interrupts teachers, and talks to peers during lessons. A functional assessment of this behavior in the fall of the prior year revealed that the function of these responses is typically to gain social attention. In contrast, the

(cont.)

FIGURE 3.1. *(cont.)*

most recent functional assessment in April also indicated that his most extreme behavior, which occurred in math, was to escape this learning context. Observations of his same-age peers show that they only become quiet during general warnings but become silent "when the teacher yells." It has been suggested by the school PBS coach to use a "stoplight." This will be a universally designed support for the entire class to signal when to be quiet. Jabrill knows where in the school his classes are but needs an adult to walk with him because he stops to talk with peers in the hallway.

Measurable Annual Goal related to meeting the student's needs:

Given support to use new social strategies, Jabrill will become when given a visual cue, arrive early to class for social time, and use negotiation skills with teachers.

Short-Term Objectives/Benchmarks:

1. Jabrill will be quiet when the teacher shows him a picture of a yellow caution light sign for:
   - 30% of the time (first quarter).
   - 50% of the time (second quarter).
   - 75% of the time (third quarter).
   He will be silent when shown a picture of a red light 100% of the time by the fourth quarter.
   Assessment: Frequency count of quieting/silent response to light.
2. Jabrill will find his class without assistance 5 minutes before the bell to have social time with the teacher and peers on 4 out of 5 days by the second quarter. *Assessment: Repeated-opportunity trials.*
3. Jabrill will use a "let's talk about it" symbol on his VOD or fold his arms to request a change of setting, materials, or activities on four out of five occasions by the third quarter. The teacher or peer will give him a list of alternatives if he does so (including resting in quiet setting). *Assessment: Frequency count of use of negotiation without noise.*

AREA: Functional Living Skills

Present Level of Educational Performance:

Jabrill enjoys grocery shopping but does not make independent purchases. The "Shoppers for Teachers Club" takes community-based shopping trips to the local grocery store to purchase items for teachers in the school. Jabrill is able to read the sight words to know what to purchase but often takes up to 15 minutes to find one item within the store. Jabrill can identify his personal information but needs an option of two choices. His family is concerned that if presented with a situation in which he needs help, he would not be able to tell someone his address and/or phone number.

Measurable Annual Goal related to meeting the student's needs:

When given opportunities to practice community skills at school and in vivo, Jabrill will purchase items and relay personal information to authorities.

Short-Term Objectives/Benchmarks:

1. When presented with a sight word of a familiar item at the grocery store, Jabrill will locate the item in 5 minutes, in three out of four trials. *Assessment: Time-based duration.*
2. When given a jig (graphic organizer) to match dollar bills, Jabrill will identify the cost of the item (e.g., $5.42), then match the correct number of dollar bills to the numbered jig (i.e., 5), and add 1 more to pay the cashier:
   - Up to $5 with 100% accuracy
   - Up to $8 with 100% accuracy
   - Up to $10 with 100% accuracy
   Assessment: Repeated opportunity across community settings.

(cont.)

FIGURE 3.1. *(cont.)*

3. When asked his address or phone number by an authority (e.g., a mall security officer or cashier), Jabrill will find his personal identification card and present it to the person asking in four out of four trials. *Assessment: Repeated trials.*

AREA: Communication

Present Level of Educational Performance:

Jabrill has strongly developed the social functions of language. He uses what articulations he can and nonverbal signals to gain attention and exchange social kidding. In the middle school context, this is highly effective for getting peers to talk with him. He is less effective in making requests and tends to wait for others to guess his needs and wants. He also does not have the function of negotiation (see section on Social Behavior.) Because his articulations are unclear, he uses a voice output communication device to augment his speech. He especially needs this device to be understood in his general education classes. Jabrill also relies on using his sounds to "joke" rather than engaging in a conversation with a clear topic.

Measurable Annual Goal related to meeting the student's needs:

When given AAC with expanded vocabulary, Jabrill will use his AAC device to maintain a topic of conversation, make his needs and preferences known, and initiate responses in general education.

Short-Term Objectives/Benchmarks:

1. When given an appropriate time to talk with a peer or teacher about a familiar topic, Jabrill will engage in conversational turn taking using both his speech and AAC to maintain a topic for at least five exchanges on 4 out of 5 days. *Assessment: Frequency count of initiations/responses on topic.*
2. In a variety of school contexts, Jabrill will gain someone's attention and ask for what he needs or wants using his speech or AAC for four out of five opportunities. *Assessment: Repeated-opportunities assessment in which the teacher or speech therapist rigs environment so Jabrill needs or wants something (e.g., "accidentally" forgetting to give him a paper passed out or placing an object of interest not quite within reach of him).*
3. In general education classes, Jabrill will raise his hand and initiate a statement of three words (e.g., "Tornados are weather") about the topic of the lesson using new content vocabulary on his AAC device with at least three, initiations in 5 days of class. *Assessment: Frequency count. (Note: if this becomes too frequent because of his preference for social attention, add a goal for maximum number of initiations later.)*

Related Services

Type of Service, Aid, or Modification			Location	Time per day/week
Assistive technology	☒ yes ☐ no		Consultation in all locations	4 hours per week
Adaptive physical education	☒ yes ☐ no		School gym	90 min/1× per week
Audiology services	☐ yes ☒ no			
Counseling	☐ yes ☒ no			
Interpreter	☐ yes ☒ no			
Medical services	☐ yes ☒ no			
Occupational therapy	☒ yes ☐ no		whole school	30 min/1× per week
Physical therapy	☒ yes ☐ no		whole school	30 min/1× per week
Psychological services	☐ yes ☒ no			
Special transportation	☒ yes ☐ no		to/from school	daily
Speech/lang. therapy	☒ yes ☐ no		whole school	30 min/2× per week

(cont.)

FIGURE 3.1. *(cont.)*

TRANSITION PLANNING/STATEMENT:

☒ Under 16, formalized transition planning not needed

☐ 16 years old and up—Outcome statement that describes a direction and plan for the student's post-high school years from the perspective of student, parent, and team members.

LEAST RESTRICTIVE ENVIRONMENT

Does this student attend the school (or, for a preschool-age student, participate in the environment) he or she would attend if nondisabled?   ☒ yes   ☐ no If no, justify:

Does this student receive all special education services with nondisabled peers?

☐ yes   ☒ no

If no, justify (justification may not be solely because of needed modifications in the general curriculum): Jabrill is able to participate with nondisabled peers for most subject areas but does need additional modifications and supports in the areas of mathematics, functional living skills, and therapy.

METHOD/FREQUENCY FOR REPORTING PROGRESS OF ATTAINING GOALS TO PARENTS

Annual Goal Progress reports will be sent to parents each time report cards are issued (every 9 weeks).

The following people attended and participated in the meeting to develop this IEP.

Position	Signature	Date
Parent	_____	_____
Parent	_____	_____
Local education agency representative	_____	_____
Special education teacher	_____	_____
General education teacher	_____	_____
Student	_____	_____
Career/Technical ed. representative	_____	_____
Other agency representative	_____	_____

FIGURE 3.1. *(cont.)*

some of the assumptions underlying the IEP. The following are our own professional interpretations of what the IEP process assumes. When these assumptions are met, we think a stronger educational program will be planned for the student with disabilities.

All Students Will Receive Instruction in the General Curriculum

One of the assumptions underlying the requirements of the IEP is that all students will have the opportunity for instruction in the general curriculum as outlined by state standards. The description of the student's current performance level includes how the disability will affect this involvement. For students with severe disabilities, this description may include a focus on an alternate level of achievement for grade-level standards. For example, a student who is in the eighth grade should have the opportunity to learn eighth-grade language arts, but rather than being expected to read and comprehend at an eighth-grade level, the student may be using accommodations such as text summaries and read-alouds, as described in Chapter 5. The IEP may briefly describe how the student's intellectual and other disabilities affect his or her achievement-level expectations. What is not appropriate is to say that because a student has severe disabilities, he or she cannot participate in the general curriculum. The requirements for participation in the general curriculum are reinforced by the requirement that the student participate in either the state's general assessment of state standards or an alternate assessment. The IEP team is the group that decides which assessment option is most appropriate. The planning document records the selection and rationale for this choice. Because AA–AAS must align with the state's academic content standards (U.S. Department of Education, 2003), students must have the opportunity to learn this content for fairness in assessment.

The Team Will Plan for Inclusion in General Education

In the early days of special education, educators sometimes assumed that students with severe disabilities needed a separate setting to meet their specialized needs. Current IDEA (2004) language for IEP planning does *not* assume that students with more severe disabilities will be in self-contained settings, but instead promotes consideration of inclusion in regular education settings and with nondisabled students. The IEP must include information on how the student will be educated with other children with and without disabilities and the extent to which the student will not participate with children who are nondisabled. Ideally, the team should begin by considering how the student can be included in general education as a full-time member of the class and plan for this inclusion. IDEA does still require that a full continuum of services be available for the delivery of special education as needed; however, there is no barrier in IDEA to including all students if their needs can be met in general education with appropriate supports. Often the extent to which a student with severe disabilities participates in inclusive settings depends on the commitment and creativity of the IEP planning team and the cultivation of the overall school environment to welcome and support students with diverse needs. Given that research shows how some schools have successfully included students with severe disabilities as members of general education classes (Agran et al., 2006; Giangreco et al., 1993; McDonnell et al., 2001), the IEP team needs a strong rationale for planning special education in a full-time self-contained setting.

The Student Will Receive Instruction and Supports to Achieve Academic and Functional Goals

As described in Chapter 1, in the early decades of special education, students with severe disabilities often received a separate, functional curriculum only. Most IEP goals were written for activities of daily living. The current expectation is that goals will address both the student's academic and functional needs. There also is an assumption that a concerted effort will be made to help the student achieve these goals. For students who take AA–AAS, benchmarks or short-term objectives (STOs) must be included, as well as annual goals. There also must be a statement of how progress toward the goals will be measured and reported (i.e., a plan for progress monitoring). The services to be provided must also be based on peer-reviewed research to the extent practicable. This is often called "evidence-based practice," as described in Chapter 4.

The Student's Unique Current and Future Needs Will Be Considered

The IEP process also addresses the student's unique educational needs. Special education is to be linked to the needs created by the student's disability. For example, if the student needs assistive technology, Braille, and a plan for PBS, each of these is included. The plan also must consider transition to adult living when the student is no older than age 16. The student must have specific goals for this transition and specified services for moving toward these goals. The older student (e.g., age 18 in many states) also must know his or her rights as an adult, referred to legally as the "age of majority." Typically, this means the student, rather than the parents, gives consent.

GUIDELINES FOR A STANDARDS-BASED IEP

From the beginning, IEPs were meant to incorporate parents' and students' input on the priorities for special education services. Because there was no established curriculum, developing the IEP was like selecting items from a store catalog. The team used ecological inventories of community, job, and home environments to list potential activities in which the student would engage. From these, the team created learning objectives based on skills needed for these activities (see Browder, 2001, and Chapter 2, this volume). In the current era of school accountability, teams also need to consider the general curriculum and, specifically, the state's standards for the student's grade level. Chapter 2 provided information on how to identify these standards and extend them for learning by students with severe disabilities. Thompson, Thurlow, Quenemoen, Esler, and Whetstone (2001) found that aligned IEPs may also focus educators on creating higher academic expectations rather than dwelling on student deficits. As McLaughlin, Nolet, Rhim, and Henderson (1999) describe, when IEPs are aligned to state standards, students receive better access to the academic content, and collaboration between general and special educators is enhanced.

When the IEP is framed by the state standards and contains goals aligned with the grade-level academic standards, it is called a "standards-based IEP" (Ahearn, 2006). Research sponsored by the National Association of State Directors of Special Education (NASDSE), reported by Ahearn (2006), found that states differ widely in their degree of emphasis and specific guidelines for creating standards-based IEPs. Some states provide teachers with goal banks that link to state standards (e.g., Arkansas). Colorado provides extensive resources on creating what is called a "standards-driven IEP" (*www.cde.state. co.us/cdesped*). Although states vary widely in their approach to standards-based IEPs, in general the IEP will be standards-based if (1) the student's current level of performance is framed in reference to grade-level standards, (2) goals on the IEP include those that specifically promote learning state academic content standards, and (3) the special education services to be provided will promote learning the general curriculum content.

There are several misconceptions about standards-based IEPs. A standards-based IEP is not the same as the curriculum. Many states have long lists of standards for each grade level. Even if these have been extended and prioritized (see Chapter 2 for information on extended standards), they cannot all be listed on the IEP. A student's daily instruction will include language arts, mathematics, science, social studies, and other subjects in the general curriculum. Figure 3.2 shows that the IEP is just a part of the student's overall curriculum. Ongoing planning is needed to prioritize this content and set weekly goals for learning the content. It is not feasible to do all of this prioritization during the IEP planning meeting. A standards-based IEP also does *not* try to include a short-term objective or even an annual goal for every state standard. (In states with many standards, this would create a very long document!) Instead, the IEP goals indicate what learning is needed to make progress in this curriculum. Some goals may be specific to the highest priority content (e.g., Jordan will identify the major branches of government). But most goals will be skills that are strategies for learning the content (e.g., "Jordan will place up to 10 pictures on a Venn diagram to compare and contrast two topics"; "Sara will choose a picture from an array of four that reflects the repeated story line in a read-aloud"). Finally, a standards-based IEP is not limited only to academic content. Students' needs for functional life skills, therapy, PBS, and other special needs should also be included. These specialized goals do not have to be cross-referenced with state standards. For example, it would be unnecessary to try to link the goal "Sara will void in the toilet when taken on

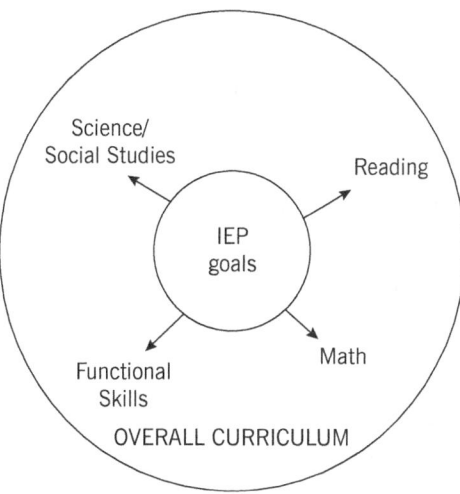

FIGURE 3.2. The IEP as one part of the student's overall curriculum.

a schedule" to an academic content standard. Most IEPs are organized by content areas (see Figure 3.2). The IEP may contain goals in each priority academic content area (i.e., math, language arts, social studies, and science) and also contain "functional goals."

FINDING THE BALANCE: INDIVIDUAL NEEDS VERSUS STATE STANDARDS

One of the challenges in creating a standards-based IEP is balancing the individual needs of the student with the expectations of the state's standards. As Ms. Lim began leading the IEP team to develop a plan for Sara, she struggled with how much time to devote to creating objectives that promote learning in topics such as mathematics and language arts versus addressing Sara's needs to develop communication and self-care skills. There is no "one size fits all" answer to this challenge. Instead, the IEP team needs to listen carefully to each member's contribution to planning and try to find consensus on what best meets the needs of the student. Balance is lost if the final IEP has only academic content when functional goals are needed or if the IEP has only functional goals, ignoring the requirements for learning state standards to prepare for the alternate assessment. Balance also is lost for students who are in the last years of high school if skills needed for adult living are not seen as a priority.

PLANNING AND ASSESSMENT FOR IEP DEVELOPMENT

As described in the opening illustration of Ms. Lim, leading a team to develop an IEP can be an overwhelming experience. Teachers need a set of steps or guidelines to follow to create an IEP. NASDSE (Holbrook, 2007) recommends a seven-step process to develop a standards-based IEP that includes (1) considering grade-level content standards, (2) determining where the student is functioning in relation to the standards, (3) developing the present level of academic and functional performance, (4) developing annual measurable goals, (5) assessing and reporting the student's progress through the year, (6) identifying specially designed instruction, and (7) determining the most appropriate assessment option for the state's large-scale assessment. In addition, the team should also make the process person-centered, and federal guidelines for IEPs for students in AA–AAS require having benchmarks or STOs for the annual goals. A step-by-step process for developing standards-based IEPs for students with severe disabilities are described next. Table 3.1 summarizes the steps for developing a standards-based IEP.

Step 1: Begin with a Student-Centered (Person-Centered Planning) Approach

In the literature on severe disabilities, there are two distinct approaches to developing IEPs—an assessment approach and a planning approach. Campbell, Campbell, and Brady (1998) describe the "assessment" approach as one that uses a diagnostic–prescriptive process. The steps in this process include delineating a sequence of skills, assessing the student's performance within this sequence, and selecting instructional objectives based on assessment results. In contrast, in a "planning" process, a team of people familiar with the student establishes curriculum goals in partnership with the student and family. This might include having a person-centered planning meeting. The terms *person-driven* and *person-controlled* have been used to emphasize that the person being served sets the

TABLE 3.1. 10 Steps for Developing a Standards-Based IEP for a Student with Severe Disabilities

Step 1. Begin with a Student-Centered (Person-Centered Planning) Approach
- Identify the student's preferences.
- Communicate with the parents and student to identify priorities (e.g., premeeting, e-mail, phone call, classroom visit).
- Determine how the student will participate in the IEP planning process (e.g., write goals, participate in the meeting, lead the meeting).

Step 2. Consider the Grade-Level Standards
- Locate the state's grade-level content standards and any extensions.
- Identify the most important standards with general educators.
- Make a list of related skills needed for these priority standards (e.g., identifying story elements).

Step 3. Identify Functional Skills Needed for Student's Current and Future Environments
- Consider skills needed for functioning in school and community.
- Obtain input on other special needs related to the disability (e.g., therapy needs; functional assessment of behavior).
- At least by age 16, consider transition needs.

Step 4. Describe the Student's Current Level of Academic and Functional Performance
- Using information from prior records (e.g., prior IEPs, multidisciplinary assessments).
- Interviewing prior educators.
- Summarizing information from direct observation.
- Using assessment outcomes.

Step 5. Develop Annual Goals for Each Content Area
- Identify the priorities for each academic content area.
  - Consider core content, self-determination, assistive technology, functional applications.
- Identify functional and other goals.

Step 6. Write Specific Short-Term Objectives or Benchmarks
- Write objectives in observable, measurable terms.
- Consider the condition and criteria for objectives.
- Sequence objectives for learning.
- Plan for generalization.

Step 7. Plan How the Student Will Access the General Curriculum
- Plan for participation in general education.

Step 8. Plan Specially Designed Instruction
- Consider assistive technology needs or other accommodations.

Step 9. Select the Appropriate State Assessment Option
- Know the state options.
- Select based on how student accesses the general curriculum (not based on student's disability).

Step 10. Develop Progress Monitoring System
- Develop appropriate type of measure.
- Schedule and implement data collection.
- Use data-based decisions.

agenda (Marrone, Hoff, & Helm, 1997). Rather than matching the person to services that already exist, services are developed based on the person's priorities and unique situation. A person-centered program can enhance self-determination skills, as students are encouraged to make decisions, set their own goals, and run their own meetings. Miner and Bates (1997) evaluated the use of a person-centered planning meeting as a means to increase student and family participation in the IEP transition planning meeting. In this person-centered planning process, the facilitator scheduled a meeting prior to the school's IEP transition meeting with the student and family to brainstorm some goals for the future that could be discussed at the school's meeting. This process increased both family participation and satisfaction with the transition planning process. There are a variety of formats for this process, which are described in Chapter 15. Although it is rarely feasible to hold a full-scale person-centered planning meeting every time an IEP is developed, the values of person-centered planning can be incorporated in three ways by (1) identifying the student's preferences, (2) communicating with the parents and student at the onset of the planning process, and (3) planning how the student will participate actively in the process.

Identifying the Student's Preferences

In a person-centered process, the IEP that is developed should be meaningful and acceptable to the person whose life it most influences—the student him- or herself. One way to promote this student-centered focus is to make a list of the student's preferences and use these in the IEP planning. For example, if a student shows a strong interest in computers, consideration may be given to what additional computer skills might be acquired to promote learning in the general curriculum. Or a student who enjoys swimming in Special Olympics might be able to participate in some way with the school's swim team. As a simple way to identify these preferences, the teacher can brainstorm a list from prior experience with the student or interview the student's past teachers. Some students may be able to respond to an interview about what they like or choose pictures to indicate their preferences. The student might present the pictures of his or her preferences at the beginning of the IEP meeting so that all members of the team can consider ways to honor his or her preferences in planning.

Sometimes a systematic preference assessment may be used in which the teacher gives the student an opportunity to sample items or events (Lohrmann-O'Rourke & Browder, 1998). The student's response to those items and events is then interpreted as a relative indicator of preference. Direct observation of the student interacting with sampling options may give more accurate results than soliciting information from third-party sources (Lohrmann-O'Rourke & Browder, 1998). Although caregivers are an excellent resource with which to begin to identify a student's preferences, research has shown that direct observation of individuals with severe disabilities sometimes conveys a different perspective (e.g., Foxx, Faw, Taylor, Davis, & Fulia, 1993; Green et al., 1988; Green, Reid, Canipe, & Gardner, 1991; Parsons & Reid, 1990). Further, when items are not disparate (e.g., most and least liked), it may be more difficult for caregivers to interpret preferences.

The steps for conducting a systematic preference assessment include (1) defining the assessment purpose, (2) selecting a range of sampling options, (3) determining what form the sampling options will take, (4) developing an assessment schedule, (5) defining a response, (6) identifying presenters and activity partners, and (g) presenting sampling options (Lorhmann-O'Rourke & Browder, 1998). For example, if the assessment purpose is to identify preferences for the IEP, the teacher may choose a range of experiences to sample that relate to how academic content may be presented (e.g., peer tutoring, cooperative learning group, seatwork, computer-assisted learning) or a range of materials to try out. Then a schedule is created that states when these options will be introduced and who will present each one in the days to come. A specific response is defined that represents the student's indication of a preference. Such responses might include showing pleasure (smiling), duration of engagement, indicating yes or no when asked "Do you like this?", or some other means of expression, such as keeping pictures of favorites. Finally, the opportunities are presented, and the teacher keeps a list of the outcomes to summarize for the IEP planning. A systematic preference assessment is time-consuming and may go beyond the time constraints of the typical IEP planning process. In contrast, it may be well worth the investment of time to find new ideas for students with behavioral and motivation problems who have made poor progress in the past or to help build the case for new opportunities (e.g., more inclusion or community-based instruction).

Knowing a person's preferences should not preempt offering choices but, rather, enrich the options for the choice. For example, if Sam's teacher knows that he likes to listen to books on tape about animals, she can have some tapes available. Because having these tapes on hand requires some preparation, the teacher needs to know Sam's preferences in advance. In contrast, knowing that Sam likes orange juice better than milk may be meaningless if Sam can choose either in the school's cafeteria line each day. Another way to make preference assessment more meaningful is to use this information to promote opportunities for self-expression and self-determination. Helping the learner to understand his or her own likes and dislikes is critical for life planning and decision making (Field & Hoffman, 1994). The student might learn to communicate likes and dislikes during conversation training or by making a scrapbook of "favorites." A third option is to create ways for the student to try out new experiences. Sampling a new experience is sometimes called a "situational assessment" (see Chapter 14). Through sampling new options, the student may acquire new or more informed preferences. Figure 3.3 is an example of a preference assessment.

Communicating with the Student's Parents

IDEA promotes having parents be full partners in the IEP planning process. This will not occur if parents are simply invited to a meeting at which a fully developed, typed IEP is presented for approval and signatures. One way to form a partnership with parents for the IEP process is to involve them early in the process. The teacher may hold a premeeting with just the parents and the student or may send an e-mail, make a telephone call, or invite parents to visit for the purpose of getting their input on priorities. The meeting itself should be a welcoming environment for parental input. Parents' schedules should be considered in setting meeting times, and parents should be given adequate prior written notice of meeting dates to make arrangements to attend. If parents cannot attend, a phone call or other communication is especially important to invite their thoughts. The school should make sure that parents understand the IEP process and have interpreters if needed. Parental involvement in the IEP should be documented, and parents should receive a copy of the IEP.

Student: Sam	Step 1 Explore each club's school website		Step 2 List clubs student is interested in joining	Step 3 Rank from most to least	Step 4 Visit top three clubs on club day	Step 5 Choose one club	Important notes about club
Person responsible	Paraeducator		Paraeducator	Paraeducator	Teacher	Teacher	Application for yearbook staff is available on the school website, no cost to join, open to juniors or seniors, Mrs. Mauck is the yearbook sponsor, Room 2025, staff meet 1st and 3rd Wednesday of each month 2nd period.
Family and Consumer Science Cooking Club	YES	NO ✓					
Band	YES ✓	NO					
BETA	YES	NO ✓					
DECA	YES	NO ✓					
FBLA	YES	NO ✓					
FCA	YES ✓	NO					
FFA	YES	NO ✓	Band	2	1st Wed/ Sept		
Key Club	YES ✓	NO	FCA	4			
STLP	YES ✓	NO	Key Club	5			
Yearbook staff	YES ✓	NO	STLP	6			
TSA	YES	NO ✓	Yearbook	1	1st Wed/ Sept	✓	
Game Club	YES ✓	NO	Game Club	3	1st Wed/ Sept		

FIGURE 3.3. Systematic preference assessment of school clubs.

In addition to these basic requirements, the process should also be conducted in ways that welcome the parents as partners and understand the family's cultural values. There are some specific strategies the teacher may use to help the family to take a lead in planning (Leal, 1998; Turnbull & Turnbull, 1997). First, the teacher can begin the meeting by having the family express what they would like to discuss. If the meeting has begun with the student sharing goals, pictures of preferences, or other things, this also sets the occasion for making the meeting a positive affirmation of the student's abilities. When parents express concerns, the teacher or other team members may restate these as possible priorities (e.g., "I hear you saying that giving Sara the chance to learn to read is important. Is that right?"). The teacher can also learn to be a sensitive and responsive listener. Parents may object to what is proposed for a variety of reasons. The proposal may conflict with their personal or cultural values, they may have had a prior negative experience, they may misunderstand what is proposed, or they may disagree with the professional assessment of their child's needs. Sometimes different professionals have given parents conflicting information (e.g., "your child can only learn functional skills"). Although specific guidelines in IDEA provide for an administrator to oversee the resolution of disputes with parents, the teacher should work in partnership to minimize the need for conflict resolution. Taking the time to build rapport with parents can have an important, positive impact on a student's educational program.

Determining How the Student Will Be Involved in the Planning Process

By law, students with disabilities have to attend their planning meeting only if appropriate. Many students with severe disabilities do not attend their meetings, but many also have never had systematic instruction in how to participate in a meeting, share goals, or lead a meeting. Arndt, Konrad, and Test (2006) have described several ways to engage students in these meetings. First, students may be asked to identify goals prior to the meeting. For example, students may choose between picture options of skills they would like to learn, or they may create an album of their preferences. One option is to teach students to present their goals as a PowerPoint presentation at the meeting. Students may practice this skill with systematic prompting and feedback until they can present with little or no assistance.

Another role students may take is to state the purpose of the meeting. This could be achieved using a voice augmentative and alternative communication (AAC) device for students who do not speak. Students might also be given an opportunity to self-evaluate by listing what they do well and what they need to do better. This might be prepared in advance of the meeting using a list of pictures or sight words. Another skill students could learn (Arndt et al., 2006) is to pose questions to others in the meeting. For example, a student might ask others what goals they would propose. During the meeting, the teacher might check for student understanding (e.g., "We are talking about your math class now. What are we talking about?"). Students may be asked what support they need, perhaps in the form of a selection (e.g., "Which of these types of help might you need in math class—a friend to help, a teacher to help, a computer, a calculator?"). The student might be asked to summarize and close the meeting. At first, the student might participate in his or her IEP meeting by using one or two of these forms. The first time a student is at the meeting, one or two of these forms of participation might be selected.

Over time, the student may learn to lead the entire meeting. For example, Koger and Bambara (1995) taught two adults with developmental disabilities to lead their own meetings by following a series of picture prompts. Students practiced in mock meetings and then applied their skills to their actual meeting. In another study, Allen et al. (2001) used a multimedia package—including a teacher manual, student workbook, and two videos—designed to teach four high school students with moderate disabilities the skills need to manage their own IEP meetings. Mock IEP meetings were held in order for students to practice their skills, followed by the real IEP meeting, in which students demonstrated the skills needed to direct their own education plans (e.g., stating the purpose of the meeting, introducing the people in attendance, communicating their interests, skills, and limitations). Involving students in the IEP planning process has recently been deemed an evidence-based practice based on 16 studies yielding a moderate level of quality by

TABLE 3.2. Promoting Student Participation in Planning Meetings

1. Plan the meeting with the student (e.g., where to meet, the time, and agenda). For students who do not have these planning skills, consider their preferences (e.g., favorite settings, most alert times of the day).
2. If the student needs support to be present and active in the meeting, identify who will provide the necessary support (e.g., teacher, paraprofessional, family member).
3. Encourage all team members to interact with the student before the meeting begins.
4. If possible, have the student call the meeting to order (e.g., ring a bell; pound a gavel) and announce the agenda (e.g., pass out written agenda). If not possible, begin the meeting by "introducing" the student and mentioning some of his or her recent achievements.
5. Encourage older students to run their own meeting (e.g., by showing pictures to initiate each new topic on the agenda). Reinforce younger students' initiations and create opportunities for them to take turns in the flow of the conversation. For students who lack conversational skills, create opportunities for the student to respond to what is being said.
6. Talk *with* the student rather than *about* the student. When reviewing the student's achievements or other information, begin by acknowledging the student directly.
7. Try to maintain the "no negative comments" rule. When discussing problems the student is encountering, do so in a way that is gentle and respectful.
8. Decide how to respond if the student tires of the meeting and wants to leave (e.g., will the meeting end?). If the team decides to continue the meeting, make notes of any decisions that will need to be reviewed later with the student.
9. For students with limited communication skills or who are passive in meetings, invite someone (e.g., advocate, peer) whose only role in the meeting is to be sure the student's participation is encouraged and acknowledged and who will remind the group of the student's preferences whenever relevant.

Note. Adapted from Browder (2001). Copyright 2001 by The Guilford Press. Adapted by permission.

the National Secondary Transition Technical Assistance Center (NSTTAC; Martin, Van Dycke, Christensen, et al., 2006). With additional studies being added to the research base of student-directed IEPs, strategies continue to be strengthened and developed (Konrad & Test, 2004; Neale & Test, 2009; Test & Neale, 2004). Table 3.2 provides some additional guidelines for making IEP meetings student friendly.

Step 2: Consider the Grade-Level Standards

To develop a standards-based IEP, it is important to identify the state standards for the student's grade level and to use these in planning. Chapter 2 provides information on how to locate these standards and extend them for students with severe disabilities. The standards should be considered for each content area in general education. Typically, this includes at least mathematics, language arts, science, and social studies. The chapters on these topics in this book can help teachers get a general overview of the strands of this content. Then the state website can be used to locate the standards for the student's assigned grade. The teacher may want to print these or have an online link bookmarked for reference in the IEP planning meeting.

Because the goal for students taking AA–AAS is alternate achievement, it will be necessary to condense and prioritize these grade-level content standards. Most states have some type of extensions or curricular frameworks for students taking AA–AAS. The teacher should locate these extensions and have hard copies or a bookmarked website for viewing in the IEP meeting. If the state has extensions, these typically form the basis for the alternate assessment. Chapter 2 provides examples of how to extend state standards for teachers who do not have this state resource.

Even these extensions may include large lists of standards. The teacher may need to review these to list the overlapping and core standards. This may require a conversation with the general education teacher in the content area. Although some of this discussion will occur in the IEP meeting itself, the realistic time constraints of most meetings make it necessary to do some preplanning of these priorities. If priorities within the content area are identified, the teacher can also begin to note what skills are needed for students to learn this content (e.g., being able to select a summary picture for informational text).

Step 3: Identify Functional Skills Needed for Student's Current and Future Environments

In addition to state standards, the team will want to consider what functional skills will be needed for the student's current and future environments. These are usually identified through an ecological inventory of the student's current and future environments. Chapter 14 provides an example of an ecological inventory. The teacher can list the environments typically accessed by the student and the skills needed for each. For example, a 12-year-old student may go to the movies with friends. Some of the skills needed for this setting are purchasing the movie ticket, purchasing snacks, locating the specific theater, using the restroom, and socializing with friends. An IEP objective that might come from this analysis might be selecting a movie title and paying the price of a ticket. One shortcut teachers may use is a checklist of functional life skills. The Life-Centered Career Education (LCCE) curriculum (Loyd & Brolin, 1997) contains lists of skills across many life domains. Examples of skills from the LCCE are shown in Figure 3.4. Having a list of potential skills for transition will be important for students who have transition plans (beginning no later than age 16). Chapter 15 provides examples of domains for transition planning.

Students may also have additional therapy and skill needs. The teacher will want to be sure that evaluations from speech therapy, occupational therapy, and physical therapy will be available for the team's consideration, along with someone who will interpret them and make recommendations. As described in Chapter 10, the best approach to meeting these therapy needs is to integrate the various therapies into the total educational program rather than relying on isolated therapies. All members of the IEP team, including the parents and the student, need to understand the goals of therapy and be involved in them. The IEP team is also required by IDEA to consider positive behavioral interventions for students whose behavior impedes their own learning or that of others. Chapter 12 provides a description of how to conduct a functional assessment that forms the foundation for planning for social behavior.

Step 4: Describe the Student's Current Level of Academic and Functional Performance

In Steps 3 and 4, the teacher is collecting information on the skills the student needs to meet the current grade-level content and for daily living (functional skills) and on other related skills and therapy needs. Now the student's current level of performance can be described using these skills lists as a frame of reference. To summarize the student's academic and functional performance, the teacher can use prior records, interviews with

LIFE-CENTERED CAREER EDUCATION
Competency Rating Scale—Modified
Record Form
DAILY LIVING SKILLS

Student Name _____ Date of Birth _____ Sex _____

School _____ City _____ State _____

Directions; Please rate the student according to his or her mastery of each item using the rating key below. Indicate the ratings in the column below the date for the rating period. Use the NR rating for items that cannot be rated. For subcompetencies rated 0 or 1 at the time of the final rating, place a check (✓) in the appropriate space in the Yes/No column to indicate the student's ability to perform the subcompetency with assistance from the community. Please refer to the CRS manual for explanation of the rating key, description of the behavioral criteria for each subcompetency, and explanation of the Yes/No column.

Rating Key: 0 = Not Competent   1 = Partially Competent   2 = Competent   NR = Not Rated

To what extent has the student mastered the following subcompetencies?	Date(s) Grade Raters							
DAILY LIVING SKILLS DOMAIN							Yes	No
1. Managing money								
1. Count money								
2. Make purchases								
3. Use vending machines								
4. Budget money								
5. Perform banking skills								
2. Selecting and maintaining living environments								
6. Select appropriate community living environments								
7. Maintain living environment								
8. Use basic appliances and tools								
9. Set up personal living space								
3. Caring for personal health								
10. Perform appropriate grooming and hygiene								
11. Dress appropriately								
12. Maintain physical fitness								
13. Recognize and seek help for illness								
14. Practice basic first aid								
15. Practice personal safety								

FIGURE 3.4. An example of skills for the Life-Centered Career Education curriculum. Based on Loyd and Brolin (1997).

professionals who have worked with the student in the past, parent interviews, and direct observations of the student.

If the student has had access to general curriculum content in the past and progress monitoring was used, the teacher will have a rich source of data from these past records to describe performance in each academic content area, as well as other IEP areas. If the student has not had prior instruction in general curriculum content, the team needs to acknowledge that current deficits in knowledge and skills may be the result of lack of opportunity. The student may have had instruction in the general curriculum, but the records of his or her progress may not have been kept clearly. In this situation, the teacher may want to interview the professionals who previously worked with the student to determine what skills the student displayed and what skills are still needed. Parents often can provide information on the student's current performance, not only in skills of daily living but sometimes in academic content as well. Parents may have kept samples of work from the prior year that helped provide a picture of the student's ability. The student's performance on the state assessment also adds information for this summary. Specific skill information (e.g., checklists) may be included in AA–AAS in some states. Other states may have only a score or rating in their records (e.g., "87%" or "proficient"). These outcomes should be included in the description of the student's current performance. Finally, to fill in the gaps in what is known about what the student can do, the teacher may use some direct observation. This may include having the student try some potential activities to see what he or she can do. Some teachers may generate their own checklists of skills that students may need to access the general curriculum for this purpose. Figure 3.5 is an example of such a checklist.

Step 5: Develop Annual Goals for Each Content Area

Once the student's current academic and functional performance has been specified, the team has the information needed to develop the annual goals. This goal setting will most likely occur in the IEP team planning meeting, but team members often bring goal suggestions based on the assessment information they have gathered. If the student has developed goals, these should be presented first in the meeting. At least one annual goal is written in each content area specified on the IEP. Some of these annual goals may link directly to a grade-level standard. Others will address multiple standards. In writing the goal, it is important to use an observable, measurable statement of performance, as shown in the following example.

Annual Goal: *"Given a variety of adapted texts and a read-aloud, Steve will identify the major elements of the story, giving examples of each for at least three different types of text."*

State Standard Link: *"Identify the major elements of text in fiction and nonfiction and support with reference to the text."* (from North Carolina Standard Course of Study)

Sometimes teams also specify the conditions for performing the skill. The conditions are the accommodations Steve will need to access books from his grade level that are adapted and read aloud. The specific performance specified in the annual goal is identifying major elements of a story. This particular goal links to a state standard for fifth-grade

Student: Roberto   **Grade Level:** Seventh Grade

Skill for accessing general curriculum	What the student can do now	What the student needs to learn
1. Participate in a read-aloud of a story.	Points to pictures when read a picture book.	Participate in the read-aloud; attend to books that are grade/age appropriate (may be adapted books).
2. Participate in read-aloud of informational text.	Attends only if text has colorful pictures and no more than two lines of text per page.	Participate in read-alouds with longer text summaries and fewer pictures (e.g., adaptations of seventh-grade textbooks).
3. Indicate answer to literal comprehension questions.	Points to picture when asked, "Show me the _____."	Choose between an array of pictures to answer a question about characters, action, and main ideas.
4. Use pictures to summarize a passage of informational text.	Selects a picture of choice and inserts it in PowerPoint with some modeling.	Select pictures that relate to topic of passage, not just preferred ones.
5. Use a concept statement to summarize the main idea in science or social studies.	Does not respond to fill-in-the-blank concept statements.	Use pictures to complete concept statements (specific concepts must be identified for each unit in the textbook).
6. Use the Internet to research a topic.	Finds familiar Internet sites using bookmarked favorites.	Follow a task analysis to find information on a chosen topic.
7. Develop a report (e.g., book report, research report).	Selects a picture of choice and inserts it in PowerPoint with some modeling.	Sequence information and convey it to teacher or class using assistive technology.
8. Follow a model to use manipulatives or models in science and math.	Requires hand-over-hand assistance to count out a math problem or set up a model (has limited fine-motor coordination).	Explore adapted materials that are easier to use; learn to imitate a model for setting up materials, as well as mastering the operation in math or concept in science.
9. Work with a cooperative learning group.	Enjoys peer work but becomes silly and does not contribute to group.	Take a turn during cooperative learning activity; generalize current skills to group context.
10. Complete seatwork such as worksheets, learning centers.	Colors the worksheet (not age appropriate); does not stay focused on learning centers.	Complete a worksheet that requires two simple independent responses (e.g., stamping picture, highlighting answer); generalize current skills to a learning center (e.g., finding picture with little to no assistance); self-monitor instructional task (place stamp of each step of task until completed).

FIGURE 3.5. An example of a teacher-made checklist to use in developing a statement of academic performance.

language arts. Note that the goal also requires generalization across types of text (e.g., short story, biography, news article).

Step 6: Write Specific Short-Term Objectives or Benchmarks

Once the annual goals are established, the teacher can develop STOs. This may also occur in the IEP team planning meeting, but again, the team members may prepare draft STOs prior to the meeting. STOs should reflect the process of shaping the student's performance toward the annual goal. As described in Chapter 4, performance can be task analyzed and taught using chaining, or different components of the skill can be taught. Here are two different ways to write STOs for Steve's annual goal in language arts. In the first example, the teacher addresses all types of text but shapes the different elements identified. In the second example, the teacher shapes each type of text one at a time.

SHORT-TERM OBJECTIVE EXAMPLE 1

Annual Goal: *"Given a variety of adapted texts and a read-aloud, Steve will identify the major elements of the story, giving examples of each for at least three different types of text."*

STO 1: Steve will identify the main character across three types of text for 2 out of 2 probes by the end of week 9.

STO 2: Steve will identify the setting of the text across three types of text for 2 out of 2 probes by the end of week 18.

STO 3: Steve will identify the conflict and resolution of the text across three types of text for 2 out of 2 probes by the end of week 24.

STO 4: Steve will identify the main idea of the text across three types of text for 2 out of 2 probes by the end of week 27.

STO 5: Steve will generalize identifying 4 out of 5 story elements across five new texts for the remainder of the school year.

SHORT-TERM OBJECTIVE EXAMPLE 2

Annual Goal: *"Given a variety of adapted texts and a read-aloud, Steve will identify the major elements of the story, giving examples of each for at least three different types of text."*

STO 1: Steve will identify the main character and setting of a short story for 2 out of 2 probes by the end of week 9.

STO 2: Steve will identify the conflict, resolution, and main idea of a short story for 2 out of 2 probes by the end of week 15.

STO 3: Steve will identify story elements of a biography for 2 out of 2 probes by the end of week 18.

STO 4: Steve will identify story elements of a news story for 2 out of 2 probes by the end of week 27.

STO 5: Steve will generalize identifying 4 out of 5 story elements across at least 5 new texts by the end of the school year.

Step 7: Plan How the Student Will Access the General Curriculum

Some students with disabilities access the general curriculum with minimal supports and accommodations. That is, they can keep pace in a regular class performing on grade level with some extra tutoring, use of assistive technology, or other accommodations, such as the opportunity to take tests in a private setting. For example, some students with significant physical challenges or ASD keep pace with grade-level achievement with such accommodations. Students with moderate and severe developmental disabilities typically are not able to keep pace with grade-level achievement even with accommodations. Instead, they will need modifications in not only instruction but also expectations. The IEP team needs to make the important decision about whether grade-level or alternate achievement of the content is expected, as this will affect what the student will learn and the type of statewide assessment to be used. If the team has defined the student's academic and functional performance well and targeted annual goals based on this definition, it should be clear whether the expectation is grade-level or alternate achievement. In contrast, this decision should be made with serious consideration of the highest possible achievement for the student, as it may affect the student's opportunities. In some states, students cannot graduate with a regular diploma unless grade-level achievement is attained.

If the student will access the general curriculum through alternate achievement, this is typically specified on the IEP. It would not be appropriate to say that the student will not access the general curriculum and plan a functional curriculum instead. In current federal legislation, all students must have the opportunity to learn the general curriculum. The team also needs to consider where and how this curriculum will be delivered. Research on the impact of including students with moderate and severe disabilities in general education classrooms has generally been supportive of these placement decisions. Early studies revealed student gains in attaining IEP objectives (Brinker & Thorpe, 1984), increased communication and social skills (Cole & Meyer, 1991), and increased peer contact both in and outside school (McDonnell, Hardman, Hightower, & Kiefer-O'Donnell, 1991). Other studies have focused on educational strategies related to high rates of student engagement (Logan, Bakeman, & Keefe, 1997), the quality and quantity of social relations between students in inclusive versus segregated settings (Fryxell & Kennedy, 1995; Grenot-Scheyer, 1994), the concerns of teachers facing inclusion (York, Vandercook, MacDonald, Heise-Neff, & Caughey, 1992), moral outcomes for general education students (Helmstetter, Peck, and Giangreco, 1994), and the impact of inclusive programming on the academic attainment of the general education students (Hunt, Staub, Alwell, & Goetz, 1994; Sharpe, York, & Knight, 1994). In almost all reported cases, inclusive programming has been linked to positive results (Hunt, Soto, Maier, & Dowering, 2003; Johnson & McDonnell, 2004; McDonnell et al., 2003).

With the literature base growing, a number of experts have outlined the models they used to facilitate the inclusion of students with severe disabilities (see, e.g., Jorgensen, 1998; Jorgensen, Schuh, & Nisbet, 2006; Lipsky & Gartner, 1989; Mastropieri & Scruggs, 2007; Villa & Thousand, 1995). Although the models vary in a number of ways, several themes emerge regarding the successful implementation of inclusion. First, it is imperative that the administration supports the movement of students with disabilities into general education and takes steps to support the changing roles of teachers. Second, professional collaboration is a frequently noted aspect of successful inclusion. Third, inclusion needs to be viewed as a process rather than an outcome. As noted by Calculator

(1994) in recounting a conversation he had with an administrator involved in inclusion, "[there was a failure] to anticipate the amount of work that would then be necessary to assure these students (and their families) that students' educational needs could be met in these . . . settings" (p. xxi).

An important part of this work is the planning needed to focus the instructional priorities of the student with moderate and severe disabilities. Inclusion is more than planning for the student to be present in general educational settings (temporal inclusion). It is also more than encouraging social membership in the class and school for students with moderate and severe disabilities (social inclusion). Students must also have the opportunity to learn from the curriculum and to address their unique instructional needs (instructional inclusion). Sometimes this will require planning how to embed systematic instruction in the general education setting, as described in Chapter 4. Table 3.3 presents some of the decisions that may be considered as the team plans how the student will access the general education setting.

Although IEP teams should give careful consideration to inclusion, the current reality is that most students with severe developmental disabilities receive services in self-contained special education classrooms (Smith, 2007). Although teachers may advocate for a school climate accepting of all students, it may take time for the needed systems-level change to occur. If the IEP team does not choose a general education placement, the reasons must be documented on the IEP, per IDEA. The planning should then focus on how the general curriculum can be delivered in the self-contained special education context. Some options may include the teacher collaborating with general education teachers on shared lesson plans that are replicated in the special education class, using published curricula that address state standards for this population (e.g., Trela, Jimenez, & Browder, 2008), and developing teacher-made lessons based on state standards using ideas provided in this book and other resources. One of the challenges of teaching the standards in a self-contained class is finding the time to address all the content. Ms. Portlock's story (that of a real teacher) illustrates how one teacher met this challenge.

FINDING THE BALANCE: "SO MANY IEP OBJECTIVES FOR DIFFERENT STUDENTS"

Ms. Portlock is a middle school teacher of students with moderate and severe disabilities. Ms. Portlock teaches her students science, math, literacy, and functional living skills every day. Over the past couple of years the daily teaching schedule in her classroom has changed. She used to look at a student's IEP and pull him or her to do one-on-one massed trials to meet the objectives. That method of teaching was strenuous, and students often did not receive daily instruction on grade-level standards or IEP objectives. Now, Ms. Portlock has divided her school day into periods based on the schedule used by the rest of the school. She teaches science, math, and literacy and still has time for community-based instruction, home and living skills, and therapy skills, as well as adapted physical education. The key to her success is thinking about the standard she is teaching in each subject area and what skills the students need to be successful. For example, this week in science the students in her class are learning about chemical reactions. Ms. Portlock has identified two new sight words and picture symbols the students need to know (i.e., *chemical reaction, solution*). While she is teaching this lesson, Ms. Portlock is able to work on students' IEP goals of "identifying new sight words." Besides working on sight-word recognition, she is also helping students who have fine-motor therapy goals that can be addressed while they participate in the experiment, behavioral goods that can be addressed in cooperative inquiry learning groups, and math IEP goals that concern measurement or numeracy.

TABLE 3.3. Decision-Making Hierarchy for Planning Adaptations in Inclusive Educational Settings

Questions to ask	If "yes," then . . .	Example	If "no," then . . .
1. Can the student participate in the class activity just like other classmates?	Student participates like classmates.	Cooperative learning group in science.	Go to 2.
2. Can the student participate in the same class activity if the environment is adapted?	Identify the student's need and strategize on adaptations to the environment.	Students have peer partners in the group.	Go to 3.
3. Can the student participate in the same class activity if the general education teacher's instruction is adapted? Or embedded systematic instruction is provided?	Identify the student's need and strategize on instructional adaptations.	Peer partner embeds systematic prompting to help student complete observation chart.	Go to 4.
4. Can the student participate in the same class activity if the general education materials are adapted?	Identify the student's need and strategize on adapted materials.	Student's observation chart simplified and color coded.	Go to 5.
5. Can the student participate in the same class activity with adapted expectations or rules?	Identify the student's need and strategize on adapted expectations or rules.	Student not expected to take a turn as group recorder.	Go to 6.
6. Can the student participate in the same class activity if given personal assistance?	Identify the student's need and strategize on personal assistance; train peer or adult.	Student's partner gives reminders to stay seated and on task.	Go to 7.
7. Can the student participate in the same class activity with goals focused on alternate achievement standards of the same content?	Identify the student's need and strategize on adaptations to incorporate different levels.	Student selects object to complete concept statement vs. written summary.	Go to 8.
8. Can the student participate in the same class activity with goals from a different curriculum content area?	Identify the student's need and strategize on adaptations to incorporate goals from a different curriculum content area.	Student works on early literacy when group reads their summaries (e.g., points to text).	Go to 9.
9. Can the student work in the general education class on a different activity related to IEP goals?	Identify the student's need and strategize on incorporating a different activity least intrusively.	When class is applying complex formula, student uses picture instructions to put science materials away.	Go to 10.
10. Can the student work in the building on a logical different activity related to IEP goals?	Identify student's needs and strategize on incorporating change of location least intrusively.	When class is taking a test, student practices using vending machine in lounge.	Go to 11.
11. Can the student work on community-based activity related to IEP goals?	Identify the student's need and strategize on incorporating change of location least intrusively.	When class is taking exams, student practices purchasing at nearby stores.	

Note. Based on Ryndak and Alper (2003).

Step 8: Plan Specially Designed Instruction

In planning specially designed instruction, the team considers accommodations and modifications the student needs to make progress in the general curriculum. For students with severe disabilities, careful consideration should be given to how to develop the student's communication system and to his or her need for assistive technology. For students to be able to "show what they know," they need both communication symbols and a mode of communication to transmit this knowledge. For example, a student who only has the symbols "eat," "toilet," "drink," and "help" on a communication system cannot communicate about math or science. Students who rely only on nonsymbolic communication also will have difficulty communicating new knowledge and need the opportunity to acquire symbol use. Most students with developmental disabilities will have "communication" as one of the domains for annual goals and STOs. Chapter 11 provides more information on how to develop a student's communication system and can provide ideas for developing goals in this area.

Besides targeting specific communication goals, the team may also want to consider other assistive technology and accommodation needs. For example, students may need adaptive equipment for writing or eating, enlarged print, special seating, or assistance in taking medication. The assessment provided by the physical therapist, occupational therapist, vision specialist, or other specialist will be especially helpful for this planning. Chapter 10 provides more information on team collaboration regarding medical, sensory, and physical challenges.

Step 9: Select the Appropriate State Assessment Option

The IEP team makes the important decision about which statewide assessment is appropriate for the student. As described in Chapter 2, these options will include the general assessment, the general assessment with accommodations, and AA–AAS. Some states may also have an alternate assessment based on modified achievement standards and/or an alternate assessment based on grade-level achievement standards. The primary criterion for determining which assessment is appropriate is the way the student accesses the general curriculum (e.g., alternate or grade-level achievement standards). The U.S. Department of Education's *Toolkit on Teaching and Assessing Students with Severe Disabilities* (2006) notes several considerations that should *not* determine the assessment. For example, the selection should not be based on the student's participation in a separate, specialized curriculum. It is not appropriate to say that a student needs the AA–AAS because he or she is in a functional curriculum. All students must have access to the general curriculum, even if they also need supplemental functional curriculum access. The decision should not be based on the student's current placement. In some states, students in inclusive settings are in AA–AAS. Nor should placement in a self-contained class be based on taking the AA–AAS. The assessment choice cannot be based on the student's disability. It would not be appropriate to decide that, because a student has both autism and a severe intellectual disability, the AA–AAS is appropriate. The decision should also not be made to boost a school's overall rating (i.e., if it is easier to get proficiency on AA–AAS). Again, the student's educational needs should determine the decision. Table 3.4 shows some examples of considerations that would lead to recommending AA–AAS based on the U.S. Department of Education *Toolkit* (2006).

TABLE 3.4. Reasons an IEP Team Might Select AA–AAS

How does the student access the general education curriculum?
• AA–AAS may be the best option if the student needs extensive prioritization within grade-level content.

How has the student responded to past academic instruction?
• AA–AAS may be the best option if the student requires ongoing systematic instruction to learn prioritized skills and needs to focus on the critical essence of the content.

How does the student interact with text?
• AA–AAS may be the best option if the student needs key words, pictures, and auditory cues embedded in adapted or controlled text; may need a reader to use these, but may have some emerging reading skills.

Do the supports the student needs change the complexity or cognitive demand of the material?
• AA–AAS may be the best option if the student needs extensive supports such as simplified symbol systems, peer models, choice making for motivation, and other strategies that may change the overall complexity or cognitive demand.

What inferences can be made about the student's generalization/transfer of learning?
• AA–AAS may be the best option if the student needs systematic instruction to generalize.

Note. Adapted from U.S. Department of Education, Office of Special Education Programs (2006).

Step 10: Develop Progress Monitoring System

Once the annual goals and STOs have been identified, the teacher can develop the progress monitoring system. IDEA requires that the IEP include a method for measuring the annual goals and a timeline for communicating outcomes to the parents. For the IEP itself, the team usually identifies the type of progress monitoring to be used. There are at least three options for progress monitoring of students with severe disabilities: (1) extending the research on curriculum-based measurement (CBM) for students with high-incidence disabilities to students with severe disabilities, (2) using a data-based decisions model, or (3) using permanent products such as the portfolio models currently in use for states' alternate assessments to track progress. CBM is characterized by direct assessment of a student's skills in the content of the curriculum that is being taught (cf. Fuchs & Fuchs, 1986; Marston, 1989; Shapiro, 1996; Shinn, 1989; Ysseldyke, Algozzine, & Thurlow, 2000). An alternative form of progress monitoring developed for students with significant disabilities focuses on making decisions about summaries of ongoing data using direct observations of performance of target skills (Belfiore & Browder, 1992; Farlow & Snell, 1994; Haring, Liberty, & White, 1980). Portfolio assessments focus on permanent student products (Allinder & Siegel, 1999; Kleinert & Kearns, 2001; Wesson & King, 1996). The following section provides more information on how to use progress monitoring for IEP objects using the data-based-decisions model.

PROGRESS MONITORING: DATA-BASED DECISIONS

Methods to Measure Skills

The teacher will need to develop a method to measure student progress on each annual goal. Sometimes the STOs will also require different forms of data, but many times these may be subsumed in one probe. There are multiple methods for conducting assessments of IEP objectives through direct observation, as shown in Table 3.5. Many priority skills can be measured by using one of these forms of measurement: (1) task-analytic assessment, (2) repeated-trials assessment, (3) permanent-product assessment, or (4) time-based assessment.

Task-Analytic Assessments

In writing a task analysis, the teacher will usually perform the skill and then write down the responses in sequence. Each step usually begins with an action verb (e.g., *Put, Fix, Clean*). These statements can be used as verbal prompts when teaching the task. Research on task-analytic assessment suggests that it may be important to break the task down into smaller, more specific responses for some students (Crist, Walls, & Haught, 1984; Thvedt, Zane, & Walls, 1984). A student who has mastered many self-care skills might be ready to learn the entire routine for eating in the cafeteria, as shown in Table 3.5; for other students it might be necessary to focus on a specific skill task analysis, such as purchasing milk. Sometimes teachers may include steps that are nonessential to the task for teaching purposes. For example, the student might read aloud the price when using the vending machine to practice number reading. These nonessential steps should be excluded when determining task mastery (Williams & Cuvo, 1986). Task-analytic assessment has wide applicability for both the academic and functional annual goals included in the IEP. Academic skills, such as participating in a read-aloud, solving a math problem, and conducting a science experiment, can all be written as task analyses to be used to monitor progress. So can such skills as performing a job task, making a purchase in the community, and getting ready for the bus.

Repeated-Trial Assessments

Some skills are not performed as a chain of responses, and task-analytic assessment is not applicable. Sometimes, when the skill does involve a chain of responses, only one or two discrete responses may be targeted for a student. For example, for a student with complex physical challenges, two discrete responses during hand washing may be choosing which scented soap to use by eye gazing and wetting his or her hands by moving them under the faucet. A discrete response during a read-aloud might be to select one of two objects to show the meaning of what was read. When discrete responses are the focus, a repeated-trial assessment is the best choice. Depending on the student's objective, these repeated trials may focus on a single response or a set of responses and may be given together at one point in time or across the day. When they are given across the day, it is called a *repeated-opportunity assessment*.

Other Options

Most teachers may find that they can measure all, or nearly all, of their students' IEP objectives using task-analytic and repeated-trial (or repeated-opportunity) assessments. These methods lend themselves well to daily data collection and data-based decisions, as described in the next sections. Other options for measuring IEP objectives include using permanent products and time-based assessments. These methods may be especially use-

TABLE 3.5. Options for Using Direct Assessment to Measure Progress on the IEP

When to use	Variations	Example
	Task-analytic assessment	
For skills that involve a chain of responding (e.g., setting a table, putting on a coat, using a photocopier, participating in a read-aloud of a story, completing a math problem)	• *Task analysis of a single skill*: Brushing teeth; solving a math problem; participating in a read-aloud • *Task analysis of an entire routine*: Having lunch in school cafeteria • *Task analysis that is repeated*: Assembly work, folding towels	• *Single-skill task analysis*: 1. Locate the author. 2. Locate the title. 3. Predict what book will be about. 4. Open book. 5. Turn the pages. 6. Point to text as reader reads aloud. 7. Locate key vocabulary word. 8. Read repeated story line. 9. Close the book. 10. Retell the story using pictures. • *Routine task analysis*: 1. Use natural cues to know when to go to lunch. 2. Collect lunchbox. 3. Wait with class. 4. Walk quietly to cafeteria. 5. Wait in line for milk. 6. Purchase milk. 7. Locate friends. 8. Socialize with friends. 9. Eat lunch. 10. Clean up table. 11. Return to class on time. • *Repeated task analysis*: Setting the table 1. Place mat on table. 2. Put plate on mat. 3. Put fork on left of plate. 4. Put knife on right. 5. Put spoon by knife. 6. Put napkin by fork. 7. Place second mat. 8. Put plate on mat. 9. Put fork on left of plate. 10. Put knife on right. 11. Put spoon by knife. 12. Put napkin by fork.
	Repeated-trials assessment	
The skill involves a discrete response (e.g., reading a word, pointing to picture, stating time, nodding "yes")	• *Single response* • *Set of responses* • *Distributed trials* • *Frequency count*	• *Single response—repeated trials*: Point to your name—"Sally" 1. Point to "Sally." 2. Point to "Sally." 3. Point to "Sally." 4. Point to "Sally." 5. Point to "Sally." 6. Point to "Sally." 7. Point to "Sally." 8. Point to "Sally." 9. Point to "Sally." 10. Point to "Sally."

(cont.)

TABLE 3.5. *(cont.)*

When to use	Variations	Example
		• *Set of responses—repeated trials*: Read these science words: 1. Evaporation 2. Condensation 3. Precipitation 4. Rain 5. Sleet 6. Snow
		• *Distributed trials*: Use schedule to initiate next activity 1. 8:00 Homeroom 2. 8:45 Science 3. 9:30 Reading 4. 10:15 Math 5. 11:00 Lunch 6. 11:45 P.E. 7. 12:30 Life Skills 8. 1:15 Community 9. 2:00 Bus
		• *Frequency count*: How many times did Bob use picture wallet? Monday: 3 Tuesday: 0 Wednesday: 4

Permanent product scoring (can be portfolios)

When to use	Variations	Example

Use when the skill produces a permanent product such as a worksheet, project, or computer printout.	• *Percent or number correct*
	• *Scoring rubric*
		• *Percent or number correct on permanent product*:
		○ Number of prices matched correctly
		○ Number of words matched to definitions
		
		• *Scoring rubric for a permanent product*:
		○ Stamp signature
		  4—Name is neat, legible and complete.
		  3—Name is legible but slightly smeared or faint.
		  2—Name is partially legible; may be smeared and faint.
		  1—Name is barely legible because too faint or smeared.
		  0—Name is not legible.

Time-based assessment

When to use	Variations	Example
Use when the purpose is to get student to perform the skill within a given time frame.	• *Rate* • *Latency* • *Duration*	• *Rate* ○ Number of correct math problems per minute • *Latency* ○ Number of seconds until buzzer pushed for help • *Duration* ○ Number of minutes to clean motel room on job site

ful for objectives in which students are gaining fluency or improving quality in already acquired skills. Table 3.5 gives examples of using permanent products and time-based assessments. Many academic skills lend themselves well to the use of permanent products. These may also be included in a portfolio of achievement. Sometimes the permanent product is rated using a rubric, as shown in Table 3.5. Time-based assessments are especially useful when the focus is on fluency. For example, by timing how long it takes a student to read a list of sight words or a short passage, the teacher may monitor increased fluency. In contrast, some students with severe disabilities need longer periods of time to produce a vocal or motoric response, and time-based measures may not provide a fair picture of what they know.

Conducting the Assessment

Once the assessment is planned, the teacher will schedule regular "probes" (i.e., a test of how well the student performs the skill). Usually these data need to be collected at least once a week to track progress. To conduct the assessment of the target skills, the teacher has two options. The first is to conduct a *test* of how well the student performs the skill *without teacher prompting or feedback*. When this test is conducted prior to beginning instruction, it is called "baseline assessment." Before teaching Betty to use the vending machine, the teacher gave her the chance to do so without help. She escorted Betty to the machine in the student commons and waited for Betty to try to purchase a soda. When Betty was not able to do a step within 5 seconds, the teacher did it for her without comment. This is called a "repeated opportunity" assessment because Betty got the opportunity to try each step. Sometimes the teacher may simply end the test when the first error occurs or when no response occurs in a given time frame. This is called a "single opportunity" assessment. The teacher scored her data sheet, putting a minus by each step Betty did not do and a plus by the step she completed (picking up the soda). The teacher repeated this same procedure the next day at the vending machine in front of the grocery store. At this site, Betty did not perform any responses correctly (see Figure 3.6). In a repeated-trial assessment, the teacher will usually present each trial and wait 3–5 seconds for the student to respond (e.g., to read each sight word). The teacher scores the data sheet for each response.

Besides testing student performance of a skill, a second option for measuring progress is to record data during instruction. Figure 3.7 shows data collection during instruction. Note that the teacher recorded the highest level of prompt needed for Cassandra to perform each step of the task analysis. On the first day of instruction, she needed physical guidance (P) to do all steps of the task analysis except cleaning up, which she did with a model (M.) The next day she was able to do more steps with a model. As the days of instruction progressed, Cassandra was able to perform some steps with a verbal prompt (V) and then with no assistance (I). Whether or not to take data during a probe or during instruction depends on the skill, the teacher, and the student. Some skills are too difficult to teach while collecting data. Some teachers prefer to use noninstructional probes for their data collection (see Figure 3.7). Some students may perform better under one method or the other (e.g., they like the challenge of being tested or do not do well when tested).

Figure 3.8 provides an example of a repeated-trial assessment. Jeremy is learning to identify the science term *landform* and to show comprehension of the term by match-

		Student Name: Betty												

Student Name: Betty

Subject/Skill: Using a vending machine

Objective: The student will independently complete all 10 of the task-analyzed steps to make a purchase from a vending machine.

Steps	%		school	grocery										
	100													
	90													
	80													
	70													
	60													
	50													
10		Checks for change	−	−	−	−	−	−	+	+	+	+	+	+
9	40	Retrieves drink or snack from machine	+	−	+	+	+	+	+	+	+	+	+	+
8		Waits for drink or snack	−	−	−	−	−	+	+	+	−	+	+	+
7	30	Makes a selection	−	−	−	−	−	+	+	+	+	+	+	+
6		Deposits money into vending machine	−	−	−	−	−	−	−	−	−	−	+	+
5	20	Takes correct amount out of purse or pocket	−	−	−	−	−	−	−	−	−	−	−	−
4		Determines amount of money needed	−	−	−	−	−	−	−	−	−	−	−	−
3	10	Decides which drink or snack to purchase	−	−	−	+	−	+	−	+	+	+	+	+
2		Scans vending machine options	−	−	−	−	−	−	−	−	+	−	−	+
1	0	Approaches vending machine	−	−	−	−	+	+	+	+	+	+	+	+
Steps	%		10	0	10	20	20	50	50	60	60	60	70	80
		Date	9/29	9/30	10/1	10/2	10/3	10/4	10/5	10/8	10/9	10/10	10/11	10/12

Mastered: Not yet **Data Pattern:** Adequate progress

Anecdotal Notes: Student is having trouble identifying the correct amount of money needed. May want to identify some opportunities for student to practice this skill throughout the day.

Decision: Student is making steady progress. Keep teaching at this level.

Key: + = Independent correct, − = Incorrect or No response or Prompted response (not independent)

FIGURE 3.6. An example of a task-analytic assessment for a functional skill.

ing the word to multiple examples of pictures of landforms during a science unit on the Earth's materials. At the beginning of instruction, Jeremy was not able to match the word with a picture in any of the five trials given; however, during the second data session, Jeremy was able perform the skill one time during the fourth trial (20%). It seemed that Jeremy was making good progress until the fifth data session, when Jeremy was not able to match the word and picture in any of the five trials. Each day data is taken, Jeremy's ability to perform the skill varies. This is an example of a skill that could be taken by the

Student Name: Cassandra

Subject/Skill: Science

Objective: The student will independently complete all 8 steps of the science experiment for 2 consecutive days.

Steps	%		11/1	11/2	11/3	11/4	11/5	11/8	11/9	11/10	11/11	11/12
	100											
	90											
	80											
	70											
	60											
	50											
	40											
8		Clean up	M	P	P	V	V	V	V	V	V	V
7	30	Compare prediction with results	P	P	P	M	P	P	P	P	M	P
6		Indicate results	P	M	M	P	M	M	M	M	M	P
5	20	Observe variables	P	M	P	P	P	M	M	V	M	V
4		Conduct experiment	P	M	V	I	M	V	V	I	V	V
3	10	Make prediction	P	M	M	M	V	V	V	M	V	V
2		Collect materials	P	P	V	M	M	M	V	M	P	M
1	0	Put on safety attire	P	P	P	P	P	P	P	P	P	P
Steps	%		O	O	O	12.5	O	O	O	12.5	O	O
		Date	11/1	11/2	11/3	11/4	11/5	11/8	11/9	11/10	11/11	11/12

Mastered: No   **Data Pattern:** No real progress

Anecdotal Notes: There are simpler means Cassandra could use for making predictions and doing the experiment.

Decision: Simplify the responses by having Cassandra use AT.

Key: P = Physical prompt, M = Model prompt, V = Verbal prompt, I = Independent correct

FIGURE 3.7. An example of task-analytic assessment for an academic skill.

			8/29	8/30	9/1	9/2	9/3	9/4	9/5	9/8	9/9	9/10	9/11	9/12
		Student Name: Jeremy												
		Subject/Skill: Science Vocabulary Words												
		Objective: The student will match the word *landform* to a picture of a landform within 4/5 trials for 3 consecutive sessions.												
	100													
	90													
	80													
	70													
	60													
	50													
10														
9	40													
8														
7	30													
6														
5	20	Trial 5—Match word to picture symbol	−	−	−	−	−	+	−	−	−	−	−	−
4		Trial 4—Match word to picture symbol	−	+	+	−	−	−	+	+	−	−	+	−
3	10	Trial 3—Match word to picture symbol	−	−	+	−	−	+	+	+	−	−	+	+
2		Trial 2—Match word to picture symbol	−	−	−	+	−	+	+	+	+	−	+	−
1	0	Trial 1—Match word to picture symbol	−	−	−	−	−	−	−	−	−	−	−	−
Steps	%		0	20	40	20	0	60	60	60	20	0	60	20
		Date	8/29	8/30	9/1	9/2	9/3	9/4	9/5	9/8	9/9	9/10	9/11	9/12

Mastered: No   **Data Pattern:** Variable data

Anecdotal Notes: Jeremy's performance fluctuates across days depending on whether he is motivated to do the skill.

Decision: Improve motivation to perform responses correctly without assistance. Action: 1. Jeremy will begin using a chart to keep track of his independent correct responses. If he gets "more than yesterday" correct, he will earn 5 extra minutes of lunch time with his peer buddy. 2. His peer buddy will embed opportunities for him to identify the landforms during the lesson, and the peer will record whether he got the answer correct.

Key: + = Independent correct, − = Incorrect or No response or Prompted response (not independent)

FIGURE 3.8. An example of a repeated-trial assessment.

teacher at a separate time in the day for testing; however, it is possible to take data during the lesson. Jeremy's teacher has chosen to use a constant time-delay procedure to provide instruction during the lesson and record whether he was able to match the term independently (+). To identify landforms is something that Jeremy's teachers will ask him several times during the science lesson; each trial was embedded during the classroom instruction by a paraprofessional (see Chapter 6 for more on embedding instruction in science).

FROM RESEARCH TO PRACTICE: "DO I REALLY HAVE TO TAKE DATA?"

Some teachers may wonder whether collecting data is necessary at all. In research with teachers, many reported that they were skeptical about how representative data were (Grigg, Snell, & Lloyd, 1989). In contrast, research has also shown that teachers' evaluations of progress are more accurate when they are based on data (Holvoet, O'Neil, Chazdon, Carr, & Warner, 1983). This may be especially true when data are variable or show a lack of progress (Munger, Snell, & Lloyd, 1989). Teachers can also enhance student progress when they learn to use their data to make instructional decisions (Belfiore & Browder, 1992; Browder, Demchak, Heller, & King, 1991; Browder, Liberty, Heller, & D'Huyvetters, 1986; Farlow & Snell, 1989).

How to Summarize Progress

Many strategies can be found in the professional literature for summarizing data. Most rely on the use of what are called "equal interval graphs." In an equal interval graph, the sessions (e.g., days) on which data are collected represent the horizontal axis, and the scale of measurement (e.g., percentage of steps correct on the task analysis) forms the vertical axis. To save time, teachers may want to develop a standard chart to graph most skills. To minimize the amount of paper needed, the data collection sheet and graph can be combined on one page. The standard chart shown in Figures 3.6, 3.7, and 3.8 (a blank revision is in Figure 3.9) provides a model for how to create a combined data sheet and graph. Snell and Lloyd (1991) found that teachers were more consistent in making instructional decisions when they viewed response-by-response data and level of assistance than when they reviewed graphed data alone. Notice that on this chart the responses are written from the bottom up. The teacher then counts the number correct and divides by the number of possible responses to get the percentage correct for that day's data.

How to Use Data to Make Decisions

Teachers who collect ongoing data also often have rules about whether and when to change programs (Farlow & Snell, 1989). The only reasons to collect data are (1) to report student progress to parents and school administrators and (2) to make instructional decisions. Investing the time to collect data becomes especially worthwhile when it can be used to make decisions that improve student progress. Having a set of guidelines or "rules" to make these decisions can be an important key to improving this progress (Browder et al., 1986; Browder et al., 1991; Farlow & Snell, 1989). The following is a description of one data-based decision system that has been extensively field tested with students with moderate and severe disabilities and evaluated through research based on real student data collected by teachers in school and adult service settings (Belfiore & Browder, 1992; Browder et al., 1986). There are three steps in using this system:

		Student Name:												
		Subject/Skill:												
		Objective:												
	100														
	90														
	80														
	70														
	60														
	50														
	40														
	30														
	20														
	10														
	0														
Steps	%														
		Date												

Mastered: **Data Pattern:**

Anecdotal Notes:

Decision:

Key:

FIGURE 3.9. Blank assessment form.

(1) analyzing the data, (2) making an instructional decision based on this analysis, and (3) deciding how to implement this decision. These steps are summarized in Table 3.6.

Step 1: Analyze the Data

In this progress monitoring system, the teacher reviews each student's progress once every 2 weeks. Students may have several charts of data for the different skills they are learning. Once teachers have mastered this system, they can review these fairly quickly. In reviewing the charts, the teacher makes sure that there are at least six data points for a review. The reason for the minimum of six is that this is the minimum number needed to draw a trend line using intersections. Most teachers who have used this system find that getting at least 6 days' worth of data out of the 10 days possible in 2 school weeks is realistic. The ideal situation is to implement the program and take data daily. Some weeks the teacher may have all 10 data points. Next, the teacher looks at the chart to see if there is a clear-cut decision. If the student has met the criteria for mastery, it is time to revise the program to focus on maintenance, fluency, or generalization of the skill. If no progress has been made, the student needs the opportunity to learn a simpler response that can achieve the same outcome. Table 3.6 offers several ideas about how to simplify the response (see "Step 3: Implement the Decision to Change Instruction").

Step 2: Use Decision Rules

The decision rules shown in Table 3.6 were originally derived from the work of Haring et al. (1980) and Browder et al. (1986). Haring et al. (1980) developed their rules by studying teachers' instructional decisions to find patterns that led to student progress. These rules were further refined by Browder et al. (1991) in their research with both school-age students and adults with severe disabilities. These rules or guidelines often seem logical to teachers as they gain experience with data summaries. With this experience teachers will discover that students who make no progress need simpler skills, that when progress is slow the reason is that the students are relying on prompting, and that when progress regresses even though the student has not been ill or absent, motivation to learn the skill may have lapsed. Until these patterns become clear to teachers, they can use Table 3.6 to find the data pattern and note the decision rule.

Step 3: Implement the Decision to Change Instruction

Once the decision is reached, the teacher needs to know how to change instruction to improve progress. The recommendations given in Table 3.6 are based on our experience in implementing the decisions and research on teaching. A similar set of recommendations was field tested in the study by Belfiore and Browder (1992). The application of these decisions is shown in Figures 3.6, 3.7, and 3.8.

In Figure 3.6, Betty is a student who is being taught to use a vending machine independently. For each assessment, Betty is asked to purchase a soda from the machine. At the beginning of learning the new skill, she is only able to take the soda out of the machine (1 step independently correct out of 10), but over time she begins to perform additional steps in the task analysis independently. After 12 days of assessment, Betty is able to perform 80% of the steps (8 out of 10) independently (adequate progress). Betty's

TABLE 3.6. Data-Based Decision Rules to Use in Determining Student Progress

Step 1: Analyze the data.

1. *Have the data been recorded on a standard chart?*

   Guideline: Collect data regularly (e.g., daily) and summarize them on a standard chart.

2. *Are the data representative of student performance?*

   Guideline: If data were collected by a substitute not trained in data collection or if the student was ill or disruptive, the data may not be accurate. If the data are not representative, continue instruction until better data can be obtained.

3. *Are there enough data to make an instructional decision?*

   Guideline: Make decisions once every 2 weeks for daily data. A minimum of 6 days of data are needed to make an instructional decision. If fewer days of data are available or if there has been a large break between the 2 weeks of data that might cause regression, note on the chart that there is "Insufficient Data for a Decision."

4. *Can a decision be made based on the daily graphed data?*

   Guideline: If the student met the criteria for mastery during this 2 weeks, or if there have been no correct independent responses, a decision can be made. Go to the "Decision Rules."

5. *What are the mean and the trend of the data?*

   Guideline: If the data are not clear-cut (i.e., showing mastery or no progress), some more summarization is needed. To summarize the data further, calculate the mean of the daily performance for the 2 weeks of review. Compare this with the mean of the prior 2 weeks. Is the mean higher by at least 5% (or whatever other criteria you set for biweekly progress)? Now summarize the trend of the data. Find the intersection of the first three points of data and mark an X and the last three points and mark an X. Connect the X's with a straight line. This line will either be going up (accelerating), going down (decelerating), or flat. When you know the mean and trend, you can go to the "Decision Rules."

Step 2: Use decision rules.

Data pattern	Conclusion	Decision
1. Reached criterion during the 2 weeks.	*Mastery*	Develop a new plan to maintain and extend performance (e.g., fluency, generalization).
2. All data points are at 0 *or* there have been no new independent responses since instruction began.	*No progress*	If this is the first 2 weeks of instruction, make no changes yet. Continue instruction. After the first 2 weeks, simplify the skill.
3. Trend: *Accelerating* Mean: *Higher by 5% or more*	*Adequate progress*	Make no changes. Continue instruction.
4. Trend: *Accelerating or flat* Mean: *Same as last decision period or higher but by less than 5%*	*Inadequate progress*	Improve antecedents (e.g., prompting strategies) so that the student makes more independent, correct responses.
5. Trend: *Decelerating (even if mean is higher)* or Mean: *Lower (even if trend is accelerating)*	*Motivation problem*	Improve motivation to perform responses correctly without assistance.

(cont.)

TABLE 3.6. *(cont.)*

Step 3: Implement the decision to change instruction.

To simplify the response	To improve antecedents	To improve motivation
Goal: Make it feasible for student to perform without assistance.	*Goal*: Increase the number of independent correct responses (+s) the student makes each day.	*Goal*: Help student recoup past performance after a regression and then continue to improve.
Strategies	*Strategies*	*Strategies*
• Use chaining: Teach only one or one portion of the task analysis. • Use a more specific task analysis: Break the task analysis down into smaller steps. • Use a simpler motor response: Use a gross motor response or one that requires less physical control or skill. • Make the discrimination simpler: Modify the materials so that it is easier to select the correct answer. • Use assistive technology. • Eliminate the need for planning and positioning: Have materials preset. • Select an alternative way to achieve the same outcome: Use an entirely different response or set of materials.	• Only use the minimal prompting needed; don't overly assist. • Wait longer before giving the prompt. • Revise the prompt to focus the learner's attention more on the natural cues. • Make sure the learner is closer to the materials than you are. • Review the task analysis to see if there are specific steps that are difficult for the learner. Simplify these steps or use more effective prompts for them. • Use nonspecific verbal cues such as "What's next?" • Use graduated guidance; that is, fade the amount of physical assistance given. • Have a peer model the response or give the prompts. • Use self-prompting with pictures or an audiotape.	• Praise only independent correct responses (+s). • Give less attention to errors—ignore and prompt the next step. • Emphasize the natural consequence for performing the response. • Embed choice in instruction (e.g., when to do the task, choice of materials, choice of seating). • Involve student in self-monitoring and graphing daily performance. • Use tangible reinforcers for performance that is better than the prior day (e.g., stickers, treats, special activity). • Vary praise statements by using different words; make statements humorous or novel; or increase enthusiasm when praising. • Eliminate all prompting and give feedback only for correct responses. • Have a peer teach the program. • Teach the student to praise him- or herself.

Note. Based on Browder (2001).

teacher did notice that she is having trouble with one of the steps consistently (identifying the correct amount of money needed), so she has planned to identify some additional opportunities for Betty to practice this skill throughout the day. No change to instruction of the task analysis will be made by the teacher, because Betty is on track for mastery of this skill.

Figures 3.7 and 3.8 represent students who are not on track for mastery. When this situation occurs, it is important to take time to review the data and make instructional decisions. In Figure 3.7, Cassandra is being taught to participate in a science lesson. She has been working on this goal since early October, and now in the month of November, she is still not able to participate in most of the steps independently (no progress). Cassandra's teachers decide to consider the response they are asking her to make to "show what she knows." They still want her to continue toward mastery of this procedure to participate independently in the science lessons, but they decide to simplify the responses they are asking her to do to demonstrate knowledge. For example, they will provide her with two options to make a prediction instead of having her generate an educated guess verbally. At the end of the lesson, instead of comparing her prediction with the results verbally, they will ask her to look at her choice for a prediction and put a checkmark if she was correct (prediction matched results) or an X if she was incorrect (prediction was different from actual results).

Figure 3.8 presents a student who can perform the skill one day, and then the next is unable to (variable progress). Jeremy is an example of a student who is having trouble with motivation. After Jeremy's teacher recognized that he was not ill and that regression did not occur across all of the skills he was being taught, she decided to pay special attention to his motivation to complete the science skill. In the repeated-trial instruction, Jeremy's teacher noticed that on days when he was working with a peer buddy in his inclusive science lesson, he would pay close attention and take the time to respond without guessing. On those days the data showed that his performance was the highest (i.e., 60% correct). The teacher and paraprofessional asked the peer if he would like to ask Jeremy to identify the land formations and pictures. The team will continue to record data to determine whether this strategy will improve Jeremy's motivation in his science class work.

Reporting Progress on the IEP to Parents

IDEA requires that parents receive regular reports of student progress on the annual goals. One of the advantages of data-based decisions is that the process yields concrete information for reporting progress. The teacher can create a form listing all annual goals and STOs. On this chart, current performance on each objective can be summarized (e.g., 60%) and compared with the STO target (e.g., 80%) to evaluate whether the student is on track for mastery or needs additional help.

CASE STUDY

Here is how Ms. Lim (introduced at the beginning of this chapter) applied the guidelines for a standards-based IEP for her student, Jabrill. First, Ms. Lim completed *Step 1: Begin with a student-centered (person-centered planning) approach* (see Table 3.1). Ms. Lim identified Jabrill's preferences by completing a simple preference assessment. She talked with Jabrill about what he liked and made a list of activities she had seen him enjoy. In completing this preference assessment, she found that Jabrill really enjoyed working with his peers. He also has a great love for sports and competitions, probably based on his experiences with the Special Olympics. Jabrill also was quite clear that he "hates math."

Ms. Lim wanted to gain as much information about Jabrill before preplanning any of his IEP goals, so she e-mailed his parents to find a time that they could talk on the phone about what they would like to see him accomplish both academically and socially during the school year. During the call, one major concern that was voiced by his parents was his participation in the general education math classroom. They were unhappy that he was leaving the math class upset almost every day. They felt that Jabrill needed a new setting and a new strategy to learn math. They attributed his behavioral outbursts in math to his frustration with this content. His parents emphasized that Jabrill had been trying to learn to count and identify number sets for the past 7 years, and they didn't want to see that goal on his IEP again ("It is time to move on!"). Jabrill's family spoke about how happy they were with his reading skills and wanted to continue to work on his reading independently. Finally, Jabrill's mother voiced a strong concern for his safety in the community. She said that now that he is getting older, it is important for him to have some ability to travel within the community setting alone or without them directly next to him and wanted to make sure that he was able tell someone his personal information if he was ever lost.

With a better understanding of Jabrill's and his parents' priorities, Ms. Lim began to consider ways Jabrill could articulate these as goals for himself and be an active participant in his IEP meeting. In prior years, Jabrill had not attended his IEP meeting. To develop Jabrill's ability to set goals, Ms. Lim presented him with pictorial options (e.g., math, social studies, computers, pencil/paper, group work) and asked questions about what classes he enjoyed the most (he said "social studies") and how he liked to learn (he said "computers"). Jabrill also vocalized his love for being with his friends and asked to keep doing that.

To help prepare Jabrill for the meeting, Ms. Lim helped Jabrill prepare a PowerPoint presentation titled "What I Like and Want." Each day they practiced as Jabrill learned to present each slide and say what he liked and wanted. She used time delay with a no-delay model to show him how to click the slide and make a statement for each slide, and then faded this to a 4-second delay until Jabrill was able to do the entire presentation with no help (see Chapter 4 for more information on time delay).

As she developed the IEP (see the next steps), Ms. Lim made a planning chart with each subject area that would be covered during the meeting and kept Jabrill updated on its development. When she developed the section on English language arts (ELA), she talked with Jabrill about what would be covered in his seventh-grade ELA class in the upcoming school year. She gave Jabrill the opportunity to use his assistive technology (AT) board to say "I like that goal," "I think that is too easy, I can do more," or "I think that is too hard for me." She repeated this as she began to brainstorm possible goals in each area. The only goals that Jabrill thought might be too hard were the ones that pertained to his social behavior in math class. Ms. Lim decided not to change the goal yet but to talk about it more in the meeting with Jabrill and the team. During the IEP meeting, Jabrill would have the opportunity to use his AT device to respond to the goals as they were proposed by the team (e.g., by saying "I like that goal" or "I think that goal is to hard for me").

To develop draft goals, Ms. Lim completed *Step 2: Consider the grade-level standards.* Because Jabrill is a seventh-grade student, Ms. Lim pulled the seventh-grade standards for ELA, math, science, and social studies off the state education department's website. She consulted with the seventh-grade team to see what standards were priorities for each content area. Because Jabrill would participate in seventh-grade ELA, science, and social studies, it was important to talk with his general education teachers to find out what plans they had for the upcoming school year. For example, when she met with the science teacher, he told her that they would be spending quite a bit of time learning how to conduct an experiment in preparation for the end-of-the-year science fair. It would be important for Jabrill to learn how to answer questions and record data so that he might participate, too. Although it was not a requirement to submit an experiment into the science fair, when Ms. Lim told Jabrill the idea, he was quite excited, as he loved to compete (e.g., in Special Olympics). Ms. Lim and Jabrill's science teacher made a list of skills needed to conduct a science experiment and content priorities from the units of instruction that would be covered in that school year—for example, identify "big idea" concepts and key vocabulary from a science unit on the properties of matter (first and second quarters); weather patterns (third quarter); and the body system (fourth quarter).

In conferring with the language arts teacher, it became clear that Jabrill was limited by relying on reading single sight words or being read aloud to. Because his decoding skills were so well developed, Ms. Lim wondered whether he might be able to read passages if the words were ones he could already decode. She planned to do an assessment of his passage reading. She also realized that Jabrill would need to comprehend some difficult themes and concepts in the seventh-grade literature as she looked at the standards and the textbook. She made a note to get a clearer idea of his comprehension skills through further assessment.

When she met with the seventh-grade math teacher, she realized from having been part of planning for his sixth-grade math that another year of frustration for all concerned would likely result. She realized that Jabrill needed a whole new approach in math, as the parents had requested. She decided to talk with the school system's AT specialist about some adaptations and accommodations and to check with the special education supervisor about what some options might be.

Next, Ms. Lim used ecological inventories to complete *Step 3: Identify functional skills needed for student's current and future environments*. She considered the activities that typical seventh graders do using an ecological inventory of the local mall. She realized that most seventh graders made purchases and ate with their friends with no assistance from parents or others. Jabrill loved to go to the mall with his friends from school, but he needed skills to make purchases. Through an ecological inventory of the middle school environment, Ms. Lim realized that Jabrill was one of the few students who walked with an adult to class. One of the complications was that Jabrill had mobility problems and had fallen once in the prior year. The physical therapist noted from her evaluation that one of the major issues with his mobility had to do with negotiating uneven pavement. Ms. Lim put Jabrill's mobility on her list of topics for the IEP meeting.

The occupational therapist introduced the idea of teaching Jabrill to use an adapted mouse to navigate content-specific computer software and the Internet. When this idea was presented to Jabrill, he responded with "I like this goal" and began to laugh. Because the computer was not always the best option in his general education classes, Ms. Lim asked about teaching him to mark his answers on a worksheet with a pencil or marker.

Ms. Lim's discussions with the AT specialist and special education supervisor also gave her some new ideas for math. She was going to propose to the team that Jabrill be taught to compensate for his lack of basic numeracy through the use of technology and to build the understanding of the mathematical concepts using his strengths in language arts. That is, she would use short stories that Jabrill would read and then teach him to find the answers using software (e.g., Excel) that provided the computation for him. Because he was so capable with symbol recognition, Jabrill would probably be able to learn to type in the numbers and select the computation symbol (such as the "sum" symbol) in a few weeks. She was going to propose doing this herself in the special education class and having a plan to rebuild his success in general math.

Next Ms. Lim worked with the full IEP team to gather information needed for *Step 4: Describe the student's current level of academic and functional performance.* Each of Jabrill's inclusion content area teachers from the previous school year (sixth grade) were asked to complete a quick survey of new skills he performed and areas of challenge. His math teacher said that "it was all challenge" because Jabrill was not able to participate in the class activities due to his behavior and lack of motivation to do the work. Jabrill's science, ELA, and social studies teachers all said he participated well with his peers but that he had issues knowing when to be quiet. They provided additional information on his skills that were included in the statements of the current level of performance (see Figure 3.1). Ms. Lim reviewed his progress from the prior year's IEP using the progress monitoring data. Jabrill had mastered 30 words in ELA, science, and math. She realized that the teachers were correct in saying that not enough was known about how well he comprehended this work. The team had been relying on Jabrill's good decoding skills in a lot of his academic planning.

Ms. Lim reviewed Jabrill's alternate assessment scores from the previous school year. Although Jabrill had been proficient in ELA and science, his scores in math were at the lowest level, "novice." Ms. Lim also knew that the expectations would be higher for Jabrill on the seventh-grade alternate assessment, as there would be some inferential comprehension questions. Ms. Lim realized that if Jabrill began to use software as an adaptation/accommodation in mathematics, this would need to be considered by the IEP team for use in the alternate assessment.

Ms. Lim also conducted some direct assessments. Using a read-aloud of a passage, she asked Jabrill several different types of comprehension questions. She discovered that he could answer only literal comprehension questions in which the answer could be located on the page of text. He could not sequence story events, connect events to his own experiences, or summarize the passage. In contrast, Jabrill surprised her with passage reading. If she created a short phrase of familiar words, he could scan it silently and answer a comprehension question. If she pointed to each word in a longer passage to help him with his silent reading, he could also answer a literal question. She decided Jabrill should have ambitious goals for learning to read passages, not just lists of sight words. In math, Ms. Lim verified that Jabrill could do one-to-one correspondence and recognize numbers. He also was able to find the number on a keyboard that she stated, but he could not identify a set of objects with a number.

Because of the behavioral concerns in the prior year, Ms. Lim had worked with the behavior support specialist and math teacher to complete a functional assessment (see Chapter 12). The team had identified his loud behaviors as escape motivated. Unfortunately, his behavior was so loud and disruptive that it interfered with the other students' learning, and so he was escorted by the paraprofessional to a conference room to do individual work, which reinforced using the loud vocalizations to escape. His PBS plan included teaching negotiation skills to end unwanted activities, but Jabrill lacked the communication skills needed to negotiate. Ms. Lim realized the PBS plan needed to include knowing when to be quiet and how to negotiate a change of activities.

Finally, each team member contributed to *Step 5: Develop annual goals for each content area* by bringing draft goals to the meeting. Because this was the first time Jabrill had attended the meeting, Ms. Lim had not tried to teach him to lead it. Instead, she had him start the meeting with his PowerPoint presentation of "What I Like and Want." She then had Jabrill demonstrate how he rated the goals, using his AT. She also had Jabrill take the lead on the goal she knew would be most difficult for him to discuss. Jabrill had the goal of improving his social behavior in his inclusion classes by being quiet when asked by the teacher and arriving early to class to socialize with his peers. His content teachers suggested this goal, Ms. Lim and Jabrill drafted the goal prior to the meeting, and Jabrill presented it at the meeting. Jabrill's AT device has also been programmed with the statement, "I want to compete in the science fair this school year," and he planned to touch the switch to let the team know his goal while discussing his science goals. (Goals for each area are shown in Figure 3.1.) During the meeting, Ms. Lim followed an agenda to keep everyone focused within the time constraints. After Jabrill's initial presentation, she summarized her notes from her preplanning, noting that the team especially needed to discuss alternatives for math and his mobility. She then had the specialists present their evaluations and recommendations. She went last, presenting her educational evaluation (i.e., the comprehension assessment and math screening). They then reviewed, revised, and confirmed the annual goals in each area.

For *Step 6: Write specific short-term objectives or benchmarks*, most of the team had drafted STOs for each of the recommended annual goals. In some cases, these were revised. There was some debate about whether Jabrill could shape his passage reading as quickly as proposed. Ms. Lim gave her reasons for wanting to try, based on both the demands of his inclusive classes and his positive response to her assessment. The team also discussed the need to emphasize comprehension in all his classes. The team also discussed ways to promote generalization of Jabrill's skills across classes and settings. For example, the occupational therapy goal to use a pencil or marker to make a selection on a worksheet or paper could be emphasized in all his classes.

One issue that arose was the need for Jabrill to do "chapter tests" if he was going to demonstrate learning of the content similar to that of his peers. Because Jabrill already had such strong listening comprehension skills, the team decided that it would be possible to create simple adapted tests, then have a peer read the questions to Jabrill, who would circle or mark the correct answer for each question. This assessment would not only allow him to participate with a peer (highly motivating) but would also provide a permanent product of his comprehension of specific content-related questions. The other benefit to this skill was its ability to be generalized across all content areas, settings, and functional applications (e.g., attendance, filling out personal info).

The team considered all of the academic skills and support needed to complete these skills as part of *Step 7: Plan for how the student will access the general curriculum*. They determined that the general education class would be the least restrictive placement for services in ELA, science, and social studies. In the area of math, the team agreed, with the parents' approval, to try a comprise by placing Jabrill in a self-contained setting for more intensive math instruction, but they also planned within that year to reintegrate him into inclusive math experiences. Even though Jabrill would receive his math instruction in a self-contained special education setting, his annual goals and objectives were still aligned to the seventh-grade standards.

To allow Jabrill to access the general curriculum, his IEP team evaluated exactly what additional supports he needed to be successful in the general curriculum. In doing this they accomplished *Step 8: Plan specially designed instruction*. Together, the occupational therapist, speech therapist, and teacher designed a plan of action to incorporate technology into most daily routines throughout Jabrill's school day. Not only was the technology a source of motivation for Jabrill, but it also allowed him to communicate both verbally and through permanent products. The use of AT via the classroom computer or voice output devices (VOD) was something that would help Jabrill become more independent within the classroom and community. The team also discussed the systematic instruction Jabrill would need to learn his IEP objectives and possible options for embedding this instruction in his general education classes (e.g., through paraprofessionals, peers, or coteaching).

Because this student accessed text by adapted forms of literature and informational text and had reached only emergent levels of literacy and mathematical computations, AA–AAS was chosen. In *Step 9: Select the appropriate state assessment option*, the team reviewed the options the state offered for assessments and found that the AA–AAS best fit Jabrill's current level of academic functioning. The alternate assessment would allow Ms. Lim to assess Jabrill on content knowledge, reading skills, and math operations using objects when needed and picture symbols to show comprehension; furthermore, it did not require Jabrill to use a paper-and-pencil test to demonstrate mastery of given content.

Finally, while developing the IEP, the team considered their plan for monitoring Jabrill's progress toward each annual goal via the STOs in *Step 10: Develop progress monitoring* system. Ms. Lim and the team made sure to write each STO with enough detail so that it would be measurable and that data could be collected on a reliable schedule. The specific type of assessment to be used for each STO was designated. As the year progressed, Ms. Lim would oversee progress to ensure that all STOs were being worked on and that the data collected were being used to make instructional decisions.

FINDING THE BALANCE

There will rarely be enough time to implement all the ideas provided in this hypothetical case study, especially for a caseload of several IEPs. Instead, this case study is meant to illustrate the guidelines of this chapter. We recommend using the 10 steps but finding ways to make the process efficient over time. We recognize that teachers will need to find a balance between time spent in developing IEPs and that needed to meet the ongoing demands of the classroom. A teacher may invest more time for the first standards-based IEP and then find ways to make the process easier. For example, some of the work Ms. Lim did in advance could be done at the IEP meeting itself once the team knows what to expect in this new planning format.

SUMMARY

This chapter provided 10 steps for developing a standards-based IEP. A standards-based IEP is one that contains goals that align to the state's standards. The IEP is not meant to restate the entire general curriculum but instead helps define priorities and strategies for learning this content. A standards-based IEP will likely have goals in science, social studies, language arts, and mathematics. Including additional social, functional, and therapy goals is also appropriate. It also is not necessary to try to "back-link" these additional goals into some academic standard. Once the annual goals and STOs are written, assessments can be planned for ongoing progress monitoring. This chapter provided examples of these teacher-made assessments and how to make instructional decisions based on these data.

APPLICATIONS

1. Pretend that you are about to write an IEP for one of your students. For each of the following standards, write an annual goal to align to each standard. Then write two short-term objectives you would use to help your student meet that annual goal. In your application, think about a specific student, so that your goals and STOs will also reflect his or her individual needs and abilities.

   State Standard 1: Describe risks and benefits of chemicals, including:
   • Medicines.
   • Food preservatives.
   • Crop yield.
   • Sanitation.

   State Standard 2: Use combinations of whole-number addition, subtraction, multiplication, and division to solve multistep problems in context.

   State Standard 3: Interact with the text before, during, and after reading, listening, and viewing by:
   • Setting a purpose using prior knowledge and text information.
   • Making predictions.
   • Formulating questions.
   • Locating relevant information.
   • Making connections with previous experiences, information, and ideas.

2. For each short-term objective you developed in #1, write the method of assessment and develop a data sheet. Use Figures 3.6, 3.7, and 3.8 as a guide.

3. Give examples of functional, social, and therapy goals the student might also need. Discuss with a partner what makes an IEP standards based and why you would not need to link these additional goals to state standards.

4. Review your state or school system website for the guidelines for IEPs. Compare and contrast this with the guidelines in this chapter and sample IEP provided.

CHAPTER 4

Evidence-Based Practices

FRED SPOONER, DIANE M. BROWDER, AND PAMELA J. MIMS

Daniella was a new teacher hired to work in Valley View School System. She provided instructional support to 12 students with disabilities. To prepare for teaching, she read the students' IEPs and considered what she had learned about planning instruction. Although the first month was challenging, she soon had the students following their schedules. The principal was pleased that the students had made a smooth transition to a new special education teacher. Daniella was not as optimistic that the transition had been a success. At the end of the first reporting period, she reviewed the students' progress. She followed the model of the prior teacher to assess progress but observed very little. She wondered what was wrong. Was the expectation that students learn material such as social studies and science too ambitious? Daniella noted that they were not making much progress in their life skills goals, either. Should she quit taking such specific data? Most teachers were not so precise in their assessment of progress, but Daniella knew it was possible to see progress in this way because her cooperating teacher had used this system. Were the IEP goals too high? Daniella was hesitant to ask for new IEP meetings to lower expectations. Daniella was working very hard, putting in long hours planning daily instruction, so she knew the reason for the lack of progress was not that she had not put in enough effort. Then Daniella went to a professional development session on systematic instruction. The presenter introduced the idea of "evidence-based practice." Daniella was encouraged to discover teaching strategies with strong support for effectiveness in promoting student progress. This chapter describes systematic instruction and provides information on evidence of effectiveness.

One of the goals of teaching is to promote student progress through applying effective strategies. These strategies can vary widely across educators depending on their preservice training, student teaching experience, personal philosophy of teaching, other background experiences, and personality. Teachers or other professionals may also learn new strategies through published resources, workshops, college courses, or trial and error in applying their own ideas. When students fail to make progress, it can be tempting to focus only on the student's challenges, the curriculum, or the goals for achievement. Although all of these variables can influence outcomes, one of the most powerful variables influencing whether students learn is the method of instruction. This variable is one that teachers can control by choosing instructional strategies that have been demonstrated by research to work. Translating research into practice can be both challenging and time-consuming for the average teacher. For this reason, some experts have begun to provide this translation through summaries of evidence-based practice. This chapter provides an overview of instructional strategies with research support. Before describing the specific teaching procedures, we offer a brief overview of how effective teaching strategies are identified.

IDENTIFYING EVIDENCE-BASED PRACTICES

At the beginning of the current millennium, federal policy promoted educators' applications of practices that have research support. The enactment of NCLB (2002) encouraged practitioners to use "evidence-based" practices to impart skills to students. For students with disabilities, the focus on evidence-based instructional strategies has also been fostered by the push for inclusion, the legal mandate of students with disabilities to be included in statewide testing, and recent evidence showing that students with disabilities could be successful in a variety of content, including academics (Cook, Tankersley, & Landurm, 2009; Odom et al., 2005). In order for evidence-based practices to be employed, these practices had to be defined by the scientific community, largely researchers in institutions of higher education who frequently engaged in research activity. To date, there have been three major efforts to describe and validate evidence-based practices in the discipline of special education ("Criteria," 2005; "Evidence-Based," 2009; Spooner, 2003). Spooner (2003) edited a collection of contributions that addressed perspectives on defining scientifically based research in the area of severe disabilities. Odom et al. (2005) set the context for the development of guidelines for defining quality indicators for research methodologies used in special education (e.g., single-subject designs; Horner et al., 2005; qualitative methodologies; Brantlinger, Jimenez, Klingner, Pugach, & Richardson, 2005; group and quasi-experimental methods; Gersten et al., 2005). Cook et al. (2009) extended the effort in the Council for Exceptional Children's (CEC) second collection ("Evidence-Based," 2009) with a set of examples on applying the quality indicator using strategies that were delineated in 2005 (e.g., severe developmental disabilities; Browder, Ahlgrim-Delzell, Spooner, Mims, & Baker, 2009; emotional and behavior disorders; Lane, Kalberg, & Shepcaro, 2009; learning disabilities; Chard, Ketterlin-Geller, Baker, Doabler, & Apichatabutra, 2009).

In the area of severe developmental disabilities the predominant methodology that has been used to substantiate research outcomes has been single-subject-design research (Browder, Ahlgrim-Delzell, et al., 2009; Horner et al., 2005; McDonnell & O'Neill, 2003; Spooner & Browder, 2003). The application of single-subject research methodology has had two underlying tenets: (1) the individual participant is the unit of analysis (e.g., the researcher reviews how each student learned the skill) and (2) visual inspection of graphed data is the primary method used to analyze behavior change (e.g., Cooper, Heron, & Heward, 2007; Gast, 2010; Johnston & Pennypacker, 1980, 1993; Tawney & Gast, 1984). The shortcoming of single-subject research is that because so few individuals participate in each study, it is difficult to infer that the outcomes will generalize to other students (what is called "external validity"). This shortcoming can be addressed by considering a compilation of studies in which a larger number of students have positive outcomes through the use of the same or a similar intervention procedure. A published review of research typically compiles studies focused on a specific method of instruction. Some derive the method of instruction by reviewing all the studies in a content area (e.g., math). Once the studies are compiled, the reviewer applies some criteria to evaluate their overall quality to determine the relative strength of the evidence for the procedure.

Horner et al. (2005) developed an initial set of criteria for the examination of quality indicators for single-subject-design research. The Horner et al. criteria specify: (1) that a minimum of five single-subject studies that meet minimally acceptable methodological criteria and document experimental control have been published in peer-reviewed journals, (2) that the studies are conducted by at least three different researchers across at least three different geographical locations, and (3) that the five or more studies include a total of at least 20 participants. The methodological criteria are evaluated by a set of quality indicators across seven major areas (e.g., description of participant, description of setting, description of dependent and independent variable, social validity). Each of these seven areas has multiple items that, collectively, sum to a total of 20 quality indicators (e.g., the indicator of social validity has four items: the dependent variable [DV] is socially important; the magnitude of change in the DV due to intervention is socially important; the independent variable [IV] is cost-effective/practical; the IV is implemented over time, typical contexts, and typical agents).

CHECK FOR UNDERSTANDING

The steps in identifying an evidence-based practice are to locate the research, evaluate its quality, and determine whether there are enough studies and participants to make the conclusion that there is sufficient evidence for the procedure. How many studies and how many participants did Horner et al. (2005) suggest? What is one example of a criterion that Horner et al. (2005) recommended be applied to evaluate the quality of a study?

Although the use of evidence-based practice is important for all students, it is especially crucial for students with disabilities. Experts have noted that even students with more mild disabilities require effective procedures to maximize learning (Dammann & Vaughn, 2001). Students with severe developmental disabilities are a population that, by definition, finds learning difficult, and so the search for effective strategies becomes even more critical (Sontag, Burke, & York, 1973; Spooner & Brown, 2009). In contrast, teachers of students with disabilities sometimes apply practices that have shown little effect on student outcomes (Cook & Schirmer, 2003; Kauffman, 1996). This may be due to not knowing what research-based strategies exist, to not realizing their importance, or to both.

Sometimes researchers are just beginning to discover what works. In general, researchers know more about teaching reading (Browder, Wakeman, et al., 2006, 128 experiments; Browder et al., 2009, 30 experiments) than mathematics (Browder, Spooner, Ahlgrim-Delzell, Harris, & Wakeman, 2008, 68 experiments) and more about teaching mathematics than science (Courtade, Spooner, & Browder, 2007, 11 experiments; Spooner, Knight, Browder, Jimenez, & DiBiase, 2009, 17 experiments). When research in an area is sparse or new, experts sometimes use the term *emerging evidence*. When no other evidence exists, the best alternative is to try a strategy with emerging evidence.

In our own reviews of academic content areas (reading, mathematics, and science), we discovered that the overarching instructional package with strong evidence of effectiveness for students with severe developmental disabilities is systematic instruction. Systematic instruction also has a robust history of effectiveness in teaching functional life skills to students with severe disabilities (Billingsley & Romer, 1983; Snell & Farlow, 1993; Spooner & Spooner, 1984; Wolery & Gast, 1984). In general, systematic instruction incorporates such components as (1) instructing students in socially meaningful skills; (2) defining target skills that are observable and measurable; (3) using data to demonstrate that skills were acquired as a result of the intervention; (4) using behavioral principles to promote transfer of stimulus control, including differential reinforcement, systematic prompting and fading, and error correction; and (5) producing behavior change that can be generalized to other contexts, skills, people, and/or materials (Collins, 2007; Snell, 1983; Spooner et al., 2009; Stokes & Baer, 1977; Wolery, Bailey, & Sugai, 1988). This chapter delineates the components of systematic instruction, which is an evidence-based practice for teaching a wide range of skills to students with severe disabilities.

Two cautions are needed in applying evidence-based practices. First, it is important to understand the procedure and to use it in the way prescribed. Implementing all the components of a defined teaching procedure is called "procedural fidelity." If a procedure does not seem to be effective, the first issue to consider is whether it was used correctly and consistently. In giving workshops, we sometimes ask an audience of teachers how many use the procedure called "time delay," and many will raise their hands. Then later we demonstrate the procedure without giving it a name and ask how many of them use what we just demonstrated. Far fewer participants raise their hands. What we illustrate by doing this exercise is that it is possible to know a term but not know how to use the actual procedure. Practicing a procedure by following a checklist of its components, seeing a procedure modeled, and getting feedback from someone who is an expert with the strategy are three ways to gain fidelity of implementation. Second, a procedure needs to be adapted and evaluated for the individual student and skill to be taught. The effectiveness of the procedure can be determined for an individual student only by assessing progress. For example, a researcher may have used verbal prompts, by a specific student may need a visual cue or other support. Chapter 3 provided information on making data-based decisions.

SYSTEMATIC INSTRUCTION

Systematic instruction is derived from principles of behavior analysis. Applied behavior analytic (ABA) principles have been successfully used with individuals with developmental disabilities for approximately 60 years (Spooner et al., 2009), dating back to the first applied study conducted by Fuller (1949). Systematic instruction was the major instructional procedure used to teach most community and domestic living skills in early research on life skills (e.g., toothbrushing; Horner & Keilitz, 1975; washing clothes; Cuvo, Jacobi, & Sipko, 1981; selecting clothes; Nutter & Reid, 1978; public telephone use; Test, Spooner, Keul, & Grossi, 1990; riding a bus; Neef, Iwata, & Page, 1978; street crossing; Vogelsberg & Rusch, 1979). As described in the previous section, these procedures are now proving effective for teaching academic content as well. The *applied component* in ABA indicates that the procedures are meant to be put to meaningful use in real-life settings such as school and the community. The *behavior component* in ABA indicates that the target behavior is operationally defined and that it can be observed and measured. The *analytic component* in ABA indicates that data are collected and analyzed to make informed decisions regarding teaching (Baer, Wolf, & Risley, 1968, 1987).

In planning interventions, a behavior analyst considers the following:

1. *Antecedent*—what happens before the behavior occurs. The antecedent sets the stage for the target behavior.
2. *Behavior*—what is targeted for change. This is the targeted behavior on which teachers will be collecting data.
3. *Consequence*—every behavior is followed by a consequence.

These terms make up a three-term contingency: ABC. The antecedent is also known as a stimulus (S), the behavior is also known as a response (R), and the consequence can either be a reinforcer, which increases the likelihood that a response will occur again in the future, or a punisher, which decreases the likelihood that a response will occur again in the future. The contingency then becomes SRC. Educators who use behavioral strategies focus on increasing behaviors that are important and meaningful for that student. In this book, we often refer to these target behaviors as the "skills" to be learned. These may include a wide range of behaviors, such as solving a math problem, summarizing a story, making a purchase, or communicating with a friend. In Chapter 12, ideas for increasing social behaviors and decreasing inappropriate behaviors using positive educative strategies are provided. Whether academic, functional, or social, these behaviors or skills can also be called the "response" that is the focus of intervention.

In planning intervention, the behavior analyst defines not only this response but also the antecedent stimulus that sets the occasion for the response and the consequence that occurs. When a certain stimulus is presented (e.g., a ball) and a focused target behavior produces a response that has previously been reinforced (e.g., student labels it "ball" and receives reinforcement), or when, in the absence of a stimulus (e.g., truck), the response has not been reinforced (e.g., student labels it "truck" and receives no reinforcement), this is known as a "discriminative stimulus," or S^D (S-dee). The S^D is the cue for the student to respond. A second type of stimulus is found when the stimulus is present (e.g., a ball) and a behavior has not received previous reinforcement. This is known as stimulus-delta, or S-delta.

In a behavioral paradigm, learning occurs when an individual consistently makes a response in the presence of a specific S^D. This is called "stimulus control." The response becomes consistent in the presence of the stimulus because of reinforcement that is provided contingent on the response. When an antecedent stimulus is either present or absent, it will affect the frequency, latency, duration, or amplitude of how behavior is changed.

In teaching, the target S^D may be words to be read, a math problem, a shoe that needs tying, the cashier's statement of the price, or any other visual, auditory, or tactile input that cues the student to make the target response (e.g., read, compute math, tie the shoe, pay for the item).

At the beginning of instruction, the student will not make the response in the presence of the S^D unless the response is known. For example, a student will not say "men" when shown the printed word *m-e-n* if this is a new sight word. To promote learning, the educator pairs the target stimulus (written word) with some other stimulus that does set the occasion for the target response (e.g., the teacher models reading "men," and the student repeats the word). This second stimulus is called a "prompt" and is described further in the next section. Because the goal of instruction is for the student to respond without teacher assistance, this prompt needs to be faded. Transferring student responding from the prompting stimulus (e.g., teacher model) to the target stimulus (e.g., sight word) is called "transfer of stimulus control."

Understanding the transfer of stimulus control is important to being able to use effective instruction. For example, the teacher who does not understand transfer of stimulus control may have a student who remains dependent on teacher guidance to make the target response. A key principle of systematic instruction is the use of systematic prompting with a defined method of fading. To plan and implement systematic instruction, teachers follow four steps: (1) Define the skills to be acquired, (2) define the methods to use in instruction, (3) implement the systematic instruction plan, and (4) review student progress to modify instruction. Each of the steps is discussed in further detail.

Step 1: Define the Skills (Responses) to Be Acquired by the Learner

Before beginning instruction, it is important to define clearly the skills the student will perform to demonstrate learning. In systematic instruction, these skills are defined as observable and measurable responses. For example, in focusing on reading, the target skill would not be to "understand" the passage, because the internal process of understanding cannot be observed or measured. Instead, the target skill might be answering comprehension questions correctly or outlining the story grammar. In addition to being observable and measurable, the target skills should also be active rather than passive for students with severe disabilities. Sometimes, because of the complex challenges of a student's disability, the teacher may inadvertently select responses that the student cannot make efficiently or independently. The result is that the student will then be taught to rely on teacher assistance long term. For example, a student with minimal voluntary arm movement may not be able to move a toothbrush to his or her mouth. A goal such as "Will brush teeth with physical guidance" creates an expectation of passive performance. Instead, the teacher could define an active response the student could make, such as "Will gaze to select toothbrush" or "will use AAC device to request assistance with brushing teeth." Although the student may need prompting, including physical guidance, to learn the response, this can be faded for independence (more on fading in the next section). In general, the target response should be one the student can do *without assistance* once transfer of stimulus control has occurred. The exception may be responses in which the goal is for the student to use some self-assistance long term (e.g., "will make recipe using picture directions") or to work with a caregiver (e.g., "will lift foot when being helped to put on pants").

Besides focusing on observable, measurable responses that are active, the educator should consider whether the target skill is a discrete response or a response chain. Discrete responses are those that involve a single step (e.g., activating a switch, saying hello). These discrete responses have a clear beginning and ending (Young, West, & MacFarlane, 1994). Some skills require multiple responses to complete them (e.g., hand washing, division). These skills are called "chained tasks." Task analysis is the process of taking a chained task, a task with multiple steps, and breaking it up into teachable components or a set of discrete steps (Spooner, 1984). Some examples of skills that can be taught using a task analysis include the following: using a drink machine, purchasing food at a fast-food restaurant, progressing through an algebraic equation, and participating in a literacy lesson.

Even when the activity requires a chained task, the target of student learning may be just one discrete response or some subset of the chain. For example, teaching all the skills needed to use the restroom to a student who needs full assistance could be so time-consuming and arduous, especially if repeated for every student, that little else could be taught. Instead, the teacher may focus on just voiding in the toilet or pulling up pants and then give assistance without instruction for all other responses.

Student learning of some responses within an activity is called "partial participation" (Baumgart et al., 1982; Ferguson & Baumgart, 1991). Sometimes the goal is for responses within the chain to be learned in some sequence until the entire activity is independent. This is called "chaining" and is described next.

Serial Chaining versus Total Task

There are three distinct ways to teach the steps of task analysis: (1) forward chaining (FC), (2) backward chaining (BC), and (3) total task presentation (TT). FC and BC are called "serial chaining procedures," as each step is trained in a serial fashion, one step at a time. The first way to teach the steps of a task analysis is through FC. In FC the student receives instruction in the first discrete step in the chain of skills, and that first step is trained to a predetermined criterion before the second step is trained (Spooner, 1984). This continues until all steps in the chain have been taught to criterion. Advantages of a serial chaining procedure such as FC have been documented in that each method in isolation (FC, BC) has been proven to be successful (McDonnell & McFarland, 1988), and comparisons of FC and BC procedures have shown no differential effects (McDonnell & Laughlin, 1989). A potential disadvantage of FC is that it may alternatively punish those steps closest to the new step because they have not been trained as long as those established at the beginning of the chain (McDonnell & McFarland, 1988).

The task analysis could also be taught through BC, in which the student receives instruction on the last discrete step in the chain of skills but the preceding skills in the chain are completed for the student. The student must meet criterion on the last step before the second-to-last skill is taught. This continues until all skills in the chain have been taught to criterion. The big advantage of using BC is that the natural reinforcement is provided sooner (e.g., when learning the last step in making a sandwich, the student gets to eat the sandwich immediately rather than having to learn the first step and then going through the additional steps before receiving the sandwich). A disadvantage of BC is that it does not match the performance demands of the environment, which require a trainee to complete all steps of the chain (McDonnell & Laughlin, 1989).

Finally, the task analysis can be taught using TT. In TT instruction, the student is instructed on each step of the chain from the beginning (Gold, 1976; Kayser, Billingsley, & Neel, 1986; Spooner, 1984). This continues until all steps in the set are mastered to a predetermined criterion (e.g., six correct completions of the task without error or assistance). Advantages of the total task procedure are (1) practice is provided on every step of the chain every trial, (2) the steps of the task are presented in their natural order, (3) avoidance of the boredom of multiple-trial instruction that arises from the repetitious presentation of a stimulus, and (4) students learn the steps at their own rate. When comparison studies of these chaining procedures have been conducted, there are documented advantages in favor of the TT procedure (e.g., Kayser et al., 1986; Martin, Koop, Turner, & Hanel, 1981; Spooner, 1984). McDonnell and McFarland (1988) indicate the relative value of TT instruction on response topography and response sequencing simultaneously and the fact that it is highly compatible with demands in community.

FROM RESEARCH TO PRACTICE

A "rule of thumb" is to teach the entire task analysis for most students and most skills. Research on teaching a response chain that has been defined through a task analysis supports teaching the entire task from the onset of instruction (e.g., Spooner, 1984). Using forward or backward chaining, or pinpointing some responses within the chain for partial participation, are options for students whose rates of learning are very slow or when a month or more of instruction produces few to no independent responses in the chain.

Step 2: Define the Specific Methods to Use in Instructing the Skills

There are three primary considerations in planning how the target skills will be taught. These include planning how the teaching "trials" will be scheduled, developing a method for systematic prompting and feedback, and planning feedback, including reinforcement, reinforcement fading, and error correction. Additional consideration needs to be given to the materials to be used and the location at which instruction will take place. These plans also are written into the systematic instruction plan (SIP) and are discussed in Step 3.

Scheduling Teaching Trials

A teaching "trial" consists of each opportunity the student has to make the target response or chain of responses if a total task is being presented. These tasks may be scheduled for massed-, spaced-, or distributed-trial instruction. In massed-trial instruction the student has multiple opportunities to make the response in rapid succession. For example, the teacher may give Andrew 10 trials in a row to find his name among an array. On each trial, the teacher presents the discriminative stimulus (the name "Andrew" with three distractor words) and the cue to respond: "Find your name." On each trial the teacher also uses some preplanned prompt and reinforcement (described in the next subsection). Sometimes massed trials may include a set of discrete responses. For example, the teacher may present a set of 10 sight words, state capitals, or addition facts. In this case there may be only one trial per sight word, but the entire set is presented in a massed-trial format. Another alternative is to present several rounds of practice with the set of 10, so that students get more than one opportunity to respond per word. For example, the teacher may review the set of 10 state capitals three times. To maintain student focus, this massed-trial instruction is usually presented rapidly with no extraneous comments. For example, the teacher could feasibly review the 10 state capitals three times (30 trials) in 5–10 minutes.

Sometimes the instructional trials are spaced. The student has some opportunity to respond and then to take a break before the next trial (Collins, 2007). This occurs naturally when a teacher is using group instruction. In reviewing the 10 state capitals, the teacher calls on Sandra. Sandra then gets a break as the teacher gives Carlos and Adrian a turn. To maximize learning, the teacher may ask Sandra to watch (and possibly repeat) Carlos's and Adrian's responses rather than simply providing downtime between trials. Sometimes the student may work alone but have spaced trials. For example, the concentration required to manipulate a new switch may be intense, and the student needs a brief rest before the next trial.

A third option is for the instructional trials to be distributed across the lesson or school day. Distributed trials work well for teaching students to use new skills during naturally occurring routines. For example, the student may receive an instructional trial to make a choice or to ask for help at five different times across the day. When using distributed trials, the teacher needs to be sure to implement the systematic prompting and reinforcement planned at this "teachable moment." A special type of distributed instruction occurs when the trials are embedded in the context of a general education lesson. For example, while teaching a lesson on state history, the teacher may pause to give the student the opportunity to name the capital. Again, this is an embedded systematic instruction trial *only if* systematic prompting and feedback are used as planned. Simply asking the question is not systematic instruction using a distributed trial.

In task-analytic instruction, the teacher may present the entire task once daily or in any of the trial formats. For example, the teacher may give the student three opportunities to perform all the steps of the task analysis to solve a math problem or tie his or her shoes (massed trials). Or the teacher may give each student in the group an opportunity to perform a brief response chain in a spaced format (each one performs the steps to solve the equation in turn). Finally, task-analytic instruction may be distributed. A student may perform the steps to make a purchase in the morning at the school store, at lunch, and on an outing to the store for community-based instruction.

FINDING THE BALANCE

The more opportunities a student has to respond, the faster learning will occur. For this reason, educators have sometimes favored massed-trial instruction for students with severe disabilities. In contrast, students may not learn when to use the response (i.e., generalize) in a massed format. Massed-trial formats may also compete with the typical format of general education lessons. To find the balance, teachers will want to be skilled in all the different options for scheduling teaching trials. At the beginning of instruction, some instruction may be embedded in an overall lesson or scheduled at the naturally occurring time. Students who need more practice can then have massed-trial tutorials. In contrast, some difficult-to-learn skills may be introduced with massed-trial instruction and then embedded in general education lessons or during daily routines.

Prompting

As described earlier, students will often not make the target response in the presence of the discriminative stimulus. For example, when shown 2 + 5, the student may not select "7" from an array of options. To promote stimulus control, the teacher introduces instructional prompts and then fades this assistance. Two ways to effectively and efficiently transfer stimulus control include response-prompting systems and antecedent-prompting systems. These methods are shown in Table 4.1.

RESPONSE-PROMPTING SYSTEMS

Response-prompting systems are those in which the prompt is delivered after, or concurrently with, the presentation of the target discriminative stimulus. Response prompts are typically actions performed by the instructor. There are at least five types of response prompts. The instructor may tell the student how to respond (verbal), indicate the material to use next (gesture), show the full desired response (model), help the student begin to make the response (partial physical), or guide the student to make the full response (physical). Teachers rarely use all of these options. Instead, one to three options are selected. To be an effective prompt, this teacher action should be a response that currently sets the occasion for the target response for the individual student. Prompts are sometimes provided before the individual has an opportunity to respond, and then they must be faded so that the individual will respond independently, without the prompt, to naturally occurring stimuli (Wolery & Gast, 1984). Five common response-prompting procedures used for students with severe disabilities are (1) the system of least prompts, (2) most-to-least prompting, (3) time delay, (4) simultaneous prompting, and (5) graduated guidance.

The *system of least prompts* (i.e., least-to-most prompt system; least intrusive prompt system) uses a prompt hierarchy in which prompts are provided as needed, from the least intrusive prompt to the most intrusive prompt. The teacher selects about three types of response prompts and sequences them in order of intrusiveness (e.g., verbal, then modeling, then physical guidance). Although "intrusiveness" is subjective, generally physical assistance is considered more intrusive than other forms of prompting. Sometimes a gesture is less intrusive than a verbal direction. Sometimes a verbal direction may give less information. Teachers also can use a hierarchy of prompts within one topography, for example, moving from less to more verbal assistance.

Once the hierarchy of prompts is chosen, the instructor plans a constant wait time (usually 3–5 seconds) to be provided after the discriminative stimulus and between prompts to provide the student a chance to respond with the least intrusive prompt possible. After the presentation of the stimulus, the instructor waits a predetermined amount of time (e.g., 4 seconds) for the student to respond independently. If the student does not respond after the predetermined amount of time, the instructor then provides the first prompt in the predetermined prompt hierarchy (e.g., verbal prompt) and again waits the predetermined time for the student to respond. This process continues (e.g., with a modeling prompt) until the student responds or until the most intrusive prompt in the hierarchy has been given (e.g., full physical guidance). If the student appears to be making an error during the instructional trial, the instructor would attempt to block (prevent) the error and redirect to the correct stimulus. If this occurs the instructional trial

TABLE 4.1. Prompt-Fading Systems for Use in SIPs

Prompt-fading system	Type of prompt used	How fading is implemented	Life skills examples	Academic examples
Simultaneous prompting	Usually one specific response prompt, such as a verbal model of the answer, is used.	Prompt is "dropped." Student is tested on ability to respond with no prompt. *Note:* This system helps to avoid prompt dependence; however, students may experience more errors with this system.	Teacher models how to put book bag on hook, then student imitates. After 3 days, teacher omits the model and waits for student to put book bag on hook.	Teacher models how to count from 1 to 5, and then the student repeats. After several repetitions, student counts from 1 to 5 without a model.
Time delay	One specific response prompt is used.	At first, teacher gives the prompt with the target stimulus (no delay). Over trials, the prompt is delayed by a few seconds. *Note:* This system assists in minimizing student errors. *Progressive time delay:* Delays are incremental. *Constant time delay:* One specific delay time interval is used.	For each step of making pizza, teacher points to step on picture recipe (0 delay gesture) and student performs the step. After 2 days, teacher waits 4 seconds before pointing to picture (constant time delay).	Teacher says, "Show me the word *bread*" as she points to the correct answer (gestural prompt). On the next trial, she says, "Show me the word *bread*," but waits 2 seconds. *Constant time delay:* Next trials continue to wait 2 seconds. *Progressive time delay:* Next trials would be 2, 4, 6, and 8 seconds.
Least to most intrusive prompts	A hierarchy of response prompts is used.	On each teaching trial, teacher waits for student to make the response with no help and then uses the hierarchy of prompts until the correct response is made.	In washing hands, teacher waits for student to turn on faucet. When no response, teacher says, "Turn on the water." When still no response, teacher models turning it on and then says, "You try, turn on the water." If still	Teacher asks student a question, "Who is President?", and waits for student to point to correct answer in a four-choice array of pictures. When student does not answer, teacher repeats the question, and states the answer (verbal prompt) "Obama."

102

			no response, teacher physically guides student while saying, "Let me help you turn on the faucet."	Find Obama." When student still does not answer, teacher touches the correct picture (model prompt) saying, "Obama, now you do it," and waits for a response. When student does not answer, teacher repeats the question, and helps student touch the picture (physical guidance).
Most to least intrusive prompts	Teaching begins with one response prompt that is highly effective but may be intrusive (e.g., physical guidance). Then a less intrusive prompt is used (e.g., verbal direction).	Teacher will usually set a specific number of days or trials to use the more intrusive prompt and then switch to a less intrusive prompt.	To teach putting hat on, first days teacher guides student to put hat on. After 2 days, taps hat and waits for student to put it on. After 2 more days, waits for student to put hat on without assistance, then uses tap if needed.	Teacher asks student a question and uses hand-over-hand guidance to teach student to press the button of the AAC (physical prompt) to respond to the question. After 10 days, teacher points to the button (gestural prompt).
Graduated guidance	Physical prompting is always used, but only with as much guidance and physical pressure as is needed.	Teacher decreases the amount of physical guidance used as student's response improves.	Teacher guides student to use a spoon so food does not spill. As student gains more motor control, teacher uses less and less physical pressure until student needs no help.	Teacher uses hand-over-hand guidance to teach correct letter formation to write the letter *M*. As student's writing improves, teacher uses less and less physical pressure until student writes the letter *M* independently.
Stimulus fading or shaping	Stimulus prompts are used. *Coding*: Use extra colors, pictures, or other features coded with correct response. *Easy-to-hard sequence*: Arrange materials in sequence.	*Coding*: Extra cues are diminished in size or brightness over time. *Easy-to-hard sequence*: Distractions become increasingly similar to the target stimulus.	Student uses a place mat with pictures drawn of plate, utensils, napkin to know how to set the table. Over time, the pictures are made lighter until it is a plain placemat (stimulus fading).	Student traces name on each paper completed. Over time, the model to trace has only dashed lines, then dots, then just an empty line so student writes name without help (stimulus fading).

Note. Based on Browder (2001).

is over. The system of least intrusive prompts is considered to be "self-fading," because the teacher uses less assistance as the student begins to respond. This self-fading can be promoted through the use of praise and other reinforcers. For example, once the student can respond with a verbal prompt, the instructor, to shape his or her progress toward independence no longer praises responses when the student waits for a model or physical guidance. The system of least prompts has been used to impart a variety of skills to individuals with developmental disabilities. For example, toothbrushing (Horner & Keilitz, 1975), clothes mending (Cronin & Cuvo, 1979), object identification (Godby, Gast, & Wolery, 1987) and restroom cleaning (Cuvo, Leaf, & Borakove, 1978), as well as other skills, have been successfully acquired by individuals with severe developmental disabilities using this prompting method. Figure 4.1 provides an example of how a teacher might use a system of least prompts to teach a student to use a vending machine, including the first two steps and the error correction procedure.

Step 1: Take out dollar.
1. Teacher waits 3 seconds for student to take out dollar. If correct, teacher praises and moves to Step 2.
2. If not correct, teacher gives verbal prompt: "Take out your dollar." Waits 3 seconds. If student is correct, teacher praises and moves to Step 2.
3. If not correct, teacher gives model: "Take out your dollar like this" (demonstrates with own dollar). "Now you try." Waits 3 seconds. If student is correct, teacher praises and moves to Step 2.
4. If not correct, teacher gives physical guidance: "Let me help you get your dollar out of your wallet" (guides hand to get dollar). Teacher praises ("Good, that's your dollar," and moves to Step 2.

Step 2: Insert dollar in money slot.
1. Teacher waits for student to insert dollar in the money slot. If correct, teacher praises and moves to Step 3.
2. If incorrect, gives verbal prompt: "Put your money in the slot." If correct, teacher praises and moves to Step 3.
3. If incorrect, gives model prompt: "Put your money in the slot like this" (teacher models with own dollar but does not put it all the way in). "Now you try." If correct, teacher praises and moves to Step 3.
4. If incorrect, gives physical guidance: "Let me help you get the dollar in the slot" (guides student's hand to put the dollar in the slot). Teacher praises and moves to Step 4. (This continues for all steps of the task analysis.)

Example of an Error Correction in Least Intrusive Prompts
After model prompt, student begins to throw dollar in the bin from which the soda is dispensed. The teacher gently covers the bin to block the error and gives the next level of prompt (physical guidance).

FIGURE 4.1. Example of what the teacher says while using least intrusive prompts.

Most-to-least prompting (i.e., system of most prompts; most intrusive prompt system) also uses a hierarchy of prompts, like the system of least prompts, but in this case the prompting starts with the most intrusive prompt and systematically moves to less intrusive prompts as the student starts to respond more independently. According to Wolery and Gast (1984), most-to-least prompting is the most widely used instructional procedure to teach response chains to individuals with developmental disabilities. A variety of skills have been trained successfully using a most-to-least prompting procedure. For example, vocational task assembly skills (Gold, 1976; Spooner, 1984; Zane, Walls, & Thvedt, 1981), dressing (Ball, Seric, & Payne, 1971; Minge & Ball, 1967), and self-feeding (Nelson, Cone, & Hanson, 1975; O'Brien & Azrin, 1972) have successfully been acquired by learners with developmental disabilities. Another major difference between the two prompt systems is that, in most-to-least prompt systems, the instructor may stay at one prompt level (e.g., partial physical prompt) for several instructional sessions before moving to a less intrusive prompt. Because this system is not "self-fading," instructors should use daily data to guide these decisions. For example, once a student responds consistently with partial physical guidance, the teacher would then fade back to a model or gesture prompt.

Time delay is a response-prompting system in which the prompt is faded using increments of time. Most often only one response prompt is chosen (e.g., model). The prompt is introduced concurrently with the target stimulus so that the student responds correctly without error (errorless responding will depend on selecting an effective prompt). For example, the teacher says, "What do we call moisture that forms in the sky?" while pointing to the correct answer ("precipitation") in an array of science terms. Over teaching trials, the instructor inserts small increments of time (e.g., 2–4 seconds) between the introduction of the target stimulus (e.g., the array of science terms and the question) and the prompt (showing the correct answer) to allow the student to "anticipate" the correct response. Time delay transfers stimulus control through this errorless learning strategy (Sidman & Stoddard, 1967; Terrace, 1963a, 1963b; Touchette, 1971). Time delay also has strong educational validity in that it has been applied to many skills with relevance to the lives of individuals with moderate and severe disabilities (Browder, Hines, McCarthy, & Fees, 1984; Collins & Griffen, 1996; Cuvo & Klatt, 1992; Koury & Browder, 1986).

FROM RESEARCH TO PRACTICE: USING TIME DELAY

To review the theoretical framework of transferring stimulus control, consider the example of a student who is learning to identify a sight word. From a behavior-analytic perspective, identifying the sight word is a discrete, observable response (e.g., saying the word, pointing to the word in an array) that is controlled by a printed stimulus. The printed stimulus (e.g., printed word) sets the occasion for the response (e.g., saying the word), and through reinforcement of the response in the presence of the stimulus (and not in the presence of other stimuli), the word itself becomes a discriminative stimulus for the reading response. When the target stimulus (printed word) does not set the occasion for the response, the teacher may use a second stimulus that does have stimulus control (e.g., her verbal model) paired with the target stimulus. This second stimulus is called the prompt. When the prompt is used, stimulus control will not be established until it is transferred from this second stimulus (e.g., verbal prompt) to the target one (e.g., saying the word). Although a variety of methods exist to transfer stimulus control, Touchette (1971) found that inserting small increments of time between the target stimulus and the prompt across trials resulted in the learner "anticipating" the correct response. In the first trial, the prompt and the target stimulus are paired concurrently. In subsequent trials, a delay is gradually inserted before the prompt (e.g., 1–2 seconds) until the student anticipates the correct response (i.e., unprompted correct response). This learning can occur with few to no errors, and so time delay is considered an "errorless learning" procedure.

There are two types of time delay (Snell & Gast, 1981), constant and progressive. In *constant time delay*, after several rounds at a zero delay, the stimulus is presented, and the instructor waits a predetermined amount of time (e.g., 4 seconds) before the controlling prompt is provided. If an error occurs during instruction, the instructor should block and redirect to the correct answer. The instructor also may repeat some of the zero-delay trials before reintroducing the 4-second delay trials, as the goal is to achieve near errorless learning. *Progressive time delay* begins at zero delay, but the wait time between the presentation of the stimulus and the delivery of the controlling prompt will progressively increase. An instructor may choose to start with a 2-second delay, move to a 4-second delay in the next round, and so on. Some preplanning will be needed to determine how many trials to remain at for each delay level. Time delay should be used only with students who exhibit a wait response. The idea is that the students should never be allowed to make an error.

Simultaneous prompting is a response-prompting system in which, on the delivery of the stimulus, the controlling prompt is immediately delivered. This is what happens during the zero-delay rounds of time delay, but with simultaneous prompting, the prompt is always delivered immediately after the stimulus at zero delay. After instruction is delivered, instructional probes are provided to see whether learning has occurred or stimulus control has been transferred. Simultaneous prompting has been used successfully with both discrete and chained tasks (Collins, 2007). Singleton, Schuster, Morse, and Collins (1999) used simultaneous prompting to train secondary school students with moderate and severe disabilities to successfully read grocery words. Parrott, Schuster, Collins, and Gassaway (2000) taught hand washing to elementary students with moderate and severe disabilities.

Graduated guidance is a response-prompting system that is often associated with responses that require a motor movement (e.g., feeding, toileting). Graduated guidance, developed by Foxx and Azrin (1973), was initially used to teach independent toileting skills to institutionalized adults with severe intellectual disability. For example, Azrin and Armstrong (1973) used graduated guidance in teaching self-feeding in their "mini-meal" procedure, and Collins, Gast, Wolery, Holcombe, and Leatherby (1991) also used graduated guidance to teach two preschool children with severe to profound multiple disabilities to use a spoon and a cup. The procedure involves the most intrusive prompt, typically hand-over-hand assistance, or what is called a full physical prompt (e.g., hand-over-hand assistance to help a student scoop food and bring it to the mouth), until the instructor feels the student starting to participate. At this point the instructor will back off the amount of assistance (e.g., the instructor will move his or her hand back to the student's wrist and continue to help the student scoop and bring food to the mouth) until the instructor feels the student is starting to participate more or initiate movement. As training continues and student progress is being reflected, the instructor can continue to lessen the level and amount of the prompt (e.g., the instructor will move his or her hand to the student's elbow). This procedure continues until the teacher has faded assistance back to just shadowing the student. At any time during this procedure that the instructor feels the student not initiating or participating, the amount of assistance can increase again. Azrin, Schaeffer, and Wesolowski (1976) used graduated guidance to teach dressing skills to individuals with profound intellectual disability.

ANTECEDENT-PROMPTING SYSTEMS

In addition to response-prompting procedures (in which the instructor guides the response), antecedent-prompting procedures can be used to change a target behavior. This procedure involves manipulating or changing the antecedent (stimulus) that is presented. Two different antecedent-prompting procedures are commonly used.

Stimulus shaping is the process of highlighting an important feature of the materials used for instruction, the relevant dimensions (Etzel & LeBlanc, 1979, Wolery & Gast, 1984). The foundation for stimulus shaping originates from the attention theory of Zeaman and House (1963). Gold and Scott (1971) provide an intellectual-disability training perspective on the complicated nuances of Zeaman and House's attention theory (e.g., redundancy, irrelevant cues, fading, clustering, overlearning, and easy-to-hard sequences). For example, to teach Sam to recognize his name, the teacher might begin by pairing the word "Sam" with shapes so that the difference is easy to discriminate. In subsequent trials, letters and words will be introduced until Sam is able to recognize all the letters in his name. See Figure 4.2 for an example of the way fading levels might look.

Stimulus fading is the procedure by which a feature of the materials (stimulus) is made more salient and then gradually faded over time to become a more generalized stimulus. In this procedure, fading involves the manipulation of any dimension of the stimulus (e.g., color, size, shape, position), not just the relevant one (Etzel & LeBlanc, 1979; Wolery & Gast, 1984). This strategy is one of the oldest methods for teaching individuals with developmental disabilities to read sight words (Dorry & Zeaman, 1973, 1975). Often the sight word will be paired with a picture or a relevant feature. For example, the word *red* is written in the color red and eventually faded so the word *red* appears in black; the word *car* is written with a picture of a car behind the word, and over time the picture of the car is faded from the material and only the word *car* remains. Figure 4.3 shows an example of stimulus fading in teaching the number 5 by manipulating size. The teacher might use several trials at each fade level.

Level 1:	***	Sam	***
	Sam	***	***
	***	***	Sam
Level 2:	Sam	T	a
	M	Sam	x
	S	b	Sam
Level 3:	put	sit	Sam
	Ask	Sam	did
	Bob	dog	Sam
Level 4:	Sam	Sue	Am
	Sat	Sam	Mam
	Tam	Sue	Sam

FIGURE 4.2. Example of fading stimulus shaping.

5   8   2

6   1   5

5   0   4

7   5   9

FIGURE 4.3. Example of stimulus fading.

The Principle of Parsimony

The principle of parsimony (Etzel & LeBlanc, 1979) involves using the most efficient or simplest intervention method that is effective. For example, it is much easier for instructors to use response prompts than to manipulate the stimulus itself (e.g., making materials that show the image of a car fading out of the word *car*; Wolery & Gast, 1984). For this reason, teachers will typically try response prompts before stimulus prompts. In addition, some response-prompting strategies are more parsimonious than others. For example, constant time delay may be easier for a paraprofessional or peer tutor to use than progressive time delay because there is only one level of fading. Table 4.2 provides a summary of the decisions teachers need to make in planning systematic prompting.

Feedback, Reinforcement, Reinforcement Fading, and Error Correction

It is also essential for instructors to identify the feedback they are going to provide during instruction. Feedback includes both reinforcement and error correction.

PRINCIPLES OF REINFORCEMENT AND REINFORCEMENT FADING

When initially teaching a skill, the instructor should reinforce every correct response (i.e., a continuous reinforcement schedule [CRF]; Cooper et al., 2007; Ferster & Skinner, 1957). Reinforcement should always include praise, but for some students or some skills it may also include tangibles (e.g., food, tokens, toys, computer time). If the praise is descriptive of the correct response, the student is more likely to make the connection between the response and instructor approval. For example, Betty's teacher would say, "Good, you put the dollar in the slot," rather than simply "Good." Sometimes the instructor may choose to use "instructive feedback," in which the teacher gives more information about the response (Werts, Wolery, Holcome, & Gast, 1995). For example, Betty's teacher might say, "Good, you put the dollar in the slot. You could also use four quarters in this slot." This descriptive feedback may help the student learn additional information.

All reinforcement, including praise statements, will need to be faded so that the student learns to complete the task without instructor attention. This fading may occur using a variable schedule of reinforcement (e.g., after an average of three responses) or a fixed ration (after every third response). Over teaching sessions, the fading schedule is lengthened (e.g., after every fifth response; after every tenth response). Once praise is faded to a lean, intermittent schedule, the student is more likely to maintain the responses. In the

TABLE 4.2. Decision Guide for Planning Systematic Prompting

Decision	Least intrusive prompting	Time delay of a response prompt	Most to least prompting	Stimulus prompts
Will more than one prompt be used?	Yes	Probably not	Yes	No
What types of prompts will be used?	A hierarchy from less to more assistance; e.g., verbal, model, physical	One prompt that is effective for student and target response (e.g., model)	A hierarchy of prompts from more to less assistance; e.g., physical, partial physical, gesture	Some modification of the discriminative stimulus (e.g., color coding; use of picture)
How much time will I wait between the discriminative stimulus and the first prompt?	Wait about 3 seconds; then, if no response, give verbal prompt; wait 3 more seconds; if no response, give model; if no response, wait 3 more seconds, give physical guidance.	On the first trial there is no time (zero delay) because prompt is given with the discriminative stimulus.	Wait about 3 seconds for student to respond, then use physical guidance. After a set number of days, fade to partial physical guidance.	Stimulus prompt is used concurrently with discriminative stimulus. Usually this requires some modification of materials in advance of teaching.
How will I fade the prompt?	This method is "self-fading." The teacher reinforces responses with least assistance student needs (e.g., if student can do it with model, teacher does not praise physical guidance).	The prompt is faded using increments of time. After the zero trials, the teacher uses some delay (e.g., 4 seconds). If progressive delay is chosen, this may increase across trials (e.g., 2 minutes, 4 minutes, 6 minutes, 8 seconds)	The prompt is faded by following a schedule to move to the lesser prompt (e.g., 2 days at each prompt level).	The prompt may be faded by reducing its salience (stimulus fading). In stimulus shaping, discrimination is made more difficult on subsequent trials. *Note:* Time delay can also be used—for example, the picture can be introduced after a 4-second delay.
What do I do to discourage errors?	If an error begins, try to block it and give the next level of prompt. Praise correct responses.	Tell student not to guess. Repeat zero-delay trials. If error occurs after the prompt, a different type of prompt or change in reinforcement for correct responses may be needed.	If an error occurs after moving to a less intrusive prompt, block the error and give a more intrusive prompt (e.g., if an error occurs on the physical assistance level, give full physical).	No error should occur at first. If it does, the choice of stimulus prompt may need to be changed, or some pretraining may be needed (e.g., to name the pictures). On subsequent trials, go back to the easier trials if errors occur (e.g., to less faded picture or easier discrimination).
How do I promote independence (transfer of stimulus control)?	Reinforce when student performs step correctly with less assistance. Give strong praise or other reinforcement for unprompted responses.	Only praise correct responses. As student begins to anticipate correct responses, only praise unprompted correct responses.	Praise correct prompted performance until the last level of fading. Then only praise correct unprompted responses.	Praise correct responses. As fading progresses, only praise responding at levels equal to, or better than, prior day.

case of Betty, the instructor will begin by praising every correct response for the first 2 weeks of instruction. She then will fade back to delivering the reinforcer only after every other independent correct response on the task analysis (a fixed ratio, FR2) and then after every fourth response. As Betty gains independence, the teacher will let receiving the soda itself serve as the natural consequence for correct responding and only occasionally offer praise.

OPTIONS FOR ERROR CORRECTION

In addition to reinforcing correct responses, the instructor should decide how errors will be treated. Usually, error correction instructs the student on the correct response and does not repeat or give attention to the error. If Betty, while learning the vending machine task, were to try to put the dollar in the coin return slot, her instructor might say, "Put the dollar in *this* slot" and model the correct response. Betty's instructor might also block the error by holding his or her hand in front of the student's hand while demonstrating the correct response. Sometimes the teacher may use a simple "no" and prompt the correct answer. For example, if the students says *cat* when the word is *can*, the teacher will say, "No, it's *can*. Say *can*." Sometimes the error correction will contain additional information or prompting, for example, "No, it's *can* . . . see the final sound /n/. Point to the letters and say it with me: *c-a-n*." What the teacher should not do is beg students to respond, give lots of hints, or scold them for wrong answers. These strategies can confuse the student about when to respond or inadvertently reinforce errors.

After defining the specific methods to use when teaching a skill, the teacher can summarize these in a written systematic instruction plan (SIP). Figure 4.4 provides an example of a completed SIP. A blank SIP form can be found in Figure 4.5.

Step 3: Implement the SIP

After developing the written SIP, the instructor will need to decide how to implement it frequently (e.g., daily). In order to implement the plan daily, it is crucial to determine who will teach the plan, when it will be taught, and where. Teachers will also need to select and develop any materials needed for the lesson. Systematic instruction can be provided in any context in which students receive instruction. For example, the research on sight word learning provides examples of students receiving time-delay instruction in community settings, in the general education class, in special education classes, and in other environments (Browder, Ahlgrim-Delzell, et al., 2009). Peers, general educators, special educators, and others have provided this instruction (Browder, Spooner, et al., 2008).

Step 4: Review Student Progress and Modify Instruction

When implementing the SIP daily, it is important to continue teaching the targeted skills daily until mastery occurs or a change is made in the plan. In order to determine whether a change needs to be made to the instructional strategies, it is important to review student progress regularly (e.g., biweekly) and modify instruction as needed. The first step to reviewing students' progress is to chart student performance. After charting student per-

Student: Marley   Date Plan Started: 8/15/10

Target Skill: Read sight words   Routine: Reading

Specific Objective: During a read-aloud, Marley will correctly find 10 vocabulary words that are embedded in a picture/word story.

Format

Materials: Story with vocabulary words embedded

Setting and Schedule for Instruction: Daily during reading class

Number of Trials: 1 trial per word for a total of 10 responses

Instructional Procedure

PROMPTING

Specific Prompt or Prompts to Be Used (list in sequence):

1. Model of pointing to word on page
2. _____
3. _____
4. _____

Type of Prompt System (check which applies):

____	System of Least Prompts				
x	Time Delay	x	Constant OR	____	Progressive
____	Most to Least Intrusive Prompts				
____	Graduated Guidance				
____	Stimulus Fading or Shaping				
____	Chaining	____	Backward OR	____	Forward
____	Other (describe):				

Fading Schedule: On the first 3 days, point to each word as it is read aloud (zero delay) and have Marley imitate doing so. Beginning on the 4th day, wait 4 seconds after reading the word for Marley to find it.

FEEDBACK

Correct Responses Praise for finding the word

Fading Schedule for Praise Only praise unprompted correct responses after the second week.

Error Correction "No, here is the word . . ." and have the student repeat, touching the word . . . .

Generalization and Maintenance Plan Use a variety of stories and have the words be at different places in the text. Have speech therapist and peer also conduct the read-alouds. After she learns to find her words, fade to only finding them occasionally during reading.

Notes: If Marley does not begin to identify the words without assistance by week 3, use a massed-trial practice reading the words prior to the read-aloud.

FIGURE 4.4. Example of a completed SIP.

Student: _____ Date Plan Started: _____

Target Skill: _____ Routine: _____

Specific Objective: _____

_____

Format

Materials: _____

Setting and Schedule for Instruction: _____

Number of Trials: _____

Instructional Procedure
PROMPTING
Specific Prompt or Prompts to Be Used (list in sequence):

1. _____
2. _____
3. _____
4. _____

Type of Prompt System (check which applies):

_____ System of Least Prompts

_____ Time Delay   _____ Constant OR   _____ Progressive

_____ Most to Least Intrusive Prompts

_____ Graduated Guidance

_____ Stimulus Fading or Shaping

_____ Chaining   _____ Backward OR   _____ Forward

_____ Other (describe): _____

Fading Schedule: _____

_____

FEEDBACK

Correct Responses _____

Fading Schedule for Praise_____

Error Correction _____

_____

Generalization and Maintenance Plan

Notes:

FIGURE 4.5. Blank SIP form.

formance, the instructor needs to review student progress (data trends) using data-based decision rules (see Chapter 3). Finally, it is important to use the decision rules discussed in Chapter 3 to modify the SIP as needed.

PLANNING OVERALL INSTRUCTIONAL SUPPORT

During the course of a day, a teacher may use a variety of forms of instructional support. Some of these will be more teacher directed; others will rely more on naturally occurring cues in the environment and student self-direction. Both for efficiency of time and to promote student learning, teachers need to consider the full spectrum of options for instructional support. Table 4.3 provides a decision model for planning instructional support. Each component of the model is described in the following sections.

Universal Design for Learning for the Whole Class

One of the most important forms of instructional support is lessons that are planned to be inclusive of all students in an entire class. Instructors should consider implementing universal design for learning (UDL). Implementing UDL involves planning for multiple means of engagement, expression, and representation. Multiple means of engagement refers to the variety of strategies used to get all learners actively involved in all aspects of the lesson. Whereas some learners may be able to read the textbook, others may need a "hands on" activity. When UDL is applied, these multiple options are not just for the student with disabilities but for all students. For example, with the use of cooperative learning groups or hands-on materials, all students may benefit from increased engagement. Multiple means of expression give students a variety of ways to show what they know. Not only will students have traditional options such as written reports or paper-and-pencil tests, but they will also have other choices, such as presentations, skits, and artwork. Sometimes the student with a disability may use a special means of expression (e.g., an object vs. a written graph) that other students do not need, but whenever possible, enough flexibility should be built into the lesson so that other students are also using alternatives. In multiple means of representation, the material is offered in ways that all students can access it. Sometimes this means using technology such as digital books. Other times, simple adaptations such as summaries and guided notes may be used. If these options are used as supplements available to all students, the student with a disability needs fewer special adaptations. Spooner, Baker, Ahlgrim-Delzell, Harris, and Browder (2007) described how teachers can learn to create a universally designed lesson.

Sometimes teachers may need to work with a grade-level general education lesson plan that has already been written and adapt it for students with severe disabilities. Again, the principles of UDL can be applied. Changes in representation may include changes to the materials (e.g., enlarged text, picture support for text) or to the way the teacher presents materials (e.g., using a light box to illuminate the book). Changes in engagement may include providing prompting and reinforcement to increase the likelihood of student success (e.g., increasing the wait time between prompts). Finally, changes in expression may include providing alternate means of allowing a student to show what he or she knows (e.g., answering comprehension questions with concrete objects). Figure

TABLE 4.3. Making Decisions about the Level of Instructional Support a Student Needs

Type of support	Example	When to use	How systematic instruction contributes
UDL for whole class	A general education lesson on whales includes multiple ways for students to access the printed material and several options for producing a report.	For all general education lessons to be inclusive of students with disabilities; special educator and general educator plan together.	Trials of systematic instruction may sometimes be embedded in the general education lesson.
Environmental supports/natural cues	Students eat lunch together and provide natural cues for when to leave and how to clean up.	For all students to increase independence from teacher assistance.	Student may receive incidental teaching on how to respond to the cue at naturally occurring times.
Student-directed learning	Student uses picture directions to know how to find information on the Internet. Student works at a work station or learning center.	For all students to increase self-determination; most general education classes require some self-directed time (e.g., seatwork, computer time).	Student may receive systematic instruction on how to use the self-directed strategy.
Small-group instruction	Teacher instructs a small group for a reading lesson.	Whenever feasible, because small-group instruction maximizes instructional time compared to 1:1.	Systematic instruction can be used in a small group by taking turns giving students trials.
Community-based instruction	Teaching occurs in typical community setting.	For generalization of skills and to teach skills that cannot be simulated at school (e.g., some jobs).	Systematic instruction can be used to teach priority community skills.
One-to-one instruction	Student works with peer or teacher in learning to put on coat or read science vocabulary.	It will not be feasible to teach all skills 1:1, so use this option when skill is not being learned with other forms of support.	Systematic instruction is often used in a 1:1 context to teach priority skills.
Special education class using 1:1, group, or whole-class instruction	Student receives extra assistance on literacy in special class.	Placement is an IEP team decision (see Chapter 3).	Systematic instruction has often been used in special education classes.

4.6 provides an example of a general education language arts lesson on *Island of the Blue Dolphins* (O'Dell, 1987) that includes principles of UDL.

Environmental and Natural Supports

When creating opportunities for students to be included in general education, community, job, and other learning contexts, it is important to capitalize on the instructional supports typically available in these contexts. These typically available resources are called "natural supports" (Nisbet, 1992). To "enhance" these natural supports simply means to: (1) identify them, (2) be sure the learner has access to them, and (3) accentuate them if necessary so that the learner can attend or respond to them more easily. The goal in most instruction is for students to learn to respond to the natural cues and consequences in their environments in performing their daily routines (Ford & Mirenda, 1984). The bell is a natural cue to go to class, and a tardy slip may be the natural consequence for not making it on time. Entering the lunchroom is the natural cue to get in line to purchase lunch. Coming to the cashier is the cue to pay, and the natural consequence of paying is sitting and eating lunch. When providing instructional support to students with moderate and severe disabilities, it is important to focus on these natural cues and consequences. In their research demonstrating how to focus prompting on natural cues, Colyer and Collins (1996) stated the price in the same way cashiers do (natural cue) before giving a prompt. They then used a prompt hierarchy to help the student respond if this natural cue was not sufficient. When using classroom or school and community simulations, teachers can incorporate natural cues and consequences (Nietupski, Hamre-Nietupski, Clancy, & Veerhusen, 1986; Westling & Fox, 1995). For example, in having students practice ordering at a restaurant, the teacher can use a copy of the actual menu.

Another form of environmental support is peer assistance. Peers can serve as tutors, buddies, or helpers with positive benefits for both the student with disabilities and the peer who is nondisabled (Hunt, Staub, Alwell, & Goetz, 1994). In recruiting peers, Eichinger and Downing (1996) recommend that participation be voluntary. They suggest recruiting peers to assist students with disabilities in the following ways:

1. Ask students if they would like to interact with a given student and give opportunities to do so.
2. Ask the teacher which students might benefit academically, socially, or emotionally from working with a student with disabilities.
3. Ask the school counselor, especially at the secondary level, for nominees.
4. Assign students to cooperative learning groups to help establish relationships.
5. Have students with disabilities join extracurricular activities and clubs.
6. Ask the school council or other school leaders if they are interested in supporting some students. (p. 130)

The specific duties the peer assistant provides can vary. They may help direct the student's attention to the teacher, help get materials ready, offer assistance with mobility (e.g., push a wheelchair), or serve as a buddy during lunch, recess, or assemblies (Downing & Eichinger, 1996). Peers may also be recruited to provide systematic instruction or to work in cooperative learning groups, as described in Chapter 1.

Inclusive General Education Lesson Plan	Homework:
Subject: *Language Arts* **Location of Lesson:** Seventh-grade Language Arts Class **Special Education Teacher:** Carlos Rivera **General Education Teacher:** Ms. Keesha Jones **Who Will Teach Lesson:** Ms. Keesha Jones **State Objective #** ELA 7.28. **Source of Lesson:** Seventh-grade novel: *Island of the Blue Dolphins*	Students will write a page about the story and how the major themes compare with their own lives. This written product may be produced with pictures from student's life.
Material/Technology Needed *(How will materials be made accessible to students with disabilities?):* Students have option of typical novel, text summaries, and novel adapted with picture support, reduced text, simplified text, added explanations and definitions, repeated storyline, physical alterations for handling, and object support when necessary	
Link to Prior Learning *(Anticipatory Set: How will you start the lesson?)* *Students will review prior chapters and introduce new chapter by viewing Internet pictures of dolphins and hearing dolphin noises (no adaptations needed).*	
Purpose/Objective of the Lesson *(What priority skills do you want the students to demonstrate in this lesson?):* *The students will outline the story grammar and identify the tone of the chapter.*	
Lesson Input/Modeling *(How will this student participate in the lesson? What responses will be used to check for this student's understanding of lesson?):* *Students will read the beginning of Chapter 3 aloud, pausing to discuss what the author is trying to achieve. To help students understand the concept of tone, we will change some key words to make the passage read differently and discuss the overall tone. Some students will use adapted text with pictures during this time. Students will then work in small groups to answer questions about tone. Some groups may choose to act out parts of the story.*	
Assessment *At end of chapter, students will outline the story grammar and write in their Language Arts journals about the author's point of view.* *Some students will follow Chapter 3 using highlighted or adapted text. Students may generate their own story grammar format or use one of several provided. Some students may cut and paste pictures to fill in key points of the plot. Some students may use the chart of "feeling words" to describe the tone of the story.*	
UDL Checklist ✓ <u>Multiple means of engagement?</u> Multisensory intro, read-alouds, small-group work, role-play option ✓ <u>Multiple means of representation?</u> Adapted text along with regular text; feelings chart; story grammar formats ✓ <u>Multiple means of expression?</u> Students can use a variety of story grammar formats, including picture option	

FIGURE 4.6. Example of applying UDL to a general education lesson plan.

A well-organized schedule is an important environmental support that can help students anticipate and prepare for each day's routine. Figure 4.7 is an example of a student's schedule.

Besides a master schedule, a second crucial form of planning that teachers use is the written weekly lesson plan. This plans outlines material to be covered during each day and at each time of the day. The special education teacher's weekly lesson plans should incorporate both the students' IEP priorities and the broader curricular areas to be addressed. When planning for inclusion, the special education teacher can obtain a copy of the general education teacher's weekly lesson plans to develop adaptations for the students with moderate and severe disabilities.

In addition to having both written schedules and weekly lesson plans, teachers can encourage learning through the physical layout of their classrooms. A model program that focuses on environmental supports for students with autism is Treatment and Education of Autistic and Related Communication-Handicapped Children (TEACCH; Schopler, Mesibov, & Hearsey, 1995). Many of the TEACCH adaptations have applicability across a broad range of students and settings. For example, the TEACCH adaptations have been used in general education classrooms and on job sites, as well as in special education classrooms. Three of the key adaptations in TEACCH are the use of visual cues in the student's environment, an individualized schedule, and work stations. The classroom environment is arranged so that the same activities occur in the same areas each day. Picture, word, and object cues are placed in these areas to assist the student in knowing the function of that area of the room. Picture and word cues are also used to help the student know what social behavior is expected. In teaching a small-group lesson, the teacher may have a symbol for taking turns and for watching quietly. As each student is called on, the teacher shows the student's name and the symbol for taking a turn. The other students are told to watch quietly. Every student has his or her own schedule. Depending on current reading skills, this schedule may include objects, picture–word combinations, or just words. The schedule may be large (a wall chart) or small enough to carry in a pocket or on a clipboard. Students refer to the schedule at the beginning of each activity, remove the card or object that depicts the activity (or check the word with a pencil), and then go to the appropriate area to start the task.

Student-Directed Learning

A third option for instructional support is student-directed learning. Whereas environmental arrangements are used to help students to perform responses in their repertoire with little or no assistance, student-directed learning strategies are designed to help students teach themselves new skills. One strategy that may be used to encourage student-directed learning is "within-stimulus prompting" (Eckert & Browder, 1997). In this strategy, visual (or auditory) prompts are placed within the materials themselves rather than delivered by the teacher. One strategy is to use what are called "permanent prompts." These may include color-coding materials or arranging materials in a certain sequence so that students can learn how to make the correct responses by responding to these stimuli. Students can also be taught to instruct themselves using scripts, pictures, or audiotapes (Wehmeyer, Agran, & Hughes, 1998) and to problem-solve when encountering a challenge such as missing materials (Hughes, Hugo, & Blatt, 1996). Another

Special education teacher's master schedule	Special education teachers' priorities for instruction	Student's schedule
7:15–7:30 Buses arrive 7:30 Homeroom	• Arrival routine • Greetings • Orientation and mobility	7:30 HOMEROOM • Goes to class with peer buddy, who escorts from bus
7:45–9:45 Language Arts Block	• Seventh-grade language arts standards • Literacy skills • Read-alouds of novels • Building decoding • Writing • Functional words	7:45 LANGUAGE ARTS • Participates in whole-class UDL lesson • Embedded SIP on using pictures to answer comprehension questions • Self-directed learning for functional words using word–picture matching
10:00–12:30 Math Block Lunch is 11:00–11:30 during this block	• Seventh-grade math standards • Money skills • Time telling with schedule	10:00 MATH • Reads time on her schedule with peer • Participates in daily UDL lesson • Embedded SIP on priority math skill (graphing)
12:30 Physical Education	• 12:30 Physical education with Mr. Hartford's class (coteaching)	12:30 PHYSICAL EDUCATION OR PT (Fridays) Working on dressing and ambulation skills from IEP
1:30 Social Studies or Science (School uses an A/B schedule to alternate these)	• Seventh-grade standards • Special focus on inquiry in science; group skills in social studies • During unit tests, use this time for community-based instruction on priority life skills.	1:30 SOCIAL STUDIES—A Day • or • SCIENCE—B Day • Participates in whole-class lesson • Embedded instruction on priority IEP skill (using KWHL chart; vocabulary; locating pictures for report on Internet)
2:00 Departure routine	• Departure skills (e.g., coat on; carry book bag; find bus)	2:00 GO TO BUS • Finds bus number with peer

FIGURE 4.7. Example of a daily schedule.

strategy is the self-determined learning model of instruction (SDLMI), which focuses on increasing opportunities to self-direct learning and improve overall opportunities for success for students both with and without disabilities (McGlashing-Johnson, Agran, Sitlington, Cavin, & Wehmeyer, 2003; Wehmeyer, Palmer, Agran, Mithaug, & Martin, 2000). SDLMI is implemented in three phases in which a problem is presented to be solved by the student. The student is taught to answer and apply four questions per phase. The first phase is to set a goal, which becomes the problem to be solved by the student. The second phase is to take action, which requires the student to identify a plan. The third phase focuses on adjusting the goal or plan by asking the student what he or she has learned. SDLMI has been shown to increase overall self-determination and to help students acquire educational goals; also, students communicate overall satisfaction with the process (Wehmeyer et al., 2000).

Another principle of the TEACCH model is to encourage students to learn to do independent work through the use of workstations. Students have their own work space, which may be separated by dividers to minimize distractions. In this space students perform independent tasks that teachers assign. Teachers may sometimes assign a series of tasks. For example, Mark will have six tasks to complete before he can play, and he has a poster with an index card in a pocket to represent each task. At the beginning of each task, he removes a card and starts to work. When all six tasks are complete and all pockets are empty, he can play with a leisure material of his choice. This work system can be constructed on a poster that creates a study carrel at the student's desk, or students may use a clipboard or small flip chart instead. The challenge in using workstations is to select work that students can do independently and that is meaningful. Critics of the TEACCH model question the value of workstations because they may not provide opportunities for students to learn new skills or even to perform functional activities (Smith, 1996). Students need the opportunity to receive direct, systematic teacher instruction to acquire new skills and should not spend their entire day in workstations. Workstations are designed to practice (maintain) previously acquired skills and help students participate in inclusive settings such as general education classrooms and jobs in which all-day one-to-one instruction may not be available or desirable. To the greatest extent possible the tasks chosen should be appropriate to the general education context (e.g., academic tasks) or should provide opportunities to practice life skills using real materials (e.g., community-validated job tasks; age-appropriate hobby materials).

Small-Group Instruction

To maximize instructional time, teachers need effective strategies for small-group instruction rather than relying on one-to-one instruction for students with severe disabilities. Students may be able to benefit from group instruction if they receive help in focusing their attention (Wolery, Cybriwsky, Gast, & Boyle-Gast, 1991; Wolery, Ault, & Doyle, 1992). For example, Schoen and Ogden (1995) had all students in a small group write a sight word before one student read it. Teachers may also focus students' attention by using a verbal prompt (e.g., "Everyone look") or by having students make a motor movement (e.g., "Raise your hand when you hear the word . . . "). Students may also need to be offered alternative ways to respond. For example, a nonverbal student might hold up a card or picture to answer a question. Some students may need ongoing individualized prompting to maintain attention in the group lesson. A paraprofessional, peer, or job coach might sit beside the student, helping him or her keep pace in the book or other materials as the teacher lectures.

Community-Based Instruction

With the appropriate support, all students, no matter what their types or levels of disability may be, can participate actively in their communities. The purpose of teaching community and leisure skills is not to get students "ready" to be part of their communities but instead to help them benefit from these experiences more fully. An important way that schools can prepare students for both current and future community and leisure opportunities is to get them directly involved in these activities through community-based instruction. Community-based instruction involves teaching students systematically and directly in community contexts. This instruction prepares students to generalize skills to environments beyond the school, to different peers, and to diverse materials (see Chapter 14 for more information on community job skills and community-based instruction).

One-to-One and Specialized Settings

Traditionally, in planning for students with severe disabilities, educators have considered special settings (e.g., self-contained class) and one-to-one instruction. One reason is that students learn rapidly with intensive, systematic instruction. In contrast, the benefits of systematic instruction are not limited to one-to-one and separate settings. As shown in Figure 4.4, systematic instruction can be used in all types of instructional arrangements. Although it is easiest to implement one-to-one instruction in a special setting, it also can be used in groups and in inclusive contexts in school and the community. Sometimes the systematic instruction is used to help the student benefit from these other instructional arrangements. For example, the student may be taught how to self-direct his or her learning with pictures. Although students may learn quickly with one-to-one instruction, this should be reserved for skills that students do not or cannot learn in other contexts. To try to teach all students all IEP objectives on a one-to-one basis limits the number of skills students can practice in a day and creates large amounts of "dead time" while students await their turns.

CASE STUDY

Jeremiah Baker is a special education teacher who coteaches in a fifth-grade general education classroom. Mr. Baker has two students with severe disabilities fully included in this classroom. The general education teacher, Mia Chu, is about to start a unit on poetry with her fifth-grade class. Before the unit starts, Mr. Baker and Ms. Chu sit together to make plans for how to include the students with disabilities in the unit. For each lesson plan that Ms. Chu has planned, Mr. Baker suggests changes to make so that his students can participate as much as possible in the unit. They consider the three components of UDL: representation, engagement, and expression. Ms. Chu likes these changes and plans for materials to help these two students to participate. Mr. Baker identifies specific skills that need to be taught within the unit for the students with disabilities. After identifying these skills, Mr. Baker writes an SIP for each skill and creates a data sheet to measure progress on each skill. The SIP identifies who is responsible for teaching each skill (e.g., a peer will point to text while a poem is read out loud). Ms. Chu provides Mr. Baker with a calendar with a plan of the unit activities and the time slots during which each lesson will be taught. During the times that Ms. Chu's students are participating in independent practice activities, Mr. Baker schedules in time to work on skills that require massed-trial instruction in a one-to-one format (e.g., time delay to teach vocabulary). Ms. Chu also decides to use some peer-partner activities to create some natural opportunities for support by a peer (e.g., reading a haiku out loud to a peer). When Ms. Chu's class is completing the unit test on poetry, Mr. Baker will give the students with disabilities an adapted form of the test, which will take about 10 minutes, and then use the remaining time and the following lunch period to work on specific community-based skills (e.g., shopping, reading safety signs).

SUMMARY

Similar to the application of alternate assessment for students with severe disabilities, evidence-based practices are another outgrowth of NCLB (2002). The quest for instructional evidence-based strategies also has been fueled by the legal mandate that students with disabilities must be included in statewide testing, the thrust for inclusion, and recent evidence showing that students with disabilities could be successful in a variety of areas, including academics (Cook et al., 2009; Odom et al., 2005). In general, these practices have been derived by the scientific community through a process of compilation and analysis, with several published studies across investigative teams from different geographic locations and many participants, and then made available to practitioners to implement in classrooms and other service settings. For students with severe disabilities, systematic instruction has been found effective in training both functional and academic skills (reading, mathematics, and science). The components of this systematic instruction include: (1) instruction of socially meaningful skills, (2) defining target skills that are observable and measurable, (3) using data to demonstrate that skills were acquired as a result of the intervention, (4) using behavioral principles to promote transfer of stimulus control, including differential reinforcement, systematic prompting and fading, and error correction, and (5) producing behavior change that can be generalized to other contexts, skills, people, and/or materials. These instructional practices should be implemented with the population of students for which they were prescribed in the manner in which they were intended to be used, and they can be adapted or modified when necessary for individual learners and content with the use of professional judgment.

APPLICATIONS

1. Find a partner and role-play (student and teacher) how to teach five sight words using time delay. (Have the first teacher use constant time delay and the second teacher use progressive time delay.)

2. Find a partner and role-play (student and teacher) how to teach a student to use a vending machine using the system of least prompts. To start, you and your partner will have to decide on the steps of the task analysis for using a vending machine and the hierarchy of prompts to be used for each step.

3. Think of a student who communicates at the concrete symbolic level. Create a systematic instruction plan for each of the following objectives for this student: Curtis will correctly read eight community/survival words in six out of eight trials; Curtis will independently complete nine of nine steps of an algebra equation.

4. Create a daily schedule that shows how a special education teacher who supports two students with severe disabilities in a fully inclusive fourth-grade classroom will spend his or her time across a typical day. The general education teacher has the following schedule:

Specials (Art/PE/Music): 8:00–9:00

Science: 9:00–10:00

Literacy: 10:00–11:00

Lunch: 11:00–12:00

English/Language Arts: 12:00–1:00

Break: 1:00–1:30

Math: 1:30–2:30

PART TWO

ADAPTING GENERAL EDUCATION CONTENT

CHAPTER 5

Literacy

DIANE M. BROWDER, FRED SPOONER, AND LYNN AHLGRIM-DELZELL

Tina is a second grader diagnosed with Rett disorder who has numerous seizures throughout the day that affect her ability to attend to and participate in instruction. She looks at those who speak to her and can smile and make vocalizations. She does not track objects but does turn toward sounds. Tina uses a wheelchair for mobility, has limited range of motion, and is encouraged to reach toward objects. She does not appear to have any intentional communication skills.

Elijah is an eighth grader in a self-contained classroom in a public school. He appears to recognize some objects as representative of activities, such as a spoon to introduce lunchtime. Although he is nonverbal, he expresses his wants and needs by smiling, vocalizing, and reaching toward things he wants or to gain attention. He expresses displeasure by pushing objects off the wheelchair tray, crying, or grimacing.

Summer is a fourth grader with Down syndrome. Summer can speak in complete sentences with some errors in articulation and grammar. Summer has a sight word vocabulary of about 100 words. She has been participating in a remedial reading program and is learning to clap out syllables of words and to locate words that rhyme. She enjoys listening to books read to her and "pretends" to read during free time at school.

Brody is a 10th grader with autism who uses a voice output device (VOD) to communicate without assistance navigating through the many levels of picture symbols paired with word and phrase lists that help him participate in academic activities. His receptive listening skills are typical of fourth graders. His reading skills are unknown.

WHAT IS LITERACY?

Broadly defined, literacy is the ability to read, write, and communicate (Armbruster, Lehr, & Osborn, 2003). Historically, literacy has been conceptualized as the ability to read and interact with books and other textual materials by reading words on a page and turning pages to continue through the document. More recently, educators and reading experts have had to rethink how these reading activities can include individuals with various disabilities who may be unable to access traditional reading materials or demonstrate reading or communication skills verbally. This chapter first presents what we know about typical reading skills and reading development, then provides suggestions and modifications to meet the needs of individuals with significant cognitive disabilities.

Skills needed to learn to read are called "emergent literacy skills." Emergent literacy skills include understanding the conventions, the purpose, and the functions of print and phonological awareness (Gunn, Simmons, & Kame'enui, 1995). Conventions of print refers to the visual structure of print, such as orientation (front vs. back of a book, reading text left to right and top to bottom, and turning pages). Purpose of print means that words convey meaning and that messages can serve multiple purposes. It also includes the understanding of basic terms associated with literacy, such as *reading, writing, drawing, page*, and *story*. Functions of print refers to the fact that print has a variety of uses in such materials as newspapers, telephone books, and signs. Phonological awareness is the ability to manipulate the sounds of language. Phonological awareness is discussed in detail later in this chapter. Whitehurst and Lonigan (1998) also include awareness of oral language and language development as emergent literacy skills. Gunn et al. (1995) agree that there is a relationship between oral and written language in that development of print skills will most likely also improve oral language skills.

Chall first developed a linear sequence of literacy skills in 1983 and refined them in a series of publications in 1995 and 1996 (Chall, 1996; Indrisano & Chall, 1995). In his sequence, these emergent literacy skills typically develop prior to entering school during the prereading stage. Figure 5.1 summarizes these stages. At the end of the prereading stage children read signs that frequently occur in their environment, read and write letters

Prereading—Reads signs, writes name and letters of the alphabet, pretends to read books, retells story previously read to them.

Stage 1: Learning to read—Learns relationship between letters and sounds and printed/spoken word; able to read simple text containing high-frequency words, sight words, phonically regular words; understands about 6,000 words but can read only about 300–500.

Stage 2: Learning to read—Reads simple familiar stories with increasing fluency; uses basic decoding skills and context cues; sight vocabulary of about 3,000 words; listening still better than reading; one-third of material understood by listening can be read.

Stage 3: Reading to learn—Reading used to learn new ideas, gain new knowledge; learning to use comprehension and study strategies; reading comprehension and listening comprehension equalized.

Stages 4 and 5: Reading to learn—Reading increasingly more abstract ideas and complex vocabulary; knowledge is reconstructed from reading new information.

FIGURE 5.1. Chall's (Chall, 1996; Indrisano & Chall, 1995) stages of reading development.

of the alphabet and their names, and pretend to read books. The early elementary school years are spent learning to read. These skills are refined and expanded during the later elementary school years through middle school. Beginning in high school and continuing into adulthood, reading skills are used to learn new information and develop ideas.

Students with significant cognitive disabilities will most likely not enter school demonstrating emergent literacy skills, nor will they likely learn to read at the same rate as their typically developing peers. They will need systematic instructional intervention and accommodation or modifications to develop these skills. The understanding of the stages of typical literacy development can assist educators in structuring their teaching in an attempt to reach the common goal of reading to learn.

Reading is a complicated process. Learning to read begins with the ability to acquire phonological skills. *Phonological skills* is a broad term used to describe the skills necessary to learn the sound structure of language. These skills include phonemic awareness, rhyming, syllabication, and onsets and rimes (Armbruster et al., 2003). Phonemic awareness appears to be the most important of these skills. The National Reading Panel (NRP, 2000) reviewed existing research on teaching reading and identified five core skills that students need in order to learn to read. These skills are phonemic awareness, vocabulary, comprehension, phonics, and fluency. Phonemic awareness is the identification and manipulation of sounds in words. Vocabulary is the words that we must know to communicate effectively and includes oral and reading vocabulary. Comprehension is an understanding of what is read. Phonics is knowledge of the relationship between individual sounds in words, called "phonemes," and the letters that represent these sounds. Knowledge of this relationship allows individuals to be able to decode unknown words. Fluency is automatic word recognition that allows individuals to read text accurately yet quickly. According to Chall's stages of literacy development, these skills are learned in stages 1 and 2 and expanded and refined in the later stages.

The *Standards for the English Language Arts* (National Council of Teachers of English and International Reading Association, 1996) also provide some guidance on literacy instruction. Twelve guiding standards "define what students should know and be able to do in the English language arts." Figure 5.2 summarizes these 12 standards. The standards were written broadly in order to provide a variety of access points for diverse learners. Students with significant cognitive disabilities are able to participate in activities that address these standards with accommodations and/or modifications that they need in order to access literature and demonstrate their knowledge.

An additional source of guidance for literacy instruction is provided by state departments of education. It is imperative that teachers know the curriculum standards set by their respective states. States offer guidance in a variety of forms to help teachers of students with significant cognitive disabilities use these curriculum standards. Chapter 2 provides a discussion of how to understand state standards and how to extend them to meet the needs of students with significant cognitive disabilities.

THE SCIENCE OF READING

Current research centers around three reading-development theories. The first, the phonological loop model (PLM; Baddeley, 2000; Baddeley & Hitch, 1974) of reading, is based in memory theory. Briefly, PLM states that our working memory is composed of four

1. Read a wide range of print and nonprint texts in order to meet the demands of society and for personal interest.

2. Read a wide range of literature in order to understand human experience.

3. Use strategies to comprehend and evaluate texts.

4. Use strategies to communicate effectively with different audiences and purposes.

5. Use strategies to write for different audiences and purposes.

6. Apply knowledge of language and media to create and discuss print and nonprint texts.

7. Conduct research by gathering and synthesizing data from different sources and communicate this information for different audiences and purposes.

8. Use different technological and informational resources to gather and synthesize information.

9. Respect diverse language use and dialects of different cultures, ethnic groups, geographic regions, and social roles.

10. English-as-a-second-language users develop competency in English in order to understand content across the academic curriculum.

11. Become a member of a variety of literacy communities.

12. Use language for learning and personal enjoyment.

FIGURE 5.2. Standards for the English Language Arts. Adapted from National Council of Teachers of English and International Reading Association (1996). Copyright 1996 by the International Reading Association and the National Council of Teachers of English. Adapted by permission.

systems. The *central executive system* supervises the performance of three subsystems: (1) visuospatial sketchpad, (2) phonological loop, and (3) episodic buffer. The *visuospatial sketchpad* stores visual information. The *phonological loop* has two subcomponents: The phonological store keeps and analyzes spoken sounds in short-term memory, and, an articulatory rehearsal component stores spoken sounds in long-term memory. The *episodic buffer* links the verbal and visual information together. As a memory theory, the PLM's premise is that reading ability or disability lies in the storage and retrieval of information stored in short- and long-term memory. The second theory, the psycholinguistic grain-size theory (Ziegler & Goswami, 2005) of reading, states that reading progresses from understanding large phonological units (words) to small phonological units (phonemes). In this theory students learn individual phonemes, phoneme combinations, and their letter combinations through repeated exposure to written vocabulary (orthography) and to the sounds associated with the written words. This theory suggests that phonological skills require direct instruction in grapheme–phoneme correspondences. Third, the lexical restructuring model (LRM; Metsala & Walley, 1998) poses that words that sound alike (similar rime patterns) are stored together in a lexical neighborhood. As vocabulary increases, these neighborhoods become more populated. Over time the words stored in these neighborhoods are increasingly segmented into smaller units in order to distinguish similar-sounding words more efficiently, and the neighborhoods are restructured. According to this theory, when a word is needed, the entire neighborhood of words is activated. Word retrieval is more accurate in smaller, more segmented neighborhoods than in larger neighborhoods. See Baddeley and Jarrold (2007), Troia (2006), and Ziegler and Goswami (2005) for more comprehensive summaries and research support for the three theories.

Although research support exists for all three of these models, very little of this research includes students with significant developmental disabilities. Some of Baddeley's work has been used to understand the reading difficulties of students with Down syndrome and indicates a possible disconnect between verbal input and the visuospatial sketchpad (Baddeley & Jarrold, 2007). So what should teachers do without a theory, and research supporting the theory, to guide their practice? It is important to begin by reviewing what we do know about teaching literacy to students with significant cognitive disabilities.

An extensive literature review of research on reading instruction for students with significant cognitive disabilities (Browder, Wakeman, et al., 2006) found that a majority of reading instruction for this population consisted of teaching vocabulary as sight words or picture identification. Very little research explored the other four NRP components of reading. Out of 128 studies on literacy in this population, only 13 studies (10%) covered phonics instruction, 5 studies (4%) covered phonemic awareness, 31 studies (24%) covered comprehension, and 36 (28%) covered fluency. In addition to informing the field about the relative vacuum of knowledge about what to teach, this review of literacy research also provided information on the effectiveness of the instructional methods used in these studies. Massed trials with systematic prompting were found to be effective practices for teaching vocabulary and comprehension. Using pictures and words in functional, meaningful ways was an effective strategy for teaching comprehension. Time delay, a specific type of systematic instruction, was found to be effective in increasing fluency. Unfortunately, not enough studies investigated effective techniques for phonemic awareness or phonics to delineate effective practices. Research is emerging in these areas indicating that students with significant cognitive disabilities can learn phonemic awareness and phonics skills (e.g., Basil & Reyes, 2003; Browder, Ahlgrim-Delzell, Courtade, Gibbs, & Flowers, 2008; Calhoon, 2001; Flores, Shippen, Alberto, & Crowe, 2004; Morgan, Moni, & Jobling, 2006).

THE CONCEPTUAL MODEL OF LITERACY

The lack of research on teaching literacy and reading skills to students with significant cognitive disabilities illustrates the lack of interest in teaching such students to actively participate in literacy activities. Several years ago, during an investigation into teachers' literacy practices, researchers asked teachers to demonstrate their literacy lessons (Browder, Ahlgrim-Delzell, Courtade-Little, & Flowers, 2006). Generally, two activities were demonstrated by all the teachers. Some teachers read books to students but did not expect students to engage with the book material, only to listen. Other teachers led researchers to "circle time" as their literacy lesson. Students were expected to learn some functional sight words, such as weather and calendar words. No teachers were teaching skills such as those identified by NRP (2000) that students would need to learn to read. Studies have documented that individuals with significant disabilities participate in more limited literacy experiences at home and at school than do their typically developing peers (Kliewer, Biklen, & Kasa-Hendrickson, 2006; Light & Smith, 1993). There are a number of possible explanations for individuals with disabilities being denied these opportunities. First, the focus for such students may be diverted to health or functional needs. Parents and teachers may spend more time addressing medical issues such as tube feeding or range of motion, than on literacy instruction. Second, parents and educators may believe that instructional time should be spent on functional skills needed to be productive in a working, independent society. A third possible reason for the reduced literacy experiences of students with significant disabilities may be lack of access to needed resources (Skotko, Koppenhaver, & Erickson, 2004). These students may need AAC devices or other adaptation to texts in order to develop literacy. The lack of access may be related to financial inability to purchase needed equipment or a lack of knowledge about how to adapt existing resources to individual needs. Some other reasons for the limited literacy experiences of students with significant cognitive disabilities are more sinister. The belief that these students are too disabled to benefit from literacy experiences results in decreased expectations that they can learn to read (Locke, 2000). Kliewer et al. (2006) provide compelling evidence of a cultural denial of the competence of individuals with cognitive disabilities. These authors suggest that society denies individuals with cognitive disabilities access to literacy through human devaluation and censure of evidence to the contrary. Regardless of the reasons used to exclude students with disabilities from literate activities, literacy is a functional skill that can be used to lead a more independent life.

It is likely that the path to literacy for students with significant cognitive disabilities will be different from that of their nondisabled peers. Browder, Ahlgrim-Delzell, et al. (2008) provide compelling arguments about why and how this path may differ. One obvious reason that this path will be altered is that many students with cognitive disabilities have communication and/or physical disabilities. Although verbal skills are not necessary in order to learn to read, traditional methods of teaching reading skills require students to respond verbally in order to demonstrate learning. Physical disabilities may limit a student's ability to hold and open a book or turn the pages. Because of these limitations, students with cognitive disabilities may require a nontraditional approach to teaching reading. More subtle reasons that this path will be altered involve the values we have about educating students with significant cognitive disabilities who learn at a slower pace. Skills that lead to greater independence and increased quality of life are highly valued. Therefore, the specific skills we might teach and the age at which they may be taught will alter the outcomes of literacy instruction for this population.

Browder, Ahlgrim-Delzell, et al. (2008) suggest that there should be two targeted outcomes for literacy instruction for this population. The first outcome is *enhanced quality of life through shared literature*. The focus of this outcome is the ability to glean information from text read aloud. Through read-alouds, information can be relayed to students who may not ever be able to read the text independently. The text may be either functional or for entertainment, but it should come from literature appropriate to the student's chronological age. These texts would need to be adapted to the student's level of understanding while retaining the main ideas of the author. The second targeted outcome of literacy for this population is *increased independence as readers*. Due to the lack of reading instruction for students with significant cognitive disabilities, we know little about what this instruction might consist of or how long it might take for them to learn to read. We should begin this journey with the assumption that the student will learn to read at least somewhat through being taught the same NRP (2000) skills identified for students without disabilities. This instruction would most likely need to be combined with systematic teaching strategies prevalent in the field of special education, such as time delay, stimulus prompting, and error correction. How long should we continue to try to teach a student with a significant cognitive disability to read? That question can be answered only by considering the specific student, the progress being made, and the age at which the reading instruction began. Typically, though, these authors suggest that although emphasis on gleaning information from text read aloud continues throughout the life cycle, it may increase in importance in later years if the student has not learned to read independently.

ACCESS TO LITERATURE

In order to meet the goal of enhanced quality of life through shared literature, students will need physical and cognitive access to books. Physical access means that students need to be able to physically handle the books being read. First, place books in an accessible space in the classroom and provide time in the daily schedule to look at them. Provide texts with a variety of different genres and themes appropriate for the chronological age of the students. As students may have had limited access to such books previously, allowing them to peruse different types of books provides them with an opportunity to learn what kinds of books they enjoy most. Some examples of different genres of literature are shown in Figure 5.3.

There are several ways to find out what books may be included in a classroom library. Consult with general education teachers, parents, and other students of the same chronological age to determine what specific books students enjoy reading. Find out which books are included in language arts instruction in the general education classroom. Search the Internet for book lists. Of key importance is to make sure that the selections are age- and grade-appropriate. Figure 5.4 lists some Internet sites that can help in locating age- and grade-appropriate books.

In addition to providing books, physical access might mean adapting the books so students can handle them. Some texts, particularly paperbacks at the upper grade levels, may be too fragile for students to open or turn pages. Even more durable books may be inaccessible to students with significant physical disabilities. An excellent resource for ideas on adapting books is *www.boston.k12.ma.us/teach/technology/emmanuel.asp*. Some adaptations for books at the preschool or early elementary school level are very simple, such as taking a book apart, laminating the pages, then rebinding it. Alternately, book pages can be placed in page protectors and a three-ring binder. Another adaptation may be to use self-laminating sheets and place them over the pages while keeping the book intact. Other adaptations, such as adhering cotton balls or popsicle sticks to pages, may be necessary to allow the student to turn the pages.

Drama	Romance
Folk/fairy tales	Mythology
Historical fiction	Autobiography
Horror	Poetry
Literary fiction	Romance
Mystery	Short stories
Science fiction	Westerns
Biography	Content-area texts

FIGURE 5.3. Examples of different literature genres.

www.barnstable.k12.ma.us/curriculum/summerreading-elem.htm
Provides a summer reading list for students in second through fourth grades.

www.emints.org/ethemes/resources/S00001316.shtml
Provides reading recommendations for students in first through fifth grades.

childrensbooks.about.com/od/agegradebooksby/Books_by_Age_Grade.htm
A directory of children's literature categorized by age and grade, preschool to high school.

www.phschool.com/curriculum_support/reading_list/middle_school.html
Provides reading recommendations for students in sixth through eighth grades.

highschoolreadinglist.com
Provides classical and contemporary reading recommendations for high school students.

FIGURE 5.4. Examples of Internet websites to locate age- and grade-appropriate book titles.

Cognitive access refers to providing access to the content of the book. Decreasing the amount of text and simplifying vocabulary can allow students with significant cognitive disabilities to grasp the main themes of a book. Preschool- and early elementary school-level books most likely need only a little adapting in this respect. Many preschool and some early elementary books already contain repeated lines that present the major theme of the book. If a repeated thematic sentence is not already present, a teacher can create one and place it in the book by writing it in or typing it on a label to adhere to pages throughout the book. Preschool and early elementary books typically also have colored pictures to represent text within the book. Objects representing the text and pictures can be used for students who do not yet use a picture communication system. By later elementary school and into middle and high school, though, pictures and repeated story lines are rarely present. Books become longer, and the content of the text at these levels also becomes more abstract, so more cognitive adaptations will be necessary for these than for preschool- and elementary-level books. Be prepared to read and rewrite books to reduce the length and vocabulary. For chapter books, a repeated story line should be created for the theme of each chapter. Pictures and objects can still be used to augment text.

Computer and digital technology can also be a valuable resource in adapting books. Students with visual and hearing impairments may particularly benefit from some type of technical adaptations. Books and pictures can be scanned onto computers for enlarging, animating, or adding sound. Software programs can be used to create and store a library of books for individual students, such as My Own Bookshelf (Soft-Touch, 2004) or Bailey's Book House (Riverdeep, n.d.). Many children's book developers offer interactive books, such as LeapFrog School (*www.leapfrogschoolhouse.com/do/findpage?pageKey=library*), Start-to-Finish books by Don Johnston (*www.donjohnston.com/products/start_to_finish/index.html*), and Capstone Press (*www.capstonepress.com/interactive/*). Augmentative communication tools such as BIGmack (AbleNet; *www.ablenetinc.com/Home/Products/Communication/tabid/56/Default.aspx*) and GoTalk (Attainment, Inc.; *www.attainmentcompany.com/xcart/home.php?cat=253*) and picture symbol software such as Boardmaker/Mayer-Johnson, Inc.; *www.mayer-johnson.com/MainBoardmaker.aspx?MainCategoryID=5419*) and Writing with Symbols 2000

(Widgit Software; *www.widgit.com/products/wws2000/index.htm*) can also be useful. The picture symbol software can be used to embed pictures into the text of the adapted books. The picture symbols can then be placed on the augmentative devices for student responding to comprehension questions. The Baltimore City School System has an excellent source of adapted elementary schoolbooks, available at *www.baltimorecity-schools.org/boardmaker/adapted_library.asp*, that requires Boardmaker. The University of North Carolina at Charlotte has a selection of middle school and high school literature and poetry, available at *education.uncc.edu/access/parenttips.htm*, that requires Writing with Symbols. Figure 5.5 illustrates some examples of how to adapt books.

Whenever one is adapting the content of a book, copyright laws must be followed. A teacher may adapt a book as described in this chapter for use in the classroom as long as each copy of the book to be adapted is purchased. For example, if a teacher is adapting only one text to read to the class, then only one copy of the book needs to be purchased. If an adapted book will be distributed to each student in the class, then the teacher must purchase each copy that will be adapted and distributed. Older books may be out of copyright, and these can be adapted without the need to purchase copies. Consult a librarian for help in understanding copyright issues for specific books.

STORY-BASED LESSONS

Story-based lessons (SBL; Browder, Gibbs, Ahlgrim-Delzell, Courtade, & Lee, 2007; Browder, Trela, & Jimenez, 2007) is a structured process to teach literature content to students. The premise behind this method of teaching literature is derived from shared story activities (also known as read-aloud events) whereby the teacher reads a story to a group of students and leads a discussion of themes, vocabulary, and events of the story. Teacher read-aloud events are considered effective teaching practices in general education across all grade levels (Dreher, 2003; Fisher, Flood, Lapp, & Frey, 2006; Richardson, 2000). In shared story activities, teachers can provide students with models of reading strategies and distinguish between various uses of language and point out how written language differs from spoken language (Hedrick & Pearish, 2003), in addition to introducing new vocabulary words and ideas. Read-aloud events also increase student motivation to read independently (Sulzby & Teale, 2003).

SBL tailors these read-aloud events to the needs of students with significant cognitive disabilities. In line with the conceptual model of reading, the structure of SBL differs based on the age of the students. Figure 5.6 provides a template of SBL at the elementary level. While reading the book, the teacher presents the student with activities related to the book, individualizing the responses to the need of the individual student. Using the template, it is possible to accommodate the communication needs of all the students in the same lesson by pairing picture symbols with words and objects as necessary. Tina is a student who is not yet communicating with intentionality. Using a system described by Browder, Mims, Spooner, Ahlgrim-Delzell, and Lee (2008), incorporating IEP team members and the principles of UDL, the IEP team decided to pair objects with sound to attract Tina's attention. A head switch was added to her wheelchair to help her say "I pick this one." Gazing at an object for more than 3 seconds was paired with activation of the head switch to indicate her answer. When Tina looked at the object for 3 seconds,

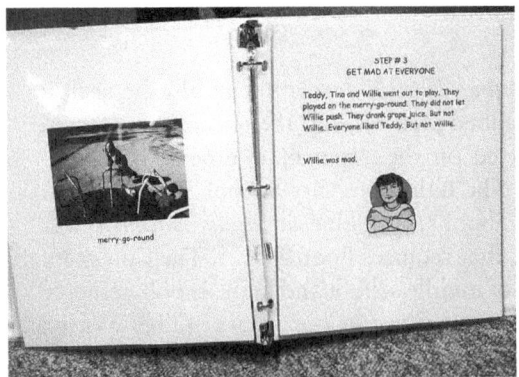

Photo by Lynn Ahlgrim-Delzell. Used with permission.

Chapter book edited for length, repeated line and clip art added, placed in page protectors and three-ring notebook.

Photo by Lynn Ahlgrim-Delzell. Used with permission.

Book unbound, laminated, and rebound, puff paint for title and author, and objects to illustrate theme of the book.

Photo by Lynn Ahlgrim-Delzell. Used with permission.

Picture symbols added for vocabulary in book.

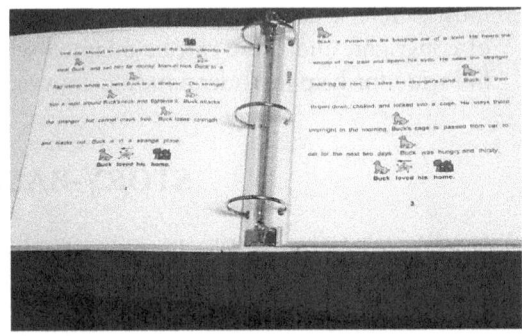

Photo by Lynn Ahlgrim-Delzell. Used with permission.

Call of the Wild rewritten with Writing with Symbols 2000, with added repeated story line for the chapter.

Photo by Lynn Ahlgrim-Delzell. Used with permission.

Original book with repeated line added and comprehension question page inserted and adhered to page with Velcro.

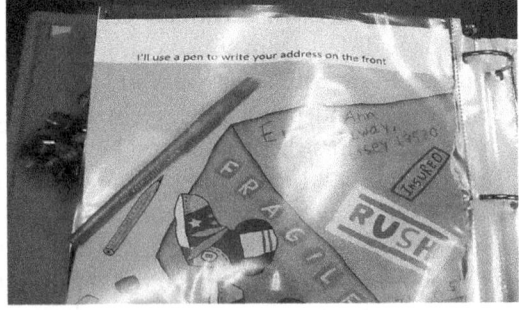

Photo by Pamela J. Mims. Used with permission.

Book unbound placed in page protectors with objects to illustrate text inserted.

FIGURE 5.5. Examples of adapted books.

Step	Description	Application to Tina and Summer (book: *Charlotte's Web* (White, 1952)
Anticipatory set	Pictures or objects related to book theme or characters, other connection to previously known information. Allow each student to interact with materials.	*Tina*—Provide objects to represent Wilbur and Charlotte and identify them as the main characters of the book. Present them with sound to make sure she looks at them. *Summer*—Present pictures of the two main characters paired with a short phrase about them that includes their written names, such as "Wilbur is a pig."
Title of the book	Read and show the title by pointing, highlighting, color coding. Have students repeat.	*Tina*—Provide a stimulus cue to help Tina distinguish the title from the author. Help her to touch the title and move her finger under the title as you say it. *Summer*—Ask her to say and point to the title after modeling it.
Author of the book	Read and show the author's name by pointing, highlighting, color coding. Have students repeat. Tell students the author is the person who wrote the book.	*Tina*—Same as above, but provide a different cue to distinguish the title from the author. *Summer*—Same as above. Ask her "What does the author do?"
Ask prediction question	Have students look at the front cover of the book, scan some pictures within the book. Ask students what they think the book is about. Provide two to four options for them to select from.	*Tina*—Make sure to place the book within her field of vision and draw her attention to it by tapping on it. Present one of the character objects and an object unrelated to the book. Ask "What do you think this book will be about?" *Summer*—Same as above, but use pictures and short phrases as choices.
Open the book	Model opening the book. Have one student open the book to get the story started.	*Tina*—With her limited mobility, the book will need to adapted by adding handles to the cover and pages. The book is presented at midline. Ask, "How do we get our story started?" *Summer*—Same as above, but book adaptations would not be necessary.
Text pointing	Students take turns throughout the book at pointing to the words as you read them. Start by sweeping from left to right, and build to word-by-word pointing.	*Tina*—Provide an enlarged repeated line so Tina can move her eyes along the line from left to right as the teacher reads and points to the words. *Summer*—Use sentences as they appear in the book to point to text. Increase to multiple lines of text.
Identify key vocabulary	Preselect up to five key vocabulary words/pictures/objects. Identify them as they are read. Have students find key vocabulary.	*Tina*—Pair words and pictures in the book with the objects. Upon reading the word, point to the picture and ask Tina to look at the corresponding object. *Summer*—After reading the word in a sentence from the book, have Summer point to the word. Present the word and ask her to read it. Present a sentence with a missing word. Ask Summer to fill in the missing word with one of the vocabulary words.

(cont.)

FIGURE 5.6. Elementary story-based lesson template and description.

Step	Description	Application to Tina and Summer (book: *Charlotte's Web* (White, 1952)
Read repeated story line	Upon reading the repeated story line throughout the book, have students read the line (if verbal), place the line on VOD, or point to a picture/word to finish the line.	*Tina*—A VOD with the line recorded on it is placed on Tina's lap tray. Whenever the line is read, the teacher guides her finger to it, saying "Your turn to say it." After repeated trials the teacher says "You read it alone next time." When the line appears next the teacher waits for Tina to respond. *Summer*—After reading the line several times, the teacher asks Summer to read the line aloud. The teacher may also ask Summer to point to the line on the page.
Turn page of the book	Each student should have the opportunity to turn the page of the book. Pose the question, "What do we need to do to keep the story going?" instead of directly telling the student to turn the page.	*Tina*—The teacher asks "What do we need to do to keep the story going?" The book is presented at midline so Tina can reach the handle. *Summer*—Same as above, but without handles.
Answer comprehension questions, review prediction.	Either during the reading or after the book is read, ask students questions regarding the book. Pose a variety of questions—some literal, such as naming characters, and some not literal, such as how the characters felt or what might happen next. Review the predictions of what the book was about and correct if necessary.	*Tina*—The teacher reminds Tina of what she had predicted the book would be about and says "Were you right? Was the book about a _____?" The same two objects are presented. *Summer*—Same as above using words or phrases.

FIGURE 5.6. *(cont.)*

the teacher guided Tina's head to hit the switch. The teacher reviewed Tina's answer with her by tapping on the object selected as an answer, saying, "You picked this one" (see Figure 5.6).

A template for SBL for middle and secondary students is provided by Browder, Gibbs, et al. (2007). Even though phonemic awareness and phonics learning typically occur at the elementary ages, they are not included in the elementary SBL. These activities occur separately, using a curriculum designed for teaching these skills. For students in middle and secondary schools, phonemic awareness and phonics will most likely not occur in separate instruction. Therefore, they are included in the template for SBL.

Teachers should select vocabulary with specific sounds to emphasize during reading of the book. Students who are verbal can repeat the sounds; others may need a VOD. Students can find words with similar sounds (rhymes), break words into syllables, and so forth—such activities are described in the next section. The phonemic awareness and phonics activities should relate to the vocabulary words from the book being read. The other steps remain the same as in the elementary-level SBL template.

Fisher et al. (2006) conducted a research study on teacher read-aloud events and found seven core components. The first component is the careful selection of texts. Select high-quality books based on the interests of the students. Locate award-winning books such as Newbery and Caldecott Medal books (a list can be found at *www.ala.org/ala/mgrps/*

divs/alsc/awardsgrants/bookmedia/newberymedal/newberywinners/medalwinners. cfm) and (*www.ala.org/ala/mgrps/divs/alsc/awardsgrants/bookmedia/caldecottmedal/ caldecotthonors/caldecottmedal.cfm*) or recipients of other book awards, such as the National Book Award (*www.nationalbook.org/nba.html*). An exhaustive list of different book awards and links to the award-winning books can be found at (*www.nationalbook. org/nba.html*). Second, it is important to practice, practice, and practice. Select vocabulary words and comprehension questions with the answer selections ahead of time. You can plan for the students' differing levels of communication by having pictures, words, sounds, and/or objects available as necessary. Plan and organize so all students are provided opportunities to participate by having VODs or other adaptations ready for independent use. Third, have a clear purpose for the SBL. A book will need to be read multiple times because each reading or each chapter may have a different purpose. The purpose of initial readings may be to increase vocabulary and literal comprehension. Later readings may work with sounds within vocabulary words or concentrate on more in-depth exploration of the book, such as characterization or a time line of main events. The fourth core component is the modeling of fluent reading. Through practice reading of the text, the book is read fluidly without errors. The fifth component is to read with appropriate expression to illustrate the text being read. This may also include facial expressions, inflections, loudness, and other expressions needed to capture the mood of the story. Book discussion is the sixth component of skilled read-aloud activities. Discussions can occur before, during, and after reading the book and at different levels of understanding, from literal questioning to evaluation. Bloom's revised taxonomy (Anderson & Krathwohl, 2001) can assist in generating questions and activities at all levels of knowledge. The seventh and final component of skilled read-aloud activities is independent reading and writing. For students with significant cognitive disabilities, independent reading may mean listening to books on tape or using a computer program, as described earlier in this chapter. It may mean creating independent access to books so students can "pretend" to read. Writing may involve the creation of name stamps, plastic letters, or jigs for letter formation. Writing may also include filling in a blank in a sentence given choices of pictures or objects, words or phrases.

FINDING THE BALANCE

- Create a book club or a lending library with other teachers to share book adaptations.
- While the teacher is presenting a small-group lesson for phonemic awareness or phonics, an assistant, speech–language therapist, or parent volunteer can be conducting an SBL for another small group.
- Use the SBL template to teach content area material, such as science or social studies. Locate a book on the content area (weather, hibernation, etc.) and follow the steps.

LEARNING TO READ

Recall that learning to read requires development of five components, as identified by the NRP (2000): phonemic awareness, phonics, vocabulary, comprehension, and fluency. SBLs provide instruction for vocabulary and comprehension within the context of reading a book. For older students, phonemic awareness and phonic activities are also embedded in SBL. For younger students just learning to read, we advocate a separate instructional time for phonemic awareness activities.

Many different activities can help develop phonemic awareness. Figure 5.7 lists activities described by Armbruster et al. (2003).

It is recommended that only a couple of these activities to teach phonemic awareness be selected, not all of them. Typically, students demonstrate these skills through verbal articulation of the sounds. The key for students with significant cognitive disabilities is to select the activities in which they can participate with the most independence. Some of these activities are more accessible to students who are nonverbal; other skills are more accessible to students with physical limitations. For example, Tina, Elijah, and Brody will need to use letter representations of the sounds to demonstrate their understanding. Tina may need enlarged letters placed near the face of the teacher, as she looks at faces. Elijah may need a three-dimensional letter placed within his range of motion on the wheelchair tray. Brody will need letters and their sounds programmed into his VOD. Summer will most likely not need letters to demonstrate her knowledge of letter sounds but may need to practice her articulation skills in producing the sounds accurately.

In order to conduct these activities, a teacher will need to be able to correctly pronounce each of the phonemes. The English language contains about 40 different phonemes, depending on the dialect in different parts of the country. These phonemes and examples of the sounds they make are listed in Figure 5.8. Sounds are categorized into *stop* and *continuous* sounds. Stop sounds are those that stop when you make them, such as the /t/ sound in *cat*. Continuous sounds are those that can be held and pronounced

Phoneme isolation—recognition of individual sounds in words.
Activity: What is the first sound in *map*? Response: /m/. What is the last sound in *cat*? Response: /t/.

Phoneme identity—recognition of the same sound in words.
Activity: What sound is the same in *can, cat*? Response: /k/.

Phoneme categorization—recognition of a word with a different sound.
Activity: What word begins with a different sound? *Man, cat, can*? Response: *man*.

Phoneme blending—combining individual phonemes together to form a word.
Activity: What word do these sounds make: /k/ /a/ /n/ [brief pause between sounds]? Response: *can*.

Phoneme segmentation—breaking a word apart into individual phonemes.
Activity: Say the sounds in *can*. Response: /k/ /a/ /n/.

Phoneme deletion—recognition of a new word when a phoneme is deleted from another word.
Activity: What is the word *lace* without the /l/? Response: *ace*.

Phoneme addition—recognition of a new word when a phoneme is added.
Activity: What is the word if we add a /p/ to the beginning of the word *lace*? Response: *place*.

Phoneme substitution—recognition of a new word by substituting one phoneme for another.
Activity: Change the /l/ to /p/ in the word *lace*. What word is it? Response: *pace*.

FIGURE 5.7. Phonemic awareness activities.

Continuous sounds

Vowels	Consonants	Letter Combinations
ape, cape	lamb, sample	they, brother
cat, apple	sit, cite	shin, plush
see, each	ran, tar	bring, ringer
head, bet	feel, loft	bird, other
if, win	have, vote	
hike, life	note, in	
rug, up	well, blow	
unit, use	yet, young	
tote, coat	zoo, prose	
food, tool	lift, kill	
pot, lock	lox, onyx	
ply, my		

Stop sounds

Consonants	Letter Combinations
tap, pin	when, where
do, lad	quip, quick
bit, tag	reach, chip
hug, hip	how, endow
can, skip, pick	tag, gem
lab, bug	gin, juggle

FIGURE 5.8. Phonetic alphabet sounds. Based on the International Phonetic Chart for English (n.d.) and Reading Mastery (2003) in Engelmann and Bruner (1995).

for a longer period of time (as long as your breath holds out!), such as the /m/ sound in *man*.

In phonics instruction students use phonemic awareness skills to pair sounds with letters. Using these skills to decode unfamiliar words is called phonics. Research has demonstrated that "systematic and explicit phonics instruction is more effective than non-systematic or no phonics instruction" (Armbruster et al., 2003, p. 13). "Systematic" implies that there is a coherent sequence of instruction. Many programs teach specific letter–sound correspondences in a specific sequence. "Explicit" instruction means that teachers are provided with specific directions for delivering the instruction. There are a number of different types of systematic and explicit phonics instruction. Figure 5.9 distinguishes between common forms of systematic and nonsystematic approaches to phonics instruction.

RESOURCES FOR LITERACY

The Early Literacy Skills Builder (ELSB; Browder, Gibbs, et al., 2007) is a systematic and explicit, research-based program specifically designed for students with significant cognitive disabilities. It combines basic literacy skills, phonemic awareness activities, and SBL to teach skills that lead into a phonics-based program. All responses are designed

Systematic approaches	Nonsystematic approaches
Synthetic phonics—letter sounds are learned in isolation, then blended to form words.	Whole-word programs—focus on word meaning and recognition while reading, may embed letter–sound knowledge into reading material.
Analytic phonics—letter–sound relationships are explored in known words.	Sight-word programs—teach recognition of individual words, may teach letter–sound knowledge as sight vocabulary increases.
Analogy phonics—teaches word families (words of same structure).	

FIGURE 5.9. Systematic and nonsystematic approaches to phonics instruction.

to accommodate nonverbal students. Lessons are divided into seven levels each, with five lessons that can be repeated. Skills are both sequential and spiraled such that earlier skills are reviewed at the higher levels. A level-based assessment provides teachers with a system to measure student progress.

The foundation level (Allor, Mathes, Roberts, Jones, & Champlin, 2010) of Early Interventions in Reading (Mathes & Torgesen, 2005) is a systematic and explicit program that includes 60 lessons utilizing the principles of direct instruction. It is designed as a bridge to Early Interventions in Reading. This program also concentrates on basic literacy and phonemic awareness activities. The program includes storybooks and lesson mastery tracking forms.

Meville to Weville (Erickson, 2004) is an early literacy and communication program that concentrates on vocabulary development and writing specifically designed for students with significant cognitive disabilities. Seventy-five lessons presented in three units use thematic-based activities to support development of self and belonging to a community, with unit titles such as "Who I Am," "Being a Student," and "What We Do." Data collection charts illustrate student learning.

APPLICATIONS

1. Do an Internet search for adapted books and information on how to adapt books. Share what you find with your colleagues.

2. Create an SBL plan by selecting a book using the principles described in this chapter. Provide for the participation of students with varying levels of support needs (physical, verbal, behavioral, etc.).

3. Practice the letter sounds.

4. Select two phonemic awareness activities and plan an activity. Make response cards for students to use.

CHAPTER 6

Comprehension across the Curriculum

DIANE M. BROWDER, FRED SPOONER, AND CANDICE MEYER

Randy opened the fifth-grade social studies book and began to read aloud fluently. Because Randy had advanced decoding skills, educators sometimes thought he could keep pace with the general class instruction with minimal support. What was not always obvious was that Randy, a student with an autism spectrum disorder, did not comprehend the passages he read so fluently. In fact, if given a short paragraph from a first-grade reader, he would not be able to answer the most basic recall questions. Comprehension is critical to success in the general curriculum. This chapter provides information about building comprehension not only for students such as Randy but also for those with few or no decoding skills.

Reading requires both decoding written text and comprehending its meaning. In today's world of technology, students who lack decoding skills may compensate with assistive technology. Students may also rely on the support of a peer or teacher who reads the passage aloud, as described in Chapter 5. What is more difficult to augment are skill deficits in comprehension. Students need to understand the meaning of a passage to gain information from it.

Comprehension can be a challenge for all students, but especially for students with disabilities (Bursuck & Damer, 2007; Gersten, Fuchs, Williams, & Baker, 2001). Surprisingly, this challenge has not been addressed well in research. In their comprehensive review of reading, Browder, Wakeman, et al. (2006) found that only a small portion of studies taught or measured comprehension. Many studies included demonstrations of students recognizing sight words without determining whether students could comprehend these words. Although students with ASD often have difficulties with reading comprehension, a surprisingly small number of studies have considered this problem (Chiang & Lin, 2007).

When comprehension has been addressed in research with students with developmental disabilities, the focus has often been severely restricted. For example, the National Reading Panel recommended (1) comprehension monitoring, (2) cooperative learning, (3) graphic and semantic organizers, (4) question answering, (5) question generating, and (6) summarizing (National Reading Panel, 2000). In contrast, Browder, Wakeman, et al. (2006) found that most comprehension interventions targeted for students with severe disabilities concerned answering questions. Because of these limitations, there is not a clear evidence-based practice for teaching comprehension to students with moderate and severe disabilities. This chapter presents information gleaned from the general reading literature and from our own experiences in applying these methods with students with autism and intellectual disability. The first part of the chapter discusses what comprehension is. The second provides specific teaching strategies.

COMPONENTS OF COMPREHENSION

Literature is composed of narrative and expository texts. Narrative text is a composition that tells a story. Examples of narrative text include novels, short stories, and biographies. The primary purpose of a narrative text is to entertain the reader. Narrative text comprises the elements of characters, setting, problem or conflict, plot (including climax), ending or resolution, main idea, theme, and author's point of view. These story elements are shown in Table 6.1. It is the first literature a novice reader learns to read and comprehend. Telling stories is a natural human experience; therefore, narrative text is a logical choice to use to introduce the process of reading. Within the general education curriculum, students learn to discern increasingly complex story elements. Young children may simply sequence the events of a story, whereas a more sophisticated reader can determine themes and the author's point of view or create alternate endings for a plot. The reader interacts with the story elements to store, match, and retrieve information that is later manipulated to solve problems (Schank, 1990).

The purposes of expository text are to inform and persuade the reader. Expository texts include the subject, or content areas, of social studies, science, mathematics, and elective subjects. Even though the formats of expository texts may differ from narrative texts, they contain many of the same elements. For example, a reader can analyze

TABLE 6.1. Story Elements

Story elements	Description
Characters	Who is in the story—main and supporting
Setting	Where and when the story takes place
Problem or conflict	The goal of the main character
Plot	Sequence of events
Ending or resolution	Goal was achieved or not achieved
Main idea	Gist of the story
Theme	Encompassing concept
Author's point of view	Perspective of the writer—to inform, persuade, or entertain

a news story using plot and author's point of view. Historical accounts may have major characters and themes. One goal for comprehension instruction is for students to learn to transfer skills acquired in reading narrative text to comprehending the elements in expository text.

BLOOM'S TAXONOMY OF KNOWLEDGE

Comprehension involves the acquisition of different forms of knowledge. Although there are many frameworks for organizing knowledge, one of the most useful to understanding reading comprehension is Bloom's taxonomy of knowledge (Bloom, Englehart, Furst, Hill, & Krathwohl, 1956). There are six basic levels of depth of knowledge according to this taxonomy (see Figure 6.1). The first level, *knowledge*, includes primarily recognizing and recalling facts. In reading comprehension, this might involve simply repeating information from a story line ("The bear found the honey. Who found the honey?"). The second level, *comprehension*, includes translating, interpreting, summarizing, and extrapolating information. The teacher might ask, "Who was hungry for honey?" The third level, *application*, involves using information in a situation that is different from the original context. The teacher might ask, "Where do we get honey?" The fourth level, *analysis*, is the breakdown of a communication into its constituent elements. It includes segmenting information into component parts to develop motives and inferences and to find evidence to support generalizations. The teacher ask query, "What could make the bear angry?" The fifth level, *synthesis*, requires putting together elements to form a whole. After the story, the teacher may have the class describe the characteristics of the bear based on actions and descriptions that occurred in the story. Finally, *evaluation* is judging the value of material and methods for given purposes. The judgments are based on some standards. The teacher might ask, "Could this story be true? Is there anything not real in the story?"

Bloom's cognitive objectives are universal and apply to all populations, whether a student with disabilities participating in a read-aloud or a person reading this textbook. Each learner will derive from the experience some depth of knowledge. All of the levels of Bloom's taxonomy are not introduced at every age. Some of the higher order thinking strategies are introduced when students are older to align with their developmental stage. For instance, the strategy of determining whether a story is real or not real is used cautiously on the first-grade level because young children have not fully developed the ability to discern between reality and fantasy (e.g., young children may believe in the tooth fairy). Differentiation of instruction across the continuum of abilities in general education

Evaluation: Judge according to some standards.

Synthesis: Combine parts into a whole.

Analysis: Break down into parts.

Application: Use materials in a new way or slant.

Comprehension: Translate, interpret, and extrapolate.

Knowledge: Recall, recognize, draw out facts.

FIGURE 6.1. Bloom's taxonomy of knowledge.

is provided by increasing the difficulty of the text, of questions within a cognitive objective or strategy, of vocabulary used, and of question format and response mode.

CHECK FOR UNDERSTANDING

Take a few minutes to check your own comprehension of Bloom's taxonomy by trying to develop a comprehension question for each level: knowledge, comprehension, application, analysis, synthesis, evaluation. Use a familiar fairytale as the text.

Research on Depth of Knowledge

The expectations for knowledge in Bloom's taxonomy may seem ambitious expectations for students with severe disabilities. Some of the research conducted on general curriculum access suggests that teachers may need help to address more complex levels of depth of knowledge. Karvonen et al. (2007) found that teachers tended to rely on the first level of Bloom's or even to use what they called an "awareness" level in which the only expectation was for students to attend to material presented in the general curriculum. Using only the first level of Bloom's taxonomy or, worse, teaching students only to show some attention to the activity (awareness), sets too low an expectation for students with severe disabilities. Flowers et al. (2006) found that states' alternate assessments addressed multiple levels of depth of knowledge even when it was lower overall than grade-level achievement. To meet the expectations of grade-level content learning, even when the depth of knowledge is reduced overall, requires that students have some skills in all levels of Bloom's taxonomy. That is, students need to be able not only to recall simple facts but also to apply, synthesize, and evaluate content.

One way to promote students' learning within a range of depth of knowledge is to gauge comprehension questions based on their entry skills. We provide examples of comprehension questions for each level of Bloom's taxonomy for students who may be at three levels of comprehension in Table 6.2. Each of Bloom's levels is described in more detail in the following subsections.

Knowledge

At the simplest level of comprehension, answers are *literal* and can be taken directly from the text. The teacher may ask the student to identify the title, author, illustrator, characters, and setting. At a beginning level, the student may recall the main character immediately after a passage is read ("Goldilocks sat on the bed. Who sat on the bed?"). As students advance, they can identify the main character at the end of the story ("Who went into the bears' house?") and may also identify supporting characters. Students can also develop comprehension at this literal level by identifying actions ("What did Wilbur do?") and descriptors ("What color was the barn?").

Comprehension

The second category, comprehension, includes the general strategies of sequencing, clarifying, identifying the problem/conflict, and identifying the ending/conclusion. Questions

TABLE 6.2. Comprehension Questions Based on Bloom's Taxonomy of Knowledge

Level	Easy	Medium	Most difficult
Knowledge: Answers can be "pulled from the page" (literal) • Title • Author • Characters • Setting • Action • Descriptors	• Point to title, author. • Point to picture of . . . • Immediate recall: "Jill went up the hill. Who went up the hill?" *or* • "The boy sat in the wagon. What did the boy do?"	• "Who is the story about?" • "What did they put in the soup?" • "Where did they find the puppy?" • "What did Wilbur do?"	• "Who else is in the story?" (supporting characters) • "What was the barn like?" (descriptors such as color, size)
Comprehension: Answers can be inferred from what is on page • Prediction • Sequencing • Identify conflict/problem • Identify ending	• "What happened last?" • "What is this story going to be about?" • "I see a cave. I feel fur . . . What is in the cave?" (from *Let's Go on a Bear Hunt*)	• "Put these events in order as first, second, last." • "Why was the girl afraid?" (conflict) • "What do you think will happen next?" • "Why did the man get arrested?" (from a news story)	• "Put these pictures in order to show what happened in the story." (more than three pictures) • "What problem did Carlos face as a young child?" (from a biography) • "How did the story end?"
Application: Requires using student's own background knowledge • Make connections • Use material in a new way	• "The bear is eating. Are you eating?" • "Sara is a girl. Are you a girl?" • "Point to a picture on the page of something that we have in our classroom."	• "Buck loved his home. How do you feel about your home?" • "The children had a scavenger hunt. What did you find on our scavenger hunt?" • "Draw a picture of this story."	• "This article is about whales. Where do whales live? What else do you know about whales?" • "Let's act out what the three pigs did."
Analysis: Breaking the information into parts • Classify • Compare • Contrast • Categorize	• "Let's put these pictures into two columns—for what Sara did in the story and what you do." • "Put these pictures into categories for the people and the actions."	• "Let's make a picture diagram for what we know about each person in our story. Who went hunting?" • "Compare what is the same and different about these two animals."	• "When the girls laughed at Renee, how did the girls feel? How did Renee feel?" • "This article is about the past. What was different in their day? How did the children get to school? How do you get to school? Now you tell me something else that was different."
Synthesis: Combining the parts into a whole • Infer • Determine main idea • Find cause and effect	• "Show me the picture of what this story was about." • "Why were the bears mad?" • "Retell the story in your own words."	• "What might be another title for this story?" • "What effect did the hurricane have?" • "How does this poem make you feel?"	• "What will happen to people if they have no jobs?" (from a news story) • "What are three things you learned from this article?"
Evaluation: Making a judgment according to some standard • Real/not real • Nonfiction/fiction • Fact/opinion • Author's point of view	• "Do pigs talk?" • "What did you think about this story?" (states an opinion) • "Which of these is a story/not a story?"	• "Did this really happen or is it fiction?" • "What is a fact in this article?" • "What is the author's opinion about this movie?" (from a review)	• "Why did the author write this?" (to persuade, entertain) • "Let's list the facts versus opinions in this article."

at this level are *textually implicit* rather than textually explicit (Vaughn & Bos, 2009). That is, the answers can be found in the text without background knowledge being needed, but they must be inferred; they cannot simply be pulled from the page. Some examples of comprehension exercises include having the student put three story facts in order (first, next, last), asking the student to predict what comes next in a story, or identifying the problem ("How did Buck get hurt?").

Application

The third category, application, requires the reader to make connections between the text and his or her background knowledge. The teacher might ask the students to recall an event in their own lives similar to those in the story (e.g., "Did you ever sleep in someone else's bed? Tell me about it."). The application may be as simple as an immediate action (e.g., "The boy is running. Are you running?"). At a more complex level, the connection will be between the text and circumstances that are beyond the student's personal experience but still in background knowledge (e.g., "This story is about a whale. Where do whales live?"). Sometimes teachers will have to develop this background knowledge— for example, by using units of instruction with related activities (e.g., viewing videos of whales; doing an art project on whales).

Analysis

The fourth category, analysis, includes classifying, categorizing, comparing, and contrasting. At the simplest level, these comparisons may be textually implicit. For example, the student may be asked to create a chart showing the actions of each character. At the most advanced level, analysis questions will require inferences using background knowledge. For example, the student may be asked to categorize sad versus happy events, which requires some understanding of these emotions. Again, the teacher may provide this background information concurrently by making connections to events in the students' lives that evoke these emotions.

Synthesis

The fifth category, synthesis, includes inferring, determining the main idea, and finding cause and effect. At this level, students will need skills in summarizing and in developing concepts such as "main idea." At the simplest level, the teacher may ask, "What is this story about?" At a more complex level, the teacher may ask the student inferential questions such as "Why did Cinderella like going to the ball?"

Evaluation

The sixth and final category, evaluation, includes evaluating real and not real, nonfiction and fiction, fact and opinion, and author's point of view. At the simplest level, students may be asked questions such as "Can pigs talk?" Once again, this requires some background knowledge of the characteristics of animals that the teacher may need to develop during the instructional unit.

Writing Objectives for Comprehension

Teachers can write objectives for comprehension write vocabulary words used for each of Bloom's cognitive objectives, shown in Figure 6.2. For example, "Given a passage from an adapted text, Johnna will *describe* the main character."

TEACHING COMPREHENSION

Selection and Preparation of the Text

A large discrepancy may exist between the chronological ages of students with severe developmental disabilities and their reading levels. Some older students may be nonreaders. In contrast, it is important for all students to have access to the literature of their peer group, that is, age- and grade-appropriate stories. Chapter 5 provided information on how to adapt text to make it more accessible for use in read-alouds or by early readers. For example, a novel may need to be rewritten as text summary with embedded pictures and repeated story lines stating the main ideas. Similarly, a chapter in a science or other textbook may need to be summarized and illustrated.

Whereas adapted text is the original text written on a lower grade level, controlled text is text composed of high-frequency and decodable words that are sequentially introduced. Controlled text is predominately used by novice readers as their primary text. An example of a controlled text is the SRA Decoding Strategies B1 student book from the Corrective Reading program (Engelmann et al., 1999). The controlled text vocabulary progresses in difficulty until it is on the level of the adapted text. The ultimate goal is to move the novice readers from reading the controlled text to reading the adapted text. In creating adapted books, teachers may want to use some controlled text to which the student can apply newly emerging decoding skills. For example, in an adaptation of *Charlotte's Web* (White, 1952), the following controlled text line might be used as a picture caption: "The rat was bad." The teacher might read the original text and then have students read the caption aloud. See Figure 6.3 for examples of the original, adapted and controlled texts from *Charlotte's Web*.

The student will . . .

Knowledge	Comprehension	Application	Analysis	Synthesis	Evaluation
define	describe	articulate	calculate	adapt	appraise
describe	discuss	assess	classify	assemble	assess
identify	estimate	compute	compare	collaborate	critique
list	explain	construct	contrast	compose	defend
name	generalize	determine	correlate	create	interpret
recall	locate	develop	diagram	design	judge
record	paraphrase	employ	differentiate	formulate	justify
relate	recognize	relate	discriminate	integrate	rate
state	restate	solve	infer	model	reframe
select	summarize	translate	outline	rearrange	support

FIGURE 6.2. Vocabulary for writing comprehension questions.

Charlotte's Web, Chapter 2

Original Text

Fern loved Wilbur more than anything. She loved to stroke him, to feed him, to put him to bed. Wilbur was what farmers call a spring pig, which simply means that he was born in springtime. When he was five weeks old, Dad said he was now big enough to sell, and would have to be sold. Next day Wilbur was taken from his home under the apple tree and went to live in a manure pile in the cellar of Farmer Zukerman's barn.

Adapted Text

Fern   said, "Let me keep the little   pig.   I can feed him. I

will name him Wilbur." Dad put down the ax.

Dad let   Fern   keep the   pig.

Fern   had the pig.

Fern   was happy.

Controlled Text

Fern   had the pig.

Fern   was happy.

FIGURE 6.3. Examples of original, adapted, and controlled text from *Charlotte's Web*.

A third option is to select books that are universally designed and that have scaffolded support. Researchers at the Center for Applied Special Technology (CAST, 1998–1999) suggested that a UDL curriculum should provide three essential qualities: (1) multiple representations of content, (2) multiple options for expression and control, and (3) multiple options for engagement and motivation. First, regarding representations of content, students with disabilities differ in their approaches to academic content. For example, students with learning or intellectual disability may require content to be delivered through auditory means as opposed to printed text. Representing content through a variety of media allows students to choose the one most appropriate for them and their learning needs. Second, students are often expected to demonstrate their knowledge and often do so through written expression; however, students with motor disabilities or those with cognitive disabilities may experience great difficulty with this task. Expression takes many forms and all of these forms are sufficient to indicate progress while expressing students' ideas and knowledge. This expression could take the form of acting, filmmaking, graphic representations (e.g., painting, photography, drawing), or music (National Center on Universal Design for Learning, 2010). Third, student engagement in learning has long been an indicator of motivation in the classroom. By using multiple representation and presentation modes, particularly those that involve digital representation and that are graphically based and incorporate video, audio, and other multimedia components, student engagement and thus motivation can be enhanced. Current technologies allow that level of individualization and thus provide greater flexibility in ways in which the student can engage in learning (CAST, 1998–1999). Some software is now available that allows teachers to create online texts with built-in scaffolded support. For example, CAST's UDL Book Builder (CAST, 2009) provides a framework in which users can adapt existing texts or create their own. The framework offers the ability to provide as much or as little support as the students need (see Figure 6.4).

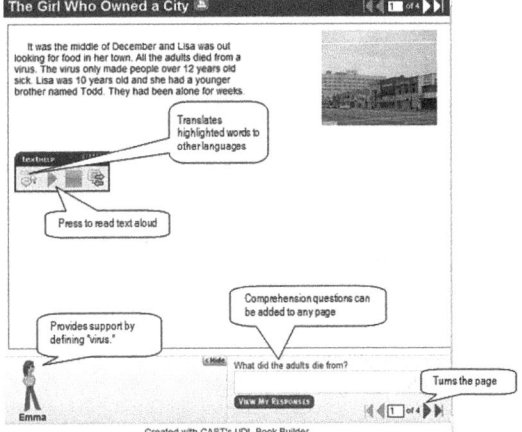

FIGURE 6.4. Example of supports offered through CAST UDL Book Builder. Copyright 2010 by CAST. Reprinted by permission.

Readability Formulas

In creating and adapting text, the teacher may consider readability level. Readability formulas estimate the difficulty of comprehending text based on a syntactic component and a semantic component. Commercial readability formula software programs can calculate the reading grade level of text, as well as provide databases of the readability of published trade books. In simplistic terms, the complexity, or difficulty, of a text is determined by the number of letters or syllables in the words, the placement of the words, and the length of the sentences (Stenner, 1996).

It is important to realize that readability formulas do not reflect all the variables that affect comprehension—such as the maturity level or life experience needed to understand the topic; the nuances, humor, and connotations of the author's voice; and the organization of the text. The selfless love of King Arthur, who allowed Sir Lancelot and Queen Guinevere to escape even though they had betrayed him, would be too mature a theme for elementary students to fully understand. In *A Modest Proposal* by Jonathan Swift (1729), the political satire directed against the apathy of Great Britain toward the Irish famine would not be grasped by a young reader or a reader who was not knowledgeable about that specific time in history. In his satire, Swift proffered eating the Irish babies as a solution to the potato famine. Regardless of their shortcomings, readability formulas provide a baseline for determining the difficulty level of text. One way to gauge the readability of text is through the application of lexiles. Figure 6.5 illustrates how lexiles are applied.

Lexile	Grade	Sentence
BR	Beginning reading	The farmer was happy.
50L	Beginning 1	The farmer was very happy.
120L	Beginning 1	The old farmer was very happy.
190L	Beginning 1	The old farmer was delighted.
250L	Beginning 1	The old farmer was very delighted.
310L	Middle 1	The farmer was happy because he won.
410L	End 1/beginning 2	The old farmer was happy because he won.
460L	Middle 2	The old farmer was delighted because he won.
840L	MIddle 5	The old farmer was delighted because his thoroughbred horse won the race.
1130L	10	The old farmer was delighted because his thoroughbred horse won the Kentucky Derby race this year.
1300L	12	Naturally, the old farmer was delighted because his thoroughbred horse, Supersonic, won the Kentucky Derby race this year.

FIGURE 6.5. Example of the lexile framework for reading. To adapt grade-appropriate literature, the teacher can use a lower lexile level. For example, the 12th-grade passage could be rewritten as "The old farmer was happy. His thoroughbred horse was named Supersonic. Supersonic won the race. His horse Supersonic won the Kentucky Derby."

Development of Background Knowledge and Other Prereading Activities

Students with severe developmental disabilities often lack the background knowledge needed to understand the themes and concepts presented in grade- and age-appropriate literature. There are several ways teachers can promote this knowledge concurrently with teaching comprehension. In presenting the story or expository text, the teacher can use a variety of activities to enrich the students' understanding of the story. For example, when teaching the novel *Island of the Blue Dolphins* (O'Dell, 1987) to a class of urban students, the teacher may need to show movie clips of island adventures and dolphins. The class might visit an aquarium and create a small model of an island using sand and water. Similarly, with expository text, the teacher may need to provide background experiences. When studying an election, the students may need to experience casting a vote and its consequences (e.g., who to elect as line leader). When learning about layers of the earth, students may need to create a model using rocks, sand, dirt, and other material. In general, as the teacher provides hands-on, multisensory experiences, students gain more understanding of the concept to be presented.

The teacher also can teach key vocabulary and concepts. The words *island* and *dolphin* can be taught using the sight-word strategies described in Chapter 5. The teacher may deepen this understanding by using a variety of pictures for each word (e.g., different pictures of dolphins) and developing an ongoing chart of "facts we learned about dolphins."

Another strategy is to use before-and-after reading strategies. Prior to reading, it is helpful to have students make predictions about the text. This may be as simple as using a picture or object to guess what the story or article will be about. It is important to review the question and make revisions in the answers so students begin to learn how to make a reasonable prediction. Before reading a new story or other text, it can also be helpful to conduct a "book walk." The student turns the pages of the text, viewing pictures and communicating about what is seen. The teacher may have the student point to pictures, guess what the character is doing, or otherwise engage with the material. This activity can be combined with asking the student to specify the purpose for reading or for making a prediction.

Using Questions to Promote Comprehension

Generating and answering questions are integral components in comprehending narrative and expository texts. An effective teacher will encourage students to develop their own questions as they read texts and attempt to answer them as they predict or encounter relevant information. Furthermore, the application and effectiveness of questioning techniques are positively correlated with the comprehension abilities of the readers. According to several meta-analyses and reviews of studies, readers who comprehend well initiate and answer questions about text better than readers who do not comprehend well (Rosenshine, Meister, & Chapman, 1996). Based on the National Reading Panel (2000) analysis of 203 studies, instruction on question generation and question answering were two of the seven effective methods to improve comprehension.

Teaching Whether Questions Are Literal or Inferential

Earlier in this chapter, strategies were provided for developing comprehension questions that promote increasing depths of knowledge based on Bloom's taxonomy. As noted in Table 6.2, questions can be literal, meaning that the information is "pulled from the page." They may be "textually inferential" in that the answer is not right on the page but can be inferred from the story alone. Inferential questions require the student to use background knowledge not contained in the text. Sometimes students may benefit from instruction in the different types of comprehension questions. Question–Answer Relationships (QAR) is a framework that guides students in finding answers relating to texts in various subjects by focusing on where the information can be found. Research in the 1980s demonstrated that QAR improved the comprehension of all students and narrowed the gap for minority students (Raphael & McKinney, 1983; Raphael & Pearson, 1985). Even though the QAR framework is not new, it continues to be widely recommended by reading experts (Mesmer & Hutchins, 2002; Roe, Smith, & Burns, 2005).

In QAR, answers are categorized as either literal answers, which are located *in the book*, or inferential answers, which are found *in my head*. "In-the-book" answers are either "right there" or "think and search."

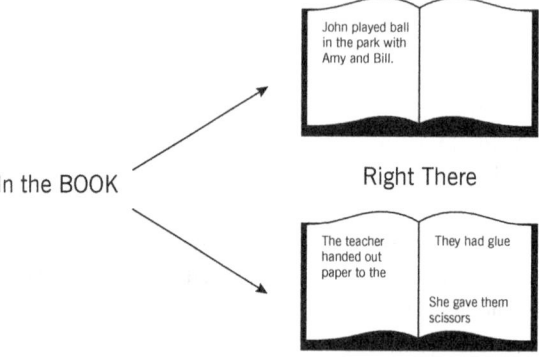

A "right-there" answer is one that is given verbatim in the text. In fact, key words within the question may be written in the same sentence as the answer in the text. For example, if the question is "Where did the kite land?" the key words are *kite* and *land*. These key words are written in the sentence that answers the question: "The kite landed in a tree." On the other hand, a "think-and-search" answer requires the reader to link sentences or words within sentences to determine the answer. "The kite sailed through the sky. Suddenly, it dove toward the earth. It came to rest on a branch." In this "think-and-search" answer, the reader is required to link the three sentences together to derive the answer.

The two subcategories for "in my head" are "author and me" and "on my own."

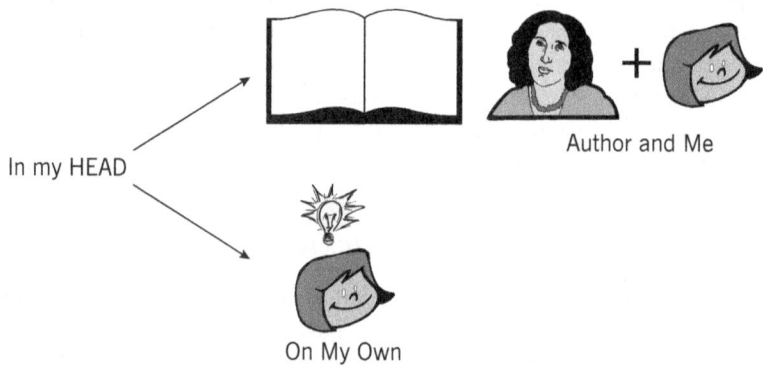

In an "author-and-me" answer, metaphors may be used. "The kite flew above the tree-tops. The trees were jealous that they could not fly and snatched it from the sky." In an "author-and-me" answer, the reader has to understand that the trees snatching the kite is a personification of the kite getting caught in the trees. "Author and me" has three types of connections: text to self, text to world, and text to theme. In this example, the text used a text-to-theme connection by incorporating a personification of trees as antagonists. In the "on-my-own" approach, the reader attempts to answer the question by reflecting on a personal experience of flying a kite. In the reader's personal experience, the kite became caught in a tree. Therefore, the personal experience assisted the reader in selecting the correct answer.

Selecting a Question Format

Questions may be set up in one of three formats: multiple choice, short answer, and free response. A multiple-choice question requires the reader to recognize the correct answer among an array of choices. This receptive format option often works well for students with developmental disabilities because it is amenable to AAC devices. For example, when asking, "Who was the main character?" the teacher can provide four word/picture options. The student points, gazes, or uses a switch to select the correct response. Figure 6.6 provides examples of receptive format comprehension questions. Whenever possible, the teacher should also use questions that require the student to compose the answer (expressive format). A short-answer question requires the reader to recall information, which is a more difficult cognitive retrieval task than a multiple-choice answer. However, a reader is able to use the semantic cues of the words surrounding the blank to aid in recalling the answer. Finally, the third type of question is a free-response question, in which the reader supplies the whole answer. It is the most difficult type of response because the reader's answer is entirely dependent on his or her ability to recall information. There is no probability of guessing the answer among choices or gleaning semantic cues from surrounding text.

FINDING THE BALANCE

Students often can show what they know more easily with a receptive question format (multiple choice). In contrast, a receptive format may also limit the amount of learning that can be demonstrated. Teachers may assume that students know only the answers presented. Whenever feasible, teachers should use some open-ended questions. Students who use AAC will then need enough variety in their response options to compose an answer.

Hamaker (1986) notes that questions can be used in four ways: (1) massed prequestions, in which all adjunct questions occur at the beginning of the text; (2) inserted prequestions, in which the adjunct questions are inserted into the text at a number of points, always preceding the text passage containing the information needed to answer them; (3) inserted postquestions, in which the adjunct questions are inserted into the text at a number of points, always following the text passage containing the information needed to answer them; (4) massed postquestions, in which all adjunct questions are placed together at the end of the text. For students with severe disabilities, the beginning

| Controlled Text |
| How did Fern feel? |
| Fern was _____. |
| sad   Dad   happy   was |

| Adapted Text |
| Who can Fern feed? |
| Fern can feed _____. |
| pig   sad   ran   Dad |

| Inferential |
| Why did Dad put down the ax? |
| Dad did not want to kill the pig.   The ax was too big. |

FIGURE 6.6. Examples of comprehension questions.

point may be to use inserted postquestions immediately after the text. This strategy is used in the Early Literacy Skills Builder (Browder, Gibbs, et al., 2007). For example, "Moe jumped over the table. Who jumped over the table?"

Prompting Students to Answer the Questions Correctly

Besides posing thoughtful questions, teachers also need strategies to help students derive the answer. One option is to use a system of least intrusive prompting (see Chapter 4 for more information on prompting). In least-to-most prompting, the teacher uses prompts on a continuum from the least intrusive to the most intrusive. Often in research using least intrusive prompts, the teacher tells the student what to do (verbal prompt), models the response, and then guides the student's hand to make the response. In contrast, for reading comprehension, the teacher should begin with the cues that are embedded in the text. For example, in a study by Mims, Browder, and Spooner (2009), the teacher used the following sequence:

Least-to-most prompting for a literal recall

- The teacher places four picture responses in front of the student and asks the comprehension question. The teacher then waits for student to find the correct comprehension response.
- If no response, the teacher rereads the text that contains the answer and waits again for the student to respond.
- If no response, the teacher rereads the text, models pointing to the answer, and waits again for the student to respond.
- If no response, the teacher physically guides the student to touch the correct picture.

When the answer is not right on the page, a different strategy, such as sustained questioning, may be needed. The following illustrates how the teacher used sustained questioning to prompt student responding.

Sustained questioning for comprehension (textually implicit)

- Question: "Why did the pioneer use trees to build a cabin?" The teacher waits for the student to answer.
- If no response, the teacher says, "I'm going to read sentences about the key words *trees* and *cabin*." The teacher reads two sentences: "The pioneer cleared a piece of land in the woods. He cut down trees and made a cabin with the logs."
- The teacher makes the first inquiry: "Where was the pioneer going to build his house?" The pioneer was going to build his house in the woods.
- The teacher makes the second inquiry: "Where are there lots of trees?" There are lots of trees in the woods.
- The teacher reasks the original question: "Why did the pioneer use trees to build a cabin?" The pioneer had lots of trees to build his house.

An important way the teacher can help students master comprehension is to reread the same story or other text daily for a week or so and ask the same comprehension questions. Over time, the student learns the answers to the questions but also may learn the strategy for finding the answer. The teacher should use the first day's reading of a passage to see whether the student has generalized these strategies to finding answers in a passage with a similar level of complexity. Otherwise, the student may simply be learning to memorize the answers based on teacher prompting without necessarily understanding the text.

Another way to help students answer questions correctly is to use a *scaffolded reading experience* (SRE). SRE is a framework for teaching that supports students' comprehension of all texts at their present ability and promotes their learning independence (Graves & Graves, 2003). In SRE, the teacher plans prereading, during-reading, and postreading activities to enable the students to effectively interact with the text. Although SRE is one specific model, scaffolding in general involves giving the reader additional information so that he or she can derive the answer. The teacher may offer some background information, help with the meaning of a word, or offer additional hints. Sometimes students with severe disabilities may become confused with this method and need a more systematic approach such as least-to-most prompting. In contrast, if students seem to be trying to derive the answer, some hints or additional information may be all the support that is needed.

Using Story Maps and Other Strategies to Teach Story Elements

All stories have basic story elements, including characters, setting, a problem or conflict, a plot (including climax), on ending or resolution, a main idea, and a theme. An important way that students gain skill in comprehension is by identifying these story elements. There are numerous strategies for teaching students story elements. One is story mapping. One form of story mapping, called semantic mapping, uses diagrams with geometric shapes and lines to show relationships between things and concepts in both narrative and expository text (Pearson & Johnson, 1978). Teachers can provide the templates, or the students can be taught to make them. The teacher assists the students in completing the templates, or the students, after repeated instruction and practice, complete them on their own.

Figure 6.7 shows a semantic map of "Little Red Riding Hood" story elements. In the narrative classic children's story, Red Riding Hood is the main character, or the protagonist, and the setting is a woods. Her mother asks Red Riding Hood to bring a basket of cookies to her sick grandmother, who lives on the other side of the woods, and warns her not to talk to strangers. The goal or problem in the story is to deliver the cookies, and the plot is the sequence of events that occur before she achieves the goal. As Red Riding Hood walks through the woods to her grandmother's house, she encounters a wolf. Little Red Riding Hood is the main character, or protagonist, and the wolf is the main character's adversary, or antagonist. The wolf asks her where she is going, and she gives her destina-

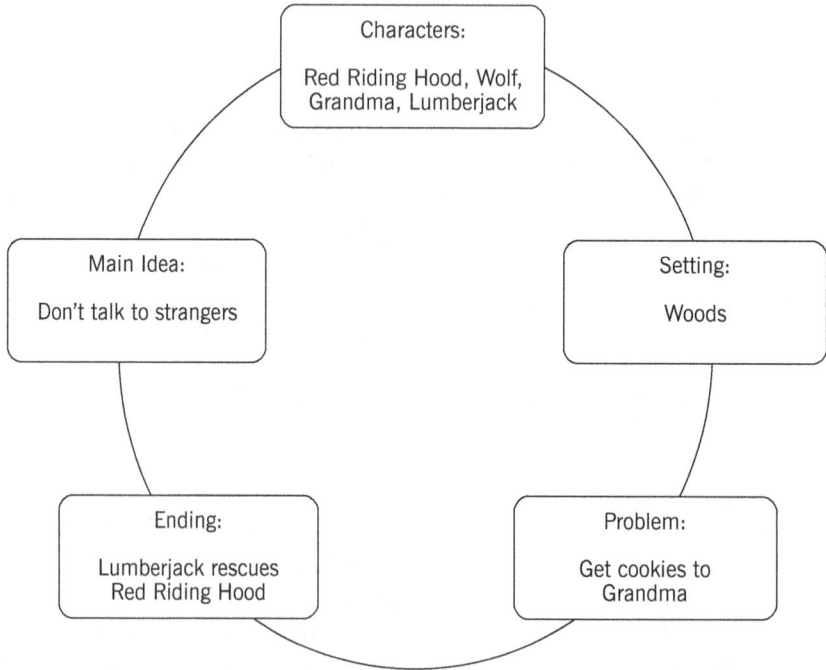

FIGURE 6.7. A semantic map with story elements of "Little Red Riding Hood."

tion. The wolf scurries ahead to the grandmother's house and ties up the grandmother. Then the wolf disguises himself as the grandmother by dressing in her nightgown and cap.

When Red Riding Hood arrives at the house, the wolf is in bed. The wolf beckons Red Riding Hood near to him. The drama or suspense of the story mounts as Red Riding Hood notices unusual features about her grandmother. She says that her grandmother has large eyes, to which the wolf responds, "The better to see you." Next, she remarks that grandmother has large ears, to which the wolf responds, "The better to hear you." Finally, she comments that her grandmother has big teeth, to which the wolf responds, "The better to eat you." The climax is the pinnacle of the drama, when the wolf jumps out of the bed to eat her. Red Riding Hood screams for help. Fortunately, a lumberjack cutting trees in the woods hears her pleas for help, breaks down the door with his axe, and rescues Red Riding Hood and her grandmother. Depending on the version, the lumberjack either kills the wolf or chases it away. The lumberjack's rescue is the resolution or ending of the story. The main idea and theme of a story are often confused or used interchangeably. One can distinguish the difference by noting that the main idea of a story is closely aligned with the goal or conflict, whereas the theme is an encompassing concept. In this story, the main idea is not to talk to strangers; the theme is good conquers all. The author's point of view is to entertain the reader while teaching a childhood lesson.

Semantic maps can also be used to teach the story elements of expository text. The Battle of Trenton, depicted in the famous painting of *Washington Crossing the Delaware*, can be used to illustrate the point. The history text could be written into the following summary:

> In the winter of 1776, Britain's general, William Howe, ordered his army of Hessian mercenaries to hold the fort at Trenton, New Jersey. The patriots' general, George Washington, had suffered a series of defeats in battle but remained undaunted. On Christmas Eve, General Washington and his troops rowed across the Delaware River to attack the fort at Trenton. The patriots won this decisive battle because they surprised the Hessians, who were sleeping after their Christmas celebration.

The story elements are shown in Figure 6.8. The main character, or protagonist, is George Washington; another character, the antagonist, is General William Howe. The setting is the winter of 1776 in Trenton, New Jersey. The sequence of events that make up the plot includes the Hessians celebrating on Christmas Eve, the patriot troops rowing across the Delaware River, the surprise attack on the Hessians while they slept, and General Washington's victory over General Howe's troops. The problem or conflict is that General Washington needs to defeat General Howe's troops; the climax is the surprise attack while the Hessians slept; and the ending, or resolution, is General Washington's victory. The main idea is that one cannot let down one's guard to celebrate during war, and the theme is that diligence and perseverance prevail.

Story maps can take a variety of forms. For example, Idol (1987) used a simple story map that included setting (characters, time, and place), the problem, the goal, the action, and the outcomes. Bos (1987), as described in Vaughn and Bos (2009), used strategy instruction to teach students to retell a story. The acronym for the strategy was "STORE" the story. First the students described the setting (S; who, what, when, where). Next the students identified the trouble (T). What did the main character need to resolve? Then

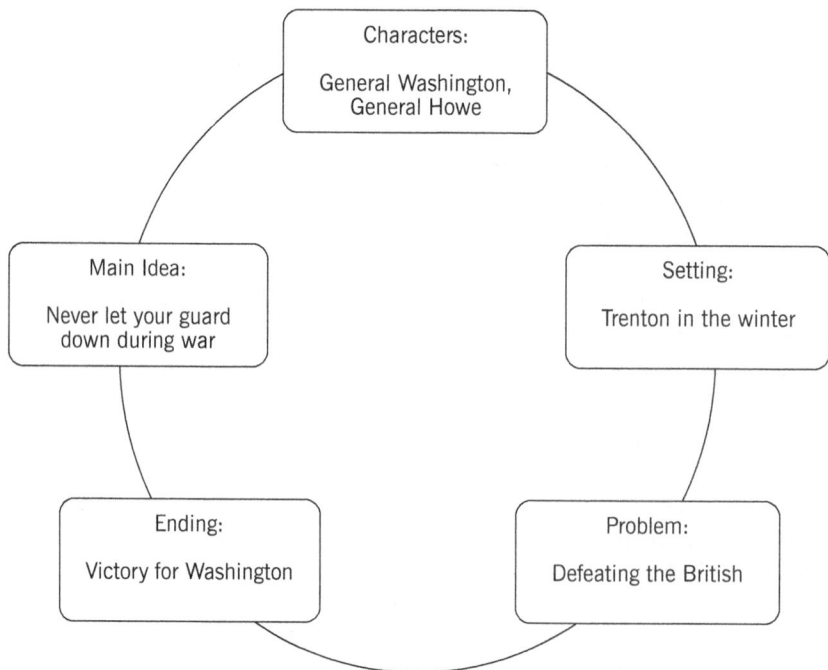

FIGURE 6.8. Semantic map for story elements in expository text.

the students listed the order (O) of action to resolve the problem. The resolution (R) was then noted, along with the ending (E) of the story. Zakas, Wood, Hicks, and Browder (2009) used a variation of a story map with students with autism that is shown in Figure 6.9. The story grammar vocabulary—*main character, setting, problem*, and *solve the problem*—were taught using a systematic scripted approach based on the principles of direct instruction. The results of this study showed that elementary-age students with autism could acquire salient story grammar terminology and complete an adapted four-step story map to demonstrate text comprehension from self-read material.

Graphic Organizers

Graphic organizers are visual templates that assist a student in grouping and categorizing information. The visual representations aid comprehension by providing a concrete picture of the organization of miscellaneous information. In this section, the well-known graphic organizers of KWL, Venn diagrams, T-charts, and semantic mapping are discussed.

KWL Charts

KWL is a graphic organizer and a teaching model developed by Ogle (1986) to encourage participation in learning from expository text. In the KWL acronym, *K* represents "know," *W* "want to know," and *L* "learned" (Hefflin & Hartman, 2002). In the original KWL method, the teacher creates a chart on a board that has three sections. In the

Story Map Worksheet

Student Name: _____

Story: _____

Chapter: _____

Date: _____

1. Identify the main character(s).

   _____

   _____

2. What is the setting of the chapter?

   _____

   _____

3. What is the problem or conflict?

   _____

   _____

4. How does _____ try to solve the problem?

                          (main character)

   _____

   _____

FIGURE 6.9. Example of a story map. Based on Carnine, Silbert, Kame'enui, and Tarver (2004).

first section, the teacher brainstorms with the students to list the things the students already know about the topic. In the middle section, the teacher writes questions for the students to answer while they read the text. Finally, in the last section, the teacher assists the students in listing the things that they have learned through reading the text. Figure 6.10 provides an example of a KWL chart. According to the *K*, or "know," section of the diagram, the students know that (1) bees can fly, (2) bees can make honey, and (3) bees have a queen. The *W*, or "want to know," section indicates that the students will try to answer the questions (1) "Where do bees live?", (2) "What do bees need to make honey?", and (3) "What is a section in the hive called?" The *L*, or "learned," section shows that the

Know What you already know	Want to Know What you want to know	Learned What you learned
1. Bees can fly.	1. Where do bees live?	1. Bees live in a hive.
2. Bees make honey.	2. What do bees need to make honey?	2. Bees need pollen to make honey.
3. Bees have a queen.	3. What is a part of a hive called?	3. A part of a hive is called a honeycomb.

FIGURE 6.10. Example of a KWL chart graphic organizer. Another variation, called a KWHL chart, can be found in Chapter 8.

students learned the following from reading the text: (1) Bees live in a hive, (2) Bees need pollen to make honey, and (3) A section in a bee hive is called a honeycomb.

Carr and Ogle (1987) extended the original teaching model and graphic organizer to include the use of summarization and mapping. The new model was called KWL Plus. Later, an additional section was added to make KWWL, so that students could note "where" they found the answers in the text (Bryan, 1998). Chapter 9 has another variation called KWHL, in which students determine "how" they will find the desired information.

Venn Diagrams

A Venn diagram (Baxendell, 2003; DiCecco & Gleason, 2002) is a graphic organizer that can be used with narrative or expository texts to compare and contrast two things. The format of the organizer consists of two intersecting circles that form two outer sections and a center section, as displayed in Figure 6.11. A Venn diagram could be used to compare and contrast the life of Laura Ingalls Wilder from the children's book *Little House on the Prairie* and the lives of students in a present-day fourth-grade classroom. The characteristics that the lives share would be placed in the center section, where the two circles overlap. The characteristics that are unique to one life or the other would be placed in the outer sections of the two circles. In this example, some similarities between the two would be that both live with their families, both go to school, and both do chores around the house. One difference would be that Laura Ingalls Wilder's family grew their own food, whereas students today buy their food at the grocery store. The visual repre-

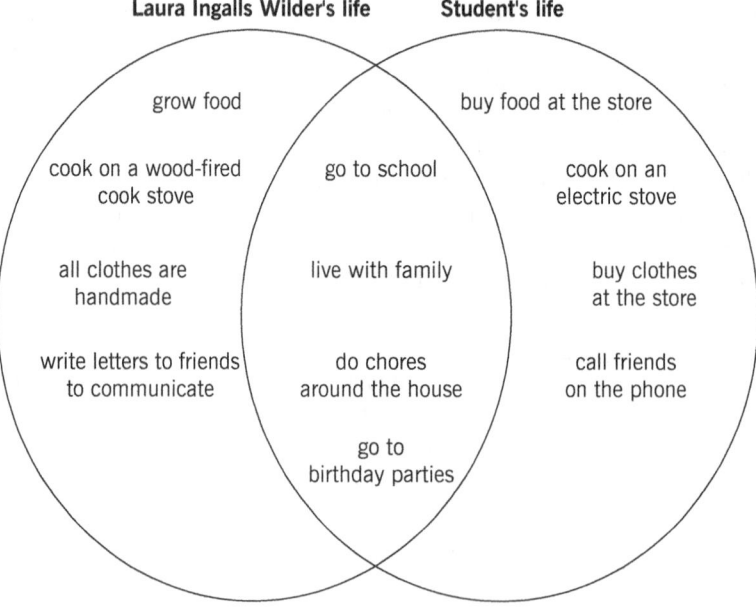

FIGURE 6.11. Example of a Venn diagram graphic organizer. Diagram provided by S. Christy Hicks.

sentation of Venn diagrams enables students to focus on each specific characteristic, one at a time. They are flexible organizers that all ability groups can use.

T-Chart

The T-chart (Baxendell, 2003; DiCecco & Gleason, 2002) is a simple chart in which two lines in the shape of the letter "T" are drawn to divide the paper into two sections. The ways in which the T-chart can be implemented are infinite. Figure 6.12 demonstrates how a T-chart can be used to categorize main characters and secondary characters in a story such as *Sarah, Plain and Tall* by Patricia Maclachlan. The left column of the T-chart is for "Main Characters" and the right column is for secondary or "Not Main Characters." From this novel, Anna, Caleb, Jacob, and Sarah Wheaton would be listed in the left column under "Main Characters," whereas Maggie, Matthew, Rose, and Violet would be listed in the right column under "Not Main Characters."[*]

Expository Text

Nearly all of the strategies presented for teaching comprehension are applicable to either narrative or expository text. Sometimes story elements do not apply well to expository text. Weaver and Kintsch (1991) suggest that expository text includes the elements of compare–contrast, classification, illustration, and procedural description. Meyer and Rice (1984) propose that expository text includes the elements of sequence, enumeration or collection, problem solution, and description but not elements such as compare–contrast and classification. Pearson and Fielding (1991) concluded that students who understand and follow the elements of expository text are able to remember the text and that, as expected, poor readers do not understand the elements of expository text. Some researchers suggest that students with disabilities may recognize narrative elements more easily (Montague, Maddux, & Dereshiwsky, 1990). When feasible, teachers may want to generalize the narrative story elements to expository text. In contrast, some expository text needs a different framework. Using a graphic organizer may help students focus on key elements in some content areas.

For example, in a science text, the students may learn about the planets in the solar system. An assignment may be to list the planets that are too hot or too cold to sustain life similar to life on Earth. A T-chart might be the most useful way to set up this information. Mercury and Venus are too hot to sustain life, and Mars, Jupiter, Saturn, Uranus,

Main character	Not main character
Anna	Maggie
Caleb	Matthew
Jacob	Rose
Sarah Wheaton	Violet

FIGURE 6.12. T-chart categorizing main characters and not main characters from *Sarah, Plain and Tall*. Chart provided by S. Christy Hicks.

---

[*] The T-chart and Venn diagram examples were contributed to this chapter by S. Christy Hicks.

Neptune, and Pluto (a dwarf planet or a plutoid) are too cold to sustain life similar to the life on Earth.

Using Collaborative Learning Groups to Promote Comprehension

When teaching content area information, teachers may also use collaborative learning groups. Collaborative strategic reading (CSR) is a cooperative-learning-group approach to understanding text by implementing four comprehension strategies (Klingner & Vaughn, 1999). The students are seated in groups of four and provided with four comprehension strategy cards: a preview card, a "clink or clunk" card, a "get the gist" card, and a wrap-up card. In addition, each student has a learning log, which can be a bound notebook or a section of his or her subject binder.

First, a student reads the title, headings, and subheadings of the text. Next, the student reads the preview card: What do we know about the topic already and what do we think we will learn about it? All of the students use cues from the title, headings, and subheadings to make predictions about the content of the text. Then, everyone brainstorms what he or she knows about the predicted topic and writes his or her comments in the learning log. Second, students read a passage from the text. As they read, they look for words or concepts that they do not understand. These unknown entities are referred to as "clinks or clunks." On the "clink" or "clunk" card are prompts to assist the students in figuring out the unknown word or idea. Third, the "get the gist" card reminds the students to find the main idea or concept when they finish the passage. This process is repeated for the subsequent passages. After all of the passages are read, the wrap-up card is played, which signals that the students should generate a list of questions and answers that demonstrate what they have learned from the text. This strategy is shown in Figure 6.13.

There are advantages to the CSR framework. It can be used for any text and content area, and it does not require teacher preparation. The disadvantage of CSR is one that is inherent in any cooperative learning technique: The teacher has to establish and consistently reinforce rules for the students to work as a team. Rules of conduct may include (1) show respect to classmates, (2) be nonjudgmental of brainstorming contributions, (3) actively participate, and (4) wait quietly for your turn to contribute. Students with severe disabilities may need additional support to participate actively in the group and to learn

Sequence	Comprehension strategy card	Request
1	Preview	What do we know about the topic already and what do we think we will learn about it?
2	Clink or Clunk	Prompts the student to assist him or her in figuring out an unknown word or idea.
3	Get the Gist	Reminds the students to find the main idea or concept when they finish the passage.
4	Wrap Up	Signals that the students should generate a list of questions and answers that demonstrate what they have learned from the text.

FIGURE 6.13. Cooperative learning for comprehension: CSR.

the content read together. This support may include assistance to complete the learning log or preteaching of the target text.

Another model for cooperative learning is concept-oriented reading instruction (CORI), which teaches students about a particular topic while they are learning an integration of four phases of learning strategies (Guthrie, Anderson, Alao, & Rinehart, 1999). The four phases include: observe and personalize, search and retrieve, comprehend and integrate, and communicate to others. In research on third- and fifth-grade language arts and science students (Guthrie et al., 1999), CORI students showed relatively high levels of conceptual learning.

To illustrate an adaptation of the CORI strategy that includes a student with moderate to severe disabilities, we use the hypothetical science theme of ocean life. In this illustration, the cooperative learning group remains together for several weeks of an instructional unit. In the first phase, observe and personalize, the students become familiar with the topic of ocean life on a personal level. Students in the Midwest who are studying the ocean have probably never been to an ocean, and the distance to a beach site makes a field trip impossible. To give the students an observation and personal experience of a beach, the teachers create a beach atmosphere in their classroom. An afternoon is designated in which the students wear swimming suits. Instead of paper and pencils, the school supplies are pails and shovels. Baby pools are filled with sand and a combination of sand and water. Artificial coral, starfish, sand dollars, and seashells are placed in the sand. A beach fragrance room freshener and an audiotape of the ocean fill the air. The students' assignment is to explore the beach and the life it supports. They feel their toes in the dry and wet sand and examine the life. Requests and inquiries are written on the board to guide the students' investigation. "Describe what you hear when you hold a conch shell to your ear." "What things can you find on the beach?" The experience is summarized in a student writing assignment about "Things Found on a Beach That Come from the Ocean."

In the second phase, search and retrieve, the students learn more about the topic through resources that include books, the Internet, videos, and experimentation. Students are heterogeneously paired according to ability to search for and retrieve information based on interest. The students have access to books about the ocean on various reading levels in the classroom. During one class, the media specialist assists the students in the media center, and another day the students search for information about starfish and sand dollars on the Internet in the computer lab. Everyone views a video about the ocean ecosystem. A local expert gives a presentation to all of the students about being a marine biologist.

In third phase, comprehend and integrate, the students use various comprehension strategies and frameworks to extract the information from the resources that they have gathered. After reading text summaries from their prior day's research, the students in general education compare and contrast starfish and sand dollars by independently completing a written Venn diagram. The students with moderate and severe disabilities find similarities and differences between starfish and sand dollars by completing a Venn diagram in which they place pictures and symbols in the appropriate location on the diagram's intersecting circles.

In the fourth phase, the students convey their findings in various ways to their classmates, parents, or the community. Some students may choose a traditional research paper format to share their newly gained knowledge. Others may use performance-based methods such as an informative presentation, play, or essay recitation. Artistic students may opt to design dioramas, puppets, diagrams, and renderings. This phase enables students to apply their creative expression. For example, two students divide the writing tasks for a research paper on the symbiotic life of a coral reef. Four students write an entire play and design costumes, which include a crab, starfish, sand dollar, and seashell. Another group of students completes the framework of a play that has been provided by the teacher, while others paint sections of paper hand puppets. The rest of the students collaboratively create a mural about life under the sea. Each student contributes to the mural based on his or her cognitive, physical, and artistic abilities.

A third option for cooperative learning is peer-assisted learning strategies (PALS), a framework in which students are taught comprehension strategies that can be transferred to other texts and situations (Fuchs, Fuchs, & Burish, 2000; Fuchs, Fuchs, Mathes, & Simmons, 1997; Mathes, Howard, Allen, & Fuchs, 1998). The strategy consists of three sessions: partner reading, paragraph shrinking, and prediction relay. See Figure 6.14 for a summary of the method.

In the partner reading session, the students are heterogeneously paired, a higher-level reader with a lower-level reader, and a text is selected at the instructional level of the lower-level reader. The students take turns being the "reader," who reads the text for 5 minutes. The higher-level reader starts first to serve as a model for the lower-level reader. Whenever the lower-performing student, or tutee, misreads a word or cannot read a word, the higher-performing student, or tutor, prompts the tutee by saying, "Stop, you missed that word. Can you figure it out?" The tutee reads the word and then repeats the sentence. After the students have each read a 5-minute session for a total of 10 minutes,

Reading	Paragraph shrinking	Predictive relay
1. Tutor reads aloud for 5 minutes.	1. Students take turns reading paragraphs.	1. Reader makes a prediction about what will happen on the next half page.
2. Tutee reads aloud same material.	2. Tutor asks tutee "who" and "what" story was about.	2. Reader reads the next half page (tutor corrects errors).
3. Tutor prompts for incorrect words.	3. Tutor asks for most important thing about the "who" or "what."	3. Reader confirms or disconfirms prediction.
4. Tutee retells the sequence of events.	4. Readers summarize main idea in 10 word or fewer. If more than 10 words, told to shrink it.	4. Reader summarizes main idea.
POINTS	POINTS	POINTS
1 = Read sentence.	1 = Identify "who" or "what."	1 = Make reasonable prediction.
10 = Retell the story.	1 = Stating most important thing.	1 = Read half page.
	1 = State main idea in 10 words or fewer.	1 = Identify "who" or "what," most important thing, and main idea.

FIGURE 6.14. Cooperative learning for comprehension: PALS model.

the tutee retells the sequence of the story. The students earn 1 point for each correctly read sentence and 10 points for correctly retelling the story.

In the second activity, paragraph shrinking, the tutee summarizes each paragraph. The students read one paragraph at a time and identify the "who" or "what" in the story and the most important thing about the "who" or "what." Then the main idea is summarized in 10 words or fewer. Whenever the tutee does not correctly summarize the paragraph, the tutor acts as a coach and prompts the tutee by saying, "That's not quite right. Skim the paragraph and try again." If the statement of the main idea is more than 10 words, the tutor says, "Shrink it." The students earn one point for correctly identifying the "who" or "what," one point for correctly identifying the most important thing about the "who" or "what," and one point for summarizing the main idea in 10 words or fewer. The students take turns trading roles.

Finally, in the last activity, prediction relay, the tutee makes a prediction about what will happen on the next half page. Then the tutee reads the half page aloud, and any reading errors are corrected by the tutor. Based on the half page, the tutor confirms or disconfirms the prediction. The tutee identifies the "who" or "what" and the most important thing about the "who" or "what" and summarizes the main idea in 10 or fewer words. Afterward, the tutee determines whether the prediction was correct or incorrect and summarizes the main idea. Whenever the person in the tutor role does not think the prediction is sound, the tutor says, "I don't agree. Think of a better prediction." The students earn one point for every reasonable prediction, one point for correctly reading each half page, one point for correctly judging the prediction, one point for "who" or "what," one point for "what mainly happened," and one point for summarizing the half paragraph in 10 words or fewer.

Research by Fuchs et al. (1997) compared the achievement of students in grades 2–6 with learning disabilities, students considered low achievers, and students who had never been referred to special education participating in PALS with that of students participating in conventional reading instruction. The results indicated that all of the students participating in PALS improved more on fluency, accuracy, and comprehension. In another study, first-grade students who had been identified as low achieving, average achieving, and high achieving participated in PALS. The results indicated that PALS had a significant effect on low-achieving students in the areas of word attack, word identification, fluency, and early reading skills.

Although research has not been conducted on including students with severe disabilities in PALS, this type of cooperative learning may be effective if the students are given an opportunity to respond at their level of literacy. Some students may simply listen to the read-alouds and answer comprehension questions rather than have a turn reading. Others may read adapted or controlled text versions of the story when it is their turn. Students may respond to comprehension questions using multiple-choice formats with pictures, objects, or sight words.

PLANNING FOR FULLER INCLUSION

Review the three examples of cooperative learning. Which one would work in your context? What would you need to preplan or do during the lesson to promote full participation by the student with severe disabilities?

CASE STUDY

Mr. Lalli teaches a fourth-grade language arts class. In his general education class, he has students who are advanced readers, apprentice readers, and novice readers. He is planning a unit to teach the novel *Charlotte's Web*. His advanced readers can read the text in its original version because they read at or above grade level. His apprentice, or struggling, readers read at an early-first-grade reading level. For them, he will use an adapted version of the text written on a lower grade level that has controlled vocabulary. His novice readers, including a student with severe disabilities, will use an adapted text with embedded pictures and repeated story lines of the main idea for each chapter. Mr. Lalli had the school's scout troop help him create these adapted novels as a special project. The adapted novels are accompanied by objects to aid in comprehension (e.g., stuffed pig, toy spider). During the presentation of the text, Mr. Lalli has the advanced readers read the original text aloud. Next, the apprentice readers summarize the key points using their controlled text. Finally, the novice readers then emphasize the "write it down" points by reading a sentence that gives the big idea of the passage. This reading may be achieved using a VOD. On some days, he has the advanced readers do silent reading while one or two students help the apprentice and novice readers with read-alouds. On other days, he has the students follow the PALS format, with the most advanced readers being the first readers. On these days, he has the readers at other levels point to the original text to the extent possible. He checks for incidental learning by the apprentice and novice readers. For example, can they find a target vocabulary word in the actual original text?

Because most of his students do not come from farm families, Mr. Lalli provided background knowledge by having the class take a field trip to a farm. He also taught information about animals in his science lessons. One of the goals is for students to be able to evaluate which parts of *Charlotte's Web* could be real and which are unreal.

Mr. Lalli uses questions in various formats to accommodate the different abilities of the students. He often asks open-ended questions to be answered verbally or in a written format. He gives all students a chance to compose the answer. Sometimes he first asks the class to tell him where they will find the information—in their heads or in the book. He also uses questions with arrays of pictures or with one-word answers for the students with moderate to severe disabilities. As needed, the paraprofessional in the class embeds systematic instruction with least-to-most-intrusive prompting or sustained questioning to help students to select the correct answer.

In the related science lesson, Mr. Lalli is using a T-chart and other graphic organizers to help students glean key facts from the book he is using about animals. To help promote understanding of real and not real, he uses a Venn diagram. Students contrast animals and people to discover that only people talk. During language arts, he refers back to this diagram to decide whether the animals' talking is real.

At the end of *Charlotte's Web*, the students will present a project to retell the story. For example, one group chooses to act out the story and another creates a picture summary. The novice readers are actively involved in these projects. Mr. Lalli monitors the groups to prompt students with severe disabilities to use their vocabulary words and express key points about the stories. They celebrate the end of the unit by watching the movie version of *Charlotte's Web*.

SUMMARY

Students need to acquire comprehension skills for text to be meaningful. Unfortunately, both researchers and teachers have sometimes focused on reading text (e.g., sight word recognition) without a concurrent focus on comprehension. This chapter provides an overview of comprehension using Bloom's taxonomy of knowledge. Teachers are encouraged to have students demonstrate understanding of text at various levels, including literal recall (knowledge), textual inference (comprehension), application, analysis, synthesis, and evaluation. To promote this comprehension, teachers can use questioning, semantic maps of story elements, and graphic organizers. Students may also need to develop the background information to understand the themes and concepts in the text. In teaching question answering, instruction may focus on how to find information (e.g., "in the book" or "in my head"). Teachers may use either receptive or expressive question formats. Students will need some systematic instruction to learn to answer questions. A least-to-most-intrusive prompting strategy may be used to teach students how to answer questions. Reading the same passage across days may be needed for students to learn how to answer questions. Students have acquired the comprehension strategy itself when they can derive the answer with new text. Semantic mapping can be used to identify the elements of a story. Expository text may also lend itself to a semantic map or may be better summarized using graphic organizers. Teachers also may use cooperative learning groups to assist with learning content area material in subjects such as science and social studies. This chapter presented three cooperative learning strategies—CSR, CORI, and PALS. Finally, teachers need to consider how to put these strategies together to differentiate instruction for diverse learners. Differentiation of text and questions are two ways to approach this goal.

APPLICATIONS

1. Select a favorite novel or children's book. Using Table 6.2, write comprehension questions for each level of Bloom's taxonomy.

2. Write a script for a least-to-most-intrusive prompting strategy to teach students to answer three of the questions you developed in #1. Select a question that would need sustained questioning instead because it is more inferential.

3. Write a systematic instruction plan for teaching students to determine whether a question is "in the book" or "in your head." What visual cues might you use to help students with these strategies?

4. Write a task analysis for filling in a semantic map for a story that you could use to teach this skill to a student with a moderate or severe disability.

5. Develop a lesson plan in a content area not covered by this book (e.g., health or business) that uses a graphic organizer to promote comprehension of a specific passage of text.

CHAPTER 7

Mathematics

DIANE M. BROWDER, FRED SPOONER, AND KATHERINE TRELA

Tony is a seventh grader who has cerebral palsy with related intellectual and physical disabilities. He reads a few sight words and is beginning to comprehend adapted novels that are read aloud. He shows his answers by either using a switch or gazing at an answer with his eyes. Tony can sometimes verbally articulate his answers. Unfortunately, Tony had minimal mathematics instruction in his school career. As a young child, a preschool teacher taught him to count to 5. His elementary teachers taught him to name coins. Even though he mastered this skill by second grade, it somehow remained an IEP objective for the next 4 years. This past year Tony's IEP team set the goal to teach Tony mathematics aligned with the grade-level standards for middle school. His teacher, Mr. Rivera, began by teaching Tony to fill in an algebraic equation based on information in a word problem read aloud to him and then to find the answer using his counting skills. Tony was excited to have the challenge of age-appropriate work. He worked hard to listen closely, articulate some answers, and use his AAC device to indicate the correct solution. Within a month, Tony could fill in and solve addition equations for sums to 10. He is now moving on to higher sums and subtraction problems. (This is based on a true story. Names and some details have been changed to protect confidentiality.)

Until recently, mathematics was underemphasized for students such as Tony with moderate and severe developmental disabilities. If students received mathematics instruction at all, it was typically limited to the use of money. Although it was important for students to learn to use money in such community activities as shopping and dining, the teacher of this skill sometimes missed this goal. Instead of being focused on purchasing, instruction sometimes stalled on teaching early childhood money skills, such as naming coins, that had little utility in community contexts.

One reason for the lack of past emphasis on mathematics was the assumption that students with severe developmental delays lacked the ability to learn mathematical concepts. This misconception paralleled the thinking of early childhood experts that typically developing young children lacked the capacity to learn mathematics. In recent years this thinking has been challenged. Both new theory and research supports the capacity of very young children to acquire substantive mathematical ideas (Sarama & Clements, 2009). Similarly, students with severe disabilities may be able to master more complex mathematical concepts than once considered possible (Jimenez, Browder, & Courtade, 2008).

Although students with severe disabilities may be able to develop higher levels of mathematical ability than once thought possible, some may question the usefulness of this outcome. Would a better goal be to teach only the skills needed for community engagement, such as purchasing? Teaching only a narrow range of purchasing skills underestimates the mathematical abilities required for daily living, as well as the capacity of students with severe disabilities to meet these demands. For example, one of the skills that students in general education mathematics develop across the school years is the use of a coordinate plane. Students begin by learning to locate points in a plane and draw line segments. With further development, students can plot points on the x- and y-axes. This skill is also applied in developing linear graphs. Using a coordinate plane may seem irrelevant to some special educators who do not use this skill in the daily demands of teaching or life in the community. What may not be apparent is that some key job opportunities require knowledge of this concept. For example, even entry-level machinists need to know how to plot points on an x- and y-axis to function in the current world of technology in which tasks are performed by computer. IEP teams rarely know what opportunities a student may have as an adult (e.g., to study machine technology in a community college). To limit these based on assumptions about the student's disability would be unfortunate. General education mathematical standards have been developed by experts with deep knowledge of what competencies are needed to be prepared for life in modern society. By teaching to these standards—even if priorities are set to teach only a few of the most important ones—teachers prepare students for a fuller range of options as adults.

STRANDS OF MATHEMATICS

Most states' standards in mathematics parallel those of the National Council of Teachers of Mathematics (NCTM, 2000). The NCTM's "equity principle" (2000, p. 12) makes clear that opportunities to learn mathematics need to be made available to all students, regardless of gender, race, or intellectual ability. Specifically, NCTM's equity principle challenged the notion that only "some students are capable of learning mathematics" (p. 12) and, instead, stated that high expectations and worthwhile opportunities for all students are essential components of mathematics curricula. Additionally, NCTM (2000) acknowledged that "some students may require accommodation" and that schools must support such individual differences with "resources for all classrooms and all students" (p. 13). Finally, NCTM's "curriculum principle" stated that math curricula should be "coherent, focus on important math, and be well articulated across the grades" (pp. 15–16). Implied in these principles is a vision of mathematics instruction that responds to the needs of all learners, develops new skills throughout the school career, and provides personally relevant learning experiences in which students can apply skills as they solve problems encountered throughout the day.

NCTM (2000) provided educators with content and process standards in order to help focus mathematics instruction. Five content areas were identified as most important to include in mathematics curricula: (1) algebra, the study of patterns and relationships; (2) geometry, the study of spatial organization; (3) data analysis, the study of organizing and interpreting facts and data; (4) measurement, the study of defining attributes in a standard format; and (5) numbers and operations, or the study of quantity and number sense. NCTM (2000) also identified five processes in learning and communicating math concepts: (1) reasoning, (2) problem solving, (3) communication, (4) connections, and (5) representation.

Content Areas of Mathematics

Algebra

Instruction in algebra enables students to recognize patterns, relations, and functions. For example, a student in second grade may be guided to recognize that the pattern, "clap, clap, step" is the same as the pattern, "blue, blue, red" (NCTM, 2000, p. 91). A fourth-grade student is then guided to both recognize an established pattern and use that information to predict subsequent data. To illustrate, students establish a relationship between the number of cubes in a tower and its surface area, then use that information to predict the surface area of towers with a larger number of cubes (NCTM, 2000, p. 160). In the middle grades (6–8), students begin to use symbols to represent relationships, with a focus on the formula for slope. Students explore how to represent information needed to solve problems in daily life (i.e., how to compare cellular phone plans) by organizing data into charts, tables, and graphs. Finally, high school students develop more sophisticated formulas to represent patterns observed in physical phenomena. For example, students may express the relation between the number of minutes of daylight from January 1 to December 30 in a city in the northern hemisphere and the number of minutes during the same period in a city in the southern hemisphere (NCTM, 2000, p. 298). Students would be guided to develop a formula that considers such variables as latitude, average daylight time, and number of months observed. Although algebra addresses more than patterns and relationships, these examples illustrate the development of thought processes that contribute to students' ability to both pose and solve problems.

Geometry

The study of geometry involves describing spatial relationships, including the use of coordinate geometry and other representational systems to organize information about their surroundings. Young children (grades K–2) may explore relationships, such as *over, near,* and *between,* when acting out stories or learning to give directions. Gradually, children learn directional words (e.g., *right, left*) to give more precise information (NCTM, 2000). In grades 3–5, students' understanding of location develops further, and maps and grids may be used to introduce the Cartesian plane (Sarama, Clements, Swaminathan, McMillen, & Gonzalez Gomez, 2003). In grades 6–8, geometric thinking and algebraic representations can be linked, as students examine line segments that form shapes on the coordinate plane. Students learn to draw parallel lines on the coordinate plane and to express their relationship algebraically using the formula for slope (NCTM, 2000). In grades 9–12, students expand use of the coordinate plane by applying transformations and using matrices to represent transformations on the coordinate plane (NCTM, 2000). Starting with a simple understanding of what is "near" or "far," students gradually develop ways to describe objects and movement in space through use of maps, grids, and representations on a coordinate plane as they study geometry.

Measurement

Measurement develops from the recognition that objects have attributes that can be described in a common language and that specific tools are used to describe those attributes. The young child (PreK–2) learns attributes by looking at, touching, or directly comparing objects (NCTM, 2000). Terms such as *large, slow*, or *deep* may be used to describe objects. Teachers then guide students to identify specific tools used to measure attributes, with a focus on linear measurement. In grades 3–5, students build on their understanding of standard measurements as they explore area, volume, weight, and size of angles to describe shapes and objects. In addition, students learn to choose appropriate units of measurement according to the problem posed (i.e., choosing to use miles rather than inches to measure distance between cities). In grades 6–8, students continue to explore volume and area, as well as applying algebraic equations to express the relationship of one measurement to another (e.g., the relationship of cubic units to square units). In high school, grades 9–12, opportunities to apply measurement concepts arise in other areas of math, as well as science, technical education, and social sciences (NCTM, 2000). At this level, students are familiar with a variety of measurement tools, including computer applications and applying measurement systems appropriate for the problem posed.

Data Analysis

Data analysis gives students opportunities to observe their surroundings in order to generate questions, choose information to answer their questions, and organize information to communicate their findings. In PreK–2, students may collect and represent data to show exact representations of their observations (e.g., a chart with each student's name and the number of pockets he or she is wearing). By grades 3–5, students may group data on a chart, for example, grouping the number of students with two, three, four, or five pockets (NCTM, 2000). In middle school (6–8), students may compare the prices and sales of jeans with specific numbers of pockets and, in grades 9–12, show the distribution of jeans sales by age group and report reasons for those preferences. Throughout a student's career, the study of data analysis helps students pose and investigate more sophisticated questions to better understand behaviors and trends in the world around them (e.g., consumer trends).

Numbers and Operations

A major emphasis for young learners in mathematics, numbers and operations may be considered a building block to all other strands of math (NCTM, 2000). To illustrate, young children (PreK–2), must develop the concept of "oneness" as they learn 1:1 correspondence in counting (Clements, Sarama, & DiBiase, 2004). In grades 3–5, students explore larger numbers, fractions, decimals, and numbers less than zero (i.e., rational numbers). Students are also introduced to composing and decomposing numbers and exploring the rules that govern operations such as addition, subtraction, multiplication, and division. In middle grades, students continue to work with large numbers, using "scientific, exponential, and calculator notation" (NCTM, 2000, p. 214). In addition, students apply operations to fractions, percentages, decimals, and negative numbers, while developing an understanding of how those numbers are used in real life (i.e., comparing temperatures below zero). In grades 9–12, students use very large and very small numbers in problem solving and develop an understanding of how to express and interpret those numbers. In high school, numbers and operations are often embedded in other subjects, such as the use of Avogadro's number in chemistry or debating the use of trillions of dollars in a national budget during a civics or economics class. Although less emphasis is placed on specifically addressing this strand of mathematics in high school, students demonstrate and apply their understanding of numbers and operations across the curriculum.

Mathematical Processes

Problem Solving

One of the most important outcomes of mathematics instruction is that students learn to apply numbers to the solution of problems. Nearly all problem solving, whether mathematical or more general, involves three steps: (1) problem identification, (2) problem analysis, and (3) problem resolution. Students often need background knowledge to understand the problem itself. The problem may be presented in such a way as to activate this background knowledge. For example, a word problem may incorporate an age-appropriate activity, such as going to the movies. Sometimes teachers may use hands-on activities to supplement this background knowledge. For example, a teacher may set up a problem in which students need to apply numbers to find a solution (see Chapter 6 for ideas to promote background knowledge). Once the problem is identified, students need to determine how to resolve it. This involves applying the appropriate mathematical operation. As students progress through the grade levels in general education, they develop a wider repertoire of concepts and reasoning to apply in solving these problems.

Reasoning and Proof

Another process that students develop through mathematics is reasoning and proof. In general education mathematics, students learn to develop and evaluate mathematical arguments and proofs. Often, the math teacher asks students to "show their work," as well as the solution to the problem. For students still developing the mathematical concepts (e.g., young children and those with developmental delay), this reasoning may be expressed through a hands-on experience. For example, students might be shown multiple examples and nonexamples of parallel items and then be asked to demonstrate the concept of parallelism or state a rule for what is parallel.

Communication

Students also learn how to communicate their mathematical thinking to others through the general curriculum. Mathematics has its own vocabulary and symbols, and students gain competence with these through the course of their school careers. In the beginning, even symbols such as "2" and "=" require gaining recognition and understanding. At a more advanced level, students learn to communicate about intercept, slope, and other mathematical concepts. For students with severe disabilities, this mathematical vocabulary typically must be taught systematically. Chapter 5 provided methods for teaching sight words and symbols that have direct applicability to mathematics vocabulary. For example, a teacher might use repeated trials with flash cards of numbers and systematic prompting/fading procedures, such as time delay, to teach number recognition. Then students might be taught to match the numbers to sets of objects. Even more advanced concepts, such as "slope," can be taught as vocabulary words by matching the words to pictures.

Connections

Although mathematics is often taught as a distinctive curricular area, the concepts can be found in many other content areas and daily experiences. Mathematics also has many connections within the content. For students with severe disabilities, teachers may need to train this generalization. When a story in language arts introduces number concepts, the teacher may embed some math practice in language arts to review what these mean. When a science experiment requires application of a math concept such as "greater than," the teacher may use the same vocabulary symbols and materials as used in math to help students make the connection.

Representations

Mathematical ideas can be represented in a variety of ways. For example, if a student wanted to summarize the outcome of a school fund-raiser by grade levels, this might be done using numbers on a chart, a pie graph, or a pictograph. One of the skills students gain in mathematics is to determine the best options for representing a concept and to use more than one method of doing so. Students with severe disabilities may especially benefit from the use of variety in representing math concepts to enhance generalization. If pennies are the only objects used for counting, students may not acquire generalized counting. By using a variety of objects for this simple skill and for more complex concepts, students learn to apply their skills more broadly.

Curriculum Focal Points

In addition to content standards and processes, the NCTM (2006) also recommends using curricular focal points. Focal points are related ideas, concepts, skills, and processes that students build across the grade levels. By using math focal points, teachers focus on a small number of key areas of mathematics for deeper understanding, math fluency, and the ability to generalize. These focal points are also sometimes used to diagnose math difficulties. Teachers can find these focal points through the NCTM website (*www.nctm.org*) or through their state's application of them. An example of an NCTM geometry focal point for kindergarten includes:

> *Measurement:* **Ordering objects by measurable attributes.** Children use measurable attributes, such as length or weight, to solve problems by comparing and ordering objects. They compare the lengths of two objects both directly (by comparing them with each other) and indirectly (by comparing both with a third object), and they order several objects according to length. (p. 12)

Teaching general mathematics to students with severe disabilities requires setting priorities within the curriculum. By beginning with these focal points, teachers can be sure to focus on the most important ideas of mathematics.

STANDARDS AND MATH RESEARCH FOR STUDENTS WITH SEVERE DISABILITIES

In a comprehensive review of mathematics research with students with moderate and severe developmental disabilities, Browder, Spooner, et al. (2008) found 68 studies of mathematics, but most focused on numbers and operations or money management and only a few focused on the other strands of mathematics identified by the National Reading Panel (2000). Because of the limited focus of prior mathematics intervention research, not enough is known about how to develop effective interventions. The evidence does reveal that students can learn what is taught. Multiple studies have shown that some students can learn number identification and counting (e.g., Lalli, Mace, Browder, & Brown, 1989; Matson & Long, 1986; Morin & Miller, 1998). Some students have learned data analysis by recording changes in their behavior (Blick & Test, 1987; McCarl, Svobodny, & Beare, 1991). Others have acquired geometry skills, such as matching shapes (Hitchcock & Noonan, 2000; Mackay, Soraci, Carlin, Dennis, & Strawbridge, 2002).

This research also provides some clues about how to develop effective instruction. Because most of the past research on math instruction has not been grade aligned or problem focused, educators will need to apply effective strategies in new ways. The meta-analysis conducted by Browder, Spooner, et al. (2008) found systematic prompting with feedback, task analysis, and generalization to real-life contexts to be evidence-based practices in mathematics. These methods are described in more detail later in this chapter. Table 7.1 summarizes the major strands and process of mathematics based on NCTM (2000).

FINDING THE BALANCE

The number and variety of grade-level standards in mathematics can seem overwhelming when planning for students with severe disabilities. Teachers of mathematics can help identify which standards are most important as building blocks to future learning or those that are the most frequently used. Some states also have extended standards developed for students who participate in alternate assessments based on alternate achievement standards (see Chapter 2 for more information on extended standards).

TABLE 7.1. Strands and Processes of Mathematics

Content standards	Process standards
• Numbers and operations • Algebra • Geometry • Measurement • Data analysis and probability	• Problem solving • Reasoning and proof • Connections • Communication • Representation

CONCEPTUAL MODEL FOR TEACHING MATHEMATICS

Figure 7.1 provides a conceptual diagram of a model for prioritizing mathematics content. As shown in the last circle on the bottom right, the ultimate goal for teaching math to students with severe disabilities is to increase autonomy in managing everyday situations. For this reason, the most important outcome students can receive from mathematics instruction is to learn to solve problems. Students need to learn to identify the problem, to represent the problem, and to solve the problem. Students may use written problems or a hands-on activity to identify a math problem to solve. The problem may involve quantitative analysis, spatial reasoning, or linear relationships. Then the problem is represented in some manner. This will include the use of mathematical symbols and vocabulary but may also include using familiar objects and symbols (e.g., pictures) to bridge understanding of these mathematical symbols. Students communicate this representation in some way (e.g., worksheet, picture graphs). Finally, the students use some specific math problem-solving method. These are learned through the content areas of math, which are shown around the "solve problem" circle. These specific operations can be taught using systematic instruction of a task analysis for the operation, as described

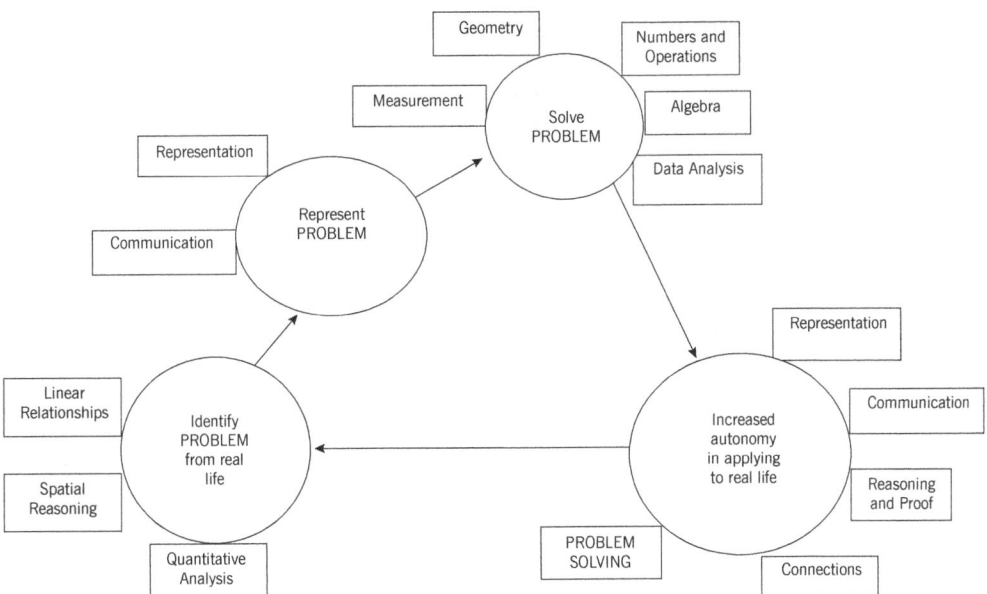

FIGURE 7.1. Conceptual model of math.

later in this chapter. Once a solution is achieved, these operations can be applied back to the real-life context from which the problem was derived (e.g., "How many more forks will be needed for a setting of six if two are already set on the table?").

METHODS FOR MATHEMATICS INSTRUCTION

Using a Math Story

Students need a way to experience the problem to be solved in mathematics. Literature in math education suggests that stories provide a natural schema in which students can organize facts (Anderson, Spiro, & Anderson, 1978; Zambo, 2005). Aligned with the National Reading Panel (2000) principle that mathematics instruction should inspire students to solve problems that are meaningful to them in settings in and outside of school, the use of literature provides a rich context in which to embed math problems. In addition, embedding problems in meaningful context may further build on the National Reading Panel's (2000) principle that effective math instruction builds on what students already know. Specifically, stories that are written within a context familiar to the student may provide a framework, or schema, on which the student may naturally organize information in order to solve the problem (Anderson et al., 1978). Furthermore, stories may provide a meaningful context by which to generalize the facts and problems to typical situations in a student's life (Pugalee, 2007). Finally, the process of following a story in order to solve a math problem can provide opportunities for students to practice early literacy skills by referencing text to identify facts, as well as to identify the nature of the problem to be solved.

Writing the Math Story

One website available to math teachers provides a resource of stories to use for contextualizing math problems for elementary students (*www.carroll.k12.org/instruction/ elemcurric/math/prompts*). Teachers can also write their own math problems. Figure 7.2 provides an example of a math story, and Table 7.2 gives some general guidelines for composing the story.

General Approach for Teaching a Math Story

Smith and Geller (2004) identified nine procedures and strategies used in previous research that have been shown to be effective with students with learning disabilities or at risk of failure. These include (1) teacher modeling, (2) self-questioning, (3) guided practice, (4) cueing prior knowledge, (5) feedback, (6) concrete, representational, and abstract (CRA) sequence of instruction, (7) hands-on experience, (8) opportunities to review, and (9) mediated scaffolding. Embedding these strategies into the framework for a story-based lesson, Pugalee (2007) suggested the following stages as one approach to developing math skills through the use of story-based lessons:

- Stage 1: Advance Organizer. Connect new skill to previously learned skills, review and practice necessary skills, and identify the new skill to be learned.
- Stage 2: Walk through a Story—Modeling the Mathematics. Use a "think aloud"

FIGURE 7.2. Sample story-based math problem used in algebra.

as the new skill is introduced. Stories may be used to bridge the abstractness of the math to a more concrete model and apply to real-world situations.

- Stage 3: Skill Building and Practice. Reuse the story context and fade modeling to allow student to apply new information.
- Stage 4: Generalization. Encourage and support students to develop story lines, scenarios or applications that embed the important concepts and skills.
- Stage 5: Assess. Document students' performance, scaffolding to correct errors, if needed.

TABLE 7.2. Guidelines for Writing Math Stories

Step	Description
Step 1: Identify the problem.	One way to do this is to summarize the problem as a brief story to be read aloud.
Step 2: Translate the problem into a math problem.	This problem is then translated into mathematical representation for ease of developing and communicating the solution. This requires using some type of mathematical representations, such as numerals or sets to represent numbers or graphic organizers to assist in creating the solution.
Step 3: Solve the problem.	During the school year, the student uses knowledge, reasoning, and skills mastered through the study of geometry, algebra, measurement, numbers and operations, and data analysis to develop and identify strategies. Many of these skills can be taught with systematic instruction of a task analysis of the problem-solving strategy.
Step 4: Apply to real life.	Once a solution is achieved, the student applies this back to the real-life context. For efficiency, the student will practice many scenarios using stories to solve problems in the classroom setting.

Using a Task Analysis to Teach the Math Story

Table 7.3 provides a task analysis for teaching a math story that incorporates some of the steps of an SBL, as described in Chapter 6. First, the teacher gets the students' attention. This attention-getter may be some object or experience related to the math story problem. For example, if the story is about buying bagels, the teacher may start by selling the students bagels in a mock bagel shop. Or if the story is about voting for a favorite movie, the teacher may begin by having the students vote and showing a movie preview. Next, the teacher gives the students a copy of the math story and asks the students to predict what the math story will be about. The students' guesses will probably relate to the lead-in activity. Then the teacher reads the story aloud. Some students may be able to help with this reading. All students should text point to follow along with the story as the teacher reads. Next, the teacher has the students read aloud the problem statement (e.g., "How many bagels did the students buy in all?"). Some students may use a voice-output AAC device for this restatement of the problem. The students then solve the problem by finding each fact and selecting the correct operation (e.g., $7 + x = 10). Finally, the teacher reviews the problem statement and the student's answers (e.g., $x = 3). These math stories may be augmented with assistive technology, including AAC devices, graphic organizers, and manipulatives. They may also be adapted for visually impaired students by adding tactile supports (e.g., outlining the graphic organizer in puffy paint or using foam board cutouts so the student can feel the signs and/or symbols).

Supplementing Stories with Assistive Technology

Recent research in the use of assistive and instructional technologies shows that such technologies support students' participation in lessons aligned with the general education curriculum (Erikson & Koppenhaver, 1997). To help students advance from concrete to abstract representations, a variety of "high-tech" assistive and instructional technologies may be used, such as online resources found at the National Library of Virtual Manipulatives for Interactive Mathematics (2009) or commercially available software such as Mathpad by Intellitools or Investigations Geo-Logo.

Additionally, use of graphic organizers and manipulatives can provide "low-tech" support to help students participate in the problem-solving process. For example, students in an elementary class may represent the number of families who own a cat, dog, or both by using a Venn diagram. Some students may need to use tangible objects to represent the items to be counted. For example, in the curriculum Teaching to Standards: Math (Trela et al., 2008), graphic organizers are used for plotting points on a plane, completing a bar graph, and solving an algebraic equation. An example of an algebraic equation graphic organizer is shown in Figure 7.3.

FROM RESEARCH TO PRACTICE

Several studies have provided evidence of the effectiveness of using graphic organizers and manipulatives in mathematical learning. Ives and Hoy (2003) used graphic organizers with high school students to organize steps to take when solving for multiple variables in a complex equation. In a review of literature on teaching algebra to students with disabilities, Gagnon and Maccini (2001) found that using graphic organizers and manipulatives was a successful intervention to aid in both the process of solving a problem and the solution of the problem, along with a review of background knowledge and explicit instruction in problem representation and solution and in self-monitoring procedures. Graphic organizers also have been used with students with moderate and severe disabilities to support learning independent living skills. For example, Gaule, Nietupski, and Certo (1985) used an adaptive shopping list to help students with significant disabilities gain independence in purchasing. The shopping list included a number line to help with estimating the amount of money needed for the purchase.

TABLE 7.3. A Task Analysis to Use for Teaching Math Stories

What the teacher will do	Materials to present	What the student will do	Examples of student responses
1. Gain student attention.	Anticipatory set	Interact with materials.	Ask questions, touch, look at materials
2. State objective of lesson. Opportunity for student to state objective of lesson.	Visual representation of objective statement	Read objective statement for lesson.	Verbal answer, touch/point, Velcro, circle, stamp, eye gaze, AAC
3. Pass individual stories to students.	Story-based lesson	Read the title.	Verbal answer, touch/point, AAC
4. Ask, "What is the story about?" Opportunity for student to make prediction.	Visual representation of predictions	Student makes a prediction.	Verbal answer, touch, Velcro, stamp, eye gaze, AAC
5. Read story without stopping.	Story-based lesson	Text point or find object on page.	Point, touch, eye gaze
6. Read problem statement. Opportunity for student to identify problem statement.	Visual representation of problem statement	Read problem statement.	Verbal answer, touch/point, Velcro, circle, stamp, eye gaze, AAC
7. Ask, "How can we solve the problem?" Find all facts. Find Fact 1. Find Fact 2. Find Fact 3.	Story-based lesson Graphic organizer Manipulatives	Identify the facts from the story.	Verbal answer, circle, touch/point, Velcro, stamp
8. Wait for student response. Record the facts.	Graphic organizer	Record the facts on individual graphic organizer.	Verbal answer, circle, touch/point, Velcro, stamp
9. Solve the problem.	Graphic organizer Manipulatives	Use manipulatives to solve problem.	Verbal answer, circle, touch/point, Velcro, stamp
10. Wait for student response. Read problem statement. State solution.	Visual representation of problem–solution	Record answer on individual organizer. State solution.	Verbal answer, circle, touch/point, Velcro, stamp

Note. This table was originally developed by the team of Project MASTERY: Diane M. Browder, Barbara Agnello, and Bree Jimenez (IES Project IES Grant No. R324A080014). Reprinted with permission from the University of North Carolina.

Equation Prompt

First fact	Sign	Second fact	Sign	Last fact
	+ –		=	

1 2 3 4 5 6 7 8 9 10

Add ———→   ←——— Subtract

$$X = \underline{\hspace{3cm}}$$

FIGURE 7.3. Example of a graphic organizer for teaching algebra. Using the task analysis in Table 7.5 [p. 178] and the math story in Figure 7.2 [pp. 176–177], a graphic organizer can allow students with significant cognitive disabilities access to algebraic concepts. From Trela, Jimenez, and Browder (2008). Copyright 2008 by Attainment Company. Reprinted by permission.

Using Systematic Instruction

Browder, Spooner, et al. (2008) found systematic instruction to be an evidence-based strategy for teaching mathematics to students with severe disabilities. Chapter 4 provides in-depth information on systematic instruction. To apply these strategies to math, the teacher would teach each step of the math story task analysis with systematic prompting and feedback. For example, the teacher would gain the students' attention using a lead-in activity. If needed, the teacher would use a verbal direction followed by a model (i.e., demonstration) and, if needed, physical guidance to show the student how to respond to the lead-in activity (e.g., raise a hand to vote for a movie). The math operation would also be prompted systematically. A script from Teaching to Standards: Math (Trela et al., 2008) is provided in Figure 7.4, which illustrates how these prompts may be worded.

   One recent study done with students with moderate disabilities showed that students could learn to independently follow the steps to solve a one-variable algebraic equation (Jimenez et al., 2008). Similar task analyses may be constructed with guidance from general education math literature to identify essential skills in data analysis, geometry, measurement, and numbers and operations.

TEACHING SPECIFIC CONTENT

Numbers and Operations

Building block skills lead to more advanced skills in numbers and operations, including counting with 1:1 correspondence and composing and decomposing numbers. These basic skills form a core of numeracy that is critical to all mathematical learning. For example, in solving an algebraic equation or computing the area of a rectangle, students will use

Story 3. Irene's friends choose a music video

SUPPORT LEVEL II

In this lesson, student support is less intensive. At key points in this lesson, students begin to solve the story problem on their own following your model and a prompting question. If a student doesn't respond to the question within 5 seconds or responds in error, model the step and have the student immediately follow your model.

MATH VOCABULARY

most, least, row, column

MATERIALS

- Concept Maps from Appendix B: most, least, row, column
- MathWork, pages 84–85
- Bar Graph 2 Poster

OPTIONAL MATERIALS

- AAC device preprogrammed with the following: most, least, row, column, Justin Timberlake, Hilary Duff, Bow Wow, 1, 2, 3, 4, 5, two problem statements
- Pointer/light pointer or eyegaze board
- Response cards: most, least, Justin Timberlake, Hilary Duff, Bow Wow, 1, 2, 3, 4, 5
- Problem statements from Appendix C

OPENING

Explain the lesson objective by saying to students: **Today we're going to learn about the math we can use to help us solve problems. Data analysis is math that helps us make choices and solve problems. We can use bar graphs to keep track of the data. We use math, like data analysis, in our lives every day.**

Task Analysis

1 Review math terms and introduce the story.

Review the data analysis terms *most, least, row,* and *column* using the Concept Maps.

Direct the students' attention to the target word (i.e., *most, least, row, column*) on each Concept Map. Point to each target word and ask: **What word is this?**

Wait for each student to respond. If no response or an incorrect response, say the word and repeat the question. Praise each correct response.

Ask students if they watch music videos. Discuss their favorite artists and what music videos they watch with friends. Explain the story, for example: **Irene and her friends planned a sleepover and they planned to have pizza and rent a music video. Irene needs to know what music video to rent. Lilli wants to see Justin Timberlake; that's the first choice.** Point to the first choice on your Bar Graph 2 Poster. When you reach the last sentence, point to it and say: **We have a problem to solve. The problem is "What music video did the friends rent?" We're going to use the bar graph to help solve the problem. Let's start.**

Ask: **What is the problem? What do we need to find out?**

Wait 5 seconds for students to respond by stating the problem. If no response or an incorrect response, model stating the problem.

Then have students check the box of the correct problem statement on their bar graphs.

3 Identify the first choice.

Now that we know what the problem is, we need to find a way to solve it. We need to find what music video Irene and her friends rented. Let's name the first choice Irene's friends have to vote on. What's the first choice?

Wait 5 seconds for students to respond by stating the first choice or pointing to the first choice in the story or on the bar graph. If no response or an incorrect response, reread the sentence and point to the first choice in the story and say: **Justin Timberlake is the first choice.**

Good, you found the first choice. The first choice in the story is Justin Timberlake. Say *Justin*.

4 Identify the second choice.

Now let's find the next choice. What's the second choice? Point to the second music video choice.

Wait 5 seconds for students to respond by stating the second choice or pointing to the second choice in the story or on the

that today the story will be about Irene and her friends choosing a music video to watch. Say: **Today we're going to read a story about Irene and her friends. They vote on the music video they want to rent.**

2 Identify the problem.

Read "Story 3: Irene's Friends Choose a Music Video" with students.

Read the story a second time and have students read along with you. As you read, think aloud as you find the facts mentioned in

bar graph. If no response or an incorrect response, reread the sentence and point to the second choice in the story and say: **Hilary Duff is the second choice.**

Great! You found the second choice: Hilary Duff. Say *Hilary*.

5 Identify the third choice.

Now let's find the next choice. What is the third choice? Point to the third music video choice.

Wait 5 seconds for students to respond by stating the third choice or pointing to the third choice in the story or on the bar graph. If no response or an incorrect response, reread the sentence and point to the third choice in the story and say: **Bow Wow is the third choice.**

Great! You found the third choice: Bow Wow. Say *Bow Wow*.

6 Record the first vote.

Now let's mark the votes that each choice received.

Read the sentence that tells the first vote, then say: **Which music video choice received the first vote?**

Wait 5 seconds for students to respond by stating *Justin Timberlake* or pointing to Justin Timberlake in the story or on the bar graph. If no response or an incorrect response, reread the sentence and point to Justin Timberlake. Say: **Irene's friend Lilli voted for Justin Timberlake. Justin Timberlake got the first vote from Lilli.**

Great! Justin Timberlake was the first vote. Now mark the vote for Justin Timberlake. Say *Justin*.

Wait 5 seconds for students to respond by marking a tally in the Justin Timberlake column on the bar graph. If no response, model marking a vote in the Justin Timberlake column.

Wonderful! You marked a vote for Justin Timberlake.

FIGURE 7.4. Script showing systematic prompting. From Trela, Jimenez, and Browder (2009). Copyright 2009 by Attainment Company. Reprinted by permission.

7 Record the next vote.

Read the sentence that tells the second vote, then say: **Which music video choice received the second vote?**

Wait 5 seconds for students to respond by stating *Hilary Duff* or pointing to Hilary Duff in the story or on the bar graph. If no response or an incorrect response, reread the sentence and point to Hilary Duff. Say: **Rose voted for Hilary Duff. Hilary Duff got the next vote from Rose.**

Great! Hilary Duff was Rose's vote. Then let's mark the vote for Hilary Duff.

Wait 5 seconds for students to respond by marking a tally in the Hilary Duff column on the bar graph. If no response, model marking a vote in the Hilary Duff column.

Awesome! You marked a vote for Hilary Duff.

8 Record the next vote.

Read the sentence that tells the next vote, then say: **Which music video choice received the next vote?**

Wait 5 seconds for students to respond by stating *Hilary Duff* or pointing to Hilary Duff in the story or on the bar graph. If no response or an incorrect response, reread the sentence and point to Hilary Duff. Say: **Nicole voted for Hilary Duff. Hilary Duff got the next vote from Nicole.**

Great! Hilary Duff was Nicole's vote. Then let's mark another vote for Hilary Duff.

Wait 5 seconds for students to respond by marking a tally in the Hilary Duff column on the bar graph. If no response, model marking a vote in the Hilary Duff column.

Wow! You marked another vote for Hilary Duff.

11 Identify the choice with the most votes.

Now we know how everyone in the story voted. Let's look at the bar graph to see which choice has the most votes. Remember, on the bar graph, the choice with the most votes will have the most boxes filled in the column. Which music video choice has the most votes?

Wait 5 seconds for students to respond by stating *Hilary Duff* or pointing to Hilary Duff in the story or on the bar graph. If no response or an incorrect response, model counting the votes and point to Hilary Duff. Say: **Hilary Duff has the most votes. The Hilary Duff video has 3 votes.**

Good work! You said *Hilary Duff*.

12 Restate the problem statement.

Now use the bar graph to solve the problem.

Direct the students to touch the problem statement while you read it: **"What music video did the friends rent?"**

9 Record the next votes.

Read the sentence that tells the next vote, then say: **Which music video choice received the next vote?**

Wait 5 seconds for students to respond by stating *Hilary Duff* or pointing to Hilary Duff in the story or on the bar graph. If no response or an incorrect response, reread the sentence and point to Hilary Duff. Say: **Irene also voted for Hilary Duff. Hilary Duff got the next vote from Irene.**

Great! Hilary Duff was Irene's vote. Mark another vote for Hilary Duff.

Wait 5 seconds for students to respond by marking a tally in the Hilary Duff column on the bar graph. If no response, model marking a vote in the Hilary Duff column.

Excellent! You marked another vote for Hilary Duff.

10 Record the next votes.

Read the sentence that tells the next vote, then say: **Which music video choice received the next vote?**

Wait 5 seconds for students to respond by stating *Bow Wow* or pointing to Bow Wow in the story or on the bar graph. If no response or an incorrect response, reread the sentence and point to Bow Wow. Say: **Sally voted for Bow Wow. Bow Wow got the next vote from Sally.**

Great! Bow Wow was Sally's vote. Mark another vote for Bow Wow.

Wait 5 seconds for students to respond by marking a tally in the Bow Wow column on the bar graph. If no response, model marking a vote in the Bow Wow column.

Excellent! You marked another vote for Bow Wow.

13 State the solution in the story context.

Reread the story and when you get to the last sentence, "What music video did the friend rent?" have students state the solution.

Wait 5 seconds for students to respond by stating *Hilary Duff* or pointing to Hilary Duff in the story or on the bar graph. If no response or an incorrect response, model counting the votes and point to Hilary Duff. Say: **Hilary Duff has the most votes. The Hilary Duff video has 3 votes.**

Then have them write or trace the words *Hilary Duff* below their bar graphs.

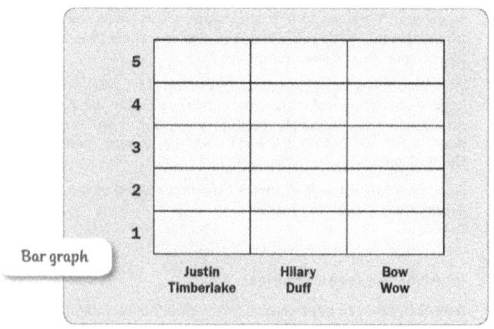

WHAT DO WE NEED TO FIND OUT? CHECK THE BOX. ☑

☐ 1. What music video did the friends rent?

☐ 2. What is Irene's favorite snack?

Bar graph

5

4

3

2

1

Justin Timberlake   Hilary Duff   Bow Wow

Video: _____

FIGURE 7.4. *(cont.)*

their knowledge of numbers and operations. Often, students with severe disabilities continue to need instruction in basic numeracy well beyond the early grades. High school students may still be learning to count accurately or add sets. These basic numeracy skills can be taught concurrently with applications to age- and grade-appropriate activities. For example, a student might work on counting objects to fill in an algebraic equation.

Table 7.4 provides a list of some of the important early numeracy skills. Ideally, students will master these in the early grades and build on this knowledge; however, these can continue to be taught concurrently with other content. One skill is called "subitizing," in which students learn to recognize the number of items in a set without counting. Interestingly, young children sometimes master some subitizing prior to learning to count (Sarama & Clements, 2009). A student may know "two shoes" or hold up five fingers for his or her age without being able to count to 2 or 5. Another skill is learning to count.

TABLE 7.4. Early Numeracy Skills

Skill	Explanation	Examples
Subitize	• Recognizing the quantity in a set without counting; students gain skill across increasingly larger sets.	• Student may recognize some sets before even learning to count: "Two shoes." At most advanced, can combine sets without adding/counting: "I saw 3 and 2 so I know it's 5."
Count	• Rote counting • Counting movable objects • Counting nonmovable objects in an array • Counting objects in random pattern • Counting up from a number • Skip counting (e.g., by 5's) • Grouping into sets (5 bundles of 4)	• An important early step is counting and then restating how many: "1, 2, 3, 4 . . . 4 books on the shelf!" Being able to count up is important for learning to use a next-dollar strategy in shopping: $4.83 is counted as "1, 2, 3, 4, . . . and one more."
Compare	• 1:1 correspondence • Which set has more/less/same? • First, second in sequence or first/next/last • Put in order small to large. • Ordinal numbers (e.g., third) • Estimates	• "Put one wash cloth with each towel" (1:1). • "Which plate has more cookies?" • "Jane is first in line; Tom is last. Who is third in line?"
Addition and subtraction	• Counts all objects in two teacher-presented sets to add • Counts out objects to solve problem. • $N + 1$ • Finds missing addend by counting up $5 + \_ = 7$. • Same as above, but decomposes (subtracts)—for example, takes 2 away from set.	• Teacher puts down three red and two blue balls; student counts and says answer. • Same as above, but student gets balls out of box. • "Here are six pencils, make it seven." • May use number line starting at 5 moving up to 7.
Place value	• Bundle items into 10 and identify how many. • Indicate how many 1's or 10's on written two-digit numeral.	• Bundle 48 popsicle sticks into bundles of 10; find 4 bundles and 8 left. • Write the number using a place value chart with 10's/1's. • Identify how many 10's/1's when given number.

Students usually begin by learning to recite the numbers. Sometimes games or songs are used to reinforce this skill. Counting movable objects is easier than counting objects that cannot be moved. Counting items in a clear array is easier than counting scattered items. By investing time in teaching students to count, teachers are also building skills for other math concepts, such as counting to add or counting the next dollar in shopping.

Students also need experience in comparing sets to determine which is relatively larger. Comparisons also help students learn sequences (e.g., first, next, last) and ordinal numbers (e.g., first, second, third). These skills have wide applications across the curriculum and may be an IEP priority. For example, in language arts, the student may sequence parts of a story by what happened first, second, and third. After conducting a science experiment, the student may summarize the sequence of the experiment.

In the primary grades, teachers often introduce the concepts of addition (composing) and subtraction (decomposing) through the use of objects and pictures. Students typically count out separate sets of objects and then combine the sets to find the sum (i.e., "How many are there in all?"). In the beginning, these objects or pictures can be paired with the appropriate math symbols. Gradually, pictures are removed, and students practice the facts represented in standard horizontal equations (i.e., $3 + 4 = 7$).

One activity that can be used to scaffold students' understanding of composing and decomposing numbers is the use of a "magic box," in which a specific number of objects is placed in a box divided into two shallow compartments (Clements et al., 2004). Students count and observe a total number of objects being placed into the box. Then, the box is closed, shaken so that the objects are arranged in the two compartments, and then opened for students to discover the combination. The combination is recorded in a math sentence (e.g., $2 + 3 = 5$), and the activity is repeated. Students then open the box again to find a new combination and record the combination. As students record their combinations, they are guided to understand that the total quantity can be subdivided into different combinations. By doing this, students build a deeper understanding of the process and properties of addition.

> As first-grade students are working at a math station in their classroom, it is Sam's turn to select (at random) how many total objects will be put into the box. Sam uses a switch to operate a spinner labeled with numbers *1* through *5*. The spinner stops on *4*. Then the group counts out four items by placing each item on a number line as they count. With the help of a fifth-grade volunteer, Sam uses a preprogrammed four-button Cheap Talk device to "say" each number as the group counts aloud. When the volunteer asks the group, "How many __ are going in the box?" the students repeat the last number, and Sam answers with his Cheap Talk device, "four." Then the items are placed into the box, the box is shaken, and the volunteer opens the box and helps the students count items that landed in each compartment. Sam counts with the group, using a teacher-designed adapted keyboard (i.e., Intellikeys) overlay with numerals *1* through *5* to type each number, and then produces a written record of the group's findings when the activity is completed. The classroom teaching assistant observes the activity to record Sam's responses, when he is asked to identify a number, as independent correct, incorrect, or prompted.

Geometry

Young children often focus on comparing and naming basic shapes. These skills build spatial understanding and are an important focus in the early elementary grades. These may not be the most important skills to teach to older students. An essential skill addressed throughout a student's school career in geometry is the use of the coordinate plane to solve problems. Clements and Battista (1992) suggest that the coordinate plane is a framework for spatial organization and the foundation of spatial–geometric thinking (Sarama et al., 2003). Sarama et al. (2003) identify the ability to use maps and understand position in two-dimensional space as a skill to build on one's understanding of grids and coordinate systems. Further, understanding two-dimensional space through the use of grid structures, planes, and maps supports the development of spatial structuring, in which students are challenged to link prior sensory experience to current problem solving. Providing representations of such real-world contexts (i.e., a map of a neighborhood) has been shown to scaffold students' early stages of geometric thought while providing a structure through which to understand their surroundings (Sarama et al., 2003). One activity that has been used to introduce young children to the coordinate plane is Investigations Geo-Logo software (TERC, 2006), in which students control the movement of a turtle by entering coordinate points, angle measurements, and directions (i.e., using the right, left, up, and down arrows on the keyboard) to guide the turtle through a digital plane.

Dharna's third-grade class has learned about right (90 degrees), obtuse (> 90 degrees), and acute (< 90 degrees) angles. In her cooperative group, Dharna is using a specially designed adapted keyboard (i.e., Intellikeys) overlay to interact with the Geo-Logo software, which gives her access to the program's activities. The group's assignment is to find the most direct route from point A to point B and to visit three preprogrammed locations on the screen. Dharna uses her DynaVox augmentative communication device to contribute to the decision making as the group plans their route. Dharna and her group then use the Intellikeys overlay to enter and produce a written record of their directions. The teacher observes the group to obtain a baseline number of the responses that Dharna initiates during the 20-minute problem-solving period.

Data Analysis

In the context of data analysis, graphs are an important component of the NCTM (2000) curriculum. In mathematics literature, understanding graphs has been described as one of the "critical moments" in mathematical learning that bridge the gap between perceptual and conceptual knowledge (Leinhardt, Zaslavsky, & Stein, 1990). For example, graphs help students *see* the relationship between factors, such as the number of students who choose pizza over hamburgers in fifth-period lunch. Furthermore, graphs help students support their reasoning about abstract concepts across the curriculum, such as the relationship between inches of snowfall and income at a ski resort, drops of solvent needed to change acidity level of different solutions, or which chapters in a novel have more happy occasions than sad occasions. In addition, the ability to understand information in a graph was identified in a 1997 survey as an essential component of adult literacy. Specifically, the term "document literacy" was used to describe the ability to locate, interpret, and use information in a graph (Organization for Economic Cooperation and Development [OECD], 1997). Given the importance of data analysis and graphing skills in the math curriculum, NCTM included "representation," or "the ability to model and interpret physical, social, and mathematical phenomena" through the use of graphs, as a process skill to be developed throughout a student's school career (NCTM,

2000, p. 66). One activity used to promote a deeper understanding of creating and interpreting information on graphs is provided in a high school computer applications course (Public Schools of North Carolina, 2002). In this project, students investigate opinions on a current events issue, design and implement a survey to collect data, and then use graphing (Microsoft Excel) and presentation (Microsoft PowerPoint) software to present their findings.

> Tevaris's computer "app" study group has decided to ask students in their high school whether they think the school should add a salad bar in the cafeteria. Tevaris uses his AAC device to help the group develop a survey and uses switch scanning to access word prediction software (i.e., Clicker 5) in order to produce a hard copy of the group's final survey. Tevaris's job in collecting data is to record answers by accessing the preprogrammed database on a laptop with switch scanning: Computer scans icon for *girl*; Tevaris hits switch to select *girl* when interviewing a girl; computer scans icon for *no*; Tevaris hits switch to record *no* when the girl answers "no" to adding a salad bar to the cafeteria. Answers are automatically entered into the database on a worksheet. Tevaris then works with his group to generate graphs using the data he entered. The group decides to show those in favor of and opposing a salad bar by total responses and by gender. The group presents their findings, with Tevaris's closing remarks (using text-to-speech feature of the presentation software), of supporting the opinion that a salad bar should be added based on the overwhelming support shown by the student body.

Algebra

Recent research in preparing students with disabilities to participate in general education algebra instruction has focused on instructional strategies for developing effective lessons (Maccini & Hughes, 2000). Gagnon and Maccini (2001) found that successful interventions included: (1) a review of background knowledge (prerequisite skills, strategies, definitions); (2) explicit instruction in problem representation and solution; (3) explicit instruction in self-monitoring procedures; and (4) use of graphic organizers and manipulatives to aid in the process of solving and finding the solution to the problem. The authors based their use of strategy instruction on previous research in teaching computational and problem-solving skills to elementary students with learning disabilities. Specifically, a mnemonic device was developed to help students remember the steps in solving a problem: Search, Translate, Answer, and Review (STAR). When provided with graphic organizers and manipulatives, students depicted the process of problem solving, progressing from concrete objects (C) to drawings of the objects (R) to finally using abstract expressions (A) using numerals and operational symbols (CRA). Using the mnemonic device (STAR) and the CRA progression, students increased their accuracy in computation, solving word problems, accurate use of strategy, and ability to independently work through the CRA sequence. In another discussion of best pedagogical practices for teaching algebra to students with disabilities, Witzel, Smith, and Brownell (2001) also cite the use of the CRA sequence of instruction as an effective tool to depict components of an algebraic equation. They note that unknown quantities must also be represented in the sequence to develop better understanding of the process of basic algebra, such as "solving for *x*."

Algebra may seem like one of the areas of math that is especially inaccessible to students with severe disabilities. Students may need systematic instruction, with many repetitions of the same operation to master these skills. Jimenez et al. (2008) taught high school students with moderate developmental disabilities to use a nine-step algebra task analysis to complete a functional task. Students were able to successfully complete the math equation and solve for x after several days of systematic instruction in using manipulatives to solve the equation. The task analysis from Jimenez et al. (2008) is shown in Table 7.5.

One activity used to help students with and without disabilities understand balancing algebraic equations uses known number quantities represented by objects and unknown number quantities represented by an opaque cup, both placed on an equation mat (Foster, 1997). Given the equation, $y + 3 = 7$, the left side of the mat has a cup (to represent the unknown quantity of y) and three objects, followed by an equal sign drawn in the middle of the mat, and seven objects on the right side of the mat. Students are then guided to understand that whatever happens on one side of the equation must also happen on the other. Thus, to balance the given equation, students must learn to isolate the variable by using the inverse operation. Although this may seem like a complicated task to teach the students, the algebra mat allows a hands-on approach to learning this concept. Students learn to start with the side of the equation with the cup. In this case, students would start on the left side. Students are directed to take away the number of objects on the left side with the cup, which in this case is three objects. Then students are directed to take away the same number of objects from the right side of the equation, because what is done to one side of the equal sign mark must be done to the other side. The equation now shows y (cup) = 4 (four objects). In this way, students have progressed from using concrete objects

TABLE 7.5. 10-Step Task Analysis Used to Teach Lesson in Algebra

Teacher	Student
1. Reads story-based problem and problem statement.	1. Identifies problem statement.
2. Asks student to identify first fact from story (if unknown quantity, use x).	2. Identifies first fact from story (if unknown quantity, use x).
3. Asks student to identify second fact from story (if unknown quantity, use x).	3. Identifies second fact from story (if unknown quantity, use x).
4. Asks student to identify last fact from story.	4. Student identifies last fact from story.
5. Gives student opportunity to mark first fact with green marker.	5. Marks first fact with green marker.
6. Gives student opportunity to mark last fact with red marker.	6. Marks last fact with red marker.
7. Gives student opportunity to identify operation needed to solve problem.	7. Identifies operation needed to solve problem.
8. Gives student opportunity to use number line to count between green and red markers.	8. Uses number line to count between green and red markers.
9. Gives student opportunity to state solution to math problem ("$4 + x = 7$"; $x = 3$")	9. States solution to math problem ("$x = 3$").
10. Restates problem statement and asks student to restate solution to story-based problem ("How much did Jordan spend on pizza?").	10. Restates solution to story-based problem ("Jordan spent 3 dollars on pizza").

(e.g., cup and objects on mat) to the symbolic representation of the equation (e.g., $y = 4$), including the process of "balancing" one side of the equation with the other.

> Katy has five equations to balance for homework. With a sixth-grade math classmate, Katy works on her homework during "study time" in the after-school enrichment program they attend together. Each student has an equation mat with the materials needed to balance each equation. For each problem, Katy uses a task analysis adapted with picture symbols to self-monitor completion of each step of the problem. Katy's equation mat is also adapted with a number line along the bottom to help her count the objects correctly. If Katy and her "study buddy" have a problem or want to check their answers, they ask the after-school monitor for permission to log onto their teacher's website. The monitor helps them check their work when finished.

Measurement

Measurement is an area of math that assigns a numerical value to attributes found in the environment (i.e., length, weight, value, time). Because measurement skills involve the use of tools to assess such characteristics, this area of math is best learned using manipulatives (NCTM, 2000; Cass, Cates, Jackson, & Smith, 2002). This area of mathematics has many applications to skills of daily living. Students may use a scale to check their weight or to weigh an item to be shipped. In planning a work or craft project, a ruler may be used to measure materials. Measurement also includes money use and telling time. Researchers have used technology and community-based instruction to help students generalize money skills to real-life settings. The following section on functional math describes how to address money management and other related functional math skills.

FUNCTIONAL MATH

Money Management

The components of money management include: (1) knowing how much money one has (computation and record keeping), (2) knowing how to gain access to one's money (banking), (3) knowing how much money one can spend (budgeting), (4) knowing how to spend it (purchasing), and (5) knowing how to use money to make money (saving and investing; Browder & Grasso, 1999). Most of the research on teaching individuals with developmental disabilities to use money has focused on teaching them to know how to count and spend their money (Browder & Grasso, 1999).

Computation and Purchasing

Students with developmental disabilities may be highly motivated to learn how to use money to purchase preferred items. Computation and purchasing are an excellent starting point for instruction in money management and in functional math in general. Depending on the complexity of the money skills taught, students with a broad range of abilities can learn to use money and make purchases independently. A skill sequence for teaching money computation and purchasing is shown in Table 7.6.

TABLE 7.6. An Easy-to-Hard Skill Sequence for Teaching Money Computation and Purchasing

Money skill	Example	Reference
1. Use a preselected amount of money to make purchase.	Teacher places two $1 bills in wallet.	McDonnell & Laughlin (1989)
2. Use response classes for types of purchases.	Student learns to use quarters for vending machine, $1 bill for convenience store, and $5 bill for lunch.	Gardill & Browder (1995)
3. Use $1 bills only and compute next-dollar amount.	If purchase is $3.45, student says next dollar is "4," and counts out 4 $1 bills.	McDonnell & Ferguson (1988)
4. Use $1, $5, or $10 bill and compute next-dollar amount.	If purchase is $6.75, student says "7," selects a $5 bill, and counts up to 7.	Frederick-Dugan et al. (1991)
5. Compute coins counting by 5's.	Student learns to count nickels, then dimes, then quarters using counting by 5's.	Lowe & Cuvo (1976)
6. Discriminate money equivalence.	Student learns that two quarters and five dimes are the same.	Frank & Wacker (1986); Stoddard et al. (1989)
7. Read price and find exact money amount.	Given price $2.56, student selects two $1 bills, two quarters, a nickel, and a penny.	Cuvo et al. (1978)

When students have no counting or money recognition skills, purchasing can still be taught by accommodating for this skill deficit through preselecting the money amount needed. Such an accommodation may be the best approach when the learner is older (e.g., an adult) or needs to learn the concept that money is needed to gain access to goods.

A support person (e.g., teacher or paraprofessional) can help the individual with disabilities who cannot count money prepare for purchasing by placing the exact money needed in his or her wallet. For example, in teaching adults with severe mental retardation to purchase a snack in a fast-food restaurant or grocery store, McDonnell and Laughlin (1989) gave the person two $1 bills. Similarly, Storey, Bates, and Hanson (1984) gave adults with mild to severe mental retardation a $1 bill to purchase coffee. If the person lacks the fine motor skills to use a wallet, the money may be carried in a pocket or given to the person at the time of the purchase. At this first step in the money and purchasing skills sequence, the person is simply learning to exchange money for desired items.

Teaching Response Class

Many people in today's fast-paced society simplify their money management by making purchases with certain types of money. For example, when going to get gas, one might use two $20 bills. Or, when going to a fast food restaurant for lunch, one might select a

$10 bill. A $5 bill may be used to purchase coffee or a soda at a convenience store. People who choose to use specific bills may save their change to convert it into dollars later at the bank.

Similarly, individuals with severe disabilities can learn to associate specific denominations of money with classes of purchases. In Gardill and Browder (1995), three classes of money were taught. Students learned to discriminate between quarters, a $1 bill, and a $5 bill. Through tabletop instruction using picture examples, the students learned to select quarters for a variety of vending machine purchases, a $1 bill when going to a convenience store, and a $5 bill to buy lunch. As prices change, these skills need to be retrained. Many vending machines now take $1 bills, and some beverages in convenience stores cost more than $1. Despite the limitation that retraining will be needed as prices increase, the response-class method of teaching money use can foster independent purchasing for students who have not been able to learn strategies that require counting or other, more complex math skills.

Next-Dollar Strategy

The next-dollar strategy, also called the "one-more-than technique," involves giving the cashier one more dollar than the stated price. For example, Ayres, Langone, Boon, and Norman (2006) used a computer to help students learn to identify the next dollar for purchasing. In a "next dollar" strategy, students count out the dollars in the price and one more to cover the cents (e.g., $8.95 would be $9 and 1 more).

In teaching the next-dollar strategy, the teacher often begins with flash card training in a classroom setting. In their study, Colyer and Collins (1996) used 75 flash cards with prices from 1¢ to $5. They also used real money ($1 bills) and a variety of items that the students could buy during instruction. They surveyed the stores and found that cashiers always stated the price. Only in some settings was the price visible on the cash register. Based on this information, the teacher trained the students to select the next dollar amount based on the stated price. The teacher used a least-intrusive-prompting hierarchy, which encouraged use of the natural cues of the stated price and printed price (if available) as follows:

1. Teacher states price and waits for student to count out next dollar amount ("Five ninety-seven").
2. If no response, the teacher shows a flashcard with the written price ($5.97) and restates it verbally ("Five ninety-seven").
3. If no response, the teacher uses an expanded verbal cue that is sometimes used by cashiers ("Five dollars and ninety-seven cents").
4. If no response, the teacher gives explicit directions on how much is needed ("Five dollars and ninety-seven cents. Give me five dollars and one more for cents").
5. If no response, the teacher models how to count out the next dollar amount ("One, two, three, four, five, and one more for cents").

Sometimes the teacher may use a number line to help the student find the number that is one more than the stated price. The next-dollar strategy can be useful across a large variety of small purchases. The accommodation needed to use the next-dollar strategy is that the person carries only $1 bills in his or her wallet. Change that accumulates each week is converted into $1 bills at the bank.

When students master the next-dollar strategy, they may be able to master the use of mixed currency. When this strategy is used for more than minor purchases, it is more convenient to carry a mix of bills (e.g., $1, $5, and $10) than a large number of $1 bills. Denny and Test (1995) taught adults with moderate mental retardation to use the next-dollar strategy using mixed currency to make purchases up to $20. Students learned to count up from the highest bill they could use. They also learned to set aside a dollar for the next-dollar amount, rather than rounding up the price. This skill sequence is shown in Table 7.6. This extra dollar was set aside as the "cents pile."

The best way to teach students to apply their next-dollar strategy is through community-based instruction. Because it rarely is feasible to teach in community settings daily, teachers will need to develop classroom simulations of purchasing. For example, Ayres et al. (2006) used a computer to help students learn to round up to the next dollar for purchasing. Students might also view videos of purchasing or practice in a classroom store.

Debit Cards

For larger purchases, the person may learn to use a debit card. A debit card functions similarly to a credit card, but the transaction is deducted from the checking account like a check. To use a debit card, the person needs to be able to enter a personal identification number (PIN) or be able to sign his or her name to the credit slip. Individuals with severe disabilities may benefit from learning to use debit cards to make periodic purchases for items such as clothing and food. Debit cards can also be used in many places, such as to obtain cash from an automatic teller machine (ATM), to pay for haircuts, to buy movie tickets, and a wide variety of other uses.

> Mr. Andrews taught his class to make purchases using store flyers and real dollars. The student would select an item to buy and then practice counting out the needed dollars. For example, if the item were "$7.28," the student counted "1, 2, 3, 4, 5, 6, 7, and one more." He then had students practice with video recordings of purchases. Students would wait for the cashier to ring the items, then repeat the price and count out the next dollar amount. Mr. Andrews's plans for the next unit were to teach use of a debit card instead of dollars.

Coin Computation

In general education, students often learn coin recognition and computation as their first money skills. In the current economy, few items can be purchased efficiently with coins, because most cost more than a dollar. Even vending machines are converting to the use of dollars. Given this economic reality, it may not be a useful investment of time to teach individuals with developmental disabilities the complex skills of coin computation. In contrast, if students have mastered the use of currency (e.g., the next-dollar strategy with mixed currency), mastery of coin computation increases their flexibility and independence in money use. For example, students may gain skills needed to work as cashiers.

Lowe and Cuvo (1976) developed a simplified method to teach coin computation by teaching students to count all coins by fives, using their fingers for self-prompting. The skill sequence they used was the following:

1. Count nickels to a dollar by 5's, using the index finger ("pointer") to move and count each coin.
2. Count dimes to a dollar by 5's, using the index and middle finger to count each dime. (Make the "victory sign" with the fingers to count dimes.)
3. Count a mix of nickels and dimes, beginning with the dimes ("victory sign") and then the nickels ("pointer").
4. Count quarters by 5's using all fingers ("hi" sign).
5. Count a mix of quarters, dimes, and nickels by 5's.
6. Count pennies with the mix by counting all silver coins first, then "counting on" pennies by 1's.

Discriminating Money Equivalence

To have the maximum flexibility with money, individuals need to be able to use money interchangeably. For example, if an item costs $12.36, a shopper could use a variety of money amounts: (1) a $20 bill; (2) two $10 bills; (3) a $10 and a $5 bill; (4) a $10 and three $1 bills; (5) three $5 bills; and (6) a $10 bill, two $1 bills, and exact change. Not all students will master this level of complexity; they still can make purchases efficiently by using the next-dollar strategy. In contrast, students who master both using currency and computing coins may benefit from moving on in their money computation and purchasing skills to learn money equivalences.

Stoddard, Brown, Hurlbert, Manoli, and McIlvane (1989) used the principle of transitivity to teach stimulus equivalence for various combinations of coins to match prices. Participants were given prices on cards (e.g., 15¢) and coins and then were asked to construct a match. Students learned to make an exact match (e.g., a quarter to a quarter) and matched the coin(s) to a price (i.e., 25¢). Then they learned: (1) two dimes and a nickel, (2) two dimes and five pennies, and (3) five nickels. This complex research primarily focused on how levels of equivalence relationships were formed. To translate this into an instructional program, the teacher could teach the student to make pairs:

- Two $5 bills = $10 ($A = B$)
- One $10 bill = $10 ($C = B$)
- Two $5 bills = one $10 bill ($A = C$)

Based on the mathematical principal of transitivity—that if $A = B$ and $B = C$, then $A = C$—students might be able to match the two $5 bills with the $10 bill after learning the first two matches. Other matches to consider that use frequently used coins and currency are:

- Five $1 bills = one $5 bill
- Two $10 bills = one $20 bill
- Four quarters = $1
- One quarter = two dimes and one nickel

Using Exact Change

If a person stands at a cash register and observes the general public making transactions, it quickly becomes apparent that most people rarely use exact change to make purchases. Students can become completely independent in making purchases without having to use exact change. Two reasons some individuals *do* use exact change are to keep close track of their money and to avoid accumulating change. Individuals with severe disabilities may have limited resources. They may not always have a $5 bill to purchase lunch every day, but it may be possible to buy lunch for $2 or $3 each day by keeping close track of change. Individuals who master the use of coins and currency and have some understanding of money equivalences have the potential to learn to count exact change. Being able to compute exact change can also be a vocational skill if the person is interested in working as a cashier. Cuvo, Veitch, Trace, and Konke (1978) taught exact-change computation up to 50¢ in four response classes: (1) 1–4¢, (2) 5–9¢, (3) 10–45¢, and (4) 11–49¢. Students learned to count back change from a purchase from the lowest to the highest coin combination. For example, if the correct change was 16¢, the person would select a penny, nickel, and dime.

Record Keeping

Although the skills described here have focused on making purchases, they can also be utilized to teach individuals to count their money to know how much they have prior to planning purchases or outings. These money skills should correspond with the money strategy being taught. For example, individuals learning to count the next-dollar amount would count their money in ones. A support person (e.g., teacher or parent) would facilitate this by converting the money to $1 bills. Counting the amount of money on hand is a step toward the next money management skill of budgeting. Besides counting the money one has on hand, a second step to beginning to follow a budget is to keep a spending record. After each monetary transaction or at the end of the day, the individual can record the amount of money spent in a notebook or by using computer software such as Microsoft Excel. By recording even the smallest purchases, the person can gain awareness of where his or her money is going. Recording purchases requires having or acquiring skills in writing or typing numbers. As skill level in writing numbers increases, students can also learn to write out numbers in words to fill out checks (e.g., "Twenty-two dollars and 50/100—").

Budgeting, Saving, and Planning Purchases

Individuals with severe disabilities need to know not only how to spend money but also how to develop a budget in order to gain control over their own personal finances. A simple way to teach budgeting, which requires few to no computation skills, is to teach the person spending habits. For example, a young child may be given a money notebook with pockets for money for lunch, school pencils, savings, and toys. In a spending-habits approach, the child learns to take out the preselected amount each day for lunch. On Monday he or she may also take the pencil money (e.g., a quarter). Once a month, after receiving the allowance, he or she can buy a small toy. Similarly, an adult with disabilities can learn to pay all bills on payday, then divide what is left into budget envelopes for a one-time purchase (e.g., clothes or pleasure item), special monthly recreational activities (e.g., movies), weekly groceries, and daily cash for a soda. A budget for an individual who is paid every 2 weeks and who has $100 after paying the bills might look like this:

Example of a Simple Budget

Week 1 Envelopes:

Groceries	$50 (use debit card)
Special purchase	$20 (two $10 bills)
Daily snack	$14 (take out two $1 bills daily)
Lunch out 1 day	$10 (one $10 dollar bill)

Another alternative in teaching budgeting is to teach planned purchases. In planning purchases, individuals use store flyers and a calculator or number line to determine whether they can buy desired items. For example, Gaule et al. (1985) taught young adults with moderate and severe mental retardation to plan their grocery purchases using a number line. As each grocery item was selected from a shopping ad with pictures and prices of food, the number line, divided into intervals of 50¢ was shaded. The participants could select items as long as they did not exceed the number of squares they had on their number line. Matson (1981) also used a shopping aid, but foods were listed in columns by price from least expensive items (e.g., under 50¢) to more expensive items (e.g., $10).

Matson and Long (1986) and Nietupski, Welch, and Wacker (1983) also focused on planning grocery purchases, but they taught participants with moderate and mild mental retardation to use a calculator. Selected items were added on a calculator and subtracted from the budgeted amount. Frederick-Dugan, Test, and Varn (1991) used a similar procedure but focused on a broad range of purchases (food, clothing, and hygiene items). The participant learned that as long as the calculator did not register a negative value, the selected items could be bought.

A simple way to begin teaching planned purchases is to have students plan a single purchase. For example, a store flyer might be used for a discount department store (e.g., K-Mart). The student cuts out or circles possible items to buy on the next trip to that store (e.g., candy, cassette tape, and shirt). Each item is subtracted from the allowance for a special purchase (e.g., $10). Those that do not yield a minus sign can be filed as "can buy." Just prior to going to the store, the student can pick something from this file to buy.

Budgeting can also be encouraged by teaching comparison shopping. To be able to comparison shop, students need to be able to determine the lesser of two prices. Sandknop, Schuster, Wolery, and Cross (1992) taught students to select the lower priced grocery item. Semiautomatic price tags found in the community grocery store were used for instruction. A number line was used with the numbers arranged vertically so the student could see which number was "lower." Students first learned to compare prices in a skill sequence of prices that required the least discrimination (i.e., different first digit) to those that required the most discrimination (i.e., all digits but the last were different). Students worked through the task analysis until they were able to determine which price was lower. The teacher used a constant time-delay procedure, beginning with no delay of a model and verbal description. Once students got all steps correct waiting for the prompt, the delay level moved to 5 seconds.

Another aspect of budgeting is paying bills. LaCampagne and Cipani (1987) taught individuals with mild mental retardation to pay bills by focusing on the three skills of: (1) writing a check, (2) recording the check in a checkbook, and (3) preparing the bill to be mailed. To teach these skills, the teacher used real materials, including actual bills and checks. Each skill was task analyzed and taught with forward chaining in a group instruction format. For example, the first step was to enter the name of the payee on the check. All students were taught to perform this skill to mastery prior to introduction of the next step (e.g., writing the date).

A difficult money management skill for many people is saving money. Individuals with developmental disabilities will need specific savings goals to understand the purpose of this aspect of money management. For example, to purchase a sweatshirt that costs $30 in the budget shown earlier, the individual might forgo making a special purchase or using money for recreation for the first 2-week pay period in order to buy the sweatshirt at the beginning of the next pay period. To help the person visualize the savings goal, a picture of a sweatshirt could be drawn on an envelope or located on the Internet. The student can then paste on three miniature pictures of $10 bills. The person would check off each picture of a $10 bill as it is placed in the savings envelope. After the third $10 is obtained, the sweatshirt could be purchased.

Banking Skills

Most people keep their money in a bank rather than making all financial transactions with cash. Individuals with severe disabilities can also learn banking skills, such as making deposits and withdrawals. For example, Bourbeau, Sowers, and Close (1986) taught students with mild intellectual disability to make deposits and withdrawals in a classroom simulation, and then the students generalized these skills to a community bank. Students may benefit from self-instruction booklets to practice such skills as deposits, withdrawals, and balancing a checkbook (Cuvo, Davis, & Gluck, 1991; Zencius, Davis, & Cuvo, 1990). The books would have picture and word instructions for each step. It also can help students to state each numeral aloud before entering it in a check register (Wacker et al., 1988).

In recent years, people have begun to use ATMs more often than cashiers to do their banking. McDonnell and Ferguson (1989) taught both cashier and automatic teller skills to individuals with moderate mental retardation, implementing all instruction in the community. In contrast, Shafer, Inge, and Hill (1986) designed a simulated ATM machine because, if mistakes were made while training in the community, the machine could take the person's ATM card. The simulation was constructed out of plywood and had paper for the videoscreen messages and painted numerals.

TIME MANAGEMENT

A second important area of functional math is time management. Just as money management involves much more than knowing how to make a purchase, time management involves more than being able to state the time. Time management involves being able to conduct advanced plans (calendar planning), to develop and adhere to a daily schedule, and to determine when to make transitions to arrive at scheduled activities on time. To master these time management skills requires knowing not only how to read a clock and a calendar but also how to plan ahead. A skill sequence for time management is shown in Table 7.7.

Picture and Object Schedules

Some individuals may not be able to read numbers or drawings of clocks but may be able to learn to manage their daily schedule using pictures or objects. If using a picture schedule, the teacher may photograph the student performing each activity or use line drawings of activities. For an object schedule, the teacher should select an object associated with an activity (e.g., a swimsuit for swimming). Some individuals may learn to use symbolic objects for activities (e.g., a refrigerator magnet of French fries for dining out or a magnet of a computer for math class). Just prior to each activity, the teacher would have the student select the object or picture for that activity. For example, Browder, Cooper, and Lim (1998) taught adults with severe mental retardation who had no symbolic communication system to associate specific objects with activities. They used a golf ball for golfing, a towel for aerobics, a library card for the library, and a name tag for attending a club. Just prior to going to the activity, the teacher showed the person the target object and a distracter (e.g., a paper clip, stapler, etc.). Using constant time delay, the teacher physically guided the person to select the correct object. This was repeated 10 times before beginning the activity. After a few training days, the teacher pointed to the correct object and waited 4 seconds before using physical guidance during each of the 10 training trials. When students selected the correct object consistently, the teacher waited 4

TABLE 7.7. A Curriculum Sequence for Teaching Time Management

Skill	Example
1. Use pictures or objects to know what to do next.	Before each activity, student is shown a picture of the activity or object associated with it and then prompted to go to that area or get needed materials.
2. Use clock hand placement to know when to make transitions.	Student is given a drawing of a clock with the hands at 3:15 (e.g., both hands on the 3). The student learns to get his or her bookbag ready for the bus when the clock hands are in this position.
3. Use clock hands or digital times to follow a full day's schedule.	An employee begins each job task by matching digital times on schedule to times on watch and performs task for that time.
4. Use a calendar to create a schedule.	A young adult looks at wall calendar in morning and enters time she will be meeting a friend for lunch in a daily schedule book (e.g., Day-Timer).
5. Follow exact times during day using a digital watch.	Individual can state time when asked (reads four-digit time) and can initiate activity at a specific time (e.g., home economics begins at 9:23).
6. Read month, days, and year. Plan activities using a calendar.	An adolescent plans activities for March by filling in soccer practices and planning to go to the movies on March 14th.
7. Tell time using an analog clock or watch.	Child can read clock to know hour and minutes (e.g., may be taught to nearest quarter hour).

seconds before pointing to the correct choice. Once the participants mastered associating objects with their activities, then they were able to choose activities by using the objects.

In the TEACCH program for students with autism, an "object schedule" is used. An object is chosen for each activity of the day and displayed on some type of object board (Schopler, Mesibov, & Hearsey, 1995). For example, a set of shelves, a large travel case with clear compartments, or boxes might all be used to house the objects for each activity. Just prior to each activity, the student is prompted to remove the object that symbolizes what to do and to proceed to the area where the activity takes place. As students gain proficiency using life-sized objects, smaller, symbolic objects are introduced (e.g., a magnet with a miniature basketball for gym or a miniature hamburger for lunch). Later, pictures and words are introduced.

Using Distinctive Clock Pictures for Transitions

If individuals are unable to read numbers and tell time, they may be able to learn to recognize distinctive clock times. For example, the hands of a clock are together and pointing up at 12:00. They form a straight vertical line at 6:00. Learning to recognize these distinctive times can be easier than reading digital clock numbers for some individuals with severe disabilities. In this approach, the teacher makes a line drawing of clocks showing the time the person needs to begin a transition. For example, if the person needs to meet a 1:00 bus, the distinctive clock hands may be 12:30 (straight vertical line) combined with a natural cue (after the noon television news ends). Teachers can teach the person to "read" these clock times using the methods suggested for sight words in Chapter 5. For example, the teacher may show the times on flash cards and use time delay. Additional prompting may be needed at first for the person to follow the times during the actual daily schedule.

Following a Full Day's Schedule

Once students can recognize a distinct time to begin an activity, they may advance to learning to follow a full day's schedule by using distinctive analog clock times, a digital clock, or a watch. The teacher prepares a schedule showing the time to begin each activity. About five minutes before the target time, the teacher can begin prompting the person to watch for the time. For example, a least-intrusive-prompts sequence to begin a transition at 9:30 may be as follows:

1. At 9:25, teacher says, "It's about time for something new. Let me know when it's close."
2. At 9:29, teacher says, "What number will be in the middle on your watch?" If no correct response, "Watch for the 3 to come up in the middle!"
3. At 9:30, teacher says, "What time is it?" If no correct response say, "See the 3 in the middle and the 0 at the end, it's 9:30."
4. If student does not begin to move to area or get materials, teacher says, "What do you do at 9:30?" If student does not respond, tell the student and help get materials.
5. At any point, the student tells time and begins transition, teacher says, "Excellent time telling! Thanks for getting ready!!"

Use a Calendar to Create a Schedule and Calendar Reading

Whether or not individuals have learned to follow a full day's schedule, they may be able to master using a calendar to plan a special activity. Bambara and Ager (1992) taught individuals with moderate mental retardation to self-schedule a leisure activity. The participants used a calendar planner. Through role play of a task analysis to do planning and prompting, the participants learned to select a picture of a desired activity, place it on the calendar at the time they wanted to do it, and contact staff if support was needed (e.g., transportation). Each day, the participants checked their calendars for special preplanned events.

If the student is going to learn to use the calendar (see skill number 6 in Table 7.7), then some sight word instruction may be needed to teach him or her to read the names of the months of the year and days of the week. If students cannot read numbers, they may also practice reading the numbers of the days.

Telling Time on Analog Clocks

One of the most difficult time management skills is telling time using analog clocks. Although this skill is taught early in math series in elementary education, individuals with severe disabilities, who do not learn time telling in these early years, may benefit from the alternatives for time management shown in Table 7.7. By wearing a digital watch, individuals can avoid the need to learn to tell time on an analog clock. In contrast, students who have mastered reading numbers to 12 and can recognize some analog configurations of the clock may be successful in learning to tell time using an analog clock. The best approach to this time-telling instruction may be to follow a skill sequence. An early resource on telling time by Thurlow and Turnure (1977) suggested using this sequence: (1) discriminating the minute and hour hands, (2) telling time to the hour (o'clock), (3) telling time to the half hour, (4) telling time to the quarter hour, and (5) telling time to the minute. Students would be taught one skill in the sequence to mastery (e.g., hour vs. minute hand) before the next skill was introduced.

FINDING THE BALANCE

Some high school teachers may wonder how much time to invest in grade-appropriate mathematics content such as geometry and algebra versus teaching everyday math skills such as purchasing and other measurement skills. The solution may be to apply grade-appropriate skills in real-life contexts. That is, if the teacher begins with the grade-level standards but then finds activities for real-life applications (e.g., with the help of the math teacher), students may learn skills with daily use but not be limited in their opportunity to build conceptual knowledge. For example, in the curriculum Teaching to Standards: Math (Trela et al., 2008), students learn how to plot points on a plane using maps of a grocery store. This activity could be combined with making the simulated purchase.

RESOURCES FOR MATH INSTRUCTION

In the curriculum Touch Math (Bullock, Pierce, & McClellan, 1989) students learn to use touch points assigned to specific numbers in order to solve addition, subtraction, multiplication, and division problems. One study showed positive effects on first- and second-grade students' achievement on weekly computation assessments (Bielsker, Napoli, Sandino, & Waishwell, 2001).

Another published curriculum, Teaching to Standards: Math (Trela et al., 2008), uses story-based problems, graphic organizers, and systematic instruction to engage students in problem solving. Each unit teaches specific skills to solve problems contextualized in stories adapted with picture symbols to support key vocabulary and facts. As students progress through each unit (data analysis, algebra, geometry, and measurement), teachers fade prompts to build independent student problem solving.

MATH Connections was developed with a grant from the National Science Foundation (Berlinghoff, Sloyer, & Hayden, 1998). This curriculum contextualizes math problems found in daily life through integrated problem solving. Students in high school take Math Connections I and II together rather than separate algebra and geometry courses in ninth and tenth grades. A field test in Connecticut (Heuer, 2005) compared scores on the state test and found that students in Math Connections scored higher than students in traditional Algebra I classes on the end-of-course algebra exam (53 vs. 43% proficient, respectively).

CASE STUDY

Mr. Tyler's fifth-grade class was learning to conduct a survey and to summarize their findings using various methods of graphing. On the first day, students chose a topic for their survey and began to create questions. Jacob, a student with severe intellectual and physical disabilities, was a member of Mr. Tyler's class. He used pictures on a voice output communication device and eye gaze to make his responses known. He had some use of his right hand to slide objects on his lap tray. Jacob was continuing to improve his numeracy skills along with the grade-appropriate math. In particular, Jacob was learning to count to 20, to use the ordinal numbers from first to third, and to count sets to add.

After several students nominated ideas for the survey, Mr. Tyler asked Jacob what he would like to survey. Jacob used his picture communication book to point to "baseball," one of his favorite sports. Mr. Tyler added this to the list of possible topics. The class then voted on their choice of sports, music, or movie stars using index cards. To begin to introduce the idea of summarizing data, Mr. Tyler decided to have the students count, chart, and graph the votes by topic. A peer used a system of least prompts to help Jacob count the votes for each topic while the other students completed a worksheet. Jacob used his VOD to read each count, and Mr. Tyler put it on the board. He then asked students to complete a bar graph. Jacob completed his by using graphing software with the help of a teaching assistant. The class then compared the graphs to decide which topic would be surveyed. Jacob was asked to indicate which bar had "more" (review skill). As the class began to write questions for the survey, Jacob composed one question by selecting between some options developed by a peer. He then used the remaining time to summarize how the class developed a survey using his ordinal numbers to sequence what they did first, second, and third.

When class was over, it was time for Jacob to go to lunch. Jacob's school offered cafeteria-style food, a grill, and vending machines. Jacob was learning to select what type of lunch he wanted to purchase and to count out the next dollar for this purchase. On

Monday he chose to order a grilled cheese sandwich and juice drink at the grill. The cost was $4.50. With the help of his lunch buddy, he counted out "1, 2, 3, 4, and one more." Jacob also was in charge of telling his lunch group when it was time to head back to class using a small digital clock on his lunch tray. When the clock showed 12:46, Jacob would tap the clock with the side of his hand.

APPLICATIONS

1. With a peer partner, try to recall each of the content areas and processes of math and give one example of what might be taught under each.

2. Select a math skill from any content area. Write a math story using the guidelines in Table 7.2. Then develop a task analysis of how to perform that math operation.

3. Create IEP objectives for some of the basic numeracy skills shown in Table 7.4. Describe how you would embed these skills to teach an upper-level math skill such as finding the slope, completing an algebraic equation, or plotting the points on a plane.

4. With a partner, try teaching the next-dollar strategy. Then together develop a task analysis for teaching ATM use.

5. Develop a schedule for a student that coincides with a typical school day.

Write a task analysis to teach the student to follow the schedule.

CHAPTER 8

❧

Science

Fred Spooner, Diane M. Browder, and Bree Jimenez

The teacher had set up two clotheslines with a balloon attached to each one. "Let's race the balloons," she said. A student volunteer pushed one balloon down the line as the teacher let the air from the second balloon. With the release of air, the balloon whooshed down the line. The students laughed and cheered. She waited for a student to ask the obvious question. She then commented, "I wonder why one balloon went faster." Someone answered that she pushed it. "No, I didn't push it." "You blew on it!" one student guessed. "No, I didn't blow on it. Let's ask a question," she prompted. "What made the balloon ____ ?" A student used his AAC device to say, "Go fast?" "What made the balloon go fast?" the teacher repeated. Then she answered, "It was some kind of force." (She held up the word *force*.) "Let's decide what we know, want to know, and how to find out about force."

Since the late 1950s and the launch of the Russian satellite Sputnik, America has put special emphasis on the education of students in scientific concepts and discovery. To help students become competitive in a rapidly changing world, the National Science Foundation funded numerous curriculum projects in the decades that followed Sputnik, but expectations for students also continued to grow. *A Nation at Risk* (National Commission on Excellence in Education [NCEE], 1983) called for science education reform based on the mediocre report of educational performance of American students in scientific areas. In the years to follow, the American Association for the Advancement of Science (AAAS) initiated a project to develop a scientifically literate society by the year 2061, titled *Project 2061: Science for all Americans* (1989). The committee chose the target year 2061 because that is the year that Halley's Comet will be visible again from Earth (the last time was 1985). In 1996, the National Research Council (NRC) published the

National Science Education Standards (NSES). The purpose of this document was to establish "science standards for all students . . . regardless of age, gender, cultural or ethnic background, disabilities, aspirations, or interest and motivation in science" (NRC, 1996, p. 2). One of the common features of all of these reforms was the expectation for all students to gain scientific literacy.

The 1996 NRC writing especially emphasized science standards for *all* students. Ironically, it would be a decade before some of the earliest resources on teaching science to students with severe disabilities would emerge (Cooper-Duffy & Perlmutter, 2006; Courtade et al., 2007; Spooner, DiBiase, & Courtade-Little, 2006). The research literature on teaching science to students with severe disabilities has been sparse (Courtade et al., 2007). Educators are just beginning to discover effective and meaningful ways to teach this content to students who have severe developmental disabilities.

WHY TEACH SCIENCE TO STUDENTS WITH SEVERE DISABILITIES?

Although educators have taught daily living skills with some links to science concepts (Courtade et al., 2007), the goal of teaching science content per se is new. When the Russians launched Sputnik in 1950, America received a "wake-up call" to focus more on science education, but these innovations bypassed students with severe disabilities who were not yet receiving a public education. When the second alarm sounded in 1983 (NCEE, 1983), science innovations again bypassed most students with severe disabilities because special educators were thinking about skills for daily living, not academic content. Although science concepts *do* have relevance for daily living, they require being intentional about teaching the science, not just the activity. For example, students can learn to wash their hands without knowing what germs are, *or* they can learn specifically about these microorganisms. No Child Left Behind (NCLB, 2002) was the "wake-up call" to teach science to students with severe disabilities. For the first time, schools were required to report adequate yearly progress for all students in science. Under NCLB, students with significant cognitive disabilities were not exempt from this requirement but were required to take alternate assessments based on alternate achievement standards that linked to the general science standards (for more information, see Chapter 2).

POINT FOR REFLECTION

Do you think it is a good policy to teach and test all students in science? What outcome should be expected for students with severe disabilities?

Jimenez, Spooner, Browder, DiBiase, and Knight (2008) described a conceptual model for teaching science that is shown in Figure 8.1. In this model, the goal of science instruction is "wonder and understanding of the natural world and my place in it." One of the exciting aspects of teaching science is that it helps students gain awareness of the world around them. When students see butterflies, they may wonder about their life cycle (e.g., "Do butterflies have babies?"). Or when golf-ball-size hail hits the roof of the building, they may wonder, "What caused these big ice pellets?" Science offers students a way

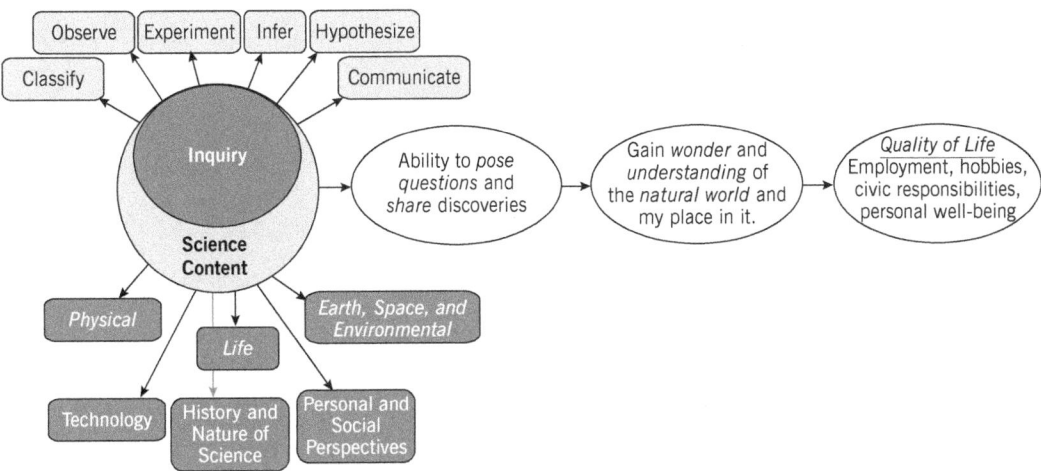

FIGURE 8.1. Conceptual diagram of science. Adapted from Jimenez, Spooner, Browder, DiBiase, and Knight (2008). Adapted with permission from the University of North Carolina.

to begin noticing the world, posing questions, and finding answers. Science can also have meaning and personal relevance to students with severe disabilities. A unit on the ocean might lead to lifelong hobbies, such as collecting shells or whale watching. A unit on the human body might provide deeper understanding of health care issues or options for a vocation. Cautions learned in chemistry might prove life saving (e.g., not to drink, smell, or mix unknown liquids). To accomplish these goals, science instruction needs to teach students to pose questions and share discoveries. As Figure 8.1 indicates, inquiry is the priority in this approach.

SCIENCE CONTENT

Figure 8.1 also indicates the primary content areas of science, which are physical science; life science; earth, space, and environment; technology; history and nature of science; and personal and social perspectives. These content areas have been articulated in the NSES published by the NRC (1996) and form the framework for most states' science standards. In general, the NSES describe the outcomes needed for scientific literacy.

In contrast, the authors of these standards (NRC, 1996) note that "different students will achieve understanding in different ways, and different students will achieve different degrees of depth and breadth of understanding depending on interest, ability, and context. But all students can develop the knowledge and skills described in the Standards, even as some students go well beyond these levels" (p. 2). To consider what to teach students with severe disabilities, educators can begin by gaining a deeper understanding of these major science standards. Table 8.1 lists the standards and content that are expected for each grade band in general education. These standards may need to be extended to make them accessible or meaningful for students with severe disabilities. For example, an eighth-grade student may encounter a physical and life science standard that calls for conducting investigations and utilizing technology and information systems to build an

TABLE 8.1. National Research Council (1996) National Science Education Standards

Unifying Concepts and Processes in Science

- Systems, order, and organization
- Evidence, models, and explanation
- Change, constancy, and measurement
- Evolution and equilibrium
- Form and function

Teaching Standard A: Science as Inquiry

K–4
- Systems, order, and organization
- Evidence, models, and explanation
- Change, constancy, and measurement
- Evolution and equilibrium
- Form and function

5–12
- Abilities necessary to do scientific inquiry
- Understandings about scientific inquiry

Teaching Standard B: Physical Science

K–4
- Properties of objects and materials
- Position and motion of objects
- The characteristics of organisms

5–8
- Properties and changes of properties in matter
- Motions and forces
- Transfer of energy

9–12
- Structure of atoms
- Structure and properties of matter
- Chemical reactions
- Motions and forces
- Conservation of energy and increase in disorder
- Interactions of energy and matter

Teaching Standard C: Life Science

K–4
- Life cycles of organisms
- Organisms and environments
- Light, heat, electricity, and magnetism

5–8
- Structure and function in living systems
- Reproduction and heredity
- Regulation and behavior
- Populations and ecosystems
- Diversity and adaptations of organisms

9–12
- The cell
- Molecular basis of heredity
- Biological evolution
- Interdependence of organisms
- Matter, energy, and organization in living systems
- Behavior of organisms

Teaching Standard D: Earth and Space Science

K–4
- Properties of earth materials
- Objects in the sky
- Changes in earth and sky

(cont.)

TABLE 8.1. *(cont.)*

5–8
- Structure of the earth system
- Earth's history
- Earth in the solar system

9–12
- Energy in the earth system
- Geochemical cycles
- Origin and evolution of the earth system
- Origin and evolution of the universe

Teaching Standard E: Science and Technology

K–4
- Abilities of technological design
- Understanding about science and technology
- Abilities to distinguish between natural objects and objects made by humans

5–12
- Abilities of technological design
- Understandings about science and technology

Teaching Standard F: Science in Personal and Social Perspective

K–4
- Personal health
- Characteristics and changes in populations
- Types of resources
- Changes in environments
- Science and technology in local challenges

5–8
- Personal health
- Populations, resources, and environments
- Natural hazards
- Risks and benefits
- Science and technology in society

9–12
- Personal and community health
- Population growth
- Natural resources
- Environmental quality
- Natural and human-induced hazards
- Science and technology in local, national, and global challenges

Teaching Standard G: History and Nature of Science

K–4
- Science as a human endeavor

5–8
- Science as a human endeavor
- Nature of science
- History of science

9–12
- Science as a human endeavor
- Nature of scientific knowledge
- Historical perspectives

Note. Data from National Research Council (1996).

understanding of chemistry. A student with a severe disability may work toward this goal by identifying chemical reactions in normal daily activities (e.g., spoilage [curdling] of milk; apple slice + air = browning; oxygen + iron = rust).

In Table 8.2, examples are provided of how to take a general education standard and teach multiple inquiry lessons to support the "main idea" or concept. The discovery statement (concept) is embedded in the lesson to provide the student an opportunity to gain concept knowledge. Students also learn key vocabulary needed to communicate about the concept. The inquiry process allows students to acquire skills for discovery. When all of these components are placed together in science instruction, the student is not only exposed to the science content but also has a chance to participate in a meaningful way to gain greater depth of understanding.

In teaching science, teachers may need to differentiate instruction for students at different levels. Chapter 2 described a method called "Work It Across" to extend a standard for students who may be beginning instruction at three levels. Figure 8.2 provides an example of differentiating expectations for a standard of recognizing that the Earth's surface is made of water, land, and living things. In this lesson, the students are specifically demonstrating their knowledge of soil, water, and rocks by comparing them using a Venn diagram. The general education expectation is that students will compare and contrast characteristics of water, soil, and rocks. Beginning with the general curriculum expectations, students will create a Venn diagram to compare and contrast the earth materials by attributes. Students at each symbolic level should be expected to perform the same targeted skills using alternate achievement standards. For students to demonstrate knowledge, instruction is differentiated so that all students will compare earth materials by attributes (e.g., hard, dry) using a graphic organizer. Some students will use words, pictures, or even actual objects to demonstrate that soil may be dry and made up of small particles, like bread crumbs.

HOW TO TEACH SCIENCE

The breadth and depth of science content as represented in state standards can be overwhelming. As described in the prior section, an important starting point is to determine priorities for student learning by choosing the "big ideas" from the different strands of content and extending the standard in collaboration with a general educator. The general education lesson plan in science also can be developed to be inclusive of students with severe disabilities by applying UDL (Center for Applied Special Technology [CAST], 1998; Orkwis, 2003). Additional strategies to promote science learning include teaching (1) vocabulary to communicate about science, (2) science concepts, and (3) the process of inquiry. Some newer research provides guidance for how to teach each of these skills.

Apply UDL

Special educators will often need to rely on the general science teachers' deep knowledge of science content in planning instruction. Through collaboration, universally designed lessons may be created that are applicable for all students (for more information on

(text resumes on page 211)

TABLE 8.2. Content Standards, Alternate Achievement, Inquiry Task Analysis, and Vocabulary Used in Science

National Standard (NSES-based on 5th–8th grade band)	Competency goal(s) from state standard course of study standards	Alternate achievement standards	Discovery statement embedded into instruction as "big idea"	Inquiry task analysis and vocabulary assessed by unit (word and picture symbols)
Science as inquiry: Abilities necessary to do scientific inquiry. Understanding about scientific inquiry.	• Identify and create questions and hypotheses that can be answered through scientific investigations. • Develop appropriate experimental procedures for: given questions, student-generated questions. • Apply safety procedures in the laboratory and in field studies: Recognize potential hazards. Manipulate materials and equipment. Conduct appropriate procedures. • Analyze variables in scientific investigations: Identify dependent and independent. Use a control. Manipulate. Describe relationships between. Define operationally. • Analyze evidence to: Explain observations. Make inferences and predictions. Develop the relationship between evidence and explanation. • Prepare models and/or computer simulations to: Test hypotheses. Evaluate how data fit.	The learner will choose questions, choose procedures with guidance, follow safety procedures, observe, collect data (use measurement tools), analyze data, and communicate results in scientific investigation.		Teacher asks/Students respond: *Engage* 1. Shows object/picture: "What is it?" 2. "What do you think it is?" 3. "What do we know about it? 4. "What do we want to know about it?" *Investigate and describe relationships* 5. "How can we find out?" 6. Prediction 7. Conduct experiment 8. "What is the same about the materials?" 9. "What is different about the materials?" *Construct explanation* 10. Scientific discovery statement *Report* 11. "What did we learn?" "Why?" 12. Summarizing question *(cont.)*

207

TABLE 8.2. (*cont.*)

National Standard (NSES-based on 5th–8th grade band)	Competency goal(s) from state standard course of study standards	Alternate achievement standards	Discovery statement embedded into instruction as "big idea"	Inquiry task analysis and vocabulary assessed by unit (word and picture symbols)
Physical science: Properties and changes in properties in matter.	• Understand that both naturally occurring and synthetic substances are chemicals. • Evaluate evidence that elements combine in a multitude of ways to produce compounds that account for all living and nonliving substances. • Identify substances based on characteristic physical properties: density, boiling/melting points, solubility, chemical reactivity, specific heat. • Identify the reactants and products of chemical reactions and balance simple equations of various types: single replacement, double replacement, decomposition, synthesis.	Observe and investigate the effects of chemicals on human health and conditions. Explore, observe, communicate, and investigate chemical/physical changes within a system: temperature, mass, volume, precipitate (iron nail in water), solubility (what dissolves in water), gas production, chemical reactions.	• Solute + solvent = solution • Some mixtures have a chemical reaction. • Solutions can cause different chemical reactions. • Solutes dissolve faster in hot solvents. • Some chemical solutions are harmful. Some chemical solutions are helpful.	*Solute* *Solution* *Solvent* *Chemical* *Chemical reaction*
Life science: Structure and function in living systems. 9–12th grade The cell	• Investigate and describe the structure and functions of cells, including cell organelles, cell specialization, communication among cells within an organism. • Investigate and analyze the cell as a living system, including maintenance of homeostasis, movement of materials into and out of cells, energy use and release in biochemical reactions. • Investigate and describe the structure and function of enzymes and explain their importance in biological systems.	Observe and demonstrate knowledge of the structure and function of the molecular and cellular basis of life: cells, maintenance of homeostasis.	• Living things have cells. • Cells have parts. • Cell division makes living things grow. • Soap helps remove bacteria that cause disease. • To stay healthy we need good nutrition. Good nutrition builds healthy cells.	*Cells* *Bacteria* *Cell division* *Disease* *Nutrition*

| Earth and space science: Structure of the Earth system, Earth's history. | • Examine evidence that atmospheric properties can be studied to predict atmospheric conditions and weather hazards: humidity, temperature, wind speed and direction, air pressure, precipitation, tornados, hurricanes, floods, storms.
• Describe how humans affect the quality of water: point and nonpoint sources of water pollution.
• Assess evidence to interpret the order and impact of events in the geological past: relative and absolute dating techniques, statistical models of radioactive decay, fossil evidence of past life.
• Evaluate the forces that shape the lithosphere, including crustal plate movement, folding and faulting, deposition, volcanic activity, earthquakes.
• Explain the model for the interior of the Earth.
• Analyze the historical development of the theory of plate tectonics.
• Investigate and analyze the importance and impact of recycling. | Observe, describe, and investigate weather. Observe, describe, and investigate water properties and human impact on water resources. Observe and describe evidence of the geological and biological past. Describe forces and processes that shape the earth. Observe and describe geological processes (volcanoes, earthquakes, tsunamis, plate tectonics, rock formation, minerals, etc.). Conservation/stewardship/maps. | • When the liquid in clouds gets too heavy, the liquid falls out as precipitation.
• When water is heated, it changes into steam; this is called evaporation.
• Steam is cooled and turns into water; this is called condensation.
• Putting something in our water that harms living things is pollution.
• Using less water is conservation.
• The Earth has layers.
• Fossils are imprints that tell us about the past.
• Plate movements cause changes in the earth's crust
• Earth's layers can help us learn a fossil's age.
• Many materials can be used again. Recycle means to use again. | *Precipitation*
Evaporation
Condensation
Pollution
Conservation
Layers
Fossil
Core
Crust
Recycle |

Note. From Courtade, Jimenez, Trela, and Browder (2008). Copyright 2008 by Attainment Company. Reprinted by permission.

Standard: Earth and Space Science: Structure of the Earth System

Essence of the standard: Identify properties of the Earth's materials.

Grade level: 2

On grade-level expectation (not adapted)	Abstract symbolic	Concrete symbolic	Beginning with symbols
		Teaching activities	
Describe characteristics of water, rocks, soil (compare and contrast using Venn diagram).	Describe different characteristics of each material (one at a time) using a bubble map and picture cues or objects for abstract representations (e.g., hard, dry). Verbal prompts and kinesthetic opportunities should be provided when needed.	Given a bubble map with no more than three bubbles and two picture cues or object representations (e.g., sand and humus for soil) at a time, identify the correct characteristic of the material (e.g., for soil, the choices could be bread crumbs or paper clips) using a model on the map if needed.	Given a bubble map with no more than three bubbles and two object representations (e.g., bread crumbs for soil) at a time, match the correct characteristic of the material (e.g., for soil, the choices could be bread crumbs or paper clips) to the material in the bubble map.
		How student shows mastery	
Complete a Venn diagram.	Complete a bubble map for each type.	Identify the characteristics for each material.	Match the characteristics.

FIGURE 8.2. "Work It Across" example for Earth and space science.

UDL, see Chapter 3). Planning may focus on (1) how to represent the material so the student can access it more fully (e.g., text summaries of chapter or objects to add understanding), (2) ways to engage the student in the lesson (e.g., having all students work in groups to create a model), and (3) alternatives for students to demonstrate learning (e.g., some students may write a summary; others may select pictures to complete a statement of the primary concepts). To further promote active engagement, the naturally existing supports in inclusive classrooms should be utilized. Experts note that adult-delivered supports may be overused and may hinder the social and academic benefits that support teams plan for students with severe disabilities (Carter & Kennedy, 2006). One of the unique opportunities inquiry science provides is for students with disabilities to participate with their peers without disabilities, with little to no adaptations. Due to the hands-on learning approach of inquiry-based science, naturally occurring peer interaction can provide an opportunity for academic learning, as well as social interaction, for all students.

Here is how a universally designed lesson with peer supports might be designed. A sixth-grade biology class was going to use observations of bread mold to infer conditions that contribute to the growth of mold. After looking up information on mold on the Internet, the student groups were to write hypotheses about what contributes to the growth of mold. The students would then plan an experiment to test their hypotheses (e.g., putting wet bread in the dark). To make the concept of mold more accessible, the teacher might create a model of bread mold that the student groups could examine closely (not real mold, because of health concerns). By working with a partner, the student with severe disabilities could be fully engaged in the Internet search. The model would provide a frame of reference for understanding pictures shown on the Internet site. The student with severe disabilities may also need some concurrent training in the key vocabulary word or symbol to be used to communicate the hypothesis (e.g., *mold, wet, dark, grows*). Whereas some students might write their hypotheses on a worksheet, others might respond by circling a picture to complete the sentence (e.g., "I think mold grows in _____ places"). Students still learning to use picture and word symbols might demonstrate where they think the mold will grow by preparing the bread for the experiment for their student group (e.g., wetting it). After several days, the student work groups would confirm or refute their hypothesis by observing the bread samples. For example, the students might write a checkmark or "X" next to their statement.

Research Example

Dymond et al. (2006) illustrated how these UDL principles can be applied in a qualitative study in a high school science class. Each week a traditional science lesson was redesigned using principles of UDL and then implemented in the classroom. The team considered several questions related to curriculum, instructional delivery, student participation, materials, and assessment. For example, to promote student participation, the team considered ways to provide choices and self-directed learning activities, to promote active engagement, and to structure the lesson so that all students could be involved in teamwork or peer teaching. One of the greatest changes that occurred as the team implemented the redesigned lessons was that the paraprofessional's role expanded from one-on-one assistance to the students with severe disabilities to helping a small group that included a student with severe disabilities.

Teach Vocabulary to Communicate about Science

All students, including those with severe disabilities, need to expand their vocabulary to be able to communicate about the information learned in science. Often this learning can be promoted for students with severe disabilities by using the same methods that have been effective for teaching sight word vocabulary (for more information on methods to teach sight words, see Chapter 5). In teaching any vocabulary, it is important for students to demonstrate the meaning of the word, as well as to recognize it. Some students may learn the vocabulary best if given a word–picture combined symbol; some may learn the word alone (without a picture); and others may use objects that have been labeled with words. To show comprehension, students may match the word to a picture or pictures (e.g., match the word *precipitation* to pictures of rain, sleet, snow) or use it in a sentence (e.g., "Rain, sleet, and snow are forms of _____"). One of the most effective ways to teach sight words is to use time delay (Browder, Ahlgrim-Delzell, et al., 2009). For example, the teacher might display four words and ask the student to point to the target word ("Show me 'precipitation'"). During the first trials, the teacher would immediately show the student the correct response to prevent errors. During subsequent trials, the teacher would delay this prompt by a few seconds (e.g., 4 seconds) to give the student the opportunity to anticipate the correct response (for a detailed illustration of time delay, see Chapter 5).

Research Examples

McDonnell et al. (2006) demonstrated how a constant time-delay procedure could be embedded in the general classroom curriculum to teach vocabulary. Four students with developmental disabilities learned to verbally define five words taken from their general education classroom curriculum through a constant time-delay procedure that was used in their inclusive context. Two of the four students focused on the acquisition of science vocabulary (e.g., *atom, biosphere, element,* and *molecule*). The embedded instruction was as effective as a comparative small-group instructional format. Similarly, Johnson and McDonnell (2004) taught general educators to embed sight word instruction in several content areas, including science, when instructing students with moderate developmental disabilities in inclusive settings.

Another alternative is to intersperse new words with known vocabulary to build student success. Browder and Shear (1996) taught weather words by intermixing new words with known vocabulary in a rapid flash-card drill. Students read aloud simple passages using the newly acquired weather words to demonstrate fluency.

Focus on Understanding

An easy mistake to make in science instruction is to teach it like a foreign language—that is, so that the focus of instruction becomes only acquiring the science sight word vocabulary. Such instruction might not even include comprehension but just science "word naming." When science instruction is at its best, students gain deep understanding of the vocabulary through hands-on experiences. For example, to teach the concept of precipitation, students might create "rain" using water to fill a sponge to understand how heavy clouds create rain (Courtade, Jimenez, Trela, & Browder, 2008). In order for the science vocabulary to be meaningful, students need to use it to communicate about their natural world as they experience it. After dissolving a powder in water, the student may label each item with newly acquired vocabulary: *solute* (powder), *solvent* (the water), and *solution* (the combination).

Teach a Generalized Concept

Students can use this newly acquired vocabulary to communicate the science concepts they are learning. Concept learning can be defined as the recognition that an object, event, action, or situation is part of a class that share the same feature or set of features (Kame'enui & Simmons, 1990). Concepts require broader generalization than simple fact statements. For example, understanding the range of hues that form the concept "red" is more complex than understanding that the stop sign is red.

One way to define a priority in a science lesson is to write a concept statement that is the "big idea" of the lesson. Some of the concept statements included in the curriculum *Teaching to Standards: Science* (Courtade et al., 2008) are shown in the next to last column in Table 8.2 as "discovery statements." To check for generalization of learning, a teacher could have a student identify a concept with a variety of materials used across an investigation. This technique is called multiple exemplar training. Multiple exemplar training has been used for students with moderate and severe disabilities to teach daily living skills (Taylor, Collins, Schuster, & Kleinert, 2002), affective behavior with children with autism (Gena, Krantz, McClannahan, & Poulson, 1996), vocational skills (Horner, Eberhard, & Sheehan, 1986), and other functional and communication skills. For example, to teach a student the concept that solutes dissolve faster in heated liquids, the teacher might use a bouillon cube in hot and cold water, sugar in hot and cold tea, and rock salt in broth.

Students may also need instruction to learn concepts that relate to attributes of materials to be described during the experiment. Being able to describe changes, size, color, and even "same" and "different" may require some direct instruction in these concepts. Kame'enui and Simmons (1990, pp. 148–197) give several guidelines for how to teach concepts. These experts recommend using a variety of materials from the concept set to be learned (e.g., a variety of big objects). Some varied objects that do not match the examples (small objects) are also selected. The teacher then sequences and presents the example objects and the other objects, followed by a check for student understanding. Figure 8.3 gives an example of a script that might be used to teach similarity and difference.

Research Example

Jimenez, Browder, and Courtade (2009) applied multiple exemplars to teach science concepts to students with moderate developmental disabilities. Three middle school students with moderate intellectual disability learned to self-direct a 12-step task analysis to complete inquiry lessons in chemistry and physical science. Students were taught to use a self-directed learning prompt (KWHL chart) to complete an inquiry lesson independently. Figure 8.4 provides an example of the KWHL chart used. All three students were able to show mastery across materials, science concepts, and instructional settings (i.e., both special education and general education classrooms.

Objective: Given one example and one nonexample of the concept, students will show whether each is an example or nonexample with 100% accuracy.

Materials: Materials will come from the lessons. For example, for teaching the concept of "different" during a lesson on rocks, the teacher will need three different-looking rocks, and three similar-looking rocks ("not different").

Tips: 1. For students who are able to respond, ask them how and why they know the answers.
2. During the "test" phase, students will be identifying the correct answer out of a total array of four (the correct answer and three distracters). Students will find an example and a nonexample for each.

Step 1: Framing

Example	Wording	Student Response
Hold up different-looking rocks.	"Today we are going to find 'different.' Listen again. Today we are going to find 'different.' What are we going to find? _____."	Student communicates "different" (says or uses AT).

Step 2: Model "My Turn"

Example	Wording	Student Response
Show one example for different (positive example, e.g., two different-looking rocks; pencil and marker; book and telephone).	"This is different."	Attends.
Show another example for different (positive example).	"This is different."	Attends.
Show a nonexample (e.g., similar rocks; two pencils; negative example).	"This is not different."	Attends.
Show a third example for different (positive example).	"This is different."	Attends.
Show a nonexample (e.g., similar rocks; negative example).	"This is not different."	Attends.

Step 3: Lead "With Me"

Example	Wording	Student Response
Show one example of different (positive example).	"This is different."	Points to object or says "different."
Show another example of different (positive example).	"This is different."	Points to object or says "different."
Show a nonexample (negative example).	"This is not different."	Points to object or says "not different."
Show a third example of different (positive example).	"This is different."	Points to object or says "different."
Show a nonexample (negative example).	"This is not different."	Points to object or says "not different."

(cont.)

FIGURE 8.3. Using direct instruction to teach students the concept of "different."

Step 4: Test "Your Turn"

Example	*Wording*	*Student Response*
Show an array of one different, and three "not different."	"Find the different one."	Points to the different item or says "different."
Show an array of three different and one "not different item."	"Find the one that is *not* different."	Points to the nondifferent item.

Error Correction

Example	*Wording*	*Student Response*	*Teacher Response*
Show an array of one different and three "not different" items.	"Find the different one."	Correct: Points to the different item or says "different."	"Different. Good!" (label the item and praise).
Show an array of one different and three "not different" items.	"Find the different one."	Incorrect: Points to the nondifferent item.	"Different. You point." (Student points to correct item or teacher guides to correct one.)

Repeat Step 3 and 4 until the student can find an example and nonexample (e.g., different and not different).

FIGURE 8.3. *(cont.)*

KWHL Chart			
What do we **K**now?	What do we **W**ant to know?	**H**ow can we find out?	What did we **L**earn?

FIGURE 8.4. An example of a KWHL chart. From Courtade et al. (2008). Copyright 2008 by Attainment Company. Reprinted by permission.

Teach the Process of Inquiry

Although having the vocabulary to communicate about science and an understanding of concepts is important, the most important goal of science is for the student to master the process of inquiry itself. By learning the process of inquiry, students have a lifelong method to use to discover phenomena in the natural world. The NRC (1996) defines inquiry as "a set of interrelated processes by which scientists and students pose questions about the natural world and investigate phenomena; in doing so, students acquire knowledge and develop a rich understanding of concepts, principles, models, and theories" (p. 214). Inquiry emphasizes an "active process" in which students are directed to make observations, pose questions, examine sources to see what they already know, plan investigations, use tools to gather data, propose predictions, and communicate results. According to the NSES, inquiry is a critical component of a science program, requiring a problem-solving process as well as hands-on activities. Because inquiry has been identified as the recommended mode of science content acquisition, it is important to prepare students with severe disabilities to gain science content through this mode.

Research Examples

Inquiry requires a "hands-on" approach to science. Mastropieri et al. (2006) used class-wide peer tutoring and compared hands-on activities with. Teacher-directed instruction for students with mild disabilities in an inclusive eighth-grade science classroom. Not only did students involved in the collaborative hands-on activities enjoy the activities, but they also performed better on middle school science content posttests than the control group. Because there has been little research on science with students with severe disabilities, there are few studies on inquiry. Courtade, Browder, Spooner, and DiBiase (2010) developed a method to prepare teachers of students with developmental disabilities to implement an inquiry-based science lesson by following a task analysis. The participating teachers were able to address a middle school science curriculum (e.g., forces of motion, chemistry) by using this inquiry-based task analysis as a framework for the lessons. The students also increased their independent responses on student versions of the inquiry task analysis. These were responses made after the teacher set up each step (e.g., asking "How are these materials the same?"). Browder et al. (2010) conducted a study in which students were taught science concepts through inquiry lessons with systematic instruction. Teachers used a task analysis to instruct students to participate in science inquiry lessons, to answer questions, and to identify new science concepts and vocabulary. Table 8.3 provides a summary of what students learned in this study, including the steps for the process of inquiry.

Directed Inquiry

When using an inquiry-based approach in science, instruction may be a teacher-directed process or open ended. For students with severe disabilities, instruction may be needed on participating in a teacher-directed process and on how to self-direct this process. To teach students to participate in inquiry, a task analysis similar to the one in Table 8.3 might be used. In this lesson, the teacher is guiding the students through each step, and the student makes a specific response. Students who are not able to generate an answer

TABLE 8.3. Inquiry-Based Science Task Analysis

Teacher	Student
1. Presents engaging materials (e.g., chrysalis of a caterpillar).	Looks/touches materials.
2. Asks student, "What is it?" or encourages student to ask the question.	Identifies the materials or asks, "What is it?" (May use voice output AAC to ask question.)
3. Asks student, "What do you know about these materials?"	Describes object. If unable to answer, teacher may give several response options from which to select (e.g., pictures for "on a stick" [correct answer], "in the water," "makes noise," "smells odd").
4. Fills in the K ("know") on KWHL chart.	Verbally answers, text points, or uses AAC.
5. Asks student, "What do you want to know about it?"	Asks a question about the material. If unable to answer, teacher models some questions (e.g., "Can we eat it?", "Where did you get it?", "What's inside?"). If student doesn't ask, "What's inside?" teacher adds this question.
6. Fills in the W ("want to know") on the KWHL chart.	Verbally answers, touches, Velcro, stamp, eye gaze, AAC.
7. Asks student to predict what will happen when he or she performs the action from #5.	Makes a prediction. If student does not guess what will happen, teacher models several guesses and has student select one.
8. Ask student "How will we find out?"	Suggests an action. If student has no ideas of what to do, teacher gives options (e.g., "Touch it," "Put it in the light," "Look inside," " Read about it"). There may be more than one right answer to try.
9. Fills in the H ("how") on KWHL chart.	Verbally answers, touches, Velcro, stamp, eye gaze, AAC.
10. Guides student through conducting the experiment	Participates in experiment (e.g., carefully peels open the chrysalis. Have another one for comparison).
11. Asks student to compare the changed material with the original. "What is the same? What is different?"	Indicates any changes. If student does not recognize what is newly discovered, teacher may model response (e.g., "This one is open. This one shows the butterfly").
12. Has student complete and read a concept statement.	Reads (points to) concept statement. "A chrysalis contains a _____" (butterfly).
13. Fills in L ("learn") on KWHL chart.	Verbally answers, touches, Velcro, stamp, eye gaze, AAC.
14. Has student relate the statement to the experiment and review experimental results.	Restates or reenacts the experiment (e.g., pantomimes opening the chrysalis).
15. Asks a question that student answers using the concept statement (e.g., "What is inside a chrysalis?").	Answers question about concept. "A chrysalis contains a butterfly."

might need a response board for science like the one shown in Figure 8.5. Some students may require actual objects to respond to questions as they build their symbolic understanding. Students may point to or gaze at objects to answer questions, indicate preferences, or make predictions throughout inquiry lessons. A directed-inquiry approach might be used with young students, for experiments that require close teacher attention, or for difficult concepts.

RESEARCH EXAMPLES

An important goal for science will be to teach students to self-direct their inquiry process. In a self-directed approach, the student is able to apply the processes, such as posing questions and summarizing outcomes. Agran et al. (2006) investigated the effects of the SDLMI on academic achievement with three junior high school students with moderate to severe disabilities. Target goals were selected by students pertaining to scientific inquiry, body system and functions, and map skills. These academic skills were measured by students' ability to identify self-directed learning strategies that would assist them in the attainment of their target goals (e.g., for science inquiry the student would identify activities done in a lab, such as gathering materials or recording information in a log).

TEACHING STUDENTS TO SELF-DIRECT THE INQUIRY PROCESS

To apply the ideas from research, the teacher should begin by deciding what aspects of the process the student will direct. Agran et al. (2006) suggests that the student might plan what to do in a future lesson (e.g., what materials to gather, which type of log to use to summarize outcomes). Or the teacher may train the student to use self-instructional materials, such as the KWHL chart, to self-direct each part of a lesson. Having skills such

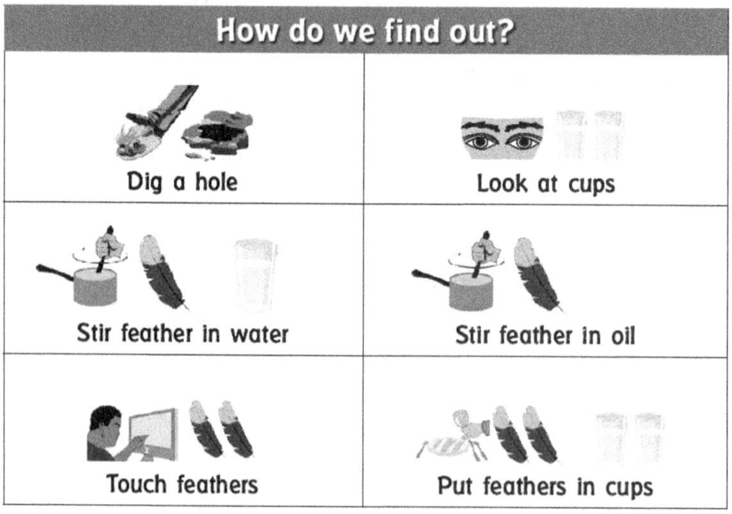

FIGURE 8.5. Inquiry lesson response board. From Courtade et al. (2008). Copyright 2008 by Attainment Company. Reprinted by permission.

as being able to fill in a KWHL chart may make it possible for a student to participate actively in a wide variety of science learning in the general education setting.

FINDING THE BALANCE: INQUIRY-BASED VERSUS ERRORLESS LEARNING APPROACH

Typically, it has been good practice to use an errorless learning approach in teaching students with severe disabilities new skills; however, when teaching inquiry-based science lessons, student discovery is promoted. To make discoveries, students need the opportunity to guess and use trial and error. For example, the student may answer questions incorrectly initially or make wrong predictions about what may happen in an experiment. In a well-designed inquiry lesson, students will learn both to hazard a guess and to correct or confirm their perceptions after gaining more information. In science education, it is possible to have rote learning and participation (e.g., "This is the sun. It is hot"). Rote responses may be appropriate at specific points in a lesson. For example, when teaching a student new vocabulary that will be used in a unit of instruction, errorless learning would be an effective strategy to use to promote sight word recognition and picture matching. Teachers might also use systematic prompting to teach students to formulate each response of a task analysis in the inquiry process (e.g., modeling how to ask questions or perform the experiment). It is key that there are some steps to the lesson at which guessing is the desired response. Inquiry is the act of problem solving and making connections. Giving students a mode in which to practice thinking and problem solving is necessary to promote student curiosity and wonder about the natural world.

CASE STUDY

Ms. McDonald (a real teacher) instructs students with moderate and severe disabilities at a local public high school. For the past several years, Ms. McDonald has been teaching her students daily science lessons based on her state's objectives using various science textbooks and general education teachers' lesson plans for ideas. Ms. McDonald will also plan hand-on inquiry experiments to help her students understand the concept. She asks them to explain what they see, what they will do, and what happens in the experiment using a KWHL chart. Her students often need picture response boards like the one shown in Figure 8.5 to respond.

During the day the students began to tell their peers who were nondisabled about the science experiments in their special education class. A science teacher approached Ms. McDonald to find out what she was using for her science experiments. Ms. McDonald decided to promote having her students learn science in a general education science class. So she and the general science teacher designed experiments to coteach, using heterogeneous student groups. Because the high school science concepts were complex and rapidly changing, Ms. McDonald continued to provide the students with disabilities with supplemental instruction related to the experiments to be conducted (e.g., key vocabulary, concept statements). In the general science class, she also promoted giving all students a KWHL chart (i.e., applying UDL), which was a tool that had helped her students self-direct their inquiry prior to inclusion. An interesting benefit of the new inclusive peer group science lessons was not only that more science learning occurred, but also that the students began to engage socially with each other in other contexts during the school day.

APPLICATIONS

1. Practice teaching the inquiry-based task analysis shown in Table 8.3. Revise the task analysis for an individual student who may use a different response mode (e.g., eye gaze).

2. Select an area of content shown in Table 8.1. Discuss how to make it usable in daily life for a student with severe disabilities.

3. Redesign a traditional science lesson using principles of UDL.

   • Target vocabulary for students with disabilities (words and how comprehension will be demonstrated). _____

   • Concept statement: _____

   • Inquiry experiment: _____

   • Universal design (adaptations in representation, engagement, and expression to make lesson accessible for all students):

   _____

   _____

Sample General Science Lesson: The Effects of Acid Rain on the Environment[*]

This is an experiment in which groups of students are given healthy plants to water with different solutions of an acid rain mixture made in class. Students will document and present their findings.

Learning outcomes

Students will gain a better understanding of the effects of acid rain on their environment, learn data collection and recording skills, correlate individual data, and create a group presentation for the class.

Time required for lesson

3–4 days

Materials/resources

Teacher will provide:

• The same type of healthy plant, one per group of three to four students (one of which will be used as a control).
• A bottle of lemon juice.
• Eye droppers, one per group of students.
• Litmus paper.
• Containers with lids, one per group of students.
• Container of pure water that has a pH of 7.
• Poster paper and markers/colored pencils/crayons as needed for each group's presentations.

---

[*] Created by Helen Beall and Heather Hughes-Buchanan, North Carolina Department of Public Instruction and LEARN NC, June and July 2004. Retrieved from *www.learnnc.org/lp/pages/2895*.

Preactivities

- Teacher introduction of an acid rain lesson coupled with illustrations showing the negative effects of acid rain on the environment.
- KWHL or other graphic organizers to assess students' prior knowledge.
- Directions on plant watering and data entry; students will water plants every other day.

Activities

- After the 2-week period of preparation, students will correlate their individual data within their group, draw or graph an appropriate visual aid, and develop an oral presentation for the class. Each member of the group must contribute to the final product.
- Groups will have time to practice their presentations.
- Each group will have 5 minutes to present their findings to the class.

Assessment

Detailed journal entries at 2-day intervals during a 2-week period comparing the condition of their plant with those of others in the class, as well as with the control plant.

Group oral presentations and visual aids on how acid levels affect plant development. Visual aids would include plant drawings, graphs, or other appropriate materials. Group presentations will be graded using a rubric.

Critical vocabulary

acid rain

pollution/pollutants

litmus paper

pH scale

environment

CHAPTER 9

Social Studies

DIANE M. BROWDER, FRED SPOONER, AND TRACIE-LYNN ZAKAS

Ms. Giovanni always had a love of social studies as a student and as teacher. To her, learning about the government, history, and culture of people throughout the world was the most important thing people could do to promote living peacefully and respectfully with each other. She had taught social studies in various upper grades over her 20-year career. During this time she had many experiences collaborating with special educators to plan for students with reading disabilities or behavioral support needs. Because of her strong commitment to social justice and multiculturalism, this planning was a natural extension of her own value system. About 10 years ago she also began to plan for students with severe disabilities to be part of her social studies classes. Although providing this new opportunity appealed to her personal values, she also was concerned that the school administration was using social studies to promote more inclusion because there was no federal or state requirement for high-stakes assessment in this content area. After talking about this inequity with her special education colleagues, she decided to support the efforts for inclusion in social studies while at the same time raising questions about why some content areas were "off limits" for inclusion. When she joined the IEP planning for Ty, a student with severe disabilities, his goal was to gain social benefits from being part of the class. Ms. Giovanni saw this new situation as an opportunity for all the students to gain more experience understanding diversity and good citizenship. Her focus with Ty was to make sure the students viewed him as a full member of the class and to be intentional about discussing with the class any situations that occurred that were inconsistent with that goal (e.g., a student mocking him).

She was surprised the next year when the special education teacher, Ms. Brown, wanted to focus on learning the social studies content and not just gaining social skills for a student named Sharon. Although Sharon seemed to have more challenges than Ty, her teacher wanted her to learn the actual 10th-grade content. Ms. Giovanni, who prided herself on being committed to a fully inclusive society, found her own belief system "rocked" by this new idea. How would a student who could not read or talk and communicated primarily with picture symbols learn about world cultures? This chapter contains ideas that the educational team could use to plan for Sharon and the very diverse spectrum of students with severe disabilities who will be learning "real" social studies content in today's schools.

As the case study illustrates, the American education system, through such legislation as No Child Left Behind (2002), focused on students meeting state standards in language arts, mathematics, and science. Unless a state also mandated competency in social studies, this content area might not receive the same priority. The first resources on teaching general curriculum content to students with severe disabilities centered around the priority areas of language arts and mathematics (Ryndak & Alper, 2003) with some also including science (Browder & Spooner, 2006). At the time this chapter was written, ideas for teaching social studies to students with severe disabilities were only beginning to be considered. For example, the national organization TASH had the first Webinar on social studies for students with severe disabilities in 2009 (Zakas, Browder, & Spooner, 2009).

Because planning in this area is new, to develop this chapter we relied on resources in social studies education, consultation with a social studies expert at our university, research on teaching this content to students with high-incidence disabilities, and the successful strategies we have observed teachers use in the schools.

OVERVIEW OF SOCIAL STUDIES

The National Council for the Social Studies (2002) defines this content as

> the integrated study of the social sciences and humanities to promote civic competence. Within the school program, social studies provides coordinated, systematic study drawing on such disciplines as anthropology, archaeology, economics, geography, history, law, philosophy, political science, psychology, religion, and sociology, as well as appropriate content from the humanities, mathematics, and natural sciences. The primary purpose of social studies is to help young people make informed and reasoned decisions for the public good as citizens of a culturally diverse, democratic society in an interdependent world. (p. 6)

According to the National Council for the Social Studies, in the past, social studies education was often associated with memorizing locations on a map or historical dates. Today the council emphasizes the teaching of social studies to provide students with information, critical thinking skills, and experiences to allow them to grow into responsible and effective citizens.

Although these goals can be applied in planning social studies for all students, educators may also want to articulate the outcomes for students with severe disabilities specifically, as teaching this content is a new area of priority. Browder, Wakeman, et al. (2007) described four reasons to teach academic content in general to students with severe disabilities. Each of these can also be a reason to teach social studies. The first reason Browder, Wakeman, et al. (2007) identify for teaching academic content is to promote educational opportunities as a means of developing competent adults. By having the opportunity to study social studies, students with severe disabilities gain the opportunity to learn about their government, history, and the world. A second reason is to respond to the rising educational expectations for students with severe disabilities. Increasingly educators have realized that students with severe disabilities can do much more than what was once thought possible. There is no way to determine how much social studies students will learn until they have access to the content. Third, teaching academics also promotes educational equality. Students who are nondisabled are not given "trials" to learn academics and then relegated to alternative content if they do not succeed. Instead, their entire school career sets expectations for learning state academic content standards. Similarly, students with severe disabilities should have sustained opportunities to learn about the society and culture in which they live. Fourth and finally, teaching academics increases opportunities for self-determination. In social studies, students may gain self-awareness about their cultural backgrounds and respect for the cultures of others, self-advocacy skills for participating in government, and ways to balance individual with group goals in a societal system.

National Social Studies Standards

The National Council for the Social Studies has named 10 themes that are addressed in the instruction of social studies: (1) culture; (2) time, continuity, and change; (3) people, places, and environments; (4) individual development and identity; (5) individuals, groups, and institutions; (6) power, authority, and governance; (7) production, distribution, and consumption; (8) science, technology, and society; (9) global connections; and (10) civic ideals and practices. Throughout the instruction of social studies, these 10 themes are addressed by teachers within and throughout the five disciplinary standards. Figure 9.1 illustrates the thematic and disciplinary standards of social studies.

The five disciplinary standards identified to complete a social studies curriculum are history, geography, civics and government, economics, and psychology (National Council for the Social Studies [NCSS], 2002). *History* is the study of the past that allows students to comprehend the time and location of specific events. History supports student learning by utilizing chronological thinking so that students can distinguish past, present, and future, and it allows students to define the history of their nation and the world. Students at all grade levels learn history through strategies such as the use of time lines and other graphic organizers; the use of visual, literary, or musical resources; and the reconstruction of literal historical passages. *Geography* is the development of spatial contexts of people, places, and environments. Within the context of geography, students learn about the Earth's physical and human systems. Geography typically involves using maps and geographical representations. A third strand in social studies is *civics and government*. The central theme of civics and government is to instruct students to be informed and responsible participants in political life and to be competent citizens committed to the furtherance of American constitutional democracy. This subject is often taught in terms of relationships between individuals and their government, using analogies of authority from families, schools, communities, and larger political systems. In *economics*, students

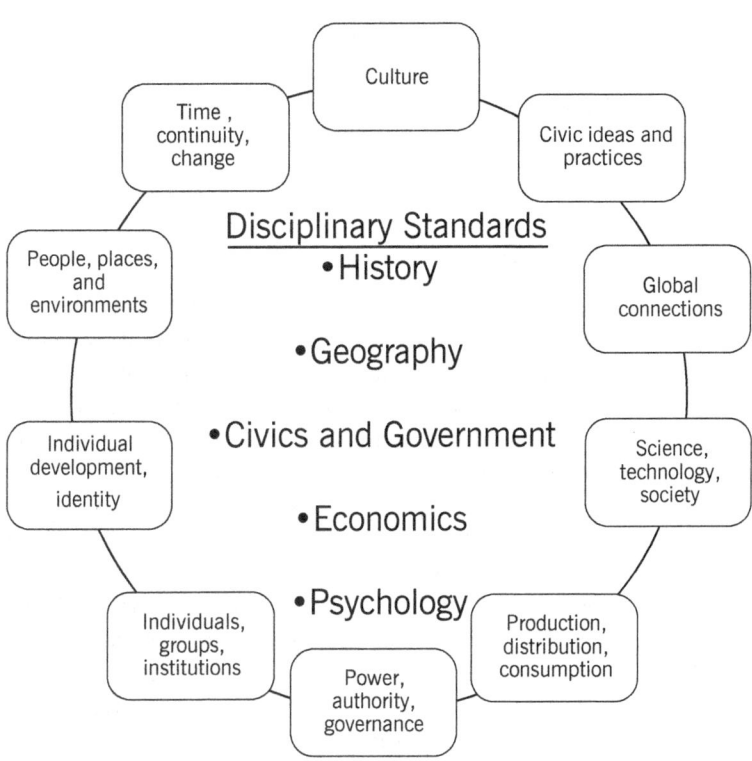

FIGURE 9.1. Thematic and disciplinary standards of social studies.

learn the basic principles of satisfying their wants and needs within the process of supply and demand. Teachers use examples of economic situations that focus on resources, desires and needs, supply and demand, goods and services, and opportunities. Finally, *psychology* is the study of human behavior that addresses thinking, learning, memory, development, personality, and behavior. This topic area is typically only addressed in high school and college-level classes and provides opportunities for students to comprehend and apply specific concepts and theories that relate to individual and group behaviors.

Research on Teaching Social Studies

In research on teaching academics to students with severe disabilities, social studies is the least understood area. Reading and mathematics have engendered the greatest number of studies. In reading, a comprehensive literature review of studies on students with autism and significant intellectual disability identified 128 experimental studies (Browder, Wakeman, et al., 2006). In a meta-analysis that focused on teaching math to students with severe disabilities, Browder, Spooner, et al. (2008) found more than 70 studies, but most focused on numbers and operations (*n* = 37) and on money (*n* = 36). Whereas reading had the most studies, followed by math, only 11 studies existed for science when Courtade et al. (2007) conducted their comprehensive review. The literature in science may be sparse, but there is virtually no literature on teaching social studies to students with moderate and severe developmental disabilities. In our search, we found only one study. In this study, students with and without autism used cooperative learning groups to learn key words and facts for social studies (Dugan et al., 1995). Given this lack of research, educators must adapt strategies from research with students with mild disabilities and must apply evidence-based practices that have been used with other content areas (e.g., systematic prompting and feedback).

Challenges with Expository Text

Social studies content can be taught using an inductive method and/or a deductive method. With the inductive method, social studies content is typically taught using textbooks that focus on expository text. Students then focus on identifying key points during questions and discussions, allowing them to draw conclusions from the data. In the deductive method, students may be presented with a hypothesis or a generalization and then use materials and assistance to verify the hypothesis (McCormick, 2008).

Using either strategy most likely requires the use of some type of instructional text. Many content-area subject textbooks can be difficult for students to negotiate (Armbruster & Anderson, 1988). Students with mild disabilities may struggle with content-area instruction and expository texts (Garjria, Jitendra, Sood, & Sacks, 2007; Gersten et al., 2001; Williams, 2005). The structure of these texts and curricula may be inconsistently organized, and the language level may prove too challenging for every student to read and comprehend its material (Frase-Blunt, 2000). One of the reasons that students may struggle with the task of comprehending content-related text is that only 1 in 10 content-area teachers is taught strategies for teaching comprehension of expository text in the content areas (Dowhower, 1999). Students with disabilities are particularly at risk to experience difficulty in learning from content-area texts (De La Paz & MacArthur, 2003). This risk may occur because of lost time in the general education classroom while receiving services to address basic skills or because of a lack of the effective accommodations and modifications needed to provide access to the curriculum prescribed.

Students with moderate to severe developmental disabilities will have even more difficulty comprehending the type of expository text that is commonly used in social studies. There also has been insufficient research on teaching reading comprehension to these students. In their comprehensive literature review of studies of students with severe disabilities, Browder, Wakeman, et al. (2006) found that few addressed comprehension of any kind and almost none targeted passage comprehension. In a second comprehensive literature review focusing specifically on text comprehension and students with autism, Chiang and Lin (2007) found that the majority of articles reviewed focused on sight word comprehension. Only four of the eleven studies reviewed in this article addressed text comprehension (Kamps, Barbetta, Leonard, & Delquadri, 1994; Kamps, Leonard, Potucek, & Garrison-Harrell, 1995; Kamps, Locke, Delquadri, & Hall, 1989; O'Connor & Klein, 2004).

Reading social studies requires a special type of comprehension—the understanding of expository text. Story-mapping strategies, computer-assisted instruction, adapted text with and without embedded graphics, study guides, mnemonic materials, and graphic organizers are among the approaches that have been used to teach expository-based reading comprehension to students with mild disabilities (Garjria et al., 2007). Chapter 6 provides more detail about how to teach comprehension of expository text. Some of these ideas are also included in the next section.

STRATEGIES TO TEACH
SOCIAL STUDIES CONTENT

To select a strategy to teach social studies, teachers need to consider what they hope to achieve. Memorizing dates or names of presidents may be achievable but may not ultimately contribute to a student's quality of life. According to Beyer (2008a), history, one of the most emphasized areas within the social studies continuum, requires the instructor to teach "thinking skills." To teach these skills, he recommends using a variety of learning activities, such as reading texts, documents, and other sources; analyzing decisions; classifying information; establishing cause-and-effect relationships; and evaluating sources for accuracy and bias. These processes require multifaceted intellectual functions, commonly called "thinking skills" (Beyer, 2001).

Beyer (2008b) also recommends making the information explicit, introducing each skill in a lesson that focuses on that skill, and guiding and supporting the skill practice. For students with severe disabilities, it may be important to target one specific type of thinking skill in the beginning and to provide many opportunities for practice. For example, the student may be asked to create a cause-and-effect diagram each day for events that occur in a historical narrative or news story.

Creating Access to the Social Studies Text

Although the overall goal of social studies is to get students to apply skills to think critically about the content, it also is important to convey knowledge of the content. For this to occur, students need to be able to use and understand the social studies text. As described in Chapter 5, teachers may choose to rewrite the text as an adapted text summary with picture symbols to support main ideas and key vocabulary. This use of considerate text, or text that provides embedded support for reading comprehension, also has been shown to increase comprehension in students with disabilities (Dimino, 2007). Some students may be able to read the text summary aloud. Others will need a peer, a teacher, or technology to provide a read-aloud, as described in Chapter 5. During the read-aloud, the student can be encouraged to participate by locating key vocabulary, rereading summary statements (using voice-output AAC if needed), and answering comprehension questions.

FINDING THE BALANCE

Creating adapted text is time-consuming and produces materials that are different from what other students read in the social studies class. In contrast, social studies texts in the upper grades are challenging even for students who are nondisabled. To what extent should teachers create adapted texts and other separate materials for social studies compared with using those typical for the context? A general rule of thumb is to always begin with the same materials that students who are nondisabled are using to see whether the student may be able to benefit from them with some minor supports. Then create adaptations to the text and other materials as needed. For example, the student may be able to follow a news story that has a descriptive picture of the big idea without needing a text summary. In contrast, a chapter in the social studies text may need to be summarized and adapted. Only in rare circumstances should the student be using completely different materials. Even tests and seat assignments can often be provided in adapted formats (e.g., picture choices.)

Teaching the Grammar of Social Studies

In addition to having a way to use the text, students need to learn systematically the "language of social studies." When this process is followed in the curricular area of English-language arts, it is commonly called story-grammar instruction. Story-grammar instruction is defined as "an attempt to construct a set of rules that can generate a structure for any story" (Rayner & Pollatsek, 1989). Terms commonly used in story grammar, especially in its simplest form, are *characters, setting, plot, resolution,* and *theme.* Story grammar can vary depending on the scope or theme of the story being read (Dymock, 2007). Students who master the concept of story grammar have a strategy that can be applied to a wide range of text. Boulineau, Fore, Hagan-Burke, and Burke (2004) found that students with learning disabilities who used the story-grammar strategy to complete a story map showed marked improvement in text comprehension and that these skills were maintained. Additional studies support the concept of teaching story grammar to students with and without disabilities to improve the comprehension of expository and narrative text (Faggella-Luby, Schumaker, & Deshler, 2007; Westerveld, & Gillon, 2008; Xin, Wiles, & Lin, 2008) in a variety of curricular areas, including math. Once again, no research exists in the area of story-grammar acquisition for students with severe disabilities.

To teach story grammar to students with severe disabilities, teachers will need to provide repeated practice in applying the terms to a text that the student reads or hears read aloud. The teacher may begin by focusing on one element of story grammar, such as identifying the characters. Once students master this element, additional elements can be added (e.g., setting, plot). Chapter 6 provides more information and examples of how to teach story grammar.

CHECK FOR UNDERSTANDING

An event is one of the elements of story grammar. What event is illustrated by the adapted text in Figure 9.2? A teacher may define the word *event* as "what happened." What words would you use to ask the student to identify this event? How would you prompt students who do not know the answer?

Teaching Geography and Mapping Skills

Besides being able to access and comprehend text, students in social studies need skills for understanding geography, especially that of reading maps. Reading a map requires being able to comprehend the text provided (e.g., the map legend) and to locate a point in a plane. During mathematics, students may learned to use a coordinate plane to locate a point, and geography provides an opportunity for generalization of this skill if the map contains a legend. Students may also find a location by locating a key sight word. The two maps shown in Figure 9.3 show the path of the Underground Railroad, on which slaves made the journey to locations where they would be free. Two key words the students might locate are *Kentucky* and *Canada.* They then might trace a finger from one to the other to consider the path of the journey. Using a map does require being able to comprehend the abstraction of a model. As described in Chapter 11, students who do not yet use abstract communication should still have the opportunity for instruction that introduces abstract symbols. A student like Sharon, introduced at the beginning of this

In 1860, there were many free African Americans. There

were many more African Americans who wanted to be free. They tried

to escape slavery by traveling on the Underground Railroad. The

Underground Railroad was a set of secret escape   routes   leading to

land where slaves could be free. There were no trains, and all

traveling happened above ground.

FIGURE 9.2. Example of adapted text used to illustrate the big ideas of the Underground Railroad.

chapter, might need to use a picture of a person who "walks" from one location to the next. She might also need to build understanding by using the words *travel* and *freedom* from her own experience and classroom activities.

Using Graphic Organizers

Graphic organizers are organizational tools that utilize visual and spatial displays that facilitate the comprehension of text through "the use of lines, arrows, and a spatial arrangement that describe text content, structure, and key conceptual relationships" (Darch & Eaves, 1986, p. 310). Historically, graphic organizers, originally known as advanced organizers, were developed to provide a way for teachers to increase the skills of their students when engaging in cognitive tasks by using visual–spatial formats to organize the information gleaned from text (Griffin, Malone, & Kame'enui, 1995). These formats may include hierarchies, flowcharts, picture charts, or Web-based maps. In a comprehensive review of research literature on the use of graphic organizers for students with learning disabilities and other mild disabilities in the area of reading comprehension for expository and narrative text, Kim, Vaughn, Wanzek, and Wei (2004) reviewed 21 studies using group designs that investigated graphic organizers. Specifically, they examined cognitive maps, semantic organizers, and framed outlines. They found that, overall, graphic organizers did promote the comprehension of expository content for the students in the varying studies, but three studies found contradictory results, so some caution should be used in applying this strategy. Graphic organizers that provided the greatest supports to students were semantic organizers and cognitive maps with and without mnemonics. Using graphic organizers can decrease the intellectual demands on students by

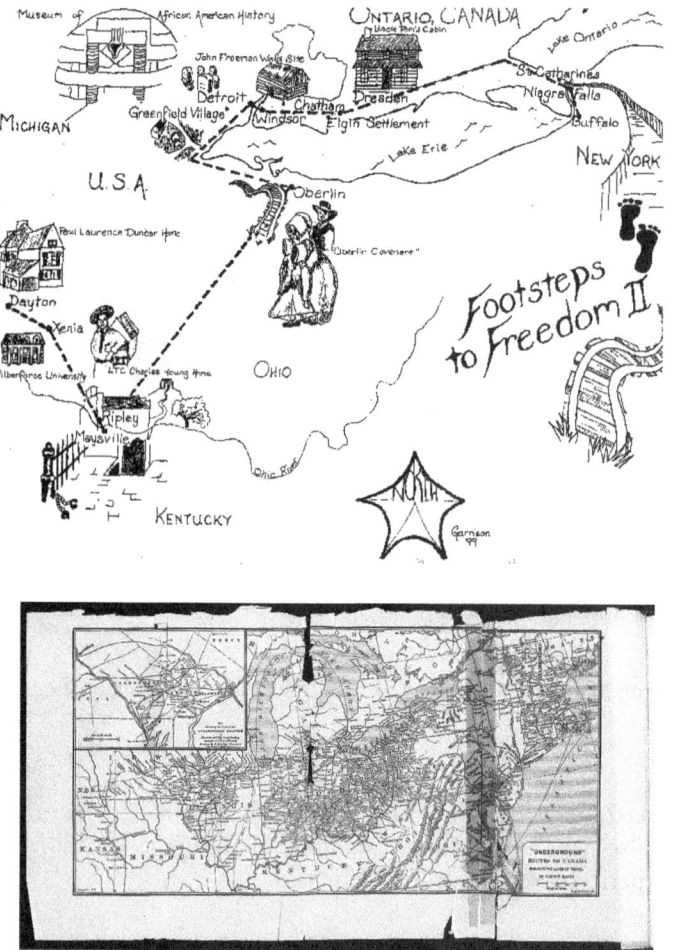

FIGURE 9.3. Examples of maps showing the path of the Underground Railroad. Reprinted with permission from Garrison Daily.

reducing the amount of semantic information that the learner will have to process (Ellis, 1994). Figure 9.4 provides several examples of graphic organizers.

Applying the Disciplinary and Thematic Standards in Instructional Units

As Figure 9.1 indicates, social studies has both disciplinary and thematic standards. To illustrate, the teacher might target a unit on the Underground Railroad. To address disciplinary standards, the teacher might include a geography lesson using maps like those shown in Figure 9.3. Students might also create their own simplified maps using two to five "stations." If applicable, students might also adapt maps of their own geographic area to show how African Americans traveled through their region from slavery to freedom. In this same unit, the teacher might address an economic disciplinary standard. Students might learn the vocabulary words *employee* (one who works for pay), *volunteer* (one who chooses to work without pay), and *slave* (one who is forced to work without pay). The

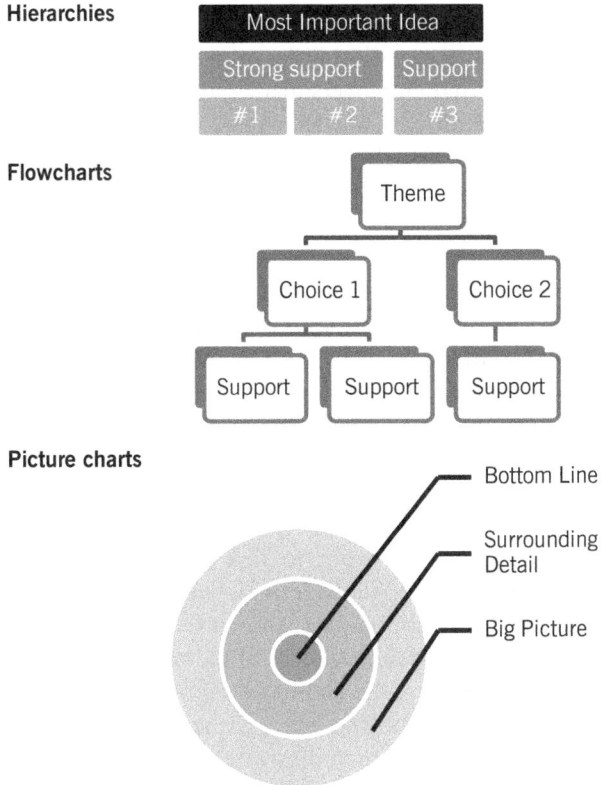

Hierarchies

Most Important Idea

Strong support | Support

#1 | #2 | #3

Flowcharts

Theme

Choice 1 | Choice 2

Support | Support | Support

Picture charts

Bottom Line

Surrounding Detail

Big Picture

FIGURE 9.4. Examples of graphic organizers.

teacher could then illustrate how much the boss makes if the worker either is not paid or is paid for one bale of cotton. The teacher may also try a brief exercise in which students do chores. Whereas some receive "pay," others can choose a job to do as a volunteer, and others must do a chore that is assigned. This exercise can lead into teaching about the thematic standard of power/authority/governance and people/places (e.g., the Emancipation Proclamation, the role of key African American leaders).

An important strategy for teachers to use in planning how to incorporate these standards is the development of thematic units. Onosko and Jorgensen (1998) identify eight essential elements for inclusive units: (1) a central unit issue or problem, (2) an opening grabber or motivator, (3) lessons that are linked to the central issue or problem, (4) richly detailed source material, (5) culminating projects, (6) varied lesson formats, (7) multiple assessments, and (8) varied modes of student expression. The central issue or theme is what creates the foundation for the unit. These typically will be suggested by the social studies text and state standards for the grade level. The theme may arise from an event or time period in history or from one of the thematic standards, such as global connections. To get students excited about the unit, the teacher should plan some kickoff and culminating event. These may include field trips, a special speaker, a simulation, drama or video, or some other activity. Sometimes the unit will include a project that students work on each day, such as creating a model of a room in which pioneer families would have lived. The teacher should articulate specific objectives for student learning during the unit and link these to an assessment. In the example of the Underground Railroad, an objective for a student with severe disabilities might be to identify the facts that slaves were forced to work for free, that employers made money on free labor, that some slaves escaped on the Underground Railroad, and that all slaves were freed by the Emancipation Proclamation. A second objective might be to state an opinion about slavery or show the Underground Railroad using a map. One way to assess factual learning might be filling in blanks with pictures or symbols. Students might express an opinion by choosing a true–false statement and an opinion to support it. Once the theme, activities, and assessments are planned, the teacher can create a series of lessons that engage students with the content. For students with severe disabilities, an adapted text summary may be created. Teachers may embed some daily practice helping students complete the key concept statements, find locations on the map, or practice giving an opinion. Figure 9.5 provides an example of an instructional unit in social studies.

Generalizing Events and Concepts into Daily Activities

Whenever possible, the teacher will want to link the new knowledge and concepts acquired in social studies to students' daily activities. This can be challenging with such historical events as the Mayflower Compact, shown in Figure 9.6. To tackle this challenge, the teacher might first reduce the big ideas of the compact to its most salient points and present these with adapted text, as shown in Figure 9.7. Salient vocabulary terms can be highlighted with picture symbols to increase the comprehension of specific words. Next the teacher provides an experience to illustrate the concept to be learned. Using the Mayflower Compact as a general outline, teachers and students might draft their own classroom "compact," determining the rules and procedures within the classroom and school environment. This will allow students to participate in a civics lesson that then directly affects their lives. To help make the link, teachers may call it their "Compact."

CASE STUDY

In the large, urban elementary school in which Ms. Tryon teaches, every student is to receive 90 minutes of social studies instruction every other day. Although Ms. Tryon feels confident in her ability to teach reading/language arts, math, and science, she is apprehensive about teaching social studies to students with autism for the first time. Initially, she begins her search for programs that will guide her through the process of teaching social studies to her students, but she find there is no commercially prepared program that meets the needs of her students and addresses the requirements of the school system.

After some planning with her school administration and the fifth-grade planning team, Ms. Tryon will coteach social studies with Mr. Harmon. Mr. Harmon's current approach is to have the student read the passage in the text; then he asks the student to answer the questions that are at the end of the passage. Occasionally, he will embed special projects, such as a role play, a report, or a cooperative group exercise. The focus of fifth-grade social studies in their state is United States history.

On the first day, Mr. Harmon begins to read to the class from the fifth-grade textbook. The students with autism squirm in their seats, and two students begin to present self-stimulatory behaviors. Mr. Harmon writes the 10 chapter questions on the board

Central Unit Issue (Theme): Ancient America

Fifth-Grade State Standards

The learner will examine how various ethnic groups influenced the development of the United States, Canada, and Mexico.

The learner will apply key geographic concepts to countries of North America.

Specific Learner Outcomes

Students will learn that:

1. Geographical factors influence civilizations through environment, economy, growth, and communication.
2. Civilizations have a rise and fall.
3. Civilization must be understood as a system.

Essential Questions

1. What can you learn from a culture?
2. What do great cultures have in common?
3. How does geography impact a civilization?
4. What happens when cultures meet?

Introducing the Unit

Through the learning activities, students will be able to answer the following topic questions:

1. When were the Aztecs, Incas, and Maya civilizations developed?
2. How did they adapt agricultural methods to suit the environment?
3. What were their contributions in math, science, and literature?
4. What factors caused their decline?

The essential questions are introduced and discussed. They are then posted in the room to revisit throughout the unit. The topic questions are then introduced and discussed as well. These are copied into the students' social studies notebooks, each on a separate page for each culture. Throughout the unit, as students discover information pertaining to a topic, they can add facts to their pages. This can serve as a growing database of information for the students to increase their knowledge base of the specific cultures.

Daily Lesson Implementation

1. **Three sessions; 45 minutes each.** Maya, Aztec, and Inca videos. This activity is strictly to build background knowledge. Aztec video title: *Indians of North America: Aztec*; Maya video title: *Ancient Civilizations for Children: Maya*; Inca video title: *Ancient Civilizations for Children: Inca*. Each video is approximately 30 minutes long and takes one class period. They are shown on three consecutive days to kick off the unit. The students have a video note-taking guide for each culture that they fill out along with the video. The video guides are copied onto one side of a page. The video guides are self-checked immediately after the video; students correct any errors.
2. **Four sessions; 45 minutes each.** Reading (in pairs) and guided note taking. Student pairs share a copy of the Pearson fifth-grade Core Knowledge book, *History and Geography*. First the students read that day's lesson with their partners. They then get the guided note-taking worksheet and reread independently, completing the guided note taking on four of the chapters. Collect the guided note-taking worksheets for both a social studies grade and a reading grade. Students are expected to spell all words correctly in the guide.

(cont.)

FIGURE 9.5. Example of a unit of instruction in social studies. Created by Susan D. Flynn. Adapted from *dspace.lasrworks.org/bitstream/10349/460/3/Aztec%20May%20Inca.pdf.*

3. **Three sessions; 45 minutes each.** *Discover Kids* magazines. Each student has his or her own magazine, which includes three scavenger hunts. They do not need to complete the scavenger hunts in any specific order, but they have 3 days to complete all three scavenger hunts. Arrange a small group to complete the scavenger hunt with students who struggle. Complete the scavenger hunt for a social studies grade. Students who finish more quickly can choose one of the essential questions and write a paragraph response in their notebooks.

4. **Three work sessions; 45 minutes each. One-day museum walk through the "Hall of Expertise"; 45-minute session.** Be an expert! Students have explored the cultures in three different resources: the videos, the books, and the *Discover Kids* magazines. They choose a specific culture and one topic about that culture to become an expert on. Some ideas are: Mayan social hierarchy, Incan terrace farming, Aztec games, a day in the life of an Incan child, Aztec decline, chocolate and the Mayans. Each student needs half a sheet of poster board to create his or her final product.

Three Work Sessions

a. All of the students who want to research the same culture work together to develop ideas they'd like to explore using the essential questions as a guide. They divide up the most compelling ideas among partners in the group. Each partner works to explore his or her assigned idea about the culture.

b. Model the layout of a poster: large letters for the title; a short phrase of explanation; an eye-catching picture viewable from a distance. Choose four or fewer marker colors to write the letters and create the picture. (More colors or too much detail creates a "busy-ness" that is distracting to the reader, and the message of the poster may be lost. Bring in a movie poster as a model.)

c. Partners research the information about their idea. They plan the poster, which includes editing and layout, on a sheet of drawing paper before they get the final-copy poster board.

d. Students come back together as a group and share their posters.

e. The group creates a time line for their culture, incorporating ideas from everyone's research into the time line.

f. The group then creates their culture's display, including the time line, in the "Hall of Expertise" (See Assessment section).

Optional art activity: Aztec calendar. Students read an article about the Aztec calendar and examine the example included. Students then create a replica of an Aztec solar calendar, choosing their own symbols for the design.

Assessment

Museum Walk: When their culture posters are complete, the students hang their expert posters in the fifth-grade hallway, which becomes the "Hall of Expertise." This assessment piece allows the fifth-graders to conduct a museum walk up and down the hallway. As they walk, they carry three sticky notes. They can choose three posters to give positive feedback on, writing the feedback on a sticky note and then placing it on the poster so that it hangs off the bottom. The teacher should model appropriate feedback before the museum walk (e.g., "That is so interesting," "Excellent drawing," "I never knew that, " "This makes me wonder . . ."). Once a poster has five stickies at the bottom, no more may be added to that poster. Make a rotation throughout the day, so that all of the kids are not in the hall at the same time. Group all of the Aztecs together, the Maya together, and the Inca together, including the time lines created by each group.

(cont.)

FIGURE 9.5. *(cont.)*

Planning for a Student with Severe Disabilities

- *People supports*: The cooperative learning groups and peer partners create natural opportunities for Sharon to receive peer support. The teacher will recruit two specific students to serve as her partners in these contexts. These partners will get additional information on how to work with Sharon.
- *Modified materials/use of technology*: Sharon will have a set of picture symbols/ words that relate to some of the concepts the group will discover about the cultural group. She will be able to give these to a peer to paste on their chart at the appropriate time. She also will find additional pictures using the Internet that she will print and contribute. Sharon will have some key vocabulary on her voice output device to use when the group reports back each day, including the name of the group and what topic they were researching that day.
- *Alternate achievement expectations*:
  - When asked about the characteristics and contributions of _____ (e.g., Aztecs), Sharon will select three pictures from an assortment of 10 possible answers.
  - When given the opportunity for a group report or project presentation, Sharon will use her AAC to give the name of the culture and each fact to be presented (e.g., where they lived).
- *Embedded instruction*: Sharon's peer will help her point to each target picture and to find the symbol on her AAC for the culture/fact to be stated using a model prompt and time-delay fading. The goal is for Sharon to have at least one opportunity to find each picture and to use each symbol on her AAC for social studies daily. (Special education teacher will train peer.)
- *Individual evaluation*: The special education teacher will probe Sharon's social studies picture identification and use of her AAC to state culture/facts on a weekly basis and graph these data for progress monitoring.

FIGURE 9.5. *(cont.)*

and asks the students to read and answer each question on a sheet of lined paper. The students with autism cannot complete the assignment, and their frustration becomes evident through inappropriate behavior.

CHECK FOR UNDERSTANDING

Before reading the rest of this case study, answer these questions. What do you think went wrong with the social studies lesson? What could the coteachers do to improve this lesson?

In the name of God, Amen. We, whose names are underwritten, the Loyal Subjects of our dread Sovereign Lord, King James, by the Grace of God, of England, France and Ireland, King, Defender of the Faith, e&. Having undertaken for the Glory of God, and Advancement of the Christian Faith, and the Honour of our King and Country, a voyage to plant the first colony in the northern parts of Virginia; do by these presents, solemnly and mutually in the Presence of God and one of another, covenant and combine ourselves together into a civil Body Politick, for our better Ordering and Preservation, and Furtherance of the Ends aforesaid; And by Virtue hereof to enact, constitute, and frame, such just and equal Laws, Ordinances, Acts, Constitutions and Offices, from time to time, as shall be thought most meet and convenient for the General good of the Colony; unto which we promise all due submission and obedience. In Witness whereof we have hereunto subscribed our names at Cope Cod the eleventh of November, in the Reign of our Sovereign Lord, King James of England, France and Ireland, the eighteenth, and of Scotland the fifty-fourth. Anno Domini, 1620.

FIGURE 9.6. The Mayflower Compact.

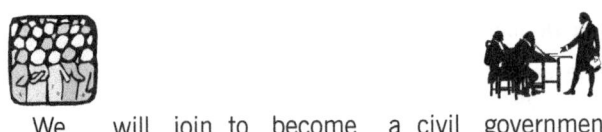

1.   We   will join to become a civil government.

2.   We   will make   laws that are fair to all   men.

3.   We   will meet together to discuss our laws and our land.

4.   We   promise to follow these   laws.

FIGURE 9.7. Example of adapted text used to illustrate the big ideas of the Mayflower Compact.

Ms. Tryon begins by creating adapted text versions of the social studies chapter. She rewrites the passage to reduce the amount of text and simplify the language. She does maintain the content of the passage. She then selects important vocabulary words from the passage and highlights these by pairing them with picture symbols. She makes a copy of this for each student with autism. She asks Mr. Harmon if she can read the summary at the beginning and end of his readings. Together they decide that the students who are nondisabled will read the summaries, and these will be called "Today's Big Ideas" for all the students. Mr. Harmon begins to assign creating the text summaries (writing 3–5 "big ideas" for this section of the chapter) as homework to the students who are nondisabled.

Ms. Tryon also revises the comprehension questions at the end of the chapter. Instead of asking her students to answer 10 questions, she reduces the number to 5 and creates multiple-choice answers with picture cues. The students with autism work on these adapted worksheets as the other students answer the questions in the book.

Although this helps Ms. Tryon support the students with autism in the early weeks of the cotaught class, she wants to make the learning experience more dynamic for all the students. She talks with Mr. Harmon about planning a unit of instruction. Together they decide to develop a unit on the American Revolution. They choose a movie as a kickoff activity and create a learning center with props to use as costumes. As students finish their work, they can act out brief scripts as some of the characters from this period. Ms. Tryon reviews Mr. Harmon's test from the prior year to develop objectives and an assessment for the students with autism. Mr. Harmon develops a series of lessons, and Ms. Tryon works with him to help make each lesson universally designed to include the students with autism. Their culminating event is a drama they perform for the other fifth-grade classes.

SUMMARY

Social studies is the content area that is focused on in literature for students with severe disabilities. Because there is almost no research on this topic, teachers need to adapt ideas used in general education and with students with mild disabilities. A beginning point for planning is the set of the disciplinary and thematic standards of social studies that are shown in Figure 9.1. A major activity in social studies is gaining information through reading expository text. Planning will be needed to make this text accessible for students with severe disabilities. This may include using adapted text summaries and comprehension questions with multiple-choice answers. More information on this instruction of comprehension can be found in Chapter 6. Besides adapting text, teachers may also teach story grammar, teach map skills, use graphic organizers, teach to both disciplinary and thematic standards, and generalize content to students' daily activities. The use of a thematic unit can be an effective way to organize social studies information. One of the important outcomes for social studies is that students will gain some critical thinking skills about the society in which they live.

APPLICATIONS

1. Pick a social studies topic. Use a graphic organizer to show how you would teach students to summarize the main ideas.

2. For a student who is just beginning to use symbols (presymbolic), how might you build understanding of the social studies topic you selected for #1?

3. Create a unit of instruction for a social studies theme. Identify the grade level and state standards you used.

PART THREE

LIFE SKILLS
AND QUALITY OF LIFE

CHAPTER 10

Sensory, Physical, and Health Care Needs

FRED SPOONER, DIANE M. BROWDER, AND PAMELA J. MIMS

Dante was a fifth grader who loved to play baseball, football, and basketball. At the end of his fifth-grade year he was involved in a serious car accident. During the accident, he sustained severe head trauma that resulted in his brain swelling. As a result, Dante had to have a section of his brain removed and was diagnosed with traumatic brain injury. He spent the rest of his fifth-grade year, all summer, and the first half of his sixth-grade year in a rehabilitation hospital. Dante had lost the ability to talk, walk, and eat. He was considered a quadriplegic and had very inconsistent eye gaze, which made it very difficult to understand any of his communicative attempts. The doctors and therapists tried to help Dante walk, talk, and eat again, but after many months with no progress, he was released from the hospital. He started back to school in the middle of his sixth-grade year in a fully inclusive general education classroom. After several meetings with the general education teacher, the special education teacher, Dante's parents, the speech therapist, the occupational therapist, the physical therapist, and the school nurse, a plan was developed for Dante. Dante would receive instruction in his fully inclusive class with his same-age peers and would receive all therapies within the context of the school day during academic periods (e.g., Dante was placed in a stander during social studies to work on bearing weight to increase bone density and to prevent his muscles from atrophy). At times, he would receive one-to-one instruction with the speech therapist and special education teacher to work on discrete skills. Other times Dante would receive embedded instruction, utilizing peers for support. The most important skill for Dante to develop was a consistent communication system because his eye gaze was inconsistent (the only observable behavior identified). The team felt it was especially important for Dante to be fully included because they could not yet determine how much he understood. In addition, it was a priority for Dante to regain his health, as he was considered medically fragile after the accident.

Many students with intellectual disability also have physical, neurological, sensory, and/ or health disabilities. It is important for teachers of students with severe disabilities to be aware of additional disabilities in addition to intellectual disability and to be properly trained to handle each student's individual needs. Teachers are not expected to be experts regarding serving students with sensory, motor, or health care needs, but they should be very knowledgeable in order to understand and work with related service providers. Related service providers are trained to assist in the removal of any possible barriers to the successful inclusion of students with special needs into the general education class-room or the setting deemed most appropriate by the IEP team (Hill, 1999).

MANAGING PHYSICAL DISABILITIES

Physical Impairments

Students with severe disabilities may possess a wide spectrum of physical impairments. These can range from mild to severe and may involve one part of the body, multiple parts of the body, or the whole body. One of the most common forms of physical impairment is the cluster of symptoms known as cerebral palsy (CP).

CP is a nonprogressive disorder of the brain that affects the way people move and their posture. It is considered a type of developmental disability because the damage to the brain occurs before it is fully mature (e.g., at birth; Best & Bigge, 2005). The damage to the brain may occur during pregnancy, at birth, or as a result of postnatal trauma or infection. Any situation in which a lack of oxygen to the brain occurs (e.g., near drown-ing, suffocation, electrocution) can impair the brain and cause the symptoms of CP. CP can affect individuals in a wide variety of ways. First, the parts of the body affected may range from all four limbs (quadriplegia) to one side of the body (hemiplegia). Or the impairment may be greater for the arms than the legs (diplegia). The impairment also differs in the motor pattern that occurs. In spastic CP, the individual has increased muscle tone (hypertonia). The tightened or "contracted" muscles can make it difficult to walk and produce a "scissor" gait. Most children with CP have a classification of spastic CP (Howle, 2002). Children with dyskinetic CP palsy have involuntary, nonpurposeful movements of their limbs and facial muscles. The individual can also become stuck in abnormal postures and require positioning to maintain normal tone. In ataxic CP, the child has impairments in balance and coordination. The child may walk with a wide gait, holding the arms out for balance (Best & Bigge, 2005). Children can also have mixed CP, with low tone in some parts of the body and spasticity in others. Additionally, for all children with CP, muscle tone can fluctuate. Infants born with CP may initially have low tone (hypotonia).

Besides CP, students may have neural tube defects in the brain, spinal cord, or ver-tebrae. The common term for the condition in which the bones of the spinal column do not close properly is *spina bifida*. There are a variety of manifestations of neural tube defects, and the results can range from mild physical impairment to paralysis. Many individuals with myelomeningocele, the most common and severe form of spina bifida, have hydrocephalus, in which blocked cerebrospinal fluid causes head enlargement, brain abnormalities, and seizures.

As described at the beginning of this chapter, students may also acquire physical impairments through traumatic brain injuries (TBI). These may include head injuries in which the skull is either fractured (open-head injury) or not (closed-head injury). Automobile or bicycle accidents, sports injuries, falls, and physical abuse are examples of events that can cause head injury. The broader term "brain injury" includes not only head injuries but also events such as infectious diseases, strokes, and near drowning or suffocation in which the brain is damaged (Best, 2001).

In muscular dystrophy (MD), the child will have progressive weakening of the muscles. Weakness usually begins in the lower legs, which may appear muscular and large, although the muscle is actually being replaced by fat and fibrous tissue. The most common form is Duchenne muscular dystrophy (DMD), which occurs due to the absence of a protein called dystrophin (Best, 2001).

Students may have other orthopedic and musculoskeletal conditions from such diseases as juvenile arthritis and osteogenesis imperfecta. Students may also have a full or partial loss of a limb from birth (congenital) or because of an accident or illness (e.g., bone tumor). Students with limb deficiencies may have therapeutic equipment, such as a prosthetic leg or arm. Table 10.1 provides a summary of the major types of physical impairments.

Therapeutic Interventions

Although physical impairments present challenges to the individual, these need not become an obstacle to full participation in school and the community. Therapeutic interventions are used to promote the child's functioning as independently as possible and to prevent possible side effects, such as muscle contractures, which can gradually reduce the child's range of motion.

The most common therapeutic interventions for students with physical impairments in the school setting are traditional physical and occupational therapies, in which the student receives interventions that involve strengthening or maintaining muscles or bone density or guidance on the use of adaptive equipment to encourage participation in educational goals. Other therapies that have become more commonplace include animal therapy and aqua therapy. In animal therapy service animals visit classrooms to decrease stress and motivate or encourage participation in physical or occupational therapy activities (Watts & Everly, 2009). Animal therapy can also include therapeutic horseback riding or swimming with dolphins. Finally, water therapy has become a very popular physical therapy for individuals with disabilities (Skinner & Thompson, 2008). A major concern with animal or water therapies is that it is often hard to incorporate the student's educational goals into these therapies if they are scheduled during the instructional day.

Physical therapy (PT) is therapy that focuses on optimal functioning of gross motor skills, weight bearing, positioning, range of motion, and mobility (Orelove & Sobsey, 2000). Occupational therapy (OT) is therapy that focuses on optimal functioning in fine motor, visual–motor and self-care skills (Orelove & Sobsey, 2000). PTs and OTs are trained to suggest or create devices or adaptations necessary for the best possible physical learning. These therapists are there to assist in providing the best possible means for the student to access his or her educational environment.

Orientation and mobility (O&M) services were traditionally provided for students with visual impairments but more recently have been offered to any student who may qualify for such services (IDEA, 1997; Neil, Bigby, & Nicholson, 2004). This service focuses on orientation and mobility skills needed to navigate as independently as possible

TABLE 10.1. Terms Used in Describing Physical Disabilities

Major category	Description	Subtypes
Cerebral palsy (CP)	A nonprogressive disability; onset occurs when the brain is not fully mature; affects movement and muscle tone	• Spastic • Dyskinetic • Ataxic • Mixed
Traumatic brain injury (TBI)	Damage to the brain as a result of a head injury, disease, stroke, near drowning, or suffocation	• Open-head injury • Closed-head injury
Muscular dystrophy (MD)	Progressive weakening of the muscles, usually beginning in the lower legs; delayed development of muscle motor skills; difficulty using one or more muscle groups; drooling, eyelid drooping; frequent falls, problems walking	• Duchenne muscular dystrophy (DMD) • Becker's muscular dystrophy (BMD) • Facioscapulohumeral muscular dystrophy • Emery–Dreifuss muscular dystrophy • Limb–girdle muscular dystrophy
Juvenile rheumatoid arthritis (JRA)	Typically appears between the ages of 6 months and 16 years; first signs often are joint pain or swelling and reddened or warm joints; the greater the number of joints affected, the more severe the disease, and the less likely that the symptoms will eventually go into total remission.	• Oligoarticular JRA • Polyarticular arthritis • Systemic JRA
Osteogenesis imperfecta	Genetic disorder characterized by bones that break easily, often from little or no apparent cause	• Type I • Type II • Type III • Type IV
Spina bifida	A developmental birth defect caused by the incomplete closure of the embryonic neural tube; some vertebrae overlying the spinal cord are not fully formed and remain unfused and open; may or may not feature the spinal cord sticking out through the opening in the bones with a fluid-filled sac surrounding the spinal cord.	• Spina bifida occulata • Spina bifida cystica • Meningocele • Lipomeningocele
	Additional syndromes associated with physical disabilities	
Angelman syndrome	A neurogenetic disorder that is often misdiagnosed as CP or autism; characteristics include developmental delays, lack of speech, seizure disorders, balance and walking difficulties, frequent laughter and happiness	N/A
Rett syndrome	A disorder of the nervous system that leads to developmental regression; under the autism spectrum disorder umbrella; normal development until 6–18 months, followed by regression of acquired speech and motor skills; often associated with breathing problems, scoliosis, seizures, sleep problems, poor circulation; affects girls	• Atypical • Classical • Provisional • Four stages • Stage 1—early onset • Stage 2—rapid destructive stage • Stage 3—plateau or pseudostationary stage • Stage 4—late motor deterioration stage

(cont.)

TABLE 10.1. *(cont.)*

Major category	Description	Subtypes
Williams syndrome	A rare genetic disorder that can lead to developmental problems; motor and perceptual disorders; feeding problems, physical abnormalities, intellectual disability	N/A
Cornelia de Lange syndrome	A congenital syndrome characterized by multiple abnormalities, including microcephaly, short stature with limb anomalies, cognitive delays, severe speech–language deficits, hearing loss, extremely low birth weight, small body stature, excessive body hair, feeding difficulties	N/A

at home, school, work, and in the community. Such services might include the use of a regular or electronic wheelchair, canes, guide dogs, or use of public transportation (Neil, Bigby, & Nicholson, 2004).

When working with the PT, OT, and O&M it is important to know and understand what goals these specialists identify for the student. It is also important that the teacher receive training from the PT and OT so they can carry out the same goals when the therapists are not available. Some of the questions a teacher may ask the therapist include:

1. How do I safely transfer the student while keeping myself safe?
2. What adaptations can I make to these materials to make them more accessible?
3. What training do I need to help my student be as successful as possible?
4. How can I integrate my students' therapies into daily academic and functional instruction?
5. How can I continue these goals in other environments, such as the community?

One of the topics to be discussed in planning for students with physical impairments is how to position the student for full access to the educational environment. Students with severe disabilities who have motor problems or muscle tone issues (i.e., hypotonia, hypertonia) may use lots of adaptive equipment such as wheelchairs, standers, wedges, adaptive chairs, and additional equipment. The PT will help the teacher identify good posture and alignment techniques to be used with students in order for them to remain comfortable and safe throughout the day. Well-planned positioning involves the student as much as possible and allows sufficient movement while not jeopardizing additional muscles in the body. Without proper positioning, students can develop side effects such as skin breakdowns, scoliosis, bone density problems, poor circulation, muscle tightness, and other problems. A student should not be left in one position for the whole day but instead should experience a variety of positions that allow access to the educational environment. A plan should be developed with the team to decide on the student's positioning schedule for the day (Heller & Forney, 2009).

Some planning may also be needed to identify safe procedures for lifting and transferring the student. Proper lifting techniques are crucial to prevent injury to the caregiver or child. Being trained by a physical therapist on each student's lifting needs is the best way to prevent injury.

It also is important to identify ways to integrate the student's therapies into daily instruction so the student is not missing critical content when being pulled out for one-to-one therapy sessions. This model of instruction is known as a transdisciplinary model in which the therapists function as consultants to the teacher and other service providers who implement the services (Orelove & Sobsey, 2000). Additionally, the therapists may also provide direct services to the student. In a transdisciplinary model, the teacher meets with the therapists to plan and review therapy goals. The team also brainstorms how the student will receive these therapies during instructional activities. For example, Isaiah, a seventh-grade student with spastic CP, has a goal to work on sitting up unassisted. Instead of the therapist removing him from the classroom to work on this skill in the therapy room, he can remain in the classroom for the ELA lesson and work on sitting unassisted with the therapist or classroom assistant (who has been previously trained by the physical therapist) during the shared story reading of a novel. This allows Isaiah to receive his critical therapy sessions without missing the ELA lesson for the day.

Transdisciplinary planning can be especially important when developing instruction for students who have multiple complex and severe disabilities. When students are poorly positioned, they may have difficulty focusing on the instructional task or making independent responses. Smith, Gast, Logan, and Jacobs (2001) provide a model to customize instruction for students with multiple disabilities. Table 10.2 summarizes their recommendations.

Sensory Impairments

Sensory impairments include visual and hearing impairments and deaf–blindness. When planning for instruction, these disabilities alone can be challenging, and extremely so in conjunction with an intellectual disability. Teachers must be cognizant of these students' strengths and work with these strengths when planning instruction.

Visual Impairments

There are a variety of visual impairments, including legal blindness, low vision, blindness, and cortical vision impairment. A student who is legally blind has 20/200 or lower vision even after corrective measures have been taken (Heller, Easterbrooks, McJannet, & Swinehart-Jones, 2009). A student who has low vision has a significant vision loss even after corrective measures have been taken, but vision may still be functional (Heller et al., 2009). A student who is blind has no vision. A student with cortical visual impairment (CVI) has suffered some damage to the visual cortex, and therefore his or her brain cannot interpret visual input, even though the eyes are intact (Best, 2001). Students with CVI have a range of vision from mild loss to blindness. It is important to know students' visual strengths and weaknesses and use this information to plan for interventions.

Interventions for students with visual impairments vary depending on their needs, but there are several strategies to consider when working with these students. First, educators can arrange the environment to enhance the visual characteristics of objects by considering color, contrast, time, illumination, and space. Second, students may benefit from the use of optical devices such as enlargers or magnifiers. Third, educators should encourage the use of residual vision and/or touch through the systematic presentation of

TABLE 10.2. Five Steps for Customizing Instruction for Students with Multiple Disabilities

Steps (after identifying an instructional goal)	Description	Example
1. Determine pre-positioning handling procedures.	If pre-positioning is required before the instructional session, it is necessary to determine all hands-on methods used to normalize muscle tone and aid in normal, upright posture, as well as normal movements.	A student with high muscle tone may require some small motor exercises to relax muscle tone before transferring to instructional positioning.
2. Determine overall body position for instruction.	For the instructional task, identify the most optimal body position for the student to access the instructional setup. This includes postural support for the following: normalizing muscle tone, maintaining alignment and posture, improving the quality and quantity of purposeful and meaningful movements of hands, arms, and head to participate in activities.	A student with poor trunk control may need to be positioned in a reclined wheelchair with proper harness placement to support proper alignment and body control.
3. Determine hand/arm and head position.	Determine hand/arm and head positions that allow the student to participate in the target behavior as independently as possible.	A student with low muscle tone may need a rolled towel or cylinder-type adaptation on his or her lap tray under the forearm and elbow to active a voice output device independently.
4. Determine instructional adaptations and materials.	Careful consideration should go into selecting the adaptations and materials necessary for the student to participate in the instructional goal. The following considerations should be taken: student's preferred sensory mode of input, preference for stimuli, and appropriate switch selection.	A student with no arm movement may need a universal mount with a spec switch attached with Velcro and placed near his or her head so he or she can use his or her head to activate the switch to participate in the instructional activity.
5. Determine handling procedures to combine with systematic instructional strategies.	Consider the prompting strategy to be used while keeping in mind the student's normal muscle tone, posture, and positioning.	Using most to least prompts with a student who is working on turning the pages of an adapted book.

Note. Based on Smith, Gast, Logan, and Jacobs (2001).

stimuli and instruction (Heller et al., 2009). For example, Ms. Thompson was helping Stella participate in a science lesson on types of rocks and minerals. She presented rock samples in a tray divided into four slots. She taught Stella to scan each slot with her hand from left to right and top to bottom as Ms. Thompson named them aloud. After scanning, she then would give Stella an opportunity to show what she learned by saying "Find the sandstone." Discussing strategies that have been helpful for the student in the past can provide a head start in helping the student gain access to the environment.

Hearing Impairments

Hearing impairments include deafness and hardness of hearing. A student who is deaf has a hearing loss that is so severe that he or she is not able to process spoken language through hearing even with an amplification device. A student who is hard of hearing is able to process some spoken language through hearing, either with or without an amplification device (Heller et al., 2009). As with visual impairments, teachers should know the strengths and weaknesses of their students with hearing impairments in order to plan interventions.

Interventions for students with hearing impairments vary depending on their needs, but there are several strategies to consider. First, educators should consider modifications to reduce background noise (e.g., carpets) or place the student with the hearing impairment away from noisy equipment (e.g., air conditioners). Second, students may benefit from strategies that enhance use of visual strengths. These may include being seated near the teacher and interpreter, using picture cues, and providing models of concepts to be described in the lesson (e.g., a model of the Earth). Families can be encouraged to consider the benefits of hearing aids, cochlear implants, and listening devices for the student. Finally, the teacher can modify materials that may be a barrier for the student (e.g., recording tapes, writing down oral questions) and use strategies that highlight important information, such as visual organizers (Heller et al., 2009).

Deaf–Blindness

Students with deaf–blindness have both vision and hearing loss that can vary from total mild. It is very rare that a student truly has no vision and no hearing. It is most important to consider the sensory strength of this student and to work with such strengths.

It is most important to identify a communication system for students with deaf–blindness. The communication system chosen for the student will depend on the vision or hearing of the student. For example, it may be possible to use a large photo communication system if the student has some functional vision. Teaching a student who is deaf–blind to successfully use a communication system will take some time, and systematic instructional strategies should be employed consistently.

Health Care Needs

Students with severe disabilities often present unique health care needs. Teachers may encounter students who need seizure care, medication administration, tube feeding, tracheostomy care, ileostomy or colostomy care, suctioning, shunt care, diabetes management, and others. It is crucial that teachers meet with the school nurse to become trained in any area of care a student may require. Teachers should never assume they know what to do because they have had a student with the same health care need before. Instead, they should receive training specific to the needs of an individual student. Additionally, teachers should receive documentation showing completion of training whenever available. In addition to teachers, paraprofessionals or anyone else working with the student also should be trained.

Seizures

A seizure occurs "when a brief, strong surge of electrical activity affects part or all of the brain" and often results in a brief change in behavior (*www.epilesyfoundation.org*, 2009). There are many different types of seizures. Spooner and Dykes (1982) described the impact of epilepsy on persons with severe disabilities for a nonmedical audience (teachers and caregivers for this population) by defining and categorizing seizures, delineating the types (e.g., partial, generalized, unilateral), and discussing treatment options (medical regimens, neurosurgery and electrical stimulation, behavior analysis). Students can experience just one or more types of seizures. The type of seizure a student has depends on the part of the brain and how much of the brain is affected by the electrical disturbance produced by the seizure. Experts separate seizures into generalized seizures (absence, atonic, tonic–clonic, myoclonic), partial (simple and complex) seizures, nonepileptic seizures, and *status epilepticus* (*www.epilesyfoundation.org*; Epilepsy Foundation, 2009). Table 10.3 provides information about each type of seizure, including the average duration and a description of what each type of seizure might look like. Because of the seriousness of seizures, it is important to monitor them by logging as much information as possible, including events that happened before and after, as well as a description of the seizure itself. Figure 10.1 provides an example of a form that might be used to log seizures.

Educators also need to know basic first aid for seizures, including the following steps:

- Do not try to stop a seizure in the middle.
- If it is a generalized tonic–clonic seizure, make sure the student is clear of all objects, and help him or her to the floor so he or she does not sustain an injury during a fall.
- Protect the student's head by placing some sort of cushion under it.
- Loosen any tight clothing the student may be wearing.
- Place a barrier between the student and the rest of the class, or have the other students leave the class so they will not become upset while watching the person having the seizure.
- Note the activities that occurred before the seizure, as well as the time the seizure occurred and the time the seizure ended.
- After the seizure is over, continue to monitor the student's breathing and level of alertness. The student most likely will be very tired and should be allowed to sleep.
- Finally, log all that you took note of during the seizure. If the student has a history of seizures, a plan of action should be identified by the student's team. The plan should include the family's wishes as to whether 911 should be called if the duration of the seizure exceeds a certain point.

Infectious Disease

Infectious disease is a term that includes illnesses that can be directly or indirectly spread from person to person and can be caused by viruses, bacteria, protozoans, and fungi. They can be particularly challenging for individuals with severe disabilities for a variety of reasons, including a lowered immune system, less physical activity, poor self-care

TABLE 10.3. Types of Seizures

Type	Duration	Description
Generalized seizures		
1. Generalized tonic–clonic (grand mal)	1–2 minutes	• Crying out • Falling • Rigidity • Jerking • Possible blue tint to skin
2. Myoclonic	Very brief (1 second)	• Rapid contractions of muscles • Usually occurring at same time on both sides of body
3. Absence (petit mal)	2–15 seconds	• Staring off • Fluttering eyes • Involuntary or automatic behaviors
4. Atonic (drop seizures)	Very brief (1 second)	• Head drops • Loss of posture • Sudden collapse • Very frequent • Protective headgear may be needed
Partial seizures		
1. Simple partial	90 seconds	• No loss of consciousness • Sudden jerking • Sensory occurrence
2. Complex partial	1–2 minutes	• Consciousness may be affected • May experience involuntary or automatic behaviors
Nonepileptic seizures		• Change person's behavior • Look like epileptic seizures • Not caused by electrical disruption in the brain
Status epilepticus	Prolonged or long spells of multiple seizures, 30 minutes in length	• Life threatening

Note. Data from Epilepsy Foundation (2009).

skills, and increased nutritional problems (Sobsey & Thuppal, 2000). Some more common infectious diseases found among children with severe disabilities are AIDS, HIV, hepatitis A, hepatitis B, scabies, colds, lice, cytomegolovirus, and influenza (Sobsey & Thuppal, 2000).

Universal precautions are a set of precautions used when providing first aid or health care intended to prevent transmission of blood-borne pathogens such as HIV or hepatitis B. Universal precautions apply to blood or body fluids that contain blood, semen, or vaginal secretions. To lessen the chance of being exposed to potentially infectious substances, protective barriers such as gloves, gowns, or masks should be used at all times

Student's Name: _____

Date	Location	Time	Length/Intensity 1 (mild) to 10 (severe)	Activities before seizure	Behavior after seizure	Anecdotal notes (e.g., breathing, skin color, eye position)

FIGURE 10.1. Seizure log.

when around blood or these other types of body fluids (Centers for Disease Control and Prevention [CDC], 2010). Teachers should also manage infection by keeping the students' environment clean and implementing careful hand washing for both staff and students. Additionally, both students and staff should consider getting any vaccine that is available to prevent the spread of infection (e.g., flu shot).

Feeding Tubes

Some students with disabilities also need to use alternate means of nourishment other than food by mouth due to their inability to swallow or difficulties in swallowing. A common alternate feeding procedure is the use of a tube. A gastrostomy feeding tube (G-tube) is a tube that directly leads to the stomach through a "button" in the abdomen. A jejunostomy tube (J-tube) is another type of tube that is implanted through the abdomen in the small intestine, just below the stomach. This allows the nutritional supplement to bypass the stomach and go directly into the intestinal tract. Some students who are able to swallow a bit without aspiration may eat some food by mouth with a G-tube or J-tube but may require additional nutrition or caloric intake supplemented through the tube (Townsley & Robinson, 1999).

Another type of tube feeding is a nasogastric (N-G) tube, which runs through the nose, down the throat, and to the stomach. This type of tube tends to be temporary and is often used during times when individuals cannot eat by mouth because of hospitalization or a serious illness that would prevent eating (Townsley & Robinson, 1999).

There are several methods of tube feeding, including the bolus method, the gravity drip method, and pump feeding. In the bolus method, a syringe is attached to the feeding tube, formula is poured into the syringe, and gravity pulls the formula through the tube. This method is very simple and is the fastest of all tube feeding methods. In the gravity drip method a gravity feeding bag or set is filled with formula and allowed to drain through the tubing. Often a clamp is used to control the flow of formula. Depending on the flow rate, it can be given in a short or long amount of time. The final method is pump feeding, in which the formula is delivered via a bag connected to an external electric or battery-operated pump that is set to deliver formula at a flow recommended by the doctor (Heller, 2009a).

When caring for a student who is tube fed, it is crucial to follow the instructions given by the caregivers and doctors. These directions will include method of delivery, position during and after feeding, amount of intake, frequency of feeding per day, care of equipment and tube site, cleaning of tube site and equipment, times of day, rate of delivery, emergency situations, water flushing after feeding, and medication delivery through tube.

Other Special Feeding Concerns

Children who do not require tube feeding may have other special feeding needs. Some may require a special way of preparing food, such as chopping or pureeing. Others may have dietary restrictions, such as in the case of lactose intolerance. Thickening of liquids or foods (e.g., with Thick-It) may be necessary to prevent aspiration. Other problems include rumination, food pocketing, and tongue thrust issues. Each of these needs or problems requires planning with the occupational and speech therapist to keep the student safe from concerns such as aspiration, which can lead to pneumonia.

Tracheostomy

A tracheotomy is a surgical procedure that opens an airway through an incision in the trachea on the neck. A tracheotomy is performed to help deliver oxygen to the lungs more easily. Students with a tracheostomy require special care and training that all educators should receive. Some of the care procedures include cleaning around the stoma (opening) and monitoring the site for pink color, irritation, drainage, and swelling. Also, be sure to clean the tracheostomy as often as the student's family or care provider requires (usually cleaning is performed every 8 hours). Prior to cleaning, suction the airway to remove secretions.

Ileostomy and Colostomy

Some children may have malformation of the intestines due to a certain condition or disease that may prevent fecal matter or urine from normally exiting the body. As a result, many of these children have to have a surgical opening created called an "ostomy." An ostomy is a place at which a connection is made through the abdomen to the intestines or part of the urinary system. An ileostomy is a surgical opening that creates a passage from the abdomen to the small intestine. Waste is disposed through this opening and collected in a bag. A colostomy is an opening from the colon to the abdomen, and a bag to collect waste may or may not be needed depending on the side of the colon on which the opening is placed. With an ileostomy or colostomy, the bag will most likely need to be emptied at some point during the school day, and proper training should take place that covers ostomy care (Heller, Bigge, & Allgood, 2001; Sobsey & Cox, 2000).

Shunts

Some children with disabilities have hydrocephalus, or excess fluid (cerebral spinal fluid) on the brain. As a result, many of these children will have to have shunts surgically implanted in the brain that allow the fluid to safely drain into other parts of the body, which relieves pressure from the brain that would otherwise cause brain damage. School staff need to be especially aware of students with shunts because shunts can become blocked or can malfunction, causing a serious medical situation. Some signs of shunt problems may include nausea, vomiting, exhaustion, headaches, blurred vision, emotional outbursts, poor schoolwork, and staring off (Heller, 2009b). It is also important to note that children with shunts are at a higher risk for developing sudden allergies to latex. Nonlatex gloves should be used with these students as a preventative measure (AbdelAziz, Vassilyadi, & Ventureyra, 2002).

Progressive Neurological Conditions

Some students with severe disabilities have progressive neurological disorders. These conditions involve a progressive deterioration in functioning that may be rapid or slow. Some progressive neurological disorders include Huntington's disease, muscular dystrophy, and Rett disorder. When educating students with progressive neurological conditions, teachers should always work toward maintaining the student's current skills, although some students can make progress on goals if their conditions progress at a slower rate.

The planning team should also consider skills that will be needed as functioning is lost (Heller & Forney, 2009). For example, a student who speaks might benefit from instruction in simple manual signs and picture use for future communication.

Death and Dying

Unfortunately, it is not uncommon for a student with severe multiple disabilities to become extremely sick or even die. When a teacher knows that a student has declining health or a progressive medical condition, he or she needs to plan in order to best serve the student, the family, and the school community. Plans should include (1) goals that should continue to be worked on or skills that should be maintained, (2) new skills that may need to be gained if current abilities are lost, (3) counseling for the student, family, and school community to prepare them for the loss of skills and overall health, and (4) reducing the side effects that might occur during this process (Rues, Graff, Ault, & Holvoet, 2006). Teachers and other members of the educational team may also need to seek counseling to process the grief that occurs with the loss of a student.

Do-Not-Resuscitate Orders

A current major issue in schools is whether or not to honor do-not-resuscitate (DNR) orders. DNRs are orders given by a doctor, based on the family's request, that resuscitation not be given if a student goes into cardiac arrest. Such orders are rare, and problems ensue when school staff members may be the ones needing to carry out the order. Emotional and legal repercussions may follow after the order is carried out. In fact, many states do not have clear guidelines about the procedures and persons responsible regarding DNR for students in schools (Sewall & Balkman, 2002). If a teacher has a student who has a DNR, it is important to find out the school's policy on honoring such orders, as well as to develop a plan in the event that such a situation should happen at school.

Preplanning

It is important that the teacher knows as much as possible about students with physical, sensory, or health impairments before the first day the student enters the classroom. Planning is essential to this process to help make the transition as smooth as possible. An important source of information is the student's prior teacher. Figure 10.2 provides a form that may be used to gather information from a student's prior teacher. The best way to obtain this information may be to meet with the teacher directly. Ideally, the receiving teacher will also plan to observe the student in his or her current setting before the student transfers to the new setting. While observing, the teacher can make notes on the student's current schedule, feeding needs, positioning needs, transferring needs, and so forth. If possible, the teacher should interview the student about his or her own perspective on future needs. Figure 10.3 provides an example of information that might be gleaned from the student. Finally, Figure 10.4 is an example of a checklist of all observations, forms, and information that should be exchanged on the transferring student.

(text resumes on page 259)

Student's Name: _____

Date: _____   Time of observation: _____

I. GENERAL

Full name of student: _____

Age: _____

Nature of disability: _____

Current food restrictions/feeding method, etc.: _____

_____

_____

_____

Medications currently taking/will take at school: _____

_____

II. EDUCATIONAL

1. Communication

Briefly describe this student's communication status.

Verbal _____   Nonverbal _____   Verbal with assistance _____

Sign language _____   Voice-output device _____   Picture book _____

Comments: _____

_____

_____

2. Health Concerns

Briefly describe any health concerns (i.e., aspiration concerns, seizures, eating issues, physical concerns, and allergies). _____

_____

_____

3. Self-Care

Briefly describe this student's level of independence regarding self-care skills.

Dressing: _____

Eating/Feeding: _____

Toileting (and equipment needed):_____

_____

Other comments: _____

(cont.)

FIGURE 10.2. Receiving teacher observation form.

4. Schedule

Object schedule _____

Photo schedule _____

Picture schedule _____

Written schedule_____

5. Other

Briefly describe necessary information in the following areas.

Sensory _____

Mobility _____

Barriers to success in my classroom _____

Physical therapy equipment needed (e.g., stander, side lyer, special chair) and number of times a day and time used. _____

_____

_____

III. SOCIAL/EMOTIONAL/BEHAVIORAL

Briefly describe this student's level of development and/or special considerations for each of the following areas.

Social skills: _____

_____

Emotional needs/development: _____

_____

Behavioral concerns/supports: _____

_____

Triggers: _____

_____

IV. STUDENT INTERESTS

V. THINGS I AM OBSERVING THAT I NEED AN ANSWER ABOUT

VI. ADDITIONAL COMMENTS

FIGURE 10.2. *(cont.)*

My name is _____, **and I am** _____ **years old.** _____
helped me fill this form out.

Interests/Hobbies
1. My favorite thing in the whole world is _____.
2. I like to _____.
3. My favorite food is _____, but I like to snack on _____.
4. The one thing I don't like the most is _____.
5. My least favorite food is _____.

Communication
6. I let people know what I want or need by (speaking, signing, using a communication device).
   Other: _____
7. I learn best (in a group, one-on-one). Other:_____

Mobility
8. I get around by (walking alone, walking with help, walker, wheelchair). Other: _____
   _____

Social/Behavioral
9. I (like, do not like) to be around other kids/people.
10. When I'm happy, I show it by _____. Here are some things that make me
    happy: _____.
11. When I'm sad, I show it by _____. Here are some things that
    make me sad: _____.
12. When I'm mad, I show it by _____. Here are some things that
    make me mad: _____.
13. When I'm scared, I show it by _____. Here are some things that make me
    scared: _____.
14. When I'm excited, I show it by _____. Here are some things that make me
    excited: _____.
15. When I'm frustrated, I show it by _____. Here are some things that
    make me frustrated: _____.
16. You can help me feel better by _____.
17. I can _____ by myself.
18. I need help with _____.
19. I don't need help with _____.

Family
20. I live (with, in a) _____.
21. I have _____ older/younger brother(s). His/their name(s) is/are _____
    _____.
22. I have _____ older/younger sister(s). Her/their name(s) is/are _____
    _____.

Medical
23. Please ask my caretaker about _____.
24. My future plans for after graduation at this time are _____.

FIGURE 10.3. Student profile for transfer/transition.

From *Teaching Students with Moderate and Severe Disabilities* by Diane M. Browder and Fred Spooner. Copyright 2011 by The Guilford Press. Permission to photocopy this figure is granted to purchasers of this book for personal use only (see copyright page for details).

Date: _____

Student's Name: _____

Please check below to indicate those documents or items you feel you will need to assist with the transfer of _____ to your classroom.

1. _____ Completed identifiable student information (name, age, category, setting, etc.)

2. _____ Student profile/interest form

3. _____ Parent form (i.e., questions, concerns, comments)

4. _____ All relevant medical information including feeding/eating restrictions/conditions

5. _____ Copy of current annual goals

6. _____ Copy of progress report

7. _____ Copy of behavioral intervention plan

8. _____ Student daily schedule

9. _____ Observation of the student

10. _____ Adaptive equipment/utensils provided specifically for this student

11. _____ This student may have special needs that go beyond these options. I need to see administration about these needs.

FIGURE 10.4. Student transfer checklist.

Planning for Teaching during Caregiving

Teaching and caring for individuals with motor, sensory, and/or health concerns may be challenging due to the need to balance instruction with care. It is most important that the student's basic needs are attended to, but there is no reason that caregiving cannot be integrated into daily instruction. Coordinating caregiving with daily instruction may require being intentional about doing so, with careful planning about when and how to provide care during the lesson. For example, physical therapy goals may be addressed during a science lesson by having the student stand in a stander while doing a science experiment with the class. Or a teacher or nurse may discreetly deliver medication via a G-tube during this time. Whatever the situation, it is not always necessary that instruction stop. Utilize your paraprofessionals, the school nurse, and the PT, PT, and orientation and mobility specialist to assist with special circumstances during the day.

FINDING THE BALANCE: CAREGIVING VERSUS TEACHING

When a teacher provides support to several students who require therapeutic and health interventions, the day can become more typical of nursing or rehabilitation than teaching without careful planning. There are several strategies to keep the focus on education. One is to share the caregiving among the staff. All members of the team should be trained in therapeutic interventions and know the student's health care needs (Heller & Forney, 2009). A second strategy is to teach while providing care and, whenever possible, provide care while teaching. Students may participate in lessons while using adaptive equipment. A student may be able to listen to a story while having a tube feeding. If the teacher is not able to address other IEP goals due to therapy or health care needs, team planning is needed to consider whether the student needs additional staff support or whether the problem can be resolved with more creative scheduling.

Planning for the Use of Assistive Technology

AT is defined in IDEA as any item or piece of equipment, whether acquired commercially, modified, or customized, that is used to increase, maintain, or improve the functional capabilities of children with disabilities. The IDEA (1997) amendments added the requirement that the IEP team consider the student's need for AT. In planning for a student's AT requirements, the team should consider whether the student has access to needed equipment and, if so, whether student or staff require instruction in its use. For example, a student may have a picture communication system or side lyer equipment, but if staff members do not know how to use this AT, the student will not benefit. The student may also need systematic instruction to learn to use specialized equipment such as a power wheelchair or a page-turning switch. Figure 10.5 provides a checklist of some of the types of AT that a planning team might consider.

SUMMARY

Many students with severe disabilities also are likely to have some other concomitant disability (e.g., sensory, neurological, physical, or health). Because of the likelihood of the involvement of these other disabilities, it is important that teachers, caregivers, parents,

I. Equipment for Mobility
1. Manual wheelchair
2. Power wheelchair
3. Travel stroller chairs
4. Walkers
5. Crutches
6. Prone scooters
7. Gait trainers

II. Equipment for Positioning
1. Side lyer
2. Wedge
3. Seating support
   a. Shoulder straps, leg separators, foot supports, trunk support
4. Standing table
5. Prone board
6. Adaptive chairs (e.g., Rifton)

III. Equipment for Daily Living
1. Lap tray
2. Adapted cup
3. Adapted spoon
4. Adaptive bowls and plates
5. Nonslip placemats
6. Adaptive dressing equipment (e.g., Velcro shoes, button hook)
7. Raised toilet seat
8. Adaptive equipment for cooking
9. Remote-control appliances

IV. Equipment for Hearing Impairment
1. Assistive listening devices (to use with or without hearing aid)
2. Telecommunication equipment to use with telephones (TDD)
3. Alerting or warning device (e.g., visual fire alarm; vibrating pager)

V. Equipment for Visual Impairment
1. Electronic or optical magnifiers
2. Large-print books
3. Closed-circuit television used to enlarge print on existing books (CCTV)
4. Screen enlargers for computers
5. Talking watch, calculator, clock
6. Raised picture books, audiotaped books, or Braille books

VI. Equipment for Instruction
1. Switches that interface with household appliances, toys, computers
2. Adapted brushes
3. Object stabilization devices (e.g., clamping base of item to table or attaching with Velcro)
4. Grasping aids (e.g., Velcro on glove and item to be picked up)
5. Book-holding device; page-turning device or adaptations (e.g., tab on page)
6. Work surface modifications (e.g., raised table)
7. Eye-gaze board (clear plexiglass to attach options for students to show response)
8. Adapted books; digitized books on computer
9. Computer adaptations (e.g., adapted computer keyboard, voice recognition software, switch with scanning, mouth stick)
10. Computer software with word prediction, talking dictionary
11. Voice output device
12. Talking calculator

FIGURE 10.5. Some possible considerations for assistive technology and adaptive equipment.

and others be knowledgeable in order to understand and work with related service providers (OT, PT, and other related medical staff).

In this chapter we have covered physical impairments (e.g., CP, spina bifida, muscular dystrophy) and described therapeutic interventions that might be helpful in remediating the condition (e.g., OT, PT), in additional to the role that transdisciplinary planning and teaming plays in the process of working with students with physical impairments. Next, we addressed sensory impairments, including visual and hearing impairments, and deaf–blindness, and touched on interventions that might be helpful in working with students with these types of conditions. Health disorders (e.g., seizures, infectious diseases, use of feeding tubes or shunts) are also frequently encountered within this population. Almost by definition, many students with severe disabilities also have feeding-related problems. Based on these concomitant conditions, these students frequently will require extensive caregiving, and that caregiving needs to be appropriately backed up with instruction; therefore, we recommend that all members of the team be trained in therapeutic interventions and know the specifics of the student's health care needs. Many times, the use of AT can be an augmentative support that can provide the interface for a communication system.

APPLICATIONS

1. You are getting ready to receive a student who has a degenerative disorder into your class. In order to plan for this student, you are going to have a planning meeting with the student's parents and therapists. Write an agenda for topics to cover during this meeting. What might you teach a student who is expected to lose physical and intellectual functioning?

2. Plan for a student with complex physical needs in an inclusive setting. Consider tube feeding, bathroom needs, medication time, therapies, and so forth.

3. Obtain additional information on basic first aid and prevention of infectious disease. Make posters to remind all staff of safety steps to follow.

CHAPTER 11

Communication Skills

DIANE M. BROWDER, FRED SPOONER, AND PAMELA J. MIMS

Randal is a 10-year-old boy with spastic cerebral palsy and a severe intellectual disability. His classroom teacher is not sure how to include Randal in the grade-level content or even how to identify what Randal's want and needs are because he is nonvocal. Because Randal's attempts to communicate are not understood, he has become increasingly frustrated, and he expresses this through inappropriate behaviors. Randal has a communication system for expressing basic needs (eating, resting, toileting) and can indicate his choice between two objects. What is missing for Randal is an appropriate way not only to communicate his wants and needs but also to "show what he knows" in the classroom activities. This chapter provides information on identifying students' communicative abilities, planning a communication system for students, and considering the best way for students to communicate learning in the general education curriculum, as well as during functional and social events.

OVERVIEW OF COMMUNICATION

Teaching communication skills should be one of the most important priorities for students with moderate and severe disabilities because the ability to communicate affects learning in all other content, as well as overall quality of life. Without an effective means of communication, individuals with severe disabilities can fall victim to the phenomenon of "learned helplessness" (Guess, Benson, & Siegel-Causey, 1985). That is, communicative attempts by individuals with severe disabilities may cease if they are unable to influence others through their attempts. In addition, when students' communicative attempts are unrecognized or ineffective, they may develop problem behaviors due to the lack of a means of self-expression (Carr et al., 1994; Durand, 1990).

There are three major components of communication: *form, content,* and *function.* When the form of communication is speech, teachers focus on syntax, including such skills as sentence structure, grammar, and inflection. When the form is an augmentative or alternative communication system, a nonspeech system, the teacher focuses on teaching the student to use this system effectively. The content of communication includes vocabulary and the topics discussed. Whatever form is used to communicate (speech or AAC), students also need to expand their vocabularies. The function of communication is the purpose of the communicative attempt. The purpose may be social, such as greeting a friend, or instrumental, such as gaining necessary items. Current best practice in communication intervention is to emphasize the functional use of communication by teaching students to make requests, initiate social routines, gain attention, and exercise other interactive skills. The form and content of communication are then selected to enhance these functions.

Besides understanding form, function, and content, educators also need to be aware of the "intentionality" of communication. As McLean and Snyder-McLean (1988) described, intentionality is an early communication skill that develops as a child interacts with others in the environment. In the beginning a child will engage in behavior that caregivers translate as having meaning, even if the individual is expressing no intent. For example, if an individual fusses in a certain way that the caregiver translates as "I'm hungry" and gives food, the individual will probably learn to use that style of fussing to get fed. This then becomes a *primitive* form of communication. Primitive forms of communication are actions that have occurred often enough to become conditioned. In some cases, a student may pull away from undesired items or interactions or close his or her eyes when overwhelmed. Again, if caregivers respond to these actions as communicative, the child learns to use them with intention. In a classic work on defining the emergence of communication, Bates (1979) called the stage in which intention is being established the *perlocutionary stage* of language development. Over time, the child learns to use communication with more intention. This level of communication is *conventional* and may include acts such as extending the hand to ask for more, turning the head to end a task, or sitting forward to ask to be moved. Bates identified this stage of communication development as the *illocutionary stage.* The third level is *referential* communication. At this level, the student can use either speech or some type of symbols to communicate. For example, the student can now ask for food by showing a picture of it or by signing "eat" or by saying "eat." Referential communication is both intentional and symbolic and is called the *locutionary stage* (Bates, 1979). Some students with moderate and severe disabilities may not use symbolic communication yet but may have a rich repertoire of intentional communication that they achieve nonsymbolically. Parents and educators' interpretation and social responsiveness to efforts to communicate are essential in shaping this intentionality. Because nonsymbolic communication can sometimes be difficult to interpret, caregivers may overlook students' expressions without careful observation. An important part of a communication assessment is to consider all the ways a student may be using communication signals.

Consider the real case of a boy named Tommy who at first seemed to have few observable, voluntary responses. He had spastic quadriplegia, was legally blind, had respiratory illness, and lived in a hospital for children who were medically fragile. His teacher, Ms. Martin, noted that he had made no progress on prior IEPs because his teachers could not find anything that he could learn to do. To plan for Tommy, Ms. Martin decided to spend 2 days writing down everything Tommy did. She then talked with the medical staff about which of these responses might be involuntary seizure activity and which were voluntary. She discovered that Tommy clucked his tongue voluntarily. He did not do so with the intention to communicate. In fact, Tommy had developed "learned helplessness" and was passive when receiving care or when caregivers spoke to him. Ms. Martin decided to respond to Tommy's tongue clucks as if they were intentional. When she fed Tommy his lunch, he had shown a preference for yogurt (swallowed it) versus applesauce (spit it out). So she would say to Tommy, "Do you want yogurt?" She modeled clucking her tongue. When he clucked, she gave him yogurt. After many trials, he clucked without her modeling. She then asked if he wanted applesauce and told him not to cluck. If he clucked, he got applesauce, and she said, "No, you don't like applesauce! Don't cluck your tongue." If he was quiet, she asked again, "Do you want yogurt?" and gave him yogurt when he clucked. After many trials he began to use the tongue cluck with clear intention as a "yes" response (Browder & Martin, 1986). Not all shaping of intentionality will be so intensely focused on one response in a massed-trial format like this. Many times the teacher or parent will simply respond to the child in the context of daily activities, such as waiting for the student to raise his or her eyes before moving him or her out of the wheelchair or for a small sound before going outside.

In addition to understanding form, function, content, and intention, it also is important to understand that communication is both *expressive* and *receptive*. Expressive communication is the production of a communication act, such as showing someone a picture, moving toward a desired object, or asking about the day's schedule. Receptive communication is the *comprehension* of someone else's communication and may be unobservable (listening in silence) or observable, such as selecting the object identified or answering a question. Students with moderate and severe disabilities do not always show even development in their expressive and receptive communication skills. For instance, students who use nonsymbolic communication may be able understand short, spoken phrases and thus understand most of what is said to them. Other students, such as some students with ASD, may speak but need concrete symbols, such as pictures or manual signs, paired with verbalizations to be able to understand. In planning for communication skills, educators need to be careful not to make assumptions about the student's receptive communication skills based on his or her expressive skills or vice versa. Table 11.1 summarizes the primary terms used to describe how students communicate.

CHECK FOR UNDERSTANDING

Two close friends are eating lunch together. Karen glances toward a boy who walks into the cafeteria and looks at her friend Jacqui. Her friend Jacqui smiles at Karen. What is the form of their communication? What is its function? Do you know the content? Who is using expressive communication? Whose is receptive? What do you think the intention of Karen's communication is? With what intention does Jacqui interpret the communication?

TABLE 11.1. Terms Used in Communication Training

Term	Application in speech	Application in AAC
Intentionality		
• Primitive (perlocutionary)	• Prespeech acts interpreted with intent	• Actions to which others will respond to encourage intentional communication
• Conventional (illocutionary)	• Prespeech acts that child uses to influence others (e.g., reaching)	• Recognized as nonsymbolic communication; may be primary mode of communication
• Referential (locutionary)	• Intentional use of speech to communicate with others	• Use of AAC systems (symbols such as pictures, words, manual signs); may be *aided* (with materials) or *unaided* (e.g., gestures, signs)
Components of communication		
• Form	• Syntax—sentence structure, grammar	• Type of system used (e.g., nonsymbolic, manual signs, picture wallet, electronic board)
• Content	• Semantics—vocabulary and meaning	• Vocabulary (symbols)
• Function	• Pragmatics—social use of language	• Pragmatics—functional/social use of communication system
Types of communication		
• Expressive	• Asking or telling information through speech	• Asking or telling information through an AAC system (e.g., pictures, gestures)
• Receptive	• Understanding spoken phrases	• Understanding concrete symbols

COMMUNICATION SYSTEMS

Understanding Students' Symbolic Levels

In an early chapter on how to plan for students' learning in the general curriculum, Browder, Ahlgrim-Delzell, Courtade-Little, and Snell (2006) introduced the idea that instruction can be differentiated based on students' current level of symbolic communication. That is, even students who are just beginning to learn to use symbols can show what they know in academic instruction using nonsymbolic means. To be able to plan ways for students to "show what they know," educators need to have deep understanding of three phases of communication development. These three levels of communication development include presymbolic, concrete symbolic, and abstract symbolic (Rowland & Schweigert, 1990). Students who are presymbolic may be at either the perlocutionary (emerging intentionality) or illocutionary (with clear intention) phase. Students who have emerging intentionality may be described as at an "awareness" level for academic planning. Browder, Flowers, and Wakeman (2008) found that teachers could identify their students' symbolic levels using descriptions of how students would respond to academic tasks.

As shown in Table 11.2, at the earliest stages (awareness), the teacher may have to give meaning to the students' responses to shape them toward intentionality. This earliest stage in planning for general curriculum access is called an "awareness" level because the goal is to identify some response that shows that the student is alert and engaged with the lesson even if he or she is not yet showing understanding. As students progress at this level, their communication will become more clearly intentional. As students gain intention but continue to rely mostly on nonsymbolic communication, they enter the "beginning with symbols" level. We call this level "beginning with symbols" to emphasize the fact that symbols are introduced even if students do not yet use them. When students rely on nonsymbolic communication, symbols are still used in instruction for two reasons. First, by pairing symbols with the student's nonsymbolic responses, symbolic communication can be shaped. Second, if symbols are not used, students' ability to learn them is unknown. That is, students cannot demonstrate that they understand a symbol if it is never introduced.

At the second level, students are beginning to use symbols in concrete ways. Typically, the symbol will need a "right here, right now" application. That is, the student can hand the teacher a picture of a cup to ask for a drink when environmental cues such as snack preparation are occurring. Or a student may be able to hand the teacher an object or picture to answer a literal comprehension question immediately after the text was read. The pictures or objects used to communicate typically must be literal representations of objects or the objects themselves (e.g., selecting a picture of a coat to ask to put coat on or a picture of a book to ask for the book). At the highest level of this stage, students begin to use everyday pictures and objects with more symbolism (e.g., a ball to ask to play) and may begin to understand models (e.g., layers of the earth). Similar to using symbols with nonsymbolic students, abstract symbols should be used for students at the concrete level. By introducing these higher level symbols in the context of daily teaching activities, students may begin to understand and use them. We like to call this level "moving forward with symbols" because students are building symbol use.

At the highest level, students understand and use abstract symbols. They understand text (e.g., sight words), symbols (e.g., +, %), abstract pictures (e.g., the picture symbol for "evaporation") and abstract objects (e.g., a model of a cell). Obviously, this level of symbol use provides the most options for planning academic instruction and promoting social interaction. Surprisingly, teachers have often planned instruction at the most basic awareness or early symbolic level even for students who have abstract symbolic skills (Karvonen, Wakeman, Browder, Rogers, & Flowers, 2009). The reason may be that models for adapting grade-level content for students with severe disabilities have only emerged in recent years.

Table 11.2 provides an example of how students at each of the symbolic levels would respond to a middle school lesson on the novel *Holes* by Louis Sachar (1998). What the students can do now reflects their current symbolic level. All students receive instruction that includes abstract symbols so as not to underestimate ability. In contrast, the teacher creates a way for the students to respond using their current symbolic levels and promotes use of a slighter higher level of communication. Figure 11.1 provides a decision model that can be used to help plan moving students to a more advanced level of symbol use.

TABLE 11.2. Example of How to Use a Student's Symbolic Level of Communication in an ELA Lesson Based on the Text *Holes* by Louis Sachar

Symbolic level	Symbols used in lesson (some abstract symbols are used for all levels)	Adaptations in presentation of materials	Symbols (or nonsymbolic responses) student currently uses	Example of a teacher's goal to promote higher symbol use
Building awareness: *Perlocutionary* (intentionality not clear)	While reading the adapted version of *Holes* (adapted with shortened text and picture symbols to represent target vocabulary and important text), salient objects are presented to reinforce concrete vocabulary and encourage engagement.	A light board may be used to highlight each object presented.	Student uses nonsymbolic responses that may or may not be intentional communication (e.g., eye gaze, facial gestures, body tension/relaxation, vocalizations).	Pair the form of the communication attempt with a symbol and reinforce all possible communication attempts (e.g., "I like how you glanced at the shovel that Stanley used to dig holes" or "You smiled! Yes, it's funny what he said!").
Beginning with symbols: *presymbolic* (primarily nonsymbolic responses)	Adapted text. Objects to represent key vocabulary. Some text is introduced (e.g., having student touch title or a story line). Student is shown pictures.	Use objects to encourage responding to simple comprehension questions (e.g., literal recall—"What did Stanley write to his family?"; show a *letter* paired with a distracter for student to answer).	Student's nonsymbolic responses have clear intent—laughs at some story lines, turns page to hear more, looks at objects, looks at teacher to hear funny line read again.	Acknowledge nonsymbolic communication as seen above, but also see whether student will respond using objects to answer comprehension questions.
Moving forward with symbols: *Concrete symbolic* (uses concrete symbols with "right here, right now" meanings)	Adapted text. Objects used for interest/vocabulary. More attention to text—text pointing.	Arrays of objects/pictures are presented when asking comprehension questions, including plausible and nonplausible distracters (e.g., three or four). All objects and pictures are also labeled with words.	Student has a large repertoire of known objects and uses them consistently. Student is starting to transition to photos or picture symbols that are "right here, right now" concepts.	In addition to concrete pictures, begin to encourage student to use abstract symbols/objects (e.g., moon as symbol for nighttime).
Going far with symbols: *Abstract symbolic* (uses words, models, symbols; may have early reading)	Adapted text and may also use some controlled text (see Chapter 6). Student participates in reading either the entire text or selected portions (e.g., repeated story line). Student primarily uses words to answer questions and may write some answers.	If more support is needed, word responses will be presented and labeled for the student.	Student uses expressive format to answer open-ended question or uses multiple-choice answers (e.g., "Why did Stanley help Zero to read?" "Because he was scared of Zero," "Because he wanted Zero to dig his holes in return," "Because he hates the camp," "Because he likes to dig holes").	Shape student's understanding of abstract comprehension questions that cannot be found on the page but require activation of background knowledge (see Chapter 6).

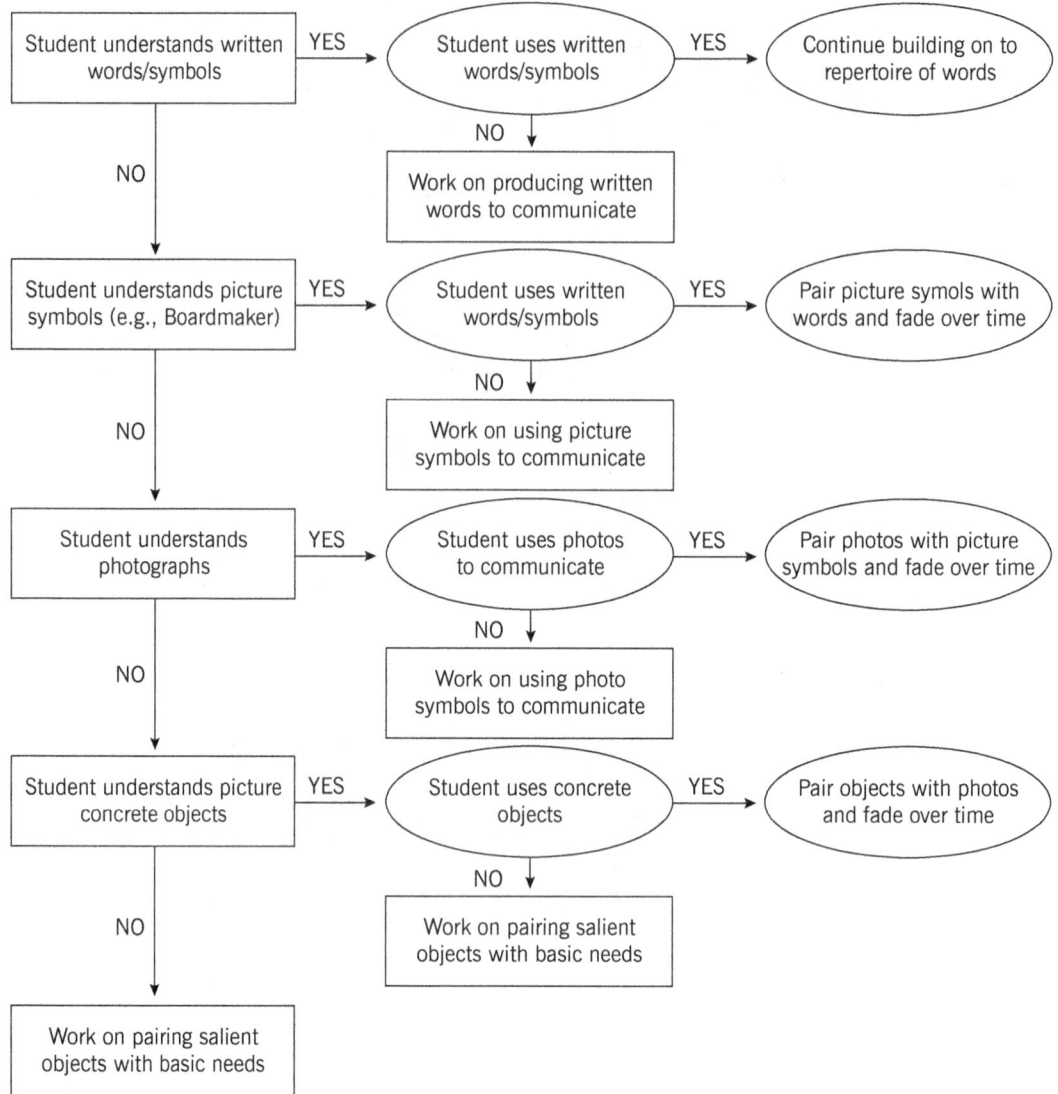

FIGURE 11.1. A decision model for promoting symbol use.

There are a few cautions in applying symbolic levels of communication to plan instruction. The first is to remember that symbolic levels are not static. That is, as instruction progresses, students should make progress in their understanding and use of symbols. A student who is presymbolic in September hopefully will have symbols and assistive technology that makes it possible to be using symbols as the year progresses. The second caution is that symbolic level does not always reflect cognitive level. A student may not yet have learned to use symbols or may have complex physical or sensory challenges that make symbol use difficult, but he or she may actually understand much of what is presented. It is better to err in presuming that the student has some understanding than not to give the student the opportunity to learn and to use symbols. There is a remarkable scene in the movie *My Left Foot* (Heller & Sheridan, 1989) in which a young man with severe physical challenges finally proves to his family his level of understanding by writing on the floor with his foot using a piece of chalk that has fallen. Students need symbols from the onset of instruction and should not have to wait for a means of communication to fall on the floor to show what they know! A third caution is to promote students' use of AAC systems so that symbols can be expanded. This is described in the next section.

CHECK FOR UNDERSTANDING

Take a few minutes to check your own comprehension of symbolic levels by trying to identify the symbolic level of each of the students in your classroom. Be careful not to underestimate what students can do! And remember that all students need access to a wide range of symbols.

Nonsymbolic Communication

Many teachers of students with severe disabilities will have at least some students who rely on nonsymbolic communication. As Table 11.2 illustrates, the goal is to introduce symbols and shape this communication. That is, a new "form" of communication (symbol use) is promoted. At the same time, the teacher needs to encourage the student to continue to expand the "function" of communication by building on current nonsymbolic responses, as well as emerging symbolic ones.

The form of nonsymbolic communication may include nearly any observable, voluntary response, such as eye gaze, body gestures, facial gestures, or sounds such as Tommy's tongue cluck. Because many students with severe disabilities here unique characteristics, it may be difficult to determine how a student uses nonsymbolic responses to communicate. Brady and Halle (1997) suggest three different strategies a teacher can use to identify how a student communicates. First, the teacher can interview the people closest to the student, such as parents and siblings, who have a long history of interpreting the student's idiosyncrasies. Next, the context in which these attempts occur should be identified as well. For example, Darius's mom reported that Darius would often arch his back when he was eating to communicate that he was full. This function must be inferred when communication is nonsymbolic. For example, for Darius, the form of nonsymbolic communication would be the arching of the back, the context would be during mealtime, and the inferred function would be to communicate that is finished eating.

A second option for learning more about how a student communicates is to conduct a direct observation. This can be achieved by keeping information on the student's responses during typical routines in the natural contexts. To organize this information, the evaluator may want to record information for each function of communication. Several experts have described the pragmatic functions of communicative utterances (Dyer & Luce, 1996; Kaiser, 1993; McLean & Snyder-McLean, 1988; Reichle & Sigafoos, 1994). Although the specific functions vary across these resources, most include behaviors that are instrumental (e.g., requesting) and social. Figure 11.2 is a direct observation form that can be used to chart all student responses in different contexts. By recording this information consistently, the evaluator is likely to find a consistent function that matches the form. For example, if during morning math time a teacher consistently charts Samuel's eye gazing toward the math manipulatives, it may be determined that eye gazing

	Muscle tone tenses	Muscle tone relaxes	Change in facial expression	Quiets	Starts vocalizing	Reaches toward materials	Pushes materials away	Eye gazes toward materials	Withdrawing or turning away	Becomes upset	Becomes aggressive	Participates in self-injurious behaviors	Starts to self-stimulate	Stops self-stimulating	Other behaviors:
Student: Setting: Context: Observer: Date:															
Instrumental functions															
Request help															
Request food/object															
Request attention															
Request action															
Request end of activity															
Protest															
Social functions															
Get social attention															
Turn taking															
Greet others															
Start conversation															
Clarify communication															
Request a routine															
Acknowledge															
Sensory functions															
Sensory															

FIGURE 11.2. Direct observation form for nonsymbolic forms and functions.

(form) during the math routine (context) is a means of requesting access to the manipulative (function).

A final option is to use structured probes when determining a student's current repertoire of forms and functions. In structured probes, all of the student's communication responses are sampled in a short period of time through activities that are used to prompt communication (Brady & Halle, 1997). These activities can also be used in teaching communication. Kaiser (1993) offers several recommendations for these activities, including (1) introducing interesting materials; (2) placing highly desired materials out of reach to see whether a student will request them; (3) giving inadequate portions or "forgetting" to serve a student when giving out snacks to see whether the student will protest or request; (4) offering choices; (5) creating situations in which the student will need assistance; and (6) creating silly situations to determine whether the student will comment or question them.

Once all voluntary responses have been identified, it is important to promote intentionality or purposeful communication. Teachers should always assume that students want to communicate and that future positive interactions will occur by improving a student's communication ability (Siegel & Wetherby, 2006).

To promote increases in intentional communication, the teacher increases the number of communication opportunities a student has, using routines throughout the day (Siegel & Wetherby, 2006). The teacher should consider naturally occurring communicative opportunities within the classroom and take advantage of these moments to help build on the student's communicative attempts (Downing, 2001). One rule of thumb is to have some target communication for every interaction with a child during the day. Upon arrival, the teacher responds to some movement or sound as a greeting (e.g., hugs student after the student pops her lips). Before going to the restroom, the teacher prompts a requesting response (e.g., looking up or patting the hips to mean "change me"). The teacher responds to some sound or movement as an attention seeker (e.g., a grumbling sound or increased movement) by moving to the student and saying, "Let's see what you need." In addition, teachers should be cognizant of changes in a student's current behavior state (e.g., from a relaxed/flaccid state to a tense/rigid state), which may signal some communication (e.g., protest/pain). Sometimes, to get students to make an intentional response, the teacher needs to wait and look expectantly at the student during the routine (e.g., teacher moves hands as if to lift student from the chair and then waits for student to turn eyes up).

To promote a transition to symbol use, the teacher pairs these responses with a picture or other symbol (Siegel & Wetherby, 2006). For example, the teacher says, "John, are you saying you are finished eating?" and holds up a picture symbol of "finished." When John looks at the picture, the teacher says, "John, you are telling me that you are finished eating?" In addition, teachers can promote acquisition and fluency by continuing to use the same symbols to represent the communicative event. John's teacher will continue to use the picture symbol of "finished" every time John exhibits the behavior. Over time John may relate meaning to the picture symbol and use it more reliably to communicate that he is full.

Another way to engage and increase communication in students with little or no intentional communication is through literacy lessons. Browder, Mims, et al. (2008) conducted a study in which they adapted grade-level texts to include a surprise element, the students' names, salient objects, and repeated storylines in order to help the students to participate in a shared story lesson. In addition, they used team planning to adapt the task analysis for participation in the shared story. Changes included providing a longer wait time for the student to respond, changing placement of AAC devices, and using light boards to help draw students' attention to the objects and text, as well as a clear prompting hierarchy. By providing these adaptations and changes, increases in all students' communication attempts were seen throughout the shared story.

AAC Systems

When students have developed intentional nonsymbolic communication and begun to attend to the symbols the teacher pairs with these responses, the next step is to introduce a symbolic communication system. If the student is nonvocal, this system may be an alternative to speech. If the student has begun to speak, these systems may augment their speech development and increase their understandability to others.

There are two main types of AAC: aided and unaided (Sigafoos & Iacono, 1993). Aided systems include those that require some type of physical equipment and can be either low tech, those consisting of no electronics or batteries (e.g., picture communication books), or high tech, those consisting of electronic or battery operated components (e.g., speech-generating devices). Unaided systems include those that do not require any type of object or those that can be demonstrated with the body (e.g., manual signs, gestures, facial expressions). To identify an appropriate AAC system for an individual with severe disabilities, an AAC assessment should be conducted. Both aided and unaided communication systems have advantages and disadvantages (Sigafoos & Iacono, 1993). First, aided high-tech systems make it easier for the general public to understand the communicative attempt of the user, but these devices are often expensive and cumbersome for the user to travel with to all settings. Aided low-tech systems are much cheaper, but the general public may not quite understand the communicative attempt the learner is trying to convey. Similarly, unaided communication systems do not cost any money, but again, the general public may not be clear about the user's intent. It is up to the planning team to weigh the advantages and disadvantages of each system while figuring out the system that is the best match for the learner and his or her needs. Figure 11.3 illustrates how a team evaluated potential systems for a learner named Jeremy. Simply providing an AAC system will not produce improved communication. Students will need systematic instruction in using their AAC systems.

Teaching AAC Use

A variety of antecedent and consequence strategies have been shown to be successful in teaching students with severe disabilities AAC use (Snell, Chen, & Hoover, 2006). One antecedent strategy is to prompt responses using the AAC system. For example, the communication partner uses verbal, gestural, model, and physical prompts to encourage the student to use a manual sign or picture to ask to go outside. Sometimes the proximity of the partner or the materials can promote use of the AAC. The communication partners place themselves, the materials, or communication systems within students' reach. Students may begin to use AAC with generalization if they receive systematic instruction across multiple stimuli (e.g., cues, people, and settings). Students may also need motiva-

Student: Jeremy Henderson   **Evaluator**: Ms. Monica LaRouche

System	Currently used by student?	If used, what symbols used?	How well does system match student's current motor, academic, and other skills?	How appropriate is system for student's social settings?
Symbols				
Nonsymbolic	Jeremy uses sounds and hand movement.	He cries or throws objects for "no"; he pulls on objects he wants; he will laugh to show preference.		Jeremy needs more age-appropriate skills.
Gestures	Does not point or use other gestures.		Resists being prompted to point.	
Manual signs	Does not use.		He might benefit from gross motor signs that can be formed easily.	School peers may not understand these signs.
Objects	Does not use except to pull on the object to ask for it.		Can grasp and release objects.	Peers and teachers may understand object use; not always practical to carry objects.
Pictures	Does not use pictures.		Has good grasp and release; consider use of picture exchange vs. board	Peers and teachers would probably understand pictures; more portable than objects
Sight words	Does not read yet.		Difficult—introduce later with sight word training	Understandable and may be more acceptable in academic settings.
Display				
One symbol at a time			A good starting point would be PECs with one picture at a time.	Easy for others to understand but limits "conversation."
Picture communication board	Has a board—not currently used.	Current board has "eat," "toilet," "Hi," "rest."	He needs motivation to use board.	As he gains pictures, use board, especially in academic classes.
Wallet or notebook	Does not use.		A next step	Can enhance conversation; offer more options.

FIGURE 11.3. Example of how a team evaluated AAC options.

tion to use their AAC system. For example, the communication partner uses turn taking, allows the student to take the lead, and shares control with the student. Enriching the environment by using items and activities that are preferred by the student may also enhance motivation. A student will not be motivated to use a symbol unless the teacher differentiates responses depending on whether or not the symbol is used. Embedding instruction in ongoing, natural, routine activities also may promote the student's use of the AAC. Similar to the activity routines described for nonsymbolic communication, the teacher may target a specific symbol for each activity during the day. For example, the student shows a picture symbol for hello, eating, going outside, using the computer, and so forth. Another strategy is to rig the environment to create desirable opportunities to respond, such as placing a desired object just out of reach but in full view. Peers or siblings may also help prompt the student to respond (Snell et al., 2006).

In addition to antecedent strategies, consequence strategies are also effective to teach AAC use to students with severe disabilities (Snell et al., 2006). Teachers may use reinforcers that are specific to the communication request (food in response to "eat," toy in response to "play," a break in response to "I need a break"). This is called reinforcer specificity. Making preferred activities or materials contingent on the AAC response could shape responding. The teacher may also use nonpunitive error correction—for example, by showing the student which picture to use to ask to go outside. The teacher should also reinforce all approximations of the desired AAC use. For example, if the student touches the picture but does not show or hand it to the teacher, this may be praised as a first step.

Picture Exchange Communication Systems

One aided AAC communication system often used with individuals with severe disabilities, including autism, who do not have a vocal repertoire is the Picture Exchange Communication System (PECS). Bondy and Frost (1994) developed this system as a means of obtaining desired items or needs (Frost & Bondy, 2002). The system is made up of several phases to teach communication. Initially, the student learns to mand, or request, items by exchanging a picture of the item for the item itself. This requires the use of a partner (e.g., teacher, parent, or peer) who will immediately accept the picture in exchange for the actual item requested. This exchange process is taught by shaping progressive approximations (e.g., touching the picture, holding the picture up, bringing the picture to the teacher). The teacher also uses prompting strategies to promote correct responding (see Chapter 4). This process continues until the student masters the exchange process with a single picture. For example, Sally is starting to learn to communicate with picture symbols for the first time. Her teacher starts by having Sally mand (request) her favorite thing, music. The teacher begins by using a physical prompt to guide Sally to give her the picture and then get a few minutes of music played on a CD. She repeats this for several trials. On the next day, the teacher uses a model prompt and, if Sally does not respond, guides her to show her the picture. On the following day, the teacher uses a verbal prompt ("Show me 'music'") and, if necessary, moves to a model prompt or physical guidance. This most-to-least-intrusive prompting hierarchy is faded to a natural cue. The teacher plays a few seconds of music and then waits for Sally to get the picture symbol and show it to her. In the past, Sally requested music time by getting upset and biting her hand. Now when Sally starts getting upset her teacher interrupts the biting by placing the picture symbol of music in Sally's hand and physically guiding her to hand it back to her. Over time, the teacher promotes requesting desired items that are farther and farther way, using an array of pictures, and requesting items from additional people and in additional settings. Over time the student learns to make choices between pictures. Figure 11.4 provides a checklist for the PECS training sequence.

Simple Voice Output Device

Simple VODs require only one press of one or a few buttons and produce a voice output or message that has been preprogrammed (e.g., BIGmack and Step-by-Step by AbleNet; GoTalk by Attainment; Cheap Talk by Enabling Devices). Such devices allow students to participate in a variety of activities, including choice making, responding to comprehension questions, participating in activities, and social activities. It is important to add a symbol of some sort on the device to help add meaning to the message the student is delivering. For example, two preprogrammed BIGmack devices may each represent one opinion of the character Stanley Yelnats from the book *Holes* by Louis Sachar. A student may be asked, "Did you *like* or *not like* Stanley Yelnats?" One BIGmack should have the picture symbol for *like* and the other the picture symbol for *not like*. This provides students with an opportunity to voice their opinions, and the labeled BIGmacks provide additional motivation for the students to respond.

As mentioned earlier, these simple VODs can also be used for answering comprehension questions. For example, after reading an adapted chapter in the novel *Island of the Blue Dolphins* and presenting a student with a preprogrammed Cheap Talk 4, the teacher may ask a sequencing question (e.g., "What happened first, second, third, and last in this chapter?"). The student will be able to respond by activating the preprogrammed response options with labeled picture symbols representing each response option.

Additionally, students can use these devices to participate in an activity. For example, during a shared story (story-based lesson), the student can activate a BIGmack to help "read" or anticipate the targeted repeated storyline. For example, in the book *Alexander and the Terrible, Horrible, No Good, Very Bad Day* by Judith Viorst (1987), a BIGmack can be preprogrammed with the last part of the repeated story line. The teacher would read "Alexander had a terrible, horrible, no good, very . . . " and wait. At this point the student could activate his or her device to fill in the end of the repeated story line, "bad day." This allows students to be actively involved in the shared story event.

Finally, students can use these devices to participate in social activities. For example, a small GoTalk can be preprogrammed with a greeting that a student can use when walking down the halls of school. This allows the student to have a voice to participate in more typical social exchanges.

Multiple-Symbol Voice Output Devices

In addition to simple VODs, more complex devices such as multiple-symbol VODs (e.g., Macaw, DynaVox) can allow students who are ready to move beyond just a single or few messages to many messages. These devices are typically used with students who are able to combine symbols to create multiple-word utterances or those who have a larger vocabulary of known words. These systems allow students to expand on known symbols and are great for students who know abstract symbols.

Pictures to train →																
PECS training sequence ↓	Picture 1	Picture 2	Picture 3	Picture 4	Picture 5	Picture 6	Picture 7	Picture 8	Picture 9	Picture 10	Picture 11	Picture 12	Picture 13	Picture 14	Picture 15	Continue Training
Mands for first item through shaping and prompting procedures.																
Student is fluent with picture exchange.																
Student generalizes pictures to new settings/people.																
Uses picture spontaneously.																
Uses picture for items that are farther away.																
Uses picture for items that are out of sight or in other settings.																

FIGURE 11.4. PECS training sequence checklist. (Work from top to bottom with first picture, then left to right.)

Sign Language

The use of manual signs such as American Sign Language (ASL) is another option for students who need a communication system. One advantage of ASL is that it is always available to the student. For example, the student can be enjoying a swim class and can sign "I need a break" or "Where is Kevin?" This option is not available with pictures and voice output systems. Students may also respond better to a communication from a teacher when it is paired with a manual sign as a referent. The disadvantage of using manual signs is that most people in society do not understand this symbol system. Teachers, peers, family members, employers, and others in the student's life will need to gain knowledge of the student's symbols or have a translator. A helpful resource for learning ASL is *Talking with Your Hands, Listening with Your Eyes: A Complete Photographic Guide to American Sign Language* by Gabriel Grayson (2003).

Promoting the Use of Spoken Language

One option for promoting students' effective communication is to use a combination of symbol systems. The student may sign some simple social exchanges, use pictures for everyday requests, and use a VOD with expanded vocabulary for academic coursework. It also is important to encourage the student to use whatever speech he or she has. Speech is the most widely understood mode of communication and the most readily available. Teachers can consult with the speech therapist to target goals to enhance the content (vocabulary) and function of the student's speech. The therapist may also recommend goals to improve its form (e.g., articulation goals). Students may also need systematic instruction to use the speech they have learned. The following are some techniques to promote the student's total communicative abilities and are applicable to both speech and AAC systems.

Naturalistic Communication Techniques

Naturalistic communication techniques (also known as milieu teaching strategies) are communication opportunities that are systematically taught throughout the day in naturally occurring events in which the student shows intention to communicate and the teacher provides meaningful forms and consequences for the student (Hancock & Kaiser, 2002). Some examples of this type of instruction were provided in the section on nonsymbolic communication. These naturalistic techniques are also especially effective for promoting student's use of their best current speech.

There are several different types of naturalistic communication techniques. First, modeling is one type of naturalistic teaching in which the teacher models and the student is expected to imitate the teacher. For example, the student looks over at the book, and the teacher says, "Book." This may encourage the student to repeat the word *book*. Another type of naturalistic teaching is incidental teaching, in which the teacher expands on communication already in the student's repertoire. For example, the student says, "Book," and the teacher says, "Yes, that is the book called *Holes*. Can you say 'holes'?"

A third type of naturalistic teaching is called mand-model and is most commonly used to build fluency with words the student currently knows (Webber & Scheuermann, 2009). If the teacher knows the student wants something (e.g., a book) but the student doesn't say the word to request it, the teacher will then say, "Tell me what you want" (mand). This is followed by an appropriate wait time. If the student still does not respond, the teacher will say "Tell me what you want," followed by desired item (mand-model; e.g., "Say 'book' ").

The final naturalistic teaching strategy is called -naturalistic time delay. This strategy involves the teacher inserting a delay of time during an activity for the student to respond. If the student does not respond within the set time delay, then the teacher models the expected behavior. For example, the teacher is reading aloud to a student and then suddenly stops reading and provides a 4-second time delay. If the student does not respond within the time delay, the teacher will say, "Tell me, 'Keep reading, please.' " In most applications of time delay, instruction begins with some no-delay trials in which the teacher prompts the student immediately. Over time, the delay before prompting is increased. In language training, these may be long pauses (e.g., 20 seconds) while the teacher waits expectantly for a student answer.

A newer form of naturalistic teaching is called enhanced milieu teaching (EMT). It is derived from both incidental and milieu instruction and has been shown to improve communication skills in students with delays in language (Hancock & Kaiser, 2002). EMT is made up of three components: environmental arrangements that encourage student engagement with activities and communicative partners, open interaction techniques, and milieu teaching procedures that will prompt and model new forms of language in functional contexts.

PROMOTING COMMUNICATION CONTENT AND FUNCTION

Content of Communication

Whatever the form of communication the student uses, it will also be important to build content, including both syntax and vocabulary. In general, children acquire vocabulary by beginning with concrete terms and moving to more abstract ones. In the beginning a child may simply indicate "bird." Over time, the child may be able to identify what a bird can do (sing, eat). The concept of "bird" may develop as the child learns to discriminate between birds and other animals. A more advanced understanding would include specific types of birds or specific habits of birds (e.g., migration patterns). There are four strategies for expanding students' vocabulary. The first is to identify the words needed for the student's current and future environments. For example, what words are needed to dine in a restaurant, to play video games with friends, or to attend a school sporting event? Students might learn words and symbols for greetings, making a purchase, giving a compliment ("good move!"), or ending the activity ("I'm tired"). This vocabulary is best taught in the context of these activities. A second option is to teach vocabulary related to the general curriculum content. Students will need to learn words to communicate knowledge that is conveyed. These may include such words as *government, voting, chemical reaction*, and *equation*. Again, some students will need picture symbols for this vocabulary. A third alternative is to use a commercial program for expanding language ability. Some of these include the Early Literacy Skills Builder by Attainment Company and Reading Mastery by SRA/McGraw-Hill. The fourth option is to teach vocabulary for underdeveloped pragmatic functions, as shown in Table 11.3. For example, a student may not have the words or symbols to protest a disliked activity or initiate a social interaction.

TABLE 11.3. How Students with Different Communication Systems May Achieve the Same Function

Pragmatic function	Nonsymbolic	AAC–picture use	Vocal
Instrumental functions			
Request help	Hands food container to teacher to open; cries.	Uses picture symbol for "help."	"Help me, please," or "Help."
Request food or object	Reaches hand toward desired food or toy.	Points to the picture for the preferred food or object from an array of options.	"May I have pretzels, please?", or simply "Pretzels."
Request attention	Taps teacher's shoulder; raises hand.	Holds up picture card for assistance or may raise hand.	Says teacher's name—"Mr. Jacoby"—or may also raise hand.
Request action	Moves toward door to ask to go outside.	Points to picture of bowling alley to ask for this activity when given an array of options.	"I want to go to the store" or "Store."
Protest	Pulls hand away when teacher tries to put on coat that is too small.	Points to symbol for "no"; may shake head "no."	"No coat" or may give reason: "No coat! Tight!"
End activity	Tries to leave seat.	Points to symbol for "break" or signs "break."	"I need a break" or "rest."
Social functions			
Get social attention "Show off"	Rolls eyes, acts coy, blows lips (raspberries).	Shows humorous picture; may pantomime action, such as pretending to be teacher.	Makes a joke: "I'm the teacher!"
Take turns	Hands object to peer.	Takes turn in a game; may point to indicate other's turn (would not necessarily use a picture).	"Your turn" and "my turn" or may simply take turn in a game.
Greet	Smiles greeting.	Waves and smiles; may say "hello" with VOD; may select picture of whom to greet.	Says, "hello" and perhaps "how are you?"
Start conversation (e.g., by directing person's attention to object or asking a question)	Hands person object to get them to talk about it or attend to it.	Points to picture of interest to get person to talk about it.	Uses a conversation starter such as "How about that football team?" May augment by sharing a picture to talk about.
Clarify communication	Persists if other person does not respond (e.g., keeps trying to hand them the object or reach an object desired).	Repeats picture selection or tries another picture if told "I don't understand."	Repeats comment more clearly or says it a different way when told "I don't understand."

(cont.)

TABLE 11.3. *(cont.)*

Pragmatic function	Nonsymbolic	AAC–picture use	Vocal
Acknowledge	Nods, smiles, or makes other response when spoken to.	Uses response pictures such as "Cool!" or "That's fun!" or "Yeah, I like that."	Acknowledges speaker using phrases such as "I like that" or "He's cool."
Negotiate a change in materials, setting, activity	Moves away from current toward preferred and looks at teacher or parent for permission.	Shakes head or symbol for "no" and shows picture of what is wanted instead.	"No more math. I want outside."
Request a social routine	Tries to get person to play a familiar game such as peekaboo.	Uses picture that starts a familiar social routine—for example, picture of dog that always makes a peer start barking and panting like a dog.	Begins a social routine such as a knock-knock joke or dance steps two friends do together.

Students' ability to use and comprehend more complex syntax also should expand over time. In the beginning a student may use simple nouns and verbs to communicate (*eat, help, toys, outside*). Over time the student can expand this to include options such as action-objects (eat lunch; go outside). Students also need to acquire words or symbols to pose questions ("What is it?"). Students also need to expand their receptive communication skills in this area. Initially students may need simple syntactical forms to respond (e.g., "Sit here; eat your food"). Over time, they may respond to more complex forms ("Put the fork here") or multiple-step commands. One mistake teachers sometimes make is to set general goals, such as that the student will ask questions or respond to "wh" questions. Obviously there are questions too complex for anyone to answer. What is better is to target questions linked to specific vocabulary, such as answering "who" the main character is after hearing a novel read aloud or answering "what happened next."

FINDING THE BALANCE

The most important goal of communication training is for students to use their skills in social contexts. For this reason, the function of communication is more important than form or content. In contrast, students may be limited in their ability to achieve these functions when symbols, vocabulary terms, and communication systems are underdeveloped. Consideration needs to be given to all three of these aspects of communication. Does the student have an adequate communication system? If not, what needs to be developed to improve the form of communication? What vocabulary needs to be taught? How can syntax be expanded? And how can these expanded options be taught within naturalistic contexts for functional use?

Function of Communication

As noted at the beginning of this chapter, what is most important is the function of communication, which is also called pragmatics. Table 11.3 provides an illustration of some of the functions of communication. As the Table shows, students who are nonsymbolic, who use AAC systems, or who use speech can all achieve the various functions of communication. Sometimes in assessing a student it becomes clear that the student lacks an age-appropriate or socially appropriate form for one of the functions. As Chapter 12 describes, students may then resort to what others consider problem behaviors to achieve these same functions. Whenever a student is relying on inappropriate behavior, some consideration should be given to how the student achieves these different communication functions. For example, a student who lacks the skills to negotiate may be able to change an activity only by running from one area to another in the classroom. To promote acquisition of a more appropriate form of communication, the teacher can use the naturalistic teaching methods described earlier. If a student begins to run from the activity, the teacher can say, "Use your pictures to tell me what you want." Then to teach negotiation the teacher might give a choice, such as "Change activities now and have 1 minute for it" or "Change when the lesson is done and have 5 minutes" (the choice might be presented in a clock face). If the student chooses to go now, the teacher honors this by giving a brief sample of the preferred activity and then redirecting him or her to a new activity—"Okay?"—and seeing if the student will say, "Yes."

In addition to these pragmatic functions, Reichle and Sigafoos (1994) also recommend giving consideration to how a student initiates, maintains, and terminates social interactions. For example, a child on the playground might initiate being pushed in a swing by taking the teacher's hand and walking to the swing set. The student might maintain the interaction by saying "more" or moving his or her body in swinging motion whenever the swing slows. When the student is tired of swinging, he or she might vocalize in protest or say "stop." In Jeremy's case, he liked the teacher trying to put his hat on (a social routine). He remembered this game the next day and took her the hat to initiate an interaction. After she went through her comic way of trying to put it on, she handed it to Jeremy, but he gave it back (maintaining the interaction). To see if Jeremy would end this, the teacher continued to play the game for a while. Finally, Jeremy became very excited and begun running in circles. To teach him to end the routine, she prompted him to sign "finished," put the hat on a shelf, and check his calendar for the next activity.

SUMMARY

This chapter introduced terms used to describe communication, including *form, content,* and *function*; level of intentionality; and receptive/expressive communication. Four levels of symbol applications are especially important in planning general education lessons: awareness, presymbolic, concrete symbolic, and abstract symbolic. For each of these levels, the teacher introduces abstract symbols but also shapes responding from a student's current level. For example, the student who responds primarily by using smiles and reaching for objects might be prompted to begin using pictures to make requests. As students begin to use nonsymbolic communication with intention, they are ready to begin using some form of AAC. This chapter provided strategies for teaching AAC with specific examples for PECS, VODs, and manual sign language. Students should also be encouraged to use whatever speech they have. Naturalistic teaching methods can be used for both AAC and speech use. What is most important is to promote the function of communication, whatever form it may take.

Goetz and Hunt (1994) have noted that there are three important points in planning communication. First, all persons communicate. This chapter illustrated how some individuals communicate nonsymbolically. Second, all communication is multimodal. This chapter described nonsymbolic, AAC, and speech, and many students will use a combination of these systems. In fact, when a person uses speech, there are also nonverbal signals and sometimes concrete referents such as an object or picture. Similarly, students with severe disabilities need the opportunity to use a combination of response forms to achieve communication functions. Third, and finally, all communication requires a partner. Communication is a social skill.

APPLICATIONS

1. Given several student case studies with a communication focus, identify the communication level of each student.

2. Discuss how to develop the communicative intent of a student who has few observable measurable responses (e.g., Tommy's example discussed in the chapter).

3. Discuss ideas of how to promote communication from one level to another (e.g., presymbolic to concrete symbolic).

4. Discuss the pros and cons of both aided and unaided communication.

CHAPTER 12

Social Skills
and Positive Behavior Support

FRED SPOONER, DIANE M. BROWDER, AND VICTORIA F. KNIGHT

Austin is a middle school student with traumatic brain injury and a severe intellectual disability who is included in the general education curriculum. Austin enjoys hanging out with his friends, joking around, and conducting science experiments. The school he attends uses schoolwide positive behavior supports in a three-tiered system. Tier 1, which is for all students, includes posting of schoolwide expectations, rules, and procedures. In addition, Austin attends a social skills group and gets counseling services in school, which is considered a Tier 2 level of support available to a smaller number of students who need more assistance. Recently, his general education math teacher, Ms. Kendrick, has informed the special education teacher that Austin has started to hit others, say "go home," and storm out of the room when she gives him independent seatwork. Ms. Kendrick has tried reviewing the class rules with him, which include keeping hands and feet to oneself, but this seems to make him angrier.

This chapter describes strategies to plan for students such as Austin who need new social skills and other positive behavior supports. Social skills encompass a wide range of behaviors, from fostering friendships to cultivating social skills to reducing inappropriate behaviors. Most individuals spend their entire lives cultivating their social skills and adapting them to new relationships and contexts. Unlike such skills as cooking or reading, social skills require engagement with others, and so are best learned in the context of positive relationships. In these relationships, we learn new ways of interacting from seeing others' models and receive affirmation for our effective strategies (smiles, laughter, conversation, cooperation) and social cues to change our inappropriate strategies (a frown, silence, resistance, a discussion about a hurtful comment). We learn not only self-advocacy but also how to respect the needs, perspectives, and preferences of others in order to develop friendships, get a job done, or help a team function. For individuals with severe disabilities, gaining these social competencies may be difficult due to both insufficient social opportunities and underdeveloped communication skills. The outcome may be that the individual relies on behavior that is inappropriate for achieving social functions. This behavior may be age inappropriate (e.g., tantrums), socially ineffective (e.g., trying to gain attention in ways others find offensive), or disruptive or dangerous to the student, others, or the environment (e.g., throwing objects).

Because social skills are best learned in the context of positive relationships, the chapter begins with a discussion of social relationships and their importance to students with developmental disabilities. Following the description of social relationships and barriers to social relationships, we review social skills for instruction, including research-based methods to promote social skills. Next, the steps of positive behavior support are explained. Finally, the idea of PBS is expanded to provide an overview of schoolwide positive behavior supports.

BUILDING SOCIAL RELATIONSHIPS

What Are Social Relationships and Why Are They Important?

The many types of interactions individuals share with others characterize social relationships. These social relationships can vary from familiar community figures that a person greets (e.g., a mail carrier) to community acquaintances with whom one has regular conversation (e.g., a hairstylist) to ongoing service providers (e.g., dentist) to work or school friendships to authority figures (e.g., teacher, employer) to close friends, family members, and romantic relationships. One of the most important ways all students learn social skills throughout their lives is through positive relationships with friends. Evidence suggests that the lack of social skills may contribute to peer rejection (e.g., Lambros, Ward, Bocian, MacMillan, & Gresham, 1998), social adjustment problems (e.g., Farmer, Irvin, Sgammato, Dadisman, & Thompson, 2009), and academic difficulties (e.g., Parke & Welsh, 1998). The presence or absence of close social relationships can have a significant impact on an individual's quality of life.

Social relationships are based on social contact, social support, and social networks (Kennedy, 2004). *Social contact* relates to the frequency and duration of interactions between two or more people. For example, one student may see one of her friends every week after school, and another student may text a friend on his cell phone every few hours. *Social support* occurs and is maintained when each party gains from their interaction. According to Kennedy, there are six types of social support: (1) emotional support (e.g., comforting during difficult events), (2) companionship (e.g., interacting within a shared environment), (3) providing access to others (e.g., introducing new acquaintances), (4) information sharing (e.g., communication about recent or upcoming events), (5) material aid (e.g., providing physical assistance or items to another), (6) decision making (e.g., helping with choices or resolutions). *Social networks* consist of the various interaction patterns among individuals. For example, some social networks are tightly connected (e.g., three best friends who interact with one another on a regular basis), whereas other social networks are more loosely associated (e.g., coworkers who interact with one another at work, but who may have different social ties outside of the workplace; Kennedy, 2004; O'Neill, 2004).

According to experts in the field, one of the most important benefits of having social relationships is feeling a sense of belonging and membership, or "connectedness" with other people (Kennedy, 2004). Membership and belonging are characterized by a sense of equality among individuals involved, mutual respect for one another, and reciprocity. Examples of membership and belonging include having a circle of friends, being a valued member of the classes and schools one attends, or feeling connected to one's family and community (Kennedy, 2004).

Barriers to Building Social Relationships

When considering instruction for students with severe disabilities, educators have historically placed more value on increasing the skills needed for independence rather than considering the importance of interdependence (Kennedy, 2004). For example, a student who only receives instruction to keep his hands to himself does not learn appropriate ways to ask for a social exchange. Although increasing independence is a critical component of instruction for students with severe disabilities, interdependence, or relationships in which students help one another and rely on one another, are equally important considerations (Kennedy & Horn, 2004).

According to Kennedy and Horn (2004), students with severe disabilities often face barriers to having social relationships. For example, students with severe developmental disabilities often face barriers in accessing typical settings, in meeting peers without disabilities in general education settings, in entering the general education curriculum, and in gaining skills for facilitating interactions. There are two major strategies for overcoming barriers to social relationships for students with severe disabilities. The first is to cultivate the environment and the second is to teach specific social skills.

Environmental Arrangements to Foster Social Relationships

To develop social relationships, students with severe disabilities need to mix with peers in both instructional and social contexts. One of the most powerful ways social relationships can be fostered is through planning ways for students to become full members of their schools. Some questions a team might consider are the following:

1. Does the student receive instruction in general education classes?
2. Does the student eat lunch with typical peers in the cafeteria?
3. Does the student participate in extracurricular activities such as sports or clubs?
4. Is the student a "member" of the general education class when class pictures are taken?
5. Does the student commute to school with peers?

Once the student is present in contexts in which social relationships can be formed, some additional environmental arrangements may be needed so that he or she does not become isolated. One option is to cultivate peer supports. This may include recruiting volunteers to invite students with disabilities to join their friendship circle for lunch or having an option for all students to sign up for lunchtime social groups that share similar interests (e.g., the "hockey table"). Peer tutors have often been employed to teach students new skills (Carter et al., 2005). Peer tutoring is what might be described as a "vertical" or helper–helped relationship. To build social relationships, students with disabilities also need opportunities for "horizontal" relationships in which all members contribute (e.g., social clubs) and vertical relationships in which they serve as helper. Another strategy is to foster the membership of all participants in a group. Schwartz, Staub, Peck, and Gallucci (2006) note that the term *membership* refers to the sense of belonging to a social group such as a classroom, cooperative work group, or friendship clique. They note that membership can be inferred when members make accommodations to include a child and when they have shared symbols (e.g., same T-shirts) and rituals that occur in the group (e.g., a special greeting). Sometimes promoting membership is a matter of advocating for a student not to be forgotten when birthdays are announced, T-shirts distributed, or teams formed.

An additional strategy with which to cultivate the environment for social relationships is to build awareness in the peer group. This may include having discussions with peers about how to include a student with disabilities in either a social or work group. The class may have some general disability awareness discussions. Schwartz et al. (2006) recommend using a class meeting in which students have a voice in setting norms and expectations for the class. This can then become a regular event and one in which discussions can be held about how to help everyone be involved more fully.

Although environmental arrangements foster social interaction, friendships cannot be "assigned" but instead develop as individuals experience the mutual benefits described earlier (e.g., sharing, emotional support). What adults can provide is support for the peers who are trying to reach out to someone with disabilities but need help in understanding differences (e.g., AAC). Adults may also help students who are developing friendships to arrange social outings. For example, when Trisha's mother picked her up during lunch one day for an appointment, she noticed that Trisha was enjoying lunch with Katie, a girl with severe disabilities. During the trip to the appointment, her mother helped Trisha brainstorm ideas for how they might have Katie over for a visit. She then contacted the teacher to convey the invitation to Katie's mother.

Adults can also help with conflict resolution skills by teaching all members of the class nonviolent ways to resolve differences. Sometimes peers without disabilities may be reluctant to give needed feedback that would solve a problem because they are trying to be "nice." For example, when Beth pulled Carla's long hair, Carla would just try to ignore it while Beth laughed. When the teacher noticed what was happening and that Carla had tears in her eyes from the pain, she told Carla to tell Beth to stop because it hurt and to try to redirect Beth's hands with a "high five" and other responses, such as pointing to pictures on the page. If this didn't work, Carla should say with a frown "not funny" and walk away so that Beth would know it was not funny to her.

FINDING THE BALANCE: PROMOTE RELATIONSHIPS OR TEACH SOCIAL SKILLS?

Most individuals learn social skills through the give and take of their daily relationships. Peer models, a friend's compliments, and discussions about values (e.g., whether to lie) are all examples of naturally occurring supports in cultivating social skills. Students with severe disabilities also need opportunities to develop social skills in relationships in which they and peers share mutual benefit and enjoyment. In contrast, many students with severe disabilities also need systematic instruction in social skills. Some balance is needed to know how to help students practice these skills (e.g., with a peer tutor) without sacrificing opportunities to be part of a social network.

Social Skills for Instruction

Social behaviors, such as saying "hello" to another student in the school cafeteria, asking for help on a school project, or asking a friend to come over for dinner, are arguably some of the most important actions for promoting quality of life. Social skills are social behaviors that help the student to communicate and socialize with others and include both verbal and nonverbal forms of communication. Interpretation and understanding of social interactions significantly affect students' behavior (e.g., Carr & Durand, 1985; Hodgdon, 1999).

Research suggests that students who have communication challenges may be at higher risk for social adjustment problems (e.g., Benner, Rogers-Adkinson, Mooney, & Abbott, 2007). Lower receptive language scores are correlated with lower social skills in students with language disorders (Benner et al., 2007). Although the relationship between communication skills and problem behaviors is not completely understood among children with severe developmental disabilities, several studies have provided evidence of a correlation between development of appropriate communication skills and a decrease in problem behaviors (e.g., Carr & Durand, 1985; Davis, Brady, Williams, & Hamilton, 1992; Durand & Carr, 1992).

According to McGinnis and Goldstein (2003), social skills can be arranged into six skill categories: (1) beginning social skills (e.g., listening, communicating "thank you"), (2) school-related skills (e.g., asking for help, following directions), (3) friendship-making skills (e.g., making eye contact, turn taking), (4) dealing with feelings (e.g., showing affection, determining how others feel), (5) alternatives to aggression (e.g., handling being teased, problem solving), and (6) dealing with stress (e.g., accepting "no"). Teachers may find the skills grouping chart and the progress summary sheet in McGinnis and Goldstein's text useful in determining which social skills to target for instruction. This chart is reprinted as Figure 12.1. Additionally, an ecological assessment can be useful in determining which social skills to target for instruction (Westling & Fox, 2000). In an ecological assessment, typical routines and skills performed by a person without a disability are directly observed and compared with the skills of the target student. The ecological assessment will include (1) information about the domain (e.g., home, school, community), (2) the specific environment (e.g., math class, kitchen), (3) subenvironments, activities, and actions needed within them (e.g., using a calculator to complete a math problem, using the washing machine for laundry), and (4) performance of the skill by the student with a disability. For example, in a science class in a school setting, typical actions may include raising hands to answer questions, working cooperatively in groups to conduct an experiment, and writing tasks on the computer to complete a written report. Components of an ecological assessment include the skills of the nondisabled peer(s), natural cues, performance criteria, and current skills of the target student. When these actions needed in a typical context are identified, the team may compare these with the current skills of the student with a disability. Skills that the student does not currently have or is experiencing difficulty with may be identified as objectives for the student with disabilities. Although an ecological assessment may be used to identify daily living, community, or job skills, it can be specifically focused on social skill needs, as shown in Figure 12.2.

It should be noted that social skills differ from culture to culture; what is considered acceptable or preferred in one culture may be considered disrespectful or rude in another culture. For example, Browder and Lim (2001) noted that gesturing with the

	Teacher pretest score Date:	Child pretest score Date:	Teacher posttest score Date:	Child posttest score Date:	Performance change Pretest–posttest Teacher	Child
I: Beginning Social Skills						
1. Listening						
2. Using Nice Talk						
3. Using Brave Talk						
4. Saying Thank You						
5. Rewarding Yourself						
6. Asking for Help						
7. Asking a Favor						
8. Ignoring						
II: School-Related Skills						
9. Asking a Question						
10. Following Directions						
11. Tring When It's Hard						
12. Interrupting						
III: Friendship-Making Skills						
13. Greeting Others						
14. Reading Others						
15. Joining In						
16. Waiting Your Turn						
17. Sharing						
18. Offering Help						
19. Asking Someone to Play						
20. Playing a Game						
IV: Dealing with Feelings						
21. Knowing Your Feelings						
22. Feeling Left Out						
23. Asking to Talk						
24. Dealing with Fear						
25. Deciding How Someone Feels						
26. Showing Affection						

Name _____

Date _____

(cont.)

FIGURE 12.1. Progress summary sheet. Scale: 1 = almost never; 2 = seldom; 3 = sometimes; 4 = often; 5 = almost always). From McGinnis and Goldstein (2003). Copyright 2003 by Ellen McGinnis and Arnold P. Goldstein. Reprinted by permission.

	Teacher pretest score Date:	Child pretest score Date:	Teacher posttest score Date:	Child posttest score Date:	Performance change Pretest–posttest Teacher	Child
V: Alternatives to Aggression						
27. Dealing with Teasing						
28. Dealing with Feeling Mad						
29. Deciding If It's Fair						
30. Solving a Problem						
31. Accepting Consequences						
VI: Dealing with Stress						
32. Relaxing						
33. Dealing with Mistakes						
34. Being Honest						
35. Knowing When to Tell						
36. Dealing with Losing						
37. Wanting to Be First						
38. Saying No						
39. Accepting No						
40. Deciding What to Do						

Scale: 1 = almost never; 2 = seldom; 3 = sometimes; 4 = often; 5 = almost always.

FIGURE 12.1. *(cont.)*

index finger is rude in some Asian cultures. Instead, to signal "come here," a downward, repeated motion of fingers toward the palm rather than an upward curl of the finger would be used. Without knowing this, a team might teach a student to gesture "come here" for assistance in a manner that would be culturally inappropriate. Whether or not a student should make eye contact when being addressed by a person in authority also varies across cultures. When planning specific social skills to teach, it is important to involve the family to be sure that these skills will be acceptable for long-term use within the extended family context. With the many priorities a student may have, teachers may struggle to find time to teach social skills in addition to general education and other life skills. A separate social skills "lesson" may not be needed; in fact, many social skills can be addressed as part of the school's overall behavior support (e.g., embedded in character education). In addition, development of social skills can occur within and across content areas. For example, in health education class, students may learn skills to cope with stress; in physical education, students may learn team relationship skills and how to cope with not winning the game. Kennedy (2004) cautions an awareness of the "readiness model." Although students may not have all of the desired social skills for interacting

Student: Jose

Environment: Oak Hill Elementary School

Subenvironment: Cafeteria

Activity: Eating lunch

Social skills of typical peers	Natural cues	Performance of the skill(s) by the target student (+/−)	Comments
Stand in line	Peers stand in line.	Tries to push forward to get food quicker.	Teach Jose to wait in line with peer; have cafeteria worker give him treat if he waited his turn.
Talk with peers in line	Peers initiate conversation.	Lacks communication skills; sometimes hits.	Teach Jose to share high-interest items in line with peer (e.g., pictures of action hero) and to give "fist bumps" (vs. hits).
Select table with peers	Peers sometimes point to seat or wave over.	Goes to same table every time and eats alone with paraprofessional.	Have peer greet Jose as he exits line and walk with him to table of boys.
Socialize while eating (talk, share food, show toys)	Peers initiate social exchange.	Eats quickly and then wants to go.	Give Jose small toys in his pockets and prompt peers to ask to see them. Peers may also share food after Jose shares toy to help maintain Jose's interest and time at table.
Stay seated until bell rings	Teacher reminds students to stay seated.	Jose currently has a paraprofessional sitting with him so he will not bolt from table.	Paraprofessional can fade distance to table gradually as Jose begins to share toys and food with peers.

FIGURE 12.2. Ecological assessment used for consideration of social skills needs.

with peers, educators should not wait for students to be "ready" prior to being allowed to interact with typical peers. All students need an opportunity to develop skills for interdependence. Interdependence is defined by Kennedy as learning "how to rely upon, relate to, and help others" (p. 100). An example of interdependence may be one student working collaboratively with other students to complete an activity or goal. When students do need systematic instruction of specific social skills, this intervention may still be embedded in general education contexts, provided by peers, used in the community, taught with small groups, or offered in one-to-one settings, as described in Chapter 4. The following section provides more information on strategies for teaching these skills across these various contexts.

Research-Based Methods to Increase Social Skills

A number of research-based interventions exist to increase or facilitate social and interpersonal skills. Many of the systematic prompting strategies discussed in the chapter on evidence-based practices, such as least-to-most prompting and stimulus fading, can be used to teach social skills to students with developmental disabilities. For example, a least-to-most prompting strategy might be used to teach Jose to share small toys with his friends at lunch (see Figure 12.2). In addition, according to the National Autism Center's (NAC; 2009) National Standards Project, social skills interventions can include: (1) joint attention interventions, (2) modeling, (3) naturalistic teaching strategies, (4) peer training packages, (5) pivotal response treatment, (6) schedules, (7) self-management, and (8) story-based intervention packages. The population of focus for most of the research studies was individuals with ASD; however, studies also included individuals with mild, moderate, and severe intellectual disability. Table 12.1 illustrates the research-based practice, definition, and examples from peer-reviewed literature according to the NAC (2009) report. To the NAC (2009) recommendations we have added functional communication training (FCT), role playing, video modeling, and visual strategies that the literature supports as research-based strategies that have been effective in promotion of social skill development for students with developmental disabilities.

To illustrate, consider the needs of Jose, which were identified in the ecological inventory of the lunchroom (Figure 12.2). The teacher might begin by recruiting a cluster of guys who sit together to include Jose and train them in taking turns standing in line with him, escorting him to the table, and prompting him to share his pocketed toys. Because Jose's entire intervention will occur in the cafeteria using the opportunities that arise to socialize with the other boys, it is a naturalistic teaching technique. If the paraprofessional needs to step in briefly to prompt Jose to remain at the table or to share a toy, this should be done as discretely as possible to avoid interfering with the groups' typical social exchanges. Jose might benefit from having the intervention introduced in a social story. The teacher would read a story in which a boy named Jose waits in line with his friends, goes to their table, and shares fun toys while waiting for everyone to leave. Or this could be introduced by showing a video model. Either introductory instruction might help Jose understand the expectations in the natural context. Jose might also benefit from having a picture schedule to help him know the sequence of what to expect: (1) wait in line, (2) get food, (3) go to a table of boys, (4) eat, (5) share toys, and (6) go when the boys go. He might self-manage this by flipping the pictures as he completes each activity. The boys provide a naturally occurring model for Jose. The paraprofessional might point to the model when he or she needs to intervene (e.g., "Sit until Rico and Bob get up"). The peers may also be trained to use pivotal response training (PRT) to assist Jose in learning pivotal skills, such as motivation. This may include gaining Jose's attention in the lunch line, giving him choices to maintain motivation (e.g., "Jose, do you want to be in front of me in line?"), and varying the toys Jose is sharing with the boys, based on what Jose is interested in. In addition, the peers would model appropriate social behavior, reinforce attempts from Jose to remain at the table or share the toy, and encourage conversation with Jose. Finally, the peers could model taking turns with Jose. The National Secondary Transition Technical Assistance Center (NSTTAC; 2009) has developed practical resources for use with students with disabilities, including research to practice lesson plans in the areas of leisure, social, communication, and safety skills. Each lesson is based on a peer-reviewed research article and includes the objective, setting, materials, content taught, teaching procedures, and evaluation procedures. One of the most important factors to consider with respect to social skill development, especially for students who have a severe disability in communication, is that the lack of such skills can lead to problem behaviors (e.g., Benner et al., 2007; Carr & Durand, 1985; Davis et al., 1992; Durand & Carr, 1992).

TABLE 12.1. Research-Based Practices and Examples from the Literature

Research-based practice	Definition according to National Autism Center (2009)	Examples	Peer-reviewed sources
Joint attention interventions	These interventions involve building foundational skills involved in regulating the behaviors of others. Joint attention often involves teaching a child to respond to the nonverbal social bids of others or to initiate joint attention interactions.	Examples include pointing to objects, showing items or activities to another person, and following eye gaze.	Drew et al. (2002); Jones, Carr, & Feeley (2006)
Modeling	These interventions rely on an adult or peer providing a demonstration of the target behavior that should result in an imitation of the target behavior by the individual with ASD. Modeling can include simple and complex behaviors. This intervention is often combined with other strategies such as prompting and reinforcement.	Examples include live modeling and video modeling.	Alcantara (1994); Apple, Billingsley, & Schwartz (2005); Bellini, Akullian, & Hopf (2007)
Naturalistic teaching strategies	These interventions involve using primarily child-directed interactions to teach functional skills in the natural environment. These interventions often involve providing a stimulating environment, modeling how to play, encouraging conversation, providing choices and direct/natural reinforcers, and rewarding reasonable attempts.	Examples of this type of approach include but are not limited to focused stimulation, incidental teaching, milieu teaching, embedded teaching, and responsive education and prelinguistic milieu teaching.	Charlop-Christy & Carpenter (2000); Grela & McLaughlin (2006); Hamilton & Snell (1993)
Peer training packages	These interventions involve teaching children without disabilities strategies for facilitating play and social interactions with children on the autism spectrum. Peers may often include classmates or siblings. When both initiation training and peer training were components of treatment in a study, the study was coded as "peer training package." These interventions may include components of other treatment packages (e.g., self-management for peers, prompting, reinforcement).	Common names for intervention strategies include peer networks, circle of friends, buddy skills package, Integrated Play Groups, peer initiation training, and peer-mediated social interactions.	Brady, McEvoy, Wehby, & Ellis (1987); Chiang, Lee, Frey, & McCormick (2004); Coe, Matson, Craigie, & Gossen (1991)
Pivotal response treatment	This treatment is also referred to as pivotal response teaching and pivotal response training. PRT focuses on targeting "pivotal" behavioral areas—such as motivation to engage in social communication, self-initiation, self-management, and responsiveness to multiple cues—with the development of these areas having the goal of very widespread and fluently integrated collateral improvements. Key aspects of PRT intervention delivery also focus on parent involvement in the intervention delivery and on intervention in the natural environment, such as homes and schools, with the goal of producing naturalized behavioral improvements.	This treatment is an expansion of natural language paradigm, which is also included in this category.	Baker-Ericzén, Stahmer, & Burns (2007); Gillett & LeBlanc (2007); Harper, Symon, & Frea (2008)

(cont.)

TABLE 12.1. *(cont.)*

Research-based practice	Definition according to National Autism Center (2009)	Examples	Peer-reviewed sources
Schedules	These interventions involve the presentation of a task list that communicates a series of activities or steps required to complete a specific activity. Schedules are often supplemented by other interventions, such as reinforcement.	Schedules can take several forms, including written words, pictures or photographs, or work stations.	Dettmer, Simpson, Myles, & Ganz (2000); Arntzen, Gilde, & Pedersen (1998)
Self-management	These interventions involve promoting independence by teaching individuals with ASD to regulate their behavior by recording the occurrence or nonoccurrence of the target behavior and securing reinforcement for doing so. Initial skills development may involve other strategies and may include the task of setting one's own goals. In addition, reinforcement is a component of this intervention, with the individual with ASD independently seeking and/or delivering reinforcers.	Examples include the use of checklists (using checks, smiley or frowning faces), wrist counters, visual prompts, and tokens.	Apple et al. (2005); Callahan & Rademacher (1999); Koegel, Koegel, Hurley, & Frea (1992)
Story-based interventions	Treatments that involve a written description of the situations under which specific behaviors are expected to occur. Stories may be supplemented with additional components (e.g., prompting, reinforcement, discussion, etc.).	Social stories are the most well-known story-based interventions, and they seek to answer the "who," "what," "when," "where," and "why" in order to improve perspective taking.	Adams, Gouvousis, VanLue, & Waldron (2003); Agosta, Graetz, Mastropieri, & Scruggs (2004); Barry & Burlew (2004)

Note. Data from Information in National Autism Center (2009).

RESEARCH TO PRACTICE: STORY-BASED INTERVENTIONS

Recently, a report from the National Autism Center's National Standards Project (2009) determined that story-based interventions, including social stories, are one of the few "established treatments" for students with autism. Story-based interventions are "treatments that involve a written description of the situation under which specific behaviors are expected to occur" (NAC, 2009, p. 15). Social stories are the most recognized of the story-based interventions. Social stories are used by educators to teach social skills to children with autism and related disabilities. Social stories provide an individual with accurate information about "who," "what," "when," "where," and "why" of the social situation in order to improve understanding. Gray (1995) has developed guidelines for producing a social story and recommends that the stories include descriptive (i.e., describing the situation or social norm), directive (i.e., telling the student what to do, rather than what not to do), and perspective (i.e., describing the feelings and thoughts of others) sentences.

Social stories can be used to assist students with disabilities in gaining knowledge about social situations (e.g., turn-taking skills) and learning new skills (e.g., toileting skills; Gray & Garand, 1993). Test, Richter, Knight, and Spooner (2010) conducted a comprehensive review and meta-analysis of the social stories literature. In contrast to the findings from NAC on story-based treatments, Test et al. (2010)

determined that social stories cannot yet be considered an evidence-based practice based on the Horner et al. (2005) criteria. The use of social stories is popular among teachers and professionals due to their practicality and wide applicability; however, teachers are encouraged to collect ongoing data to evaluate the benefits for individual students. In addition, recommendations from both sources support the use of social stories with additional components (e.g., prompting, reinforcement, discussion, etc.). Finally, although social stories are recommended by Gray and her colleagues (Gray & Garand, 1993; Test et al., 2010) found that adherence to Gray's guidelines alone may not result in designing an effective intervention. See Figure 12.3 for an example of a social story.

POSITIVE BEHAVIOR SUPPORT

Students who have problem behaviors can be affected socially, emotionally, and cognitively. For example, problem behaviors can interfere with a student's ability to form friendships and with his or her overall inclusion in the school community (e.g., Hanson & Carta, 1996; Kauffman, Lloyd, Baker, & Riedel, 1995). In fact, problem behaviors are usually the primary reason students are placed in alternate settings, such as special schools or residential facilities (Kauffman et al., 1995). Students with severe disabilities display both *externalizing*, or outward, displays of behavior (e.g., tantrums, hitting, property destruction) and *internalizing*, or internal, displays of problem behavior (e.g., social withdrawal, self-stimulation). In the past, schools and communities sometimes have used methods to *manage* challenging behaviors, including aversive interventions, such as punishment, seclusion, and time out. Research in the past 20 years suggests that the use of more positive approaches that *support students* rather than *manage behaviors* are effective in reducing problem behaviors and increasing desired behaviors (e.g., Didden, Duker, & Korzilius, 1997; Horner et al., 1990; Sugai, Simonsen, & Horner, 2008). Collectively, these approaches are called *positive behavior support* (PBS). PBS is a collaborative, problem-solving approach to understanding the reasons for problem behavior (Bambara & Kern, 2005). The PBS approach aims at designing comprehensive interventions that improve the quality of life by making problem behavior less effective, efficient,

Getting Food in the Cafeteria
I line up in the cafeteria line.
There is a friend in front of me.
There is a friend behind me.
I follow the friend in front of me in line.
I am quiet.
My hands are to my sides.
I get the tray and put it on the counter.
I slide the tray as I walk, and my tray does not touch another tray.
I tell the person behind the counter what I want to eat.
She puts the food on my plate.
I put the plate on my tray.
I slide the tray to the end of the counter.
I tell the cashier my name.
I wait for her to say "OK" or to nod.
I carry my tray to the table with the rest of my class.

FIGURE 12.3. Example of a social story.

and relevant, while at the same time making the desired behavior more functional. The goal of PBS is not only to reduce problem behaviors in the short term but also to create lasting changes by teaching alternative skills and designing environments that contribute to the problem behavior. PBS blends behavioral technology and research-based methods with person-centered values to achieve outcomes that are socially meaningful and relevant to the person, family, and others involved in the students' life (Bambara & Kern, 2005). Before we discuss the process of PBS, it may be helpful to review basic principles of behavior.

Understanding Basic Principles of Behavior

PBS is rooted in *behaviorism*, or the philosophy of the science of behavior (Cooper et al., 2007; Skinner, 1974). The key point of behaviorism is that what individuals do—their behavior—can be understood (Cooper et al., 2007). Both PBS and behavior analysis maintain that behavior is functional, communicative, and context-based (Dunlap, Harrower, & Fox, 2005). In other words, the behavior serves a *function* for the individual engaged in the behavior. Problem behavior continues to occur because it is consistently followed by the individual's obtaining something or escaping or avoiding something. Behavior is communicative in that it serves to act on the social environment. For example, the function of the behavior may be to request assistance or to avoid a task demand, both of which are examples of communication, as can be seen in Table 12.2. Finally, behavior is related to the environmental context (Baer et al., 1968, 1987). Environments can be arranged such that the desirable behaviors can be increased and the problem behaviors can be reduced.

The Process of PBS

PBS can be thought of as a five-step process, which includes: (1) defining the problem behavior, (2) assessing the problem behavior, (3) developing a hypothesis statement, (4) designing a support plan, and (5) implementing, evaluating, and revising the support plan (Bambara & Kern, 2005; Horner, Albin, Todd, & Sprague, 2006). The following paragraphs illustrate the five-step process. Figure 12.4 provides an overview of the PBS process.

Define the Problem Behavior

The first step in developing an individualized PBS process is to determine whether or not the problem behavior requires more support than is provided to the majority of students as part of schoolwide PBS (Horner et al., 2006). If so, the problem behavior (or set of problem behaviors) is identified by describing it in observable, measurable terms. At this stage, the team describes the *topography* of the problem behavior (or what the behavior "looks like"; Cooper et al., 2007). Additionally, at this stage, the team may want to consider the severity of the problem behavior. Students may also have several behavioral challenges occurring simultaneously, in which case PBS teams may need to prioritize support based on the seriousness of behavior (Bambara & Kern, 2005). For example, *destructive behaviors*, or behaviors that are considered harmful or threatening to the safety of others, should receive first priority for intervention when teams are planning for PBS. If this is the

TABLE 12.2. Identifying the Communicative Function of the Behavior

Function	Questions for the team	Example for a student named Krissy	Communicative message
Obtain attention/ social interaction	Is the behavior a method to gain social attention?	The teacher is speaking with another student, and Krissy starts to engage in self-injurious behaviors.	"I want your attention." "Look at me!"
Obtain materials or activities	Is the behavior a form of obtaining preferences?	Another student is playing with a toy, and Krissy starts to scream.	"I want this."
Escape or avoid attention or social interaction	Is the behavior nonsocial or used to avoid people?	The speech therapist walks into the room, and Krissy runs out of the classroom.	"Leave me alone." "Please don't bother me."
Escape or avoid materials or activities	Is the behavior used to refuse what is disliked or no longer appealing?	The teacher asks Krissy to complete a math activity, and Krissy starts hitting the student next to her.	"I don't want to do this." "No." "This is too hard." "I need help." "I need a break."
Obtain or escape or avoid sensory stimulation	Does the behavior occur throughout the day even when the student is alone? Does the student appear to be in pain?	Krissy vocalizes when she is alone, with peers, and with teachers.	"I am bored." "I am hurt." "I enjoy this." "I am tense."

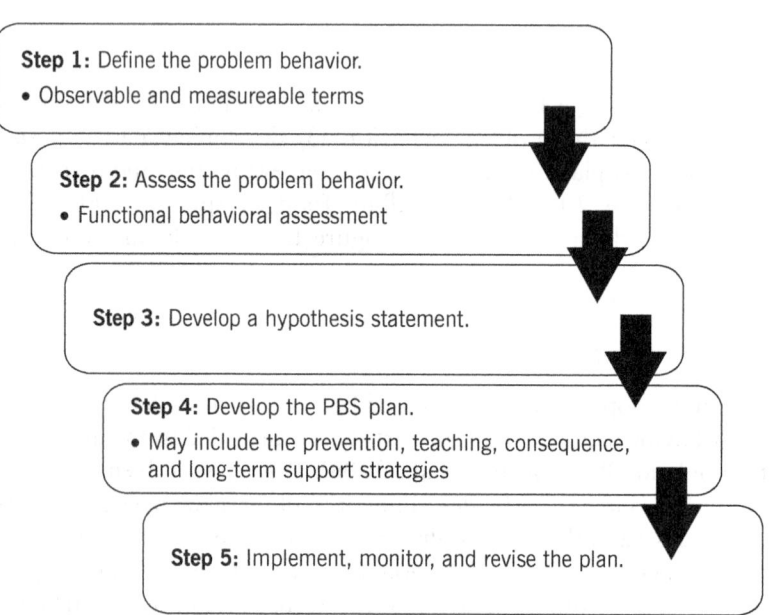

FIGURE 12.4. Steps of the PBS process.

case, the team should implement a crisis management plan through a comprehensive PBS plan. Further, if teams are considering a change in educational placement due to disruptive behavior, they are required by IDEA (1997) to review a student's existing behavior management plan and conduct a functional behavioral assessment (see the next subsection).

The second level of priority would be given to *disruptive behaviors*, those that interfere with learning, that prevent students from fully participating in home, school, and community activities, and that may prevent positive social relationships from developing. Finally, the third level of priority should be given to *distracting behaviors* (e.g., tapping on the desk, needing to follow a certain routine, engaging in one-way conversations), or behaviors that "deviate from what is typically expected from a student of the same age, but [do] not substantially interfere with learning and participation in daily activities" (Bambara & Kern, 2005, p. 52). Throughout the process, the team must consider the supports needed by the individual so that he or she can be successful, rather than focusing on simply reducing or eliminating the problem behavior.

Formally Assess the Problem Behavior

The second step is to assess the problem behavior within the context of the environment to determine why the behavior is occurring. The most important part of a PBS plan is to develop a *functional behavioral assessment* (FBA), in which information about an individual and his or her environment is gathered and analyzed. Research indicates that the use of FBAs is associated with an increase in effectiveness of PBS interventions (e.g., Didden et al., 1997; Marquis et al., 2000). Further, IDEA (1997) requires the use of FBAs and PBS by schools.

The process of conducting an FBA involves gathering broad and specific information through both direct and indirect methods. Examples of *indirect methods* include record reviews, interviews (with peers, parents, teachers, and the student), and checklists. One research-based tool for determining why problem behaviors persist is called the Motivation Assessment Scale (MAS; Durand, 1988). The MAS is a practical, individualized questionnaire that assesses the functions or motivations of problem behaviors by determining the influence of social attention, tangibles, escape, and sensory consequences on the problem behavior. It includes 16 questions, organized into four categories of reinforcement (e.g., social attention). When completed, the MAS yields a numerical score for each function, with the highest score representing the most probable function of the behavior in question. Research has shown formal methods such as the MAS to be more effective in generating a hypothesis of behavior than simply asking teachers which function (e.g., social attention) is maintaining the problem behavior (Durand, 1988).

Direct methods help to validate the information collected during indirect assessments. *Direct methods* are evaluated and recorded at the time the behaviors happen. Examples of direct methods include anecdotal notes as the behavior is occurring, an *antecedent–behavior–consequence* (ABC) analysis, and a functional assessment observation (FAO; O'Neill et al., 1997). Anecdotal notes can be helpful for the FBA, especially if it includes information about occurrences before and after the behavior of concern; however, this method is considered an informal measure of behavior. An ABC analysis provides a structured format for evaluating the problem behavior and consists of a data sheet arranged into three columns. The first column includes a description of what happens before the problem behavior (i.e., antecedent), the second column indicates the behavior (i.e., behavior), and the third column describes what happens after the problem behavior (i.e., consequence; see Figure 12.5 for an example of an ABC observation form). From the indirect and direct assessments, the FBA will consist of a clear statement defining: (1) the topography of behavior; (2) when it is most and least likely to occur; and (3) why the problem behavior is maintained (Horner et al., 2006).

Develop a Hypothesis Statement

The third step of the PBS process is for the team to develop a hypothesis of the *function* (i.e., purpose) of the behavior with the goal of understanding why the behavior is occurring (Cooper et al., 2007). The *hypothesis* is a plausible explanation of the behavior based on the relationship between the problem behavior and the environment, such as the conditions that establish and maintain the problem behavior.

Consider these two examples. Pamela is a 3-year-old who discovers that when she yells, her teacher rushes over to find out what is wrong (i.e., getting social attention). Allison is a 19-year-old who screams when tasks in the classroom become too challenging for her and is sent to the principal's office (i.e., escaping the challenging work). Although the topography of the behaviors is identical in these two examples (i.e., yelling), the functions of the behaviors are very different. Therefore, when developing a PBS plan, the topography of the behavior may be of little value if the team does not determine the underlying reasons for the problem behavior. A useful format when developing a hypothesis statement is the four-term contingency.

The *four-term contingency* is a behavioral equation that includes the (1) setting events, (2) antecedent events, (3) behavior, and (4) maintaining consequences of the problem behavior (Cooper et al., 2007). *Setting events* are events, circumstances, or stimuli that temporarily alter the value of reinforcers that maintain problem behaviors. For example, illness is a setting event that may decrease the value of social praise. The result may be that the illness increases the value of escaping from an academic task. In other words, if a student has the flu, he or she may not be as "motivated" to work on algebra even if the teacher says "Nice work!" It is important that the team determine information about the student's general medical status, social interactions, sleeping and eating patterns, and other setting events that may affect the behavior's maintaining consequences and antecedent conditions. *Antecedent events* are conditions that occur before the behavior. When determining antecedent conditions, the team should include information on when, where, and with whom the problem behaviors occur. Carr (1994) and Carr et al. (2002) encourages teams to focus as much or more on what happens *between* the incidents of problem behavior (e.g., when a person is doing well) as they do on what is happening *during* or *before* a bout of problem behavior. The information gathered from situations in which the person is successful can help teams identify how to support the student during more difficult situations.

As discussed previously in the chapter, problem behavior is functional in that it serves a *purpose* for the individual. Consequences following the problem behavior are usually *maintaining consequences*, and therefore they give information about the purpose of the behavior (Cooper et al., 2007). For example, a child throws a tantrum in the store because he wants a toy, resulting in the mother's embarrassment and subsequent buying of the toy (thus the child obtains a tangible object as a result of crying). In this case, the maintaining consequence is the buying of the toy. This process can be seen in

Student Name:	Observation Date:
Observer:	Time:
Activity:	Class Period:

Behavior:

ANTECEDENT	BEHAVIOR	CONSEQUENCE

FIGURE 12.5. ABC Observation Form.

Figure 12.6. Using the information from the FBA, the team can develop a hypothesis of the problem behavior. Hypothesis statements parallel the four-term contingency format and usually begin by identifying the setting events and the antecedent events ("when this happens"), illustrating the problem behavior ("the student does"), and describing the function(s) of the behavior ("to get or avoid . . . "; see, e.g., Carr, Langdon, & Yarbrough, 1999). For example, direct and indirect assessments of Charlie, a 4-year-old student with autism, reveal that he has many behaviors considered to be problem behaviors: hitting, crying, crawling under the desk, pinching, and pulling hair. However, the results of the FBA indicate that there are two primary "functions" of his behavior—escape from activities and social attention from peers. Examples of the hypothesis statements that may be developed are summarized as:

- Hypothesis 1: When Charlie is asked to complete a writing task, he will hit, cry, and crawl under the desk to avoid/escape completing the assignment.
- Hypothesis 2: When Charlie sees his friends playing, he will pinch or pull a peer's hair to gain peer attention.

Once the team has developed a testable hypothesis statement, they can validate the hypothesis by directly observing the student in the environment(s) in which the behavior(s) occur. This can be done using an ABC form (described previously; see Figure 12.5), a scatterplot analysis (Doss & Reichle, 1991), and/or an FAO form (O'Neill et al., 1997; see Figure 12.6).

A *scatterplot analysis* is a grid on which a teacher can plot the occurrence of a problem behavior within designated time periods (e.g., half-hour time periods) across multiple days (Doss & Reichle, 1991). The data from the scatterplot reveals information about when the behaviors are likely to occur, as well as when the behaviors are *not* likely to occur. When the team begins the PBS process, they can focus on interventions that alter the environmental conditions during the time periods in which the problem behavior is occurring to reduce the problem behaviors. The team may use the information gathered during periods in which the problem behavior did not occur to inform them of the changes needed during periods in which the problem behavior does occur.

An FAO (O'Neill et al., 1997) integrates the ABC observation form and the scatterplot to provide team members with information about the relationships between the antecedent and consequence conditions of the problem behavior. Identification of these relationships can inform the team about possible "triggers" of the behavior, as well as consequences that may be maintaining or increasing the problem behavior. In all cases of direct observation methods, one can determine only the correlational relationships between environmental variables and behaviors; one cannot conclude causal relationships between environmental variables and behaviors.

Setting events +	Antecedent events →	Behavior →	Maintaining consequences
Student wakes up with a headache.	Teacher requests homework.	Student throws head on desk and refuses to give teacher the homework.	Student is sent outside of the classroom to consider his or her actions.

FIGURE 12.6. Four-term contingency.

The final outcomes of a completed FBA should be the following: (1) a description of the problem behavior within the context/environment; (2) direct and indirect assessments; (3) information about the setting events of the problem behavior; (4) antecedents that increase the behavior (i.e., "trigger") and information about antecedents that decrease the problem behavior; (5) possible consequences that maintain the behavior; and (6) a hypothesis of the problem behavior synthesizing the aforementioned information (Horner et al., 2006).

Develop a PBS Plan

The fourth step uses information gathered from the FBA to create the PBS plan. Contrary to behavior management plans, in which the focus is only stopping the problem behaviors, the purpose of a PBS plan is to develop *prevention, teaching, and consequence* strategies that produce long-lasting changes for the student, family, and others. Comprehensive PBS plans involve the following components: *prevention strategies* (that make the problem behavior irrelevant), *teaching strategies* (that make the problem behavior inefficient), *consequence strategies* (that make the desired behavior more effective) and *long-term supports* (that include lifestyle changes and strategies to sustain support; Horner, Sugai, Todd, & Lewis-Palmer, 1999–2000; Horner et al., 2006). Table 12.3 shows examples and

TABLE 12.3. Behavior Support Plan Components with Examples

Type of strategy	What it does	Examples
Prevention strategies	• Modify or eliminate problem behaviors by making them irrelevant. • Change antecedent or setting events.	• Provide student with a schedule. • Give medication at night, rather than before school. • Change teacher/parent prompts (e.g., from "Time for bed" to "Want to read a bedtime story?")
Teaching strategies	• Teach replacement skills serving the same function as the problem behavior, making the behavior inefficient. • Teach new adaptive skills to expand overall competence.	• Teach a student to use a "break" card. • Implement functional communication training (FCT). • Teach a social skill, such as a greeting. • Teach play skills. • Teach problem solving, such as requesting help.
Consequence strategies	• Respond to problem behavior (determine strategies that increase desired behavior and decrease problem behavior). • Develop a crisis management plan, as needed.	• Reinforce attempts at desired behavior. • Ignore problem behavior. • Student self-monitors appropriate behaviors. • Teacher uses token systems.
Long-term supports	• Make lifestyle changes. • Team sustains support long term.	• Provide a circle of friends. • Encourage participation in community events and activities. • Ensure desired behaviors are part of transition planning. • Provide communication between teachers from year to year.

Note. Based on Bambara and Kern (2005) and Horner, Sugai, Todd, and Lewis-Palmer (1999–2000).

definitions of prevention, teaching, consequence, and long-term support strategies. Team members may want to use a competing behavior analysis (CBA) to design the comprehensive positive behavior support plan from the information collected during the FBA. A CBA involves the following four steps: (1) synthesizing the FBA information to develop a hypothesis of the problem behavior(s), with a separate hypothesis for each response class; (2) identifying a desired and alternative behavior that is considered acceptable though it may be not ideal; (3) identifying potential intervention strategies such as prevention, teaching, consequence, and long-term supports; and (4) selecting the strategies that are likely to make the problem behavior irrelevant, ineffective, and inefficient (Horner et al., 2006). An example of a CBA is in Figure 12.7.

Interventions may involve all or some of the components, but teams should consider preventative and teaching methods rather than consequence strategies alone. The intent of PBS is to ensure that interventions related to the problem behavior are proactive and supportive, rather than reactive. One benefit of using prevention interventions for educators and students is getting fast-acting results, which can in turn create a positive atmosphere for the student in which to learn replacement and coping skills. In addition, prevention strategies can be a relief for teachers and parents because they work so quickly and effectively. On the other hand, most students with developmental disabilities will also need to learn socially acceptable replacement behaviors for the targeted behavior problem through teaching strategies. Fortunately, when the functions of the problem behavior are well understood through an FBA, there are often abundant teaching methods that can address the same behavior across settings. Finally, teams need to consider how skills will be maintained and generalized over time to provide long-term supports (Bambara & Kern, 2005).

Implement, Evaluate, and Revise the PBS Plan

The goal of the PBS plan is to promote desired behavior while simultaneously making the problem behavior *irrelevant, inefficient,* and *ineffective* (Carr et al., 2002). To accomplish this goal, the team will need to complete a written statement of the plan to ensure implementation, evaluation, and modifications to the existing plan. Coordination of team members is essential to ensure that the written PBS plan is being carried out across settings and with a variety of people (e.g., Carr et al., 2002).

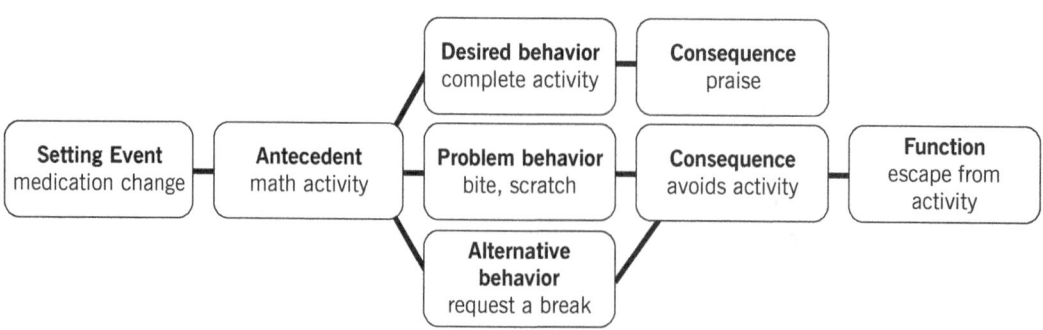

FIGURE 12.7. Competing behavior analysis.

IMPLEMENTING

According to Horner et al. (2006), in order to implement a PBS plan, the team should start with a *written PBS plan*. First, academic and lifestyle contexts for behavior support should be defined. For example, the written PBS plan should include a summary of the person-centered planning and vision planning for the student. Second, operational definitions of the problem behavior (i.e., clear definitions of the topography in observable and measurable terms) will assist team members in deciding the nature and severity of the problem behaviors. The operational definition should focus on both individual behaviors and response classes (i.e., groups of behaviors that serve the same function). Third, problem routines need to be identified (i.e., define problem behaviors within the context of the environment), which will reduce the likelihood that the behavior is "blamed" on a personality trait of the student (e.g., "Cayden is just lazy"). Fourth, hypotheses from the functional assessment are stated, serving as a reminder to the team of the plan's goals and objectives. Fifth, foundational issues affect the problem behavior and cut across routines and should therefore be described in the written PBS plan. Examples of foundational issues include a person's health and physical well-being, ability to communicate, capacity to express choice and control, skills in building social relationships, and activity patterns. Sixth, prevention, teaching, and consequence strategies are considered and developed (see examples in Table 12.3). Seventh, evaluation and assessment strategies will include the behaviors to be examined, any relevant data collection forms, procedures, and persons responsible. Finally, measures must be taken to ensure contextual fit over time. To promote contextual fit, the PBS plan must be implemented with fidelity and consistency across settings and team members to ensure sustainability. The PBS plan should be relatively easy for teachers, parents, and support personnel to implement across typical routines and activities (Bambara & Kern, 2005; Carr et al., 2002; Horner et al., 2006).

EVALUATING

One of the most important questions about the PBS plan, once in place, is, How successful is the plan? The team can use the written plan to evaluate the progress of the student based on the individualized PBS goals and objectives. An evaluation plan, developed by Bambara and Kern (2005), may be useful in this stage of the PBS process. Statements of meaningful outcomes, student expectations, measurement methods, responsible person(s), and expected time lines should be part of the evaluation plan. Team members will need to meet on a regular basis to evaluate the written plan and to problem-solve for the next steps in the plan.

REVISING

During the ongoing evaluation of the PBS plan, the team may need to make changes to the existing plan based on the team's satisfaction with the outcomes. Success should not be judged by the absolute elimination of the problem behavior, as this is usually next to impossible, especially for students who have difficulty with communication as part of a developmental disability. Rather, the team should evaluate the success of the PBS plan based on (1) reduction in the problem behaviors, (2) an increase in replacement and other adaptive skills, and (3) improvement in broad social and learning outcomes (e.g., membership/belonging, peer acceptance, friendship development).

FINDING THE BALANCE: TEACHING VERSUS MANAGING BEHAVIOR PROBLEMS

Teachers may sometimes feel that they have insufficient time to teach academic content because they seem to be always handling behavior problems. Substantial research has found a correlation between academic challenges and behavior problems (e.g., Fleming, Harachi, Cortes, Abbott, & Catalano, 2004; Nelson, Benner, Lane, & Smith, 2004). One solution, discussed in the chapter, may be as simple as developing an FBA and implementing a PBS plan. By decreasing some of the problem behaviors addressed in the PBS plan, academically engaged time may increase. In addition, some of the problem behaviors may be a result of the student not feeling academically challenged or, alternatively, frustrated by academic tasks.

Another solution may be to use video modeling. Reviews of this practice suggest that video modeling may be an effective instructional approach for students with developmental disabilities, especially students with ASDs (e.g., McCoy & Hermansen, 2007). Video modeling is an instructional technique in which the targeted behaviors are recorded on video in order to increase the students' ability to imitate and generalize the targeted behaviors (Hitchcock, Dowrick, & Prater, 2003). Video modeling has been used successfully to teach a variety of social, academic, and functional skills. For example, videos can be created in which salient social cues are emphasized, specific social and communication behaviors are highlighted, and sequences for task completion are presented (Quill, 2000). Finally, video models may incorporate adults, peers, oneself, and even visual point of view.

Video modeling may be appealing to teachers because live modeling, although effective, can be time-consuming. In fact, video modeling may be more effective than live modeling; in one study, students acquired the skill faster and generalized to other settings more frequently than in the live-modeling condition (Charlop-Christy, Le, & Freeman, 2000). Additionally, video modeling is cost-effective and efficient—once the target behavior is recorded, it can be used over and over, with a variety of students and across settings (Graetz, Mastropieri, & Scruggs, 2006). By using video models or other antecedent strategies (e.g., social stories, classroom rules) to prevent problems from occurring, teachers may find that they may be able to spend more time focused on content instruction.

SCHOOLWIDE POSITIVE BEHAVIOR SUPPORT

Problem behavior (e.g., aggression, bullying, noncompliance, truancy) has been a primary concern for educators for over 20 years (e.g., Horner, Diemer, & Brazeau, 1992). Unfortunately, traditional responses to problem behavior in school communities have been exclusion and punishment (Gottfredson, Gottfredson, & Hybl, 1993). In the past, research on PBS has evaluated outcomes related to individuals with severe disabilities; however, in recent years researchers and practitioners have realized that providing a full continuum of instructional and behavioral supports for all students improves the fidelity and consistency of specialized plans for individual students. School communities have begun to apply PBS to a broader systemwide approach called schoolwide positive behavior support (SWPBS). SWPBS increases the applicability of PBS from the individual student to the entire school community by expanding the tenets of prevention, skill building, and environmental modifications (Bambara & Lohrmann, 2006). SWPBS can be defined as a data-driven, decision-making framework that guides selection, integration, and implementation of evidence-based strategies to assist schools in decreasing problem behavior and increasing academic performance (Sugai et al., 2008).

SWPBS addresses the concern of the "wait to fail" model of many school communities by proactively addressing students' social behavior needs and preventing both social and academic failure (Simonsen, Sugai, & Negron, 2008). SWPBS requires the integration of four emphasized elements: (1) decisions based on *data*; (2) clear and measurable *outcomes* supported and determined by data; (3) *evidence-based practices* to support student outcomes, and (4) investment in *systems* that efficiently and effectively support implementation of these practices with fidelity over time. SWPBS is a systemic approach within the context of a three-tiered prevention framework: Tier 1, or the primary intervention tier (provided to all students); Tier 2, or the secondary intervention tier (for students whose behaviors are not responsive to the primary intervention tier); and Tier 3, or the tertiary intervention tier (for students whose behaviors are not responsive to primary and secondary intervention tiers; Sugai et al., 2008).

The goal of Tier 1 interventions is to provide schoolwide supports delivered by staff in a consistent and positive manner to teach prosocial behaviors and prevent problem behaviors. In Tier 2, specialized group strategies may be implemented to assist students who are at risk for learning or behavior challenges and who are unresponsive to Tier 1 interventions. Tier 3 interventions consist of specialized, individualized supports for students who are at high risk for behavioral and academic problems (Sugai et al., 2008; see Figure 12.8 for the continuum of schoolwide instructional and positive behavior support).

SWPBS is currently being implemented in over 7,000 schools in more than 37 states ("What is School-Wide Positive Behavior Support?" 2009). When implemented as prescribed, schools can expect that most students (89%, 74%, and 71% of elementary, middle, and high school students, respectively) will respond favorably to the Tier 1 interventions (Simonsen et al., 2008). Measurable outcomes of successful implementation of SWPBS systems in schools include: decreases in discipline referral suspensions and expulsions, improvement in students' academic performance, and improvement in supports for students who require specialized behavioral supports (Sugai et al., 2008).

CASE STUDY

The beginning of this chapter introduced the case of Austin, who was having difficulties during seatwork in mathematics. The general education teacher started to collect data on the number of times he was refusing to do his seatwork and running from the class, and the number seemed to be increasing. Ms. Hofsess, the special education teacher, evaluated the data from Ms. Kendrick, along with other information about how well Austin was doing with just Tier 1 and 2 supports.

At this point, Austin needed Tier 3 interventions. Ms. Hofsess suggested that Austin's team meet to conduct a brief FBA. From the direct observations, Ms. Hofsess noticed that Ms. Kendrick gave Austin math worksheets that were from a preschool-level curriculum (a possible setting event). In addition, she noted that Austin may have tried to communicate that he would like to work with a peer by tapping on that student's arm (which was interpreted as a hit). When other students were allowed to work in pairs, no one worked with Austin. Both the types of worksheets and lack of a peer partner seemed to set the occasion for Austin to begin to yell "go home" and run from the room. The FBA indicated that his behavior seemed to be escape motivated (to escape working alone on worksheets of low preference). The team also learned that another setting event may have been a reduction in Austin's medication. Although this may have helped explain Austin's intolerance for a nonpreferred activity, it did not prevent the team from planning a school-based intervention. The PBS plan developed by the team first brainstormed ways to use antecedent strategies. The special education teacher helped create math worksheets

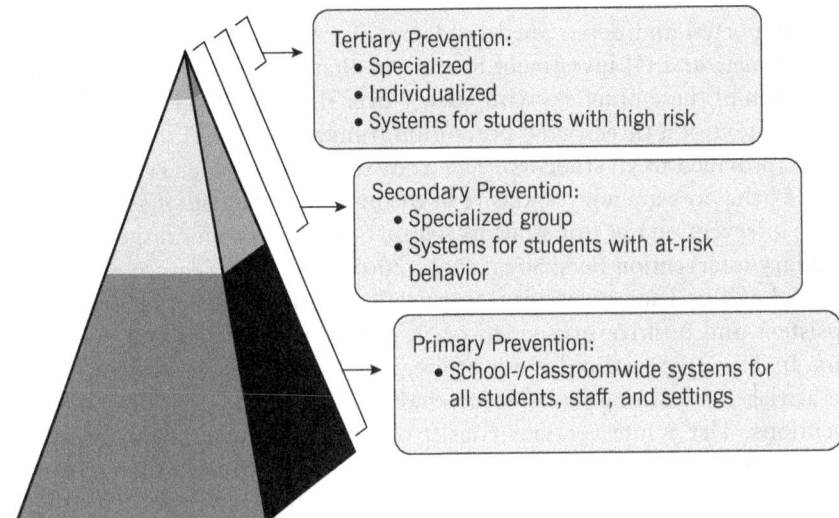

FIGURE 12.8. Continuum of schoolwide instructional and PBS. From Sugai (2009), *www.pbis. org.*

that were comparable to the content of those used by others in the class (grade appropriate) but adapted for Austin's level of understanding. The plan also called for Austin to learn to negotiate when the work assigned was intolerable. He would receive systematic prompting to choose between one of four options on a communication response overlay for his AAC: (1) "OK" (2) "A friend to help" (3) "A teacher to help" or (4) "I need a break." The consequence strategy to be used would be verbal praise for using the AAC and for completing his seatwork. If he did the seatwork alone (the hardest option) on days all students worked alone, he would also be able to have some time on the computer (a high-preference activity). If he began to yell "go home," before he bolted from the room, the teacher would prompt him to use his AAC to pick "I need a break" and allow him to put his head down. Finally, to facilitate long-lasting changes, Austin would receive instruction to self-evaluate his seatwork completion and would be given the opportunity to generalize his response options to other classes. Because there were a lot of changes to be made, the intervention was introduced to Austin using a video model of one of his favorite peers demonstrating each of his four options (work alone, friend to help, teacher to help, need a break). As Austin watched the video, he practiced pointing to the overlay. This video could be reviewed with Austin daily until he began to use the system consistently.

SUMMARY

The development of positive social relationships is critical for students with severe disabilities, as a lack of social skills can lead to problems with peers, social adjustment, and academics. Without training, students with severe disabilities may have difficulty socializing and communicating their wants and needs.

In this chapter we have described how social relationships are of specific importance to students with severe disabilities. Certain barriers to social relationships exist for students with severe disabilities, including a lack of access to typical settings, peers, and grade-appropriate curriculum. Fortunately, practical strategies are available to teachers and students for overcoming these barriers; these were explained in the chapter. Next, we discussed the environmental arrangements used to foster social relationships. Teachers are required to use research-based methods to promote social skills, and several of these research-based strategies are offered in this chapter. Often, students with severe disabilities have challenges in communication and socialization, leading to problem behavior. Students with challenging behaviors may require implementation of a positive behavior intervention plan. Teams should have a basic understanding of the principles of behavior before developing a plan for students with challenging behavior. The chapter reviews the basic tenets of behavior, along with a five-step process for applying a PBS plan. PBS plans should promote the desired behavior while simultaneously making the problem behavior *irrelevant*, *inefficient*, and *ineffective*. The chapter concludes with a review of schoolwide positive behavior support (SWPBS). SWPBS addresses problem behavior at a three-tired systemic level by proactively addressing students' social behavior needs. SWPBS requires that teams make decisions based on *data*, determine clear and measurable *outcomes*, use *evidence-based practices*, and invest in *systems* that implement practices with fidelity.

APPLICATIONS

1. Give some examples of social skills you might teach in your classroom or school. What methods would you use to teach social skills? (Provide examples of research-based and/or established interventions).

2. In a group, create a case study of a student with a problem behavior (be sure to have parental permission). Provide information about what is happening in the home and school environment, as well as information about what happens directly before and after the behavior occurs. Create a "mini" FBA based on this study and include the guidelines on pages 297–298. The final FBA will include: (1) a description of the problem behavior within the context/environment; (2) direct and indirect assessments; (3) information about the setting events of the problem behavior; (4) antecedents that increase the problem behavior (i.e., "trigger") and that decrease the problem behavior; (5) possible consequences that maintain the behavior; and (6) a hypothesis of the problem behavior synthesizing the aforementioned information.

3. With a partner, develop a competing behavior analysis for a student in your class (or a case study you create) who has a problem behavior.

4. As a group, have each member write a social story for a student who needs to ride the bus to school safely. Share the individual stories as a group, and discuss similarities and differences. If you used this story for a student in your classroom, how would you know whether or not it was working?

5. Develop a video model to use to help students learn a behavior that is often challenging (e.g., walking in the hall to the cafeteria). You may recruit one of your current students or another student to serve as the model. Narrate the video to praise the student's skills.

CHAPTER 13

Personal and Daily Living Skills

FRED SPOONER, DIANE M. BROWDER, AND JOSHUA BAKER

Sarah is a middle school student who enjoys swimming, popular music, and being with her peers. Sarah has a severe intellectual disability and communicates through vocalizing delight (e.g., laughs, says "bah!") or disapproval (e.g., buzzes her lips; cries). After years of training in using the toilet, washing her hands, and food preparation, she still needs help to carry out these skills. She will select the clothes she wants to wear if given two choices. She has also learned to put on her hat and carry her book bag or lunch tray. Meals are difficult because Sarah has an intense interest in food, grabs food, and overstuffs her mouth. Sarah is in a club that goes to movies, has sleepovers, and schedules other after-school events. Although Sarah goes to the club meetings at school, she has not joined the social events because of the logistics of personal care. Her teacher and parents want to plan a way for Sarah to be able to participate with her club in after-school events. This chapter provides ideas for teaching home and personal living skills not only for students who will master self-care and independent living but also for students like Sarah who may need ongoing support.

Many students with severe disabilities will need systematic instruction to master personal care and other daily living skills. Students are more likely to gain some degree of independence in their personal care if given opportunities to learn and apply these skills. In their meta-analysis of the research on deinstitutionalized adults with severe and profound intellectual disability who moved into community placements, Lynch, Kellow, Thomas, and Willson (1997) found that the most pronounced gains occurred in self-care. In contrast, Uehara, Silverstein, Davis, and Geron (1991) found more intense medical needs as well as adaptive behavior, self-care, and self-preservation needs among individuals with developmental disabilities who had been placed in nursing home settings. The acquisition of personal care skills also is often a parental priority. In a survey of family members of young adults with severe disabilities, Thorin and Irvin (1992) discovered that self-care, sexuality, and getting along with others were the most frequently mentioned concerns. As described in the opening case study, a lack of personal care skills can create barriers to participating in community opportunities. Although individuals who need ongoing support for personal care *can* be active members in the community and hold competitive jobs, the more personal independence the person acquires and retains, the easier it becomes to gain access to these opportunities.

When the first public school services for students with severe disabilities emerged in the mid-1970s, there was intense professional interest in how best to teach personal and daily living skills. A large body of research now exists on how to teach skills such as eating, dressing, using the toilet, brushing teeth, housekeeping, food preparation, and laundry skills (Konarski & Diorio, 1985; Westling & Fox, 1995). Although this research continues to provide important information on how to apply systematic instruction to these skills, there are some important new advances in teaching personal and daily living skills. Recent research has started to emphasize how technology can be used to enhance these skills (e.g., Bellini et al., 2007; Mechling, Gast, & Fields, 2008). With new technology such as Palm personal devices, portable DVDs, portable cameras, and MP3 players, it is possible for the teacher to provide a variety of realistic models and self-instructional strategies. Another recent addition to the research since their inception in the 1970s are models for partial participation (e.g., Bosner & Belfiore, 2001). Not all students will become independent in their daily routines but instead will rely on lifelong caregiver support. Guidelines are needed to select skills that will encourage autonomy and personal dignity even when lifelong care may be necessary. Newer resources on personal and daily living also promote self-determination and cultural diversity. Home and personal care skills are indeed "personal." The way individuals perform these routines is influenced by their cultural background, family traditions, and personal preferences. The teacher needs to consult with each child's caregiver in order to respect these traditions and cultural routines. Educators need to take person-centered and family-centered perspectives when teaching home and personal care skills.

Educators also need to consider how to address personal and daily living skills in inclusive school settings. Personal care skills are typically mastered in the early preschool years, and so teaching them to school-age students can be stigmatizing. Some personal living and daily living skills (e.g., toileting, sex education) are among the most private issues in our society. Educators need to plan ways to teach needed skills and provide support for personal care in ways that respect the dignity and preferences of the individual. Table 13.1 summarizes some guidelines to follow in planning personal care. The next section describes each of these guidelines.

TABLE 13.1. Guidelines for Planning Personal Care and Daily Living Skills Instruction

1. Plan with the family to identify priorities and respect cultural values (e.g., what to teach first, family food preferences, family's values regarding food, privacy, and other issues).

2. Identify ways to promote the student's self-determination in personal care and home routines (e.g., choice making, goal setting, self-direction).

3. Use systematic instruction to increase student independence.

4. Plan for partial participation and nonintrusive supports, especially for older students who lack personal care skills.

GUIDELINES FOR PLANNING INSTRUCTION FOR PERSONAL AND DAILY LIVING SKILLS

Plan with the Family

Although planning with families is important for all aspects of the IEP (see Chapter 3), this input is essential for personal and daily living skills. Students may have allergies or other health issues that have implications for instruction (e.g., a need to avoid foods that cause allergies). Families' cultural values may also influence instructional decisions. For example, some religions avoid specific types of food. Parents may have preferred methods for managing the child's diet or toileting schedule. Educators may not understand the implications that teaching or not teaching some skills may have for the family unless there is joint planning. For example, one teacher taught her students to unfasten their seatbelts. Then one student's mother reported that she could no longer safely drive her child without a second adult in the car because he repeatedly unfastened his seatbelt. The teacher had taught the child to unfasten his seatbelt but had not taught him to do so only after the vehicle had stopped. If the teacher had talked with the mother prior to planning this instruction, she might have taught the skill a different way or not taught it at all until the student had acquired more passenger safety skills. In another true story, a teacher expressed frustration with Charlie's mother because she would not give Charlie the opportunity to generalize his newly acquired grocery shopping skills. Once they talked, it became clear that shopping was the activity that the mother used to take a break from child care, and so she was resistant to including any of her children in this activity. In contrast, the child's aunt volunteered to provide shopping opportunities when Charlie came to her house. An example of a clash in cultural values occurred when a teacher asked the parents to send in money for all the students to go out for hamburgers once a week as their community-based instruction. One set of parents did not respond to the request. When the teacher called the mother, she learned that they considered fast food unhealthy and did not eat beef. Figure 13.1 provides questions that educators may use in interviewing parents to plan instruction.

Another reason to plan with the family is that some students may have intense support needs in personal care. For example, Margaret took multiple medications for seizure control and to improve her respiratory function. These medications increased her urinary output and decreased her appetite. Because Margaret was underweight, the teacher needed to be careful to feed Margaret her full lunch every day if possible. She had to be careful with any classroom snacks because Margaret had peanut allergies and was on a gluten-free diet. Margaret also resisted any hard foods (e.g., celery, beans), possibly due to a bad experience with nuts. Figure 13.2 shows how the teacher summarized the notes from her meeting with Margaret's mother. After identifying Margaret's care needs, the teacher then collaborated with the occupational therapist to plan how to address Margaret's eating challenges (see Chapter 10 on working with therapists).

Identify Ways to Promote Student Self-Determination in Daily Routines

Students and their parents may not always have the same perspectives on priorities for their lives. In a study on vocational skills, Martin, Woods, Sylvester, and Gardner (2005) compared the choices made between caregivers and students with severe disabilities. The authors found that the caregivers of students with severe disabilities often made different

1. *Tell me about your son's/daughter's mealtimes.*
   - Who prepares the food? _____ Does your son or daughter help? _____
   - How well does your son or daughter eat? _____
   - What assistance, if any, do you give to help him or her eat? _____
   - What are his or her favorite foods? _____
   - What does he or she dislike? _____
   - Are there certain foods that are off limits because of allergies, a special diet, or religious customs? __
     _____
   - Are there any medical concerns related to your child's eating? _____
   - Can he or she follow a recipe? _____ With pictures? _____ With media? _____

2. *Let's talk about how your child's toileting needs.*
   - Does your child indicate the need to use the toilet? _____ To be changed? _____
   - Does your child use diapers? _____ If so, is this all the time or at certain times? _____
   - How often does he or she need to be changed? _____ Are there any special concerns? _____
   - If not in diapers, does your child ask to use the toilet? _____
   - Do you take your child to the toilet on a schedule? _____ How often? _____
     Have you charted the occurrences? _____
   - Does your child have toileting accidents? _____ How often? _____
   - What does your child do for himself or herself in the restroom? _____
   - Are there any special concerns related to toileting? _____

3. *Let's talk about how your child gets dressed.*
   - How does your child get dressed and ready for school? _____
   - If you dress your child, does he or she do anything for himself or herself? _____
   - Who chooses your child's outfits? _____
     Can your child choose his or her clothing? _____
   - Are there any special concerns related to dressing? _____

4. *What other skills should we emphasize in your child's daily routine?*
   - Chores and housekeeping? _____ If so, what specific skills? _____
   - Grooming skills such as hair, nail care, and/or makeup? _____
   - Telephone or cell phone use? _____
   - Internet use? _____ Social networks? _____
   - Other? _____

5. *Are you interested in having your child receive sex education at school?*
   - What topics should be addressed in this sex education? _____
   - Are there topics that you prefer not be taught at school or at this age? _____

6. *Does your child have opportunities to express choices or preferences during these daily routines?* _____
   _____ *If so, how?* _____
   - Do you sometimes disagree with your child on his or her choices? _____
     What are the issues on which you have recently disagreed? _____

7. *Is there anything else you would like to share that will help me meet your child's unique needs and respect your family's customs?* _____

FIGURE 13.1. Planning instruction with the family for personal and daily living skills

Student: Margaret Chu   **Teacher:** Ms. Baxter

Medication Notes: Diamox (anticonvulsant; may cause thirst and increased urine output); Beconase (anti-inflamatory respiratory tract medication; may cause sneezing and nose irritation); Depakote (vomiting, loss of appetite).

Allergy Notes: Severe to nuts; peanuts can be life threatening.

Dietary Restrictions: No peanuts or recipes with peanut oil; on a gluten-free diet (see list of food restrictions including wheat products); lactose intolerant (no dairy products).

Other Medical Notes: Has been seizure free for almost 1 year; takes seizure meds after breakfast; will not need to administer during the school day; susceptible to urinary tract infections.

Family Preferences: Parents will send a lunch that is consistent with her gluten-free diet; need to create a list of acceptable school snacks; parents eat a traditional Asian diet and not many sweets; concern that last teacher used candy as a daily reward.

Student's Preferences: Margaret does not like food with hard texture like beans, celery (may be related to a bad experience with nuts); pureed carrots are her favorite food.

FIGURE 13.2. Summary of family planning notes for a student with intense support needs.

choices than did the students. Similarly, students may have different perspectives on what they want to learn or do (e.g., to cook but not to do dishes; to wear the same clothes as their peer group). Educators must be careful to respect students' relationships with their parents. Parents are often the primary long-term source of support for individuals with severe disabilities. In contrast, educators may be able to help a parent accept his or her child's unique interests and growing maturity.

During the caregiver interview it is important to include questions (see Figure 13.1, item 6) about the students' opportunities to use self-determination skills. Sometimes educators and family members provide too much support in personal and daily living skills because it is faster or easier to do so, not realizing that one day the child will need to be more independent. Teachers need to consider the overall goal of encouraging student self-determination (Wehmeyer, 1992). For example, the student might make choices in each of his or her daily routines, such as what type of toothpaste she wants or which shirt he will wear to school. The student might set goals for learning, such as whether he or she will discard his or her trash after lunch. Many daily living skills lend themselves well to self-instruction, such as using pictures to prepare a meal or set the table.

FINDING THE BALANCE: PERSONAL PREFERENCE VERSUS THE SOCIAL NORM

Promoting self-determination skills is encouraged and should be taught to students with severe intellectual disability. Sometimes teachers find themselves at a crossroads whenever students with disabilities make choices that are not typical of the social norm. For example, what if a high school student insists on wearing a cartoon character sweatshirt and carrying a cartoon character lunch box everywhere he goes? This style is not age-appropriate and may result in negative attention from same-age peers. It is awkward for the teacher to discuss with the caregivers the chronologically appropriate way to dress, but it is important to do so, as the students will be included with their same-age peers throughout the school day. Spooner and Wood (2004) suggest that a flyer can be made to send home to the caregivers to inform them that their child is growing up. The flyer can be made for all of the caregivers of the students in a class in order to address common styles among students in the schools. Spooner and Wood (2004) also suggest that similar flyers can be sent home on a regular basis to assist with conversational topics, such as movies and sports, as well as addressing "growing up" and the need for less "baby talk." It is also extremely important for teachers to understand and respect all students' cultural backgrounds and styles. The teacher may need to learn different customs in order to help the child dress with respect to his or her culture. Discussing cultural differences at the beginning of the school year with the caregivers can give the teacher a better understanding of how to address these needs.

Another way to promote self-determination is to plan ways for students to be more active participants in their daily routines. Even if students cannot become fully independent, "partial participation" goals need to be acknowledged (Ferguson & Baumgart, 1991). That is, students can learn to make some independent responses within their daily living routines. It is important that teachers target specific, measurable *independent* responses that students will eventually be able to make without teacher guidance. If IEP objectives focus on responses made with teacher guidance, students remain passive in their daily routines. The teacher may work strenuously guiding the student through the routine while the student learns little to nothing about what to do. Although physical guidance and other forms of support may be used initially to teach correct responding, *it is essential that the target response be one that the student is physically capable of making without teacher assistance.* These observable, measurable responses that the student is physically capable of making can be called "active responses."

Students also need to be able to "take charge" of their daily routines as they mature into adulthood. An adult can require extensive personal care but still be "in charge" of that care by directing the caregiver's actions. Helping students take charge can be done by creating opportunities for choice in personal routines and by allowing them to initiate or terminate the steps of the activity. Students' personal dignity can also be encouraged by respecting their privacy and using materials appropriate to their chronological age and setting. Figure 13.3 provides an example of how a teacher planned a student's active participation during school arrival, lunch, and restroom use.

Use Systematic Instruction to Teach Personal and Daily Living Skills

As described earlier in this chapter, research on applying systematic instruction to effectively teach personal care and daily living skills has been ongoing for more than 40 years. One of the first steps is to task-analyze the steps needed to perform the specific activity. For example, Table 13.2 shows the steps needed for first aid (Spooner, Stem, & Test, 1989). Similarly, a task analysis might be used for operating a washer to clean clothes, loading a dishwasher, putting on a coat, packing a book bag, making pudding, sweeping the floor, or nearly any other activity of daily living. As described in Chapter 4, the task may be taught using all steps (whole task) or by teaching a step at the beginning or end of the task and gradually adding other steps (forward or backward chaining). In general, whole-task instruction should be used, with chaining as an alternative if progress is slow.

Student: Karen McDaniel **Age**: 13   **Teacher**: Ms. Samuelson

Routine	More active responses	Choice-making responses	Student's responses "take charge"	Age and setting appropriateness
Arrival				
1. Go from bus to classroom.	• Help with transfer to chair.		• Nod for book bag to be put on chair. Look up to ask to be wheeled.	
2. Take off coat.	• Lift right arm as coat is removed.	• Choose whether to put coat on chair or hook.	• Vocalize when ready to take coat off.	
3. Put belongings away.	• Grasp/release refrigerator door to help put lunchbox away.		• Nod to indicate take lunchbox out.	
Mealtime				
1. Get lunch.	• Grasp refrigerator door.	• Use eye pointing to indicate choice of seat.	• Indicate lunchtime by pointing to object schedule.	
2. Open containers.		• Eye-point to indicate container to open first (order in which to eat lunch).		
3. Eat.	• Scoop food after spoon is placed in bowl.		• Use eye contact to indicate when ready for next bite of food.	• Use spare T-shirt (not a bib) for spills.
4. Clean up lunch.	• Release containers in lunchbox after placed in hand.		• Vocalize to indicate when finished with lunch.	
Restroom				
1. Go to restroom.			• Point to picture of "Women" for restroom to indicate when ready to go.	• Use universal sign for "women," not picture of a toilet.
2. Use toilet.	• Help lift buttocks for pants down. Help with transfer on/off toilet.		• Indicate when ready to get off toilet by vocalizing.	• Use single-person restroom for privacy.
3. Wash hands.	• Turn water on. Move hands toward water. Release paper towel in trash.	• Choose wall or pump soap; paper towel or hot air dryer.		

FIGURE 13.3. Planning active participation for students who may need ongoing support in their daily routines.

TABLE 13.2. Task Analysis of First Aid

Communicating an emergency	Applying a plastic bandage
1. Locate phone.	1. Look at injury.
2. Pick up receiver.	2. Find bandages needed.
3. Dial 9.	3. Select proper size.
4. Dial 1.	4. Find outside tabs of wrapper.
5. Dial 1.	5. Pull down tabs to expose bandage.
6. Put receiver to ear.	6. Find protective covering on bandage.
7. Listen for operator.	7. Pull off by tabs, exposing gauze portion.
8. Give full name.	8. Do not touch gauze portion.
9. Give full address.	9. Apply to clean, dry skin.
10. Give phone number.	
11. Explain emergency.	
12. Hang up after operator does.	

Taking care of minor injuries	First aid for choking
1. Let it bleed a little to wash out the dirt.	1. Let the person cough and try to get object out of throat.
2. Wash with soap and water.	2. Stand behind victim.
3. Dry with clean cloth.	3. Wrap your arms around victim.
4. Open plastic bandage.	4. Make a fist with one hand, placing the thumb side of the clinched fist against the victim's abdomen—slightly above the navel and below the rib cage.
5. Cover injury with bandage (hold by edges).	
6. Call 911 if severe and no adult available.	5. Press fist into abdomen with a quick upward thrust.
	6. Repeat Step 5 as needed.

Note. Based on Spooner, Stem, and Test (1989).

Once the skill has been task-analyzed, the teacher needs to select a method for systematic prompting and fading. Researchers have successfully used both the system of least prompts (Arnold-Reid, Schloss, & Alper, 1997; Mechling & Gast, 1997) and time delay (Hall, Schuster, Wolery, Gast, & Doyle, 1992; Miller & Test, 1989). In the system of least intrusive prompts, the teacher follows a hierarchy of prompts at each step of the task analysis. For example, the teacher may wait for the student to measure the laundry detergent; if there is no response, the teacher may then gesture to the measuring cup; if there is still no response, the teacher may then model the response and have the student repeat the action. In time delay, the teacher will use one prompt for all steps of the task analysis with no delay and then fade to some delay interval on subsequent presentations of the task analysis. For example, on the first day, the teacher may model each step of loading the washer, with the student then imitating each step. On the third day, the teacher waits 5 seconds for the student to perform the step before using the model, if needed. Both of these procedures are described and illustrated in Chapter 4. With these systematic prompting procedures, the teacher also uses reinforcement for correct responding (e.g., praise for each step) that is faded over instructional sessions. Errors can be corrected by giving a higher level of prompt. Sometimes teachers provide extra information as part of the feedback for responding. For example, Jones and Collins (1997) embedded safety skills information (e.g., to turn off the microwave if smoke is seen).

Daily living skills also lend themselves well to student self-instruction. For example, Pierce and Schriebman (1994) taught children with autism to self-manage chores. The instructions were in the form of a photo album with one step of the task analysis on each page. The students learned to identify the pictures. Then they learned to point to the picture, perform the step, and self-reinforce. In the final phase of learning, the instructor was able to leave the student to perform the entire chore without assistance. Students learned to use the book to set a table, make a bed, make a drink, get dressed, and do laundry without an adult nearby. Picture recipes are another option for this type of self-instruction (Singh, Oswald, Ellis, & Singh, 1995). Some researchers have demonstrated the usefulness of self-operated auditory recordings (Post & Storey, 2002). For example, in Briggs et al. (1990) students learned to perform chores while wearing a tape player with a prerecorded script. When a bell sounded, the student turned off the tape and performed the step.

RESEARCH NOTES

Recent research on teaching personal care and daily living skills has demonstrated new techniques, such as video modeling (Bellini et al., 2007; Mechling et al., 2008) and social stories (Gray, 2000). Both of these strategies have had a great amount of success in the research literature and can be deemed "evidence-based practices" (see Chapter 4). Bellini et al. (2007) defined video modeling as a technique that usually involves the student watching a video demonstration and then imitating the behavior of the model. Bellini et al. (2007) found that video modeling helped students with autism increase social engagement skills and maintain these skills over time. In a similar study using video modeling, Mechling et al. (2008) found that three students with moderate intellectual disability could master three cooking tasks with the use of a portable DVD player. Social stories are short, personalized stories that can be written by the teachers to help the students gain a better understanding of daily routines and expectations (Gray, 2000). In a review of the research on social stories, Ali and Frederickson (2006) found social stories being used for a wide range of skills, including decreasing disruptive behaviors (Scattone, Wilczynki, Edwards, & Rabian, 2002) and increasing hand washing (Hagiwara & Myles, 1999) and social behaviors (Thiemann & Goldstein, 2001). Although Ali and Frederickson (2006) question whether social stories are an "evidence-based practice," they do state that the positive results of most of the studies allow professionals to justify the use of social stories with children with autism and other developmental disabilities. Again, it is important to personalize the curriculum based on each individual. With social stories, some students may require a multimedia approach, others may need them written, and some may not be able to understand them at all.

Using new tools and technologies can create a positive classroom experience. These techniques are inexpensive, easy to make, and fun for the learner. Although more research is needed on the use of video modeling and social stories, these strategies may be considered and used to personalize the personal and daily living skills for each individual student.

Sometimes students can be more independent in responding if stimulus cues are used. For example, Sarber and Cuvo (1983) taught students to plan balanced meals by using boards that were color coded for the different food groups. Similarly, students may learn to set a table by using place mats with the place settings drawn on them. Selecting clothes that match might be achieved by hanging clothes on hangers with picture tags to show the paired items. Commercial materials may be available to help with this instruction. For example, the Select-a-Meal curriculum published by Attainment Company uses a strategy similar to that of Sarber and Cuvo (*www.attainment.com*).

In planning systematic instruction, it also is important to plan for how students will generalize the newly acquired skills. One important strategy is to give students the opportunity to use new skills as frequently as possible. For example, if the student has learned to put on her or his hat or brush her or his teeth, all caregivers at home and school should give the student the opportunity to do these things. Sometimes the family will need to train for generalization to the home. Teachers can share their task analysis and show parents how they wait for independent responding before prompting the student to respond. Another strategy is to use what is called general case instruction. For example, Horner, Williams, and Steveley (1987) taught students to make a variety of phone calls by teaching variations such as the type of phone, its location, the person being called, and topic of conversation. Chapter 14 provides more information on general case instruction.

Sometimes the challenge is not generalization to the home but finding ways to teach personal and daily living skills in the school routine. To plan this instruction, the teacher can review the daily schedule to learn when personal care skills are needed (e.g., on arrival, at lunchtime, when getting ready to leave). Some of these can simply be taught in the natural context (e.g., the student might receive systematic instruction in packing a book bag while all students are getting packed for the day). Others may require some privacy (e.g., the student uses a private restroom for toileting). Sometimes additional opportunities can be created without being intrusive on the students' day (e.g., having the student help clean a break area to learn some housekeeping skills; asking parents to send a lunch item that requires use of the microwave each day; changing clothes in a private area before and after physical education).

Plan for Partial Participation and Nonintrusive Supports When Needed

When students lack most personal care skills and are passive in daily routines, it can be difficult to know what to target as priorities. To teach every skill in every routine is not feasible given the time pressure of a school day. For example, a teacher helping seven students with no skills to use the restroom could spend the entire morning teaching these skills. Instead, the teacher may set priorities for what to teach first and then use chaining of responses. For example, hand washing can be taught in a backward chain; teaching the student first to throw a towel away, then to turn water off, then to rinse hands, and so forth. Parental and student preferences and self-determination considerations can help in setting priorities. Any skills that are not a current priority can be performed by the teacher for the student as efficiently as possible (e.g., the teacher washes the student's hands up to the point of rinsing and then teaches the last three steps).

Sometimes the student has physical challenges that will require lifelong personal assistance. A student who has no use of his or her limbs (quadriplegic) will probably need some assistance to dress and eat. When this is the case, specific responses can be chosen for partial participation. This partial participation can be made especially meaningful by putting the student in charge of the routine (self-determination). The student may choose what materials are to be used, who will provide assistance, when the activity will take place, or where it will be completed. For example, when it is time for the student's teeth to be brushed, the teacher asks, "Do you want Ms. Hill or me to help you with your teeth today? Which flavor toothpaste? Brush or sponge? Orange cup or blue cup for rinsing?" Another way the student may meaningfully participate is by performing responses that make the caregiving routine more efficient. For example, a student with limb control may lift his leg or arm while being dressed, which makes dressing the person less strenuous and faster. Or the student who is quadriplegic may open her mouth or turn her head to help with tooth brushing (Snell, Lewis, & Houghton, 1989). In addition to these goals for partial participation, some consideration may be given to the types of supports that will make the activity easier. These may include using adapted equipment or improved positioning, as described in Chapter 10. Figure 13.4 provides an example of three different levels of expectations for a morning routine. In the first, the student will learn the entire routine. In the second, the student will be chaining skills to work toward independence. In the third, the student is learning to direct his own caregiving routine.

EXAMPLES OF HOME
AND PERSONAL LIVING CURRICULA

Educators can glean ideas for home and personal living curricula by using an ecological inventory or by reviewing published curricula. This section of the chapter also provides ideas in several skill areas. In an ecological inventory, the teacher considers each of the major environments in a student's life, the activities performed in these environments, and skills needed for current and future participation in these activities. In this example, the teacher considered both Joey's school and home environments. Although it would not be feasible to teach all of these skills, this inventory helps provide ideas for IEP planning in this area. A second option is to refer to a published life skills curriculum (e.g., Ford et al., 1989; Giangreco, Cloninger, & Iverson, 1998; Loyd & Brolin, 1997; Wilcox & Bellamy, 1987). These curricula usually list skills by life skills domain. In the following sections, we provide some examples of skills in these major domains, with examples from research of how they may be taught.

Skill	**Greg:** Full independence in entire routine.	**Joe:** Chaining skills toward independence.	**Bob:** Self-direct his care (does not have physical ability to perform tasks alone).
Dressing	Learning to match clothes and select clothes appropriate to activity and personal tastes; dresses without assistance.	Knows how to put on socks. Learning to choose and put on T-shirt. Next will learn to put on pants.	Currently vocalizes protest if a shirt is too tight. Learning to use eye gaze to select shirt; vocalizes consent when shirt is on correctly.
Mealtime	Learning to prepare and plan balanced meal; eats without assistance and uses microwave.	Knows how to use a spoon; learning to spear with a fork and use napkin; learning to operate microwave.	Needs assistance to eat; learning to look at food to indicate what he wants to eat next and to operate a blender.
Use of restroom	Working on self-monitoring of hand washing; otherwise independent.	Learning to use toilet by being taken on a schedule; throws towel away; learning to turn water on/off.	Currently indicates needs to be changed by whining; learning to look at caregiver to indicate when ready to be lifted from changing table.
Household chores	Can perform essential chores; learning to follow picture schedule to know when to do chores; improving laundry sorting.	Knows how to empty trash; learning to follow picture task analysis to wipe table and chairs.	Learning to use eye gaze to indicate when ready for tray to be cleared; currently thanks caregiver with a smile.

FIGURE 13.4. How expectations may differ for daily living skills instruction.

Eating Skills

Perske, Clifton, McLean, and Stein (1977) described the ideal mealtime as having the following characteristics:

- Feeling of comradeship and belonging.
- Relaxing and being less defensive.
- Communicating in many ways with voice, eyes, body, taste, smell, and touch.
- Laughing and feeling joyful.
- Being accepted exactly as you are and being glad you are *you*.
- Making choices.
- Having all the time you need.
- Heightening all the senses.
- Feeling full, satisfied, and relaxed.
- Taking in nutrition for growth and good health.

Having an ideal mealtime can be difficult for an individual with severe disabilities because of deficits in both eating and social skills. Learning skills in this area may make it easier for students to focus on the social context of mealtimes, such as during school lunch periods. In contrast, students who will need long-term assistance to eat also need the opportunity for peer socialization at lunch instead of eating in the classroom. Teachers should seek balance between the goals of socialization and nutrition during school lunch periods. This can be done by reserving direct, systematic instruction for only the highest priority skills. This direct instruction might also occur in some private tutoring sessions rather than at lunchtime. Being with peers who model eating skills is a form of natural support during school lunches. The teacher may use environmental arrangements, such as giving the student spoons with an enlarged grip, a plate with raised edges, and a rubber mat to make it easier to eat. Sometimes the teacher or a peer can simply prepare the food further for simplified eating. A sandwich might be cut into bite-size pieces. Students may also use self-instruction. For example, wiping the mouth after each bite is one way for a student to pace him- or herself so as to avoid stuffing the mouth with food.

Some students may need to eat in private to preserve lunchtime as a social context (e.g., the student who is tube fed or who gags easily when eating). Other students will need direct, systematic instruction to learn some basic eating skills. This direct instruction need not occupy the entire meal. The teacher and student might go to the cafeteria early to work on eating whatever menu item needs a spoon (e.g., applesauce), and then the student is free to eat the remainder of lunch (e.g., finger foods such as burritos and carrot sticks) with friends. Some students who need to be fed may enjoy having a peer who is nondisabled provide this assistance. This assistance may be provided just before everyone gets into the cafeteria or during the busy activity of the regular lunchtime, depending on the student's needs and preferences. When a student needs direct instruction, the teacher will probably use a task analysis of the skill and systematic prompting as described in Chapter 4. For example, to teach self-feeding, Collins and colleagues (1991) used this task analysis:

1. Grasp spoon.
2. Scoop food.

3. Raise spoon to lips.
4. Open mouth.
5. Put spoon in mouth.
6. Remove spoon.
7. Lower spoon.

Collins et al. (1991) used constant time delay to teach eating with a spoon, drinking from a cup, and napkin use. Eating skills also lend themselves well to the use of graduated guidance, in which physical assistance is gradually withdrawn as the student masters each motor response. For example, in Azrin and Armstrong's (1973) study, the teacher began by molding her hand around the student's hand to help the student lift the spoon to and from the mouth. As the student began to master the movement with the spoon, the teacher faded this physical pressure to a gentle touch. The guidance was then faded to touches on the forearm, elbow, upper arm, and, finally, the shoulder.

Systematic instruction might also be used to teach a mealtime routine such as eating lunch in the cafeteria. Kohl and Stettner-Eaton (1985) created a 32-step task analysis for going through the cafeteria line. They also task-analyzed eating and cleaning up. These researchers then demonstrated how fourth graders who were nondisabled could serve as trainers of cafeteria skills. The peers used a "feedback only" method of instruction in which they praised or corrected each response as it occurred. Task analyses and systematic prompting can also be used to teach students family-style dining. Wilson, Reid, Phillips, and Burgio (1984) used a system of least intrusive prompting to teach students to set the table, pass and serve themselves food, and clear the table.

Eating Problems

Sometimes an assessment will reveal that a student has eating problems. These problems may reflect the need for specific skill instruction. A student who grabs others' food may need to learn the concept of table or cafeteria boundaries, as Sarah did (see example below).

> Sarah's teachers had a difficult time with her during lunchtime. Sarah was always reaching across other students and taking food from their plates. A lot of times she would spill things or make a mess. Also, many of the students did not want to sit by her because they thought she would touch their food. When her teacher assessed her eating skills, she discovered that Sarah did not seem aware of the boundaries of her own plate. She also lacked the skill to ask for a food item not put on her plate by the cafeteria staff because she had few communication skills. To assist Sarah, the teacher got her a bright, distinctive place mat to use at school and home. As Sarah ate, the teacher would frequently point to Sarah's place setting and say, "Look, you have more potato salad," or "Here, you still have juice to drink." She also taught Sarah to extend her hand in the direction of the food that she wanted. For example, when she wanted margarine for her bread, she would "hover over" the margarine dish with her hand until served. The teacher also discovered that Sarah sometimes did not recognize that she still had food on her plate because it became mixed together as she tried to eat everything with a spoon. The teacher organized Sarah's food with separate dishes for finger foods, items to eat with a spoon, and items to be speared with

a fork. She taught Sarah to eat one food at a time using the method that worked best. Sarah could still be in charge of her meal by selecting the order in which to eat each item. Once she had learned to ask for food by extending her hand, to eat food within the boundary of her place mat, and to keep foods separate, Sarah began to eat her meals without grabbing food.

In research conducted with a student who grabbed food, Smith, Piersel, Filbeck, and Gross (1983) found that seating the student alone and reinforcing her with favorite foods for not stealing food was effective. Over time, the student was able to rejoin her peers. Some researchers have found that students' table manners improve when the dining environment is made more appealing. Hendrickson, Akkerman, and Speggen (1985) and VanBiervliet, Spangler, and Marshall (1981) demonstrated that skills improved in family-style dining compared with large, residential cafeterias.

Students who eat too rapidly or gorge themselves with food risk choking. Both Luiselli (1988) and Knapczyk (1983) found that teacher-delivered pacing prompts were effective with students in slowing their rate of eating. In this method, the teacher cues the student when to take the next bite, and these cues are gradually faded. Teachers can also help students use self-pacing. Wayne learned to pace his eating by setting a 10-second timer between each bite. While waiting for the timer to ring, Wayne would chew. When the timer sounded, he swallowed and took another bite. The teacher rewarded Wayne for eating his lunch while using self-pacing by giving him a special treat at the end of the meal. After several weeks, Wayne was able to eat at a safe pace without using the timer. Eventually, the teacher was also able to fade the use of the treat. Sometimes teachers will need to use reinforcement to increase the rate of eating for students who eat extremely slowly (Luiselli, 1988).

Other students' eating problems focus on the quantity or types of food that they will eat. For example, a student with Prader–Willi syndrome may constantly crave food because he or she is always hungry. Sarah, the student described earlier, rarely indicated that she had had enough to eat. Instead, she would continue eating large quantities of food with resultant weight gain. At home, her parents discovered that if they gave her a low-fat, high-fiber diet and dry popcorn or fresh vegetables to eat at the end of a meal until the family finished, Sarah was willing to stop eating when the family did. Some students refuse food or will eat only a limited number of foods (e.g., only cereal). Sometimes the problem of eating limited types of food can be resolved by giving the student a bite of a highly preferred food after each bite of a nonpreferred food (Riordan, Iwata, Finney, Wohl, & Stanley, 1984). Over time the student can be required to take more bites of the nonpreferred food to get the preferred food. Students who do not show any food preferences might need some other form of reinforcement, such as toy play after each bite of food (Riordan et al., 1984). Figure 13.5 provides an example that can be used to chart a student's current eating and drinking needs.

Some inappropriate behaviors may occur that are specific to a school cafeteria. As mentioned before, it may take time to slowly transition some students into the regular, noisy cafeteria environment. It may also be difficult for some students to understand the specific rules of the cafeteria (e.g., waiting to line up for recess in elementary settings). A number of activities must be taught when entering a typical lunch room, such as waiting in line, carrying your tray, choosing food, selecting a seat, and sitting until dismissed. Some students may not understand why they must remain seated although they have

	Mastery	Partial mastery	Not mastered
Eating skills			
1. Takes food from a spoon and swallows.			
2. Chews food.			
3. Chooses between two food items.			
4. Indicates when full/finished eating.			
5. Expresses desire to eat.			
6. Feeds self finger foods.			
7. Uses a napkin.			
8. Uses a spoon.			
9. Eats a sandwich.			
10. Paces eating (does not stuff mouth).			
11. Spears with a fork.			
12. Eats without spilling.			
Drinking skills			
1. Swallows from cup held by someone.			
2. Chooses between two drinks.			
3. Holds own glass to drink.			
4. Drinks from a soda can.			
5. Drinks from a mug.			
6. Drinks from water fountain.			
7. Drinks through a straw.			

FIGURE 13.5. Checklist of eating and drinking skills.

finished their lunch. Timed intervals of idle time may be introduced to the student before he or she gets up from the lunch seat. For example, the teacher may have a timer beside the student set for 1 minute. The student will need to remain seated for 1 minute after completing lunch before he or she can go to recess. As the student understands the concept, the time can slowly increase until the student can remain in his or her seat the entire expected time of the other students. Ozdemir (2008) used social stories (Gray, 2000) to help reduce the disruptive behavior of a student with autism while waiting in the lunch line. The social story was eventually faded, and the desired behavior was maintained.

Food Preparation

Learning to prepare food is important not only because of the nutrition it provides but also because of the personal enjoyment and socialization associated with food. Families and friends often celebrate important events with food. Most individuals have specific food likes and dislikes. Food preferences also may reflect individuals' cultural heritage. To consider these many functions of food in the lives of students, teachers should begin by conferring with the family about ideas for instruction. The family may identify some of the student's favorite foods and share ideas from the family's typical menus or snack items. The student's parents can also provide information on food restrictions. The teacher should identify foods that the student may be allergic to or special diets (e.g., gluten-free) that have been suggested by the student's doctor. The teacher can then further assess the student's food preferences through systematic preference assessment (Lohrmann-O'Rourke & Browder, 1998). To conduct this assessment the teacher can select several potential foods that the student may like. Then, by introducing two foods at a time, the teacher can record which food the student chooses. After several trials of sampling food, some specific food likes and dislikes may emerge.

To assess and teach specific food preparation skills, the teacher may want first to prepare easy-to-follow directions to encourage the student's self-direction. Researchers who have taught individuals with moderate and severe disabilities to prepare food have used sight word instruction books (Browder, Hines, McCarthy, & Fees, 1984), picture books (Griffin, Wolery, & Schuster, 1992), a cassette tape player with audiotaped directions (Trask-Tyler, Grossi, & Heward, 1994), and a communication board with picture overlays and voice output (Mechling & Gast, 1997). A recent review of the research found that new technologies such as palmtop personal computer-based systems and video-based systems (e.g., portable DVD players and laptops), as well as the traditional picture-based and auditory systems, are currently being used to teach cooking (Mechling et al., 2008). These high-tech devices are mobile and usually grasp the interest of the students and provide them auditory, as well as visual, stimuli. Mechling et al. (2008) researched the effectiveness of using a portable DVD player to complete multiple cooking tasks with three students with moderate intellectual disability. All three students were successful in completing the task analyses independently using the DVD player. As advances in technology increase, it will be easier to adapt instruction, making an individualized and personalized cooking curriculum for each student. In fact, Mechling and Stephens (2009) used a video camera to record corresponding steps of task analyses designed for students with moderate intellectual disability. In the videos, an adult modeled the correct procedure to complete each step of the task analyses. The students would then watch each cooking skill being performed on a portable DVD player using the "play" and "pause" buttons. The data from this study showed that the video instruction was more effective than the traditional static picture prompts.

In addition, adapted cookbooks can be created, or commercial cookbooks (e.g., *Home Cooking*; *www.attainment.com*) may be used for individuals with limited reading skills. Singh et al. (1995) demonstrated how to teach individuals with profound cognitive disabilities to follow a picture cookbook. They task-analyzed each step of the recipe preparation and provided systematic prompting.

Food preparation can also be an excellent opportunity to teach additional knowledge, such as the basic food groups, the nutritional value of food, and safe food handling. Jones and Collins (1997) embedded extra information about safe food handling and nutrition in the instructive feedback they gave while teaching adults with moderate mental retardation to prepare food. For example, after telling the participant to fill the cup with water to make a hot chocolate mix, they said something like "Drink at least six glasses of water a day for your health." Later they assessed the students' mastery of this additional information by asking them such questions as "How much water should you drink?" Using food preparation can be a creative way to teach these more complex concepts. Figure 13.6 provides a list of skills that are most likely to be used during food preparation.

Dressing and Grooming Skills

Dressing and grooming are important ways in which individuals portray their personal style. This personal style may change over time, with the middle school years being a time when students are keenly aware of their appearance. Often, in teaching dressing and grooming, teachers have focused on mechanics, such as how to brush teeth, comb hair, or put on a shirt. Although these mechanics are important, students also need the opportunity to make choices about their appearance. By taking a self-determination focus, the teacher can encourage students to take pride in their appearance. Even students who rely on caregivers to be dressed can direct that care through choosing clothes and accessories to create a personal style.

To encourage the development of a personal style, the teacher can begin assessment for dressing and grooming through systematic preference assessment. For students who can discriminate pictures and can communicate symbolically, the teacher might use clothing catalogs and magazines to explore preferences. The student might develop a scrapbook of favorite styles. In collaboration with the family, the teacher can then focus community-based instruction on shopping for clothing items or accessories that create this style. For students who do not recognize pictures and use nonsymbolic communication, the teacher should create opportunities to sample different options. For example, does the student like smooth or textured fabrics? Sweatshirts or velour? Does the student visually attend longer to certain colors or accessory items? Andrea was a young adult with severe physical and cognitive disabilities who showed a keen interest in things that sparkled. Her teacher collaborated with her mother to help Andrea purchase bracelets, hair accessories, shirts with sequins, and other items that Andrea seemed to enjoy. When the teacher styled Andrea's hair during the day, she gave her a choice of hair accessories by holding up two options to see which Andrea chose by reaching toward it. In these ways, people who provided support to Andrea helped translate her preference for objects that sparkle into a personal style of dressing.

Food preparation skills	Mastery	Partial mastery	Not mastered
1. Chooses between two foods to prepare by asking, pointing, nodding, looking, or other means of communication.			
2. Plans simple snack of food and beverage.			
3. Plans meal using major food groups.			
4. Uses blender to make beverage by pressing button or using adaptive switch.			
5. Rinses fresh fruit and vegetables.			
6. Helps prepare food by pouring contents from package and stirring (e.g., pudding, cake mix, drink mix).			
7. Prepares snack or sandwich that requires stacking and spreading (e.g., peanut butter crackers, chicken sandwich).			
8. Uses microwave for food or beverage (e.g., prepares hot dog, hot chocolate, popcorn). • Reads and sets cooking time. • Uses matching to set time. • Uses coding to set time. • Needs assistance to set time.			
9. Follows simple recipe using: • Photographs • Audiotape • Sight words • Directions on package • Picture cookbook • Portable DVD using the "pause" button in between steps • Palmtop portable device			
10. Pours beverages.			
11. Sets the table.			
12. Bakes frozen item in oven (e.g., frozen casserole, pie). • Reads and sets temperature. • Uses matching to set temperature. • Uses color coding. • With assistance, sets oven temperature.			
13. Prepares "heat and eat" stovetop item (e.g., soup, canned pasta).			
14. Chops and cuts (e.g., fresh fruit or vegetables, refrigerator cookies).			
15. Prepares convenience food following package or picture instructions (e.g., stir-fry meal).			
16. Coordinates preparing several foods at once to serve a meal.			
17. Measures ingredients.			

FIGURE 13.6. Food preparation checklist.

After giving first priority to the student's style preferences, the teacher can consider what mechanics of dressing and grooming to teach. Collaborating with the family on this planning is essential. Sarah's mother was hesitant when the teacher suggested instructing Sarah in how to take off her shirt; her mother feared that she would begin doing so in public. Because Sarah was 12, and larger than her mother, dressing her was becoming increasingly difficult. Together, the teacher and Sarah's mother selected some responses that Sarah could make that would make dressing her less physically demanding (e.g., raising her leg when putting on pants). They also selected responses that helped put Sarah more in charge of dressing.

Nearly all of the research on teaching dressing and grooming skills has focused on the mechanics of these skills, rather than on choice or style. The contribution of this research is that it provides important clues for defining the specific responses to be taught and how to teach them. Alberto, Jobes, Sizemore, and Doran (1980) taught students to put on a pullover sweater and elastic outer pants using forward chaining. That is, they taught the student one specific response (the first response) in putting on the clothing item. When this was mastered, they had the student do the first step and then taught the second. In contrast, Sisson, Kilwein, and Van Hasselt (1988) taught students the entire task analysis of putting on socks, elastic waist pants, and pullover shirts but used graduated physical guidance to help the student perform each step. These physical prompts were systematically faded. They used three clothing items and found that students were able to generalize to three similar items. Reese and Snell (1991) were also able to teach the entire task analysis for putting on and taking off coats and jackets, but they used oversized garments as well as graduated guidance to help students succeed. Over time the size of the garments was reduced and the physical guidance was faded until the students were independent. Some students have physical challenges that make it impossible for them to dress and groom themselves. For such students, specific responses can be chosen to encourage their active participation in these routines. For example, Snell et al. (1989) taught students with multiple disabilities to partially participate in a toothbrushing routine. They had a student (1) open his or her mouth wide, (2) keep it open while the teacher brushed one area, and (3) close the mouth with lips touching. This routine was repeated four times as the teacher brushed four areas of the mouth. Then the student dropped his or her head toward the basin, spit, and lifted his or her head. Finally, the teacher had the student help with drying his or her face by first turning his or her head to one side and then turning it to the other side as the teacher held the towel against his or her mouth. This partial participation might also include responses such as having the student look up to ask to have the next section of his or her mouth brushed and to choose the flavor of toothpaste. Figure 13.7 provides checklists that can be used for assessing specific dressing and grooming skills.

Students may do more when in the presence of peers who perform these skills for themselves. Schoen, Lentz, and Suppa (1988) demonstrated that students with Down syndrome made some gains in using a water fountain and washing their faces simply by observing their peers. Alberto et al. (1980) also found greater gains in dressing skills in a group instruction format. Some dressing skills lend themselves well to group contexts. For example, adolescent girls often enjoy grooming when around peers who are doing the same (e.g., trying new hairstyles and makeup). In contrast, some dressing and grooming skills are personal. Performing them in a group might inhibit responding and violate the student's privacy. Students may also demonstrate more skill if assessed at the appropriate time and in the right context for using these skills. Freagon and Rotatori (1982) found that adults with moderate to profound intellectual disability learned such skills as deodorant use, toothbrushing, and hand washing faster when they were taught during the natural times and contexts compared to artificial times. Students may be much more proficient in washing hands when they are anticipating lunch than if they are simply taken to the restroom at an artificial time for an assessment of this skill (see Figure 13.7).

Using the Toilet

Societal expectations of the age at which children master bowel and bladder control vary culturally, but nearly all cultures expect complete continence by the time a child reaches school age. Although incontinence can occur at any age due to illness or physical or mental changes, if it is not managed well it can be both highly stigmatizing and unhealthy for the individual and others in the environment. The reasons for delayed or arrested bowel and bladder control in individuals with moderate and severe disabilities are varied. They can include neurological damage, slower awareness of internal cues to the need to void, less ability to learn from others' prompts to use the toilet, and difficulty in communicating to others the need for assistance in using the toilet (Snell & Farlow, 1993).

There are three options for bowel and bladder management: (1) learning to use the toilet based on internal cues about bladder and bowel fullness, (2) going to the toilet on a time schedule that prevents accidents, and (3) using sanitary products or alternatives (e.g., catheterization) in lieu of using the toilet. If at all possible, teaching students to use the toilet on their own initiative is the ultimate goal, because it encourages personal dignity. Several studies have demonstrated that some students with severe disabilities can master toilet training (Azrin & Foxx, 1971; Hobbs & Peck, 1985). Students can be prompted to use the toilet on a schedule and also be allowed to make extra trips (Richmond, 1983). Not all students master using the toilet and may need the support of incontinence products (e.g., disposable underpants or diapers) to avoid the stigma of public incontinence. Whichever option for bowel and bladder management is chosen, the student may receive various levels of assistance and instruction, as shown in Figure 13.8. In using this chart to plan support for toileting needs, the teacher first selects the method of management. The goal for Kane is to learn to use the toilet on a schedule. Because he is a preteen (age 12) and has frequent accidents, he will also wear a sanitary product (pull-up disposable underpants) until he masters the toilet training schedule. The teacher then plans support needs related to the method selected. The goal is for Kane to ask for help to go to the toilet by using a picture when told it is time. In the restroom, Kane will learn to assist himself by pulling his pants up and down (the teacher will help with fastening and zipping for now). He also will be in charge of throwing away his disposable underpants when soiled and will learn to put on new ones. Because Kane seems to be reinforced by the attention he receives when he voids in public, the use of disposable underpants will also resolve this problem.

If the goal of the bowel or bladder management program is using the toilet based on either internal cues or a schedule, the teacher will need to determine when to take the student to the toilet. If the goal is attending to internal cues, it is best to prompt the child to go just before an accident would typically occur. To determine at what point this might happen, the teacher can keep daily data for a week or two by checking the student every 15 minutes to determine whether he or she is dry or has voided. In contrast, with schedule

Skill	Mastery	Partial mastery	Not mastered
Dressing and undressing			
1. Chooses between two clothing options.			
2. Selects outfit for the day.			
3. Chooses accessories for personal style.			
4. Moves arm and lifts leg to help in dressing.			
5. Communicates to caregiver when needing help in dressing (e.g., looks up to get shirt on; vocalizes to get sweater off; asks for help with fastening pants).			
6. Pulls down pants in restroom.			
7. Takes off clothing: • Shoes • Socks • Jacket or sweater • Pants • Shirt • Unfastens Velcro • Unsnaps • Unbuttons • Unzips			
8. Dresses • Puts jacket, coat on. • Puts on elastic waist pants, underpants. • Puts on large T-shirt; sweatshirt. • Puts on tube socks. • Puts on jeans (may not zip them). • Fastens Velcro fasteners. • Snaps. • Zips. • Buttons.			
Toothbrushing			
1. Chooses between two toothpastes.			
2. Asks for help with toothbrushing (e.g., looks at/points to toothbrush).			
3. Participates with caregiver in toothbrushing by opening/closing mouth.			
4. Spits out toothpaste.			
5. Brushes own teeth.			

(cont.)

FIGURE 13.7. Checklist of dressing and grooming skills.

Skill	Mastery	Partial mastery	Not mastered
Washing hands or face			
1. Asks for help with washing hands or face (e.g., points to sink).			
2. Chooses between two types of soap.			
3. Determines whether water is comfortable temperature (e.g., nods, smiles).			
4. Participates in washing by: • Moving hands toward water. • Moving face back and forth against cloth.			
5. Grasps and releases paper towel in trash.			
6. Washes own hands when told.			
7. Initiates washing hands and face.			
Other grooming			
1. Asks for help with combing/styling hair.			
2. Combs/styles own hair.			
3. Uses makeup (optional).			
4. Cares for nails.			
5. Leaves restroom groomed for public. • Clothing straight • Zippers and fasteners closed • Hair neat • Hands washed • Face clean • Makeup on neatly (optional)			
6. Showering or bathing • Chooses bath products to use (e.g., soap, shampoo). • Washes body. • Shampoos hair. • Shaves. • Applies deodorant.			

FIGURE 13.7. *(cont.)*

Directions: Identify the method of bowel and bladder management to be used in the top row. Then read down the column to plan the level of assistance needed.

Name: _Kane Hartwell_   **Date:** _November 4_

Method →	Uses toilet based on internal cues.	Uses toilet on a specific time schedule.	Does not use toilet. Uses . . .
↓ **Support needs**		_Goal is for Kane to be schedule trained._	_X_ Incontinence products _Kane will stay in disposable underpants until accident free._ _____ Catheterization _____ Other: _____
1. _Initiation_ • Takes care of needs without prompting. • Prompt student to do on his/her own. • Asks for help. • Prompt student to ask for help. • Caregiver initiates.		_Prompt Kane to show picture for toilet when it is time to go._	
2. _Using the toilet or changing diaper_ • Performs all steps independently. • Prompt student with goal of becoming independent. • Interactive: Student will do these steps without prompts. • Interactive: Prompt student to do these steps. • Caregiver does all assistance.		_Prompt Kane to help push pants down and to sit down on his own._	_Kane can remove and discard disposable underpants without assistance. Prompt him to put these on with goal of independence._
3. _Accident management_ • Manages his/her own cleanup. • Use prompting to manage cleanup with goal of independence. • Interactive: Student will do these steps without prompts. • Interactive: Prompt student to do these steps. • Caregiver should provide cleanup.		_Attention to accidents seems to have increased incontinence. By using disposable underpants, he can be limited to restroom cleanup._	

FIGURE 13.8. Example of plan for bowel and bladder management.

training, the teacher may begin with a frequent schedule of going to the toilet (e.g., every 30 minutes) with reinforcement if the student voids. The schedule is then increased by 15-minute increments up to about 2 hours. Some students will not achieve a 2-hour pattern and will need a more frequent voiding schedule. An alternative method of training to schedule is to pick one time of day for the student to use the toilet (e.g., after lunch) and then to add additional time periods during the day (Fredericks et al., 1981). Students may also need training and support to generalize their toilet skills across community and other environments. This can be done by making sure all those who provide support to the student are following the management plan for toileting (Dunlap, Koegel, & Koegel, 1984).

Sometimes in assessing a student's toileting needs, the teacher will identify problems related to this routine. Gray and Boswell (1999) recommend solutions from their work with students with autism. A few of these include:

Problem	*Potential solution*
1. Resists sitting on toilet.	• Practice sitting with clothes on; fade to underwear; then none. • Help child understand how long to sit by playing a tape or using timer.
2. Fears flushing toilet or is overinterested in it.	• Use visual or verbal signal when it is time to flush: "Ready, set, go." • Flush when child is away from toilet; gradually transfer to child flushing.
3. Child plays in toilet water.	• Let child hold a toy as a distraction. • Give child padded lap desk while seated.
4. Does not aim in toilet when standing (boy).	• Use a target, like a piece of cereal.
5. Uses large quantities of toilet paper.	• Use facial tissue or put clothespin to show where to tear off.
6. Resists being cleaned.	• Try different material (e.g., wipes).

Housekeeping and Laundry

For many individuals with and without disabilities, mastering housekeeping and laundry skills involves not only learning to perform specific tasks but also acquiring the habit of doing them on a regular basis. In many families, these tasks are shared by each member. In planning for students with moderate and severe disabilities, the teacher can plan with the student and family what the student's responsibility will be in contributing to the upkeep of the home. Consideration can also be given to the skills that have potential for career development. For example, learning to fold towels might lead to a job in a commercial laundry.

Most researchers who have focused on housekeeping and laundry skills have used task analyses of specific sets of skills, such as bedmaking (McWilliams, Nietupski, & Hamre-Nietupski, 1990), using a key (Ivancic & Schepis, 1995), or using a washing machine (Browder et al., 1984; Miller & Test, 1989). The teacher may want to begin with a more broad-based assessment, such as the checklist shown in Figure 13.9. It may be helpful to share this checklist with the student and family to determine not only what the student can do but also what is most relevant for instruction at this time. Then, when specific skills have been chosen, a task analysis can be used for ongoing monitoring of the student's progress. Students who cannot master the entire task can still be active participants by learning specific responses such as carrying dishes to the sink, wiping the table, or grasping soiled clothes and releasing them into the washer.

Teachers may also want to assess whether students can manage completing chores on a given schedule. Following a chores schedule can be useful not only for home living but also as a step toward job training. Pierce and Schriebman (1994) taught children with autism to use a picture album to complete chores such as setting the table, making the bed, making a drink, getting dressed, and doing laundry. Once the student learned the meaning of each picture and how to perform the task, the therapist was able to leave the area, and the child could complete each step of the task by following the pictures. Anderson, Sherman, Sheldon, and McAdam (1997) taught adults with mental retardation to self-schedule their activities for after-work hours by sequencing photos in an album.

Sex Education

One of parents' primary concerns about their older children's transition to adulthood is the issue of sexuality (Wolfe & Blanchett, 1997). Two important reasons that students with severe disabilities need sex education are to manage their own sexuality and to avoid abuse or harassment. Given the confusion and mixed messages in American society about sexuality, students with developmental disabilities may find it especially difficult to learn acceptable behaviors for inclusive settings. McCabe and Cummins (1996) found that adults with mild intellectual disability, compared with college students who were nondisabled, were less knowledgeable and more negative about sex but also had more experience with pregnancy and sexually transmitted disease.

The challenge of teaching sex education to individuals with severe disabilities is that care must be taken that educational activities do not themselves become abusive or a violation of privacy. In school settings, teachers who provide sex education to students who are nondisabled use lectures and audiovisuals. Some students with developmental disabilities are not able to comprehend the material in these formats. However, using one-to-one instruction or more specific materials might violate the student's legal rights or offend parents. Some planning teams may decide to include more explicit sexuality training in collaboration with parents and school authorities. A questionnaire given to guardians of women with intellectual disability revealed that 29% of the women with intellectual disability had not been taught or been given the opportunity to manage their own menstrual care (Rodgers & Lipscombe, 2005). Although this study found a large percentage of women who had not been given the opportunity, it did note that there were some women with severe disabilities who were able to care for themselves independently. In one case, Epps, Stern, and Horner (1990) used a task analysis and systematic prompting to teach young women with intellectual disability menstrual care. Lumley,

Housekeeping and laundry skills	Mastery	Partial mastery	Not mastered
Kitchen/lunchroom			
1. Wipe table or tray after eating.			
2. Carry dishes to sink (or tray to cleanup area).			
3. Wash dishes in sink.			
4. Load dishwasher.			
5. Clean sink.			
6. Clean floor.			
Living areas			
1. Dust with choice of dusters (e.g., feather, cloth).			
2. Straighten living area.			
3. Vacuum. • Vacuum entire room; under furniture. • Vacuum main floor area. • Help by turning vacuum on/off.			
4. Strip bed. • Help by putting pillow on chair.			
5. Make bed. • Help by pulling covers up. • Help by putting pillow on bed.			
Bathroom			
1. Clean tub.			
2. Clean toilet.			
3. Clean sink.			
4. Clean floor.			
Laundry			
1. Put clothes in hamper.			
2. Sort clothes for washing.			
4. Use washer and dryer. • Help by putting clothes in. • Help by pulling clothes out. • Do all steps except setting dial. • Perform all steps without help.			
5. Fold towels and washcloths.			
6. Fold clothes.			

FIGURE 13.9. Checklist of housekeeping and laundry skills.

Miltenberger, Long, Rapp, and Roberts (1998) taught avoiding abuse using a "No, Go, Tell" sequence. With the review and approval of a human rights committee, they also probed the participants' reactions to simulated harassment in natural settings.

Some students may need help in learning the concept of privacy. This may be addressed by teaching them to discriminate between the private and nonprivate zones of their body. They may also need to learn differential social responses. For example, students may learn to give a wave, not a hug, to acquaintances and to reserve hugs for close friends and family. The CIRCLES Program (Parents Helping Parents, 2007) provides color-cue training and videos that can be useful in teaching social and sexual boundaries. This program may be acceptable to parents who do not want explicit sexual content taught. In contrast, Sexuality Education for Persons with Severe Developmental Disabilities (Brekke, 1988) provides explicit slides to help teach students behaviors that are private versus public. Figure 13.10 offers ideas that might be considered in assessing the need for a sex education program.

Exercise and Nutrition

It has been found that people with disabilities are more at risk to be overweight than people without disabilities (Patrick, 2003); furthermore, a study in the United States (Jones & Lollar, 2008) found that high school students with physical disabilities reported more behaviors that put their weight at risk. In a recent study (Maaskant, van Knijff-Raeven, van Schrojenstein Lantman-de Valk, & Veenstra, 2009) data were collected on a cohort of participants with intellectual disability who were identified as being at risk of becoming obese. This study found that over 30% of the participants became overweight at the end of a 5-year span. This study further showed that women with intellectual disability may be more prone to being overweight than men with intellectual disability. Another study showed similar results and also found that overweight and obesity are more prevalent in adults with intellectual disability when compared with the general population (Melville et al., 2008).

All students, including those with significant developmental disabilities, need to be involved in the planning of their exercise, leisure, and nutrition. Similar self-determination strategies to those used to involve students in their IEP meetings, transition plans, and other personal and daily living skills should be taught to students to promote future independence and active participation in their own personal lives. For example, the U.S. Department of Agriculture provides a website specific to the food pyramid (*www.mypyramid.gov*) that can be adapted for students with intellectual disability. Figure 13.11 provides an example of how the food pyramid can be adapted into a visual format. In Figure 13.11 the water, pasta, and fruit portions from the pyramid have boxes beside the pictures so the students can self-monitor their eating. A more detailed chart can be made to provide the students with a checklist of the foods they want to eat (see the bottom of Figure 13.11). If the students can recognize the number of servings of each subcategory of foods, then a more detailed checklist may be used, such as the one found in Figure 13.12. The teacher may need to assist the child with this chart at first to help him or her mark the appropriate box.

Most students with severe intellectual disability participate in the general education physical education class; however, many of the activities are not thought out or designed to meet the individual needs of the students with disabilities. By using the principles of universal design for learning (UDL; CAST, 1998), discussed in previous chapters, the

1. Why is sex education being considered at this time?
   - Age of student: *How old is the student?* _____
   - Concern about specific behaviors: *What are these behaviors?* _____

   - Community risks: *Describe these risks.* _____

   - Parental request: *What have the parents requested?* _____

   - Other: _____
2. What is the school district's policy on sex education?
   - Have you talked with an administrator about this policy? _____
   - How is sex education provided for students who are nondisabled? _____

   - Can this student be included in this general program? _____
     If so, how? If not, why not? _____
3. What are the parents' and student's preferences?
   - What are the parents' preferences regarding sex education? _____

   - To what extent has the student shown interest in sexual issues? _____

4. Which of the following should be included in the student's sex education program?
   - Names of private body parts and their function. _____
   - Social expectations for private body zones (e.g., don't touch others in these areas; keep these areas covered). _____
   - How to avoid abuse or harassment ("No, go, tell"). _____
   - Social interactions appropriate for different relationships (e.g., wave, don't hug). _____
   - Specific behaviors that are private versus public. _____
   - Intercourse and reproduction. _____
   - Birth control. _____
   - Avoiding sexually transmitted disease. _____
   - Other: _____
5. How should the sex education program be designed?
   - Who, where, what materials? _____

   - Procedural safeguards (human rights protection): _____

FIGURE 13.10. Questions to consider in planning a sex education curriculum for students with moderate and severe disabilities.

From *Teaching Students with Moderate and Severe Disabilities* by Diane M. Browder and Fred Spooner. Copyright 2011 by The Guilford Press. Permission to photocopy this figure is granted to purchasers of this book for personal use only (see copyright page for details).

FIGURE 13.11. Example of a picture checklist following the food pyramid.

general and special education teachers can plan together on ways to include all students in some activities. The UDL chart (see Figure 13.13) shows a lesson plan for elementary-age students on playing "human foosball."

Nutrition and exercise may also be introduced through a literacy exercise. In Figure 13.14 the daily menu is in the form of a story (similar to those introduced in Chapter 5). The teacher can provide choices for the students on these schedules or can begin by keeping a preference assessment on the activities that the student may enjoy. Figure 13.15 shows an example of a short picture schedule for a daily exercise routine. If a more specific schedule is needed, then the teacher may provide the student with a checklist of activities to follow (see Figure 13.16). It is important to introduce new activities so that different muscles are worked and also to keep the students' interest.

8							
7							
6							
5							
4							
3							
2							
1							
	Water (8)	Rice, Pasta, and Bread (6)	Fruit (2)	Vegetable (3)	Meat, Poultry, Fish, Beans (2)	Milk, yogurt, Cheese (3)	Fats, Oils, and Sweets

FIGURE 13.12. Example of a self-monitoring checklist of the food pyramid (eat fats, oils, and sweets sparingly). Adapted from *www.mypyramid.gov.*

Purpose of lesson: To engage the students in an activity working on passing skills and teamwork.

Description: The students will be placed onto two separate teams simulating a large foosball table. Floor tape will be place on the ground and the students must stay on their tape. The students will practice passing the ball to each other.

Concept	What does it mean?	Barriers	How do I provide equal access?
Representation	The presentation of information that will provide equal access for all learners. Modifications that can be made to classroom materials that would make them more accessible to students with disabilities.	• Small soccer ball • Large playing field • Small goals	• Use a larger (soft) inflatable. • Everyone must stay in a hula hoop instead of the taped area. • Shorten the length between the cones for the goals.
Expression	Alternatives of communication in order to provide equal access of expression to all learners.	• Nonverbal	• All students will only be allowed to throw their hands up to get the ball.
Engagement	To increase the opportunity and motivation to provide equal access in engagement to all learners.	• Fine motor skills • Wheelchair • Some students may not get the opportunity to touch the ball	• Provide a smaller playing area for everyone. • Every 2 minutes the students will rotate to different positions. Students may use their hands if needed. • In order for the goal to count, every member of the team must touch the ball at least once
Notes:			

FIGURE 13.13. The UDL "at-a-glance" for "human foosball." Lesson plan based on *www.pecentral.org.*

CASE STUDY

At the beginning of this chapter, a middle school student named Sarah was introduced. Although she was active in a school club, her personal care deficits limited her participation in after-school activities. The following describes what the team planned, applying the guidelines in this chapter:

Planning with Family to Identify Priorities and Honor Cultural Values

Sarah's parents had three primary concerns. First, they requested that food preparation activities take into consideration Sarah's tendency to gain weight easily. If she became obese, it might become physically impossible for her parents to provide her care. Second,

FIGURE 13.14. Example of a picture schedule for daily menu.

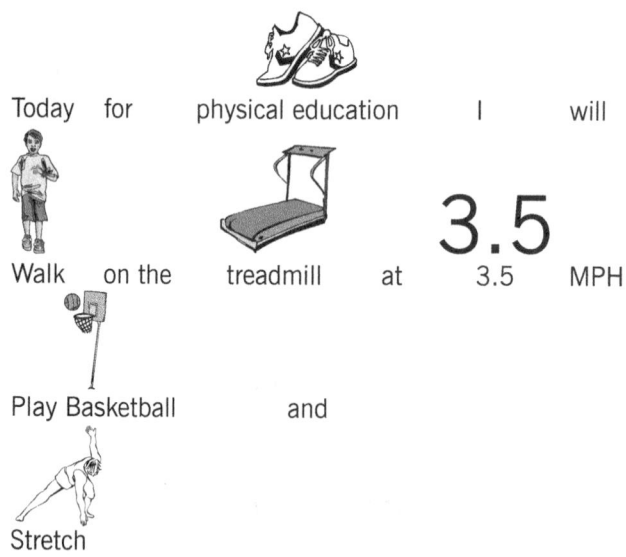

FIGURE 13.15. Example of a picture schedule for daily exercises.

Activity	Monday	Tuesday	Wednesday	Thursday	Friday
Walking: Treadmill	X	X	X	X	X
Walking: Outside		X			
Elliptical trainer	X			X	
Stair stepper	X		X		
Swimming					
Bicycling					
Weight Training			X		
Basketball					
Tennis					
Other:					
Pickle Ball		X			
Stretching	X	X	X	X	X

FIGURE 13.16. Example of a completed checklist of physical activities.

they were concerned with how difficult mealtimes have become, with her grabbing food and overstuffing her mouth. Her parents were also concerned that Sarah become "accident free" by using the toilet consistently. Because she had no way to indicate the need to use the toilet, her mother had her urinating on a 2-hour schedule but had to "guess" when the bowel movements would occur. Given Sarah's age and desire to be a full participant in her club, the team decided that Sarah would use a disposable undergarment during community activities to avoid the stigma of accidents. This strategy also would simplify planning for her menstrual care on days that outings are planned. The team also targeted the priority that Sarah would learn to indicate the need to toilet. Because Sarah did not comprehend pictures and could not make manual signs, she would be taught to use the gesture of patting her waist to indicate this need. Sarah's inappropriate mealtime behaviors would be addressed using the special place mat and food preparation strategies described earlier in this chapter. The team also targeted having Sarah learn to be around food without grabbing it by teaching her to prepare some simple foods (e.g., microwave a low-fat hotdog; use air popper for popcorn). When asked about sex education, Sarah's parents were wary about what the teacher would address. They had strong personal values in this area related to their religious heritage. When the teacher suggested that Sarah's sex education at this time might focus on learning to respect others and her own personal boundaries, her parents agreed that this would be important. Some target skills were learning new ways to greet others (handshakes and "high five" slaps vs. bear hugs) and social customs regarding privacy (e.g., keeping her shirt down).

Promoting Student Self-Determination

Sarah could be not only active but also more in charge of her daily routines as she made the transition to adult living. The team decided to give Sarah opportunities to choose clothing, lunch entrees, and toiletry items. Sarah also began the process of directing her own care. For example, she was taught to ask for help to dress and to nod when she was ready to be dressed. She would find her own seat in the lunchroom and would put her glass down to show when she was finished with lunch. Her preferences were also encouraged. For example, because Sarah loved hot dogs, she would have the opportunity to learn how to prepare them. She loved water, so the team thought that she might enjoy learning to rinse the dishes. The teacher decided to try using a video model to help Sarah instruct herself in these skills.

Using Systematic Instruction to Increase Student Independence

Sarah had a full school schedule, including language arts, mathematics, science, and social studies. She also took a life skills class that was offered as part of the general curriculum. In this class, she had opportunities to work on food preparation and housekeeping and to practice some money management skills. The life skills teacher agreed to have Sarah make popcorn for the class on Fridays. A peer helped Sarah to follow a video clip on an MP3 player to make the popcorn. Similarly, she used a clip to microwave a hot dog about once a week when the class prepared a snack, as well as participating in the group cooking lesson. Sarah received support to go to the toilet in a private school restroom every 2 hours and after lunch. Just prior to going, she was prompted to pat her side to indicate the need to toilet. The support person showed her a picture of the restroom on her daily schedule and modeled patting her side. After the first week, she waited four seconds to see whether Sarah would initiate this communication response. In the restroom, the instructor used backward chaining by having Sarah dry her hands and throw away the towel. She used least intrusive prompts, including verbal, model, and physical prompts, for these steps, with praise for each correct response. As Sarah learned each step, she added the next step in the backward-chaining sequence. Sarah's special education teacher provided practice meals for her, using a snack in a small-group setting and least intrusive prompts to encourage her to eat from her place mat or to ask for food by raising her hand. Sarah had daily opportunities to generalize this skill in the cafeteria when eating with a peer who received training in how to prompt her to eat her own food or ask to share food. Sarah had many other skills in her IEP related to her academics and social and communicative needs. One skill the teacher generalized to Sarah's life skills needs is the use of read-alouds, including social stories about eating with friends. She also worked on building a picture vocabulary for Sarah and included picture symbols relevant to Sarah's priorities (e.g., popcorn, hot dog, other snack choices, restroom, and the sign "please" to ask to share food).

Planning for Partial Participation and Nonintrusive Supports

Sarah will probably need lifelong aid in her daily routines. Despite intensive instruction for most of her life, Sarah still needs assistance to dress, eat, and use the toilet. This ongoing need for support is partly due to her physical challenges, which make it difficult for her to perform some of the motor responses needed to perform these skills. Despite these limitations, Sarah can be more active in her care by lifting her arm and leg to assist with dressing, using a spoon and fork, performing some of the steps to wash her hands, and putting her soiled clothes in a bag or hamper. Sarah may need some support to participate in the community outings, such as help with toileting and preparing her food for appropriate eating (e.g., cutting it into bite-size pieces). Having a second adult volunteer available as needed to colead the outings might be the best option (vs. having a middle school peer assist with toileting). This coleader can provide support to all the children so that they will not be overshadowed by Sarah's interactions with her peers.

SUMMARY

Persons with severe disabilities by definition, in most cases, will require specific training in personal care skills. Failure to acquire personal care skills potentially could serve as a barrier to community placement. Documentation on the successful acquisition of personal care skills such as toilet training, hand washing, toothbrushing, dressing, eating, and food preparation dates back to the 1960s, and with the recent focus on teaching academic skills (i.e., reading, mathematics, science) to this population, research on the application of systematic instructional procedures to teach these important skills has not been the thrust of scientific investigation. On the other hand, what has found its way into the literature has been the role of new technological applications (e.g., Palm personal devices, portable DVDs, portable cameras, and MP3 players) in teaching personal care skills. There also have been extensions of partial participation, self-determination, and cultural influence on teaching these personal care skills.

Because of the importance of personal care skills, we have included this chapter in the book, even though much of the research investigating the acquisition of these skills by students or persons with severe disabilities was typically conducted more than a decade ago. We have reviewed guidelines for planning instruction, identified ways to promote self-determination using systematic instruction to teach these skills, and provided a plan for partial participation. We also have provided examples of home and personal living curricula (e.g., eating, food preparation, dressing, toileting, housekeeping, exercise and nutrition). Based on the nature and needs of this population, personal care skills will still be necessary, as the field continues to emphasize independent functioning in community and school settings.

APPLICATIONS

1. Practice writing a task analysis for a personal or daily living skill. How can this task analysis be designed to address the students' individualized needs? Can you incorporate technology, such as video modeling, to help the student better understand and complete the skill? What other systematic instruction strategies are needed?

2. Talk with a family about their priorities for their child using the questions in Figure 13.1. From this interview, decide what personal and daily living skills priorities might be included in an IEP.

3. Develop materials a student might use for self-instruction in "preparing a favorite dish" (e.g., macaroni and cheese). You may use media such as Boardmaker, Writing with Symbols, or Microsoft Word to incorporate pictures into your task analysis. *Extra*: Also think about the recent chapters on literacy and the procedures on adapting a book. How could you adapt a cookbook using some of these techniques?

CHAPTER 14

Community and Job Skills

Fred Spooner, Diane M. Browder, and Sharon Richter

Raymond Johnson celebrated his 16th birthday. Ray had a moderate intellectual disability and Down syndrome. During a planning meeting with his school staff and parents, he presented a picture Power Point of his future goals. He wanted to work with animals, earn money, go to professional sports events, and spend time with friends. His planning team talked about how Ray could begin working toward those goals in the year to come. They talked with him about the option of working with animals at a local shelter as a volunteer. The team also considered what skills Ray might want to have to enjoy a professional sports event, such as planning the date, taking the bus, and purchasing a ticket. They also considered how this instruction could be incorporated into Ray's school schedule. One of the first steps was to plan an outing with friends to a high school sports event and purchase the tickets in advance from the athletics office. In the month to come, he would learn about taking the bus to the arena from his home through a video simulation and then actually go to the arena for a tour.

Linda Parker was a 14-year-old who also presented her PowerPoint to her school team. Linda had a severe intellectual disability and Rett syndrome. Linda developed her PowerPoint with the help of her teacher. She chose pictures of her preferences by gazing between picture choices. She also indicated preferences for some of the options by listening to tapes with sound effects and smiling to show the ones she liked best. Based on Linda's preferences, the team agreed that Linda's interests were musical activities of any kind, swimming, hearing stories read aloud, and spending time with girls her age. The team considered ways to build swimming and music into her school schedule and to cultivate some school friends. They also realized Linda needed some opportunities for job tryouts, as she did not yet indicate a preference for any particular type of work.

One of the important outcomes of education is to have all students able to function in the community and become successfully employed. The Individual with Disabilities Education Improvement Act (IDEA, 2004) was created "to ensure that all children with disabilities have available to them a free appropriate public education that emphasizes special education and related services designed to meet their unique needs and prepare them for further education, employment, and independent living" (Section 300.1[a]). Some students with severe disabilities such as Linda may need lifelong support in several life domains, but even if this is necessary, well-designed instruction in community and job skills can enhance options and minimize this level of support. For example, as Linda experiences different jobs, she may show both interest and ability not yet realized. This chapter provides an overview of community and job skills for students with severe developmental disabilities, including evidence-based instructional strategies, essential content for students with severe developmental disabilities, and barriers to successful involvement.

OVERVIEW OF THE NEED TO DEVELOP COMMUNITY AND JOB SKILLS

A strong rationale for teaching skills that foster community participation and employment can be found in postschool outcome data for students with disabilities. Adult life includes a variety of essential experiences, including "living, working, playing, and learning" (Lohrmann-O'Rourke & Gomez, 2001, p. 158), yet graduates of special education programs have historically experienced low rates of meaningful participation in each of these areas. Typically, adults with disabilities are unemployed, live dependently on others, do not participate in postsecondary education or recreation activities, and experience social isolation (Blackorby & Wagner, 1996). Although the recent National Longitudinal Transition Study—2 (NLTS-2) (see Newman, 2005) has indicated modest improvements in adult success among graduates of special education programs, students with disabilities continue to struggle with unsuccessful adult outcomes (Cameto, 2005; Levine & Wagner, 2005; Newman, 2005; Wagner, 2005a, 2005b).

Individuals with severe developmental disabilities experience even greater challenges in adult life than people with more mild disabilities (Blackorby & Wagner, 1996; Cameto, 2005; Levine & Wagner, 2005; Newman, 2005; Wagner, 2005a, 2005b). Adults with severe developmental disabilities commonly experience unsuccessful outcomes residentially, educationally, vocationally, and recreationally (Cameto, 2005; Levine & Wagner, 2005; Newman, 2005; Wagner, 2005a, 2005b, 2005c).

USING COMMUNITY-BASED AND COMMUNITY-REFERENCED INSTRUCTION

A variety of common tasks take place in the community, such as buying groceries, working at job, using the public library, taking public transportation, attending a sporting event, going to the dentist, and eating out with friends. In order to facilitate successful community participation, educators must design instruction for students with severe developmental disabilities that includes both *community-referenced instruction* and *community-based instruction*.

Community-referenced instruction is instruction that is designed to support students' use of skills in their current and subsequent community settings. Snell and Browder (1986) suggest that community-referenced instruction is built on the philosophy of normalization (Wolfensberger, 1972) and applied behavior analysis (Baer et al., 1968, 1987). Normalization sets the tenets that community living is for *all persons*, including those with disabilities; and applied behavior analysis is the technology for measuring and influencing behavior change. Together they provide a balanced framework for planning and evaluating community-referenced instruction. Community-referenced instruction refers to *teaching instructional content* that is essential to students' success in community settings. Although the content of community-referenced instruction is based on the expectations and consequences that occur naturally in community settings, this type of instruction may take place in a variety of settings, such as the classroom, the school campus, and the students' homes, as well as in community settings. Examples of community-referenced instruction include teaching students to (1) purchase a variety of items and services, (2) get around in their communities, (3) use a bank and budget their money, (4) get and maintain a job, (5) enjoy free time, (6) exhibit appropriate safety skills, and (7) participate as contributing members of their communities.

A variety of instructional strategies are effective in teaching students with significant cognitive disabilities, as described in Chapter 4. However, community-based instruction is one instructional strategy that is particularly important in preparing students with skills needed to be active members of their communities. Community-based instruction refers to the *setting* in which instruction takes place. Community-based instruction provides instruction in one specific setting: the community. Potential community-based instruction sites include many of the places people frequent each week, including clothing stores, drugstores, grocery stores, restaurants, movie theaters, sports arenas, doctor's offices, libraries, post offices, cultural events, job sites, public transit depots, and many community settings. Although community-based instruction takes place exclusively in the community, research indicates that community-based instruction paired with instruction in a simulated setting is more effective than either simulated instruction alone or community-based instruction alone (Cihak, Alberto, Kessler, & Taber, 2004). Simulated instruction involves teaching community skills using classroom materials that approximate the community context. These may include videos of the activity, computer simulations, photographs, and props. For example, a teacher may make an ATM from a cardboard box or create a video of someone making a purchase at a store. While using these materials, the student can have repeated practice of the steps to complete the activity with systematic prompting and feedback from the teacher.

DECIDING WHAT TO TEACH

To provide students with severe developmental disabilities with skills needed for meaningful participation in community settings, teachers must use their communities as a guide or reference when making decisions regarding *what to teach*. Four main strategies are useful in designing community-referenced instruction, including: (1) ecological inventories, (2) situational assessments, (3) discrepancy analyses, and (4) community-referenced curriculum guides.

Ecological Inventories

Conducting an ecological inventory involves assessing the skills a student needs to be successful in his or her current and future environments in order to identify specific instructional targets. Ecological inventories should be conducted for all arenas of a student's current life, including education (e.g., general education classroom, special education classroom, total school environment); employment and training (e.g., school-based enterprises, on-campus jobs, community-based vocational training and shadowing experiences); and independent living, which includes both where a student will live (e.g., student's home, neighborhood) and how a student will have fun (e.g., extra curricular activities, school clubs, community sports teams, concerts, theaters, YMCA). In addition to assessing the skills needed to fully participate in the settings a student currently frequents, ecological inventories must also evaluate the skills needed in postsecondary life. To prepare students for adult life, teachers should review students' postsecondary goals, which are developed annually and documented in the transition component of the IEP, and conduct ecological inventories in the settings in which students plan to learn, work, live, and have fun as adults.

One way to conduct this survey for leisure skills is to use Ford et al.'s (1989) five categories: (1) school and extracurricular activities, (2) home or neighborhood activities that can be done alone, (3) home or neighborhood activities that can be done with family or friends, (4) community activities with family and friends, and (5) activities for physical fitness. Another way to conduct ecological inventories is visit sites to identify needed skills. Moon, Komissar, Friedlanger, Hart, and Kiernan (1994) recommended traveling around the student's neighborhood looking for places where students the same age are playing, places with activities that may be of interest to the student, and places that just might be fun.

Browder (1991) described an ecological inventory process that involves visiting a site to gain information to plan community-based instruction. This process involves both viewing the site and interviewing people who work or spend time in the location. Figure 14.1 provides an example of an ecological inventory that was used in planning for Jacob, a 17-year-old student with moderate intellectual disability who plans to attend an 18–21 program at his local community college after high school. In the 18–21 Program, he will learn new skills related to academics and employment on a college campus, just like other students his age without disabilities. To identify the skills Jacob will need to be successful in the 18–21 Program, Jacob's transition specialist interviewed Debra Fenning, the 18–21 Program teacher at Central Community College. Jacob was excited to attend community college, as his older brother did when he graduated from high school, but Jacob's mother was concerned for Jacob's safety navigating a college campus alone. Jacob's transition specialist visited the site and shared the information she gathered with Jacob and his mother so they could make an informed decision.

Situational Assessments

After identifying community sites for students' potential participation sites, special education teachers then evaluate the sites to identify those skills essential for participation via ecological inventory. Next, it is important to give students the opportunity to try out the activities in these sites and conduct situational assessments through observation, that is, an assessment that is conducted to evaluate skills in the natural situations and

Site: Central Community College

Interviewee: Debra Fenning, 18–21 Program Teacher

Date: May 17, 2009

Student: Jacob

1. **Describe the site.**

   The 18–21 Program holds classes in two classrooms on the first floor of Johnson Hall. Johnson Hall is on the west side of campus, next to the Student Union and across the street from the Student Athletic Center. From the main entrance, the two 18–21 Program classrooms are located at the end of the hallway on the left, across from the restrooms. An instructor provides 2 hours of instruction in a whole-group, small-group, or individual format in the classroom, and students participate in lectures, complete assignments, work on group projects, and use the computer for a specific purpose. Students also take general courses within the college.

2. **What activities occur in this site?**

   Sitting at desks, taking notes, socializing with peers at the tables, using computers.

3. **What is the schedule of the 18–21 Program?**

   Classes on life skills are held on Mondays and Wednesdays from 1 P.M. until 3 P.M.; students can plan other courses with the help of a counselor.

4. **How accessible is the site? What orientation and mobility skills are required?**

   Johnson Hall is brand new, and it meets ADA accessibility standards. The main entrance has automatic revolving doors that spin slowly when a person approaches. Some mobility is needed to get to the vending machines, the public phone, or the snack bar; they are located at the far end of the building. There are stairs and elevators to the basement, second, and third floors of the facility. The remainder of the campus is easy to navigate, with buildings well marked.

5. **What safety considerations need to be considered for the 18–21 Program?**

   Ms. Fenning says that the students who attend the 18–21 Program are treated just like other college students. The 18–21 Program teachers meet the students in the classrooms at the beginning of class and leave class when the session is complete. Students are expected to get to campus and get around campus independently. Additionally, students who demonstrate behavior problems are disciplined in the same manner in which a typical college student would be. Therefore, aggression toward others and self-injury of any kind are not tolerated in the classroom. The campus police patrol the campus and the school buildings, and several "Blue Box" safety phones are located throughout the campus in case of emergencies. Additionally, the 18–21 Program staff does not provide any assistance to students after class as they wait for the bus or for a ride. Most students in the 18–21 Program go shopping or out with friends as a group after classes are complete by walking or using public transportation.

5. **Is any special equipment or clothing required?**

   Casual clothing is appropriate for the 18–21 Program.

6. **What types of communication and social skills are required?**

   Interacting appropriately with known and unknown students on campus and asking for help when needed are two important skills. Most students have cell phones and know how to use them independently to call friends and family when needed. When students walk across campus alone, most keep to themselves, talk on their cell phones, or listen to their iPods as they walk.

(cont.)

FIGURE 14.1. Example of an ecological inventory of a community college.

7. What natural reminders (cues) and rewards (contingencies) are available?

The students are graded on assignments and progress toward goals. Students who attend the 18–21 Program are expected to exhibit age-appropriate prosocial behavior. Other natural rewards that exist are making friends and having a part-time job and money to spend.

8. Will any assistance be provided in the restrooms or cafeterias?

No assistance is typically provided. Students must have independent self-care skills, or special arrangements must be made for a personal attendant.

9. What is the recommendation for Jacob?

The 18–21 Program at Central Community College seems like a good fit for Jacob. He has indicated that he is excited about attending Central Community College. He meets most of the requirements: he is independent in self-care, has good social skills, and consistently demonstrates age-appropriate behavior. The site seems safe and accessible. Jacob will need some additional instruction in taking a bus home, managing unsupervised time between classes or while waiting on the bus, finding classes, and meeting new people.

FIGURE 14.1. *(cont.)*

settings in which they are typically used. For example, a situational assessment could be conducted in the workplace to determine the appropriateness of students' interactions with coworkers, in addition to conducting one to evaluate a student's ability to use public transportation.

For example, for Jacob, the next step would be scheduling an opportunity for him to attend an 18–21 Program class session and to meet with a college counselor. Offering Jacob the opportunity to participate in a class session is important for a number of reasons. First, Jacob can use the information gained in this experience to determine whether his postsecondary plans to attend Central Community College align with his preferences and desires for adult life. Second, situational assessments are unique because the planning team can evaluate a student's skills in accordance with the expectations and challenges that are inherent in natural settings. Some challenges but may not be realistically simulated in a classroom setting. For example, in the community college setting, Jacob would be expected to find his classes in Johnson Hall independently. Such a challenge cannot be replicated realistically in his high school building because Johnson Hall is unfamiliar to him. Situational assessments can be completed in a variety of ways. One common procedure is to identify the skills needed for the situation or setting, create a checklist, and use it during the situational assessment to evaluate the extent to which student performance aligns with skills required for the situation. Results of a situational assessment conducted for Jacob at Central Community College are presented in Figure 14.2.

Discrepancy Analysis

Another way to summarize the findings of a situational assessment is to analyze a student's performance in comparison with the expected performance of a same-age peer without a disability, as shown in Figure 14.3. This procedure is known as *discrepancy analysis*. This procedure would be particularly helpful in identifying pertinent instructional targets for a student who is preparing for postsecondary employment. During job sampling activities, situational assessment paired with discrepancy analysis would identify students' preferences, strengths, needs, and interests in comparison with those of workers who currently hold similar employment positions.

Site: *Central Community College*

Observer: *Joann Reynolds, Transition Specialist*

Date: *May 21, 2010*

Student: *Jacob*

Transportation to Site:
- ✓ Rides safely in car from home to campus.
- __ Gathers items needed for class.
- ✓ Exits car at curb or in parking lot.
- ✓ Walks onto sidewalk or grassy area.

Navigating on Campus:
- ✓ Walks safely out of way of traffic.
- ✓ Maintains belongings.
- ✓ Displays appropriate social interactions with unfamiliar people.
- ✓ Displays appropriate social interactions with familiar people.
- __ Walks at typical appropriate pace.
- na If talking on cell phone, uses appropriate volume.

Locating Building:
- ✓ Locates Johnson Hall.
- __ If confused, uses campus map for guidance.
- ✓ Enters through revolving door at main entrance.

Locating and Entering Appropriate Classroom:
- ✓ Enters main foyer of Johnson Hall.
- __ Locates classroom 103.
- ✓ Uses bathroom before class if needed.
- ✓ Enters classroom.
- __ Arrives at class on time.

Classroom Participation:
- ✓ Sits at desk.
- __ Organizes materials needed for session.
- ✓ Stays alert.
- ✓ Participates in class activities.
- __ Raises hand for questions/responses.

Behavioral Observations:
- ✓ Displays appropriate student behavior.
- ✓ Refrains from talking about unrelated topics during class sessions.
- __ Stays in classroom for class session.
- ✓ Participates in class activities with appropriate volume.

Social Interactions:
- ✓ Is polite to teacher.
- ✓ Shows respect for others.
- ✓ Listens when others are speaking.
- ✓ Participates in turn-taking conversation.
- __ Speech is understood by others.
- __ Does not touch others unless appropriate.
- ✓ Makes eye contact with others.
- ✓ Avoids confrontation.
- __ Maintains appropriate personal space.

Safety Skills:
- ✓ Maintains belongings.
- ✓ Stays in well-lit areas.
- __ Stays in populated areas.
- ✓ If lost, asks official for assistance.
- ✓ Does not approach strangers.
- ✓ Does not leave campus with strangers.
- na If witnessing an emergency, uses Blue Box telephone.
- na If seriously hurt, uses Blue Box telephone.
- na If sick, calls family member for ride home.

Actions after Class:
- ✓ Waits for ride at agreed-upon area.
- na Calls family member if ride is more than 15 minutes late.

Recommended Instructional Targets

1. Gather materials needed for class.	7. Stay in classroom for class session.
2. Walk at appropriate pace to arrive at class on time.	8. Speak in a manner understood by others.
3. Use a campus map.	9. Not touching others unless appropriate.
4. Locate classroom 103.	10. Maintain appropriate personal space.
5. Organize materials for class session.	11. Stay in populated areas.
6. Raise hand for questions/responses.	12. Meet new people.

FIGURE 14.2. Situational Assessment Results for Jacob.

Skills needed in community college setting	Jacob's performance	Peer's performance	Instructional implications for Jacob
Getting to campus	Brother drives Jacob to campus.	Brian takes public bus to campus.	Travel training
Navigating on campus	Walked too slow, walked into student union and sat for a few minutes.	Walked to class building, made quick phone call outside, entered building.	Appropriate pace instruction
Locating building	Could not use map to locate building.	Knew where his class was.	Map reading instruction
Locating and entering appropriate classroom	Did not know which classroom to enter, was late for class.	Arrived at appropriate class on time.	Map reading instruction, instruction regarding promptness
Classroom participation	Did not have paper to write on in class, did not raise hand to ask questions or provide responses, left classroom three times to use bathroom and check cell phone for messages.	Had all materials to take notes and participate in class session, raised hand to ask questions and provide responses, stayed in class for entire session.	Appropriate student behavior instruction
Social interactions	Speaking not understood by others, hugged teacher and other students upon entering classroom, sat too close to male friend in class.	Shook hands with one male student, waved and smiled at one female student, said "Good afternoon" to the instructor.	Social skills instruction
Safety skills	Walked in isolated area near loading docks at back of building.	Stayed in areas near other students.	Instruction regarding safe and unsafe areas
Actions after class	Waited for ride at agreed-upon area.	Waited for bus at bus stop with friends.	Travel training

FIGURE 14.3. Discrepancy analysis for Central Community College based on situational assessment.

Community-Referenced Curriculum Guides

Finally, community-referenced curriculum guides are helpful in identifying the community settings and the corresponding skills that are valuable for meaningful student participation in community settings. First, The Syracuse Community-Referenced Curriculum Guide for Students with Moderate and Severe Disabilities (Ford et al., 1989) is a curriculum that aims to prepare students with significant cognitive disabilities for the "real world." Instructional topics include collaborating with families, community living, functional academics, social, communication, and motor skills, and strategies for implementing instruction. The Council for Exceptional Children endorsed a second community-referenced curriculum, Life-Centered Career Education (LCCE; Brolin, 1989). The LCCE includes instructional recommendations related to community and employment skills. The main components of LCCE are daily living skills, personal and social skills, and occupational guidance and preparation (Brolin, 1989).

Assessing the skills necessary for students' community and employment success is an essential step in identifying instructional targets across a variety of community settings. Conducting ecological assessments, situational assessments, and discrepancy analysis and using community-referenced curriculum guides will simplify decisions regarding what to teach for students' successful participation and independence in four areas of community instruction: (1) getting around in the community, (2) being a consumer, (3) working competitively, and (4) having fun.

FOUR AREAS FOR COMMUNITY INSTRUCTION

Getting Around in the Community

Pedestrian skills and travel skills are essential to participation in the community and in the workplace among students with disabilities. Given effective training in both simulated and *in vivo* settings, many students with disabilities will exhibit appropriate pedestrian and travel skills. A number of important pedestrian and transportation skills are included in Table 14.1.

Pedestrian skills include using sidewalks when possible, walking around obstructions, responding to information and caution signs, crossing streets and parking lots, identifying intersections, and using pedestrian signs and traffic signals. All students need to learn to cross streets safely; however, some students may not display independent pedestrian skills. For these students, learning to cross streets with an escort is an important alternative. This goal might include learning to stop at curbs to wait for an escort's (or service dog's) signal to cross. Other students may become independent in crossing streets with repeated instruction. This instruction may begin in less crowded streets and then progress to busier intersections. For safety, teachers may also want to use videos or computer simulations to practice attending to the cues for safe crossing, such as an absence of cars or the presence of a walk signal or green light. Since 1976, several successful strategies have emerged from the research literature for teaching pedestrian skills to individuals with developmental disabilities—including using task analysis (Page, Iwata, & Neef, 1976), most-to-least prompting (Batu, Ergenekon, Erbas, & Akmanoglu, 2004), and progressive time delay in simulated and in vivo settings (Collins, Stinson, & Land, 1993). For example, the steps to cross a street can be written as a task analysis. Most to least prompting may be the safest alternative to teach the student to cross. The teacher

TABLE 14.1. Pedestrian and Transportation Skills

Pedestrian skills	Transportation skills
• Using sidewalks when possible.	• Safe passenger behavior.
• Walking around obstructions.	• Reading bus timetable.
• Responding to signs.	• Waiting at the appropriate place.
• Crossing streets and parking lots.	• Identifying appropriate bus.
• Identifying intersections.	• Boarding the bus.
• Using pedestrian signs.	• Paying the fare.
• Using traffic signals.	• Demonstrating acceptable, safe social skills.
	• Identifying appropriate bus stop.
	• Alerting the driver to stop if necessary.
	• Exiting the bus.
	• Using pedestrian skills to get to destination.

and student may begin by crossing arm in arm. As students gain practice crossing safely, the teacher may give less and less assistance (e.g., in descending order, hand on arm, verbal cue alone, no prompt).

FINDING THE BALANCE

Teaching street crossing requires managing the safety risks to students. Teachers need to find a balance between promoting students' increased independence in navigating through the community and maintaining student safety. Before beginning a street-crossing program, teachers should develop a safety plan that is shared with administrators, parents, and the student. The plan may include how risks will be minimized, a plan for emergencies, and how decisions will be made to fade teacher assistance.

In addition to pedestrian skills, students need travel training. Travel training is "short-term, comprehensive, intensive instruction designed to teach students with disabilities how to travel safely and independently on public transportation" (Groce, 1996a, p. 2). Travel training is not a new idea—the special education community has recognized the importance of travel for individuals with disabilities for over 50 years. In 1957, Lown indicated that travel training could alleviate reservations "in the minds of the family, friends, and the public" (1957, p. 179) and, most important, provide individuals with disabilities with "general sense of freedom" (1957, p. 179).

Travel training should focus on the types of transportation available to students in the communities in which they live. Although some individuals with developmental disabilities learn to operate cars, car passenger safety and public transportation skills will more often be the focus for this group. In many communities, the primary mode of transportation is cars, and so students need to learn to ride safely in a variety of cars, including wearing a seatbelt. Sometimes the skill of wearing a seatbelt needs to be taught using differential reinforcement to build toleration for being fastened for longer and longer periods of time (i.e., longer car rides).

In addition to safe passenger behavior, instruction about using public transportation will likely include reading bus timetables, waiting at the appropriate bus stop or depot, identifying the appropriate bus to take to travel to a destination, boarding the bus, paying the fare, demonstrating acceptable and safe social skills, identifying the appropriate bus stop, alerting the driver to stop if necessary, exiting the bus, and using appropriate pedestrian skills to arrive at the destination. Besides buses, students may also need to learn to take subways, trains, planes, and ferries, depending on their community options.

A number of travel training resources are available to guide educators in designing travel instruction. Groce (1996a) provides travel-training basics, including who should be included in travel training, who should provide instruction, and how instruction should be provided. Voorhees (1996) describes a comprehensive seven-step training sequence: (1) teaching basic community skills and knowledge of transportation routes, stops, and costs; (2) observing the student; (3) teaching behavior in unexpected circumstances; (4) observing the student's social behavior; (5) observing the travel skills of the student when he or she is aware of observation; (6) observing the travel skills of the student when he or she is unaware of observation; and (7) observing the travel skills of the student when he or she is unaware of observation to assess maintenance of travel skills over time. Additionally, Wissick and Schweder (2007) describes how social stories combined with community-based instruction can be used effectively to increase students' skills related to travel and leisure (for more information on social stories, see Chapter 12).

A number of community groups and service agencies provide travel training directly to consumers. The New York City Board of Education Travel Training Program (Groce, 1996b) is a program in which specially trained paraprofessionals provide travel training to students with disabilities in an urban setting. The Maryland Department of Disabilities, like many other states, provides training for professionals who plan to provide travel-related instruction and instruction for individuals with disabilities in need of travel training. Finally, Easter Seals Project ACTION also offers valuable resources for special educators and individuals with disabilities.

Consumer Skills for the Community

To be able to participate in a variety of community activities, people must be able to complete a number of tasks associated with their role as consumers. Like pedestrian skills, consumer skills are important for students with disabilities to learn, both in the classroom and in the community. Given effective training in both simulated and invivo settings, students with disabilities will gain consumer skills, including identifying coins and bills, selecting items for purchase, paying for items, saving money, banking, budgeting money, and many others. A number of consumer skills that are important to participation in community settings are displayed in Table 14.2.

Consumer skills are important to students' independence, as well as their self-determination. By teaching consumer skills, teachers of students with severe disabilities empower students to experience greater autonomy in decision making regarding financial decisions. For students to become prepared consumers, a wide array of instructional targets must be covered, including skills related to paying for items, shopping, eating out, banking, and budgeting.

Paying for Items

Paying for items is a skill that is essential to meaningful community participation across a variety of settings. Whether seeing a movie with friends, buying groceries in a supermarket, or eating at a fast-food restaurant, paying for items is an important skill that is worthy of instruction. Additionally, students have increased independence in a number of community settings when they understand how to make purchases effectively.

TABLE 14.2. Consumer Skills for Community Settings

• Counting single dollar bills.	• Reading cost of items on menu.
• Counting mixed bills.	• Paying check at table in restaurant.
• Adding mixed groups of coins and bills.	• Keeping money in a wallet or purse.
• Determining how much money you have.	• Storing bills and coins separately.
• Determining cost of items desired.	• Waiting on line to speak to teller at bank.
• Determining whether desired items are within budget.	• Opening a bank account.
• Using coins and bills in vending machines.	• Making a withdrawal or deposit in person.
• Using coins and bills for purchases in community.	• Making a withdrawal or deposit using an ATM.
• Waiting for change.	• Selecting items for purchase.
• Using an ATM card for purchases.	• Comparing prices among similar items.
	• Adding to identify sum of prices of purchases.

Research indicates that students with disabilities have successfully used four strategies for paying for items in the community, including using (1) a set amount of money that is provided by another individual for the purchase, (2) a class system to make purchases, (3) the calculator method, and (4) the "one-more-than" strategy.

First, Bates, Cuvo, Miner, and Korabek (2001) found that participants with mild and moderate intellectual disability were able to improve their purchasing skills in a grocery setting via instruction that included providing each participant with a $10 bill, a shopping list (including pictures and labels of hot dogs, buns, catsup, mustard, beans, and chips), and verbal directions to "buy the things on the list."

Second, Gardill and Browder (1995) indicated that students learned to pay for items by classifying purchase types by the typical cost associated with the item. The three classes of purchases were a vending machine item, a snack, and lunch. Researchers taught specific money types that should be used for each of the three types of purchases. For example, given that vending machine items usually cost less than $1, the specific money type used for vending machine purchases would be quarters.

Third, a number of researchers have taught students to use calculators to identify the total cost of items for purchase (Frederick-Dugan et al., 1991; Matson & Long, 1986; Nietupski et al., 1983; Smeets, 1978). Using this strategy, students were taught either to pay the exact cost of items (Smeets, 1978) or pay more than the cost (Matson & Long, 1986). Additionally, Nietupski et al. (1983) taught students to use calculators but also taught them to use visual prompts to calculate sales tax.

Fourth, a popular and easy-to-use purchasing strategy is the "one-more-than" strategy, which is also known as the "next-dollar" strategy. To use this strategy, students listen to the price that the clerk requests and look at the cash register to identify the number of dollars required for the purchase. Next, to provide enough money for the purchase, the students give the clerk the number of dollars required and *one more dollar* to cover the change. For example, for a purchase cost of $4.51, the student would provide the clerk with four dollars *and* one more dollar (to cover the change), for a total of $5 (for more information on teaching the next-dollar strategy, see Chapter 7).

Recently, a few studies have identified successful strategies for teaching students with intellectual disability how to use a debit card for purchases. First, Mechling, Gast, and Barthold (2003) taught participants to make purchases with a debit card using an interactive computer program that simulated steps via video depiction. Next, Cihak et al. (2004) taught purchasing skills using a system of least prompts in simulated and community settings on consecutive days. In the simulated setting, participants learned to use a debit card to make purchases by identifying appropriate steps in a photo album. In the community setting, participants practiced the skill at a register at a community store.

Shopping

Shopping can focus on purchasing essentials, such as groceries and clothing, or items related to recreation, such as CDs and games. Regardless of the purpose of the item purchased, a number of skills related to shopping are essential. Many researchers who have taught shopping usually focus on the entire routine, from entering the store until the purchase is complete (McDonnell & Horner, 1985), but they may also select steps using "backward chaining," in which students learn the last steps and then add new steps until the entire routine is learned (McDonnell & Laughlin, 1989).

Researchers have identified a number of unique yet effective strategies for teaching shopping skills to individuals with cognitive disabilities. First, Gaule et al. (1985) taught students to prepare a shopping list, locate items in the store, and purchase the items using modeling and corrective feedback. Second, Mechling, Gast, and Langone (2002) taught students to read grocery aisle signs and to locate items using computer-based instruction. Additionally, keep in mind that shopping provides an excellent opportunity for students to generalize sight word and money skills, as described in Chapters 5 and 7. Table 14.3 gives a task analysis of shopping skills.

Eating Out

Dining at a restaurant or buying a snack can be a leisure activity as well as a means to eat. Traditionally, researchers have focused on the steps needed to make and consume the food. Teachers can be creative in using school settings to help prepare students for purchasing food in public. First, Gardill and Browder (1995) taught middle school students to use specific money amounts for food purchases by using a school vending machine, the cafeteria, classroom simulations, and community trips to fast-food restaurants. School simulations can be made realistic by obtaining materials from the community site, such as menus, paper cups, place mats, trays, and other items. In school, the student can practice the communication and money skills that often take more practice than community outings allow. Second, Sowers and Powers (1995) not only used a simulation but also invited parents to school to learn how to implement the training in their family trips to restaurant settings. Finally, Mechling and Cronin (2006) successfully taught students with intellectual disability to use AAC devices to order meals in fast-food restaurants via computer-based video instruction that included video recordings, still photographs, and voice recordings. Table 14.4 lists some of the skills for purchasing meals and snacks.

Banking

Banking skills can include skills that commonly occur at home, including writing checks, balancing a checkbook, using online banking features, and assessing account balances. Additionally, many banking skills are used primarily in community settings, such as cashing checks, making a bank deposit, interacting with the bank teller, and withdrawing money from the teller or a bank machine.

Alberto, Cihak, and Gama (2005) found that students with intellectual disability learned to effectively withdraw $20 using a debit card when in vivo instruction was paired with simulated instruction that included a depiction of steps via either static picture prompts or video modeling. Although both strategies were effective, students made

TABLE 14.3. Shopping Skills

• Entering the store.	• Placing item in the basket.
• Using a cart or basket.	• Waiting in the checkout line.
• Locating items.	• Greeting cashier.
• Asking for help if items are not found.	• Paying for the item(s).
• Choosing specific item(s).	• Carrying package.
• Taking item from shelf.	• Leaving the store.

TABLE 14.4. Purchasing Meals and Snacks

• Choosing where to go.	• Interacting with companions while eating or drinking.
• Selecting money needed for outing.	• Disposing of trash.
• Choosing food items.	• Choosing when to leave.
• Expressing choice to waiter or cashier.	• Using vending machine.
• Paying for food.	• Generalizing across variety of restaurants.
• Choosing where to sit or expressing preference to restaurant hostess.	

fewer errors and attained mastery in fewer instructional sessions when static pictures were used in simulated instruction rather than video modeling.

Budgeting

Budgeting skills are obviously critical to students' financial independence, but these skills are also related to skills of self-determination (e.g., planning to make desired purchases, making choices between various goods and services). To truly gain control over personal finances, individuals with intellectual disability need to know not only how to spend money but also how to develop a budget. A simple way to teach budgeting that requires few to no computation skills is to teach the person spending habits. For example, a young child may be given a money notebook with money pockets that are identified for specific purposes, including lunch money, school pencils, savings, and toys. In a spending-habits approach, the child learns to take out the preselected amount each day for lunch. Once a week, he or she may also use some of the school pencil money to purchase a pencil. Once a month, he or she may buy a toy. Similarly, an adult with an intellectual disability can learn to pay bills on payday and then divide what is left for a one-time purchase (e.g., clothes, DVD), a monthly recreational event (e.g., movies), weekly groceries, and daily cash for a soda. Another alternative in teaching budgeting is to teach planned purchases. In planning purchases, individuals use store flyers and a calculator or number line to determine whether they can buy desired items. For example, Gaule et al. (1985) taught young adults with moderate and severe intellectual disability to plan their grocery purchases on a number line divided into 50-cent intervals as each item was selected from a shopping aid with pictures and prices of food. The participants colored the appropriate number of intervals they had on their number lines. Matson (1981) also used a shopping aid, but foods were listed in columns by price from small items (under 50¢) to more expensive items (over $10).

Choices

Besides learning the logistics of using community resources, students also need opportunities to make choices in these contexts. Cooper and Browder (1998) demonstrated how these choices could be embedded in a community purchasing routine. The young adults with severe disabilities who participated were given choices before each of five different steps of the purchasing task analysis. The teacher conducted a baseline assessment to determine how many choices the participants would make. For example, before entering the restaurant, the teacher would stand back to see which door the participant chose (e.g., by touching it or trying to open it). Other choices the students made were menu items (from pictures), condiments, and seating. Once the instructor determined which choices the learner could make, choice-making instruction was used to teach participants how to make the other choices. In this instruction, the teacher made two options clear (e.g., "Which door?" while pointing to two doors). The showing of these specific options was faded using time delay (Chapter 4 provides more information on time delay). If the student made a choice, the teacher commended this choice. If not, the teacher said, "I'm not sure which one. I'll help you choose," and guided the student's hand to indicate a choice.

Working Competitively in the Community

Most adults seek the benefits associated with working competitively in a community setting. For people with and without disabilities, holding a job has a number of benefits above and beyond the paycheck. Working individuals experience advantages associated with (1) working toward financial independence, (2) setting and achieving economic goals, (3) building relationships with others, (4) gaining skills and knowledge, (5) having resources with which to pursue preferred activities and purchase desired items, and (6) experiencing a sense of accomplishment in a job well done.

Individuals with disabilities gain skills for the workplace in many of the same ways they acquire other skills, such as those associated with math, reading, socialization, and laundry skills. Evidence-based instructional procedures (as discussed in Chapter 4) should be used to teach skills for employability among individuals with intellectual disability. For example, a task analysis may be used to teach students a daily living skill with many steps, such as using a washing machine, or a multistep math problem such as reducing fractions to the simplest form.

Similarly, task analyses have been used to teach a variety of vocational skills to individuals with intellectual disability. For example, Bates et al. (2001) taught janitorial skills to transition-age students with mild and moderate intellectual disability using a task analysis illustrated in a photo album and a least-to-most prompting strategy. Additionally, Riffel et al. (2005) taught four students with intellectual as well as other disabilities (autism, Prader–Willi syndrome) to set cafeteria and dining room tables using a task analysis delivered via a palmtop personal computer. More recently, Mechling and Ortega-Hurndon (2007) taught three transition-age students with moderate intellectual disability to deliver office mail, water a plant, and change paper towels using a task analysis delivered via computer-based video paired with the teacher feedback.

To determine the most appropriate jobs to teach, it is important to conduct an ecological inventory, as described earlier in this chapter. The teacher may begin by listing major employers in the area and scanning the classified ads to identify job opportunities. The teacher may also want to tour a community or technical college to learn what opportunities exist for additional training in a trade. These jobs can then be simulated in the school context or taught in vivo using volunteer opportunities. For example, the teacher may use a school store to teach retail skills and also help students volunteer in food pantries, charitable clothing stores, and other contexts to extend these skills. Younger students need the opportunity for a variety of job tryouts. These may include working with plants, caring for animals, managing store stock (e.g., removing or affixing labels), clerical work (photocopying, mailings), cleaning, and food preparation. School simulations may also be linked to trades trained in area colleges, such as use of simple tools, basic auto maintenance, and health care (e.g., changing sheets, refilling water; for more information on job tryouts, see Chapter 15).

The workplace also serves as an additional setting in which students can use many skills associated with academics (as discussed in Chapters 5–9), communication (Chapter 11), social skills (Chapter 12), and personal and daily living skills (Chapter 13). For example, in the workplace, students have an opportunity to use language skills. This clearly links to a standard identified by the National Council of Teachers of English (NCTE) and the International Reading Association (IRA), which states that students "adjust their use of spoken, written, and visual language (e.g., conventions, style, vocabulary) to communicate effectively with a variety of audiences and for different purposes" (NCTE & IRA, 1998, 2009).

Having Fun in the Community

Community participation is an important consideration in designing plans for recreation activities. Although recreation can certainly take place in the home, students also need opportunities for community outings. Browder, Cooper, and Lim (1998) assessed setting preference by measuring participants' engagement time in activities in two settings, including those with people with disabilities and without disabilities and found that all participants preferred inclusive community settings. Next, Browder et al. (1998) taught participants to use objects that represented a setting for an activity. Participants overwhelmingly selected community settings. As this study illustrates, students with severe disabilities can learn to use objects or other communicative symbols to express both what they want to do and where they want to go. Having this opportunity for choice is especially important for leisure activities.

Lieberman and Stuart (2002) surveyed 51 adults who were deaf–blind to determine their current participation in leisure activities and the activities they would prefer to take part in in the future. Researchers asked 10 questions, including both closed-ended and open-ended questions. In response to items related to leisure time preferences, a majority of respondents indicated that they preferred activities with other people (65%), health-related activities (65%), dancing (63%), boating (63%), outside activities (61%), computer activities (57%), water activities (55%), and board games (53%). Respondents also indicated the challenges they faced in participating in preferred leisure activities, including a lack of community ties and supports, of information about advantages of health-related activities, and of information about opportunities in the local area. Similar to job sampling, students with severe disabilities may need to sample leisure activities to discover what is available and what they enjoy.

To teach leisure skills, teachers may need to target instruction toward how to choose an activity, plan an outing, and perform the skills for the activity. At the simplest level, students can learn to choose between two objects or pictures related to activities. These may begin with classroom options, such as viewing books or playing computer games. Students may then learn to generalize this instruction to choosing community activities such as going to the park or shopping at the mall. Some students may need objects related to these activities to build understanding (e.g., a tree branch for the park; a wallet for the mall). Some activities require advanced planning. Students may also learn to plan an outing by selecting the activity, scheduling it on the calendar, and following a list of preparation for the activity (e.g., arranging transportation, purchasing tickets). Finally, students may need instruction in how to perform the activity itself. For example, students may need systematic instruction to learn to play ultimate Frisbee in the park or attend a ball game.

An important consideration in developing leisure skills is to choose some that encourage physical fitness. Group fitness activities can also foster social interaction. Ellis, Wright, and Cronis (1996) observed students with moderate and severe disabilities in regular gym classes and found that more interactions occurred in group activities. Initially, the student may need direct instruction to participate in the exercise program. Cooper and Browder (1998) taught adults with severe disabilities to perform a specific water exercise and then encouraged peers who were nondisabled to help the participants maintain their skills. Other students may prefer a self-managed exercise routine. Ellis, Cress, and Spellman (1992) taught students with moderate mental retardation to walk either in the school hallways or on a treadmill using self-monitoring. To keep track of their distance, the students put a baton in a basket after completing each lap in the hallway or set a timer on the treadmill. These participants improved the duration of their exercise over time by setting increasingly higher goals for themselves (e.g., more batons in the basket). Whereas some individuals like to focus on one specific fitness activity, such as walking or swimming, others prefer cross-training. To encourage a diversified fitness plan, Zhang, Gast, Horvat, and Dattilo (1995) taught four students with severe disabilities bowling, throwing, and putting in a school gym. Besides increased fitness, exercise can have other benefits. In training students to play basketball in the Special Olympics in Turkey, Gencoez (1997) observed concurrent reductions in their problem behavior. Special Olympics has a long tradition of promoting fitness for athletes with disabilities, and for some students, participation in this program is highly valued. In contrast, students also need the opportunity to be active in inclusive school and community fitness programs. Schleien, Green, and Heyne (1993) describe how inclusive opportunities can be created in three ways: (1) students with disabilities can be integrated into generic recreation programs (e.g., Little League, dance classes, physical education at school), (2) students who are nondisabled can be recruited to participate in a special program ("reverse mainstreaming"), or (3) a new program can be developed that includes all students from the onset ("zero exclusion"). Whatever type of program is selected, students with moderate and severe disabilities will often need systematic instruction to learn how to participate in the activities.

TEACHING COMMUNITY PARTICIPATION AND EMPLOYMENT SKILLS VIA COMMUNITY-BASED INSTRUCTION

As described earlier in this chapter, community and job skill training should be community referenced (i.e., directly tied to what is available in the student's own community) and, when possible, community based (i.e., taught in the community setting). In the past four decades, strategies for teaching individuals with developmental disabilities skills in and for the community have been well established through research. Several of these strategies for community-based instruction and its alternatives are described next.

Use Community-Based Instruction plus Simulated Instruction

Teaching community and job skills in *either* a simulated (e.g., classroom) or a community (e.g., grocery store) setting is less effective than teaching community and job skills in *both* the simulated and the community setting (Bates et al., 2001). When students have the opportunity to practice skills at school using simulations and then to apply them to the

the real community setting, they are more likely to achieve mastery. Bates et al. (2001) found that individuals with mild or moderate intellectual disability were more successful in performing laundry, janitorial, restaurant, and grocery tasks when provided with both simulated and community instruction. For simulated instruction, researchers asked participants to point to pictures depicting the steps in the task analysis for the tasks. In the community setting, researchers asked participants to perform steps in the task analysis in stores, restaurants, Laundromats, and public restrooms. Pictures provide one alternative for simulations, and live-action video can also be a powerful tool for practice. Students may practice with materials while seeing the skill performed in the actual setting.

Use Inconspicuous Strategies and Materials

When teaching community and job skills in community settings, it is important to select inconspicuous materials and instructional strategies. That is, materials and instructional strategies should not attract unnecessary attention to an individual with disabilities or diminish the perceived competence of an individual with disabilities. For example, if a student needs verbal prompting to select the appropriate number of bills needed to pay a cashier, the teacher can provide needed supports quietly. Additionally, for a student who uses a picture schedule as a visual prompt to complete all components of a dishwashing task, a pocket-sized schedule that a student could refer to when needed would be more appropriate than a schedule that would hang on the wall at all times.

Maintain the Characteristics of the Community

As teachers plan for community-based instruction, many experience challenge in designing Community-Based Instruction sessions that closely maintain the characteristics and challenges of the community. When one instructor simultaneously teaches five students with intellectual disability how to give money to a cashier, the expectations and problems vary dramatically from those that would be present for a student performing the task independently. For example, when performing the task independently, the following challenges may be present: (1) a lack of assistance from a teacher, (2) unfamiliar individuals in line behind the student who may be impatient, (3) few or no individuals modeling the skills required for purchasing, and (4) a responsibility to communicate and respond independently to questions or statements posed by the cashier (e.g., "Would you like to donate one dollar to a local charity?" "Did you find everything you were looking for today?"). To maintain the characteristics of the community, the teacher may want to fade proximity to the students or have only one student go through the line at a time. It is also important to encourage the student to relate to the cashier and attend to other natural cues (e.g., the price shown on the register). Similarly, in job contexts, the teacher should promote focusing on the job supervisor and relating to coworkers.

Teach Self-Management and Self-Monitoring

One way to fade the amount of teacher prompting and presence is to teach students to self-manage their community experience. One option is for students to use items or devices that help them to be successful. For example, many people carry a list to the grocery store so that they can remember the items that should be purchased. Also, many people use a "to-do" list or write themselves notes to remember an errand. Similarly, in community settings, people with developmental disabilities can also benefit from lists or other printed reminders. For example, a student may use a written checklist of steps to complete all necessary tasks for a job such as cleaning a hotel room. A small device such as an iPod with headphones might be helpful. For example, a hostess at a restaurant might have the cue, "Is there anyone at the door waiting to be seated?"

Incorporate Assistive Technology

According to IDEA (2004), an AT device is "any item, piece of equipment, or product system, whether acquired commercially off the shelf, modified, or customized, that is used to increase, maintain, or improve functional capabilities of a child with a disability." AT devices can be essential to students' acquisition of skills and knowledge; however, for transition-age students, special considerations are warranted. When teaching skills for adult life, be sure that the materials used during instruction, including AT devices, will be available to students after graduation. In cases in which AT devices will not be available to a student, teach the student to perform skills with only those materials that will be available to them in adult life. For example, if a student uses a pocket-sized VOD to order a meal in a restaurant but does not own the device, school personnel should both increase efforts to identify a funding source to assist the family in purchasing the device and teach the student to order meals and communicate clearly with unfamiliar people either without the assistance of any device or with the assistance of a device that is available to the student after graduation.

Issues in Community-Based Instruction

Although community-based instruction continues to be important for students with moderate and severe disabilities, many professionals now see the need to plan this time carefully so that it does not compete with school inclusion and learning general curriculum content. Removing only children with disabilities to learn community skills can stigmatize them and emphasize their differences from peers. When children with disabilities are removed from the regular education class, they may miss valuable instruction and socialization time. Also, it is unusual to see children in the community during typical school hours, which may work against the goal of helping students "blend" into their community contexts.

Given these issues, it may be tempting for administrators to eliminate community-based instruction and, by doing so, reduce costs and potential risks to student safety. This would be a serious loss for students with moderate and severe disabilities who may not generalize skills from school to community contexts unless directly trained to do so (Snell & Browder, 1986). Community-based instruction may also be a highly preferred and motivational activity for many students. As schools encourage students' self-determination, it is important to listen to students' choices about their school activities. Community-based instruction provides a way for schools to form partnerships with area businesses. For example, educators can work with business leaders in planning this instruction (Aveno, Renzaglia, & Lively, 1987). Rather than discontinuing this important resource, schools should update their approach to minimize the competition between school inclusion and community-based instruction.

To update this approach, educators can use four strategies: (1) reconsidering who participates in community-based instruction, (2) focusing on generalization, (3) involving peers who are nondisabled, and (4) expanding the school day or working with after-school programs. First, school districts may want to reconsider who participates in community-based instruction by using a set of criteria rather than a blanket policy that all students receive this training. It may be appropriate for some elementary students to have *no* community-based instruction beyond what incidental learning occurs in school field trips. Other elementary students may have behavioral challenges in community contexts or special skill needs that make this a high priority for them and their families. In updating community-based instruction policies, educators may want to use criteria such as the following to determine who participates in this program:

1. How important is this instruction to the family?
2. To what extent is community-based instruction a preferred activity for the student?
3. How many years does the student have left in school to learn community skills?
4. Are there specific skill deficit issues that need to be addressed in community settings (e.g., problem behavior in a grocery store)?
5. Can these skills be addressed by training the student across more environments within the school?
6. Is the student beyond the typical age to be in public school (19–21)?
7. What will the student miss at school when he or she is in the community?

Community-based instruction programs can be also updated by focusing on generalization. If students are instructed to generalize, they will be able to use the skills taught in untrained contexts. Horner, McDonnell, and Bellamy (1986) demonstrated how to achieve generalization by careful planning of settings to use in training in an approach called *general case instruction*. Teachers train the *general case* by selecting settings that sample the range of variation found in the community. For example, training in settings that have students use automated doors as well as those that are pushed or pulled open may help the student be able to use any door he or she may encounter in the community in the future. Figure 14.4 provides an example of an assessment of a student's ability to generalize. Although general case instruction focuses on training in multiple community settings, Westling and Floyd (1990) found that students can sometimes learn to generalize from just *one* community context if this is augmented by school practice. This school-based practice can be designed as a close simulation of what occurs in the community.

To update community-based instruction, teachers can also include children who do not have disabilities as a unique form of cooperative learning (Moon et al., 1994; Schleien et al., 1993). During these small-group activities all students work together to achieve a common goal. A science class may go to the park to take water samples. This class activity may also offer an opportunity for the student with severe disabilities to practice skills such as street crossing and wearing a wallet with emergency information. Leisure activities provide another alternative to participate with children who are nondisabled (Moon et al., 1994). These may include after-school activities, school clubs, and community outings, such as taking a gym class to the YMCA to swim.

The fourth option for updating community-based instruction is to expand the school day to incorporate these after-school activities. This option can be expensive and may not be feasible for some districts. In contrast, other districts that have already expanded their school day for older students or have provided after-school care for younger students may be able to incorporate community-based instruction during this time.

Student: _Randy S._   **Skill:** _Purchase at concession stand_

Generic task analysis	Settings				
	High school football stadium	Pete's hot dog stand	Community fundraisers (e.g., church)	Jackson Arena	Implications for Instruction and Accommodations
1. Approach stand.	Stands are on perimeter. Randy could not negotiate walking through the crowd. (−)	Has large hot dog on top. Randy walked to it. (+)	Volunteers knew Randy and invited him to their table. (+ with natural support)	Stands are in hallway. Randy could not negotiate crowd. (−)	Weave through crowd with companion.
2. Wait in line.	Long wait; began to vocalize loudly. (−)	No waiting. (omit step)	Volunteers served him ahead of others. (omit step)	Long wait; sat on floor. (−)	Go at "off" times. Practice standing and waiting.
3. Make choice.	Bobbed head toward someone's hot dog. (− made choice but was stigmatizing)	Looked at hot dogs intently. (+)	Grabbed bag of hot dog buns. (− made choice but was inappropriate)	Did not choose. (−)	Point to options and have him gaze.
4. Inform cashier.	Teacher told cashier. (−)	Pete recognized his eye gaze as an order. (+)	Volunteers recognized grabbing. (− not appropriate)	Teacher told cashier. (−)	Use picture order card.
5. Take out money.	Teacher physically guided. (−)	Teacher guided. (−)	Volunteers gave it to him. (omit step)	Teacher guided. (−)	Learn to take dollar from pocket.
6. Give money.	Handed money to cashier. (+)	Handed money to Pete. (+)	Not applicable. (omit step)	Handed money to cashier. (+)	Generalized
7. Take food items.	Grasped hot dog on tray. (+)	Grasped hot dog on napkin. (+)	Grasped hot dog alone. (+)	Hot dog in bag; took bag. (+)	Generalized
8. Find place to sit/stand to eat	Stood and ate in line—would not move. (−)	Ate while standing at Pete's counter. (−)	Stood at table and ate. (−)	Followed escort to tables. (+)	Walk with food away from counter.
No. of steps correct	2/8	5/7	3/5	3/8	

FIGURE 14.4. Assessing a student's generalization skills.

CASE STUDY

Mr. Harmon was planning for Linda's community and job instruction for the coming year. To cultivate Linda's interest in music, he decided to focus on encouraging her to join the school choir, express her preferences for songs, and learn to purchase a CD. He conducted ecological inventories of the local music stores and noted the skills that other 14-year-olds displayed, including listening to sample tracks, scanning the racks, and paying for a purchase. Other teens also socialized in the store and in the mall. To help her express her preferences for songs, Mr. Harmon had Linda sample a wide variety of music from Internet websites. He taught her to "mark" her favorite songs by vocalizing as the song was played and then putting a picture of the CD cover in a "favorites" album. Following a task analysis, she learned to find the CD in the music store and pay for the purchase. When her parents gave her an iPod for her birthday, Mr. Harmon taught her the steps of a task analysis to download a song online. Mr. Harmon arranged for students from Linda's life science class to join some of the community outings and help her download songs in the computer lab at school.

Mr. Harmon also wanted Linda to experience job options. He kept a large display of plants on the windowsills of his class and began to teach Linda to care for them. He also had her photocopy items needed for class. He had Linda join the Pep Club, whose frequent fund-raising activities called for some job-related skills, such as washing cars, selling candy, and making banners. When he considered his community's largest employers, he realized that there were job opportunities in health care. He taught Linda to play stories on tape during volunteer community outings to a local retirement center. Through these experiences Linda began to cultivate job-related skills.

APPLICATIONS

1. List the major employers in your community and the types of jobs each provides. Select one job and discuss how it might be taught using a school simulation and community-based instruction.

2. Conduct an ecological inventory of your neighborhood mall. What types of activities occur in this setting? What skills would students need for these activities? Take this activity another step by conducting a discrepancy analysis for a specific student compared with a peer who is nondisabled.

3. Write down your five favorite leisure activities. How did you cultivate these interests? For each activity, plan how a student with developmental disabilities could: (1) try out the activity, (2) express a preference for the activity (e.g., what picture or object would be used), and (3) plan the activity (list all the steps needed for planning). If there also is a skill to be learned, write a task analysis for this skill.

4. Design simulated instruction to teach students to order a meal in a fast-food restaurant. What materials would you use? Write the task analysis.

5. Create an employment plan for a student in one of the jobs you identified in #1. Write the task analysis for performing the job. What related social or academic skills might be needed? What self-management skills?

CHAPTER 15

Transition to Adult Living

Fred Spooner, Diane M. Browder, and Nicole Uphold

This year Mr. Jablonski has three students for whom he has provided support preparing to transition to adult opportunities. Margo has a severe intellectual disability and mild cerebral palsy, and she relies mostly on nonsymbolic communication. Because Margo's parents recently moved to the school system, this will be Mr. Jablonski's first, and only, year with Margo. He has discovered that she continues to need some support for her personal care (e.g., schedule trained to use the toilet; needs some supervision while eating). Margo's parents have expressed strong interest in having her find a home of her own and a job. In Margo's transition planning meeting, her mother talked about the things they plan to do as a couple when Margo, their youngest child, leaves home and they are "empty nesters." Mr. Jablonski worries that they have not accepted the challenges ahead in finding Margo services. He tried to explain that there is no entitlement for adult services and that they will need to work as a team with Margo to find her the best possible opportunities. Most important, the team still does not have a clear picture of Margo's priorities and preferences. His challenge in supporting Jacob's transition is quite different. Jacob has a moderate intellectual disability and can converse using speech. Through community-based job training, he has shown aptitude for and interest in working in a grocery store. In fact, his current employer wants to hire Jacob full time. Jacob also has made rapid progress in gaining skills for independence at home and in the community in recent years. He lives alone with an elderly mother who is looking forward to having Jacob "retire" from school and be home with her full time to keep her company. The third student, Neerav, also has unique circumstances. Neerav is a young man with autism who has a history of engaging in high rates of self abusive behavior (hitting himself), which he displays primarily to escape low-preference tasks and settings. He communicates using picture symbols and follows a picture schedule. Neerav has shown some skill at a community job emptying used vases for a florist. He has a high preference for all types of plants and flowers and for being outside. Neerav comes from a strong extended family whose cultural tradition is for unmarried adult members to live with their parents or a sibling. Neerav, like his twin sister who is not disabled, will live with his parents after graduation. Because Neerav's current job is an internship, the challenge for the year ahead will be to find a job placement that meets Neerav's preferences and abilities. Neerav also may need long-term support in this job. This chapter provides information on planning for transition to adult services for individuals with severe disabilities.

The emphasis on transition planning for students with severe disabilities began in the 1980s, when new initiatives in supported employment demonstrated that individuals with disabilities, including those with severe disabilities, could succeed in competitive jobs (Wehman et al., 1987). In contrast, the unemployment rate for this population was found to be extremely high, over 60% (Wagner, Cadwallader, & Marder, 2003; Wehman, Kregel, & Seyfarth, 1985a). Students and families who had reaped the benefits of a free public education found that they had no "entitlement" to adult services. For many individuals, reaching age 21 meant either finding no options or having to accept segregated day services as their only option. In response to the bleak postschool outcomes students with disabilities faced, Congress passed Public Law 98-199, which put a priority on transition services by providing money for research and demonstration projects related to transition. Congress also passed the Developmental Disabilities Act of 1984, which stipulated that employment of individuals with disabilities be made a priority and offered guidelines for providing supported employment services. *Supported employment* is paid employment in a competitive job setting with ongoing support services. In this same era (1984), the Carl D. Perkins Vocational Education Act expanded the vocational education and assessment services available to students with disabilities to include transition services. As amended in 1990 and 1998, this act mandated that students be informed of their vocational opportunities at least 1 year prior to graduation and that equal access to all vocational services be given to students with disabilities. In addition to laws passed by Congress, experts in the field began to define transition services. Madeline Will, the director of the Office of Special Education and Rehabilitative Services, and Andrew Halpern, a leader in special education research at the time, both published papers providing models of transition from school to adult life (Halpern, 1985; Will, 1984). Will's model emphasized the transition from school to employment, and Halpern added residential environment and social/interpersonal networks as postschool outcomes (see Figure 15.1). In an early resource on transition, Wehman et al. (1988) recommended that transition planning focus on:

- Employment
- Postsecondary education
- Residential plans
- Financial/income needs
- Recreation/leisure needs
- Medical needs
- Counseling/case management (e.g., sex education, respite care, counseling)

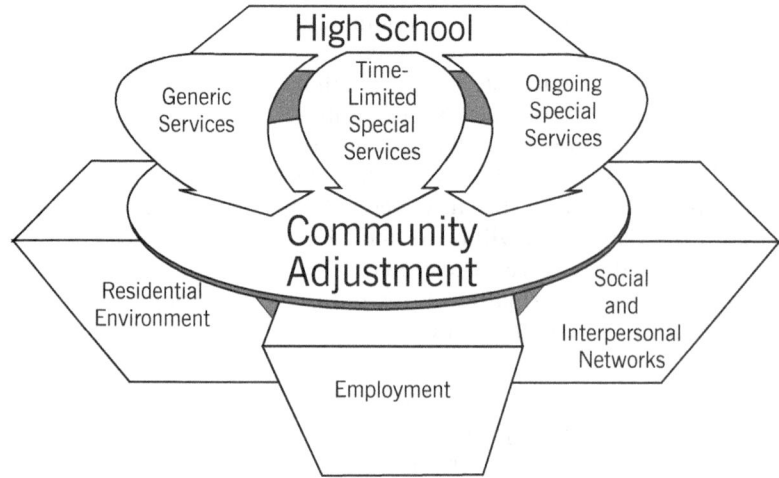

FIGURE 15.1. A model for transition. From Halpern (1985). Copyright 1985 by The Council for Exceptional Children. Reprinted by permission.

- Transportation needs
- Advocacy/legal needs
- Personal/home/money management

The focus on transition that emerged in the 1980s continued into the next decade. The reauthorization of the Individuals with Disabilities Act (Public Law 101-476) in 1990 defined transition planning and mandated individualized transition plans in IEPs. Transition was defined as a coordinated set of services to promote movement from school to postschool activities. Transition activities must be based on the student's needs and preferences and include the development of employment and other adult living objectives. Since the reauthorization of IDEA (2004), this transition planning must begin at age 16 as part of the student's IEP. By age 16, or earlier if deemed appropriate by the IEP team, these transition service needs are defined to include any interagency responsibilities or linkages and appropriate postsecondary goals.

Transition has been defined by the federal government in IDEA (2004, Section 602.34) as

a coordinated set of activities for a child with a disability that:

- Is designed to be within a results-oriented process, that is focused on improving the academic and functional achievement of the child with a disability to facilitate the child's movement from school to post-school activities, including postsecondary education, vocational education, integrated employment (including supported employment); continuing and adult education, adult services, independent living, or community participation
- Is based on the individual child's needs, taking into account the child's strengths, preferences, and interests; and
- Includes instruction, related services, community experiences, the development of

employment and other post-school adult living objectives, and, if appropriate, acquisition of daily living skills and functional vocational evaluation.

"A coordinated set of activities" refers to activities that assist the student with transitioning from high school and are provided by the school and adult service providers. An
outcome-oriented process means that the focus of the activities is on the adult outcome,
what the student wants to do after high school. Based on the student's needs, taking into
account the student's preferences and interests refers to asking the student (or assessing
to determine) what the student is interested in and wants to do, along with accounting
for what the student needs. The seven areas mentioned (e.g., instruction, related services,
community experiences) are the categories in which transition activities should be considered.

Instruction is the means by which students learn a skill. Related services are the support services (e.g., transportation, physical therapy, and mobility training) provided to
the student to help him or her be successful in school and outside of school. Community
experiences are the opportunities to learn and practice skills in the community. Employment refers to the activities that can help students decide on a career and obtain the skills
necessary for that career. Postschool adult living activities help the student become an
independent adult (e.g., rent an apartment, obtain prescriptions, register to vote). Daily
living skills are those activities that an adult performs at home and in the community on a
regular basis (e.g., dressing, cooking, grocery shopping). Finally, a functional vocational
evaluation assesses a student's aptitudes and employment skills in a work setting. Each of
these areas is shown in Figure 15.2.

TRANSITION-FOCUSED EDUCATION

In transition-focused education, the student's education is focused on his or her future.
Although a formal transition plan is required beginning at age 16, transition planning,
or planning for the future, should begin early in a student's life and encompass all phases
of the child's life. Thinking about the future can help IEP teams set priorities for academic and daily living skills and consider ways to promote self-determination skills.
Many studies have been done to determine which school indicators lead to better post-

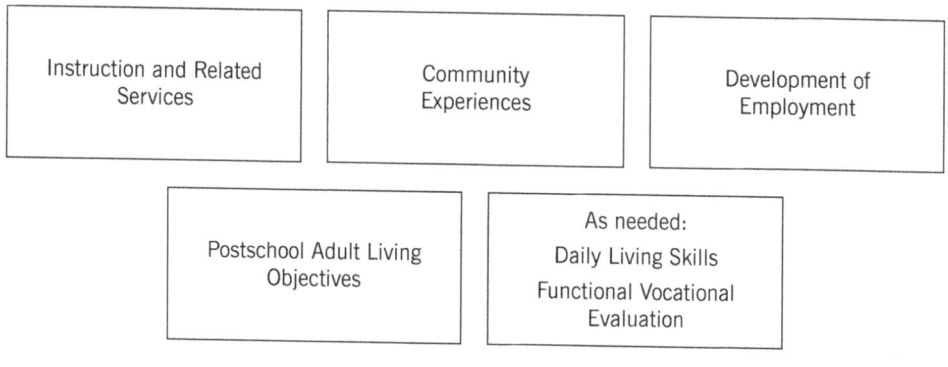

FIGURE 15.2. What transition services include.

school outcomes for individuals with disabilities (Blackorby, Hancock, & Siegel, 1993; Bullis, Davis, Bull, & Johnson, 1995; Halpern, Yovanoff, Doren, & Benz, 1995; Heal & Rusch, 1995; Roessler, Brolin, & Johnson, 1990). Using these indicators, Kohler (1996) developed the taxonomy for transition programming, a model to help schools provide transition-focused education; this is shown in Figure 15.3. There are five categories in the taxonomy: (1) student-focused planning, (2) student development, (3) family involvement, (4) interagency collaboration, and (5) program structure.

Student-Focused Planning

Student-focused planning places the student, not current school practices, at the center of transition planning. This is also called "person-centered" planning (Holburn & Vietze, 2002). Each student is assessed to determine his or her strengths and areas of needs, and IEPs are then developed to assist the student in reaching his or her postschool goals.

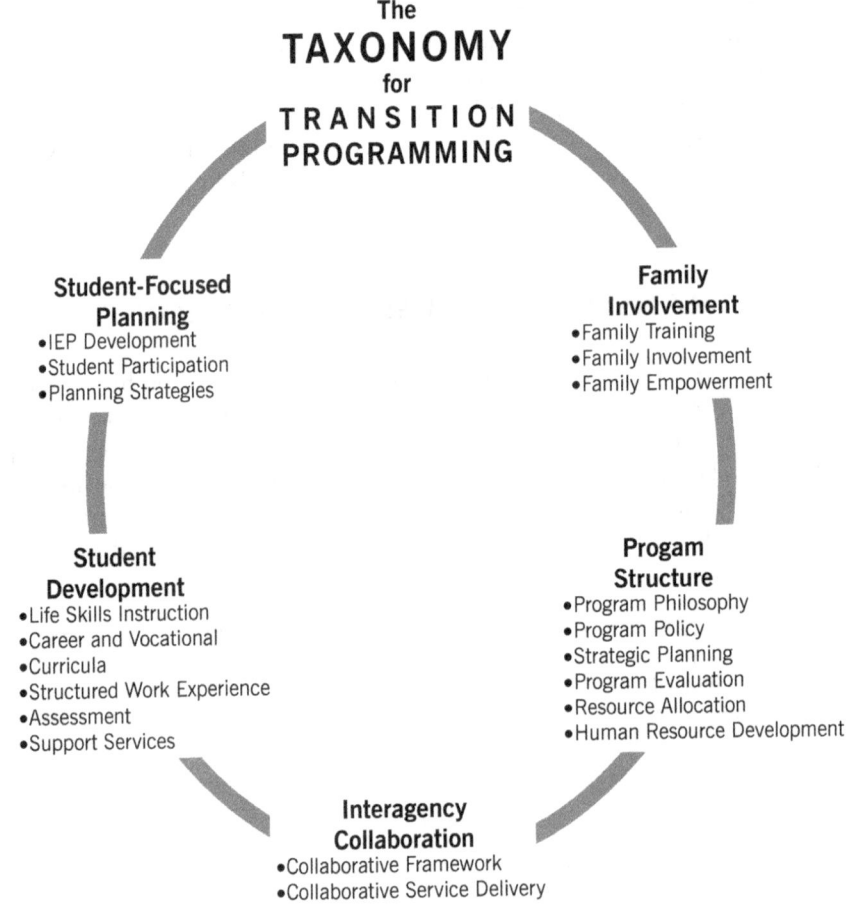

FIGURE 15.3. Kohler's taxonomy for transition programming. From Kohler (1996). Copyright 1996 by the University of Illinois, Transition Research Institute. Reprinted by permission.

Students should also be involved in their transition planning from age 16, as federal law mandates (although the age is younger in many states). Students should not only attend their IEP meetings but also be actively involved in all aspects of the IEP, including plan development and implementation. Chapter 3 provides examples of ways to involve students in their own meetings.

Student Development

Student development is the school programming that teaches students the skills needed to be successful adults. The previous chapters of this book have discussed evidence-based practices to teach students skills, including assessment activities, systematic instruction, and school and community-based instruction.

Family Involvement

Family involvement is critical to transition planning. Families bring knowledge of the student that the schools may not see. In addition, they will provide support to the student as he or she transitions from school to adult life. Educators need to encourage family involvement and provide parents with information related to adult life, including available adult services.

Interagency Collaboration

Adult service agencies provide many services to individuals with disabilities. Educators need to learn what services are available and who provides them. In addition, educators need to collaborate with these agencies to ensure that their students are going to receive assistance during school and once the students leave school.

Program Structure

Program structure refers to the way transition services are provided to the student. For example, students will need opportunities to learn skills in, as well as for, the community, as described in Chapter 14. Educators need an understanding of long-term transition planning and program evaluation. Educators need to determine the structure of their long-range transition programming. In addition, educators need to evaluate whether the program they are providing for a student is helping the student achieve his or her post-school goals.

PLANNING FOR THE MAJOR COMPONENTS OF TRANSITION

One of the important ways students receive transition services is through instruction that is targeted to preparing them for areas of adult transition. Three areas that are especially important are independent living, employment, and opportunities for higher education or career training.

Independent Living

When the student with severe disabilities leaves school, he or she will begin independent living. The majority of individuals with disabilities live with their parents or other family members (Newman et al., 2009). Most young adults in American society have the goal of living independently of their parents. For individuals with severe disabilities, some ongoing support may be needed to achieve this goal. Sometimes families provide financial support for a home, and either the family or an agency provides in-home assistance (e.g., for meal preparation; cleaning). The advantage of this model of supported living is that the dwelling is the individual's own home, and personal preferences (e.g., whether to have a roommate, when to eat, how clean to be) can be honored. In contrast, many individuals without disabilities have to make compromises about their living situations due to financial and other constraints—for example, by sharing a home with a roommate or living for a temporary period in a college dormitory. A group home may be a short-term or long-term option for an individual with severe disabilities. Typically the group home is owned by the service provider, roommates are chosen by the provider, and there are some ground rules for the operation of the home (e.g., when meals are scheduled). In contrast, some adults live with their extended families by choice. Some cultures or families strongly value living with family rather than with strangers. When helping students with severe disabilities consider future living arrangements, the option of continuing to live at home should be respected.

Assessment and Instruction

Besides helping students identify their options as to where they will live as adults, planning needs to include identifying and teaching skills needed to maintain a home. Even students who continue to live with their parents as adults can contribute more to the ongoing functioning of the home. To identify needed skills, the teacher may observe students performing a variety of daily living activities and keep track of strengths and of areas needing additional instruction. Interviewing the parents also allows a teacher to determine whether the student performs the skill in one location but not at others (e.g., washes his or her hands before eating at home but not at school) or if the student performs skills at home that are not typically performed at school (e.g., bathing). See Table 15.1 for examples of different types of assessment.

For example, Ms. Johnson sends home a skills checklist to Tommy's parents and asks them to complete information about his skills to maintain a home. From the checklist, she learns that Tommy needs the opportunity to learn to prepare his own food and to clean areas of the home besides his own room. Once skills have been identified, the teacher considers how to incorporate these into the school routine. Many of these skills can be taught in the classroom or at school during natural times. For example, students may help with classroom chores or receive instruction to refine hygiene skills in a private restroom. Some skills can be cultivated at school with some creative planning of new activities. A weekly school fund-raiser with special snacks gives students the opportunity to learn some food preparation, safe food handling, and money skills. Other skills will require the use of a realistic home setting. Some school programs included instruction in a home living setting in the school or community in which students practice housecleaning, cooking, and other independent living skills.

TABLE 15.1. Independent Living Assessments

Type	Useful for	Example	Sample assessment
Checklist	Determining whether student has skill or needs to learn skill	• Student showers or bathes regularly. • Student keeps hair clean and neat. • Student dresses in reasonably clean clothing.	Ansell Casey Life Skills Assessment (Casey Family Programs, n.d.)
Rating scale	Determining how independently student can perform a skill	• Student selects and modifies recipes. • Student cares for clothing.	*Transition and Independent Living Skill Assessment*
Observation	Validating that student performs skill	• Observe student use restroom. • Observe student clean in the kitchen.	*The Syracuse Community-Referenced Curriculum Guide*

FINDING THE BALANCE:
TEACHING SKILLS IN AND FOR THE HOME AT SCHOOL OR AT HOME?

Many skills that students will need to live in a home of their own can be addressed in normally occurring school routines. Students can learn to use restroom eating, and personal cleanliness skills in the typical school day. In contrast, many skills needed to care for a home are simply not typical in the general education context. For example, most high school students do not vacuum, wash their clothes, or plan meals during their school day. Sometimes the general curriculum offers a life skills class for all students in which these domestic skills can be learned and practiced. Or the high school special education class may be set up like a small apartment where students can learn these skills. In other cases, the need may exist for some time out of school practice of these skills in a real home setting.

Employment

To prepare for employment, students will need instruction in their possible career options. Career education should have a longitudinal approach, encompassing a student's entire career. There are four phases of career education (Brolin, 1997; see Table 15.2). The first phase is career awareness and begins in elementary school. During this phase, students begin to understand that there is a world of work. Students realize that their parents go to work every day. Students become exposed to people in different jobs, such as firefighters, doctors, dentists, teachers, and grocery clerks. Students during this time are learning basic vocational skills such as responsibility, teamwork, and requesting help.

The second phase of career education is career exploration. This phase begins in middle school and is the time students explore various jobs. Students start to realize that there are many more jobs than what they see every day. Students are learning their strengths and weaknesses and how these might relate to a career choice. For example, a student who does not interact with others might realize that working in a grocery is not a good job choice. A student who enjoys being outside might decide to work in landscaping. During career exploration, students learn more advanced vocational skills, such as problem solving, critical thinking, and punctuality.

TABLE 15.2. Phases of Career Education

Career awareness

- Begins in elementary school.
- Students begin to understand the concept of work.
- Students learn general vocational skills, such as responsibility, teamwork, problem solving.

Career exploration

- Begins in middle school.
- Students explore various jobs.
- Students begin to understand their strengths and weaknesses and how these relate to a job.
- Students begin to work in the community to learn about the world of work and jobs.

Career preparation

- Begins in middle school.
- Students narrow down job possibilities based on their strengths and weaknesses and what they know about each job.
- Students gain real-life experience at their job choices.

Career assimilation

- Begins in high school.
- Students decide on a job and finalize preparations for that job.
- Students link with adult services to ensure continued support.

The third phase of career education is career preparation. This phase begins in late middle school and continues into high school. Students in this phase are starting to narrow down their career choices based on their strengths, weaknesses, and knowledge about different jobs. Students also gain real-life experience at their job choices through volunteer work, job sampling, and paid employment.

The final phase of career education is career assimilation. This often occurs in high school, but sometimes students do not reach this phase until much later. Students in this phase have decided on a career and finalize their preparations for that career. For example, a student might decide she wants to work as a veterinary assistant. She volunteers at the local animal shelter on the weekends and shadows a veterinary assistant during the school day. Students in this phase link with adult service agencies to ensure continued support to help them reach their chosen careers.

In addition to selecting a type of job through career education, some consideration needs to be given to the type of postschool employment support students will need. Postschool employment support for students with disabilities includes a wide range of options. There are several types of employment outcomes for students with disabilities, including competitive employment, supported employment, self-employment, volunteer work, and sheltered employment or adult day programs. Competitive and supported employment have the most advantages for the individual, as they can honor the student's choice of jobs and provide competitive wages and as they typically occur in inclusive contexts. In competitive employment, the individual is on the company payroll, receives full pay, and does not receive any additional support (except accommodations as required under the Individuals with Disabilities Act of 1990). This can be either full- or part-time employment. In supported employment, the individual receives support in order to maintain a job. Volunteer work and some adult day programs that are community based may have the advantage for the individual with disabilities of social inclusion with adults who are nondisabled who engage in the same activities, but they do not have the advantage of payment. Sheltered work provides payment but typically takes place in a self-contained setting with other workers with disabilities.

There are several types of supported employment. The first is *individual placement*, in which the individual is placed at one job site and receives assistance for that job, typically from a job coach. Some supported employment providers also cultivate natural supports (e.g., training the existing supervisor) and paid coworkers to help individuals maintain their jobs. In *enclaves* and *mobile work crews*, a group of individuals with disabilities are placed at a job site and perform job tasks. There is a job coach or other support person assisting the individuals with the tasks. Enclaves are placed at one job site and remain there to do the job. For example, a printing company might have an enclave of three individuals with disabilities and one job coach on site. Mobile work crews travel to different job sites as needed and perform various job tasks. For example, a mobile work crew might focus on lawn maintenance or window cleaning and travel to the job each day. Regardless of the type of supported employment, all workers earn at least minimum wage. Sometimes the job support is time limited; that is, a job coach is provided until the individual masters the job. At other times, long-term support is anticipated. The need for long-term support is one reason that enclaves and mobile work crews are used—so that the maximum number of individuals can receive needed job support with existing financial resources.

Self-employment offers a nontraditional route to employment. This type of employment matches an individual's unique skills and interests with work opportunities. The individual works for him- or herself, and, similar to all self-employment, wages can vary. Sample self-employment opportunities include opening a gift shop, child care, dog grooming, and small-engine repair. Self-employment can be combined with supported employment. That is, an individual with severe disabilities might be able to provide a dog grooming service with the help of a coworker who is paid to provide assistance.

Volunteer work is unpaid employment in which the individual performs tasks for an organization. Legally and ethically, volunteer work should not consist of work that would normally be done by a paid employee. Volunteer work is typically performed at community service organizations, such as a hospital, library, or non-for-profit agency. Individuals can be candy stripers, or can reshelve books at the library, make copies, and put together mailings.

The final employment outcome is sheltered employment or an adult day program. In this setting, individuals with disabilities work with other individuals with disabilities. Individuals usually earn less than minimum wage and perform a variety of job tasks. Job tasks include placing stickers on books, collating paper, packaging items, sorting, and assembly. An adult day program may not technically be an employment option if the focus is only on leisure activities. In an adult day program, the individual attends each day on a set schedule similar to school. Some adult day programs provide opportunities for volunteer or paid work.

Customized employment is a new support option designed to assist individuals with disabilities in obtaining competitive work. There are four elements to customized employment: (1) meeting the individual's needs and interests, (2) using another person for assistance with obtaining a job, (3) negotiating job tasks with employers, and (4) providing supports to the individual to be successful on the job (U.S. Department of Labor, 2005). Customized employment often involves job carving or job sharing. Job carving modifies a job by taking out one or more of the tasks and reassigning these tasks to a new job. Job sharing means that one or people share the job tasks for one particular job.

Assessment and Instruction

There are several approaches to conducting assessment on the needs of individual students. Interest inventories, surveys, interviews, aptitude tests, observations, ecological inventories, and situational assessments can all be used to help students determine their interests and abilities related to employment. Interest inventories, surveys, and interviews ask students and their families about the student's job-related interests and abilities. Sample questions include: What type of job interests you? Do you like to work with people? Do you like to work indoors or outdoors? Are you good at math? Aptitude tests assess the student's knowledge and skills related to work. These are pencil-and-paper tests designed to determine an individual's abilities related to the world of work.

Ecological inventories are an examination of the local community to determine what employment and support opportunities exist for students with disabilities. Teachers or other support personnel can meet with employers, tour businesses, or network with others to discover the jobs that are available in the community. This knowledge allows teachers to determine the types of jobs that their students may have. Teachers can then begin to teach skills needed in these jobs to their students.

In a situational assessment, a student is placed on a job for a short period of time and given the opportunity to try out the job. Students are assessed to determine how well they perform the job and additional skills that need to be taught. These assessments should look not only at completion of vocational tasks but also at the informal aspects of a job, such as requesting assistance, arriving on time, and social skills.

For example, John is a 10th-grade student in Mr. Jones's class. John has never worked in the community; however, he has performed jobs around the school, such as shredding paper, collecting the daily attendance sheets, and cleaning in the cafeteria. John does not know what type of job he would like to have. He is very social, and his teacher thinks he would like to work with people. Mr. Jones conducts an ecological inventory to determine what local jobs are available in the community and involve working with people. Mr. Jones identifies five different jobs based on John's strengths and interests. John then spends a few days at each job undergoing a situational assessment. Mr. Jones is looking at whether John can follow directions, how well he interacts with coworkers, and how quickly he learns the job tasks. Based on this assessment, Mr. Jones determines that John needs to learn how to ask for help and how to appropriately greet people and follow directions.

Employment instruction should be school based and community based. School-based instruction can focus on the generic job skills needed for all jobs, such as responsibility, punctuality, asking for assistance, and requesting time off. Students can also learn skills that can generalize to other jobs. One way to teach these generic job skills is through school-based enterprises. This means that the students will sell items that they have either made or purchased. Students learn skills such as following instructions, listening, communicating with the public, counting money, giving change, and tracking stock. The advantages of school-based enterprises are that jobs can be tailored toward students' interests and skills and students can try out a variety of jobs. Another way to teach employment skills is through community-based instruction. Students go to a job site with a job coach and perform certain aspects of a job. Chapter 14 provides a more detailed discussion of community-based instruction.

For example, after John's assessment, Mr. Jones places John at job site at the local humane society. At this job site, John needs to greet customers and show them animals available for adoption. Mr. Jones uses a task analysis to teach John each step of greeting the customer, viewing the animals, letting a customer hold an animal, and returning the animal to its cage. Before John works with the public, Mr. Jones teaches John this skill for several days using systematic prompting. From his ecological inventory observing the site, Mr. Jones also knows that the customers will ask John questions that he cannot understand. Mr. Jones teaches John to say "I will need to get someone else to help you" and then to get his supervisor. By the end of the first week, John is ready to interact with the public. Mr. Jones continues to shadow John in this work site, providing intermittent prompts and feedback as needed in a discreet manner. After a month, Mr. Jones helps a coworker learn how to help John when he needs this intermittent prompt, and he begins to reduce his time on site.

Education and Training

The variety of options for postsecondary education and training for individuals with severe disabilities is expanding. In the past, a student with intellectual disability would receive at most some type of job training, such as on-the-job or employment skills training. Recently, schools have partnered with colleges to offer an on-campus learning environment for students with cognitive disabilities who are older than the traditional high school student (i.e., 18–22 years old). Although there are not many of these arrangements across the United States (Hart, Grigal, Sax, Martinez, & Will, 2006), they offer students the chance to learn skills in an environment that is typical for students ages 18–21. There are three models of postsecondary education for individuals with cognitive disabilities. The first is a mixed or hybrid model. Students learn life skills with other students with disabilities and socialize and/or take academic classes with students without disabilities. The second model is a substantially separate model. Students attend life skills classes only with other students with disabilities; however, students do have the option of participating in social activities offered through the campus, although no formal arrangement may exist. The third postsecondary education model is the inclusive individual support model. There is no formal program in this model; the students take college courses for audit or credit and receive any support services (e.g., tutor, technology) needed to be successful.

Assessment and Instruction

Areas to assess in planning for postsecondary education include academic strengths, social skills, maturity, problem-solving skills, and independent living skills. The students' preferences should also play a key role in this planning. Sometimes these interests may not emerge until students try some college classes. She is currently 16 years old. Her parents would like her to attend an 18–21 program at the local college. Linda's teacher,

Ms. Miller, conducts a comprehensive assessment to determine what skills Linda needs to learn before moving to this program. In addition, Ms. Miller observes Linda during her academic classes to determine future class needs. Ms. Miller determines that Linda needs to learn to manage her daily schedule rather than waiting for the teacher to tell her where to go next. She also needs to learn a method of taking class notes. Ms. Miller will use systematic instruction to teach Linda to initiate the next activity on her schedule and to use a template for guided notes. She also will do some community-based instruction with Linda, going to the college campus to eat in the cafeteria and attend some special events.

SELF-DETERMINATION

One of the most important outcomes of transition planning is self-determination. Although the school team can help the student begin to transition into adult living, the student also needs skills to continue negotiating the many changes that will come with adulthood. Self-determination is defined as "a combination of skills, knowledge, and beliefs that enable a person to engage in goal-directed, self-regulated, autonomous behavior" (Field et al., 1998, p. 2). The component skills of self-determination are choice making, decision making, goal setting and attainment, problem solving, self-awareness, self-advocacy, self-regulation, and self-efficacy (Powers, Singer, & Sowers, 1996; Wehmeyer & Schwartz, 1998a). Research has shown that students with higher levels of self-determination perform better in school, are more likely to have higher paying jobs, have some financial freedom, and live independently (Wehmeyer & Palmer, 2003; Wehmeyer & Schwartz, 1997). There are at least three ways that self-determination can be included as part of a transition plan. The first is to identify specific self-determination goals for the student to learn. The second is to provide opportunities for the student to practice these skills during transition planning. The third is to provide opportunities for the student to practice self determination during other instructional activities.

Identifying and Teaching Self-Determination Goals

Using instructional methods discussed in Chapter 4, individual self-determination skills such as choice making and problem solving can be taught to students with disabilities. Algozzine et al. (2001) and Wood et al. (2005) conducted reviews of the literature published from 1975 to 2006 and found that 35 (out of 72) studies across the two reviews included people with significant cognitive disabilities. The most common self-determination skills being taught to students with significant cognitive disabilities were choice making ($n =$ 19 studies) and self-management ($n = 11$ studies). Systematic instruction, including time delay, least-to-most prompting, and modeling, was used to teach self-determination skills. During transition planning, specific IEP goals may be targeted for the student to increase self-determination skills, such as setting a goal, self-advocating for support needs (e.g., with a general education teacher), and making decisions.

It is important to remember that students need not only instruction to learn these skills but also the opportunity throughout the school day to practice. Teaching a student to make choices is not beneficial if the student is never provided the *opportunity* throughout the school day to make choices. Once a student is taught how to make choices, the teacher can provide the opportunity to practice the skill in the school setting. Examples include allowing the student to choose his or her own lunch, which activity to complete first, and where to sit in the classroom.

Providing Opportunities to Use Self-Determination during Transition Planning

As described earlier, the transition planning process should be student centered. Another term for this is *person-centered planning*. Person-centered planning is an ongoing process that helps students first dream about their future, then locate the supports needed to reach their goals, and finally work on attaining their goals. Sometimes person-centered planning involves having a special meeting or series of meetings to help the student think more about the future. The student and his or her family decide on a team of people who they think will not only assist the student with goal attainment but also provide the support that is necessary to reach those goals. This team of people meets to discuss the student's dreams, current supports, and future support needs. The goal of the group is to assist the individual in becoming more independent and realizing his or her full potential in the community. Figure 15.4 provides an example of how one team illustrated this planning process.

Students can also take a more active role in the IEP and transition planning meetings at school. Konrad and Test (2004) identified four ways that students can be involved in the IEP process: planning the IEP, drafting the IEP, meeting to revise the IEP, and implementing the IEP. Planning the IEP includes determining strengths and needs, establishing goals, and organizing materials for the meeting. This would include assessing students' likes and dislikes and strengths and needs.

Drafting the IEP refers to choosing and writing goals and objectives, assessing present level of performance, and other aspects of the IEP. Both published curricula and teacher-developed curricula can be used to help draft the IEP. Konrad and Test (2004) examined the effects of an instructional program on the ability of students to complete an IEP template. A template is a six-page open-ended assessment divided into three sections: (1) vision statement/strengths, (2) needs/goals, and (3) services/least restrictive environment. After instruction, all students learned how to complete the IEP template, and students scored statistically significantly higher on their IEP awareness. This template has been used with students with multiple disabilities to draft the IEP. Konrad, Trela, and Test (2006) evaluated the effects of GO FOR IT . . . NOW! on student ability to write IEP goal paragraphs. Four high school students with orthopedic impairments, mild mental retardation, or multiple disabilities were individually taught how to write paragraphs about goals and objectives. Results indicated that students increased their scores on both the content and quality of their IEP goal paragraphs.

Students can be involved in their IEP meetings. Participation can take on several different forms, from simply attending the meeting to answering questions posed by the teacher to leading the meeting. There are published curricula available to help teachers teach their students to participate in their IEP meetings. One such curriculum is Self-Directed IEP (Martin, Marshall, Maxon, & Jerman, 1996). The Self-Directed IEP is an empirically based strategy that uses multimedia to teach students to lead their IEP meet-

Develop a Personal Profile

1. Draw the student's "support circles" (four concentric circles).

   Middle: Student's name
   Circle 1: Closest and most important people (e.g., Mom, Sally)
   Circle 2: Close, but not quite as close (e.g., neighbor—Mrs. Fields)
   Circle 3: People from church, sports teams, clubs, or other associations (e.g., Sam)
   Circle 4: People paid to be in student's life (e.g., teacher, bus driver)

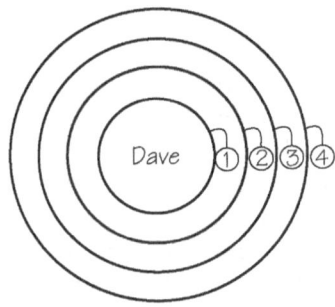

2. Draw a "community presence map": Include the community settings that the student uses daily, weekly, or occasionally.

Grocery store

Church

Restaurant

Uncle Bill's House

3. List the student's preferences.

Likes	Dislikes
Ice cream	Vegetables
Kind people	Being teased
Cars	Cold weather
Being outside	

(cont.)

FIGURE 15.4. Agenda for a person-centered planning meeting. (This agenda is based on the person-centered planning process used in the research of Miner & Bates, 1997. Dave's case is fictitious.) From Browder (2001). Copyright 2001 by The Guilford Press. Reprinted by permission.

4. List the student's capacities.

What Do People Like about Dave?

Great smile!　　　　　Works hard　　　　　　　Great listener

Describe a Desirable Future

1. Future living situations?
2. Community participation?
3. Employment?
4. Recreation/leisure?

Dave's Future

Work around cars
Outdoor fun—ski, hikes
Deliver newspapers like Uncle Bill
Join the football booster club

Action Plan

Goal	Action	Person responsible	Next step
1. Get a job	Job tryouts	Transition specialist	Schedule tryout.
2. Be outside more	Go hiking	Dave and Sam	Dave will set date.
3. Be in booster club	Sign up	Dave with Uncle Bill	Get the form.

Note Any Systems Change Needed

Currently job tryouts are only offered to students with mild disabilities—will need to advocate for Dave to have this chance.

The booster club currently has no members with mental retardation. Dave will be a "trailblazer."

Summarize the Meeting

Review goals, activities required to move toward a desirable future, and person responsible for each activity. Consider future meetings to continue planning process: Whom to invite? when to meet? where to meet?

FIGURE 15.4. *(cont.)*

ing. This curriculum consists of 11 steps: (1) begin the meeting by stating the purpose, (2) introduce everyone, (3) review past goals and performance, (4) ask IEP members for feedback on goals, (5) identify goals for this school year, (6) ask questions, (7) deal with differences in opinion, (8) state supports needed to meet goals, (9) summarize goals and supports, (10) thank everyone for attending, and (11) summarize decisions made at the meeting. This curriculum is evidenced based and has been used with students with severe disabilities (Allen et al., 2001).

Implementing the IEP occurs after the IEP meeting has ended. This phase involves teaching students strategies to assist them in meeting their IEP goals. German, Martin, Marshall, and Sale (2000) evaluated the effects of Take Action on the goal attainment skills (e.g., having a bus pass, locating five items at the supermarket, not interrupting a conversation) of high school students with mild to moderate mental retardation. Take Action consists of four steps: plan, act, evaluate, and adjust. Students chose daily goals and were taught how to set a strategy to reach their goals, how to decide on support they would need to meet goals, how to evaluate their progress toward goal attainment, and how to adjust their goals based on their evaluations. All students attained their daily goals after intervention. For more examples of how students can be involved in their IEP planning, see Chapter 3.

Providing Opportunities for Self-Determination during Other Instruction

Another way to teach self-determination skills is to infuse this instruction into the teaching of other skills (Konrad, Walker, Fowler, Test, & Wood, 2008). Konrad and colleagues have created a model to align self-determination instruction with academic instruction. Teachers decide which academic and self-determination skills the student needs to learn and how they will teach these skills. For example, the teacher decides that the student needs to learn how to tell time and self-regulation skills. The teacher will use systematic instruction to teach time telling and at the same time have the student practice by following a schedule.

CASE STUDIES

At the beginning of this chapter, we described three students who were in their last year of high school. This is what transpired through their transition planning. In Margo's case, Mr. Jablonski contacted Margo's prior transition teacher and was able to get much more detail on her abilities and preferences. He discovered that even though she required ongoing support for personal care, she had learned to assist her caregivers and direct this care. She had learned to signal when she was ready to go to the restroom, helped to put on her own clothes, and washed her hands alone or vocalized if she needed help. She could eat completely independently if her food was cut in bite-size pieces. Although nonverbal, she had developed many ways to socialize with others and enjoyed people. She would joke with others by imitating their mannerisms, laugh on cue, and wave greetings. Finding work Margo could and would do was more challenging. She preferred socializing to getting tasks done. Mr. Jablonski decided to capitalize on this strength by finding a job in which socializing was the task (e.g., being a greeter). To his surprise, her parents turned out to have not only high expectations for Margo's future but also strong advocacy skills. Although Mr. Jablonski had not been able to find a residential provider who would consider Margo, her parents took the opposite view that Margo was selecting the provider and that not just anyone would be acceptable. Her parents made appointments for Margo to interview the available providers. As they asked questions related to Margo's needs and preferences, they watched to see how each interacted with her and whether Margo enjoyed their company and the home they visited. One of the providers interviewed was impressed with Margo and the parents' perspective and decided to support Margo. So she became a trailblazer with this service provider as the first individual with severe disabilities to be supported in a community home. Her two new roommates had mild intellectual disability. Mr. Jablonski did not find Margo a paying job by the time she graduated, but the residential provider found her a day program that had a strong community-based leisure program.

Mr. Jablonski discovered that Jacob's sister shared Jacob's goal to work and live in the community. She became an active member of his transition team and helped Jacob's mother consider the reasons that having a job might be best for Jacob. Jacob did take the job with the grocer on graduation and gained increased independence by getting a ride to work with a coworker. He developed friendships with the owner of nearby deli, where he ate lunch, and with the town's sheriff, who also offered to give Jacob a ride when needed. When Jacob's mother died unexpectedly, his sister needed to help Jacob make a decision about where to live. Using some of the skills he learned with Mr. Jablonski for decision making, he told his sister he wanted to stay in the house where he grew up. His sister helped him find a way to make this work financially by helping him find a roommate who agreed to provide some of the support Jacob needed with meals and finances in exchange for a reduced rent.

Mr. Jablonski worked with a new adult service provider who was implementing innovative new services to plan creatively for Neerav's job opportunities. The new provider contracted to do some of Neerav's transition assessment, including trying a wide variety of paid jobs, leisure opportunities, and other adult opportunities. The provider recommended having Neerav attend the community college with support to take courses in horticulture. The team also developed a creative schedule that would be predictable to Neerav but that would give him a range of inclusive opportunities. Mondays included lunch, an afternoon in the college gym, and applying for jobs with florists. On Tuesday and Thursday afternoons, he worked at a part-time job in a recycling center. On Wednesdays, he took the bus uptown and did some touring (e.g., museums). On Fridays, he did a leisure activity that he chose and arranged on Monday (e.g., movies). Neerav needed ongoing support for all these activities. This support included a combination of provider paid support, which was sometimes one on one (to attend class) and sometimes a small group (e.g., three men went to the gym together). Some activities were supported with the help of volunteers who worked with the provider agency (e.g., to attend a Friday-night sporting event). A goal for Neerav was to cultivate adult peer relationships that would also become part of his support system. (These case studies are based on true stories of three students' transition outcomes. Their names and some details have been changed to protect their privacy.)

SUMMARY

The emphasis on transition planning for students with severe disabilities grew out of the 1980s, based on initiatives in supported employment that documented that members of this population could be placed successfully in competitive employment. Although students and family had been able to benefit from free public educational programs, there was no entitlement to adult services. Early resources on transition planning focused on such areas as employment, postsecondary education, residential plans, medical needs, transportation needs, and personal, home, and money management.

Based on the importance of planning transition to adult life for students with severe disabilities as a significant part of the curriculum process, we have included it as an element throughout the chapters in the book, even though there are several independent sources on the topic. We have covered topical content on transition-focused education (e.g., student-focused planning, family involvement, interagency collaboration), planning for the major components of transition (e.g., independent living, assessment and instruction, employment), and self-determination (e.g., identifying and teaching goals, providing opportunities for self-determination during transition planning and instruction). For components of transition that require instruction (e.g., employment, independent living, self-determination), we suggest that systematic instruction be used. We also have provided some case studies to be used as examples as to how transition planning can and should be implemented.

APPLICATIONS

1. Interview a person who leads transition planning in your school system. Find out how the planning focuses on the students' needs and preferences. What areas of planning are the typical focus? What agencies typically participate?

2. Identify the agencies that provide employment support in your region. Find out which of the employment models they offer (supported employment, customized employment, sheltered workshop, adult day program.) Interview one of the directors to find out what opportunities exist for students with severe disabilities.

3. Where do most students with disabilities live when they graduate from schools in your school system? What group homes exist in the area? What are the criteria for acceptance? Are there providers who offer support in the individual's own home? Which providers serve individuals with severe disabilities?

4. Contact disability services at the local community college. Ask if there are services for individuals with intellectual disability. Do these include support to attend inclusive classes or a separate program? Does your school system offer an 18- to 21-year-old program at an area college?

References

AAIDD Ad Hoc Committee on Terminology and Classification. (2010). *Intellectual disability: Definition, classification, and systems of supports* (11th ed.). Washington, DC: American Association on Intellectual and Developmental Disabilities.

AbdelAziz, H., Vassilyadi, M., & Ventureyra, E. C. G. (2002). Late-onset erythema along a sterile functioning ventriculoperitoneal shunt: Case report and review of the literature. *Child's Nervous System, 18,* 235–237.

Achieve, Inc. (2002). Measuring up: A standards and assessments benchmarking report for Oklahoma. Retrieved June 29, 2005, from *www.achieve.org/dstore.nsf/Lookup/OKLA-HOMA%202002/$file/OK%20Benchmark.pdf*

Adams, L., Gouvousis, A., VanLue, M., & Waldron, C. (2003). Social story intervention: Improving communication skills in a child with Autism Spectrum Disorder. *Focus on Autism and Other Developmental Disabilities, 19,* 87–94.

Agosta, E., Graetz, J., Mastropieri, M., & Scruggs, T. (2004). Teacher–researcher partnerships to improve social behavior through social stories. *Intervention in School and Clinic, 39,* 276–287.

Agran, M., Blanchard, C., Wehmeyer, M., & Hughes, C. (2001). Teaching students to self-regulate their behavior: The differential effects of student vs. teacher-delivered reinforcement. *Research in Developmental Disabilities, 22,* 319–332.

Agran, M., Cavin, M., Wehmeyer, M. W., & Palmer, S. (2006). Participation of students with moderate to severe disabilities in the general curriculum: The effects of the self-determined learning model of instruction. *Research and Practice for Persons with Severe Disabilities, 31,* 230–241.

Ahearn, E. (2006). Standards-based IEPs: Implementation in selected states. Retrieved from / *www.projectforum.org/index.cfm*

Alberto, P. A., Cihak, D. F., & Gama, R. I. (2005). Use of static picture prompts versus video modeling during simulation instruction. *Research in Developmental Disabilities, 26,* 327–339.

Alberto, P., Jobes, N., Sizemore, A., & Doran, D. (1980). A comparison of individual and group instruction across response tasks. *Journal of the Association for Persons with Severe Handicaps, 5,* 285–293.

Alcantara, P. R. (1994). Effects of videotape instructional packaging on purchasing skills of children with autism. *Exceptional Children, 61,* 40–55.

Algozzine, B., Browder, D., Karvonen, M., Test, D. W., & Wood, W. M. (2001). Effects of interventions to promote self-determination for individuals with disabilities. *Review of Educational Research, 71,* 219–277.

Ali, S., & Frederickson, N. (2006). Investigating the evidence base of social stories. *Educational Psychology in Practice, 22,* 355–377.

Allen, S. K., Smith, A. C., Test, D. W., Flowers, C., & Wood, W. M. (2001). The effects of Self-Directed IEP on student participation in IEP meetings. *Career Development for Exceptional Individuals, 24,* 107–120.

Allinder, R. M., & Siegel, E. (1999). "Who is Brad?" Preservice teacher's perception of summarizing assessment information about a student with moderate disabilities. *Education and Training in Mental Retardation and Developmental Disabilities, 34,* 157–169.

Allor, J. H., Mathes, P. G., Roberts, K. R., Jones, F. G., & Champlin, T. (2010). Teaching students with moderate intellectual disabilities to read: An experimental examination of a comprehensive reading intervention. *Education and Training in Developmental Disabilities, 45,* 3–22.

Almond, P., & Bechard, S. (2005, April). *Alignment of two performance-based alternate assessments with combined content standards from eight states through expanded benchmarks.* Paper presented at the meeting of the National Council on Measurement in Education, Montreal, Quebec, Canada.

Alper, S., & Ryndak, D. L. (1992). Educating students with severe handicaps in regular classes. *Elementary School Journal, 92,* 373–387.

Alper, S., & Ryndak, D. L. (1996). *Curriculum content for students with moderate and severe disabilities in inclusive settings.* Needham, MA: Allyn & Bacon.

American Association for the Advancement of Science. (1989). *Project 2061: Science for all Americans.* Washington, DC: Author.

American Association on Mental Retardation. (2002). *Mental retardation: Definition, classification, and systems of supports* (10th ed.). Washington, DC: Author.

Anderson, L. W., & Krathwohl, D. R. (Eds.). (2001). *A taxonomy for learning, teaching, and assessing: A revision of Bloom's taxonomy of educational objectives.* New York: Longman.

Anderson, M. D., Sherman, J. A., Sheldon, J. B., & McAdam, D. (1997). Picture activity schedules and engagement of adults with mental retardation in a group home. *Research in Developmental Disabilities, 18,* 231–250.

Anderson, R. C., Spiro, R. J., & Anderson, M. C. (1978). Schemata as scaffolding for the representation of information in connected discourse. *American Educational Research Journal, 15,* 433–440.

Apple, A. L., Billingsley, F., & Schwartz, I. S. (2005). Effects of video modeling alone and with self-management on compliment-giving behaviors of children with high-functioning ASD. *Journal of Positive Behavior Interventions, 7,* 33–46.

Armbruster, B. B., & Anderson, T. H. (1988). On selecting considerate content textbooks. *Remedial and Special Education, 9,* 47–52.

Armbruster, B. B., & Howe, C. E. (1985). Educators team up to help students learn. *NASSP Bulletin, 69,* 82–86.

Armbruster, B. B., Lehr, F., & Osborn, J. (2003). *Put reading first: The research building blocks for teaching children to read.* Washington, DC: Center for the Improvement of Early Reading Achievement and National Institute for Literacy.

Arndt, S. A., Konrad, M., & Test, D. W. (2006). Effects of Self-Directed IEP on student participation in planning meetings. *Remedial and Special Education, 27,* 194–207.

Arnold-Reid, G. S., Schloss, P. J., & Alper, S. (1997). Teaching meal planning to youth with mental retardation in natural settings. *Remedial and Special Education, 18,* 166–173.

Arntzen, E., Gilde, K., & Pedersen, E. (1998). Generalization of schedule following in a youth with autism. *Scandinavian Journal of Behaviour Therapy, 27,* 135–141.

Ault, M. J., Wolery, M., Doyle, P. M., & Gast, D. L. (1989). Review of comparative studies in instruction of students with moderate and severe handicaps. *Exceptional Children, 55,* 346–356.

Autism Society of America. (n.d.). What are autism spectrum disorders? Retrieved January 19, 2010, from *www.autism-society.org/site/PageServer?pagename=about_whatis*

Aveno, A., Renzaglia, A., & Lively, C. (1987). Surveying community training sites to insure that instructional decisions accommodate the site as well as the trainees. *Education and Training in Mental Retardation, 22,* 167–172.

Ayres, K. M., Langone, J., Boon, R. T., & Norman, A. (2006). Computer-based instruction for purchasing skills. *Education and Training in Developmental Disabilities, 41,* 253–263.

Azrin, N. H., & Armstrong, P. M. (1973). The "mini-meal": A method for teaching eating skills to the profoundly retarded. *Mental Retardation, 11,* 9–11.

Azrin, N. H., & Foxx, R. M. (1971). A rapid method of toilet training the institutionalized retarded. *Journal of Applied Behavior Analysis, 4,* 89–99.

Azrin, N. H., Schaeffer, R. M., & Wesolowski, M. D. (1976). A rapid method of teaching profoundly retarded persons to dress by a reinforcement-guidance method. *Mental Retardation, 14*(6), 29–33.

Baddeley, A. D. (2000). The episodic buffer: A new component of working memory? *Trends in Cognitive Science, 4,* 417–423.

Baddeley, A. D., & Hitch, G. (1974). Working memory. In G. H. Bower (Ed.), *The psychology of learning and motivation: Advances in research and theory* (Vol. 8, pp. 47—90). New York: Academic Press.

Baddeley, A., & Jarrold, C. (2007). Working memory and Down syndrome. *Journal of Intellectual Disability Research, 51,* 925–931.

Baer, D. M., Wolf, M. M., & Risley, T. R. (1968). Some current dimensions of applied behavior analysis. *Journal of Applied Behavior Analysis, 1,* 91–97.

Baer, D. M., Wolf, M. M., & Risley, T. R. (1987). Some still-current dimensions of applied behavior analysis. *Journal of Applied Behavior Analysis, 20,* 313–327.

Baer, R. M., McMahan, R. K., & Flexer, R. W. (2004). Transition models and promising practices. In R. W. Flexer, T. J. Simmons, P. Luft, & R. M. Baer (Eds.), *Transition planning for secondary students with disabilities* (2nd ed., pp. 53–82). Upper Saddle River, NJ: Merrill/Prentice Hall.

Baker-Ericzén, M., Stahmer, A. C., & Burns, A. (2007). Child demographics associated with outcomes in a community-based pivotal response training program. *Journal of Positive Behavior Interventions, 9,* 52–60.

Ball, T. S., Seric, K., & Payne, L. E. (1971). Long-term retention of self-help skill training in the profoundly retarded. *American Journal of Mental Deficiency, 76,* 378–382.

Bambara, L. M., & Ager, C. (1992). Using self-scheduling to promote self-directed leisure activity in home and community settings. *Journal of the Association for Persons with Severe Handicaps, 17,* 67–76.

Bambara, L. M., Browder, D. M., & Koger, F. (2006). Home and community. In M. E. Snell & F. Brown (Eds.), *Instruction of students with severe disabilities* (6th ed., pp. 526–568). Upper Saddle River, NJ: Merrill/Prentice Hall.

Bambara, L. M., & Kern, L. (2005). *Individualized supports for students with problem behaviors: Designing positive behavior plans.* New York: Guilford Press.

Bambara, L. M., & Lohrmann, S. (2006). Introduction to special issue on severe disabilities and school-wide positive behavior support. *Research and Practice for Persons with Severe Disabilities, 31,* 1–3.

Barry, L. M., & Burlew, S. B. (2004). Using social stories to teach choice and play skills to children with autism. *Focus on Autism and Other Developmental Disabilities, 19,* 45–51.

Bartlett, L. (2000). Medical services: The disputed related service. *Journal of Special Education, 33,* 215.

Basil, C., & Reyes, S. (2003). Acquisition of literacy skills by children with severe disability. *Child Language Teaching and Therapy, 19*(1), 27–48.

Bates, E. (1979). *The emergence of symbols: Cognition and communication in infancy.* New York: Academic Press.

Bates, P. E., Cuvo, T., Miner, C. A., & Korabek, C. A. (2001). A simulated and community-based instruction involving persons with mild and moderate mental retardation. *Research in Developmental Disabilities, 22,* 95–115.

Batu, S., Ergenekon, Y., Erbas, D., & Akmanoglu, N. (2004). Teaching pedestrian skills to individuals with developmental disabilities. *Journal of Behavioral Education, 13*(3), 147–164.

Baumgart, D., Brown, L., Pumpian, I., Nisbet, J., Ford, A., Sweet, M., et al. (1982). Principle of partial participation and individualized adaptations in educational programs for severely handicapped students. *Journal of the Association of Persons with Severe Handicaps, 7,* 17–27.

Baxendell, B. (2003). Consistent, coherent, creative: The 3 Cs of graphic organizers. *Teaching Exceptional Children, 35*(3), 46–53.

Beall, H., & Hughes-Buchanan, H. (2004). The effects of acid rain on the environment. Retrieved from *learnnc.org/lp/pages/2895*

Belfiore, P. J., & Browder, D. M. (1992). The effects of self-monitoring on teacher's data-based decisions and on the progress of adults with severe mental retardation. *Education and Training in Mental Retardation, 27,* 60–67.

Bellini, S., Akullian, J., & Hopf, A. (2007). Increasing social engagement in young children with autism spectrum disorders using video self-modeling. *School Psychology Review, 36,* 80–90.

Benner, G. J., Rogers-Adkinson, D., Mooney, P., & Abbott, D. A. (2007). An investigation of the relationship between receptive language and social adjustment in a general sample of elementary school children. *Journal of At-Risk Issues, 13,* 13–21.

Berlinghoff, W. P., Sloyer, C., & Hayden, R. W. (1998). *Math connections: A secondary mathematics core curriculum.* Armonk, NY: It's About Time.

Best, S. J. (2001). Physical disabilities. In J. L. Bigge, S. J. Best, & K. W. Heller (Eds.), *Teaching individuals with physical, health, or multiple disabilities* (4th ed., pp. 34–64). Upper Saddle River, NJ: Pearson.

Best, S. J., & Bigge, J. L. (2005). Cerebral palsy. In S. J. Best, K. W. Heller, & J. L. Bigge (Eds.), *Teaching individuals with physical or multiple disabilities* (5th ed., pp. 87–109). Upper Saddle River, NJ: Pearson.

Beyer, B. K. (2001). Infusing thinking in history and the social studies. In A. L. Cost (Ed.), *Developing minds: A resource book for teaching thinking* (pp. 317–325). Alexandria, VA: Association for Supervision and Curriculum Development.

Beyer, B. K. (2008a). How to teach thinking skills in social studies and history. *Social Studies, 98,* 196–201.

Beyer, B. K. (2008b). What research tells us about teaching thinking skills. *Social Studies, 99,* 223–232.

Bielsker, S., Napoli, L., Sandino, M., & Waishwell, L. (2001). Effects of direct teaching using creative memorization strategies to improve math achievement (Masters of Arts Action Research Project, St. Xavier University and Skylight Professional Development Field-Based Masters Program). ERIC Document Reproduction Service. (ED460855)

Billingsly, F. F., & Romer, L. T. (1983). Response prompting and the transfer of stimulus control: Methods, research, and a conceptual framework. *Journal of the Association for the Severely Handicapped, 8,* 3–12.

Blackorby, J., Hancock, G. R., & Siegel, S. (1993). *Human capital and structural explanations of post-school success for youth with disabilities: A latent variable exploration of the National Longitudinal Transition Study.* Menlo Park, CA: SRI International.

Blackorby, J., & Wagner, M. (1996). Longitudinal postschool outcomes of youth with disabilities: Findings from the National Longitudinal Transition Study. *Exceptional Children, 62,* 399–413.

Blick, D. W., & Test, D. W. (1987). Effects of self-recording on high school students' on-task behavior. *Learning Disability Quarterly, 10,* 203–213.

Bloom, B. S., Englehart, M. B., Furst, E. J., Hill, W. H., & Krathwohl, D. R. (Eds.). (1956). *Taxonomy of educational objective: The classification of educational goals: Handbook I. Cognitive domain.* New York: McKay.

Board of Education of the Hendrick Hudson Central School District, Westchester County, et al. v. Rowley, 458 U.S. 176 (1982).

Bolt, S. E., & Roach, A. T. (2009). *Inclusive assessment and accountability: A guide to accommodations for students with diverse needs.* New York: Guilford Press.

Bondy, A., & Frost, L. (1994). The Picture Exchange Communication System. *Focus on Autistic Behavior, 9,* 1–19.

Bosner, S. M., & Belfiore, P. J. (2001). Strategies and considerations for teaching an adolescent with Down syndrome and type 1 diabetes to self-administer insulin. *Education and Training in Mental Retardation and Developmental Disabilities, 36,* 94–102.

Boulineau, T., Fore, C., Hagan-Burke, S., & Burke, M. D. (2004). Use of story-mapping to increase the story-grammar text comprehension of elementary students with learning disabilities. *Learning Disability Quarterly, 27,* 105–121.

Bourbeau, P. E., Sowers, J. A., & Close, D. W. (1986). An experimental analysis of generalization of banking skills from classroom to bank settings in the community. *Education and Training in Mental Retardation, 21,* 98–107.

Brady, M. P., McEvoy, M. A., Wehby, J., & Ellis, D. (1987). Using peers as trainers to increase an autistic child's social interactions. *Exceptional Children, 34,* 213–219.

Brady, N. C., & Halle, J. W. (1997). Functional analysis of communicative behaviors. *Focus on Autism and Other Developmental Disabilities, 12,* 95–104.

Brantlinger, E., Jimenez, R., Klingner, J., Pugach, M., & Richardson, V. (2005). Qualitative studies in special education. *Exceptional Children, 71,* 197–207.

Brekke, B. (1988). *Sexuality education for persons with severe developmental disabilities.* Santa Monica, CA: Stanfield.

Briggs, A., Alberto, P., Sharpton, W., Berlin, K., McKinley, C., & Ritts, C. (1990). Generalized use of a self-operated audio prompt system. *Education and Training in Mental Retardation, 25,* 381–389.

Brinker, R. P., & Thorpe, M. E. (1984). Integration of severely handicapped students and the proportion of IEP objectives achieved. *Exceptional Children, 51,* 168–175.

Brolin, D. (Ed.). (1989). *Life-centered career education: A competency-based approach* (3rd ed.). Reston, VA: Council for Exceptional Children.

Brolin, D. (1997). *Life-centered career education: A competency-based approach* (5th ed.). Reston, VA: Council for Exceptional Children.

Browder, D. M. (1991). *Assessment of individuals with severe disabilities: An applied behavioral approach to life skills assessment* (2nd ed.). Baltimore: Brookes.

Browder, D. M. (2001). *Curriculum and assessment for students with moderate and severe disabilities.* New York: Guilford Press.

Browder, D. M., Ahlgrim-Delzell, L., Courtade, G., Gibbs, S. L., & Flowers, C. (2008). Evaluation of the effectiveness of an early literacy program for students with significant developmental disabilities using group randomized trial research. *Exceptional Children, 75,* 33–52.

Browder, D. M., Ahlgrim-Delzell, L., Courtade-Little, G., & Flowers, C. (2006, April). *Training teachers of students with significant cognitive disabilities to develop literacy lessons.* Paper presented at the annual meeting of the American Educational Research Association, San Francisco, CA.

Browder, D. M., Ahlgrim-Delzell, L., Courtade-Little, G. R., & Snell, M. (2006). Access to the general curriculum. In M. Snell & F. Brown (Eds.), *Instruction of students with severe disabilities* (6th ed., pp. 489–525). Upper Saddle River, NJ: Merrill/Prentice-Hall.

Browder, D. M., Ahlgrim-Delzell, L., Spooner, F., Mims, P. J., & Baker, J. N. (2009). Using time delay to teach literacy to students with severe developmental disabilities. *Exceptional Children, 75,* 343–364.

Browder, D. M., Cooper, K., & Lim, L. (1998). Teaching adults with severe disabilities to express their choice of settings for leisure activities. *Education and Training in Mental Retardation and Developmental Disabilities, 33,* 226–236.

Browder, D. M., Demchak, M. A., Heller, M., & King, D. (1991). An in vivo evaluation of data-based rules to guide instructional decisions. *Journal of the Association for Persons with Severe Handicaps, 14,* 234–240.

Browder, D. M., Flowers, C., Ahlgrim-Delzell, L., Karvonen, M., Spooner, F., & Algozzine, R. (2004). The alignment of alternate assessment content to academic and functional curricula. *Journal of Special Education, 37,* 211–223.

Browder, D. M., Flowers, C., & Wakeman, S. Y. (2008). Facilitating participation in assessments and the general curriculum: Level of symbolic communication classification for students with significant cognitive disabilities. *Assessment in Education: Principles, Policy and Practice, 15,* 137–151.

Browder, D. M., Gibbs, S. L., Ahlgrim-Delzell, L., Courtade, G., & Lee, A. (2007). *Early literacy skills builder.* Verona, WI: Attainment.

Browder, D. M., & Grasso, E. (1999). Teaching money skills to individuals with mental retardation: A research review with practical applications. *Remedial and Special Education, 20,* 297–308.

Browder, D. M., Hines, C., McCarthy, L. J., & Fees, J. (1984). A treatment package for increasing sight word recognition for use in daily living skills. *Education and Training of the Mentally Retarded, 19,* 191–200.

Browder, D. M., Karvonen, M., Davis, S., Fallin, K., & Courtade-Little, C. (2005). The impact of teacher training on state alternate assessment scores. *Exceptional Children, 71,* 267–282.

Browder, D. M., Liberty, K., Heller, M., & D'Huyvetters, K. (1986). Self-management to improve teachers' instructional decisions. *Professional School Psychology, 1*(3), 165–175.

Browder, D. M., & Lim, L. (2001). Family-centered planning: A multicultural perspective. In D. M. Browder (Ed.), *Curriculum and assessment for students with moderate and severe disabilities* (pp. 116–147). New York: Guilford Press.

Browder, D. M., & Lohrmann-O'Rourke, S. (2001). Promoting self-determination in planning and instruction. In D. Browder (Eds.), *Curriculum and assessment for students with moderate and severe disabilities* (pp. 148–178). New York: Guilford Press.

Browder, D. M., & Martin, D. K. (1986). A new curriculum for Tommy. *Teaching Exceptional Children, 18*(4), 261–265.

Browder, D. M., Mims, P., Spooner, F., Ahlgrim-Delzell, L., & Lee, A. (2008). Teaching elementary students with profound disabilities to participate in shared stories. *Research and Practice in Severe Disabilities, 33,* 3–12.

Browder, D. M., & Shear, S. M. (1996). Interspersal of known items in a treatment package to teach sight words to students with behavior disorders. *The Journal of Special Education, 29,* 400–413.

Browder, D. M., & Spooner, F. (2006). *Teaching language arts, math, and science to students with significant cognitive disabilities.* Baltimore: Brookes.

Browder, D. M., Spooner, F., Ahlgrim-Delzell, L., Flowers, C., Algozzine, B., & Karvonen, M. (2003). A content analysis of the curricular philosophies reflected in states' alternate assessments. *Research and Practice for Persons with Severe Disabilities, 28,* 165–181.

Browder, D. M., Spooner, F., Ahlgrim-Delzell, L., Harris, A., & Wakeman, S. (2008). A meta-analysis on teaching mathematics to students with significant cognitive disabilities. *Exceptional Children, 74,* 407–432.

Browder, D. M., Spooner, F., Algozzine, B., Ahlgrim-Delzell, L., Flowers, C., & Karvonen, M. (2003). What we know and need to know about alternate assessment. *Exceptional Children, 70,* 45–61.

Browder, D. M., Spooner, F., Wakeman, S. Y., Trela, K., & Baker, J. (2006). Aligning instruction with academic content standards: Finding the link. *Research and Practice for Persons with Severe Disabilities, 31,* 309–321.

Browder, D. M., Trela, K., Courtade, G. R., Jimenez, B. A., Knight, V., & Flowers, C. (2010, April). Teaching mathematics and science standards to students with moderate and severe developmental disabilities. *The Journal of Special Education.* Advance online publication: doi:10.1177/0022466910369942

Browder, D. M., Trela, K., & Jimenez, B. (2007). Training teachers to follow a task analysis to engage middle school students with moderate and severe developmental disabilities in grade-appropriate literature. *Focus on Autism and Other Developmental Disabilities, 22,* 206–219.

Browder, D. M., Wakeman, S. Y., & Flowers, C. (2009). Alignment of alternate assessment with state standards. In W. Shafer & R. W. Lissitz (Ed.), *Alternate assessments based on alternate achievement standards: Policy, practice, and potential.* Baltimore: Brookes.

Browder, D. M., Wakeman, S. Y., Flowers, C., Rickelman, R. J., Pugalee, D., & Karvonen, M. (2007). Creating access to the general curriculum with links to grade level content for students with significant cognitive disabilities: An explication of the concept. *Journal of Special Education, 41,* 2–16.

Browder, D. M., Wakeman, S. Y., Spooner, F., Ahlgrim-Delzell, L., & Algozzine, B. (2006). Research on reading instruction for individuals with significant cognitive disabilities. *Exceptional Children, 72,* 392–408.

Brown, F., Belz, P., Corsi, L., & Wenig, B. (1993). Choice diversity for people with severe disabilities. *Education and Training in Mental Retardation, 28,* 318–326.

Brown, L., Nietupski, J., & Hamre-Nietupski, S. (1976). The criterion of ultimate functioning and public school services for severely handicapped children. In M. A. Thomas (Ed.), *Hey, don't forget about me!* Reston, VA: Council for Exceptional Children.

Bryan, J. (1998). K–W–W–L: Questioning the known. *Reading Teacher, 51,* 618–620.

Bullis, M., Davis, C., Bull, B., & Johnson, B. (1995). Transition achievement among young adults with deafness: What variables relate to success? *Rehabilitation Counseling Bulletin, 39,* 130–150.

Bullock, J., Pierce, S., & McClellan, L. (1989). *Touch Math.* Colorado Springs, CO: Innovative Learning Concepts.

Bursuck, W. D., & Damer, M. (2007). *Reading instruction for students who are at risk or have disabilities.* Boston: Pearson.

Byrnes, M. (2008). Writing explicit, unambiguous accommodations. *Intervention in School and Clinic, 44,* 18–24.

Calculator, S. N. (1994). Introduction. In N. W. Nelson (Series Ed.) & S. N. Calculator & C. M. Jorgensen (Vol. Eds.), *Including students with severe disabilities in schools: Fostering communication, interaction, and participation* (pp. xxi). San Diego, CA: Singular.

Calhoon, J. A. (2001). Factors affecting the reading of rimes in words and nonwords in beginning readers with cognitive disabilities and typically developing readers: Explorations in similarities and differences in word recognition cue use. *Journal of Autism and Developmental Disabilities, 31,* 491–504.

Callahan, K., & Rademacher, J. A. (1999). Using self-management strategies to increase the on-task behavior of a student with autism. *Journal of Positive Behavior Interventions, 1,* 117–122.

Cameto, R. (2005, April). The transition planning process. *NLTS Data Brief, 4*(1). Retrieved August 8, 2006, from *www.ncset.org/publications/ viewdesc.asp?id=2130*

Campbell, P. C., Campbell, C. R., & Brady, M. P. (1998). Team Environmental Assessment Mapping System: A method for selecting curriculum goals for students with disabilities. *Education and Training in Mental Retardation and Developmental Disabilities, 33,* 264–272.

Carl D. Perkins Vocational and Applied Technology Education Act, 20 U.S.C. § 2301 *et seq.* (1984).

Carnine, D. W., Silbert, J., Kame'enui, E. J., & Tarver, S. G. (2004). *Direct instruction reading* (4th ed.). Upper Saddle River, NJ: Pearson Prentice Hall.

Carr, E. G. (1994). Emerging themes in the functional analysis of problem behavior. *Journal of Applied Behavior Analysis, 27,* 393–399.

Carr, E. G., Dunlap, G., Horner, R. H., Koegel, R. L., Turnbull, A., Sailor, W., et al. (2002). Positive behavior support: Evolution of an applied science. *Journal of Positive Behavior Interventions, 4,* 4–17.

Carr, E. G., Dunlap, G., Horner, R. H., Turnbull, A. P., McLaughlin, D. M., Ruef, M. B., et al. (1999). *Positive behavior support for people with developmental disabilities: A research synthesis.* Washington, DC: American Association on Mental Retardation.

Carr, E. G., & Durand, V. M. (1985). Reducing problem behaviors through functional communication training. *Journal of Applied Behavior Analysis, 18,* 11–126.

Carr, E. G., Langdon, N. A., & Yarbrough, S. C. (1999). Hypothesis-based intervention for severe problem behavior. In A. C. Repp & R. Horner (Eds.), *Functional assessment of problem behavior: From effective assessment to effective support* (pp. 9–31). Belmont, CA: Wadsworth.

Carr, E. G., Levin, L., McConnachie, G., Carlson, J. I., Kemp, D. C., & Smith, C. E. (1994). *Communication-based intervention for problem behavior.* Baltimore: Brookes.

Carr, E. G., & Ogle, D. M. (1987). K–W–L Plus: A strategy for comprehension and summarization. *Journal of Reading, 30,* 626–631.

Carter, E. W., Cushing, L. S., Clark, N. M., & Kennedy, C. H. (2005). Effects of peer support interventions on students' access to the general curriculum and social interactions. *Research and Practice for Persons with Severe Disabilities, 30,* 15–25.

Carter, E. W., & Kennedy, C. H. (2006). Promoting access to the general curriculum using peer support strategies. *Research and Practice for Persons with Severe Disabilities, 31,* 284–292.

Casey Family Programs. (n.d.). Ansell Casey Life Skills Assessment. Retrieved from *www.caseylifeskills.org/pages/assess/assess_aclsa.htm*

Cass, M., Cates, D., Jackson, C. W., & Smith, M. (2002, March). Facilitating adolescents with disabilities understanding of area and perimeter concepts via manipulative instruction. In *No Child Left Behind: The Vital Role of Rural Schools: Annual National Conference Proceedings of the American Council on Rural Special Education (ACRES),* Reno, NV.

Center for Applied Special Technology. (1998). What is universal design for learning? Wakefield, MA: Author. Retrieved from *www.cast.org/research/udl/index.html*

Center for Applied Special Technology. (1998–1999). The national center on accessing the general curriculum. Retrieved January 13, 2005, from *www.cast.org/ncac*

Center for Applied Special Technology. (2009). The national center on accessing the general curriculum. Retrieved November 30, 2009, from *www.cast.org/bookbuilder*

Centers for Disease Control and Prevention. (2010). Bloodborne pathogens in healthcare settings. Retrieved from *cdc.gov/ncidod/dhep/bp.html*

Chall, J. S. (1983). *Stages of reading development.* New York: Harcourt Brace.

Chall, J. S. (1996). *Stages of reading development* (2nd ed.). Fort Worth, TX: Harcourt Brace.

Chan, S. (1986). Parents of exceptional Asian children. In M. K. Kitano & P. C. Chinn (Eds.), *Exceptional Asian children and youth* (pp. 36–53). Reston, VA: Council for Exceptional Children.

Chard, D. J., Ketterlin-Geller, L. R., Baker, S. K., Doabler, C., & Apichatabutra, C. (2009). Repeated reading interventions for students with learning disabilities: Status of the evidence. *Exceptional Children, 75,* 263–281.

Charlop-Christy, M. H., & Carpenter, H. M. (2000). Modified incidental teaching sessions: A procedure for parents to increase spontaneous speech in their children with autism. *Journal of Positive Behavior Interventions, 2*(2), 98–112.

Charlop-Christy, M. H., Le, L., & Freeman, K. A. (2000). A comparison of video modeling with in vivo modeling for teaching children with autism. *Journal of Autism and Developmental Disorders, 30,* 537–552.

Chen, D., & Miles, C. (2004). Working with families. In F. P. Orelove, D. Sobsey, & R. K. Silberman (Eds.), *Educating children with multiple disabilities* (4th ed., pp. 31–65). Baltimore: Brookes.

Chiang, H. M., & Lin, Y.-H. (2007). Reading comprehension instruction for students with autism spectrum disorders: A review of the literature. *Focus on Autism and Other Developmental Disorders, 22*, 259–267.

Chiang, I.-T., Lee, Y., Frey, G. C., & McCormick, B. P. (2004). Testing the situationally modified social rank theory on friendship quality in male youth with high-functioning autism spectrum disorder. *Therapeutic Recreation Journal, 38*, 261–274.

Childre, A. L. (2004). Families. In C. H. Kennedy & E. M. Horn (Eds.), *Including students with severe disabilities* (pp. 78–99). Boston: Pearson.

Cihak, D. F., Alberto, P. A., Kessler, K., & Taber, T. A. (2004). An investigation of instructional scheduling arrangements for community based instruction. *Research in Developmental Disabilities, 25*, 67–88.

Clements, D. H., & Battista, M. T. (1992). Geometry and spatial reasoning. In D. A. Grouws (Ed.), *Handbook of research on mathematics teaching and learning* (pp. 420–464). New York: Macmillan.

Clements, D. H., Sarama, J., & DiBiase, A. M. (2004). *Engaging young children in mathematics: Standards for early childhood mathematics education.* Mahwah, NJ: Erlbaum.

Coe, D. A., Matson, J. L., Craigie, C. J., & Gossen, M. A. (1991). Play skills of autistic children. *Child and Family Behavior Therapy, 13*(3), 13–40.

Cole, D. A., & Meyer, C. L. (1991). Social integration and severe disabilities: A longitudinal analysis of child outcomes. *Journal of Special Education, 25*, 340–351.

Collins, B. C. (2007). *Moderate and severe disabilities: A foundational approach.* Upper Saddle River, NJ: Prentice Hall.

Collins, B. C., Gast, D. L., Wolery, M., Holcombe, A., & Leatherby, J. G. (1991). Using constant time delay to teach self-feeding to young students with severe/profound handicaps: Evidence of limited effectiveness. *Journal of Developmental and Physical Disabilities, 3*, 157–179.

Collins, B. C., & Griffen, K. A. (1996). Teaching students with moderate disabilities to make safe responses to product warning labels. *Education and Treatment of Children, 19*, 30–45.

Collins, B. C., Stinson, D. M., & Land, L. (1993). A comparison of in vivo and simulation prior to in vivo instruction in teaching generalized safety skills. *Education and Training in Mental Retardation, 28*, 128–142.

Colyer, S. P., & Collins, B. C. (1996). Using natural cues within prompt levels to teach the next dollar strategy to students with disabilities. *Journal of Special Education, 30*, 305–318.

Cook, B. G., & Schirmer, B. R. (Eds.). (2003). What is special about special education [Special issue]. *Journal of Special Education, 37*(3).

Cook, B. G., Tankersley, M., & Landurm, T. J. (2009). Determining evidence-based practices in special education. *Exceptional Children, 75*, 365–383.

Cooper, J. O., Heron, T. E., & Heward, W. L. (2007). *Applied behavior analysis* (2nd ed.). Upper Saddle River, NJ: Pearson Prentice Hall.

Cooper, K. J., & Browder, D. M. (1998). Enhancing choice and participation for adults with severe disabilities in community-based instruction. *Journal of the Association for Persons with Severe Handicaps, 23*, 252–260.

Cooper-Duffy, K., & Perlmutter, D. G. (2006). Developing math and science skills in general education contexts. In D. M. Browder & F. Spooner (Eds.), *Teaching language arts, math, and science to students with significant cognitive disabilities* (pp. 245–265). Baltimore: Brookes.

Council of Chief State School Officers. (2002). Models for alignment analysis and assistance to states. Washington, DC: Author. Retrieved October 20, 2009, from *www.ccsso.org/content/ pdfs/AlignmentModels.pdf*

Courtade, G., Browder, D. M., Spooner, F., & DiBiase, W. (2010). Training teachers to use an inquiry-based task analysis to teach science to students with moderate and severe disabilities. *Education and Training in Developmental Disabilities, 45*, 378–399.

Courtade, G., Jimenez, B., Trela, K., & Browder, D. M. (2008). *Teaching to standards: Science: An inquiry-based approach for middle and high school students with moderate and severe disabilities.* Verona, WI: Attainment.

Courtade, G., Spooner, F., & Browder, D. M. (2007). A review of studies with students with significant cognitive disabilities that link to science standards. *Research and Practice for Persons with Severe Disabilities, 32,* 43–49.

Crist, K., Walls, R. T., & Haught, P. (1984). Degree of specificity in task analysis. *American Journal of Mental Deficiency, 89,* 67–74.

Criteria for Evidence-Based Practice in Special Education. (2005). [Special issue]. *Exceptional Children, 71*(2).

Crockett, J. B. (2000). Viable alternatives for students with disabilities: Exploring the origins and interpretations of LRE. *Exceptionality, 8*(1), 43–60.

Crockett, J. B., & Kaufmann, J. M. (1999). *The least restrictive environment: Its origins and interpretations in special education.* Mahwah, NJ: Erlbaum.

Cronin, K. A., & Cuvo, A. J. (1979). Teaching mending skills to mentally retarded adolescents. *Journal of Applied Behavior Analysis, 12,* 401–406.

Cushing, L. S., & Kennedy, C. H. (1997). Academic effects on students without disabilities who serve as peer supports for students with disabilities in general education classrooms. *Journal of Applied Behavior Analysis, 30,* 139–152.

Cushing, L. S., & Kennedy, C. H. (2004). Facilitating social relationships in general education settings. In C. H. Kennedy & E. M. Horn (Eds.), *Including students with severe disabilities* (pp. 206–216). Boston: Allyn & Bacon.

Cuvo, A. J., Davis, P. K., & Gluck, M. S. (1991). Cumulative and interspersal task sequencing in self-paced training for persons with mild handicaps. *Mental Retardation, 29,* 335–342.

Cuvo, A. J., Jacobi, E., & Sipko, R. (1981). Teaching laundry skills to mentally retarded adults. *Education and Training of the Mentally Retarded, 16,* 54–64.

Cuvo, A. J., & Klatt, K. P. (1992). Effects of community-based videotape and flash card instruction of community-referenced sight words on students with mental retardation. *Journal of Applied Behavior Analysis, 25,* 499–512.

Cuvo, A. J., Leaf, R. B., & Borakove, L. S. (1978). Teaching janitorial skills to the mentally retarded: Acquisition, generalization, and maintenance. *Journal of Applied Behavior Analysis, 11,* 345–355.

Cuvo, A. J., Veitch, V. D., Trace, M. W., & Konke, J. L. (1978). Teaching change computation to the mentally retarded. *Behavior Modification, 2,* 531–548.

Dammann, J. E., & Vaughn, S. (2001). Science and sanity in special education. *Behavioral Disorders, 27,* 21–29.

Darch, C., & Eaves, R. (1986). Visual displays to increase comprehension of high school learning disabled students. *Journal of Special Education, 20,* 309–318.

Davis, C. A., Brady, M. P., Williams, R. E., & Hamilton, R. (1992). Effects of high probability requests on the acquisition and generalization of responses to requests in young children with behavior disorders. *Journal of Applied Behavior Analysis, 25,* 905–916.

De La Paz, S., & MacArthur, C. A. (2003). Knowing the how and why of history: Expectations for secondary students with and without learning disabilities. *Learning Disability Quarterly, 26,* 142–154.

Demchak, M. A. (1990). Response prompting and fading methods: A review. *American Journal on Mental Retardation, 94,* 603–615.

DeMitchell, T. A., & Kerns, G. M. (1997). Where to educate Rachel Holland? Does least restrictive environment mean no restrictions? *Clearing House, 70,* 161–166.

Denny, P. J., & Test, D. W. (1995). Using the one-more-than technique to teach money counting to individuals with moderate mental retardation: A systematic replication. *Education and Treatment of Children, 18,* 422–432.

Dettmer, S., Simpson, R. L., Myles, B. S., & Ganz, J. B. (2000). The use of visual supports to facilitate transitions of students with autism. *Focus on Autism and Other Developmental Disabilities, 15,* 163–169.

Developmental Disabilities Act of 1984, 42 U.S.C. § 6000 *et seq.*

DiCecco, V., & Gleason, M. (2002). Using graphic organizers to attain relational knowledge from expository text. *Journal of Learning Disabilities, 35,* 306–321.

Didden, R., Duker, P. C., & Korzilius, H. (1997). Meta-analytic study on treatment effectiveness for problem behaviors with individuals who have mental retardation. *American Journal of Mental Retardation, 101,* 387–399.

Dimino, J. (2007). Bridging the gap between research and practice. *Journal of Learning Disabilities, 40,* 183–189.

Donnellan, A. (1984). The criterion of the least dangerous assumption. *Behavioral Disorders, 9,* 141–150.

Donnellan, A., & Neel, R. S. (1986). New directions in educating students with autism. In R. H. Horner, L. H. Meyer, & H. D. B. Fredericks (Eds.), *Education of learners with severe handicaps: Exemplary service strategies* (pp. 99–126). Baltimore: Brookes.

Dorry, G. W., & Zeaman, D. (1973). The use of fading technique in paired-associate teaching of a reading vocabulary with retardates. *Mental Retardation, 11,* 3–6.

Dorry, G. W., & Zeaman, D. (1975). Teaching a simple reading vocabulary to retarded children: Effectiveness of fading and nonfading procedures. *American Journal of Mental Deficiency, 79,* 711–716.

Doss, S., & Reichle, J. (1991). Replacing excess behavior with an initial communicative repertoire. In J. Reichle, J. York, & J. Sigafoos (Eds.), *Implementing augmentative and alternative communication* (pp. 215–237). Baltimore: Brookes.

Dowhower, S. (1999). Supporting a strategic stance in the classroom: A comprehension framework for helping teachers help students to be strategic. *Reading Teacher, 52,* 672–688.

Downing, J. E. (2001). Meeting the communication needs of students with severe and multiple disabilities in general education classrooms. *Exceptionality, 9,* 147–156.

Doyle, P. M., Wolery, M., Ault, M. J., & Gast, D. L. (1988). System of least prompts: A review of procedural parameters. *Journal of the Association for Persons with Severe Handicaps, 13,* 28–40.

Drasgow, E., Yell, M. L., & Robinson, T. R. (2001). Developing legally correct and educationally appropriate IEPs. *Remedial and Special Education, 22,* 359–373.

Dreher, S. (2003). A novel idea: Reading aloud in a high school English classroom. *English Journal, 93,* 50–53.

Drew, A., Baird, G., Baron-Cohen, S., Cox, A., Slonims, V., Wheelwright, S., et al. (2002). A pilot randomized control trial of a parent training intervention study for pre-school children with autism: Preliminary findings and methodological challenges. *European Child and Adolescent Psychiatry, 11,* 266–272.

Dugan, E., Kamps, D., Leonard, B., Watkins, N., Rheinberger, A., & Stackhaus, J. (1995). Effects of cooperative learning groups during social studies for students with autism and fourth-grade peers. *Journal of Applied Behavior Analysis, 28,* 175–188.

Dunlap, G., Harrower, J., & Fox, L. (2005). Understanding the environmental determinants of problem behaviors. In L. Bambara & L. Kern (Eds.), *Individualized supports for students with problem behaviors* (pp. 25–46). New York: Guilford Press.

Dunlap, G., Koegel, R. L., & Koegel, L. K. (1984). Continuity of treatment: Toilet training in multiple community settings. *Journal of the Association for Persons with Severe Handicaps, 9,* 134–141.

Durand, V. M. (1988). The Motivation Assessment Scale. In M. Hersen & A. Bellack (Eds.), *Dictionary of behavioral assessment techniques* (pp. 309–310). Elmsford, NY: Pergamon.

Durand, V. M. (1990). *Functional communication training: An intervention program for severe behavior problems.* New York: Guilford Press.

Durand, V. M., & Carr, E. G. (1992). An analysis of maintenance following functional communication training. *Journal of Applied Behavior Analysis, 25,* 777–794.

Dyer, K., & Luce, S. C. (1996). Teaching practical communication skills. In D. Browder (Ed.), *Innovations* (pp. 345–358). Washington, DC: American Association on Mental Retardation.

Dymock, S. (2007). Comprehension strategy instruction: Teaching narrative text structure awareness. *Reading Teacher, 61,* 161–167.

Dymond, S. K., Renzaglia, A., Rosenstein, A., Chun, E. J., Banks, R. A., Niswander, V., et al. (2006). Using a participatory action research approach to create a universally designed inclusive high school course: A case study. *Research and Practice for Persons with Severe Disabilities, 31,* 293–308.

Eckert, T. A., & Browder, D. M. (1997). Stimulus manipulations: Enhancing materials for self-directed learning. In D. M. Baer & E. M. Pinkston (Eds.), *Environment and behavior* (pp. 279–288). Boulder, CO: Westview Press.

Education for All Handicapped Children Act of 1975, 20 USC §1401 *et seq.*

Eichinger, J., & Downing, J. E. (1996) Instruction in the general education environment. In J. E. Downing (Ed.), *Including students with severe and multiple disabilities in typical classrooms* (pp. 15–34). Baltimore: Brookes.

Elementary and Secondary Education Act of 1965, 20 U.S.C. § 6301 *et seq.* (1965).

Ellis, D., Cress, P., & Spellman, C. (1992). Using timers and lap counters to promote self-management of independent exercise in adolescents with mental retardation. *Education and Training of the Mentally Retarded, 27,* 51–59.

Ellis, D. N., Wright, M., & Cronis, T. G. (1996). A description of the instructional and social interactions of students with mental retardation in regular physical education. *Integrated Physical Education, 31,* 235–241.

Ellis, E. (1994). Integrating writing strategy instruction with content-area instruction: Part I. Orienting. *Intervention in School and Clinic, 29*(3), 169–180.

Engelmann, S., & Bruner, E. C. (1995). *Reading mastery classic I.* Columbus, OH: SRA/McGraw-Hill.

Engelmann, S., Meyer, L., Carnine, L., Becker, W., Eisele, J., & Johnson, G. (1999). *Corrective Reading program.* Columbus, OH: Science Research Associates.

Epilepsy Foundation. (2009). About epilepsy. *www.epilepsyfoundation.org/*

Epps, S., Stern, R. J., & Horner, R. H. (1990). Comparison of simulation training on self and using a doll for teaching generalized menstrual care to women with severe mental retardation. *Research in Developmental Disabilities, 11,* 37–66.

Erickson, K. (2004). *Meville to Weville.* Roseville, MN: Ablenet.

Erikson, K. A., & Koppenhaver, D. A. (1997). Integrated communication and literacy instruction for a child with multiple disabilities. *Focus on Autism and Other Developmental Disabilities, 12,* 142–151.

Etscheidt, S. (2003). An analysis of legal hearings and cases related to individualized education programs for children with autism. *Research and Practice for Persons with Severe Disabilities, 28,* 51–69.

Etzel, B. C., & LeBlanc, J. M. (1979). The simplest treatment alternative: The law of parsimony applied to choosing appropriate instructional control and errorless-learning procedures for the difficult-to-teach child. *Journal of Autism and Developmental Disorders, 9,* 361–382.

Evidence-Based Practices for Reading, Math, Writing, and Behavior. (2009). [Special issue]. *Exceptional Children, 75*(2).

Faggella-Luby, M., Schumaker, J. B., & Deshler, D. D. (2007). Embedded learning strategy instruction: Story-structure pedagogy in heterogeneous secondary literature classes. *Learning Disability Quarterly, 30,* 131–147.

Farlow, L. J., & Snell, M. E. (1989). Teacher use of student performance data to make instructional decisions: Practices in programs for students with moderate to profound handicaps. *Journal of the Association for Persons with Severe Handicaps, 14,* 13–22.

Farlow, L. J., & Snell, M. E. (1994). *Making the most of student performance data.* Washington, DC: American Association on Mental Retardation.

Farmer, T. W., Irvin, M. J., Sgammato, A. N., Dadisman, K., & Thompson, J. H. (2009). Interpersonal competence configurations in rural Appalachian fifth graders: Academic achievement and associated adjustment factors. *Elementary School Journal, 109,* 301–321.

Ferguson, D., Meyer, G., Jeanchild, J., Juniper, L., & Zingo, J. (1992). Figuring out what to do with the grown-ups: How teachers make inclusion "work" for students with disabilities. *Journal of the Association for Persons with Severe Handicaps, 17,* 218–228.

Ferguson, D. L., & Baumgart, D. (1991). Partial participation revisited. *Journal of the Association for Persons with Severe Handicaps, 16,* 218–227.

Ferster, C. B., & Skinner, B. F. (1957). *Schedules of reinforcement.* Englewood Cliffs, NJ: Prentice Hall.

Field, S., & Hoffman, A. (1994). Development of a model of self-determination. *Career Development for Exceptional Individuals, 17,* 159–169.

Field, S., Martin, J., Miller, R., Ward, M., & Wehmeyer, M. (1998). *A practical guide for teaching self-determination.* Reston, VA: Council for Exceptional Children.

Fisher, D., Flood, J., Lapp, D., & Frey, N. (2006). Interactive read-alouds: Is there a common set of implementation practices? *Reading Teacher, 58*(1), 8–17.

Fleming, C. B., Harachi, T. W., Cortes, R. C., Abbott, R. D., & Catalano, R. F. (2004). Level and change in reading scores and attention problems during elementary school as predictors of problem behavior in middle school. *Journal of Emotional and Behavioral Disorders, 12,* 130–144.

Flores, M. M., Shippen, M. E., Alberto, P., & Crowe, L. (2004). Teaching letter–sound correspondence to students with moderate intellectual disabilities. *Journal of Direct Instruction, 4*(2), 173–188.

Flowers, C., Ahlgrim-Delzell, L., Browder, D., & Spooner, F. (2005). Teachers' perceptions of alternate assessments. *Research and Practice for Persons with Severe Disabilities, 30,* 81–92.

Flowers, C., Browder, D. M., & Ahlgrim-Delzell, L. (2006). An analysis of three states' alignment between language arts and mathematics standards and alternate assessment. *Exceptional Children, 72,* 201–216.

Flowers, C., Wakeman, S., Browder, D., & Karvonen, M. (2007). *Links for academic learning: An alignment protocol for alternate assessments based on alternate achievement standards.* Charlotte: University of North Carolina at Charlotte.

Flowers, C., Wakeman, S., Browder, D., & Karvonen, M. (2009). An alignment protocol for alternate assessments based on alternate achievement standards. *Educational Measurements: Issues and Practice, 28*(1), 25–37.

Ford, A., & Mirenda, P. (1984). Community instruction: A natural cues and corrections decision model. *Journal of the Association for Persons with Severe Handicaps, 9,* 79–87.

Ford, A., Schnorr, R., Meyer, L., Davern, L., Black, J., & Dempsey, P. (1989). *The Syracuse community-referenced curriculum for students with moderate and severe disabilities.* Baltimore: Brookes.

Foster, A. (Ed.). (1997). *Algebra I* (4th ed.). New York: Glencoe/McGraw-Hill.

Fowler, L. (1998). Native American communities: A more inclusive society? *TASH Newsletter, 24,* 21–22.

Foxx, R. M., & Azrin, N. H. (1973). The elimination of autistic self-stimulatory behavior by over-correction. *Journal of Applied Behavior Analysis, 6,* 1–14.

Foxx, R. M., Faw, G. D., Taylor, S., Davis, P. K., & Fulia, R. (1993). "Would I be able to . . . ?": Teaching clients to assess the availability of their community lifestyle preferences. *American Journal of Mental Retardation, 98,* 235–248.

Frank, A. R., & Wacker, D. P. (1986). Analysis of a visual prompting procedure on acquisition and generalization of coin skills by mentally retarded children. *American Journal of Mental Deficiency, 90,* 468–472.

Frase-Blunt, M. (2000). High stakes testing: A mixed blessing for special students. *CEC Today, 7,* 1–15.

Freagon, S., & Rotatori, A. F. (1982). Comparing natural and artificial environments in training self-care skills to group home residents. *Journal of the Association for the Severely Handicapped, 7,* 73–86.

Frederick-Dugan, A., Test, D. W., & Varn, L. (1991). Acquisition and generalization of purchasing skills using a calculator by students who are mentally retarded. *Education and Training in Mental Retardation, 4,* 381–387.

Fredericks, H. D. B., Grover, D. N., Baldwin, V. L., Moore, W. G., Toews, J., Aschbacher, V., et al. (1981). *Toilet training the handicapped child* (4th ed.). Monmouth, OR: Instructional Development.

Frost, L., & Bondy, A. (2002). *The Picture Exchange Communication System training manual.* Newark, DE: Pyramid Educational.

Fryxell, D., & Kennedy, C. H. (1995). Placement along the continuum of services and its impact on students' social relationships. *Journal of the Association for Persons with Severe Handicaps, 20,* 259–269.

Fuchs, D., Fuchs, L. S., & Burish, P. (2000). Peer-assisted learning strategies: An evidence-based practice to promote reading achievement. *Learning Disabilities Research and Practice, 15,* 85–91.

Fuchs, D., Fuchs, L. S., Mathes, P. G., & Simmons, D. C. (1997). Peer-assisted learning strategies: Making classrooms more responsive to diversity. *American Educational Research Journal, 34,* 174–206.

Fuchs, L. S., & Fuchs, D. (1986). Effects of systematic formative evaluation: A meta-analysis. *Exceptional Children, 53,* 199–208.

Fuller, P. R. (1949). Operant conditioning of a vegetative human organism. *American Journal of Psychology, 62,* 587–590.

Gagnon, J. C., & Maccini, P. (2001). Preparing students with disabilities for algebra. *Teaching Exceptional Children, 34*(1), 8–15.

Gardill, M. C., & Browder, D. M. (1995). Teaching stimulus classes to encourage independent purchasing by students with severe behavior disorders. *Education and Training in Mental Retardation and Developmental Disabilities, 30,* 254–264.

Garjria, M., Jitendra, A. K., Sood, S., & Sacks, G. (2007). Improving comprehension of expository text in students with LD: A research synthesis. *Journal of Learning Disabilities, 40,* 210–225.

Gartner, A., Lipsky, D., & Turnbull, A. (1991). *Supporting families with a disability: An international outlook.* Baltimore: Brookes.

Gast, D. L. (2010). *Single subject research methodology in behavioral sciences.* New York: Routledge.

Gaule, K., Nietupski, J., & Certo, N. (1985). Teaching supermarket shopping skills using an adaptive shopping list. *Education and Training of the Mentally Retarded, 20,* 53–59.

Gena, A., Krantz, P. J., McClannahan, L. E., & Poulson, C. L. (1996). Training and generalization of affective behavior displayed by youth with autism. *Journal of Applied Behavior Analysis, 29,* 291–304.

Gencoez, F. (1997). The effects of basketball training on the maladaptive behaviors of trainable mentally retarded children. *Research in Developmental Disabilities, 18,* 1–10.

German, S. L., Martin, J. E., Marshall, L. H., & Sale, R. P. (2000). Promoting self-determination: Using *Take Action* to teach goal attainment. *Career Development for Exceptional Individuals, 23,* 27–38.

Gersten, R., Fuchs, L. S., Compton, D., Coyne, M., Greenwood, C., & Innocenti, M. S. (2005). Quality indicators for group experimental and quasi-experimental research in special education. *Exceptional Children, 71,* 149–164.

Gersten, R., Fuchs, L. S., Williams, J. P., & Baker, S. (2001). Teaching reading comprehension strategies to students with learning disabilities: A review of research. *Review of Educational Research, 71,* 279–320.

Giangreco, M. F. (2006). Foundational concepts and practices for educating students with severe disabilities. In M. E. Snell & F. Brown (Eds.), *Instruction of students with severe disabilities* (6th ed., pp. 1–27). Upper Saddle River, NJ: Pearson Education/Prentice-Hall.

Giangreco, M. F., Cloninger, C. J., & Iverson, V. S. (1998). *Choosing options and accommodations for children* (2nd ed., pp. 29–95). Baltimore: Brookes.

Giangreco, M. F., Dennis, R., Cloninger, C., Edelman, S., & Schattman, R. (1993). "I've counted Jon": Transformational experiences of teachers educating students with disabilities. *Exceptional Children, 59*, 359–372.

Gillett, J., & LeBlanc, L. A. (2007). Parent-implemented natural language paradigm to increase language and play in children with autism. *Research in Autism Spectrum Disorders, 1*, 247–255.

Goals 2000: Educate America Act of 1994, 20 U.S.C. § 5811 (1994).

Godby, S., Gast, D. L., & Wolery, M. (1987). A comparison of time delay and system of least prompts in teaching object identification. *Research in Developmental Disabilities, 8*, 283–305.

Goetz, L., & Hunt, P. (1994). Augmentative and alternative communication. In E. C. Cipani & F. Spooner (Eds.), *Curricular and instructional approaches for persons with severe disabilities* (pp. 263–288). Boston: Allyn & Bacon.

Gold, M. W. (1976). Task analysis of a complex assembly task by the retarded blind. *Exceptional Children, 43*, 78–84.

Gold, M. W., & Scott, K. G. (1971). Discrimination learning. *Training the developmentally young.* New York: John Day.

Gottfredson, D. C., Gottfredson, G. D., & Hybl, L. G. (1993). Managing adolescent behavior: A multiyear, multischool study. *American Educational Research Journal, 11*, 97–115.

Graetz, J. E., Matropieri, M. A., & Scruggs, T. E. (2006). Show time: Using video self-modeling to decrease inappropriate behavior. *Teaching Exceptional Children, 38*(5), 43–48.

Graves, M. F., & Graves, B. (2003). *Scaffolding reading experiences: Designs for student success.* Norwood, MA: Christopher-Gordon.

Gray, C. (1995). Teaching children with autism to "read" social situations. In K. A. Quill (Ed.), *Teaching children with autism: Strategies to enhance communication and socialization* (pp. 219–241). New York: Delmar.

Gray, C. A. (2000). *The new social story book: Illustrated edition.* Arlington, TX: Future Horizons.

Gray, C. A., & Garand, J. D. (1993). Social stories: Improving responses of students with autism with accurate social information. *Focus on Autistic Behavior, 8*(1), 3–10.

Gray, D., & Boswell, S. (1999). Applying structured teaching principles to toilet training. *Spectrum, 15*(3), 6–9.

Grayson, G. (2003). *Talking with your hands, listening with your eyes: A complete photographic guide to American Sign Language.* Garden City Park, NY: Square One.

Green, C. W., Reid, D. H., Canipe, V. S., & Gardner, S. M. (1991). A comprehensive evaluation of reinforcer identification process for persons with profound multiple handicaps. *Journal of Applied Behavior Analysis, 24*, 537–552.

Green, C. W., Reid, D. H., White, L. K., Halforn, R. C., Brittain, D. P., & Gardner, S. M. (1988). Identifying reinforcers for persons with profound handicaps: Staff opinion versus systematic assessment of preferences. *Journal of Applied Behavior Analysis, 2*, 31–43.

Grela, B. G., & McLaughlin, K. S. (2006). Focused stimulation for a child with autism spectrum disorder: A treatment study. *Journal of Autism and Developmental Disorders, 36*, 753–760.

Grenot-Scheyer, M. (1994). The nature of interactions between students with severe disabilities and their friends and acquaintances without disabilities. *Journal of the Association for Persons with Severe Handicaps, 19*, 253–262.

Griffin, A. K., Wolery, M., & Schuster, J. W. (1992). Triadic instruction of chained food preparation responses: Acquisition and observational learning. *Journal of Applied Behavior Analysis, 25*, 257–279.

Griffin, C. C., Malone, L. D., & Kame'enui, E. J. (1995). Effects of graphic organizer instructing on fifth-grade students. *Journal of Education Research, 89*, 98–107.

Grigg, M. C., Snell, M. E., & Lloyd, B. H. (1989). Visual analysis of student evaluation data: A qualitative analysis of teacher decision making. *Journal of the Association for Persons with Severe Handicaps, 14*, 13–22.

Groce, M. (1996a). An introduction to travel training. *NICHY: Transition Summary, 9,* 2–5.

Groce, M. (1996b). A model of a travel training program: The New York City Board of Education Travel Training Program. *NICHY: Transition Summary, 9,* 10–13.

Guess, D., Benson, H. A., & Siegel-Causey, E. (1985). Concepts and issues related to choice-making and autonomy among persons with severe disabilities. *Journal of the Association for Persons with Severe Handicaps, 10,* 79–86.

Gunn, B., Simmons, D., & Kame'enui, E. (1995). *Emergent literacy: Synthesis of the research* (Technical Report No. 19). Retrieved May 8, 2007, from *idea.uoregon.edu/~ncite/documents/techrep/tech19.html*

Guthrie, J. T., Anderson, E., Aloa, S., & Rinehart, J. (1999). Influences of concept-oriented reading instruction on strategy use and conceptual learning from text. *Elementary School Journal, 99,* 343–366.

Hagiwara, T., & Myles, B. S. (1999). A multimedia social story intervention: Teaching skills to children with autism. *Focus on Autism and Other Developmental Disabilties, 14,* 82–95.

Hall, M. G., Schuster, J. W., Wolery, M., Gast, D. L., & Doyle, P. M. (1992). Teaching chained skills in a non-school setting using a divided half instructional format. *Journal of Behavioral Education, 2,* 257–279.

Halpern, A. (1985). Transition: A look at the foundations. *Exceptional Children, 58,* 202–211.

Halpern, A. S., Yovanoff, P., Doren, B., & Benz, M. R. (1995). Predicting participation in postsecondary education for school leavers with disabilities. *Exceptional Children, 62,* 151–164.

Hamaker, C. (1986). The effects of adjunct questions on prose learning. *Review of Educational Research, 56,* 212–242.

Hamilton, B. L., & Snell, M. E. (1993). Using the milieu approach to increase spontaneous communication book use across environments by an adolescent with autism. *Augmentative and Alternative Communication, 9,* 259–272.

Hancock, T. B., & Kaiser, A. P. (2002). The effects of trainer-implemented enhanced milieu teaching on the social communication of children with autism. *Topics in Early Childhood Special Education, 22,* 39–54.

Handleman, J. S. (1986). Severe developmental disabilities: Defining the term. *Education and Treatment of Children, 9,* 153–167.

Hanson, M. J., & Carta, J. J. (1996). Addressing the challenges of families with multiple risks. *Exceptional Children, 62,* 200–212.

Hanson, M. J., Lynch, E. W., & Wayman, K. I. (1990). Honoring the cultural diversity of families when gathering data. *Topics in Early Childhood Special Education, 10*(1), 112–131.

Haring, N. G., Liberty, K. A., & White, O. R. (1980). Rules for data-based strategy decisions in instructional programs: Current research and instructional implications. In W. Sailor, B. Wilcox, & L. Brown (Eds.), *Methods of instruction for severely handicapped students* (pp. 159–192). Baltimore: Brookes.

Harper, C. B., Symon, J. B. G., & Frea, W. D. (2008). Recess is time-in: Using peers to improve social skills of children with autism. *Journal of Autism and Developmental Disorders, 38,* 815–826.

Harry, B. (1992). *Cultural diversity, families, and the special education system: Communication and empowerment.* New York: Teachers College Press.

Hart, D., Grigal, M., Sax, C., Martinez, D., & Will, M. (2006). Postsecondary education options for students with intellectual disabilities. *Institute for Community Integration Research to Practice, 45,* 1–4.

Hazelkorn, M., Packard, A. L., & Douvanis, G. (2008). Alternative dispute resolution in special education: A view from the field. *Journal of Special Education Leadership, 21,* 32–38.

Heal, L. W., & Rusch, F. R. (1995). Predicting employment for students who leave special education high school programs. *Exceptional Children, 61,* 472–487.

Hedrick, W. B., & Pearish, A. B. (2003). Good reading instruction is more important than who provides the instruction or where it takes place. In P. A. Mason & J. S. Schumm (Eds.), *Prom-*

ising practices for urban reading instruction (pp. 6–24). Newark, DE: International Reading Association.

Hefflin, B. R., & Hartman, D. K. (2002). Using writing to improve comprehension: A review of the writing-to-reading research. In C. Block & L. Gambrell (Eds.), *Comprehension instruction: Building on the past and improving instruction for today's students*. San Francisco, CA: Jossey-Bass.

Heflin, L. J., & Simpson, R. L. (1998). Interventions for children and youth with autism: Prudent choices in a world of exaggerated claims and empty promises: Part I. Intervention and treatment option review. *Focus on Autism and Other Developmental Disabilities, 13,* 194–211.

Heller, K. W. (2009a). Monitoring students' disabilities and individualized health care plans. In K. W. Heller, P. E. Forney, P. A. Alberto, S. J. Best, & M. N. Schwartzman (Eds.), *Understanding physical, health, and multiple disabilities* (2nd ed., pp. 349–366). Upper Saddle River, NJ: Pearson.

Heller, K. W. (2009b). Traumatic spinal cord injury and spina bifida. In K. W. Heller, P. E. Forney, P. A. Alberto, S. J. Best, & M. N. Schwartzman (Eds.), *Understanding physical, health, and multiple disabilities* (2nd ed., pp. 95–117). Upper Saddle River, NJ: Pearson.

Heller, K. W., Bigge, J., & Allgood, P. (2001). Adaptations for personal independence. In J. L. Bigge, S. J. Best, & K. W. Heller (Eds.), *Teaching individuals with physical, health, or multiple disabilities* (4th ed., pp. 34–64). Upper Saddle River, NJ: Pearson.

Heller, K. W., Easterbrooks, S., McJannet, D., & Swinehart-Jones, D. (2009). Vision loss, hearing loss, and deaf-blindness. In K. W. Heller, P. E. Forney, P. A. Alberto, S. J. Best, & M. N. Schwartzman (Eds.), *Understanding physical, health, and multiple disabilities* (2nd ed., pp. 191–218). Upper Saddle River, NJ: Pearson.

Heller, K. W., & Forney, P. (2009). Understanding disabilities and effective teaming. In K. W. Heller, P. E. Forney, P. A. Alberto, S. J. Best, & M. N. Schwartzman (Eds.), *Understanding physical, health, and multiple disabilities* (2nd ed., pp. 3–17). Upper Saddle River, NJ: Pearson.

Heller, P. (Producer), & Sheridan, J. (Director). (1989). *My left foot* [Motion picture]. United Kingdom: Ferndale Films.

Helmstetter, E., Peck, C. A., & Giangreco, J. F. (1994). Outcomes of interactions with peers with moderate and severe disabilities: A statewide survey of high school students. *Journal of the Association for Persons with Severe Handicaps, 19,* 253–262.

Hendrickson, K. C., Akkerman, P. S., & Speggen, L. (1985). Dining arrangements and behavior of severely mentally retarded adults. *Applied Research in Mental Retardation, 6,* 379–388.

Heuer, C. M. (2005). Comparison of performance on the Connecticut academic performance test by students enrolled in a standards-based mathematics program with students enrolled in a traditional mathematics program (Master's thesis). Retrieved from *eprints.ccsu.edu/archive/00000226/01/FullText.htm*

Hill, J. L. (1999). *Meeting the needs of students with special physical and health care needs*. Upper Saddle River, NJ: Prentice Hall.

Hitchcock, C. H., Dowrick, P. W., & Prater, M. A. (2003). Video self-modeling intervention in school-based settings: A review. *Remedial and Special Education, 24,* 36–46.

Hitchcock, C. H., & Noonan, M. J. (2000). Computer-assisted instruction of early academic skills. *Topics in Early Childhood Special Education, 20,* 145–158.

Hobbs, T., & Peck, C. A. (1985). Toilet training people with profound mental retardation: A cost effective procedure for large residential settings. *Behavioral Engineering, 9,* 50–57.

Hodgdon, L. (1999). *Solving behavior problems in autism*. Troy, MI: Quirk Roberts.

Holbrook, M. D. (2007). A seven-step process to creating standards-based IEPs. Retrieved from the National Association of State Directors of Special Education website, *www.projectforum.org/index.cfm*

Holburn, S., & Vietze, P. M. (2002). *Person-centered planning: Research, practice, and future directions*. Baltimore: Brookes.

Holvoet, J., O'Neil, G., Chazdon, L., Carr, D., & Warner, J. (1983). Hey, do we really have to take data? *Journal of the Association for the Severely Handicapped, 8*, 56–70.

Horner, R. H., Albin, R. W., Todd, A. W., & Sprague, J. (2006). Positive behavior support for individuals with severe disabilities. In M. E. Snell & F. Brown (Eds.), *Instruction of students with severe disabilities* (6th ed.). Upper Saddle River, NJ: Merrill Prentice Hall.

Horner, R. H., Carr, E. G., Halle, J., McGee, G., Odom, S., & Wolery, M. (2005). The use of single-subject research to identify evidence-based practice in special education. *Exceptional Children, 71*, 165–180.

Horner, R. H., Carr, E. G., Strain, P. S., Todd, A. W., & Reed, H. K. (2002). Problem behavior interventions for young children with autism: A research synthesis. *Journal of Autism and Developmental Disorders, 32*, 423–446.

Horner, R. H., Diemer, S. M., & Brazeau, K. C. (1992). Educational support for students with severe problem behaviors in Oregon: A descriptive analysis from the 1987–88 school year. *Journal of the Association for Persons with Severe Handicaps, 17*, 154–169.

Horner, R. H., Dunlap, G., Koegel, R. L., Carr, E. G., Sailor, W., Anderson, J., et al. (1990). Toward a technology of "nonaversive" behavioral support. *Journal of the Association for Persons with Severe Handicaps, 15*, 125–132.

Horner, R. H., Eberhard, J. M., & Sheehan, M. R. (1986). Teaching generalized table bussing. *Behavior Modification, 10*, 457–471.

Horner, R. H., & Keilitz, I. (1975). Training mentally retarded adolescents to brush their teeth. *Journal of Applied Behavior Analysis, 8*, 301–309.

Horner, R. H., McDonnell, J. J., & Bellamy, G. T. (1986). Teaching generalized skills: General case instruction in simulation and community settings. In R. H. Horner, L. H. Meyer, & H. D. Fredericks (Eds.), *Education of learners with severe handicaps: Exemplary service strategies* (pp. 289–314). Baltimore: Brookes.

Horner, R. H., Sugai, G., Todd, A. W., & Lewis-Palmer, T. (1999–2000). Elements of behavior support plans: A technical brief. *Exceptionality, 8*, 205–216.

Horner, R. H., Williams, J. A., & Steveley, J. D. (1987). Acquisition of generalized telephone use by students with moderate and severe mental retardation. *Research in Developmental Disabilities, 8*, 229–247.

Howle, J. M. (2002). *Neuro-developmental treatment approach: Theoretical foundations and principles of clinical practice*. Laguna Beach, CA: Neuro-Developmental Treatment Association.

Hughes, C., Hugo, K., & Blatt, J. (1996). Self-instructional intervention for teaching generalized problem-solving within a functional task sequence. *American Journal on Mental Retardation, 100*, 565–579.

Hunt, P., Soto, G., Maier, J., & Dowering, K. (2003). Collaborative teaming to support students at risk and students with severe disabilities in general education classrooms. *Exceptional Children, 69*, 315–332.

Hunt, P., Staub, D., Alwell, M., & Goetz, L. (1994). Achievement by all students within the context of cooperating groups. *Journal of the Association for Persons with Severe Handicaps, 19*, 290–301.

Idol, L. (1987). Group story mapping: A comprehension strategy for both skilled and unskilled readers. *Journal of Learning Disabilities, 20*, 196–205.

Improving the Academic Achievement of the Disadvantaged, 34 C.F.R. §200.1 *et seq.* (2003).

Improving America's Schools Act of 1994, 20 U.S.C. § 8001 (1994).

Individuals with Disabilities Act of 1990, PL 101-476, 1201 U.S.C et seq.

Individuals with Disabilities Education Act Amendments of 1997, 20 U.S.C. §1400 *et seq.* (1997).

Individuals with Disabilities Education Improvement Act of 2004, 20 U.S.C. §1400 *et seq.* (2004).

Indrisano, R., & Chall, J. S. (1995). Literacy development. *Journal of Education, 177*(1), 63–83.

Inge, K., & Moon, S. (2006). Vocational preparation and transition. In M. Snell & F. Brown

(Eds.), *Instruction of students with severe disabilities* (6th ed., pp. 569–609). Columbus, OH: Pearson Merrill Prentice Hall.

Irving Independent School District v. Tatro, 104 S. Ct. 3371 (1984).

Ivancic, M. T., & Schepis, M. M. (1995). Teaching key use to persons with severe disabilities in congregate living settings. *Research in Developmental Disabilities, 16*, 415–423.

Ives, B., & Hoy, C. (2003). Graphic organizers applied to higher-level secondary mathematics. *Learning Disabilities: Research and Practice, 18*, 36–51.

Jimenez, B. A., Browder, D. M., & Courtade, G. R. (2008). Teaching an algebraic equation to high school students with moderate developmental disabilities. *Education and Training in Developmental Disabilities, 43*, 266–274.

Jimenez, B. A., Browder, D. M., & Courtade, G. R. (2009). An exploratory study of self-directed science concept learning by students with moderate intellectual disabilities. *Research and Practice for Persons with Severe Disabilities, 34*(2), 33–46.

Jimenez, B., Spooner, F., Browder, D. M., DiBiase, W., & Knight, V. (2008). *A conceptual model for science for students with significant cognitive disabilities.* [Brochure]. Retrieved from *education.uncc.edu/access/*

Johnson, E., & Arnold, N. (2004). Validating an alternate assessment. *Remedial and Special Education, 25*, 266–275. doi: 10.1177/07419325040250050101

Johnson, J. W., & McDonnell, J. (2004). An exploratory study of the implementation of embedded instruction by general educators with students with developmental disabilities. *Education and Treatment of Children, 27*, 46–63.

Johnston, J. M., & Pennypacker, H. S. (1980). *Strategies and tactics for human behavioral research.* Hillsdale, NJ: Erlbaum.

Johnston, J. M., & Pennypacker, H. S. (1993). *Strategies and tactics for human behavioral research* (2nd ed.). Hillsdale, NJ: Erlbaum.

Jones, E. A., Carr, E. G., & Feeley, K. M. (2006). Multiple effects of joint attention intervention for children with autism. *Behavior Modification, 30*, 782–834.

Jones, G. Y., & Collins, B. C. (1997). Teaching microwave skills to adults with disabilities: Acquisition of nutrition and safety facts presented as nontargeted information. *Journal of Developmental and Physical Disabilities, 9*, 59–78.

Jones, S., & Lollar, D. J. (2008). Relationship between physical disabilities or long-term health problems and health risk behaviors or conditions among U.S. high school students. *Journal of School Health, 78*, 252–257.

Jorgensen, C. M. (1998). *Restructuring high schools for all students: Taking inclusion to the next level.* Baltimore: Brookes.

Jorgensen, C. M. (2005). The least dangerous assumption: A challenge to create a new paradigm. *Disability Solutions, 6*(3), 1, 5–9.

Jorgensen, C. M., Schuh, M. C., & Nisbet, J. (2006). *The inclusion facilitator's guide.* Baltimore: Brookes.

Kaiser, A. P. (1993). Parent-implemented language intervention: An environmental perspective. In A. P. Kaiser & D. B. Gray (Eds.), *Enhancing children's communication: Research foundations for intervention* (pp. 63–84). Baltimore: Brookes.

Kame'enui, E. J., & Simmons, D. C. (1990). *Designing instructional strategies: The prevention of academic learning problems.* Columbus, OH: Merrill.

Kamps, D. M., Barbetta, P. M., Leonard, B. R., & Delquadri, J. (1994). Classwide peer tutoring: An integration strategy to improve reading skills and promote peer interactions among students with autism and general education peers. *Journal of Applied Behavior Analysis, 27*, 49–61.

Kamps, D. M., Leonard, B., Potucek, J., & Garrison-Harrell, L. (1995). Cooperative learning groups in reading: An integration strategy for students with autism and general classroom peers. *Behavioral Disorders, 21*, 89–109.

Kamps, D., Locke, P., Delquadri, J., & Hall, R. (1989). Increasing academic skills of students with autism using fifth grade peers as tutors. *Education and Treatment of Children, 12*, 38–51.

Karvonen, M., Flowers, C., Browder, D. M., Wakeman, S. Y., & Algozzine, B. (2006). Case study of the influences on alternate assessment outcomes for students with disabilities. *Education and Training in Developmental Disabilities, 41*, 95–110.

Karvonen, M., Wakeman, S., Browder, D. M., Rogers, M. A. S., & Flowers, C. (2009). *Academic curriculum for students with significant cognitive disabilities: A decade after IDEA 1997.* Manuscript submitted for publication.

Karvonen, M., Wakeman, S. Y., Flowers, C., & Browder, D. M. (2007). Measuring the enacted curriculum for students with significant cognitive disabilities. *Assessment for Effective Intervention, 33*(1), 29–38.

Katsiyannis, A., & Maag, J. W. (2001). Manifestation determination as a golden fleece. *Behavioral Disorders, 68*, 85–96.

Kauffman, J. M. (1996). Research to practice issues. *Behavioral Disorders, 22*, 55–60.

Kauffman, J. M., Lloyd, J. W., Baker, J., & Riedel, T. M. (1995). Inclusion of all students with emotional and behavioral disorders? Let's think again. *Phi Delta Kappan, 76*, 542–546.

Kayser, J. E., Billingsley, F. F., & Neel, R. S. (1986). A comparison of in-context and traditional instructional approaches: Total task, single trial versus backward chaining, multiple trials. *Journal of the Association of Persons with Severe Handicaps, 11*, 28–38.

Kennedy, C. H. (2004). Social relationships. In C. Kennedy & E. Horn (Eds.), *Including students with severe disabilities* (pp. 100–118). Boston: Pearson Education.

Kennedy, C. H., & Horn, E. M. (2004). *Including students with severe disabilities.* Boston: Allyn & Bacon.

Kim, A.-H., Vaughn, S., Wanzek, J., & Wei, S. (2004). Graphic organizers and their effects on the reading comprehension of students with LD: A synthesis of the research. *Journal of Learning Disabilities, 37*, 105–118.

Kleinert, H. L., & Kearns, J. F. (Eds.). (2001). *Alternate assessment: Measuring outcomes and supports for students with disabilities.* Baltimore: Brookes.

Kleinert, H. L., Kearns, J. F., & Kennedy, S. (1997). Accountability for all students: Kentucky's alternate portfolio assessment for students with moderate and severe cognitive disabilities. *Journal of the Association for Persons with Severe Handicaps, 22*, 88–101.

Kleinert, H. L., Kennedy, S., & Kearns, J. F. (1999). The impact of alternate assessment: A statewide teacher survey. *Journal of Special Education, 33*, 93–102.

Kliewer, C., Biklen, D., & Kasa-Hendrickson, C. (2006). Who may be literate? Disability and resistance to the cultural denial of competence. *American Education Research Journal, 43*(2), 163–192.

Klingner, J. K., & Vaughn, S. (1999). Promoting reading comprehension, content learning, and English acquisition through collaborative strategic reading. *Reading Teacher, 52*, 738–747.

Knapczyk, D. R. (1983). Use of teacher-paced instruction in developing and maintaining independent self-feeding. *Journal of the Association for Persons with Severe Handicaps, 8*, 10–16.

Koegel, L. K., Koegel, R. L., Hurley, C., & Frea, W. D. (1992). Improving social skills and disruptive behavior in children with autism through self-management. *Journal of Applied Behavior Analysis, 25*, 341–353.

Koger, F., & Bambara, L. M. (1995, May). *Teaching adults to direct their own planning meeting.* Paper presented at the annual meeting of the Association for Behavior Analysis, Washington, DC.

Kohl, F. L., McLaughlin, M., & Nagle, K. (2006). Alternate achievement standards and assessments: A descriptive investigation of 16 states. *Exceptional Children, 73*, 107–123.

Kohl, F. L., & Stettner-Eaton, B. A. (1985). Fourth graders as trainers of cafeteria skills to severely handicapped students. *Education and Training of the Mentally Retarded, 20*, 229–245.

Kohler, P. (1996). *A taxonomy for transition programming.* Champaign: University of Illinois, Transition Research Institute.

Konarski, E. A., & Diorio, M. S. (1985). A quantitative review of self-help research with the severely and profoundly mentally retarded. *Applied Research in Mental Retardation, 6*, 229–245.

Konrad, M., & Test, D. W. (2004). Teaching middle-school students with disabilities to use an IEP template. *Career Development for Exceptional Individuals, 27,* 101–124.

Konrad, M., Trela, K., & Test, D. W. (2006). Using IEP goals and objectives to teach paragraph writing to high school students with physical and cognitive disabilities. *Education and Training in Developmental Disabilities, 41,* 111–124.

Konrad, M., Walker, A. R., Fowler, C. H., Test, D. W., & Wood, W. M. (2008). A model for aligning self-determination and general curriculum standards. *Teaching Exceptional Children, 40*(3), 53–64.

Koppenhaver, D. A., & Yoder, D. E. (1993). Classroom literacy instruction for children with severe speech and physical impairments (SSPI): What is and what might be. *Topics in Language Disorders, 13*(2), 1–15.

Koury, M., & Browder, D. M. (1986). The use of time delay to teach sight words by peer tutors classified as moderately mentally retarded. *Education and Training of the Mentally Retarded, 21,* 252–258.

LaCampagne, J., & Cipani, E. (1987). Training adults with mental retardation to pay bills. *Mental Retardation, 25,* 293–303.

Lachman v. Illinois State Board of Education, 852 F.2d 290 (7th Cir. 1988).

Lalli, J. S., Mace, F. C., Browder, D. M., & Brown, D. K. (1989). Comparison of treatments to teach number matching skills to adults with moderate mental retardation. *Mental Retardation, 27,* 75–83.

Lambros, K. M., Ward, S. L., Bocian, K. M., MacMillan, D. L., & Gresham, F. M. (1998). Behavioral profiles of children at risk for emotional and behavioral disorders: Implications for assessment and classification. *Focus on Exceptional Children, 30*(5), 1–16.

Lane, K. L., Kalberg, J. R., & Shepcaro, J. C. (2009). An examination of the evidence base for functional-based interventions for students with emotional and/or behavioral disorders attending middle and high schools. *Exceptional Children, 75,* 321–340.

Leal, L. (1998). *A family-centered approach to people with mental retardation.* Washington, DC: American Association on Mental Retardation.

Learning Clinic. (2006). *Transition and independent living skill assessment.* Brooklyn, CT: The Learning Clinic.

Leinhardt, G., Zaslavsky, O., & Stein, M. K. (1990). Functions, graphs, and graphing: Tasks, learning, and teaching. *Review of Educational Research, 60,* 1–64.

Levine, P., & Wagner, M. (2005). The household circumstances and emerging independence of out-of-school youth with disabilities. In M. Wagner, L. Newman, R. Cameto, N. Garza, & P. Levine (Eds.), After high school: A first look at the postschool experiences of youth with disabilities: A report from the National Longitudinal Transition Study-2 (NLTS2). Menlo Park, CA: SRI International. Retrieved from *www.nlts2.org/pdfs/afterhighschool_ chp6. pdf*

Lieberman, L., & Stuart, M. (2002). Self-determined recreational and leisure choices of individuals with deaf-blindness. *Journal of Visual Impairment and Blindness, 96,* 724–735.

Light, J., & Smith, A. K. (1993). The home literacy experiences of preschoolers who use augmentative communication systems and of their nondisabled peers. *Augmentative and Alternative Communication, 9,* 10–25.

Lipsky, D. K., & Gartner, A. (1989). The current situation. In D. K. Lipsky & A. Gartner (Eds.), *Beyond a separate education: Quality education for all* (pp. 3–24). Baltimore: Brookes.

Locke, P. A. (2000). *Literacy: Everyone can benefit (regardless of the severity of the disability).* Washington, DC: International Society for Augmentative and Alternative Communication.

Logan, K. R., Bakeman, R., & Keefe, E. B. (1997). Effects of instructional variables on engaged behavior of students with disabilities in general education classrooms. *Exceptional Children, 63,* 481–497.

Lohrmann-O'Rourke, S., & Browder, D. M. (1998). Empirically based methods of preference assessments for individuals with severe disabilities. *American Journal on Mental Retardation, 103,* 146–161.

Lohrmann-O'Rourke, S., & Gomez, O. (2001). Integrating preference assessment within the transition process to create meaningful school-to-life outcomes. *Exceptionality, 9*, 157–174.

Lowe, M. L., & Cuvo, A. J. (1976). Teaching coin summation to the mentally retarded. *Journal of Applied Behavior Analysis, 9*, 483–489.

Lown, A. (1957). Freedom through travel training: Out of the classroom. *Exceptional Children, 24*(4), 178–179.

Loyd, R. J., & Brolin, D. E. (1997). *Life centered career education: Modified curriculum for individuals with moderate disabilities* (rev. ed.). Reston, VA: Council for Exceptional Children.

Luckasson, R., Coulter, D. L., Polloway, E. A., Reiss, S., Schalock, R. L., Snell, M. E., et al. (1992). *Mental retardation: Definition, classification, and systems of support* (9th ed.). Washington, DC: American Association on Mental Retardation.

Luckasson, R., & Reeve, A. (2001). Naming, defining, and classifying in mental retardation. *Mental Retardation, 39*, 47–52.

Luiselli, J. K. (1988). Improvement of feeding skills in multihandicapped students through paced-prompting interventions. *Journal of the Multihandicapped Person, 1*, 17–30.

Lumley, V. A., Miltenberger, R. G., Long, E. S., Rapp, J. T., & Roberts, J. A. (1998). Evaluation of a sexual abuse prevention program for adults with mental retardation. *Journal of Applied Behavior Analysis, 31*, 91–101.

Lynch, E. W., & Hanson, M. J. (Eds.). (1998). *Developing cross-cultural competence: A guide for working with young children and their families* (2nd ed.). Baltimore: Brookes.

Lynch, P. S., Kellow, J., Thomas, J., & Willson, V. L. (1997). The impact of deinstitutionalization on the adaptive behavior of adults with mental retardation: A meta-analysis. *Education and Training in Mental Retardation and Developmental Disabilities, 32*, 255–261.

Maaskant, M. A., van Knijff-Raeven, A. G. M., van Schrojenstein Lantman-de Valk, H. M. J., & Veenstra, M. Y. (2009). Weight status of persons with intellectual disabilities. *Journal of Applied Research in Intellectual Disabilities, 22*, 426–432.

Maccini, P., & Hughes, C. A. (2000). Effects of problem-solving strategy on the introductory algebra performance of secondary students with learning disabilities. *Learning Disabilities Quarterly, 15*, 10–21.

Mackay, H. A., Soraci, S. A., Carlin, M. T., Dennis, N. A., & Strawbridge, C. P. (2002). Guiding visual attention during acquisition of matching-to-sample. *American Journal on Mental Retardation, 107*, 445–454.

Mandlawitz, M. R. (2002). The impact of the legal system on educational programming for young children with autism spectrum disorder. *Journal of Autism and Developmental Disorders, 32*, 495–508.

Marchese, T. J. (1991, November). "TQM reaches the academy." *AAHE Bulletin*, 3–9.

Marion, R. L. (1980). Communicating with parents of culturally diverse exceptional children. *Exceptional Children, 46*, 616–623.

Marquis, J. G., Horner, R. H., Carr, E. G., Turnbull, A. P., Thompson, M., Behrens, G. A., et al. (2000). A meta-analysis of positive behavior support. In R. M. Gerston & E. P. Schiller (Eds.), *Contemporary special education research: Synthesis of the knowledge base on critical instructional issues* (pp. 137–178). Mahwah, NJ: Erlbaum.

Marrone, J., Hoff, D., & Helm, D. T. (1997). Person-centered planning for the millennium: We're old enough to remember when PCP was just a drug. *Journal of Vocational Rehabilitation, 8*, 285–297.

Marston, D. B. (1989). A curriculum-based measurement approach to assessing academic performance: What it is and why do it. In M. R. Shinn (Ed.), *Curriculum-based measurement: Assessing special children* (pp. 18–78). New York: Guilford Press.

Martin, G., Koop, S., Turner, G., & Hanel, F. (1981). Backward chaining versus total task presentation to teach assemblyline tasks to severely retarded persons. *Behavior Research of Severe Developmental Disabilities, 2*, 117–137.

Martin, J. E., Marshall, L. H., Maxson, L., & Jerman, P. (1996). *Self-directed IEP*. Longmont, CO: Sopris West.

Martin, J. E., Van Dycke, J. L., Christensen, W. R., Greene, B. A., Gardner, J. E., & Lovett, D. L. (2006). Increasing student participation in their transition IEP meetings: Establishing the self-directed IEP as an evidence-based practice. *Exceptional Children, 72,* 299–316.

Martin, J. E., Van Dycke, J. L., Greene, B. A., Gardner, J. E., Christensen, W. R., Woods, L. L., et al. (2006). Direct observation of teacher-directed IEP meetings: Establishing the need for student IEP meeting instruction. *Exceptional Children, 72,* 187–200.

Martin, J. E., Woods, L. L., Sylvester, L., & Gardner, J. E. (2005). A challenge to self-determination: Disagreement between the vocational choices made by individuals with severe disabilities and their caregivers. *Research and Practice for Persons with Severe Disabilities, 30,* 147–153.

Mary, N. L. (1990). Reactions of black, Hispanic, and white mothers to having a child with handicaps. *Mental Retardation, 28*(1), 1–5.

Mastropieri, M. A., & Scruggs, T. E. (2007). *The inclusive classroom: Strategies for effective instruction* (3rd ed.). Upper Saddle River, NJ: Merrill.

Mastropieri, M. A., Scruggs, T. E., Norland, J. J., Berkeley, S., McDuffie, K., Tornquist, E. H., et al. (2006). Differentiated curriculum enhancement in inclusive middle school science: Effects on classroom and high-stakes tests. *Journal of Special Education, 40,* 130–137.

Mathes, P. G., Howard, J. K., Allen, S. H., & Fuchs, D. (1998). Peer-assisted learning strategies for first-grade readers: Responding to the needs of diverse learners. *Reading Research Quarterly, 33,* 62–94.

Mathes, P., & Torgesen, J. (2005). *Early interventions in reading.* New York: McGraw Hill/SRA.

Matson, J. L. (1981). Use of independence training to teach shopping skills to mildly mentally retarded adults. *American Journal on Mental Deficiency, 86,* 178–183.

Matson, J. L., & Long, S. (1986). Teaching computation/shopping skills to mentally retarded adults. *American Journal of Mental Deficiency, 91,* 98–101.

McCabe, M. P., & Cummins, R. A. (1996). The sexual knowledge, experience, feelings, and needs of people with mild intellectual disability. *Education and Training in Mental Retardation and Developmental Disabilities, 31,* 13–21.

McCarl, J. J., Svobodny, L., & Beare, P. L. (1991). Self-recording in a classroom for students with mild to moderate mental handicaps: Effects on productivity and on-task behavior. *Education and Training in Mental Retardation, 26,* 79–88.

McCormick, T. M. (2008). Fear, panic, and injustice: Executive Order 9066 a lesson for grades 4–6. *Social Education, 72,* 268–271.

McCoy, K., & Hermansen, E. (2007). Video modeling for individuals with autism: A review of model types and effects. *Education and Treatment of Children, 30,* 183–213.

McDonnell, J. J., & Ferguson, B. (1988). A comparison of general case in vivo and general case simulation plus in vivo training. *Journal of the Association for Persons with Severe Handicaps, 13,* 116–124.

McDonnell, J. J., & Ferguson, B. (1989). A comparison of time delay and decreasing prompt hierarchy strategies in teaching banking skills to students with moderate handicaps. *Journal of Applied Behavior Analysis, 22,* 85–91.

McDonnell, J. J., Hardman, M., Hightower, J., & Kiefer-O'Donnell, R. (1991). Variables associated with in-school and after-school integration of secondary students with severe disabilities. *Education and Training in Mental Retardation, 26,* 243–257.

McDonnell, J. J., & Horner, R. H. (1985). Effects of in vivo versus simulation plus in vivo training on the acquisition and generalization of grocery item selection by high school students with severe handicaps. *Analysis and Intervention in Developmental Disabilities, 5,* 323–343.

McDonnell, J. J., Johnson, J. W., Polychronis, S., Riesen, T., Jameson, M., & Kercher, K. (2006). Comparison of one-to-one embedded instruction in general education classes with small group instruction in special education classes. *Education and Training in Developmental Disabilities, 41,* 125–138.

McDonnell, J. J., & Laughlin, B. (1989). A comparison of backward and concurrent chaining strategies in teaching community skills. *Education and Training in Mental Retardation, 24,* 230–238.

McDonnell, J. J., Mathot-Buckner, C., Thornson, N., & Fister, S. (2001). Supporting the inclusion of students with moderate and severe disabilities in junior high school general education classes: The effects of classwide peer tutoring, multi-element curriculum, and accommodations. *Education and Treatment of Children, 24*, 141–160.

McDonnell, J. J., & McFarland, S. (1988). A comparison of forward and concurrent chaining strategies in teaching laundromat skills to students with severe handicaps. *Research in Developmental Disabilities, 9*, 177–194.

McDonnell, J. J., & O'Neill, R. (2003). A perspective on single/within-subject research methods and "scientifically based research." *Research and Practice for Persons with Severe Disabilities, 28*, 138–142.

McDonnell, J. J., Thorson, N., Disher, S., Methot-Buckner, C., Mendel, J., & Ray, L. (2003). The achievement of students with developmental disabilities and their peers without disabilities in inclusive settings: An exploratory study. *Education and Treatment of Children, 26*, 224–236.

McGinnis, E., & Goldstein, A. (2003). *Skill-streaming in early childhood: New strategies and perspectives for teaching prosocial skills.* Champaign, IL: Research Press.

McGlashing-Johnson, J., Agran, M., Sitlington, P., Cavin, M., & Wehmeyer, M. (2003). Enhancing the job performance of youth with moderate to severe cognitive disabilities using the self-determined learning model of instruction. *Research and Practice for Persons with Severe Disabilities, 28*, 194–204.

McLaughlin, M., Nolet, V., Rhim, L., & Henderson, K. (1999). Integrating standards: Including all students. *Teaching Exceptional Children, 31*(3), 66–71.

McLean, J., & Snyder-McLean, L. (1988). Application of pragmatics to severely mentally retarded children and youth. In R. Schiefelbusch & L. Lloyd (Eds.), *Language perspectives: Acquisition retardation and intervention* (pp. 255–288). Austin, TX: Pro-Ed.

McWilliams, R., Nietupski, J., & Hamre-Nietupski, S. (1990). Teaching complex activities to students with moderate handicaps through the forward chaining of shorter total cycle response sequences. *Education and Training in Mental Retardation, 25*, 292–298.

Mechling, L. C., & Cronin, B. (2006). Computer-based video instruction to teach the use of augmentative and alternative communication devices for ordering at fast food restaurants. *Journal of Special Education, 39*, 234–245.

Mechling, L. C., & Gast, D. L. (1997). Combination audio/visual self-prompting system for teaching chained tasks to students with intellectual disabilities. *Education and Training in Mental Retardation and Developmental Disabilities, 32*, 138–153.

Mechling, L. C., Gast, D. L., & Barthold, S. (2003). Multi-media computer-based instruction to teach students with moderate intellectual disabilities to use a debit card to make purchases. *Exceptionality, 11*, 239–254.

Mechling, L. C., Gast, D. L., & Fields, E. A. (2008). Evaluation of a portable DVD player and system of least prompts to self-prompt cooking task completion by young adults with moderate intellectual disabilities. *Journal of Special Education, 42*, 179–190.

Mechling, L. C., Gast, D. L., & Langone, J. (2002). Computer-based video instruction to teach persons with moderate intellectual disabilities to read grocery aisle signs and locate items. *Journal of Special Education, 35*, 224–240.

Mechling, L. C., & Ortega-Hurndon, F. (2007). Computer-based video instruction to teach young adults with moderate intellectual disabilities to perform multiple step job tasks in a generalized setting. *Education and Training in Developmental Disabilities, 42*, 24–37.

Mechling, L. C., & Stephens, E. (2009). Comparison of self-prompting of cooking skills via picture-based cookbooks and video recipes. *Education and Training in Developmental Disabilities, 44*, 218–236.

Melville, C. A., Cooper, S. A., Morrison, J., Smiley, E., Allan, L., Jackson, A., et al. (2008). The prevalence and incidence of mental ill health in adults with autism and intellectual disabilities. *Journal of Autism and Developmental Disorders, 38*, 1676–1688.

Mesmer, H. A. E., & Hutchins, E. J. (2002). Using QARs with charts and graphs. *Reading Teacher,* 56, 21–27.

Metsala, J., & Walley, A. (1998). Spoken vocabulary growth and segmental restructuring of lexical representations: Precursors to phonemic awareness and early reading ability. In J. Metsala & L. Ehri (Eds.), *Word recognition in beginning reading* (pp. 89–120). Mahwah, NJ: Erlbaum.

Meyer, B. J. F., & Rice, G. E. (1984). The structure of text. In P. D. Pearson, R. Barr, M. L. Kamil, & P. Mosenthal (Eds.), *Handbook of reading research* (Vol. 1, pp. 319–351). Mahwah, NJ: Erlbaum.

Meyer, L. H., Eichinger, J., & Park-Lee, S. (1987). A validation of program quality indicators in educational services for students with severe disabilities. *Journal of the Association for Persons with Severe Handicaps, 12,* 251–263.

Miller, U. C., & Test, D. W. (1989). A comparison of constant time delay and most-to-least prompts in teaching laundry skills to students with moderate retardation. *Education and Training of the Mentally Retarded, 24,* 363–370.

Mims, P. J., Browder, D. M., & Spooner, F. (2009). *Increasing comprehension during a shared story students with moderate and severe intellectual disabilities.* Manuscript submitted for publication.

Miner, C. A., & Bates, P. E. (1997). The effect of person centered planning activities on the IEP/transition planning process. *Education and Training in Mental Retardation and Developmental Disabilities, 32,* 105–112.

Minge, M. R., & Ball, R. S. (1967). Teaching of self-help skills to profoundly retarded patients. *American Journal of Mental Deficiency, 71,* 864–868.

Mirenda, P., & Iacono, T. (2009). *Autism spectrum disorders and AAC.* Baltimore: Brookes.

Montague, M., Maddux, C. D., & Dereshiwsky, M. I. (1990). Story grammar and comprehension and production of narrative prose by students with learning disabilities. *Journal of Learning Disabilities, 23,* 190–197.

Moon, S., Komissar, C., Friedlanger, R., Hart, D., & Kiernan, W. (1994). Finding or creating fun in your community. In S. Moon (Ed.), *Making school and community recreation fun for everyone: Places and ways to integrate* (pp. 63–84). Baltimore: Brookes.

Morgan, M., Moni, K. B., & Jobling, M, A. (2006). Code-Breaker: Developing phonics with a young adult with an intellectual disability. *Journal of Adolescent and Adult Literacy, 50*(1), 52–65.

Morin, V. A., & Miller, S. P. (1998). Teaching multiplication to middle school students with mental retardation. *Education and Treatment of Children, 21,* 22–36.

Munger, G. F., Snell, M. E., & Lloyd, B. H. (1989). A study of the effects of frequency of probe data collection and graph characteristics on teachers' visual analysis. *Research in Developmental Disabilities, 10,* 109–127.

National Alternate Assessment Center. (2005, June). *Access and alignment to grade-level content for students with the most significant cognitive disabilities: A training module for large-scale use.* Presentation at the annual meeting of the Council for Chief State School Officers Large-Scale Assessment Conference, San Antonio, TX. Available online at: *www.naacpartners.org/products/workshops/CCSSOseminars/16600/slide7.htm*

National Autism Center. (2009). *National Standards Project: Addressing the need for evidence-based practice guidelines for autism spectrum disorders.* Randolf, MA: Author.

National Center on Universal Design for Learning. (2010). UDL guidelines—version 1.0. Retrieved October 14, 2010, from *http://www.udlcenter.org/aboutudl/udlguidelines/introduction*

National Commission on Excellence in Education. (1983). *A nation at risk: The imperative for educational reform.* Washington, DC: Government Printing Office.

National Council for the Social Studies. (2002). *National standards for social studies teachers.* Washington, DC: Author. Available at *www.socialstudies.org*

National Council of Teachers of English and International Reading Association. (1996). *Standards for the English language arts*. Urbana, IL: Author.

National Council of Teachers of English and International Reading Association. (2009). The standards for the English language arts. Retrieved July 8, 2009, from *www.ncte.org/standards*

National Council of Teachers of Mathematics. (2000). *Principles and standards for school mathematics*. Reston, VA: Author.

National Council of Teachers of Mathematics. (2006). Curriculum focal points for prekindergarten through grade 8 mathematics: A quest for coherence. Retrieved from *www.nctmmedia. org/cfp/focal_points_by_grade.pdf*

National Library of Virtual Manipulatives. (2009). Virtual library. Retrieved from *nlvm.usu.edu*

National Reading Panel. (2000). *Teaching children to read: An evidence-based assessment of the scientific research literature on reading and its implications for reading instruction*. Washington, DC: U. S. Department of Health and Human Services. (NIH Publication No. 00-4754).

National Research Council. (1996). *National science education standards*. Washington, DC: National Academy Press.

National Secondary Transition Technical Assistance Center. (2009). *Research to practice lesson plan starter library*. Retrieved October 20, 2009, from *www.nsttac.org/LessonPlanLibrary/ Main.aspx*

Neal, J., Bigby, L., & Nicholson, R. (2004). Occupational therapy, physical therapy, and orientation and mobility services in public schools. *Intervention in School and Clinic, 39*, 218–222.

Neale, M., & Test, D. W. (2010). Effects of the *I CAN USE EFFORT* strategy on quality of student verbal contributions and IEP participation with third- and fourth-grade students with disabilities. *Remedial and Special Education, 31*, 184–194. doi:10.1177/0741932508327462

Neef, N. A., Iwata, B. A., & Page, T. J. (1978). Public transportation training: In vivo versus classroom instruction. *Journal of Applied Behavior Analysis, 11*, 331–334.

Neef, N. A., Iwata, B. A., & Page, T. J. (1980). The effects of interspersal training versus high-density reinforcement on spelling acquisition and transition. *Journal of Applied Behavior Analysis, 13*, 153–158.

Nelson, G. L., Cone, J. D., & Hanson, C. R. (1975). Training correct utensil use in retarded children: Modeling vs. physical guidance. *American Journal of Mental Deficiency, 80*, 114–122.

Nelson, J. R., Benner, G. J., Lane, K., & Smith, B. W. (2004). Academic achievement of K–12 students with emotional and behavioral disorders. *Exceptional Children, 71*, 59–73.

Newman, L. (2005). Changes in postsecondary education participation of youth with disabilities. In M. Wagner, L. Newman, R. Cameto, & P. Levine (Eds.), Changes over time in the early postschool outcomes of youth with disabilities: A report from the National Longitudinal Transition Study—2 (NLTS2). Menlo Park, CA: SRI International. Available at *www. nlts2. org/pdfs/str6_ch4_postsec.pdf*

Newman, L., Wagner, M., Cameto, R., & Knokey, A. M. (2009). The post-high school outcomes of youth with disabilities up to 4 years after high school: A report of findings from the National Longitudinal Transition Study—2 (NLTS2). Menlo Park, CA: SRI International. Available at *www.nlts2.org/reports/2009_04/nlts2_report_2009_04_complete.pdf*

Nietupski, J., Hamre-Nietupski, S., Clancy, P., & Veerhusen, K. (1986). Guidelines for making simulation an effective adjunct to in vivo community instruction. *Journal of the Association for Persons with Severe Disabilities, 11*, 12–18.

Nietupski, J., Welch, J., & Wacker, D. (1983). Acquisition, maintenance, and transfer of grocery item purchasing skills by moderately and severely handicapped students. *Education and Training in Mental Retardation, 18*, 279–286.

Nisbet, J. (1992). *Natural supports in school, at work, and in the community for people with severe disabilities*. Baltimore: Brookes.

No Child Left Behind Act of 2001, 20 U.S.C. §§ 6301 *et seq.* (2002).

Nolet, V., & McLaughlin, M. J. (2000). *Accessing the general curriculum.* Thousand Oaks, CA: Corwin Press.

Norlin, J. W. (2007). What do I do when—: *The answer book on special education law.* Horsham, PA: LRP.

Nutter, D., & Reid, D. H. (1978). Teaching retarded women a clothing selection skill using community norms. *Journal of Applied Behavior Analysis, 11,* 475–487.

Oberti v. Board of Education of the Borough of Clementon School District, 995 F.2d 1204 (3rd Cir. 1993).

O'Brien, G., & Azrin, N. H. (1972). Developing proper mealtime behaviors of the institutionally retarded. *Journal of Applied Behavior Analysis, 5,* 389–399.

O'Connor, I. M., & Klein, P. D. (2004). Exploration of strategies for facilitating the reading comprehension of high functioning students with autism spectrum disorders. *Journal of Autism and Developmental Disorders, 34,* 115–127.

O'Dell, S. (1987). *Island of the blue dolphins.* New York: Yearling.

Odom, S. L., Brantlinger, E., Gersten, R., Horner, R. H., Thompson, B., & Harris, K. R. (2005). Research in special education: Scientific methods and evidence-based practices. *Exceptional Children, 71,* 137–149.

Ogle, D. M. (1986). K–W–L: A teaching model that develops active reading of expository text. *Reading Teacher, 38,* 564–570.

O'Neill, R. E. (2004). Positive behavior supports. In C. Kennedy & E. Horn (Eds.), *Including students with severe disabilities* (pp. 141–158). Boston: Pearson.

O'Neill, R. E., Horner, R. H., Albin, R. W., Sprague, J. R., Storey, K., & Newton, J. S. (1997). *Functional assessment for problem behavior: A practical handbook* (2nd ed.). Pacific Grove, CA: Brooks/Cole.

Onosko, J., & Jorgensen, C. (1998). Unit and lesson planning in the inclusive classroom: Maximizing learning opportunities for all students. In C. Jorgensen (Ed.), *Restructuring high schools for all students* (pp. 71–105). Baltimore: Brookes.

Orelove, F. P., & Sobsey, D. (2000). *Educating children with multiple disabilities: A transdisciplinary approach* (3rd ed.). Baltimore: Brookes.

Organization for Economic Cooperation and Development. (1997). *Employment outlook.* Paris: Author.

Orkwis, R. (2003). *Universally designed instruction.* Arlington, VA: Council for Exceptional Children. (ERIC Document Reproduction Service No. ED468709)

Ozdemir, S. (2008). The effectiveness of social stories on decreasing disruptive behaviors of children with autism: Three case studies. *Journal of Autism and Developmental Disorders, 38,* 1689–1696.

Page, T. J., Iwata, B. A., & Neef, N. A. (1976). Teaching pedestrian skills to retarded persons: Generalization from the classroom to the natural environment. *Journal of Applied Behavior Analysis, 9,* 443–444.

Parents Helping Parents. (2007). The CIRCLES program. Retrieved from *www.php.com/services/circles*

Parke, R. D., & Welsh, M. (1998). Social relationships and academic success. *Thrust for Educational Leadership, 20*(1), 32–34.

Parrott, K. A., Schuster, J. W., Collins, B. C., & Gassaway, L. J. (2000). Simultaneous prompting and instructive feedback when teaching chained tasks. *Journal of Behavioral Education, 10,* 3–19.

Parsons, M. B., & Reid, D. H. (1990). Assessing food preferences among persons with profound mental retardation: Providing opportunities to make choices. *Journal of Applied Behavior Analysis, 23,* 183–195.

Patrick, D. L. (2003). Overweight and obesity among people with disabilities in Washington State. *Proceedings of the 131st Annual Meeting of APHA,* Seattle, Washington.

Pearson, P. D., & Fielding, L. (1991). Comprehension instruction. In R. Barr, M. L. Kamil, P.

Mosenthal, & P. D. Pearson (Eds.), *Handbook of reading research* (Vol. 2, pp. 815–860). White Plains, NY: Longman.

Pearson, P. D., & Johnson, D. D. (1978). *Teaching reading comprehension.* Austin: TX: Holt, Rinehart, and Winston.

Pennsylvania Department of Education, Bureau of Special Education and Bureau of Assessment and Accountability. Guidelines for IEP teams: Assigning students with IEPs to state tests (ASIST). (2010). Retrieved from *www.pde.state.pa.us/special_edu/lib/special_edu/pssa-m_ iep_team_guideline_september_24_2009_revised_____f....pdf*

Perske, R., Clifton, A., McLean, B. M., & Stein, J. I. (Eds.). (1977). *Mealtimes for severely and profoundly handicapped persons: New concepts and attitudes.* Baltimore: Brookes.

Pierce, K. L., & Schriebman, L. (1994). Teaching daily living skills to children with autism in unsupervised settings through pictorial self-management. *Journal of Applied Behavior Analysis, 27,* 471–481.

Post, M., & Storey, K. (2002). Review of using auditory prompting systems with persons who have moderate to severe disabilities. *Education and Training in Mental Retardation and Developmental Disabilities, 37,* 317–327.

Powell, D. S., Batsche, C. J., Ferro, J., Fox, L., & Dunlap, G. (1997). A strength-based approach in support of multi-risk families: Principles and issues. *Topics in Early Childhood Special Education, 17,* 1–26.

Powers, L. E., Singer, G. H. S., & Sowers, J. (1996). *Promoting self-competence in children and youth with disabilities: On the road to autonomy.* Baltimore: Brookes.

Public Schools of North Carolina. (2002). Career and technical education. In *North Carolina Standard Course of Study.* Retrieved from *www.dpi.state.nc.us/cte/curriculum/*

Pugalee, D. K. (2007). *Developing students' mathematical and scientific literacy through text: Effective content-related reading practices.* Norwood, MA: Gordon.

Quill, K. A. (2000). *Do–Watch–Listen–Say: Social and communication intervention for children with autism.* Baltimore: Brookes.

Raphael, T. E., & McKinney, J. (1983). An examination of 5th and 8th grade childrens' question-answering behavior: An instructional study in metacognition. *Journal of Reading Behavior, 15,* 67–86.

Raphael, T. E., & Pearson, P. D. (1985). Increasing students' awareness of sources of information for answering questions. *American Educational Research Journal, 22,* 217–236.

Rayner, K., & Pollatsek, A. (1989). *The psychology of reading.* Hillsdale, NJ: Erlbaum.

Reading mastery classic. (2003). New York: SRA/McGraw-Hill.

Reese, G. M., & Snell, M. E. (1991). Putting on and removing coats and jackets: The acquisition and maintenance of skills by children with severe multiple disabilities. *Education and Training in Mental Retardation, 26,* 398–410.

Reichle, J., & Sigafoos, J. (1994). Communication intervention for persons with developmental disabilities. In E. Cipani & F. Spooner (Eds.), *Curricular and instructional approaches for persons with severe disabilities* (pp. 241–262). Boston: Allyn & Bacon.

Richardson, J. S. (2000). *Read it aloud! Using literature in the secondary content classroom.* Newark, DE: International Reading Association.

Richmond, G. (1983). Shaping bladder and bowel continence in developmentally retarded preschool children. *Journal of Autism and Developmental Disorders, 13,* 197–205.

Riffel, L. A., Wehmeyer, M. L., Turnbull, A. P., Lattimore, J., Davies, D., Stock, S., et al. (2005). Promoting independent performance of transition-related tasks using a palmtop PC-based self-directed visual and auditory prompting system. *Journal of Special Education Technology, 20*(2), 5–14.

Riordan, M. M., Iwata, B. A., Finney, J. W., Wohl, M. K., & Stanley, A. E. (1984). Behavioral assessment and treatment of chronic food refusal in handicapped children. *Journal of Applied Behavior Analysis, 17,* 327–341.

Riverdeep. (n.d.). Bailey's book house [computer software]. Retrieved September 11, 2008, from *web.riverdeep.net/portal/page?_pageid=818,1383495,818_1383542&_dad=portal&_ schema=PORTAL*

Roach, A. T., & Elliott, S. N. (2006). The influence of access to general education curriculum on alternate assessment performance of students with significant cognitive disabilities. *Educational Evaluation and Policy Analysis, 28*, 181–194. doi: 10.3102/01623737028002181

Roach, A. T., Elliott, S. N., & Webb, N. L. (2005). Alignment of an alternate assessment with state academic standards: Evidence for the content validity of the Wisconsin alternate assessment. *Journal of Special Education, 38*, 218–231.

Rodgers, J., & Lipscombe, J. (2005). The nature and extent of help given to women with intellectual disabilities to manage menstruation. *Journal of Intellectual and Developmental Disability, 30*, 45–52.

Roe, B. D., Smith, S. H., & Burns, P. C. (2005). *Teaching reading in today's elementary schools.* Boston: Houghton Mifflin.

Roeber, E. (2002). Setting standards on alternate assessments (Synthesis Report No. 42). Minneapolis, MN: University of Minnesota, National Center on Educational Outcomes. Retrieved October 19, 2009, from *education.umn.edu/NCEO/OnlinePubs/Synthesis42.html*

Roessler, R. T., Brolin, D. E., & Johnson, J. M. (1990). Factors affecting employment success and quality of life: A one-year follow-up of students in special education. *Career Development for Exceptional Individuals, 13*, 95–107.

Rosenshine, B., Meister, C., & Chapman, S. (1996). Teaching students to generate questions: A review of the intervention studies. *Review of Educational Research, 66*, 181–221.

Rowland, C., & Schweigert, P. (1990). *Tangible symbol systems: Symbolic communication for individuals with multisensory impairments.* Tucson, AZ: Communication Skill Builders. (ERIC Document Reproduction Service No. 319154)

Rues, J. P., Graff, J. C., Ault, M. M., & Holvoet, J. (2006). Special health care procedures. In M. E. Snell & F. Brown (Eds.), *Instruction of students with severe disabilities* (6th ed., pp. 251–290). Upper Saddle River, NJ: Pearson.

Ryndak, D. (1996). Education teams and collaborative teamwork in inclusive settings. In D. L. Ryndak & S. Alper (Eds.), *Curriculum content for students with moderate and severe disabilities in inclusive settings* (pp. 77–96). Boston: Allyn & Bacon.

Ryndak, D. L., & Alper, S. (2003). *Curriculum and instruction for students with significant disabilities in inclusive settings* (2nd ed.). Boston: Allyn & Bacon.

Sachar, L. (1998). *Holes.* New York: Macmillan.

Sacramento City Unified School District v. Rachel H., 14 F.3d 1398 (9th Cir. 1994).

Sailor, W., & Roger, B. (2005, March). Rethinking inclusion: Schoolwide applications. *Phi Delta Kappan, 86*, 503–507.

Sandknop, P. A., Schuster, J. W., Wolery, M., & Cross, D. P. (1992). The use of an adaptive device to teach students with moderate mental retardation to selected lower priced grocery items. *Education and Training in Mental Retardation, 27*, 219–229.

Sarama, J., & Clements, D. H. (2009). *Early childhood mathematics education research.* New York: Routledge.

Sarama, J., Clements, D. H., Swaminathan, S., McMillen, S., & Gonzalez Gomez, R. M. (2003). Development of mathematical concepts of two-dimensional space in grid-environments: An exploratory story. *Cognition and Instruction, 21*, 285–324.

Sarber, R. E., & Cuvo, A. J. (1983). Teaching nutritional meal planning to developmentally disabled clients. *Behavior Modification, 7*, 503–530.

Scattone, D., Wilczynki, S. M., Edwards, R., & Rabian, B. (2002). Decreasing disruptive behaviours of children with autism using social stories. *Journal of Autism and Developmental Disorders, 32*, 535–543.

Schank, R. C. (1990). *Tell me a story.* New York: Macmillan.

Schleien, S., Green, F., & Heyne, L. (1993). Integrated community recreation. In M. Snell (Ed.) *Instruction of students with severe disabilities* (4th ed.). New York: Merrill.

Schoen, S. F., Lentz, F. E., & Suppa, R. J. (1988). An examination of two prompt fading procedures and opportunities to observe in teaching handicapped preschoolers self-help skills. *Journal of the Division for Early Childhood, 12,* 349–358.

Schoen, S. F., & Ogden, S. (1995). Impact of time delay, observational learning, and attentional cuing upon word recognition during integrated small-group instruction. *Journal of Autism and Developmental Disorders, 25,* 503–519.

Schopler, E., Mesibov, G. B., & Hearsey, K. (1995). Structured teaching in the TEACCH system. In E. Schopler & G. B. Mesibov (Eds.), *Learning and cognition in autism* (pp. 243–268). New York: Plenum Press.

Schwartz, I. S., Staub, D., Peck, C. A., & Gallucci, C. (2006). Peer relationships. In M. E. Snell & F. Brown (Eds.), *Instruction of students with severe disabilities* (pp. 365–404). Upper Saddle River, NJ: Merrill Prentice Hall.

Sewall, A. M., & Balkman, K. (2002). DNR orders and school responsibility: New legal concerns and questions. *Remedial and Special Education, 23,* 7–14.

Shafer, M. S., Inge, K. J., & Hill, J. (1986). Acquisition, generalization, and maintenance of automated banking skills. *Education and Training in Mental Retardation, 21,* 265–272.

Shapiro, E. S. (1996). *Academic skills problems* (2nd ed.). New York: Guilford Press.

Sharpe, M. N., York, J. L., & Knight, J. (1994). Effects of inclusion on the academic performance of classmates without disabilities. *Remedial and Special Education, 15,* 281–287.

Shinn, M. R. (Ed.). (1989). *Curriculum-based measurement: Assessing special children.* New York: Guilford Press.

Sidman, M., & Stoddard, L. T. (1967). The effectiveness of fading in programming a simultaneous form discrimination for retarded children. *Journal of the Experimental Analysis of Behavior, 10,* 3–15.

Siegel, E., & Wetherby, A. (2006). Nonsymbolic communication. In M. E. Snell & F. Brown (Eds.), *Instruction of students with severe disabilities* (6th ed., pp. 489–525). Upper Saddle River, NJ: Pearson.

Sigafoos, J., & Iacono, T. (1993). Selecting augmentative communication devices for persons with severe disabilities: Some factors for educational teams to consider. *Australia and New Zealand Journal of Developmental Disabilities, 18,* 133–146.

Simonsen, B., Sugai, G., & Negron, M. (2008). School-wide positive behavior supports: Primary systems and practices. *Teaching Exceptional Children, 40*(6), 32–40.

Singh, N. N., Oswald, D. P., Ellis, C. R., & Singh, S. D. (1995). Community-based instruction for independent meal preparation by adults with profound mental retardation. *Journal of Behavioral Education, 5,* 77–92.

Singleton, D. K., Schuster, J. W., Morse, T. E., & Collins, B. C. (1999). A comparison of antecedent prompt and test and simultaneous prompting procedures in teaching grocery words to adolescents with mental retardation. *Education and Training in Mental Retardation and Developmental Disabilities, 34,* 182–199.

Sisson, L. A., Kilwein, M. L., & Van Hasselt, V. B. (1988). A graduated guidance procedure for teaching self-dressing skills to multihandicapped children. *Research in Developmental Disabilities, 9,* 419–432.

Skinner, A., & Thompson, A. (2008, July). Aquatics therapy and the Halliwick concept. *Excptional Parent,* 76–77.

Skinner, B. F. (1974). *About behaviorism.* New York: Knopf.

Skotko, B. G., Koppenhaver, D. A., & Erickson, K. A. (2004). Parent reading behaviors and communication outcomes in girls with Rett syndrome. *Exceptional Children, 70,* 145–166.

Smeets, P. M. (1978). Teaching retarded adults monetary skills using an experimental calculator. *Behavioral Engineering, 5,* 51–59.

Smith, A. L., Jr., Piersel, W. C., Filbeck, R. W., & Gross, E. J. (1983). The elimination of mealtime food stealing and scavenging behavior in an institutionalized severely mentally retarded adult. *Mental Retardation, 21,* 255–259.

Smith, K. S., & Geller, C. (2004). Essential principles of effective mathematics instruction: Methods to reach all students. *Preventing School Failure, 48,* 22–29.

Smith, P. (2007). Have we made any progress? Including students with intellectual disabilities in regular education classrooms. *Intellectual and Developmental Disabilities, 45*, 297–309.

Smith, P. D., Gast, D. L., Logan, K. R., & Jacobs, H. A. (2001). Customizing instruction to maximize functional outcomes for students with profound multiple disabilities. *Exceptionality, 9*, 135–145.

Smith, T. (1996). Are other treatments effective? In C. Maurice, G. Green, & S. C. Luce (Eds.), *Behavioral intervention for young children with autism* (pp. 45–62). Austin, TX: Pro-Ed.

Snell, M. E. (Ed.). (1983). *Systematic instruction of the moderately and severely handicapped* (2nd ed.). Columbus, OH: Merrill.

Snell, M. E. (2005). Fifteen years later: Has positive programming become the expected technology for addressing problem behavior? A commentary on Horner et al. (1990). *Research and Practice for Persons with Severe Disabilities, 30*, 11–14.

Snell, M. E., & Browder, D. M. (1986). Community-referenced instruction: Research and issues. *Journal of the Association for Persons with Severe Handicaps, 11*, 1–11.

Snell, M. E., & Brown, F. (Eds.). (2006). *Instruction of students with severe disabilities* (6th ed.). Upper Saddle River, NJ: Pearson Merrill/Prentice Hall.

Snell, M. E., Chen, L., & Hoover, K. (2006). Teaching augmentative and alternative communication to students with severe disabilities: A review of intervention research 1997–2003. *Research and Practices for Persons with Severe Disabilities, 31*, 203–214.

Snell, M. E., & Farlow, L. J. (1993). Self-care skills. In M. E. Snell (Ed.), *Instruction of individuals with severe disabilities* (4th ed., pp. 380–441). New York: Macmillan.

Snell, M. E., & Gast, D. L. (1981). Applying time delay procedure to the instruction of the severely handicapped. *Journal of the Association for the Severely Handicapped, 6*, 3–14.

Snell, M. E., Lewis, A. P., & Houghton, A. (1989). Acquisition and maintenance of toothbrushing skills by students with cerebral palsy and mental retardation. *Journal of the Association for Persons with Severe Handicaps, 14*, 216–226.

Snell, M. E., & Lloyd, B. H. (1991). A study of the effects of trend, variability, frequency, and form of data on teachers' judgments about progress and their decisions about program change. *Research in Developmental Disabilities, 12*, 41–62.

Sobsey, D., & Cox, A. W. (2000). Integrating health care and educational programs. In F. P. Orelove & D. Sobsey (Eds.), *Educating children with multiple disabilities: A transdisciplinary approach* (3rd ed., pp. 217–251). Baltimore: Brookes.

Sobsey, D., & Thuppal, M. (2000). Children with special health care needs. In F. P. Orelove & D. Sobsey (Eds.), *Educating children with multiple disabilities: A transdisciplinary approach* (3rd ed., pp. 161–216). Baltimore: Brookes.

SoftTouch. (2004). *My own bookshelf* [computer software]. Retrieved September 11, 2008, from *http://www.softtouch.com/myownbookshelf.aspx*

Sontag, E., Burke, P., & York, R. (1973). Considerations for serving the severely handicapped in the public schools. *Education and Training of the Mentally Retarded, 8*, 20–26.

Sowers, J., & Powers, L. (1995). Enhancing participation and independence of students with severe physical and multiple disabilities in performing community activities. *Mental Retardation, 33*, 209–220.

Spooner, F. (1984). Comparisons of backward chaining and total task presentation in training severely handicapped persons. *Education and Training in Mental Retardation, 19*, 15–22.

Spooner, F. (Ed.). (2003). Perspectives on defining scientifically based research [Special issue]. *Research and Practice for Persons with Severe Disabilities, 28*(3).

Spooner, F., Baker, J., Ahlgrim-Delzell, L., Harris, A., & Browder, D. M. (2007). Effects of training in universal design for learning (UDL) on lesson plan development. *Remedial and Special Education, 28*, 108–116.

Spooner, F., & Browder, D. M. (2003). Scientifically based research in education and students with low-incidence disabilities. *Research and Practice for Persons with Severe Disabilities, 28*, 117–125.

Spooner, F., & Brown, F. (in press). Educating students with significant cognitive disabilities:

Historical overviews and future projections. In J. M. Kauffman & D. P. Hallahan (Eds.), *Handbook of special education*. London, UK: Routledge/Taylor & Francis/Informa.

Spooner, F., DiBiase, W., & Courtade-Little, G. (2006). Science standards and functional skills: Finding the links. In D. M. Browder & F. Spooner (Eds.), *Teaching language arts, math, and science to students with significant cognitive disabilities* (pp. 229–243). Baltimore, MD: Brookes.

Spooner, F., & Dykes, M. K. (1982). Epilepsy: Facts and impact upon severely and profoundly handicapped persons. *Journal of the Association for the Severely Handicapped, 7*(3), 87–96.

Spooner, F., Dymond, S. K., & Kennedy, C. H. (Eds.). (2006). Accessing the general curriculum [Special issue]. *Research and Practice for Persons with Severe Disabilities, 31*(4).

Spooner, F., Dymond, S. K., Smith, A., & Kennedy, C. H. (2006). What we know about accessing the general curriculum for students with significant cognitive disabilities. *Research and Practice for Persons with Severe Disabilities, 31*(4), 277–283.

Spooner, F., Knight, V., Browder, D. M., Jimenez, B., & DiBiase, W. (2009). *Evaluating evidence-based practices in teaching science content to students with severe developmental disabilities*. Manuscript submitted for publication.

Spooner, F., & Spooner, D. (1984). A review of chaining techniques: Implications for future research and practice. *Education and Training of the Mentally Retarded, 19*, 114–124.

Spooner, F., Stem, B., & Test, D. W. (1989). Teaching first aid skills to adolescents who are moderately mentally handicapped. *Education and Training in Mental Retardation, 24*, 341–351.

Spooner, F., & Wood, W. M. (2004). Teaching personal care and hygiene skills. In P. Wehman & J. Kregel (Eds.). *Functional curriculum for elementary, middle, & secondary age students with special needs*. Pro-Ed: Austin, TX.

Stenner, A. J. (1996). *Measuring reading comprehension with the Lexile Framework*. Durham, NC: MetaMetrics.

Stoddard, L. T., Brown, J., Hurlbert, B., Manoli, C., & McIlvane, W. J. (1989). Teaching money skills through stimulus class formation, exclusion, and component matching methods: Three case studies. *Research in Developmental Disabilities, 10*, 413–439.

Stokes, T. F., & Baer, D. M. (1977). An implicit technology of generalization. *Journal of Applied Behavior Analysis, 10*, 349–367.

Storey, K., Bates, P., & Hanson, H. B. (1984). Acquisition and generalization of coffee purchasing skills by adults with severe disabilities. *Journal of the Association for Persons with Severe Disabilities, 9*, 178–185.

Sugai, G., Simonsen, B., & Horner, R. H. (2008). Schoolwide positive behavior supports: A continuum of positive behavior supports for all students. *Teaching Exceptional Children, 40*(6), 5–10.

Sulzby, E., & Teale, W. H. (2003). The development of the young child and the emergence of literacy. In J. Flood, D. Lapp, J. Squire, & J. Jensen (Eds.), *Handbook of research on teaching the English language arts* (2nd ed., pp. 300–313). Mahwah, NJ: Erlbaum.

Swift, J. (1729). *A modest proposal*. Retrieved November 1, 2009, from *art-bin.com/art/omodest.html*

Tawney, J. W., & Gast, D. L. (1984). *Single subject research in special education*. Columbus, OH: Merrill.

Taylor, P., Collins, B. C., Schuster, J. W., & Kleinert, H. (2002). Teaching laundry skills to high school students with disabilities: Generalization of targeted skills and nontargeted information. *Education and Training in Mental Retardation and Developmental Disabilities, 37*, 172–183.

TERC, The Investigations Curriculum. (2006). *Geo-Logo* (1st ed.) [Computer software]. Glenview, IL: Pearson Scott Foresman.

Terrace, H. S. (1963a). Discrimination learning with and without "errors." *Journal of the Experimental Analysis of Behavior, 6*, 1–27.

Terrace, H. S. (1963b). Errorless transfer of a discrimination across two continua. *Journal of the Experimental Analysis of Behavior, 6*, 223–232.

Test, D. W., Mazzotti, V. L., Mustian, A. L., Fowler, C. H., Kortering, L. J., & Kohler, P. H. (2009). Evidence-based secondary transition predictors for improving post-school outcomes for students with disabilities. *Career Development for Exceptional Individual's, 32*, 160–181.

Test, D. W., & Neale, M. (2004). Using *The Self-Advocacy Strategy* to increase middle graders' IEP participation. *Journal of Behavioral Education, 13*, 135–145.

Test, D. W., Richter, S., Knight, V., & Spooner, F. (2010). A comprehensive review and meta-analysis of the social stories literature. *Focus on Autism and Other Developmental Disabilities.* Advance online publication. doi: 10.1177/1088357609351573

Test, D. W., Spooner, F., Keul, P. K., & Grossi, T. (1990). Teaching adolescents with severe disabilities to use the public telephone. *Behavior Modification, 14*, 157–171.

Thiemann, K. S., & Goldstein, H. (2001). Social stories, written text cues and video feedback: Effect on social communication of children with autism. *Journal of Applied Behavior Analysis, 34*, 425–446.

Thomas, S. B., & Rapport, M. J. K. (1998). Least restrictive environment: Understanding the direction of the courts. *Journal of Special Education, 32*, 66–78.

Thompson, S. J., Johnstone, C. J., Thurlow, M. L., & Altman, J. R. (2005). *2005 state special education outcomes: Steps forward in a decade of change.* Minneapolis: University of Minnesota, National Center on Educational Outcomes. (ERIC Document Reproduction Service No. ED495882)

Thompson, S. J., & Thurlow, M. (2001). *2001 state special education outcomes: A report on state activities at the beginning of a new decade.* Minneapolis: University of Minnesota, National Center on Educational Outcomes.

Thompson, S. J., Thurlow, M. L., Quenemoen, R. F., Esler, A., & Whetstone, P. (2001). *Addressing standards and assessments on state IEP forms* (Synthesis Report No. 38). Minneapolis: University of Minnesota, National Center on Educational Outcomes.

Thorin, E. J., & Irvin, L. K. (1992). Family stress associated with transition to adulthood of young people with severe disabilities. *Journal of the Association for Persons with Severe Handicaps, 17*, 31–39.

Thousand, J. S., & Villa, R. A. (2000). Collaborative teaming: A powerful tool in restructuring. In R. A. Villa & J. S. Thousand (Eds.), *Restructuring for caring and effective education: Piecing the puzzle together* (2nd ed., pp. 254–292). Baltimore: Brookes.

Thurlow, M. L., & Turnure, J. E. (1977). Children's knowledge of time and money: Effective instruction for the mentally retarded. *Education and Training of the Mentally Retarded, 12*, 203–212.

Thvedt, J. E., Zane, T., & Walls, R. T. (1984). Stimulus functions in response chaining. *American Journal of Mental Deficiency, 88*, 661–667.

Touchette, P. E. (1971). Transfer of stimulus control: Measuring the moment of transfer. *Journal of the Experimental Analysis of Behavior, 15*, 347–354.

Towles-Reeves, E., Kearns, J., Kleinert, H., & Kleinert, J. (2007, April). Learner Characteristics Inventory: Describing the characteristics of students taking the alternate assessment based on alternate achievement standards (AA–AAS). Paper presented at the meeting of the American Educational Research Association, Chicago, IL. Retrieved from *www.naacpartners.org/products.aspx*

Towles-Reeves, E., Kleinert, H., & Muhomba, M. (2009). Alternate assessment: Have we learned anything new? *Exceptional Children, 75*, 233–252.

Townsley, R., & Robinson, C. (1999). What rights for disabled children? Home external tube feeding in the community. *Children and Society, 13*, 48–60.

Trask-Tyler, S. A., Grossi, T. A., & Heward, W. L. (1994). Teaching young adults with developmental disabilities and visual impairments to use tape-recorded recipes: Acquisition, generalization, and maintenance of cooking skills. *Journal of Behavioral Education, 4*, 283–311.

Trela, K., Jimenez, B. A., & Browder, D. M. (2008). *Teaching to standards: Math: A literacy-based approach for students with moderate and severe disabilities.* Verona, WI: Attainment.

Troia, G. (2006). Meaningful assessment of content-area literacy for youth with and without disabilities. *Assessment for Effective Intervention, 31*(2), 69–80.

Turnbull, A. P., & Turnbull, H. R. (1997). *Families, professionals, and exceptionality: A special partnership* (3rd ed.). Upper Saddle River, NJ:. Merrill.

U.S. Department of Education. (2003, December 9). *Title I—Improving the academic achievement of the disadvantaged; Final rule,* 68 Fed. Reg. 236.

U.S. Department of Education, Office of Special Education Programs. (2006). Toolkit on teaching and assessing students with severe disabilities: A decision framework for IEP teams related to methods for individual student participation in state accountability assessments. Retrieved from *osepideasthatwork.org/index.asp*

U.S. Department of Education. Title 1: Improving the academic achievement of the disadvantaged; Final rule, 68 Fed. Reg. 236 (December 9, 2003).

U.S. Department of Labor. (2005). Customized employment: Practical solutions for employment success. Retrieved from *www.dol.gov/odep/pubs/custom/index.htm*

Uehara, E. W., Silverstein, B. J., Davis, R., & Geron, S. (1991). Assessment of needs of adults with developmental disabilities in skilled nursing and intermediate care facilities in Illinois. *Mental Retardation, 29,* 223–231.

Van Reusen, A. K., & Bos, C. S. (1990). IPLAN: Helping students communicate in planning conferences. *Teaching Exceptional Children, 22*(4), 30–32.

VanBiervliet, A., Spangler, P. F., & Marshall, A. M. (1981). An ecobehavioral examination of a simple strategy for increasing mealtime language in residential facilities. *Journal of Applied Behavior Analysis, 14,* 295–305.

Vaughn, S. R., & Bos, C. S. (2009). *Strategies for teaching students with learning and behavior problems.* Boston: Allyn & Bacon.

Vergason, G. A., & Anderegg, M. L. (1997). *Dictionary of special education and rehabilitation.* (4th ed.). Denver, CO: Love.

Villa, R. A., & Thousand, J. S. (Eds.). (1995). *Creating an inclusive school.* Alexandria, VA: Association for Supervision and Curriculum Development.

Viorst, J. (1987). *Alexander and the terrible, horrible, no good, very bad day.* New York: Atheneum.

Vogelsberg, R. T., & Rusch, F. R. (1979). Training three severely handicapped young adults to walk, look, and cross uncontrolled intersection. *AAESPH Review, 4,* 264–273.

Voorhees, P. J. (1996). Travel training for persons with cognitive or physical disabilities: An overview. *NICHY: Transition Summary, 9,* 7–9.

Wacker, D. P., Berg, W. K., McMahon, C., Templeman, M., McKinney, J., Swarts, V., et al. (1988). Evaluation of labeling-then-doing with moderately handicapped persons: Acquisition and generalization with complex tasks. *Journal of Applied Behavior Analysis, 21,* 369–380.

Wagner, M. (2005a). Changes in the engagement in school, work, and preparation for work of out-of-school youth with disabilities. In M. Wagner, L. Newman, R. Cameto, & P. Levine (Eds.), Changes over time in the early postschool outcomes of youth with disabilities: A report of findings from the National Longitudinal Transition Study (NLTS2) and from the Natioal Longitudinal Transition Study—2 (NLTS2). Menlo Park, CA: SRI International. Available at *www.nlts2.org/pdfs/str6_ch6_engage.pdf*

Wagner, M. (2005b). Changes in the household arrangements and social activities of out-of-school youth with disabilities. In M. Wagner, L. Newman, R. Cameto, & P. Levine (Eds.), Changes over time in the early postschool outcomes of youth with disabilities: A report of findings from the National Longitudinal Transition Study (NLTS) and the National Longitudinal Transition Study—2 (NLTS2). Menlo Park, CA: SRI International. Available at *www.nlts2.org/reports/2005_06 /nlts2_report_2005_06_ complete.pdf*

Wagner, M. (2005c). The leisure activities, social involvement, and citizenship of youth with disabilities after high school. In M. Wagner, L. Newman, R. Cameto, N. Garza, & P. Levine (Eds.), After high school: A first look at the postschool experiences of youth with disabilities: A report from the National Longitudinal Transition Study—2 (NLTS2). Menlo Park, CA: SRI International. Available at *www.nlts2.org/pdfs/afterhighschool_chp7.pdf*

Wagner, M., Cadwallader, T., & Marder, C. (with Cameto, R., Cardoso, D., Garza, N., et al.). (2003). Life outside the classroom for youth with disabilities. A report from the National Longitudinal Transition Study—2 (NLTS2). Menlo Park, CA: SRI International. Available at *www.nlts2.org/reports/2003_04-2/nlts2_report_2003_04-2_complete.pdf*

Wagner, M., Marder, C., Blackorby, J., Cameto, R., Newman, L., Levine, P., et al. (2003). The achievements of youth with disabilities during secondary school: A report from the National Longitudinal Transition Study—2 (NLTS2). Menlo Park, CA: SRI International. Available at *www.nlts2.org/reports/2003_11/nlts2_report_2003_11_complete.pdf*

Wakeman, S., Bechard, S., Karvonen, M., & Almond, P. (2009). Principles for aligning alternate assessment based upon alternate academic achievement standards with grade-level academic content standard: A self-study guide for state departments of education. Dover, NH: Measured Progress. Retrieved from *www.measuredprogress.org/resources/inclusive/research/grants/pa/StudyGuideEducators.pdf*

Watt, M. G. (2005). *Standards-based reforms in the United States of America: An overview.* (ERIC Document Reproduction Service No. ED490562)

Watts, K., & Everly, J. S. (2009). Helping children with disabilities through animal-assisted therapy. *Exceptional Parent, 39,* 34–35.

Weaver, C. A., III, & Kintsch, W. (1991). Expository text. In R. Barr, M. L. Kamil, P. Mosenthal, & P. D. Pearson (Eds.), *Handbook of reading research* (Vol. 2, pp. 230–244). White Plains, NY: Longman.

Webb, N. L. (1997). *Criteria for alignment of expectations and assessments in mathematics and science education* (Research Monograph No. 6). Washington, DC: Council of Chief State School Officers.

Webber, J., & Scheuermann, B. (2009). Using naturalistic teaching strategies to build communication skills in students with severe disabilities. In W. L. Heward (Ed.), *Exceptional children: An introduction to special education* (9th ed., pp. 476–477). Upper Saddle River, NJ: Pearson.

Wehman, P., Hill, J. W., Wood, W., & Parent, W. (1987). A report on competitive employment histories of persons labeled severely retarded. *Journal of the Association for Persons with Severe Handicaps, 12,* 11–17.

Wehman, P., Kregel, J., & Seyfarth, J. (1985a). Outlook for young adults with mental retardation. *Rehabilitation Counseling Bulletin, 25,* 90–99.

Wehman, P., Kregel, J., & Seyfarth, J. (1985b). Transition from school to work for individuals with severe handicaps: A follow-up study. *Journal of the Association for Persons with Severe Handicaps, 10,* 132–136.

Wehman, P., Moon, M., Everson, J., Wood, W., & Barcus, J. (1988). *Transition from school to work: New challenges for youth with severe disabilities.* Baltimore: Brookes.

Wehmeyer, M. (1992). Self-determination and the education of students with mental retardation. *Education and Training in Mental Retardation, 27,* 302–314.

Wehmeyer, M. L. (2005). Self-determination and individuals with severe disabilities: Re-examining meanings and misinterpretations. *Research and Practice for Persons with Severe Disabilities, 30,* 113–120.

Wehmeyer, M. L., Agran, M., & Hughes, C. (1998). *Teaching self-determination to youth with disabilities: Basic skills for successful transition.* Baltimore: Brookes.

Wehmeyer, M. L., & Palmer, S. B. (2003). Adult outcomes for students with cognitive disabilities three years after high school: The impact of self-determination. *Education and Training in Developmental Disabilities, 38,* 131–144.

Wehmeyer, M. L., Palmer, S. B., Agran, M., Mithaug, D. E., & Martin, J. E. (2000). Promoting causal agency the self-determined learning model of instruction. *Exceptional Children, 66,* 439–453.

Wehmeyer, M. L., & Schwartz, M. (1997). Self-determination and positive adult outcomes: A follow-up study of youths with mental retardation or learning disabilities. *Exceptional Children, 63,* 245–255.

Wehmeyer, M. L., & Schwartz, M. (1998a). The relationship between self-determination and quality of life for adults with mental retardation. *Education and Training in Mental Retardation and Developmental Disabilities, 33*, 3–12.

Wehmeyer, M. L., & Schwartz, M. (1998b). The self-determination focus of transition goals for students with mental retardation. *Career Development for Exceptional Individuals, 21*, 75–86.

Werts, M. G., Wolery, M., Holcombe, A., & Gast, D. L. (1995). Instructive feedback: Review of parameters and effects. *Journal of Behavioral Education, 5*, 55–75.

Wesson, C. L., & King, R. P. (1996). Portfolio assessment and special education students. *Teaching Exceptional Children, 28*(2), 44–48.

Westerveld, M. F., & Gillon, G. T. (2008). Oral narrative intervention for children with mixed reading disability. *Child Language Teaching and Therapy, 24*, 31–54.

Westling, D. L., & Floyd, J. (1990). Generalization of community skills: How much training is necessary? *Journal of Special Education, 23*, 386–406.

Westling, D. L., & Fox, L. (1995). *Teaching students with severe disabilities.* Upper Saddle River, NJ: Prentice-Hall.

Westling, D. L., & Fox L. (2000). *Teaching students with severe disabilities* (2nd ed.). Upper Saddle River, NJ: Prentice Hall.

Westling, D., & Fox, L. (2004). *Teaching students with severe disabilities* (3rd ed.). Upper Saddle River, NJ: Prentice Hall.

What is school-wide positive behavior support? (2009, March). School-wide Positive Behavior Support (SWPBS). Retrieved from *pbskansas.org/swpbs/schoolwide/Training/files/Kansas_School-Wide_Positive_Behavior_Support_Newsletter.pdf*

White, E. B. (1952). *Charlotte's web.* New York: HarperCollins.

White, J., & Weiner, J. S. (2004). Influence of least restrictive environment and community-based training on integrated employment outcomes for transitioning students with severe disabilities. *Journal of Vocational Rehabilitation, 21*, 149–156.

Whitehurst, G. J., & Lonigan, C. J. (1998). Child development and emergent literacy. *Child Development, 69*, 848–872.

Wilcox, B., & Bellamy, G. T. (1987). *The activities catalog: An alternative curriculum for youth and adults with severe disabilities.* Baltimore: Brookes.

Will, M. (1984). *OSERS programming for the transition of youth with disabilities: Bridges from school to working life.* Washington, DC: U.S. Office of Education, Office of Special Education and Rehabilitation Services.

Williams, G. E., & Cuvo, A. J. (1986). Training apartment upkeep skills to rehabilitation clients: A comparison of task analytic strategies. *Journal of Applied Behavior Analysis, 19*, 39–51.

Williams, J. P. (2005). Instruction in reading comprehension for primary-grade students: A focus on text structure. *Journal of Special Education, 39*, 6–18.

Wilson, P. G., Reid, D. H., Phillips, J. F., & Burgio, L. D. (1984). Normalization of institutional mealtimes for profoundly retarded persons: Effects and noneffects of teaching family style dining. *Journal of Applied Behavior Analysis, 17*, 189–201.

Wissick, C. A., & Schweder, W. (2007). Column: Using community-based social stories to enhance instruction for high school students with moderate disabilities. *Journal of Special Education Technology, 22*, 59–64.

Witzel, B., Smith, S. W., & Brownell, M. T. (2001). How can I help students with learning disabilities in algebra? *Intervention in School and Clinic, 37*, 101–104.

Wolery, M., Ault, M. J., & Doyle, P. M. (1992). *Teaching students with moderate to severe disabilities: Use of response prompting strategies.* New York: Longman.

Wolery, M., Bailey, D. B., & Sugai, G. M. (1988). *Effective teaching: Principles and procedure of applied behavior analysis with exceptional students.* Boston: Allyn & Bacon.

Wolery, M., Cybriwsky, C. A., Gast, D., & Boyle-Gast, K. (1991). Use of constant time delay and attentional responses with adolescents. *Exceptional Children, 57*, 462–474.

Wolery, M., & Gast, D. L. (1984). Effective and efficient procedures for the transfer of stimulus control. *Topics in Early Childhood Special Education, 4*, 52–77.

Wolfe, P. S., & Blanchett, W. J. (1997). Infusion of sex education curricula into transition planning: Obstacles and solutions. *Journal of Vocational Rehabilitation, 8*, 143–154.

Wolfensberger, W. W. (1972). *The principle of normalization in human services.* Toronto, Ontario, Canada: National Institute on Mental Retardation.

Wood, W. M., Fowler, C. H., Uphold, N. M., & Test, D. W. (2005). A review of self-determination interventions with individuals with severe disabilities. *Research and Practice for Persons with Severe Disabilities, 30*, 121–146.

Xin, Y. P., Wiles, B., & Lin, Y. Y. (2008). Teaching conceptual model-based word problem story grammar to enhance mathematics problem solving. *Journal of Special Education, 42*, 163–178.

Yell, M. L. (1995). Least restrictive environment, inclusion, and students with disabilities: A legal analysis. *Journal of Special Education, 28*, 389–404.

Yell, M. L. (2006). *The law and special education* (2nd ed.). Upper Saddle River, NJ: Merrill/Prentice Hall.

Yell, M. L., & Drasgow, E. (1999). A legal analysis of inclusion. *Preventing School Failure, 43*(3), 118–126.

Yell, M. L., & Drasgow, E. (2000). Litigating a free appropriate public education: The Lovaas hearings and cases. *Journal of Special Education, 33*, 205–214.

York, J., Vandercook, T., MacDonald, C., Heise-Neff, C., & Caughey, E. (1992). Feedback about integrating middle-school students with severe disabilities in general education classes. *Exceptional Children, 58*, 244–258.

Young, K. R., West, R. P., & MacFarlane, C. A. (1994). Program development, evaluation, and data-based decision making. In E. C. Cipani & F. Spooner (Eds.), *Curricular and instructional approaches for persons with severe disabilities* (pp. 50–80). Boston: Allyn & Bacon.

Ysseldyke, J. E., Algozzine, B., & Thurlow, M. L. (2000). *Critical issues in special education* (3rd ed.). Boston: Houghton Mifflin.

Ysseldyke, J., Dennison, A., & Nelson, R. (2003). Large-scale assessment and accountability systems: Positive consequences for students with disabilities (Synthesis Report No. 51). Minneapolis: University of Minnesota, National Center on Educational Outcomes. Retrieved October 19, 2009, from *education.umn.edu/NCEO/OnlinePubs/Synthesis51.html*

Zakas, T. L., Browder, D., & Spooner, F. (2009, November 3). Social studies: Let's get organized [Webinar 2]. Retrieved December 21, 2009, from *www.tash.org/dev/tashstore/prod.aspx?prodid=52&catid=4*

Zakas, T. L., Wood, C. L., Hicks, S. C., & Browder, D. M. (2009). *Effects of story grammar instruction on story mapping for students with autism.* Manuscript in preparation.

Zambo, R. (2005). The power of two: Linking math and literature. *Mathematics Teaching in the Middle School, 10*, 394–400.

Zane, T., Walls, R. T., & Thvedt, J. E. (1981). Prompting and fading guidance procedures: Their effect chaining and whole task teaching strategies. *Education and Training in Mental Retardation, 16*, 125–130.

Zeaman, D., & House, B J. (1963). The role of attention in retardate discrimination learning. In N. R. Ellis (Ed.), *Handbook of mental deficiency* (pp. 159–223). New York: McGraw-Hill.

Zencius, A. H., Davis, P. K., & Cuvo, A. J. (1990). A personalized system of instruction for teaching checking account skills to adults with mild disabilities. *Journal of Applied Behavior Analysis, 23*, 245–252.

Zhang, J., Gast, D., Horvat, M., & Dattilo, J. (1995). The effectiveness of a constant time delay procedure on teaching lifetime sports skills to adolescents with severe to profound intellectual disabilities. *Education and Training in Mental Retardation and Developmental Disabilities, 30*, 51–64.

Ziegler, J. C., & Goswami, U. (2005). Reading acquisition, developmental dyslexia, and skilled reading across languages: A psycholinguistic grain size theory. *Psychological Bulletin, 131*, 3–29.

Index

421